Computer Applications in Management

Computer Applications in Management

Sanjay Saxena
Managing Director, Total Synergy Consulting Pvt. Ltd.,
New Delhi.

Prabhpreet Chopra
Technology Consultant
Total Synergy Consulting Pvt. Ltd.,
New Delhi.

VIKAS®
VIKAS® PUBLISHING HOUSE PVT LTD

VIKAS® PUBLISHING HOUSE PRIVATE LIMITED
E-28, Sector-8, Noida-201301 (UP), India
Phone: +91-120-4078900 • Fax: +91-120-4078999
VIKAS® Registered Office: A-27, 2nd Floor, Mohan Co-operative Industrial Estate, New Delhi-110044
E-mail: helpline@vikaspublishing.com • Website: www.vikaspublishing.com

SALES AND MARKETING OFFICES OF VIKAS® AND S CHAND AND COMPANY LIMITED

Chennai	:	Ph: 044-2363 2120, chennai@schandpublishing.com
Guwahati	:	Ph: 0361-2738 811, 2735 640, guwahati@schandpublishing.com
Hyderabad	:	Ph: 040-4018 6018, hyderabad@schandpublishing.com
Jalandhar	:	Ph: 0181-4645 630, jalandhar@schandpublishing.com
Kolkata	:	Ph: 033-2335 7458, 2335 3914, kolkata@schandpublishing.com
Lucknow	:	Ph: 0522-4003 633, lucknow@schandpublishing.com
Mumbai	:	Ph: 022-2500 0297, mumbai@schandpublishing.com
Patna	:	Ph: 0612-2260 011, patna@schandpublishing.com

Computer Applications in Management
ISBN: 978-81259-2060-1

Product Code: V8CAM60COMP10ENAA06O

First Published 2006
Reprinted several times between 2006 and 2021, 2023
Reprint 2025

PRINTED IN INDIA
By Vikas Publishing House Private Limited, Plot 20/4, Site-IV, Industrial Area Sahibabad, Ghaziabad-201010 and Published by Vikas Publishing House Private Limited, E-28, Sector-8, Noida-201301

Preface

Computers have today changed the face of the world of business and management. It is today essential for a successful manager to be comfortable in the use of computers and aware of the great potential it offers in improving efficiency and productivity in all aspects of business.

Our attempt in this book is to provide a sound theoretical as well as practical basis for understanding the subject. We have tried to present a clear conceptual understanding of computer concepts and, to help students, an easy to follow visual style for the practical usage of various packages has been followed. Basically, if the reader follows this book in a sequential manner, s/he would have covered the entire syllabi of these papers. For the more interested and committed, additional 'Do-it-yourself' exercises have been given at the end of the relevant chapters.

We would greatly appreciate your comments and suggestions. Please write to us either at our publisher's address or mail us at sanjaysaxena@tscpl.com and prabh@tscpl.com

Sanjay Saxena
Prabhpreet Chopra

Acknowledgements

It is impossible to thank everybody, but a few people need special mention.

First and foremost Piyush Chawla our friend and publisher whose patience in dealing with authors is exceeded only by his great sense of humour!

Our parents and family for always being there and providing us the necessary emotional and moral support.

Special thanks to Monica, without whose help the book would not have seen the light of the day.

Thanks are also due to all the colleagues at Total Synergy and Vikas publishing, and friends who directly or indirectly contributed towards making this book a reality.

Sanjay Saxena
Prabhpreet Chopra

Contents

CHAPTER 1 Understanding Computers

INTRODUCTION

The significance of Information Technology (IT) is well recognised today. It has become a must for the survival of business houses, with constantly growing need for qualitative information technology. One of the major components of information technology, that has gained increased popularity, is the computer. The presence of computer technology can be seen in every sphere of modern life: rail / air reservations, weather forecasting, medical diagnosis, banking, hotels, office automation, and many more.

COMPUTER: A DEFINITION

The word 'computer' literally means 'something that computes' or 'calculates'. But considering a computer to be merely a calculating device would be to severely limit its powers. It may be defined as a device that can operate upon information or data. This is done through the execution of a program (a sequence of instructions which operate on data to perform certain tasks).

The dictionary definition of a computer is:

"An automatic electronic apparatus for making calculations or controlling operations that are expressible in numerical or logical terms."

CHARACTERISTICS OF COMPUTERS

Speed

Internal processes of computers operate at the speed of light, limited only by the programs that control these processes, and the quantum of data under process. The speed with which computers perform is way beyond human capabilities. To express it differently, a computer does in one minute what a human being could take a lifetime.

While referring to the speed of computers, we do not talk in terms of seconds or even milliseconds (10^{-3}). The units of speed are in microseconds (10^{-6}), nanoseconds (10^{-9}), and even picoseconds (10^{-12}). A powerful computer is capable of performing about 3–4 million simple instructions per second.

Accuracy

The accuracy of a computer is consistently high. Errors can occur, but these are almost always due to human error rather than technological weaknesses. Imprecise thinking by the programmer, inaccurate data, or poorly designed systems are the origins of error. Computer errors arising due to incorrect data input or unreliable programs are often referred to as GIGO (garbage-in-garbage-out).

Diligence

Unlike human beings, a computer does not suffer from limitations associated with living beings like tiredness and lack of concentration, and hence can work for hours at a stretch without errors arising from the above (non-existent) faults. As a result, computers score over human beings in performing routine tasks that require a high degree of accuracy. If a million calculations need to be performed, a computer will perform the millionth calculation with exactly the same accuracy and speed as the first one.

Versatility

Computers are capable of performing almost any task, provided the task can be reduced to a series of logical steps. For example, a task such as preparing a payroll can be broken down into a logical sequence of operations, and is therefore ideal for computerised processing.

Notwithstanding all this, the computer itself has only limited ability and actually performs only four basic operations:

- exchange of information with the outside world via Input/Output (I/O) devices
- transfer of data internally within the Central Processing Unit (CPU)
- performance of the basic arithmetic operations
- performance of operations of comparison

In one sense, the computer is not versatile because it is limited to the above-mentioned basic functions. Yet, since so many everyday activities can be reduced to interplay between these functions, it means that computers are effectively, highly ingenious and versatile devices.

Intelligence

A computer does not possess any intelligence of its own. It can perform only those tasks that can be broken down into a series of logical steps. Therefore, it needs to be told what it has to do and in what sequence.

Storage

The speed with which computers can process large amounts of information has led to the large scale information generation, resulting in the information explosion.

Storage of information in a human brain and a computer happens differently. Using its intelligence the human brain subconsciously sifts through new knowledge and selects what it feels is important and retains it in the memory, and the unimportant information is relegated to the back of the mind or just forgotten. Computers, on the other hand, can store and recall any amount of information by using secondary storage capability (a type of detachable memory). Information can therefore be retained as long as desired and recalled as and when required.

EVOLUTION OF COMPUTERS

A glance at the history of computers gives us the basic understanding of the technological development computers have gone through in the past, and leads us to its projections in the future.

The 'Abacus' is the earliest known device that qualifies as a digital computer. This device represents numbers by the position of the beads on a rack. Simple and rapid addition and subtraction can be carried out by positioning the beads appropriately.

Figure 1.1 Abacus–earliest known digital computer

Ancestors of the modern age computer were the earlist mechanical and electro-mechanical devices. These can be traced as far back as the 17th century.

The first attempt towards automatic computing was made by *Blaise Pascal*, a French mathematician. He invented the Mechanical Adding machine in 1642. This device consisted of a number of gears and chains and performed repeated additions and subtractions. It was called Pascaline. Later many attempts were made in this direction but the inventions of *Charles Babbage*, a professor at Cambridge University, is worth mentioning. He is considered to be the *father of modern digital computers*. He designed two computers:

- the 'Difference Engine' (1822) based on the mathematical principle of finite differences and used to solve calculations on large numbers. It was also used to solve trigonometric functions and polynomials.
- the 'Analytical Engine' (1842) a general purpose computing device intended to be completely automatic. This could perform any mathematical operation and at a speed of 60 additions per minute.

Some Well-known Early Computers

Mark I: After World War II, there was a need for advanced calculations. By that time, many mechanical desk calculators had been developed with a high degree of reliability. Howard A. Aiken of Harvard University, while working on his doctorate in physics, in the year 1937, designed a machine that could automatically perform a sequence of arithmetic operations. Completed in 1944, it was named Mark I. The time taken for average multiplication and division was about four and eleven seconds, respectively. The results were printed at the rate of one result per five seconds.

ENIAC: The Electronic Numeric Integrator and Calculator was completed in 1946 and was the first electronic computer. It owes its origin to a design team led by Professors J. Presper Eckert and John Mauchly at the Moore School of Engineering of the University of Pennsylvania, USA. It could store and manipulate only a very limited amount of information, and its programs were wired on boards. The ENIAC performed 5000 additions per second, consumed 150 kilowatts of power, and needed to be water cooled!

EDVAC: Between 1947 and 1950, the More School personnel and the Ballistics Research Laboratory of the US Army built a computer named EDVAC (The Electronic Discrete Variable Automatic Computer) which was based on John Von Neuman's concept of 'stored program'. The basic idea behind the stored program concept is that data as well as sequence of instructions can be stored in the computer's memory to enable automatic flow of operations.

UNIVAC I: The Universal Automatic Computer (UNIVAC), developed in 1951, was the first digital computer to be produced and was installed in the Census Bureau. However, the first business use of a computer was done by General Electric Corporation in 1954, using UNIVAC I.

In 1952, International Business Machines (IBM) introduced various improved models of the UNIVAC I in rapid succession, thereby making digital computers commercially available for business and scientific applications.

COMPUTERS: THEN AND NOW

The history of computer development can be divided into distinct phases which are often referred to as generations of computing devices. 'Generation' in computer terminology is a 'step' in technology. Each generation of computers is characterised by a major technological development that fundamentally changes the way computers operate, resulting in increasingly smaller, cheaper, more powerful efficient and reliable devices with decreasing energy consumption and lesser generation of heat.

Originally, the term 'generation' was used to distinguish between varying hardware technologies only. But nowadays, it has been extended to include both hardware and software.

Read about each generation and the developments that led to the current devices that we use today.

First Generation (1940–1956): Vacuum Tubes

The first computers used vacuum tubes in their circuitry and magnetic drums for memory. A vacuum tube was a fragile glass device that used filaments as a source of electrons and could control and amplify electronic signals.

These computers could perform computations in milliseconds but were enormous in size, taking up almost an entire room. They were very expensive to operate and in addition to using a great deal of electricity, generated a lot of heat resulting in malfunctioning.

Figure 1.2
A vacuum tube

First generation computers relied on machine language (binary-coded programs) to perform operations and could solve only one problem at a time. Input was based on punch cards and paper tape, and output was displayed on printouts.

Early computers like ENIAC, EDVAC, UNIVAC I can all be classified as first generation computers.

Second Generation (1956–1963): Transistors

Transistors developed in 1947 replaced vacuum tubes and ushered in the second generation computers. The transistor was far superior to the vacuum tube, allowing computers to become smaller, faster, cheaper, more energy-efficient and more reliable than their first-generation predecessors. Although transistors also generated a great deal of heat that could damage the computer, it was a substantial improvement over the vacuum tube. Second-generation computers still relied on punched cards for input and printouts for output.

The cryptic binary machine language gave way to symbolic or assembly language that allowed programmers to specify instructions in words. High-level programming languages like COBOL and FORTRAN were also being developed at this time.

These were also the first computers that stored their instructions in their memory, which moved from magnetic drum to magnetic core technology.

The first computers of this generation were developed for the atomic energy industry.

Third Generation (1964–1971) : Integrated Circuits

Transistors were clearly an improvement over the vacuum tube but were still characterized by a great deal of heat generation resulting in computer damage.

The development of integrated circuit by Jack Kilby, an engineer with Texas Instruments, in 1958, was the hallmark of the third generation of computers.

Figure 1.3 An IC chip

Instead of punched cards and printouts, users interacted with third generation computers through the devices like keyboards and monitors. They also interfaced with an operating system that allowed the device to run many different applications at one time with a central program that monitored the memory.

For the first time, computers became accessible to the masses audience because they were substantially smaller and cheaper than their predecessors.

Fourth Generation (1971– Present): Microprocessors

After integrated circuits, the only place to go was down–in size, that is. Large Scale Integration (LSI) could fit hundreds of components onto a single chip. By the 1980's, Very Large Scale Integration (VLSI) squeezed hundreds of thousands of components onto a single chip. Ultra Large Scale Integration (ULSI) increased that number to millions.

The ability to fit so much processing capability in an area so small, helped to diminish the size and price of the computers. It also increased its power, efficiency and reliability.

Initially the IC technology was used only for constructing the processor, but it was soon realised that the same technology could also be used for the construction of memory. The first memory chip was constructed in 1970 and could hold 256 bits.

As more and more components were fabricated on a single chip, fewer and fewer chips were needed to construct the processor. What in the first generation filled the entire room could now fit in the palm of the hand. The Intel 4004 chip, developed in 1971, located all the components of the computer – from Central Processing Unit and memory to Input/Output controls – on a single chip. This was the first microprocessor.

Figure 1.4 The intel pentium microprocessor chip

In 1981 IBM introduced its first computer for the home user, and in 1984 Apple introduced the Macintosh. Microprocessors also moved out of the realm of desktop computers and into many areas of life as more and more everyday products began to use microprocessors.

As computers increased in computing power, it was possible to link them together to form networks, which eventually led to the development of the Internet. Fourth generation computers also saw the development of GUIs, the mouse and various handheld devices.

Fifth Generation (Present and Beyond): Artificial Intelligence

Fifth generation computing devices based on artificial intelligence are still developing. One does see glimpses of these today in the form of voice recognition systems. The use of parallel processing and supercomputers is helping to make artificial intelligence a reality. Quantum computation and molecular technology will radically change the face of computers in the years to come. The goal of fifth-generation computing is to develop devices that respond to natural language input and are capable of learning and self-organisation.

The horizon is far off, and the end is nowhere in sight; the possibilities are immense, as is the potential of computer technology to revolutionise human life.

BASIC ANATOMY OF THE COMPUTER

As seen in earlier sections, the size, shape, cost, and performance of computers have changed over the years, but the basic logical structure has not changed. Any computer system essentially consists of three important parts, namely, input device, central processing unit (CPU) and output device. The CPU itself consists of the main memory, the arithmetic logic unit, and the control unit.

In addition to the five basic parts mentioned above, computers also employ secondary storage devices (also referred to as auxiliary storage or backing storage) which are used for storing data and instructions on a long-term basis.

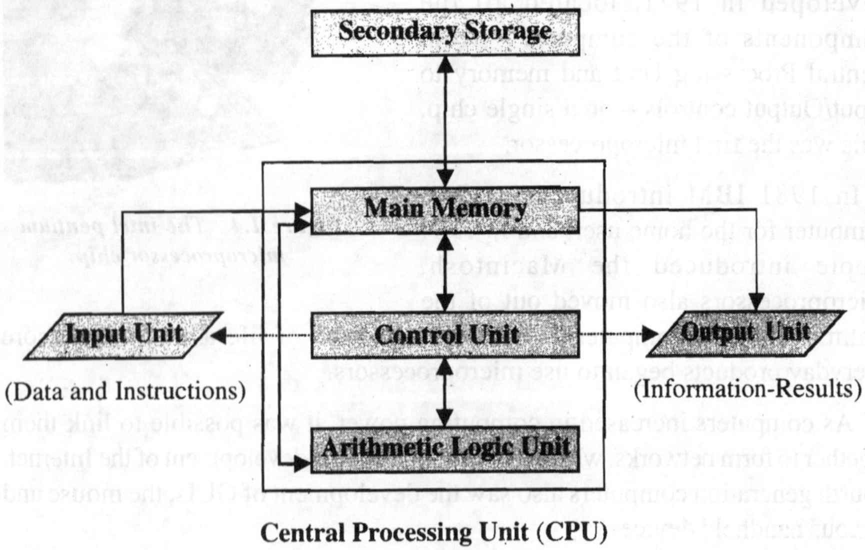

Figure 1.5 Schematic representation of a computer system

All computer systems perform the following five basic operations for converting raw data into relevant information:

1. **Inputting**: The process of entering data and instructions into the computer system.
2. **Storing**: The process of saving data and instructions so that they are available for use as and when required.
3. **Processing**: Performing arithmetic or logical operations on data, to convert them into useful information. Arithmetic operations include operations of add, subtract, multiply, divide etc., and logical operations are operations of comparison like equal to, less than, greater than, etc.
4. **Outputting**: This is the process of providing the results to the user. These could be in the form of visual display and/or printed reports.
5. **Controlling**: Refers to directing the sequence and manner in which all the above operations are performed.

Let us now familiarise ourselves with the various computer units that perform these functions:

Input Unit

Both program and data need to be in the computer system before any kind of operation can be performed. Program refers to the set of instructions which the computer is to carry out, and data is the information on which these instructions are to operate. For example, if the task is to rearrange a list of telephone subscribers in alphabetical order, the sequence of instructions that guide the computer through this operation is the program, whilst the list of names to be sorted is the data.

The process of transferring data and instructions from the external environment into the computer system, is performed by the Input Unit. Instructions and data enter the input unit depending upon the particular input device used (keyboard, scanner, card reader etc.). Regardless of the form in which the input unit receives data, it converts these instructions and data into computer acceptable form (Binary Codes). It then supplies the converted data and instructions to the computer system for further processing.

Main Memory (Primary Storage)

Data and instructions are stored in the primary storage before processing and are transferred as and when needed to the Arithmetic Logic Unit (ALU) where the actual processing takes place. Once the processing is completed, the final results are again stored in the primary storage till they are released to an output device. Also, any intermediate results generated by the ALU are temporarily transferred back to the primary storage until needed at a later time. Thus data and instructions may move many times back and forth between the primary storage and the ALU before the processing is completed.

It may be worth remembering that no processing is done in the primary storage.

Arithmetic Logic Unit (ALU)

After the input unit transfers the information into the memory unit the information can then be further transferred to the ALU where comparisons or calculations are done and results sent back to the memory unit.

Since all data and instructions are represented in numeric form (bit patterns), ALUs are designed to perform the four basic arithmetic operations: add, subtract, multiply, divide, and logic/comparison operations such as equal to, less than, greater than.

Output Unit

Since computers work with binary code, the results produced are also in binary form. The basic function of the output unit therefore is to convert these results into human readable form before providing the output through various output devices like terminals, printers etc.

Control Unit

It is the function of the control unit to ensure that according to the stored instructions, the right operation is done on the right data at the right time. It is the control unit that obtains instructions from the program stored in the main memory, interprets them, and ensures that other units of the system execute them in the desired order. In effect, the control unit is comparable to the central nervous system in the human body.

Central Processing Unit

The control unit, Arithmetic Logic Unit along with the main memory are together known as the Central Processing Unit (CPU). It is the brain of any computer system.

Secondary Storage

The storage capacity of the primary memory of the computer is limited., Often, it is necessary to store large amounts of data. So, additional memory called secondary storage or auxiliary memory is used in most computer systems.

Secondary storage is storage other than the primary storage. These are peripheral devices connected to and controlled by the computer to enable permanent storage of user data and programs. Typically, hardware devices like magnetic tapes and magnetic disks fall under this category.

THE SYSTEM CONCEPT

A computer is referred to as a 'computer system' because of the very definition of a 'system'. A system is typically referred to as a group of elements, logically related, having a common goal to achieve.

Since a computer is made up of integrated components (input/output devices, CPU, storage), working together to achieve a goal (as per the instructions to be executed), it is classified as a 'system'. Other examples of commonly known 'systems' are respiratory system and digestive system.

KEY POINTS

- Computers are characterised by speed, accuracy, diligence, versatility, storage, and intelligence.
- Mark I, ENIAC, EDVAC, UNIVAC I are some well-known early computers.
- Computers can be classified into various generations based on their technological enhancements.

First Generation	Second Generation	Third Generation	Fourth Generation	Fifth Generation
• Use of vacuum tubes • Limited storage capacity • Slow speed • Machine and assembly languages • Problems of over-heating	• Use of transistors and diodes • Increased storage capacity • Faster speed • Reduction in size and heat generation • High level programming languages (COBOL, FORTRAN)	• Use of integrated circuits (ICs) • More flexibility with input/output • Smaller in size and better performance • Extensive use of high level languages • Remote processing and time sharing	• Use of large scale and very large scale integrated circuits (LSI, VLSI) • Increased storage • Considerably faster and smaller • Modular design, versatility and compatibility • Sophisticated programs and languages for special applications • Increased use of micro - computers (PCs)	• Use of ICs with ULSI technology • Based on artificial intelligence • Larger capacity storage (RAID, Optical disks) • Support for more complex applications • Still under development

- All computer systems convert raw input data into useful information by performing the five basic operations of inputting, storing, processing, outputting, and controlling.
- The main components of the computer system (Figure 1.5) along with their functions:

Computer Element	Function
Input Unit	To receive data and instructions in a form that can be understood by the computer.
Output Unit	To present information via a suitable output device like terminal or a printer.
Storage 1. Main Memory (Primary Storage)	To hold data and instructions after input, until needed. Also to hold information awaiting output. The instructions (provided by the programmers) specify the actions to be taken on the data.
2. Secondary Storage (Auxiliary or Backing Storage)	To supplement main storage. Used to store large amounts of data or instructions permanently. Much cheaper than main storage.
Arithmetic Logic Unit (ALU)	To carry out calculations and comparisons based on the instructions.
Control Unit	To take the stored instructions in sequence, one at a time. To interpret each instruction and prompt its execution by one of the units like input, output, storage or ALU.

REVIEW QUESTIONS

1. Choose the appropriate answer:

i. Transistor-based computers are

(a) First generation (b) Second generation
(c) Fifth generation (d) Hoover generation

ii. The outstanding characteristic of computer that lets it perform large quantities of work with the same accuracy and speed is referred to as

(a) Speed (b) Accuracy
(c) Diligence (d) Versatility

iii. The output unit

(a) Converts data and instructions to machine readable form
(b) Ensures that the right operation is done on the right data at the right time
(c) Stores data and instructions till needed
(d) Represents information in human readable form

2. Match the following:

X	Y
1. First Generation computers	a. Input unit
2. Performs calculations and comparisons	b. Integrated chips
3. Interprets and ensures that instructions are carried out in the desired sequence	c. Control unit
4. Third Generation computers	d. Vacuum tubes
5. Converts data and instructions to machine readable form	e. Arithmetic logic unit

3. Fill in the blanks with the appropriate choices listed below:

(i) UNIVAC I (ii) CPU (iii) Microseconds (iv) Mark I (v) ICs

1. ____________ was the first electronic computer made in 1944.
2. ____________ was the first digital computer developed in 1951.
3. While talking about the speed of computers we talk in terms of ________.
4. The new technology used in third generation computers was ____________.
5. The Control Unit, Arithmetic Logic Unit along with the main memory is together known as the ____________.

CHAPTER 2

Data Representation

DATA REPRESENTATION WITHIN THE COMPUTER

Information is handled in the computer by electrical components such as transistors, integrated circuits, semiconductors and wires, all of which can indicate only two states or conditions. Transistors are either conducting or non-conducting; magnetic materials are either magnetised or non-magnetised in a direction; a pulse or voltage is either present or not present. All information can therefore be represented within the computer by the presence (ON) or absence (OFF) of these various signals.

Thus, all data to be stored and processed in computers are transformed or coded as strings of two symbols, one symbol to represent each state. The two symbols normally used are 0 and 1. These are known as BITS, an abbreviation for BInary digiTS.

Let us now understand some commonly used terms:

Value	*Meaning*
0	Off
1	On

BITS A bit is the smallest element used by a computer. It holds one of the two possible values.

A bit which is OFF is also considered to be FALSE or NOT SET; a bit which is ON is also considered to be TRUE or SET.

Since a single bit can only store two values, there could possibly be only 4 unique combinations namely,

00 01 10 11

Bits are therefore, combined together into larger units in order to hold greater range of values.

NIBBLE A nibble is a group of FOUR bits. This gives a maximum number of 16 possible different values.

$$2^4 = 16 \text{ (2 to the power of the number of bits)}$$

BYTES Bytes are a grouping of 8 bits (Two Nibbles) and are often used to store characters. They can also be used to store numeric values.

$$2^8 = 256 \text{ (2 to the power of the number of bits)}$$

WORD Just like we express information in words, so do computers. A computer 'word' is a group of bits, the length of which varies from machine to machine, but is normally pre-determined for each machine. The word may be as long as 64 bits or as short as 8 bits.

NUMBER SYSTEMS

A number is made of individual digits (e.g., 905 consists of the digits 9, 0 and 5). The value of each digit in a number is determined by three considerations:

(a) The digit itself;

(b) The position of the digit in the number;

(c) The base or radix of the number system (where base is defined as the number of digits which can occur in any position).

The number system that we use in our day-to-day life is called the Decimal Number System. In the decimal system, the base is equal to 10 since any position can contain one of ten digits (0 1 2 3 4 5 6 7 8 9). The system therefore has a carry factor of 10 and each digit indicates a value that depends on the position it occupies:

In 5,421	The digit 5 signifies	5 × 1000	5000	Thousands position
In 5,421	The digit 4 signifies	4 × 100	400	Hundreds position
In 5,421	The digit 2 signifies	2 × 10	20	Tens position
In 5,421	The digit 1 signifies	1 × 1	1	Units position
		Total	**5421**	

The notation used to express numbers as shown above is known as **Positional System.**

Binary Numbers

If the number system has only two symbols, then its base is 2. Such a system is known as a Binary System. Here we have only two digits 0 and 1. Therefore, the binary equivalent of the decimal number 2 has to be stated as 10 (a 0 with a one carry, read as 'one, zero'). (See Table on next page)

Numbers in this system are represented in strings of bits. For example, a binary number is shown below:

1 0 1 0 1

↓ Most significant Bit ↓ Least significant

The bit to the extreme right is called the **least significant bit** and the bit to the extreme left is the **most significant bit**. The weights assigned to bits in this system are powers of 2, namely,

$2^0 = 1$

$2^1 = 2$

$2^2 = 4$ etc.

Decimal Number	Binary Equivalent
0	0
1	1
2	10
3	11
4	100
5	101
6	110
7	111
8	1000
9	1001
10	1010

Converting binary to decimal For converting the value of binary number to its decimal equivalent, we need to find its quantity by multiplying each digit with its place value. Thus, the decimal value of the binary number 10101 is calculated as shown below:

$$\begin{array}{ccccccccccl} 1 & & 0 & & 1 & & 0 & & 1 & & \\ 1 \times 2^4 & + & 0 \times 2^3 & + & 1 \times 2^2 & + & 0 \times 2^1 & + & 1 \times 2^0 & & \\ 16 & + & 0 & + & 4 & + & 0 & + & 1 & & = 21 \text{ in decimal} \end{array}$$

Octal Numbers

An octal system has eight digits represented as 0,1,2,3,4,5,6,7.

e.g. octal number $(23)_8$

Note the subscript 8. This indicates it is an octal number. Similarly, a subscript of 2 will indicate a binary number, 10 a decimal number, and H a hexadecimal number. In case no subscript is specified, then the number is treated as a decimal number.

Converting octal to decimal The conversion is similar to the one shown for binary to decimal conversion except the place values.

Converting $(23)_8$ to its decimal equivalent,

$$\begin{array}{cccl} 2 & & 3 & \\ 2 \times 8^1 & + & 3 \times 8^0 & \\ 16 & + & 3 & = 19 \text{ in decimal} \end{array}$$

Hexadecimal Numbers

The hexadecimal system has sixteen digits which are represented as 0, 1, 2, 3, 4, 5, 6, 7, 8, 9, A, B, C, D, E, F.

e.g. hexadecimal number $(F2)_H$

Converting hexadecimal to decimal Converting $(F2)_H$ to its decimal equivalent,

$$\begin{array}{ccccl} F & & 2 & & \\ F \times 16^1 & + & 2 \times 16^0 & & \\ 240 & + & 2 & & = 242 \text{ in decimal} \end{array}$$

Note: F is equivalent of 15 in decimal.

Conversion of decimal number to binary number As mentioned above, external to the computer we use decimal numbers whereas internally we use binary representation. We thus need to convert decimal to binary. The method of converting a decimal integer to its binary equivalent is based on the fact that any decimal integer can be expressed as a sum of powers of 2 as shown below:

$$(23)_{10} = (1 \times 2^4) + (0 \times 2^3) + (1 \times 2^2) + (1 \times 2^1) + (1 \times 2^0)$$
$$= (10111)_2$$

The easiest method to find the coefficients of the powers of two is to divide the given number by 2. Division is stopped when the quotient becomes zero.

Example: The binary equivalent of $(23)_{10}$

Divisor	Quotient	Remainder	
2	23		
2	11	1	⟶ Least significant bit
2	5	1	
2	2	1	
2	1	0	
	0	1	⟶ Most significant bit

The binary equivalent of the decimal number is determined by the sequence of remainders obtained during division. The least significant bit of the binary number is the first remainder obtained and most significant bit is the last remainder.

The binary equivalent of the above number (23) is thus: $(10111)_2$

Decimal to hexadecimal conversion is similar except 16 is used as the divisor instead of 2.

Example: The hexadecimal equivalent of $(23)_{10}$

16	23		
16	1	7	→ Least significant bit
	0	1	→ Most significant bit

The hexadecimal equivalent of the above number (23) is thus : $(17)_{16}$

Converting from One Number System to Another

Since we use decimal numbers in our everyday lives, numbers expressed in decimals are much more meaningful than values expressed in any other numbering system. Because the input and final outputs are to be in decimal, computer professionals are required to convert numbers from other number systems to decimal and vice versa.

Converting to decimal from another base As has been explained in the earlier sections, converting a number from any other base to decimal requires the following three steps:

1. Determine the place value for each digit i.e. the position of the digit depending on the base of the number system.
2. Multiply the obtained place values by the digits in the corresponding columns.
3. Sum the products calculated in step 2. This will give the resultant value in decimal.

Example: The decimal equivalent of $(1010)_2$

Step 1: Determine the position values (Note there are 4 digits in the number)

2^3	2^2	2^1	2^0
= 8	= 4	= 2	= 1

Step 2: Multiplying the obtained place values by digits in the corresponding columns

8	4	2	1
× 1	× 0	× 1	× 0
8	0	2	0

Step 3: Sum the products (as calculated in step 2)

$$8 + 0 + 2 + 0 = 10$$

Hence, $1010_2 = 10_{10}$

Converting from decimal to a new base (Remainder technique) Converting a decimal number to another base can be done using the remainder technique. This has been explained using the following four steps:

1. Divide the quotient of the number to be converted with the value of the new base.
2. Separate the remainder got from step 1.
3. Repeat steps 1 and 2 till we get 0 as the quotient.

   Note: the first remainder is the least significant bit while the last remainder is the most significant bit.
4. The number to the new base is achieved by writing the remainder values from the most significant bit to the least significant bit (i.e. Remainders in the reverse order)

Example: The hexadecimal equivalent of $(428)_{10}$

			Remainder	
Step 1:	16	428		
Step 2:	16	26	12 = C	→ Least significant bit ↑
Step 3:	16	1	10 = A	
		0	1 = 1	→ Most significant bit

Step 4: 1AC

Hence, $428_{10} = 1AC_{16}$

Converting of binary to octal and hexadecimal The conversion of binary to octal or hexadecimal is fairly straightforward.

For converting binary to octal:

1. The binary number is divided into groups of **three** (starting from the right).

2. Each of these groups is then combined by place value to generate the equivalent octal.

Example: Converting 110101_{12} to its octal equivalent

	1	101	011
can also be written as	001	101	011

Note: The number has not changed, we have just added zeroes to complete the grouping.

Then
$$011 = 0 \times 2^2 + 1 \times 2^1 + 1 \times 2^0 = 0 + 2 + 1 = 3$$
$$101 = 1 \times 2^2 + 0 \times 2^1 + 1 \times 2^0 = 4 + 0 + 1 = 5$$
$$001 = 0 \times 2^2 + 0 \times 2^1 + 1 \times 2^0 = 0 + 0 + 1 = 1$$

Hence, $1101011_2 = 153_8$

For converting binary to hexadecimal:

1. The binary number is divided into groups of **four** (starting from the right).
2. Each of these groups is then combined by place value to generate the equivalent hexadecimal digit.

Example: Converting 1101011_2 to its hexadecimal equivalent

	110	1011
can also be written as	0110	1011

Note : Once again zeroes have been added to complete the grouping.

Then $1011 = 1 \times 2^3 + 0 \times 2^2 + 1 \times 2^1 + 1 \times 2^0$

$= 8 + 0 + 2 + 1 = 11$ or B

$0110 = 0 \times 2^3 + 1 \times 2^2 + 1 \times 2^1 + 0 \times 2^0$

$= 0 + 4 + 2 + 0 = 6$

Hence, $1101011_2 = 6B_H$

CHARACTER REPRESENTATION

Binary data is not the only data handled by the computer. We also need to process alphanumeric data like alphabets (upper and lower case), digits (0 to 9) and special characters like + – * / ( ) space or blank etc. These also must be internally represented as bits.

BCD

Binary Coded Decimal (or BCD) is one of the early memory codes. It is based on the concept of converting each digit of a decimal number into its binary equivalent rather than converting the entire decimal value into a pure binary form. It further uses 4 digits to represent each of the digits. The table below shows the BCD equivalent of the decimal digits.

Decimal Number	Binary Equivalent
0	0000
1	0001
2	0010
3	0011
4	0100
5	0101
6	0110
7	0111
8	1000
9	1001

Converting 42_{10} into its BCD equivalent, would result in:

$$42_{10} = \frac{0100}{4} \quad \frac{0010}{2} \quad \text{or} \quad 01000010 \text{ in BCD}$$

As seen, 4-bit BCD code can be used to represent decimal numbers only. Since 4 bits are insufficient to represent the various other characters used by the computer, instead of using only 4-bits (giving 16 possible combinations), computer designers commonly use 6 bits to represent characters in BCD code. In this the 4 BCD numeric place positions are retained, but two additional zone positions are added. With 6 bits it is possible to represent 2^6 or 64 different characters. This is therefore sufficient to represent the decimal digits (10), alphabetic characters (26), and special characters (28).

EBCDIC

The major drawback with the BCD code is that allows only 64 different characters to be represented. This is not sufficient to provide for decimal numbers (10), lowercase letters (26), uppercase letters (26), and a fairly large number of special characters (28 plus).

The BCD code was therefore extended from a 6-bit to an 8-bit code. The added 2 bits are used as additional zone bits, expanding the zone bits to 4. This resulting code is called the Extended Binary-Coded Decimal Interchange Code (EBCDIC). Using the EBCDIC it is possible to represent 2^8 or 256 characters. This takes care of the character requirement along with a large quantity of printable and several non-printable control characters (movement of the cursor on the screen, vertical spacing on printer etc.).

Since EBCDIC is an 8-bit code, it can easily be divided into two 4-bit groups. Each of these groups can be represented by one hexadecimal digit (explained earlier in this chapter). Thus, hexadecimal number system is used as a notation for memory dump by computers that use EBCDIC for internal representation of characters.

Developed by IBM, EBCDIC code is used in most IBM models and many other computers.

ASCII

A computer code that is very widely used for data interchange is called the 'American Standard Code for Information Interchange' or ASCII. Several computer manufacturers have adopted it as their computers' internal code. This code uses 7 digits to represent 128 characters. Now an advanced ASCII is used having 8-bit character representation code allowing for 256 different characters. This representation is being used in Micro Computers.

Let us look at the encoding method. The table below shows the bit combinations required for each character.

	00	01	02	03	04	05	06	07	08	09	0A	0B	0C	0D	0E	0F
00	NUL	SOH	STX	ETX	EOT	ENQ	ACK	BEL	BS	TAB	LF	VT	FF	CR	SO	SI
10	DLE	DC1	DC2	DC3	DC4	NAK	SYN	ETB	CAN	EM	SUB	ESC	FS	GS	RS	US
20		!	"	#	$	%	&	'	(	)	*	+	,	-	.	/
30	0	1	2	3	4	5	6	7	8	9	:	;	<	=	>	?
40	@	A	B	C	D	E	F	G	H	I	J	K	L	M	N	O
50	P	Q	R	S	T	U	V	W	X	Y	Z	[	\	]	^	_
60	`	a	b	c	d	e	f	g	h	i	j	k	l	m	n	o
70	p	q	r	s	t	u	v	w	x	y	z	{	|	}	~	DEL

Thus, to code a text string 'Hello.' in ASCII using hexadecimal digits:

H	e	l	l	o	.
48	65	6C	6C	6F	2E

The string is represented by the byte sequence 48 65 6C 6C 6F 2E.

Error-detecting Codes

Errors may occur while recording data on magnetic surfaces due to bad spots on the surface. They may also be introduced during data transmission between units, due to electrical disturbances. Most of these errors result in change of a bit from 0 to 1 or 1 to 0. One of the simplest and most commonly used error detection code is called the **Parity bit.**

A parity bit is an extra bit added to the binary data such that it makes the total number of 1's in the data either odd or even. In case of **Even parity,** a bit is added to each character in such a way that the total number of 1s in each character code is even. Similarly, in case of **Odd parity,** the bit added to each character makes the number of 1s in the character code odd.

For example, in a 7-bit data 0110101 let us add the eighth bit, which is a parity bit. In case of even parity, the added bit, should be 0 since there are already four 1s in the given 7-bit number. While in case of odd parity, the added bit would be a 1 making the total number of 1's odd (5 in number).

All characters would then have 8-bits including the parity check bit. Whenever a character is read from storage or received from a remote location, the number of bits in its code is counted. It has to be even (in case of even parity). If it is odd, then at least one bit is wrong. A single error in any eight bits of the code will definitely be detected. However, two errors cannot be detected by this scheme, as the total number of 1s will remain even after two bits change. The probability of more than one error occurring at a time is usually very small that is why this scheme is commonly accepted as adequate.

Codes have also been devised which use more than one check bit in order to not only detect but also correct errors. These are called **error-correcting codes**. We will not be discussing these codes in this book.

KEY POINTS

- All code or data is stored and processed in computers using two symbols 0 and 1. These are called 'binary digits' or 'bits'.
- The number of unique strings possible in a code with 2 bits is 4 (00, 01, 10, 11). In general the number of unique strings possible with n bits in each string is 2^n.
- A nibble is a group of four bits having a maximum of 16 possible different values (2^4).
- A byte is a group of eight bits and is often used to store characters.
- A Word is a group of bits, the length of which varies from machine to machine. It may be as long as 64 bits or as short as 8 bits.
- Binary numbers are determined using the positional notation. Powers of 2 are used as weights in the binary number system. A binary number 10011, for example, has a decimal value of ($1\times2^4 + 0\times2^3 + 0\times2^2 + 1\times2^1 + 1\times2^0 = 19$).
- Conversion of a decimal number into its binary equivalent is done by dividing the number by 2 and storing the remainder. This process is repeated with the quotient, till the quotient becomes 0. For example, the binary equivalent of the decimal number 9 is 1001.
- High-valued binary numbers require long sequences of 0s and 1s. A more concise representation is obtained using the hexadecimal notation. This has a base of 16 and uses the symbols 0, 1, 2, 3, 4, 5, 6, 7, 8, 9, A, B, C, D, E, F for data representation.
- The American Standards Institution has evolved a standard code to represent characters by computers. This code is called ASCII and uses 7 bits to represent each character. ASCII defines codes for English Alphabets (uppercase and lowercase), decimal digits (0 - 9), 32 special characters, and a number of control characters.
- Errors may occur while recording and reading data and when data is transmitted from one unit to another, in a computer. For detection of errors, a parity bit is usually added to the character string. If the bit is chosen such that the total number of 1s in the new code is even, it is termed as even parity. While, if the bit chosen is such that the total number of 1s in the new code is odd, it is termed as odd parity.

REVIEW QUESTIONS

1. Choose the appropriate answer:

i. The binary equivalent of the decimal number 892 is

(a) 1001111100 (b) 1101101100
(c) 1101111100 (d) 1101100010

ii. The decimal equivalent of binary 11111 is

(a) 65 (b) 63
(c) 36 (d) 56

iii. Which of the following is not a coding scheme

(a) BCD (b) EBCDIC
(c) ASCIC (d) ASCII

iv. Binary number 01111100110111100011 in hexadecimal would be represented as

(a) 7CDE3 (b) 6CDE3
(c) 7BCD3 (d) 7CDF3

v. Even parity means adding a parity check bit so that

(a) The number of 0s in the new code are even
(b) The number of 1s in the new code are odd
(c) The number of 1s in the new code are even
(d) The number of 0s in the new code are odd

2. State whether True or False:

i. The decimal equivalent of the binary number 110 is 7.
ii. In the octal number system, the symbols used are 0,1,2,3,4,5,6,7.
iii. 'American Standard Computer for Information Interchange' is the full form of ASCII.
iv. 10000111000 is the binary equivalent of the decimal number 1000.

3. Match the following:

X		Y
1. The smallest element of information used by a computer	a.	Octal system
2. A group of 8 bits	b.	Nibble
3. Base 16	c.	Hexadecimal system
4. A group of 4 bits	d.	Bit
5. Base 8	e.	Byte

4. Fill in the blanks with the appropriate choices listed below:

(i) 15 (ii) Parity (iii) IBM (iv) 0 or 1 (v) ASCII

1. A bit holds one of the two possible values ____________.
2. The decimal equivalent of the binary number 1111 is ____________.
3. ____________ uses 7 bits to represent each character.
4. The bit used for error detection is called the ____________ bit.
5. The Extended Binary Coded Decimal Interchange Code is used in computers manufactured by ____________.

CHAPTER 3

The Central Processing Unit

Execution of programs is the main function of the computer. The program to be executed is a set of instructions that are stored in the computer's memory. The central processing unit (CPU) executes the instructions of the program to complete a task. Also, all the major calculations and comparisons are carried out inside the CPU. Additionally, the CPU is responsible for activating and controlling the operations of various units of the computer system. It activates the peripherals to perform input or output.

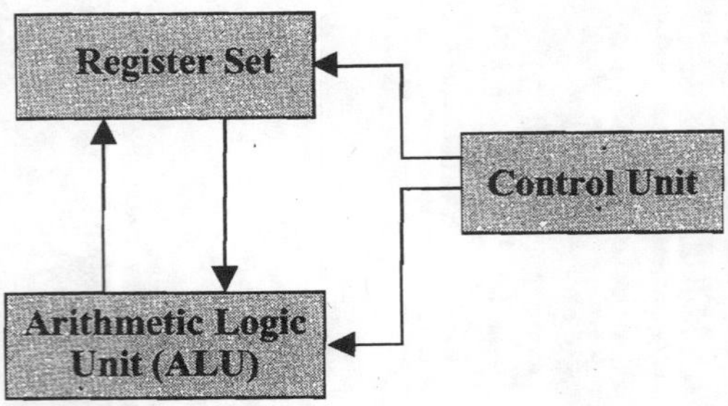

Figure 3.1 Major components of CPU

The CPU is made up of three major components (as seen in Figure 3.1): the register set (associated with the main memory) that stores the intermediate data during the execution of instructions, the arithmetic logic unit (ALU) which performs the required micro-operations for executing the instructions, and the control unit that supervises the transfer of information among the registers and instructs the ALU as to which operation to perform.

CONTROL UNIT

The Control Unit plays an important role for the functioning of the CPU itself and transfer of data/information from a device to the CPU or vice versa. It does not perform the actual processing on the data but manages and coordinates the entire computer system including the input and the output devices. It retrieves and interprets the instructions from the program stored in the main memory, and issues signals that cause other units of the system to execute them.

It does this through some special purpose registers and a decoder. The special purpose register called the **Instruction register** holds the current instruction to be executed, and the **Program control register** holds the next instruction to be executed. The decoder interprets the meaning of each instruction supported by the CPU. Each instruction is also accompanied by a **Microcode,** i.e., the basic directions to tell the CPU how to execute the instruction.

ARITHMETIC LOGIC UNIT (ALU)

The ALU provides arithmetic and logic operations. This means that when the control unit encounters an instruction that involves an arithmetic operation (add, subtract, multiply, divide) or a logic operation (equal to, less than, greater than), it passes control to the ALU. The ALU has the necessary circuitry to carry out these arithmetic and logic operations.

As an example, a comparison of two numbers (a logical operation) may require the control unit to load the two numbers in the requisite registers and then pass on the execution of the 'compare' function to the ALU.

The figure below represents the basic structure of a CPU.

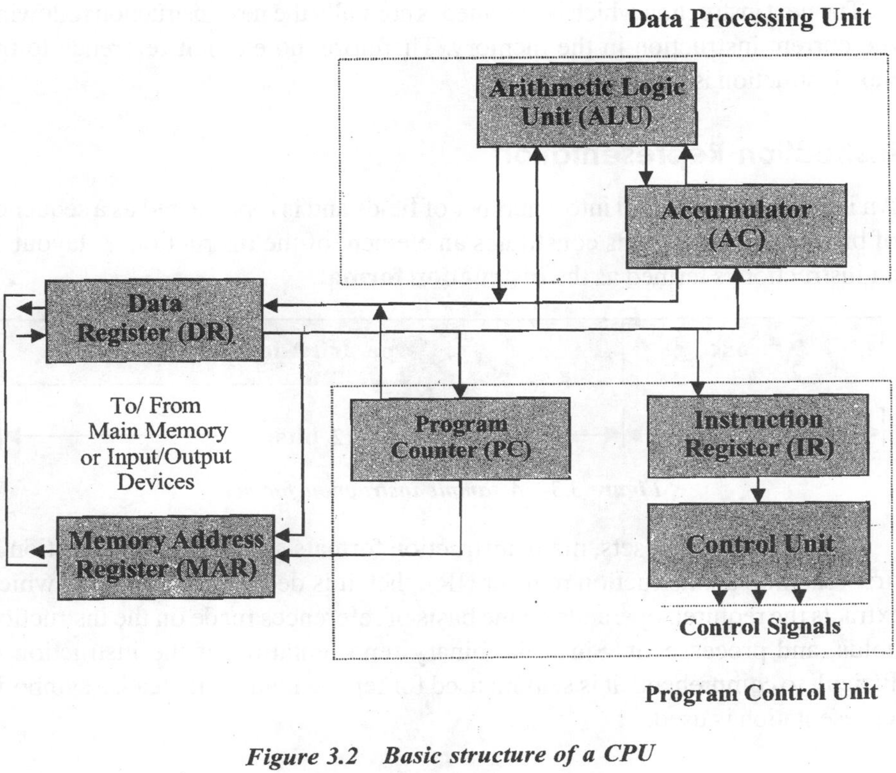

Figure 3.2 Basic structure of a CPU

INSTRUCTION SET

The primary function of the processing unit in the computer is to interpret the instructions given in a program and carry out the instructions. Processors are designed to interpret a specified number of instruction codes. Each instruction code is a string of binary digits. All processors have input/output instructions, arithmetic instructions, logic instructions, branch instructions and instructions to manipulate characters. The number and type of instructions differ from processor to processor. The list of specific instructions supported by the CPU is termed as its **Instruction set.**

An instruction in the computer should specify the following:

- The task or operation to be carried out by the processor. This is termed as the **opcode.**
- The address(s) in memory of the operand(s) on which the data processing is to be performed.
- The address in the memory that may store the results of data processing operation performed by the instruction.
- The address in the memory for the next instruction, to be fetched and executed.

The next instruction which is executed is normally the next instruction following the current instruction in the memory. Therefore, no explicit reference to the next instruction is provided.

Instruction Representation

An instruction is divided into a number of fields and is represented as a sequence of bits. Each of the fields constitutes an element of the instruction. A layout of an instruction is termed as the **instruction format.**

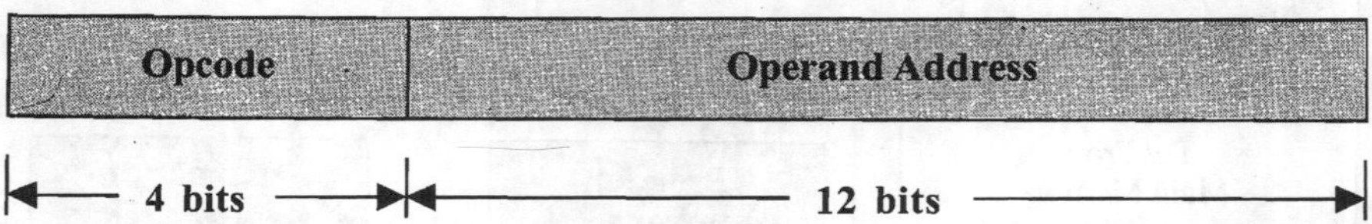

Figure 3.3 A sample instruction format

In most instruction sets, many instruction formats are used. An instruction is first read into an instruction register (IR), then it is decoded by the CPU which extracts the required operands on the basis of references made on the instruction fields, and processes it. Since the binary representation of the instruction is difficult to comprehend, it is seldom used for representation. Instead, a symbolic representation is used.

Examples of typical instructions:

Instruction	Interpretation	Number of Addresses
ADD A,B,C	Operation A = B + C is executed	3
ADD A,B	A = A + B. In this case the original content of operand location is lost	2
ADD A	AC = AC + A. Here A is added to the accumulator	1

Typically, CPUs manufactured by different manufacturers have different instruction sets. This is why machine language programs developed for a particular CPU do not run on a computer with a different CPU (having a different instruction set).

Registers

The basic task performed by the CPU is instruction execution. Each instruction is executed using several small operations called micro-operations. Therefore, the basic issues relating to a CPU can be expressed as:

- it should be as fast as possible.
- the capacity of the main memory needed by the CPU is very large.

To understand further, let us define two relevant terms:

Cycle time of the CPU: time taken by the CPU to execute a well-defined shortest micro-operation, and

Memory cycle time: speed at which the memory can be accessed by the CPU.

It has been found that the memory cycle time is approximately 1–10 times higher than the CPU cycle time. That is why temporary storage is provided within the CPU in the form of CPU registers. The CPU registers are termed as fast memory and can be accessed almost instantaneously.

Further, the number of bits a register can store at a time is called the length of the register. Most CPUs sold today have 32-bit or 64-bit registers. The size of the register is also called the word size and indicates the amount of data that a CPU can process at a time. Thus, the bigger the word size, the faster the computer can process data.

The number of registers varies among computers, but typical registers found in most computers are:

Memory Address Register (MAR): specifies the address of memory location from which data is to be accessed (in case of read operation) or to which data is to be stored (in case of write operation).

Memory Buffer Register (MBR): receives data from the memory (in case of read operation) or contains the data to be written in the memory (in case of write operation).

Program Counter (PC): keeps track of the instruction that is to be executed next, after the execution of the current instruction.

Accumulator (AC): interacts with the ALU and stores the input or output operand. This register, therefore, holds the initial data to be operated upon, the intermediate results and final results of processing operations.

Instruction Register (IR): instructions are loaded in the IR before their execution, i.e., the instruction register holds the current instruction that is being executed.

The simplest form of instruction processing can be defined as a two-step process:

1. The CPU reads (fetches) instructions (codes) from the memory one at a time.
2. It executes or performs the operation specified by this instruction.

The fetching of the instruction is done using the program counter (PC) that keeps track of the next instruction to be fetched. Normally, next instruction in sequence is fetched, as programs are executed in sequence. The fetched instruction is in the form of binary code and is loaded into an instruction register (IR), in the CPU. The CPU then interprets the instruction and performs the required action. In general, these actions can be divided into the following categories:

- *Data transfer* from CPU to memory or memory to CPU or from CPU to I/O or I/O to CPU.
- *Data processing* an arithmetic or logic operation may be performed on the data by the CPU.
- *Sequence control* this action is typically required for altering the sequence of execution. For example, if an instruction from location 50 specifies that the next instruction to be fetched should be from location 100, then the program counter will need to be modified to contain the location 100 (which otherwise would have contained 51).

Execution of an instruction may involve any combination of these actions.

Processor Speed

The term processor has replaced the term central processing unit (CPU). The processor in a personal computer or embedded in small devices is often called a **Microprocessor.**

The speed at which the processor executes commands is called the processor speed or **clock speed.** Every computer contains an internal clock (known as the system clock) that regulates the rate at which the instructions are executed and synchronises the various computer components. The processor requires fixed number of clock cycles (electric pulses per second) to execute each instruction. Clock cycles are required to fetch, decode, and execute a single program instruction. Thus, the shorter the clock cycle, the faster the processor.

In a computer, clock speed, therefore refers to the number of pulses per second generated by an oscillator that sets the tempo for the processor. It is usually measured in MHz (**Megahertz** - Million of pulses per second) or GHz (**Gigahertz** - Billions of pulses per second).

Computer clock speed has been roughly doubling every year. The Intel 8088, common in computers around the year 1990, ran at 4.77 MHz. Today's personal computers run at clock speeds of a 100–1000 MHz and some even exceed one gigahertz.

Although the processing speed in personal computers is measured in terms of megahertz, the processing speed of mini computers and mainframe systems is measured in terms of MIPS (millions of instructions per second) or BIPS (billions of instructions per second). This is because personal computers generally employ a single microprocessor chip as their CPU while other classes of computers employ multiple processors to speed up their overall performance. Thus a minicomputer having a speed of 500 MIPS is capable of executing 500 million instructions per second.

Clock speed is a measure of computer 'power,' but it is not always directly proportional to the performance level. If you double the speed of the clock, leaving all other hardware unchanged, you will not necessarily double the processing speed. The type of microprocessor, the bus architecture, and the nature of the instruction set all make a difference. In some applications the amount of random access memory (RAM) is important too.

CISC vs RISC

The term 'CISC' (complex instruction set computer or computing) refers to computers designed with a full set of computer instructions that were intended to provide needed capabilities in the most efficient way. Later, it was discovered that by reducing the full set to only the most frequently used instructions, the computer could get more work done in a shorter amount of time for most applications. Since this was called reduced instruction set computing (RISC), there was now a need for a name for full set instruction computers, hence the term CISC.

RISC (reduced instruction set computer or computing) is a microprocessor designed to perform a smaller number of types of computer instructions so that it can operate at higher speed. Since each instruction type that a computer must perform requires additional transistors and circuitry, a larger list would mean the microprocessor being more complicated and slower in operation.

John Cocke of IBM Research in Yorktown, New York, originated the RISC concept in 1974 when he stated that about 20% of the instructions in a computer perform 80% of the work.

While a number of microchips today use the RISC concept – typically found in Sun Microsystems SPARC microprocessors and other medium-sized computers like IBM RS/6000 – Intel's Pentium microprocessors are CISC microprocessors.

KEY POINTS

- The CPU executes the instructions of a program to complete a task. The main components of the CPU are the control unit and the arithmetic logic unit.
- The Control Unit performs the function of transferring data/information from a device to the CPU or vice versa. It obtains instructions from the program stored in the main memory, interprets the instructions and issues signals so that other units of the system can execute them.
- The Arithmetic Logic Unit is the place where arithmetic operations (add, subtract, multiply, divide) or logic operations (equal to, less than, greater than) are performed.
- Each CPU has the built-in ability to execute a particular set of machine instructions called the 'Instruction set'.
- Each instruction is executed using several small operations called micro- operations. During the execution process, information flows between the various units in the computer system. In order to handle this process satisfactorily, as well as speed up the rate of transfer, the computer uses special memory units called registers. These hold information temporarily and are a part of the CPU.
- Registers are high-speed memory and can be accessed almost instantaneously.
- Processor speed is determined by the clock speed, which is the number of pulses generated in a second by an in-built electronic clock, and is measured in Megahertz (MHz) or Gigahertz (GHz).
- The processor speed in case of mini computers and mainframes is measured in terms of MIPS (millions of instructions per second) or BIPS (billions of instructions per second).

- The typical registers found in most of the computers include:

Register Name	Function
Memory Address Register (MAR)	Holds the address of the memory location from where data is to be retrieved or to which data is to be stored
Memory Buffer Register (MBR)	Holds information on its way to and from memory
Program Counter (PC)	Holds the address of the next instruction to be executed
Accumulator (AC)	Accumulates the results and data to be operated upon
Instruction Register (IR)	Holds the current instruction

- CISC (Complex instruction set computer or computing) defines computers designed with a full set of computer instructions that were intended to provide needed capabilities in the most efficient way. Intel's microprocessors are CISC units.
- RISC (Reduced instruction set computer or computing) is a microprocessor designed to perform smaller number of types of instructions so that it can operate at higher speed. Sun SPARC microprocessors, IBM RS/6000 are typical RISC machines.

REVIEW QUESTIONS

1. Choose the appropriate answer:

i. The Control Unit

(a) Performs the arithmetic operations
(b) Manages and coordinates the entire computer system
(c) Executes the logic operations
(d) Performs the actual processing on the data

ii. The Memory Address Register

(a) Specifies the address of the memory from which data is to be accessed
(b) Is the register that receives data from the memory
(c) Specifies the address of the memory to which data is to be stored
(d) Both a and c

iii. Which of the following is not a commonly known register?

(a) MBR (b) AU
(c) PC (d) IR

iv. RISC computers were designed to:

(a) Perform smaller number of types of computer instructions
(b) Operate at higher speed
(c) Have a simpler CPU design
(d) All of the above

2. State whether True or False:

i. Each instruction is executed using several small operations called micro-operations.

ii. Clock speed is the speed at which the processor executes the commands.

iii. Registers are a part of the main memory.

iv. Sequence control is the action required to alter the sequence of execution.

3. Match the following:

X		Y
1. Millions of pulses per second	a.	PC
2. Millions of instructions per second	b.	CISC
3. Complex instruction set computing	c.	MIPS
4. Keeps track of which instruction is to be executed next	d.	IR
5. Holds the current instruction being executed	e.	MHz

4. Fill in the blanks with the appropriate choices listed below:

(i) Registers (ii) Cycle time of CPU (iii) Instruction set (iv) Accumulator (v) Memory cycle time

1. The list of specific instructions supported by a CPU is called its __________.

2. The CPU ______________ are termed as fast memory.

3. The time taken by the CPU to execute the shortest micro-operation is ____________.

4. ________________ is the speed at which memory can be accessed by the CPU.

5. ________________ accumulates the results and the data to be operated upon.

CHAPTER 4 Memory Organisation

Memory in the computer system is required for storage and subsequent retrieval of instructions and data. We saw in the earlier chapter that the CPU contains several registers for storing data and instructions. But these can store only few bytes. If all the instructions and data being executed by the CPU would reside in Secondary storage (like magnetic tapes and disks), and loaded into the registers of the CPU as the program execution proceeded, it would lead to CPU being idle for most of the time since the speed at which the CPU processes data is much higher than the speed at which data can be transferred from disks to registers. Every computer thus requires storage space where instructions and data of a program can reside temporarily when the program is being executed. This temporary storage area is built into the computer hardware and is known as the primary storage or main memory. Devices that provide backup storage (like magnetic tapes and disks) are called secondary storage or auxiliary memory.

Thus, a memory system can be considered to consist of three groups of memories:

(a) ***Internal processor memory*** consists of a small set of high-speed registers that are internal to a processor and are used as temporary locations where actual processing is done.

(b) ***Primary storage or main memory*** is a large memory, which is fast, but not as fast as internal processor memory. This memory communicates directly with the CPU and is mainly based on integrated circuits.

(c) ***Secondary storage or auxiliary memory or backing store*** is much larger in size than the main memory but is slower than the main memory. It typically stores all the system programs and other software.

Another kind of memory that is increasingly being used in modern computers is called the cache memory. It is logically positioned between the internal memory (registers) and the main memory. It stores and caches some of the content of the main memory that is currently in use by the processor.

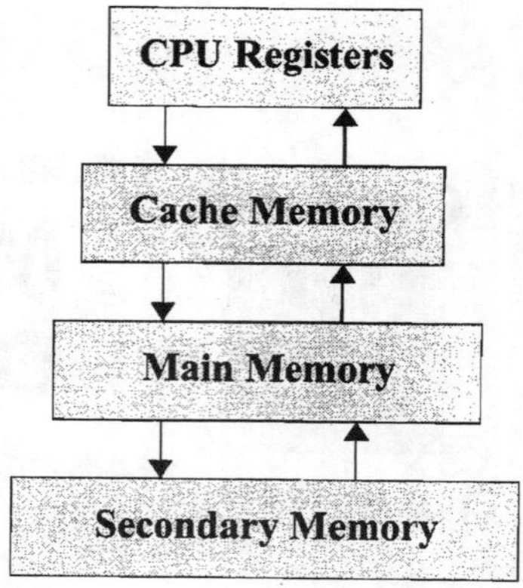

Figure 4.1 The memory hierarchy

The total memory capacity of the computer can therefore be visualised as being a hierarchy of components consisting of all storage devices employed in a computer system from the slow but high-capacity auxiliary memory to a relatively faster main memory, to an even smaller and faster cache memory accessible to the high-speed processing logic. Thus, as one goes down in the hierarchy, the following conditions occur:

1. decreasing cost per bit
2. increasing capacity
3. increasing access time
4. decreasing frequency of access of the memory by the processor

STORAGE EVALUATION CRITERIA

The most common properties used for characterising and evaluating the storage unit of the computer system are expressed below:

1. ***Storage capacity:*** Represents the size of the memory. It is the amount of data that can be stored in the storage unit. Primary storage units have less storage capacity as compared to secondary storage units. While the capacity of internal memory and main memory can be expressed in terms of number of words or bytes, the capacity of external or secondary storage is measured in terms of bytes.
2. ***Storage cost:*** Another key factor that is of prime concern in a memory system is cost. It is normally expressed per bit. It is obvious that lower costs are desirable. It is worth noting that as the access time for memories is increasing, the cost is decreasing.
3. ***Access time:*** The time required to locate and retrieve the data from the storage unit. It is dependant on the physical characteristics and access mode used for that device.

   Primary storage units have faster access time as compared to secondary storage units.
4. ***Access mode:*** Memory is considered to be consisting of various memory locations. Access mode refers to the mode in which information is accessed

from the memory. Memory devices can be accessed in any of the following ways:

(a) *Random access memory (RAM):* It is the mode in which any memory location can be accessed in any order in the same amount of time. Ferrite and semiconductor memories, which generally constitute the primary storage or main memory, are of this nature.

(b) *Sequential access:* Memories that can be accessed only in a pre-defined sequence are sequential access memories. Here since sequencing through other locations precedes the arrival at a desired location, the access time varies according to the location. Information on a sequential device can be retrieved in the same sequence in which it was stored. Songs stored on a cassette, that can be accessed only one by one, is an example of sequential access. Typically, magnetic tapes are sequential access memory.

(c) *Direct access:* In certain cases the information is neither accessed randomly nor in sequence but something in between. In this kind of access, a separate read/write head exists for each track, and on a track the information can be accessed serially. This semi-random mode of access exists in magnetic disks.

5. ***Permanence of storage:*** If the storage unit can retain the data even after the power is turned off or interrupted, it is termed as non-volatile storage. While, if the data is lost once the power is turned off or interrupted, it is called Volatile storage. It is obvious from these properties that the primary storage units of the computer systems are volatile, while the secondary storage units are non-volatile. A non-volatile storage is definitely more desirable and feasible for storage of large volumes of data.

Memory Capacity

Capacity, in a computer system, is defined in terms of the number of bytes that it can store in its main memory. This is usually stated in terms of kilobytes (kB) which is 1024 bytes or Megabytes (MB) which is equal to 1024 KB (10,48,576 bytes). The rapidly increasing memory capacity of computer systems has resulted in defining the capacity in terms of Gigabytes (GB) which is 1024 MB (1,07,37,41,824 bytes).

Thus a computer system having a memory of 256 MB is capable of storing (256 × 1024 × 1024) 26,84,35,456 bytes or characters.

MAIN MEMORY

Static and Dynamic RAM

The main memory is the central storage unit in a computer system. It is a relatively large and fast memory and is used to store programs and data during computer operations. The principal technology used for the main memory is based on semiconductor integrated circuits. Integrated circuit RAM chips are available in two possible modes, static and dynamic.

The static RAM (SRAM) stores binary information using clocked sequential circuits. The stored information remains valid only as long as power is applied to the unit. On the other hand, dynamic RAM (DRAM) stores binary information in the form of electric charges that are applied to capacitors inside the chip. The stored charge on the capacitors tends to discharge with time and so must be periodically recharged by refreshing the dynamic memory. The dynamic RAM offers larger storage capacity and reduced power consumption. Therefore, large memories use dynamic RAM, while static RAM is mainly used for specialised applications.

The different types of memory discussed above are both of the read/write type. What about a memory where only one of the operations is possible, e.g., if we allow only reading from the memory (cannot change the information in the memory)? The memory might have some major importance, like an important bit of the computer's operating system which normally does not change, can be stored in this kind of memory. Such a memory is called ROM (Read Only Memory).

Read-Only Memory (ROM)

Most of the memory in a general-purpose computer is made of RAM integrated circuit chips, but a portion of the memory may be constructed using ROM chips. Originally, RAM was used to refer to random-access memory, but now we use the term read/write memory to distinguish it from read-only memory (since ROM is also random access). RAM is used for storing bulk of the programs and data that are subject to change, while ROM is used to store programs that are permanently resident in the computer and do not change once the production of the computer is completed.

Among other things, the ROM portion of the main memory is used for storing an initial program called the bootstrap loader. The bootstrap loader is a program whose function is to start the computer software operating when power is turned on. Since RAM is volatile, its contents are destroyed when power is turned off. The contents of ROM remain unchanged even after the power is turned off and on again.

Read-only memories can be manufacturer-programmed or user-programmed. When the data is burnt into the circuitry of the computer by the manufacturer, it is called manufacturer-programmed ROM. For example, a personal computer manufacturer may store the boot program permanently in the ROM chip of the computers manufactured by it. Note that such chips are supplied by the manufacturer and are not modifiable by users. This is an inflexible process and requires mass production. Therefore, a new kind of

ROM called PROM (Programmable Read-only Memory) was designed. This is also non-volatile in nature and can be written only once using some special equipment. The writing process in PROM can be performed electrically by the supplier or the customer.

In both ROM and PROM, the write operation can be performed only once and whatever is written cannot be changed. But what about the cases where you mostly read but also write a few times? Another type of memory chip called EPROM (Erasable Programmable Read-only Memory) was developed to take care of such situations. EPROMs are typically used by R&D personnel who experiment by changing micro-programs on the computer system to test their efficiency.

Further, EPROM chips are of two types: EEPROMs (Electrically EPROM) in which high voltage electric pulses are used to erase stored information, and UVEPROM (Ultra Violet EPROM) in which stored information is erased by exposing the chip for some time to ultraviolet light.

The figure below summarises the various types of Random Access Memories.

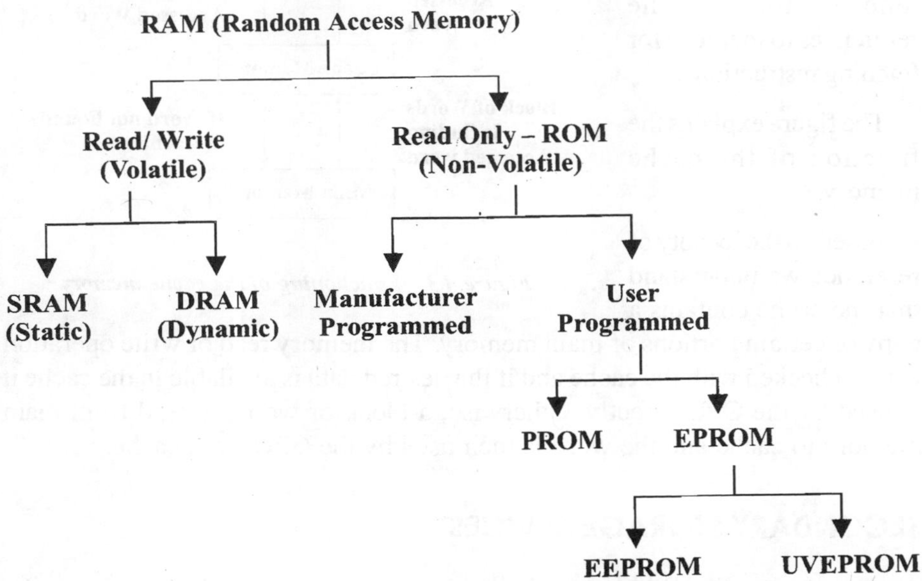

Figure 4.2 Types of random access memories

Cache Memory

Cache memories are small, fast memories placed between the CPU and the main memory. They are faster than the main memory with access times closer to the speed of the CPU. Although caches are fast, they are also very expensive and so are used only in small quantities. For example, caches of size 64K, 128K are normally used in PC-386 and PC-486, where can have 1 to 8 MB of RAM or even more. Cache memories are therefore intended to provide *fast speed* memory retrieval without sacrificing the size of the memory.

If the memory is so small, how can it be advantageous in increasing the overall speed of memory? The answer to this lies in the phenomenon known as locality of reference. Let us examine what this means.

Locality of reference Analysis of a large number of typical programs has shown that memory references at any given interval of time tend to be confined to a few localised areas in the memory. This phenomenon is known as the property of locality of reference. This is true because most of the programs typically contain iterative loops (like 'for' or 'while' loops). During the execution of such programs, the same set of instructions (within the loop) are executed many times. The CPU repeatedly refers to the set of instructions in the memory that constitute the loop. Every time a specific subroutine is called, its set of instructions is fetched from the memory. Thus loops and subroutines tend to localise the references to memory for fetching instructions.

The figure explains the function of the cache memory.

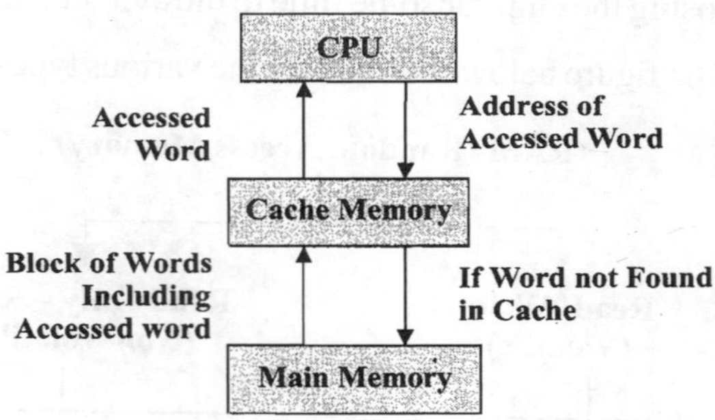

Figure 4.3 Functioning of the cache memory

Based on the locality of reference we understand that the cache contains a copy of certain portions of main memory. The memory read or write operation is first checked with the cache and if the desired data is available in the cache it is used by the CPU directly. Otherwise, a block of words is read from main memory to cache and the word is then used by the CPU from cache.

SECONDARY STORAGE DEVICES

As discussed earlier, RAM is a volatile memory having limited storage capacity. The cost of RAM is also relatively higher as compared to secondary memory. Logic dictated that a relatively cheaper media, showing some sort of permanence of storage, be used. As a result additional memory called *external* or *auxiliary memory* or *secondary storage* is used in most computers.

The magnetic medium was found to be long lasting and fairly inexpensive, therefore, became an ideal choice for large storage requirements. Magnetic tapes and disks are commonly used as storage media. With the advancements in optical technology, optical disks are making inroads as one of the major secondary storage devices. Characteristics of all these are discussed in detail in this section.

Magnetic Tapes

Magnetic tapes are used for storing files of data that are sequentially accessed or not used very often and are stored off-line. They are typically used as backup storage for archiving of data.

In case of magnetic tapes, a tape (plastic ribbon usually 1/2 inch or 1/4 inch wide and 50 to 2400 feet long) is wound on a spool and its other end is threaded manually on a take-up spool. The beginning of the tape (BOT) is indicated by a metal foil called a *marker*. When a write command is given, a block of data (records are usually grouped in blocks of two or more) is written on the tape. The next block is then written after a gap (called Inter Block Gap or IBG). A series of blocks are written in this manner. The end of tape (EOT) is indicated by an end-of-tape marker which is a metal foil stuck in the tape. After the data is written, the tape is rewound and kept ready for reading.

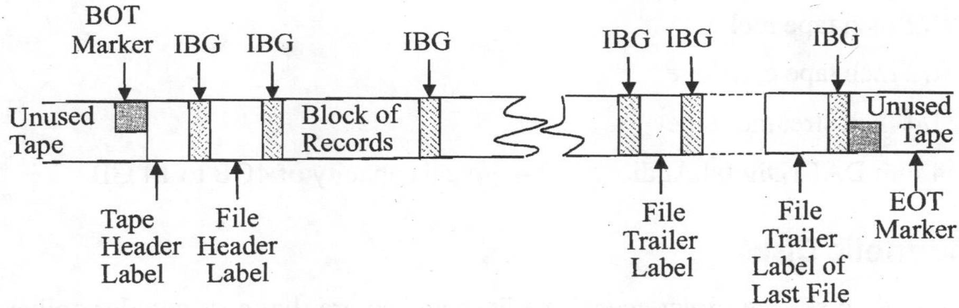

Figure 4.4(a) Data organisation on a magnetic tape

Figure 4.4(b) Magnetic tape reel

Figure 4.4(c) Magnetic tape cartridge

The tape is read sequentially, i.e., data can be read in the order in which the data has been written. This implies that if the desired record is at the end of the tape, all the earlier records have to be read before it is reached. A typical example of a tape can be seen in a music tape cassette where to listen to the 5th song one must listen to, or traverse, the earlier 4 songs. The access time of information stored on tape is therefore, very high as compared to that stored on a disk.

The storage capacity of the tape depends on its data recording density and the length of the tape. The data recording density refers to the amount of data that can be stored or the number of bytes that can be stored per linear inch of tape. The data recording density is measured in BPI (Bytes per inch).

Thus,

Storage capacity of a tape = Data recording density × Length of tape

It is worth noting that the actual storage capacity for storing user data, is much less owing to the file header labels, file trailer labels, BOT and EOT markers, and the use of IBGs.

Some commonly used magnetic tapes are:

- 1/2 inch tape reel
- 1/2 inch tape cartridge
- 1/4 inch streamer tape
- 4 mm DAT (Digital Audio Tape) – typical capacity of 4GB to 14 GB

Magnetic Disks

Magnetic disks are direct-access medium and so are the most popular online secondary storage devices. Direct-access devices are also called random-access devices because information is literally available at random or in any order. Access to any location on the device is direct and so approximately equal access time is required for each location. An example of this is a music CD where if you wish to listen to the 5th song, you can directly select the 5th track. It does not require you to fast forward the previous 4 songs.

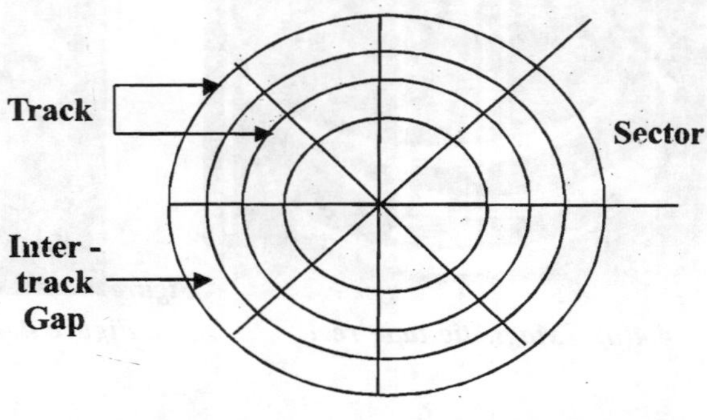

Figure 4.5 Logical layout of a magnetic disk

A magnetic disk is a circular plate made of metal or plastic, coated with magnetised material. Often both sides of the disk are used. Data is recorded on the disk in the form of magnetised and non-magnetised spots (not visible to the naked eye) representing 1s and 0s.

Data is stored in concentric rings or *tracks*. To minimise the interference of magnetic fields, the adjacent tracks are separated by *inter-track gaps*. Tracks are commonly divided into sections called sectors. In most systems, the minimum quantity of information that can be transferred is a sector. Usually 8 or more sectors per track are found.

A track in a given sector near the circumference is longer than the track near the centre of the disk. If bits are recorded with equal density, some tracks would contain more bits than the other tracks. To ensure that each sector can store equal amounts of data, some disks use variable recording density with higher density on tracks near the centre than on tracks near the circumference.

Multiple disks are usually stacked and used together to create disk storage systems having large capacities. In this case, multiple disks are fixed on a central shaft, one below the other to form a *disk pack*. This is then mounted on a disk drive that has a motor to rotate this disk pack about its axis. The disk drive also has an access arm assembly with a separate read/write head for each surface of the disk pack. The access arms for all the disks surfaces move together. A disk system, is thus addressed by the disk number, the disk surface, the sector number and the track within the sector.

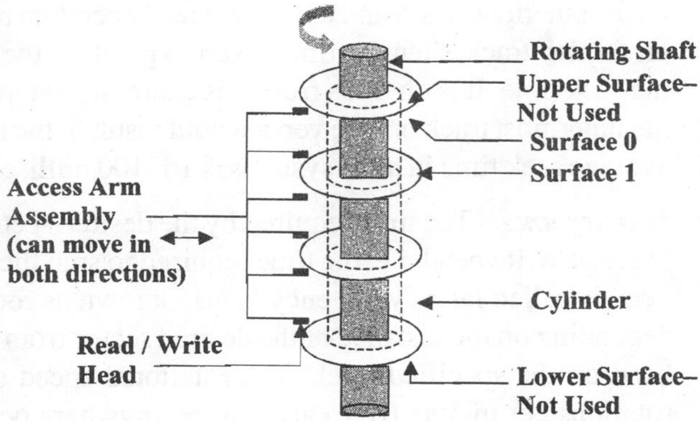

Figure 4.6 A Disk Pack with Four Disks

Usually, the upper surface of the topmost disk and the lower surface of the bottom-most disk are not used since these are prone to getting scratched easily. For faster access of data from disk packs, a concept called cylinders is used. As can be seen in Figure 4.6, a set of corresponding tracks on all the recording surfaces of the disk pack together form a cylinder. Thus if there are 100 tracks on each disk surface, there are 100 cylinders in the disk pack.

Cylinder-based organisation provides for faster data access. The related records of file can be stored on the same cylinder (on multiple disks of a disk pack) and subsequently with one movement of the access arm, all records on say cylinder 5 (5th track of every recording surface) can be simultaneously read.

The storage capacity of a disk system can be determined as follows:

Storage capacity = Number of recording surfaces × Number of tracks per surface × Number of sectors per track × Number of bytes per sector

Example: If a disk pack consists of 4 plates each having 2655 tracks having 125 sectors per track. Also, each sector can store 512 bytes, then

Storage capacity = 6 × 2655 × 125 × 512 = 1,01,95,20,000 bytes = 1×10^9 bytes approximately or 1 GB or 1 Gigabyte

Note: We have 6 recording surfaces since there are 4 disk plates.

Access time on disks As detailed earlier, the disk address is specified in terms of the surface number, track or cylinder number, and the sector number. The read/write heads need to be first positioned on the track on which the data are to be recorded or from which data needs to be read. Information is always written from the beginning of a sector and can be read only from the beginning of the desired track. Thus, the disk access time depends on the following factors:

- ***Seek time:*** The time taken to position the head on a specific track. The seek time would vary depending upon the position of the access arms at the time the read/write command was received, i.e., if the access arm was positioned on the outermost track and the current read operation required it to be positioned on the 5th track, then the time taken to position the access arm on track 5 is the seek time. It is obvious from this example that moving from outermost to the innermost track or vice versa would result in the maximum seek time. The average seek time in most systems is 10–100 milliseconds.
- ***Latency time:*** The time required by the desired sector to be positioned under the read/write head, i.e. the time required to spin the desired sector under the head is called latency. Latency is also known as rotational delay and varies depending on the distance of the desired sector from the initial position of the head on the specified track. The rotational speed of a disk is measured in rotations per minute (rpm) and can be anywhere between 300 to 7200 rpm. On an average, latency is equal to half the time taken for a rotation by the disk.

In addition to these two times, the time taken to read a block of words (Transfer rate) can also be considered. But this is usually too small in comparison to seek and latency time, and disk access time is generally considered to be a sum of seek time and latency time. Further, since access times to disk are large, a sizable portion of the data is read in a single go. That is why disks are referenced in blocks.

Based on the size and packaging of the disks, they can be classified into two types – floppy disks and hard disks. Further, disks that are permanently attached to the unit assembly and cannot be removed by the occasional user are called hard disks. A drive using removable disks is called a floppy disk drive.

Floppy Disks

The disks used with a floppy disk drive are small removable disks made of plastic coated with magnetic recording material. There are two sizes commonly used, with diameters of 5¼ and 3½ inches.

- The 5¼ inch disk is a 5¼ inch diameter floppy disk. Earlier such disks recorded data only on one side and were called single-sided (SS) disks. Today both the surfaces are used for recording and are called double-sided (DS) disks. These are available in two capacities – double density (DD), and high density (HD), where density refers to the number of bits that can be stored per square inch area.
- The 3½ inch disk is a disk of 3½ inch diameter. These record data on both sides and are therefore double sided disks. These disks come in three differentapacities – double density, high density, and very high density. These are smaller and can store more data than can the 5¼ inch disks.

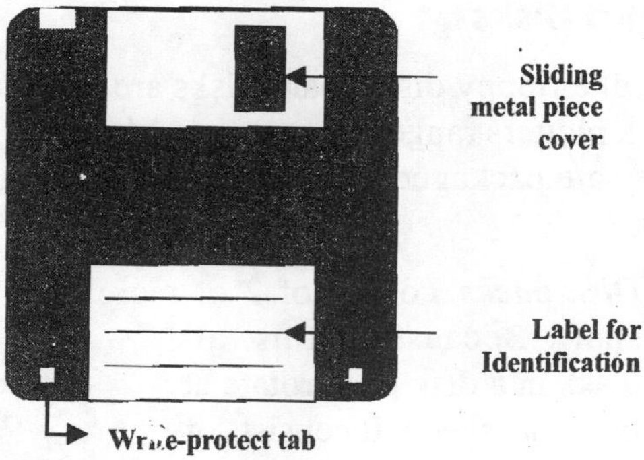

Figure 4.7 A 3½ inch floppy disk

The storage capacity for any disk can be calculated as:

Storage capacity = *Number of recording surfaces × Number of tracks per surface × Number of sectors per track × Number of bytes per sector*

Thus, for a 3-1/2 inch high density disk which has 80 tracks, 18 sectors/track, and 512 bytes/sector, the disk storage capacity can be calculated as follows:

$$2 \times 80 \times 18 \times 512 = \text{14,74,560 bytes or 1.4 MB (approximately)}$$

The table below provides the necessary details and associated storage capacities of various kinds of floppy disks.

Floppy disks are extensively used in personal computers as a medium for distributing software to computer users.

Size (diameter in inches)	No. of Recording Surfaces	No. of Tracks	No. of Sectors/ Tracks	No. of Bytes/ Sector	Storage Capacity (approx)
5 ¼	2	40	9	512	3,68,640 bytes or 360kB
5 ¼	2	80	15	512	12,28,800 bytes or 1.2 MB
3 ½	2	40	18	512	7,37,280 bytes or 720 kB
3 ½	2	80	18	512	14,74,560 bytes or 1.4 MB
3 ½	2	80	36	512	29,49,120 or 2.8 MB

Hard Disks

Unlike floppy disks, hard disks are made up of rigid metal. The sizes for the disk platters range between 1 to 14 inches in diameter. Depending on the way they are packaged, hard disks can be categorised as disk packs or Winchester disks.

- ***Disk packs*** consist of 2 or more hard disks mounted on a single central shaft. Because of this, all disks in a disk pack rotate at the same speed. It consists of separate read/write heads for each surface (excluding the upper surface of the topmost disk platter and the lower surface of the bottommost disk platter, as mentioned earlier in this chapter). Disk packs are removable in the sense that they can be removed and kept offline when not in use (typically stored away in plastic cases). They have to be mounted on the disk drive before they can be used. Thus different disk packs can be mounted on the same disk drive at different instances, thereby providing virtually unlimited (modular) storage capacity.

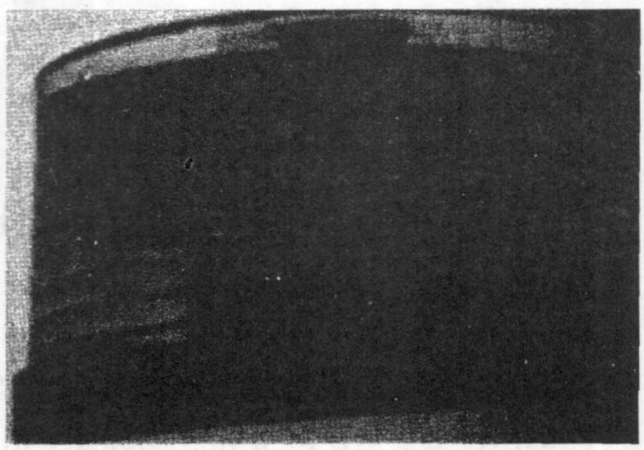

Figure 4.8 A disk pack

- ***Winchester disks*** also consist of 2 or more hard disk platters mounted on a single central shaft but are of the fixed type. The disk platters are sealed in a contamination-free container. Due to this fact all the disk platters, including the upper surface of the topmost disk platter and the lower surface of the bottommost platter, are used for storing data. So, even though Winchester disks have limited storage capacity as opposed to disk packs, they can store larger amounts of data as compared to the same number of disk platters.

Figure 4.9 A Winchester disk

Another kind of disk called the zip disk is very common today. This consists of a single hard disk platter encased in a plastic cartridge. Such a disk typically has a capacity of about 100 MB. The zip drive can further be fixed or portable. The fixed zip drive is permanently connected to the computer system while the portable ones can be carried around and connected to any computer system for the duration of its use. In both cases however, the zip cartridge (the actual storage medium) is portable just like a floppy, albeit with a nearly 100 times larger storage capacity.

Figure 4.10 Zip disks and zip drive

Optical Disks

Optical disks are storage devices with huge storage capacity. It is a relatively new storage medium and uses laser beam technology for writing and reading of data.

Optical disks consist of one large track that starts from the outer edge and spirals inward towards the centre (this is unlike the magnetic disk in which tracks are concentric circles on the disk platter). An optical disk is also split up into sectors but these are of the same length regardless of its location on the track. Data is therefore packed at maximum density over the disk.

The storage capacity of an optical disk is determined as follows:

Storage Capacity = Number of sectors × Number of bytes per sector

(Note that we do not consider the number of tracks since there is only one track in this case)

Thus, a 5.25 inch optical disk having 3,30,000 sectors and storing 2,352 bytes per sector, will have a storage capacity

$$3,30,000 \times 2352 = 77,61,60,000 \text{ bytes or } 740 \text{ MB (approx.)}$$

The technology used in optical disks uses laser beams to write and read data as opposed to the read /write head used in magnetic disks. Data is recorded by etching microscopic pits (burnt surface) on the disk surface. A high intensity laser beam is used to etch the pits while a low intensity laser beam is used for data retrieval.

Figure 4.11 An optical disk and disk drive

Three optical memory devices that are becoming increasingly popular in various computer applications are CD-ROM, WORM, and Erasable Optical disks. We shall discuss these below.

CD-ROM The CD-ROM (Compact disk read-only memory) is a direct extension of the audio CD. It is usually made from a resin named polycarbonate that is coated with aluminium to form a highly reflective surface. The information on a CD-ROM is stored as a series of microscopic pits on the reflective surface (using a high-intensity laser beam). The process of recording information on these disks is known as 'mastering'. This is so-called because this master disk is then used to make a die, which is used to make copies.

The information is retrieved from a CD-ROM using a low-powered laser, which is generated in an optical disk drive unit. The disk is rotated and the laser beam is aimed at the disk. The intensity of the laser beam changes as it encounters a pit. A photo-sensor detects the change in intensity, thus recognizing the digital signals recorded on the surface of the CD-ROM and converts them into electronic signals of 1s and 0s.

As the name suggests, information stored in CD-ROM can be read only. It cannot be modified in any way. It is therefore useful for applications in which there is a database of information that is useful as it is and does not need changing in any way, e.g., a directory such as Yellow Pages. CD-ROMs are very useful for distributing large amounts of information to a large number of users. The advantages of CD-ROMs lie in the fact that they provide for:

- large storage capacity for information/data.
- fast and inexpensive mass replication.
- suitable for archival storage since they are removable disks.

The disadvantages of CD-ROMs are:

- they are read-only and cannot be updated.
- access time is greater than that of a magnetic disk.

WORM The drawbacks of CD-ROM were partially resolved by the introduction of WORM ('write-once, read many').

In certain applications, only a few copies of compact disks are required to be made which makes the CD-ROM production economically unviable from a commercial point of view. This is because manufacturers do CD-ROM duplication by using expensive duplication equipment. For such cases, write-once read-many CDs have been developed.

WORM disks allow users to create their own CDs by using a CD-Recordable (CD-R) drive. This can be attached as a peripheral device to the computer system. WORM disks recorded like this, can be read by any CD-ROM drive.

Erasable optical disk The most recent development in optical disks is the erasable optical disk. The data in these can be changed repeatedly as in case of magnetic disks. Erasable optical disks are therefore also known as rewritable optical disks.

These disks integrate the magnetic and optical disk technologies to enable rewritable storage with the laser-beam technology and so are also called magneto-optical disks. In such systems, a laser beam is used along with a magnetic field to read or write information on a disk, which is coated with a magnetic material.

To write, the laser beam is used to heat a specific spot on the magnetic coated material. At this elevated temperature, a magnetic field is applied so that the polarisation of that spot can be changed thereby recording the desired data. This process does not cause any physical changes in the disk and so can be repeated many times. Reading is done by detecting the degree of rotation of the polarised laser beam reflected from the surface. This implies that as the disk spins, the polarised spots pass under the laser beam and depending on their orientation or alignment some of them reflect the light while others scatter it. This produces patterns of 'on' and 'off' that are converted into electronic signals of binary 1s and 0s.

The capacity of an erasable disk is very high in comparison to a magnetic disk. For example, a 5¼ inch optical disk can store around 650 MB of data while Winchester disks normally can store a maximum capacity of 320 MB. This is why magneto-optical disks are ideal for multimedia applications that require large storage capacities.

MASS STORAGE DEVICES

Any physical storage media has a limit to its capacity and performance. There is a constant effort towards improving such media and as a result, larger capacity secondary storage devices have emerged. These are characterised by using multiple units of the same storage media, as a single unit, to provide for higher storage capacities. Disk Arrays (Multiple disks), Tape Libraries (Multiple tapes), and CD-ROM Jukebox (Multiple CDs) are the three most commonly used mass storage devices.

Mass data storage devices are characterised by relatively slow access time. This is because additional time in terms of first locating the desired disk, tape, or CD-ROM (as the case maybe) needs to be accounted for. However, they are more cost effective in case of applications that require huge storage capacity and for which rapid access to data is not the prime consideration.

They can also be used for off-line or archival storage of information/data since they can support huge volumes of information/data to be backed up.

Disk array (RAID) RAID (Redundant Array of Inexpensive Disks) is an acronym for a disk array and consists of a number of hard disks and disk drives with a controller in a single box.

The basic idea of RAID was to combine multiple small, inexpensive disk drives into an array of disk drives which yields performance exceeding that of a Single Large Expensive Drive (SLED). Additionally, this array of drives appears to the computer as a single logical storage unit or drive.

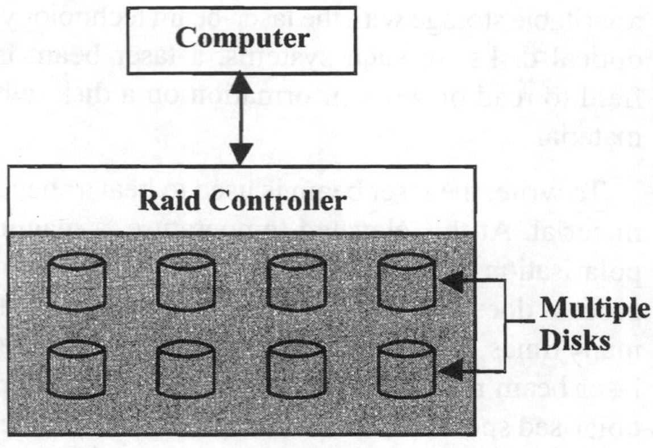

Figure 4.12 A RAID consisting of 8 disks

The concept was pioneered through academic research funded by Digital Equipment Corporation and has now become a standard in the computing industry for applications requiring fast, reliable storage of large volumes of data.

There are several different types of RAID configurations that are described in terms of 'levels'. The various levels of RAID storage are as follows:

- ***RAID 0:*** Data is split across drives, resulting in higher data throughput. Since no redundant information is stored, performance is very good, but the failure of any disk in the array results in data loss. This level is commonly referred to as striping.
- ***RAID 1:*** It provides redundancy by writing all data to two or more drives. The performance of a level 1 array tends to be faster on reads and slower on writes compared to a single drive, but if either drive fails, no data is lost. This level is commonly referred to as mirroring. Mirroring is the most expensive RAID option (since it doubles storage requirements), but it offers the ultimate in reliability.
- ***RAID 0+1:*** It is a combination of striping and mirroring. This configuration provides optimal speed and reliability, but possesses the same cost problem as RAID1.
- ***RAID 5:*** It employs a combination of striping and parity checking. The use of parity checking provides redundancy without the overhead of having to double disk capacity. Simply put, parity checking involves determining whether each given block has an odd or even value. These values are summed across the stripe sets to obtain a parity value. With this parity value, the contents of a failed disk can easily be determined and rebuilt on a spare drive.

There are other RAID configurations in addition to the ones described, but these are the ones most commonly used in the industry.

As can be noticed, RAID configurations result in higher reliability due to the use of multiple disks. In addition to this, both mirroring and striping (techniques used in distributing data across the disks) also result in speeding up the read process since different parts of the same file, residing on different disks, can be read at the same time.

Tape libraries Network administrators are hungry for technologies that will allow them to efficiently and economically manage the explosive growth in data stored on networks. As the amount of data increases, the backup process takes longer. Simply adding another tape drive to reduce the backup time doesn't really help. Further, systems operated in this manner, represent one of the largest operational costs of a data centre and also typically represent the predominant need for human intervention.

The solution to this problem is the multi-drive automated tape library. These libraries consist of a set of magnetic tapes with a controller mounted in a single unit. The unit may have one or more tape drives to read and write data on the tapes in the tape library. Automated tape libraries allow random access to large numbers of tape cartridges and concurrent use of two or more drives, rather than manually loading one tape after another. The unit typically has robotic arms to retrieve the appropriate tape from the tape library and mount it on one of the tape drives for processing.

Automated tape libraries can be designed to provide extremely precise control and support for tape drives. Properly implemented, library automation can significantly enhance the operational reliability of tape drives by eliminating the highly variable human/machine interface. In this particular case, the objective of the system design is to avoid failures rather than to tolerate them, as is the case in RAID systems.

Automated tape libraries are typically used for data archiving purposes and as an online data backup device for automated backup.

CD-ROM jukebox The CD-ROM jukebox is much like the automated tape library but consists of a set of CD-ROM disks instead of the magnetic tapes. The set of CD-ROM disks along with a controller are mounted in a single unit. Once again, the unit can have one or more drives to read data from the disks in the jukebox. The unit has robotic arms to retrieve the appropriate CD and mount it on one of the CD-ROM drives for processing. At the end of processing, the CD is automatically returned to the appropriate slot.

CD-ROM jukeboxes are typically used for archiving read-only data that can be accessed online, e.g., online encyclopedias, online directories, etc. A large CD-ROM jukebox may consist of hundreds of disks providing a storage capacity of terabytes.

Data Backup

Data stored on an online storage device, such as a hard disk, can be damaged or lost due to any one of the following reasons:

- a disk crash
- virus attack
- accidental deletion by users
- hardware malfunction, or
- natural calamity (e.g., earthquake, fire, floods etc.)

Useful and sensitive data needs to be protected against such eventualities. Data should therefore be copied from online storage devices to secondary storage devices (like magnetic tapes, floppy disks, zip disks) and stored in safe locations. This process is known as backing up of data.

Data Backup now constitutes an essential part of IT policies in most of the organizations. Different types of backup media may be appropriate for different users and applications, depending upon the volumes, periodicity, accessibility, security, sensitivity etc. However, determining the appropriate backup policy, which would depend on the unique requirements of each organisation, is outside the scope of this book.

KEY POINTS

- Memory in the computer system is required for storage and subsequent retrieval of instructions and data. The temporary storage built into the computer hardware is known as the primary storage or main memory.
- Devices like magnetic tapes and disks provide for backup storage and are termed as secondary storage or auxiliary memory.
- The internal processor memory consists of the small set of high-speed registers that are internal to a processor and are used as temporary locations where actual processing is done.
- Cache memory is extremely fast and small memory, logically positioned between the CPU registers and the main memory and stores very active data and instructions during process. The access time of cache memory is closer to processing speed of the CPU.
- The storage unit of a computer system is characterised and evaluated on properties like storage capacity, storage cost, access time, access mode, and permanence of storage.
- Capacity of the main memory refers to the number of bytes that it can store in its main memory. It is measured in terms of Kilobytes (1024 bytes) or Megabytes (1024 kilobytes) or Gigabytes (1024 megabytes).
- Memory devices may be accessed in random, sequential or direct mode.
- Random access allows access to any memory location, in any order, in the same amount of time.
- In sequential access, memory can be accessed only in a predefined sequence. The access time therefore varies according to the location.
- In the direct access mode, information is neither accessed randomly, nor in sequence but something in between. A separate read/write head exists for each track, and on the track the information can be accessed serially.
- The computer's main memory is built up of volatile RAM chips. These RAM chips are of two types namely, static and dynamic. In static RAM (SRAM) information remains valid only as long as power is applied to the unit, while dynamic RAM (DRAM) uses external circuitry to refresh or 'regenerate' the storage charge in order to retain the stored data.
- ROM is a special type of RAM and is non-volatile in nature. There are two types of ROM–manufacturer-programmed and user-programmed. While

manufacturer-programmed ROMs have data burnt into the circuitry, user-programmed ROMs can have the user load and then store read-only programs (PROM or Programmable ROM).

- Information once stored on the ROM or PROM chip cannot be altered. However, another type of memory–called EPROM or Erasable PROM–allows a user to erase the information stored on the chip and reprogram it with new information. The two types of EPROM chips are – EEPROM or Electrically EPROM and UVEPROM or Ultra Violet EPROM.
- Since the primary storage of a computer system is volatile and is limited in capacity, secondary storage devices are used to store data and instructions permanently.
- Secondary storage is non-volatile, provides for larger storage capacity, has lower cost per bit stored, but has an operating speed much slower than the primary storage.
- Magnetic tapes are sequentially accessed storage devices and are used as backup storage for archiving data.
- Magnetic disks are a direct access medium and so are most popular online secondary storage devices.
- The storage capacity of a disk can be determined as follows:

  Storage capacity = *Number of recording surfaces × Number of tracks per surface × Number of sectors per track × Number of bytes per sector*
- Seek time refers to the time taken to position the head on a specific track on a disk. The average seek time in most systems is 10–100 milliseconds.
- Latency time refers to the time required by the required sector to be positioned under the read/ write head. It is also known as rotational delay. The rotational speed of a disk is between 300–7200 rpm.
- Floppy disks are small removable disks made of plastic coated with magnetic recording material. These are commonly found in two sizes–5¼ inch diameter, and 3½ inch diameter. Floppy disks are used as a medium for distributing software to computer users.
- Hard disks are made of rigid material. They can be categorized as disk packs, Winchester disks and zip disks.
- Optical disks are storage devices having huge storage capacity. They use laser beam technology for reading and writing of data.
- Optical disks have a single large track starting from the outer edge and spiraling inwards towards the center, split into sectors of the same length regardless of location on the track.

- The storage capacity of an optical disk can be determined as follows:

  Storage capacity = Number of sectors × Number of bytes per sector
- The most commonly used optical storage devices include CD-ROM, WORM, and erasable optical disks.
- CD-ROMs are read-only, WORM is write-once read many, and Erasable optical disks are rewritable optical disks.
- Since any physical storage media has a limit to capacity and performance, constant efforts towards improving such media has resulted in larger capacity storage devices called mass storage devices. They use multiple units of the same storage media, as a single unit, to provide for higher storage capacity. The three most commonly used mass storage devices are the Disk arrays, Tape Libraries, and CD-ROM jukeboxes.
- Disk arrays consist of a number of hard disks and disk drives with a controller in a single box. Also known as RAID (Redundant Array of Inexpensive Disks) are available in various configurations. The most commonly used configurations include RAID 0, RAID 1, RAID 0+1, and RAID 5.
- Tape libraries consist of a set of magnetic tapes with a controller mounted in a single unit. The unit may have one or more tape drives to read and write data on the tapes in the tape library. Automated tape libraries allow random access to large numbers of tape cartridges and concurrent use of two or more drives, rather than manually loading one tape after another. Such libraries are typically used for data archiving purposes and as online data backup device or automated backup.
- The CD-ROM Jukebox is a set of CD-ROM disks, having a controller, mounted in a single unit. Once again, the unit can have one or more drives to read data from the disks in the jukebox. CD-ROM jukeboxes are typically used for archiving read-only data that can be accessed online.
- Data must be copied from online storage devices to secondary storage devices like magnetic tapes and disks, to provide for any loss of data during eventualities. This process is called data backup and has become an essential part of the IT strategy of most organisations.

REVIEW QUESTIONS

1. Choose the appropriate answer:

i. Instructions and data during execution reside in the:

(a) Auxiliary memory (b) Processor memory

(c) Cache memory (d) Primary memory

ii. RAM is:

(a) Read-write memory

(b) Volatile

(c) Can be used by user programs and system programs

(d) All of the above

iii. Which of the following terms is not associated with magnetic tapes:

(a) EOT (b) BOT

(c) IBG (d) None of the above

iv. Magnetic Disks:

(a) Are sequential access devices

(b) Are read-only devices

(c) Have data recorded in the form of magnetised and non-magnetised spots

(d) Consist of a single track

v. A magnetic disk having 80 tracks, 15 sectors per track, and storing 512 bytes per sector will have a storage capacity of:

(a) 1.2 MB (b) 360 KB

(c) 720 KB (d) 1.4 MB

vi. The storage capacity of an optical disk is determined using:

(a) Number of tracks on the disk

(b) Number of recording surfaces, number of tracks per surface, and number of sectors per track

(c) Number of sectors, and number of bytes per sector

(d) Number of recording surfaces, number of tracks per surface, number of sectors per track, and number of bytes per sector

2. State whether True or False:

i. Memory hierarchy is built into the computer system as the main memory cannot store very large amount of data.

ii. Secondary memory is slower than the main memory, but has larger storage capacity.

iii. In random access memory, any location can be accessed independently.

iv. ROM is volatile memory.

v. Magnetic disks are characterised by tracks and sectors.

vi. Data backup is required to safeguard data in case of catastrophic eventualities.

vii. RAID configuration is used to enhance access speed.

viii. Storage cost in a computer system refers to the per bit storage cost.

3. Match the following:

X	Y
1. Low cost, low speed devices	a. Volatile memory
2. Relatively large and fast memory	b. Magnetic disks
3. Power required all the time	c. Main memory
4. Small fast memories between the CPU and main memory	d. Magnetic rapes
5. Direct access devices	e. Auxiliary storage
6. Permanent storage	f. Non-volatile memory
7. Sequential access devices	g. RAID
8. Mass storage device	h. Cache

4. Fill in the blanks with the appropriate choices listed below:

(i) Storage capacity (ii) Latency time (iii) DRAM (iv) Non-volatile (v) Seek time (vi) CD-ROM Jukebox (vii) Optical devices (viii) Locality of reference

1. ______________ memory is referred to as permanent storage.
2. ______________ use laser beam technology to read and write data.
3. The time delay in positioning the desired sector under the read/write head is termed as ____________.
4. ______________ is the time required to position the specified track under the head.
5. ______________ is typically measured in terms of kilobytes, megabytes or gigabytes.
6. Laye memories use______________ because it offers larger storage capacity and reduced power consumption.
7. In typical programs, memory references at any given interval of time tend to be confined to a few localised areas in memory. This phenomenon is known as ______________.
8. A set of CD-ROM disks, having a controller, mounted in a single unit, is known as _______.

CHAPTER 5 Input Devices

The computer will be of no use if it is not able to communicate with the external world. A computer must therefore, have a system to receive information from the outside world (users and other computers) and must be able to communicate results to the external world. Computers have an input-output sub-system, referred to as I/O sub-system, which provides an efficient mode of communication between the central system and the outside world. Programs and data must be entered into the computer memory for processing, and results obtained from computations must be displayed or recorded for the user's benefit.

This can be explained with a very common scenario where the average marks of a student need to be calculated, based on the marks obtained in various subjects by the student. The marks would typically be available in the form of a document containing the student's name, roll number, and marks scored in each subject. This data must first be stored in the computer's memory after converting it into machine – readable form. The data will then be processed (average marks calculated) and sent from the memory to the output unit, which will present the data in a form that can be read by users.

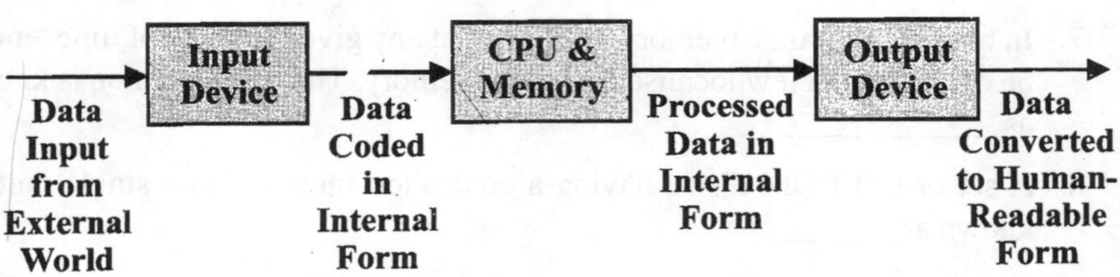

Figure 5.1 Role of I/O devices in a computer system

The I/O devices that provide a means of communication between the computer and the outside world are known as peripheral devices. This is because they surround the CPU and the memory of a computer system. While input devices are used to enter data from the outside world into the primary storage, output devices are used to provide the processed results from primary storage to users.

In this chapter, we will discuss the various input devices available for data input. Output devices will be the topic of discussion of the subsequent chapter.

As mentioned earlier in this section, input devices are used to transfer user data and instructions to the computer. The most commonly used input devices can be classified into the categories of:

- keyboard devices (general and special purpose, key-to-tape, key-to-disk, key-to-diskette)
- point-and-draw devices (mouse, trackball, joystick, light pen, touch screen etc.)
- scanning devices (optical mark recognition, magnetic ink character recognition, optical bar code reader, digitiser, electronic-card reader etc.)
- voice recognition devices
- vision-input devices (webcam, video camera etc.)

KEYBOARD DEVICES

Keyboard devices allow input into the computer system by pressing a set of keys, mounted on a board connected to the computer system. Keyboard devices are typically classified as general-purpose keyboards and special-purpose keyboards.

General-purpose Keyboard

The most familiar means of entering information into a computer is through a typewrite-like keyboard that allows a person to enter alphanumeric information directly.

The most popular keyboard used today is the 101-keys with a traditional QWERTY layout, having an alphanumeric keypad, 12 function keys, a variety of special-function keys, numeric keypad, and dedicated

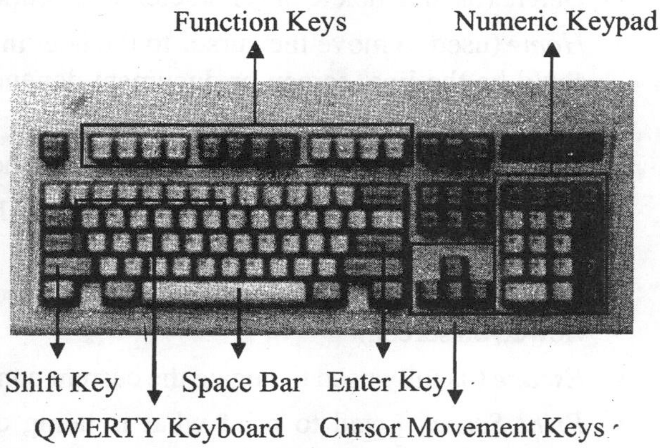

Figure 5.2 QWERTY keyboard layout

cursor-control keys. It is so called because the arrangement of its alphanumeric keys in the upper left row (as seen in the Figure 5.2).

- **Alphanumeric Keypad:** Contains keys for the English alphabets, 0 to 9 numbers, special characters like * + – / [ ] etc.
- **12 Function Keys:** These are keys labeled F1, F2 ... F12 and are a set of user programmable function keys. The actual function assigned to a function key differs from one software package to another. These keys are also called soft keys since their functionality can be defined by the software.
- **Special-function Keys:** Have special functions assigned to each of these keys. For example, the enter key is used to send the keyed – in data into the memory. Other special keys include:
    - *Shift* (used to enter capital letters or special characters defined above the number keys)
    - *Spacebar* (used to enter a space at the cursor location)
    - *Ctrl* (used in conjunction with other keys to provide added functionality on the keyboard)
    - *Alt* (like Ctrl, it is used to expand the functionality of the keyboard)
    - Tab (used to move the cursor to the next tab position defined)
    - *Backspace* (used to move the cursor one position to the left and also delete the character in that position)
    - *Caps Lock* (to toggle between the capital letter lock feature – when 'on', it locks the keypad for capital letters input)
    - *Num Lock* (to toggle the number lock feature on and off – when 'on', it inputs numbers when you press the numbers on the numeric keypad)
    - *Insert* (used to toggle between the insert and overwrite mode during data entry – when 'on', entered text is inserted at the cursor location)
    - *Delete* (used to delete the character at the cursor location)
    - *Home* (used to move the cursor to the beginning of the work area which could be the line, screen or document depending on the software being used)
    - *End* (used to move the cursor to the end of the work area)
    - *Page Up* (used to display the previous page of the document being currently viewed on screen)
    - *Page Down* (used to view the next page of the document being currently viewed on screen)
    - *Escape* (usually used to negate the current command)
    - *Print Screen* (used to print what is being currently displayed on the screen)

- **Numeric Keypad:** Consists of keys having numbers (0 to 9) and mathematical operators (+ – * /) defined on them. It is usually located on the right side of the keyboard and supports quick entry of numerical data.
- **Cursor-control Keys:** Defined by the arrow keys used to move the cursor in the direction indicated by the arrow (top, down, left, right)

Another well-known key arrangement is the Dvorak system, which was designed to be easier to learn and use. The Dvorak keyboard has the most common consonants on one side of the middle or home row and the vowels on the other side, so that typing tends to alternate keystrokes back and forth between hands. Although the Dvorak keyboard has never been widely used, it has it's adherents.

Special-Purpose Keyboard

These are standalone data entry systems used for computers deployed for specific applications. These typically have special purpose keyboards to enable faster data entry. A very typical example of such keyboards can be seen at the Automatic Teller Machines or the ATMs where the keyboard is required for limited functionality (support for some financial transactions) by the customers. Point-of-Sale or POS terminals at fast food joints, Air / Railway reservation counters are some other examples of special-purpose keyboards, etc.

These keyboards are specifically designed for special types of applications only.

Key-to-tape, key-to-disk, key-to-diskette

These are standalone data entry stations. These units usually have a small processor attached to a keyboard and a visual display unit. The processor checks for the accuracy of data at the time of entry. The screen displays data as it is being entered. These facilities are very useful and desirable during mass data entry and are therefore becoming very popular in data processing centres.

POINT-AND-DRAW DEVICES

The keyboard facilitates input of data in text form only. While working with display based packages, we usually point to a display area and select an option from the screen (fundamentals of GUI applications). For such cases, the sheer user-friendliness of input devices that can rapidly point to a particular option displayed on screen and support it's selection, resulted in the advent of various point-and-draw devices.

Mouse

A mouse is a small device that a computer user pushes across a desk surface in order to point to a place on a display screen and to select one or more actions possible from that position. The mouse first became a widely used computer tool when Apple Computer made it a standard part of the Apple Macintosh. Today, the mouse is an integral part of the graphical user interface (GUI) of any personal computer. The mouse apparently got its name by being about the same size and color as a toy mouse.

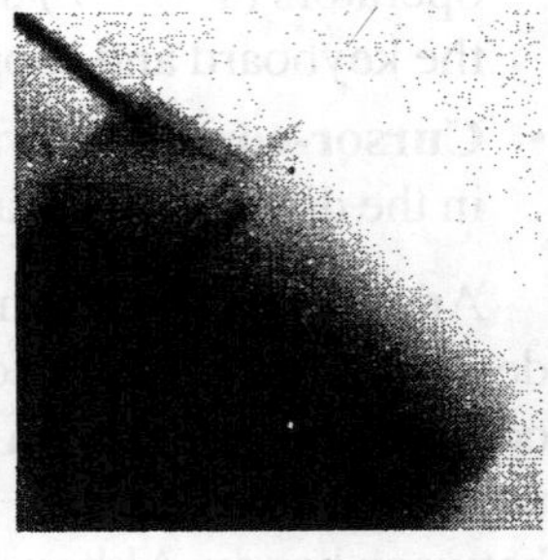

Figure 5.3 Mouse

The most conventional kind of mouse has two buttons on top: the left one is used most frequently. In the windows operating systems, it lets the user click once to send a "Select" indication that provides the user with feedback that a particular position has been selected for further action. The next click on a selected position or two quick clicks on it causes a particular action to take place on the selected object. For example, in Windows operating systems, it causes a program associated with that object to be started. The second button, on the right, usually provides some less-frequently needed capability. For example, when viewing a Web page, you can click on an image to get a pop-up menu that, among other things, lets you save the image on your hard disk. Some models have a third button for additional capabilities. Some mouse manufacturers also provide a version for left-handed people.

Trackball

The trackball is a pointing device that is much like an inverted mouse. It consists of a ball inset in a small external box, or adjacent to–and in the same unit as–the keyboard of some portable computers.

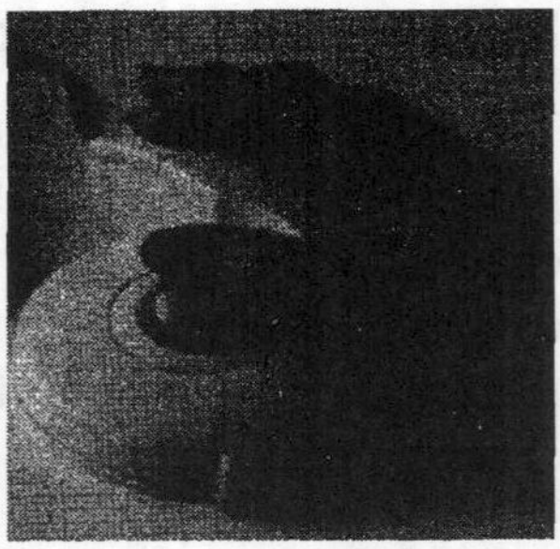

Figure 5.4 Trackball

It is more convenient and requires much less space than the mouse since here the whole device is not moved (as in the case of a mouse). Trackball comes in various shapes but supports the same functionality. Typical shapes used are a ball, a square, and a button (typically seen in laptops).

Joystick

The joystick is a vertical stick that moves the graphic cursor in the direction the stick is moved.

It consists of a spherical ball, which moves within a socket, and has a stick mounted on it. The user moves the ball with the help of the stick that can be moved left or right, forward or backward, to move and position the cursor in the desired location. Joysticks typically have a button on top that is used to select the option pointed by the cursor.

Figure 5.5 Joystick

Video games, training simulators, and control panels of robots are some common uses of a joystick.

Light Pen

The light pen is a pen-shaped device allowing natural movement on the screen. It is made up of a light sensitive cell and a lens assembly designed in such a way that it focuses onto itself any light in its field of view. The pen contains a light receptor and is activated by pressing the pen against the display screen. The receptor is the scanning beam that helps in locating the pen's position (X and Y coordinates on screen). Suitable system software is provided to initiate the desired action once the area on the display screen is located with the help of the light pen.

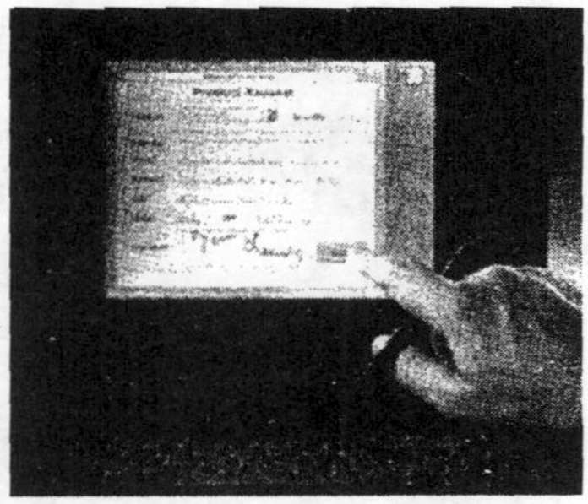

Figure 5.6 Light pen

Light pens are typically used in CAD (Computer Aided Design) applications to directly draw on screen.

Touch Screen

A touch screen is probably one of the simplest and most intuitive of all input devices. It uses optical sensors in, or near, the computer screen that can detect the touch of a finger on the screen. Once the user touches a particular screen position, sensors communicate the position to the computer. This is then interpreted by the computer to understand the user's choice for input.

The most common usage of touch screens is in information kiosks where users can receive information at the touch of a screen. These devices are becoming increasingly popular today.

SCANNING DEVICES

Scanning devices are input devices used for direct data entry from the source document into the computer system. Scanners facilitate the capturing of information and storing it in a graphical format for displaying it back on the graphical screen. They consist of two components, one to illuminate the page so that the optical image can be captured and the other to convert the graphical image into a digital format for storing. The graphical images thus scanned can be seen and processed directly by the computer.

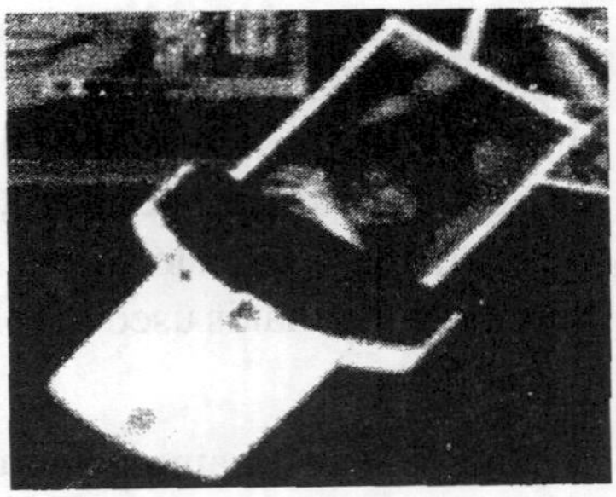

Figure 5.7(a) ***Hand-held scanner***

There are two types of scanners, CONTACT and LASER. Both bounce a beam of light off an image, and then measure the reflected light to determine the value of the image. Hand-held contact scanners make contact as they are brushed over the printed matter to be read. Laser-based scanners are more versatile and can read data passed near the scanning area.

Figure 5.7(b) ***Flat-bed scanner***

H:.nd-held scanners are used where the information to be scanned or the volume of documents to be scanned is very low. They are much cheaper as compared to the flat-bed scanners.

Capturing information using scanners reduces the possibility of human error typically seen during large data entry. The reduction in human intervention improves the accuracy of data and provides for timeliness of the information processed.

Most recent trends for data input is towards source data automation. The equipments used for source data automation capture data as a by-product of a business activity thereby completely eliminating manual input of data. Some common examples of these are described below.

Optical Mark Recognition (OMR)

OMR devices can sense marks on computer readable paper. This kind of device is typically used by academic institutions to grade aptitude tests where candidates need to mark the correct option from a number of alternatives, on a special sheet of paper. These answer sheets can then be directly read by the optical mark recognition device and can be used for further processing by the computer.

The actual technique used by an

OMR device once again involves focusing a light on the page being scanned thereby detecting the reflected light pattern for the marks. Pencil marks made by the user reflect the light determining which responses are marked.

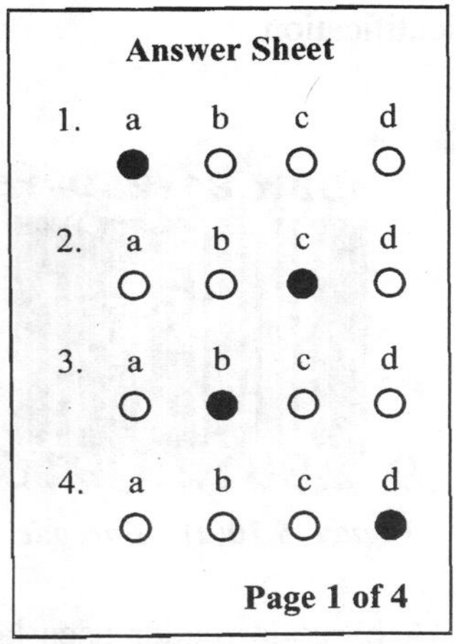

Figure 5.8 An example of a pre-printed answer sheet that can be read by an OMR device

Magnetic Ink Character Recognition (MICR)

Magnetic ink character recognition (MICR) is similar to optical mark recognition and is used exclusively by the banking industry. MICR devices are used by the banking industry to read the account numbers on cheques directly and subsequently do the necessary processing.

Banks using the MICR technology print cheque books on special types of paper. The necessary details of the bank (like the bank's identification code, relevant account number, and cheque number) are pre-printed on the cheques using an ink that contains iron oxide particles that can be magnetised.

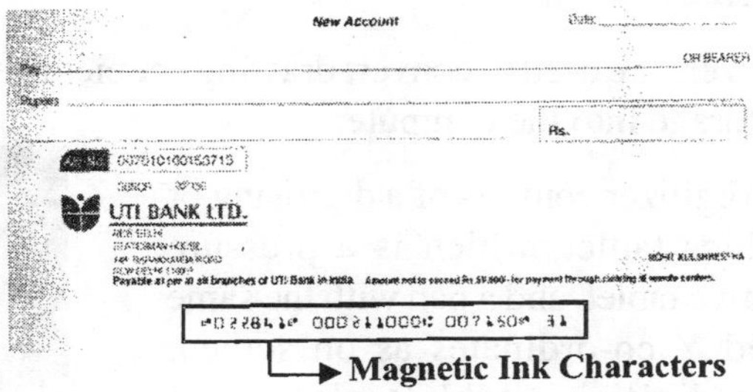

Figure 5.9 A bank cheque using MICR technology

MICR readers are used to read and sort cheques and deposits. An MICR reader-sorter reads the data on the cheques and sorts the cheques for distribution to other banks and customers or for further processing.

Optical Bar Code Reader (OBR)

Data coded in the form of small vertical lines forms the basis of bar coding. Alphanumeric data is represented using adjacent vertical lines called Bar codes. These are of varying widths and spacing between them used to uniquely identify books, merchandise in stores, postal packages etc.

Below is an example of a bar code used on one of the books for its unique identification.

Figure 5.10(a) Barcode example

Figure 5.10(b) Barcode reader

A barcode reader uses laser beam technology. The laser beam is moved across the pattern of bars in a bar code. These bars reflect the beam in different ways. The reflected beam is then sensed by a light-sensitive detector, which then converts the light patterns into electrical pulses thereby transmitting them to logic circuits for further conversion to alphanumeric value.

Barcode devices are available as hand-held devices.

Digitizer

Digitizers are used to convert drawings or pictures and maps into a digital format for storage into the computer.

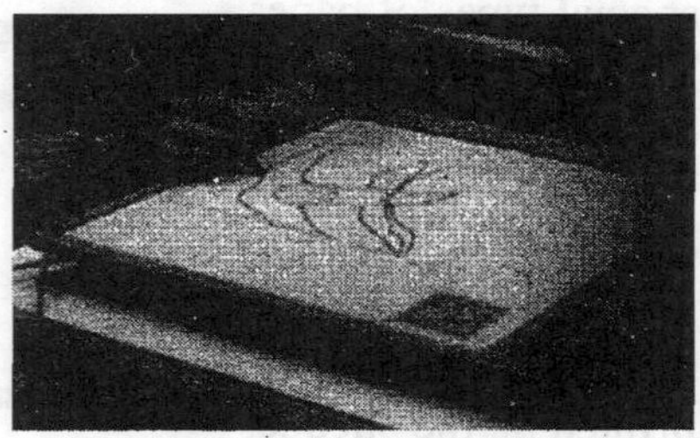

Figure 5.11 Digitizing tablet

A digitizer consists of a digitising or graphics tablet, which is a pressure sensitive tablet, and a pen with the same X and Y co-ordinates as on screen. Some digitising tablets also use a crosshair device instead of a pen. The movement of the pen or crosshair is reproduced simultaneously on the display screen. When the pen is moved on the tablet, the cursor on the computer's screen moves simultaneously to the corresponding position on screen (X and Y coordinates). This allows the user to draw sketches directly or input existing sketched drawings easily.

Digitizers see most common usage by architects and engineers as a tool for Computer Aided Designing (CAD).

Electronic-card Reader

Card readers are devices that also allow direct data input into a computer system. The electronic-card reader is connected to a computer system and reads the data encoded on an electronic card and transfers it to the computer system for further processing.

Electronic cards are plastic cards with data encoded on them and meant for a specific application. Typical examples of electronic cards are the plastic cards issued by banks to their customers for use in Automatic Teller Machines or ATMs. Electronic cards are also used by many organizations for controlling access of various types of employees to physically secured areas.

Figure 5.12 Access card security system

Depending on the manner in which the data is encoded, electronic cards may be either magnetic strip cards or smart cards. Magnetic strip cards have a magnetic strip on the back of the card. Data stored on magnetic strips cannot be read with the naked eye, a useful way to maintain confidential data.

Smart cards, going a stage further, have a built-in microprocessor chip where data can be permanently stored. They also possess some processing capability making them suitable for a variety of applications. For example, to gain access, an employee inserts a card or badge in the reader. This device reads and checks the authorisation code before permitting the individual to enter a secured area. Since smart cards can hold more information as compared to magnetic strip cards, they are gaining in popularity.

VOICE RECOGNITION DEVICES

One of the most exciting areas of research involves the recognising of an individual human voice as the basis of input to the computer system. Eliminating the keying in of data, basic commands can very easily be given, facilitating at quick operation.

Voice recognition devices consist of a microphone attached to the computer system. A user speaks into the microphone to input data. The spoken words are then converted into electrical signals (this is in the analog form). A digital-to-analog converter then converts the analog form to digital form (0s and 1s) that can be interpreted by the computer. The digitised version is then matched with existing pre-created dictionary to perform the necessary action.

Voice recognition devices have limited usage today because they have several problems associated with it. Not only do they require the ability to recognise who is speaking, but also what is being said (the message). This difficulty arises primarily because people speak with different accents and different tone pitches. The computer requires a large vocabulary to be able to interpret what is being said. Today's voice recognition systems are therefore successful in a limited domain. They are limited to accepting words and tasks within a limited scope of operation and can handle only small quantities of data.

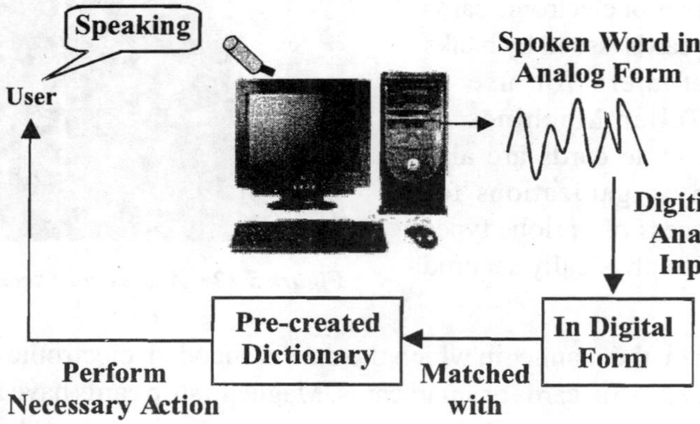

Figure 5.13 Steps in a voice recognition system

Most speech-recognition systems are SPEAKER-DEPENDENT, that is, they respond to the unique speech of a particular individual, a feature not recessarily inconvenient but never the less limiting in generalised applications. It therefore requires creating a database of words for each person using the system.

VISION-INPUT DEVICES

Vision input devices allow data input in the form of images. It usually consists of a digital camera, which focuses on the object whose picture is to be taken. The camera creates the image of the object in digital format, which can then be stored within the computer. The system then compares the digitised image to be interpreted to the pre-recorded digitised images in the computer's database, much like a speech-recognition system does with voice input. The computer identifies the image by matching the structure of the input image with those images in the database. Based on whether on not the match is found, the appropriate action is taken.

Video input or capture is the process of entering full-motion recording into a computer and storing the video on a hard disk or some other medium. Video capture cards are needed for entering video information in the computer. The video files thus created usually take up huge amounts of space on a hard disk (3 minutes of high quality video can occupy one gigabyte of space) and so are usually compressed before storage. The most popular standard used for compression is the MPEG (Motion Pictures Expert Group).

Webcams and *Video Cameras* are most commonly used to input visual data.

KEY POINTS

- Input-Output (or I/O) devices provide a means of communication between the computer and the outside world. They are also known as peripheral devices.
- An input device accepts data from the outside world and transforms it into a form the computer can interpret.
- Keyboards are the most commonly used input devices. They can be classified as general-purpose and special-purpose keyboards. While general-purpose keyboards are standard keyboards meant for general applications, special-purpose keyboards are meant for special-purpose applications to enable faster data entry and user interaction.
- Point-and-draw devices are input devices used to point to, and select menu items or icons displayed on screen. They provide a means for Graphical user interface (GUI). The mouse, trackball, joystick, light pen, and touch screen are commonly used point-and-draw devices.
- Scanning devices provide for direct data input from source documents and are of two types – CONTACT and LASER.
- The optical mark reader (OMR) is a scanner capable of recognising specific types of marks made by a pen or pencil. Data of the nature of choice or selection is typically used as input to the OMR.
- The Magnetic-Ink Character Recognition (MICR) technology is used by the banking industry for processing large volumes of cheques. It uses special ink with which information is pre-printed on the cheques.
- Data represented as vertical lines of varying width and spacing is referred to as bar-code representation of data. An Optical Bar-Code reader (OBR) is a scanner used for decoding bar-coded data. Bar code are especially useful in billing and inventory.
- Maps and drawings can be inputted into the computer system using a digitiser. It provides for recreation of the drawing from the stored information and incorporation of any changes as and when required.
- Electronic card readers read the data encoded on electronic cards and convert it to machine readable form, for further processing.
- Depending on the manner in which data is encoded, electronic cards can be either of the two types – magnetic strip cards and smart cards. Magnetic strip cards store data encoded on a magnetic strip attached to the back of the card. Smart cards have a built-in microprocessor that stores encoded data permanently in the chip's memory.

- Voice recognition devices input data in the form of human voice thereby providing an easy means of data input. They are currently successful in a limited domain.
- Vision input devices allow a computer to accept data by focusing a camera on the object of concern. The data input is usually an image created from the objects' shape and features. Webcams and video cameras are commonly used devices for video input.

REVIEW QUESTIONS

1. Choose the appropriate answer:

i. Tick the odd one out:

(a) Trackball (b) Joystick
(c) Mouse (d) Webcam

ii. Special-purpose keyboards are meant for:

(a) Quick and easy entry of user data
(b) All kinds of applications
(c) Checking accuracy of data at the time of data entry
(d) All of these

iii. Electronic card reader:

(a) Reads graphic data existing on cards
(b) Reads encoded data on an electronic card
(c) Converts drawings and pictures into a digital form
(d) None of hese

iv. Hand-held scanners:

(a) Are used to scan large amount of data
(b) Are more versatile of the scanning devices
(c) Input data when they are brushed over the matter to be read
(d) Input data when they are passed near the scanning area

2. State whether True or False:

i. Keyboard is one of the most common input devices.
ii. Mouse should not be used in cases where graphical user interface is common.
iii. Scanners are devices used for outputting pictures.
iv. Peripheral devices provide a medium for communication between the computer system and the outside world.

3. Match the following:

X		Y
1. Used as a tool in CAD	a.	OBR
2. Reads data coded in the form of small vertical bars	b.	MICR
3. Used exclusively by the banking industry	c.	Digitiser
4. Senses marks on computer readable paper	d.	OMR

4. Fill in the blanks with the appropriate choices listed below:

(i) Source (ii) Vision-input (iii) Voice-recognition (iv) Numeric

1. ______________ keypad supports quick entry of numeric data.
2. Scanners are used to input data directly from ______________ documents.
3. Images can be input into the computer system using ______________ devices.
4. Speech recognition is a feature of ______________ devices.

CHAPTER 6

Output Devices

An output device is an electromechanical device that accepts data from the computer and translates into a form that can be understood by the outside world. The processed data, stored in the memory of the computer, is sent to an output unit, which then transforms the internal representation of data into a form that can be read by the users.

The output can normally be produced in two ways – on a display unit/device, or on paper. Other kinds of output like speech output and mechanical output are also used in certain applications. Output produced on display units or speech output that cannot be touched, is referred to as softcopy output while output produced on paper or material that can be touched, is known as hardcopy output.

A wide range of output devices are available today and can be broadly classified under the categories of:

- display devices (monitors, multimedia projectors, terminals – dumb, smart, intelligent, X terminals)
- printers (dot matrix, inkjet, laser)
- plotters (flatbed, drum)
- Computer output microfilm (COM)
- voice response systems (voice reproduction system, speech synthesizer)

DISPLAY DEVICES

One of the most common and important peripherals in a computer system is the display device. Conventional computers used display terminals known as alphanumeric terminals. These used a form of multi-dot (7 × 5 or 9 × 7) array to display characters. These were used to read text information displayed on screen.

The increasing demand for displaying graphs and pictures, for visual presentation of information (more effective for user interaction), brought about the advent of graphic display devices.

Graphic display is typically made up of a series of dots called 'pixels' (picture elements) whose pattern produces the image. Each dot on the screen can be addressed uniquely and directly. Owing to the fact that each dot can be addressed as a separate unit, it provides greater flexibility for drawing pictures.

Display screen technology may be one of the three categories:

Cathode ray tube (CRT) The main components of a cathode ray terminal are the electron gun, the electron beam controlled by an electromagnetic field, and a display screen which is phosphor-coated. The screen's phosphor-coating is organised into a grid of dots called pixels.

The electron gun emits an electron beam, which is directed towards the phosphor-coated display by the electromagnetic field, and this in turn creates the image.

There are two types of CRT displays:

- ***Vector CRT display:*** In which the electron beam is directed only to places where the image is to be created.
- ***Raster scan display:*** In which image is projected on screen by directing the electron beam across each row of the picture elements from top to the bottom of the screen. This type of display provides a high dynamic capability since the image is continuously refreshed. It offers full colour display at a relatively low cost and is therefore becoming increasingly popular.

The quality of display is indicated by the resolution of the display device. The number of horizontal and vertical pixels determines resolution. Typical resolutions in graphic display range from (800 × 600) to (640 × 768) to (1024 × 1024) pixels.

Based on the resolution and the number of colours supported, several standards for colour monitors have evolved. The most popular of these include:

- Color graphics adapter (CGA), which has a resolution of (320 × 200) and supports up to 16 colours.
- Extended graphics adapter (EGA) has a resolution of (640 × 350) and supports up to 16 colours.
- Video graphics adapter (VGA) has a resolution of (640 × 480) and supports up to 256 colours.
- Super VGA having a resolutions ranging (800 × 600) to (1280 × 1024) and supporting up to 256 or more colours.

Note that each one of these is implemented by installing an add-on card in the computer, commonly known as graphics adapter or the video card. This card is then connected to the appropriate monitor.

Liquid crystal display (LCD) Introduced in watches and clocks in the 1970s and is now applied to the display terminals. In this, the cathode ray tube was replaced by liquid crystal to produce the image. It does not have colour capability and the image quality is relatively poor. The main advantage of LCD is its low energy consumption. It finds its most common usage in portable devices where compactness and low energy requirements are of prime importance.

Projection display Projection display technology is characterised by replacing the personal size screen with large screens upon which the images are projected. These systems are connected to the computer and whatever appears on the computer terminal gets enlarged and projected on a large screen. These are being used today for large group presentations.

Monitors

Monitors use a cathode ray tube (CRT) to display information. It resembles a television screen and is similar to it in other respects.

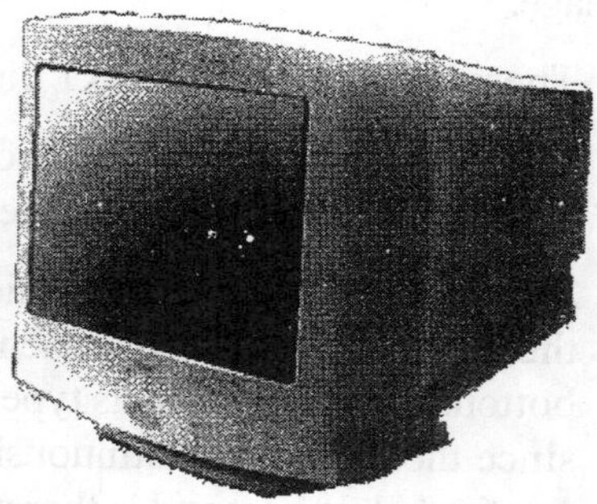

Figure 6.1 CRT monitor

The monitor is typically associated with a keyboard for manual input of characters. The screen displays information as it is keyed in, enabling a visual check of input before it is transferred to the computer. It is also used to display the output from the computer and hence serves as both an input and an output device.

The monitor along with the keyboard is called a Visual Display Unit (VDU).

This is the most commonly used input/output device today and is also known as a soft copy terminal. A printing device is usually required to provide a hard copy of the output.

Multimedia Projectors

A multimedia projector is an output device used to project information from the computer onto a large screen so that it can be viewed by a large group of people. Prior to this, the standard mode of giving presentations was to make transparencies and projecting them using an overhead projector. This was a tedious and time-consuming activity, since for every change in the subject matter a new transparency had to be prepared. And of course, since electronic cut, copy and paste was not possible this, meant additional work.

A multimedia projector can directly be plugged into the computer system and information projected on a large screen thereby making it possible to present information to a large audience. The presenter can also use a pointer to emphasise specific areas of interest in the presentation.

Another popular method used today is to connect the computer to an LCD flat screen and then project the LCD image using an overhead projector.

Owing to its convenience and applicability, multimedia projectors are increasingly becoming popular in seminars, presentations, classrooms etc.

Terminals–Dumb, Smart, Intelligent

Terminals are classified as dumb, smart, and intelligent based on their processing capability. These are being used as online, remote data entry devices.

Dumb terminal consists of a terminal and a keyboard for data input. The data entered is sent directly to the main computer. The terminal itself does not possess any processing capability. Data entered through dumb terminals is referred to as 'dirty' data since it is sent to the main computer along with any errors. This may lead to delays in processing data since data needs to be first 'cleaned' before processing can be done.

Smart terminal is characterised by additionally having a microprocessor and limited internal storage. It, therefore, supports editing inputted data before sending it to the main computer. This means that it supports preliminary processing of data locally thereby assuring that only 'clean' data is transmitted to the main computer for further processing. However, smart terminals cannot be programmed by users.

Intelligent terminal computers having a built-in microprocessor, memory and which can be programmed by users, are termed intelligent terminals. Such terminals also have their own online secondary storage devices like disks. Data can be stored locally and small jobs can be processed by the terminal itself without the need to interact with the CPU of the main computer.

Current technology has brought about a low price differential between dumb, smart and intelligent terminals. This has increased the use of intelligent terminals.

X Terminals

X terminals are graphic terminals supporting a wide variety of commands. These encompass a rich set of commands to draw graphics and images along with display of characters. They support managing areas on the screen also known as 'Windows'. Opening a new window, resizing the existing window, closing an existing window, are typical commands available for handling windows. X terminals (typically used with servers) are very commonly used today.

PRINTERS

Printers are used for producing output on paper. There are a large variety of commercially available printers today (estimated to be 1500 different types). These printers can be classified into categories based on:

- Printing technology
- Printing speed
- Printing quality

Printing technology Printers can be classified as impact or non-impact printers, based on the technology they use for producing output.

Impact printers use variations of standard typewriter printing mechanism where a hammer strikes the paper through an inked ribbon. These printers have a mechanism that touches the paper in order to create an image. Dot matrix printers and character printers fall under this category.

Non-impact printers do not touch the paper when creating an image. They use chemical, heat or electrical signals to etch symbols on paper. Many of these require special coated or treated paper. Inkjet, laser and thermal printers fall under this category of printers.

Printing speed Refers to the number of characters printed in a unit of time. Based on speed these may be classified as character printer (prints one character at a time), line printers (print one line at a time), and page printers (print the entire page at a time). Printer speeds are therefore measured in terms of characters-per-second or cps for a character printer, lines-per-minute or lpm for a line printer, and pages-per-minute or ppm for a page printer.

Printing quality Is determined by the resolution of printing and is characterised by the number of dots that can be printed per linear inch, horizontally or vertically. It is measured in terms of dots-per-inch or dpi. Printers can be classified as near-letter-quality or NLQ, letter-quality or LQ, near-typeset-quality or NTQ, and typeset-quality or TQ based on their printing quality. NLQ printers of resolutions of about 300 dpi, LQ of about 600 dpi, NTQ of about 1200 dpi, and TQ of about 2000 dpi. NLQ and LQ printers are used for ordinary printing in day-to-day activities, while NTQ and TQ printers are used to produce top-quality printing, typically required in the publishing industry.

The section that follows explains the working of some commonly used printers.

Dot Matrix

Dot matrix printers were the most popular impact printers used in personal computing. These printers use a print head consisting of a series of small pins to strike a ribbon coated with ink, causing the ink to transfer to the paper at the point of impact. Characters thus produced are in a matrix format. The shape of each character, i.e. the dot pattern, is obtained from information held electronically.

Figure 6.2(a) Characters formed using dots

Figure 6.2(b) Dot matrix printer

The speed, versatility and ruggedness, combined with low cost, tend to make such printers particularly attractive in the personal computer market.

Typical printing speeds in case of dot matrix printers range between 40 – 1000 cps (characters-per-second). The one major disadvantage of this technology is that the print quality is low.

Inkjet

Inkjet printers use a series of nozzles to spray drops of ink directly on the paper. These therefore fall under the category of non-impact printers.

Figure 6.3 Inkjet printer

The print head of an inkjet printer consists of a number of tiny nozzles that can be selectively heated up in a few microseconds by an IC register. When this happens, the ink near it vapourises and is ejected through the nozzle to make a dot on the paper placed in front of the print head. The character is printed by selectively heating the appropriate set of nozzles as the print head moves horizontally.

If you have ever looked at a piece of paper that has come out of an inkjet printer, you would have noticed that:

- the dots are extremely small (usually between 50 and 60 microns in diameter), so small that they are tinier than the diameter of a human hair (70 microns).
- the dots are positioned very precisely, with resolutions of up to 1440×720 dots per inch (dpi).
- the dots can have different colors combined together to create photo-quality images.

Inkjet printers are slower than dot-matrix printers (40 - 300 cps), cheaper to buy but are more expensive in running costs (the ink cartridge cost is considerably higher than that of the DMP ribbon) and are used by people/organisations where speed of printing is not the most important factor.

Laser

Laser printers use dry ink (toner), static electricity, and heat to place and bond the ink onto the paper. They use a combination of laser and photocopier technology. Printing is achieved by deflecting laser beam onto the photosensitive surface of a drum after which the latent image attracts the toner to the image. The toner is then electro-statistically transferred to the paper and fixed into a permanent image.

Figure 6.4 Laser printer

Laser printers are capable of converting computer output into print, page by page. Since characters are formed by very tiny ink particles, they can produce very high quality images (text and graphics), generally offer a wide variety of character fonts, and are silent and fast in use.

Laser printers are faster in printing speed than other printers discussed above. Their speeds can range from 10 pages a minute to about 200 pages per minute, depending upon the make/model.

Laser is high quality, high speed, high volume, and non-impact technology that works on plain paper or pre-printed stationary. This technology is relatively expensive but is becoming very popular because of the quality, speed and noiseless operations.

PLOTTERS

Plotters are used to produce graphical output on paper. It is a device capable of producing charts, drawings, graphics, maps etc. It is much like a printer but is designed to print graphs instead of alphanumeric characters.

Based on the technology used, plotters may be pen plotters or electrostatic plotters. While pen plotters have an ink pen attached to draw the images, electrostatic plotters work similar to a laser printer. Image is produced by charging the paper with a high voltage. This voltage attracts the toner, which is then melted on the paper with heat. Electrostatic plotters are fast, but the quality is generally considered to be poor when compared to pen plotters. This is why pen plotters are more extensively used as compared to electrostatic plotters.

Flatbed plotters and drum plotters constitute the most commonly used plotters.

Flatbed Plotters

Flatbed plotters have a flat base like a drawing board on which the paper is laid (as shown in Figure 6.5(a)). One or more arms, each of them carrying an ink pen, moves across the paper to draw. The arm movement is controlled by a microprocessor (chip). The arm can move in two directions, one parallel to the plotter and the other perpendicular to it (called the x and y directions). With this kind of movement, it can move very precisely to any point on the paper placed below.

The computer sends the commands to the plotter which are translated into x & y movements. The arm moves in very small steps to produce continuous and smooth graphics.

The size of the plot in a flatbed plotter is limited only by the size of the plotter's bed.

The advantage of flatbed plotters is that the user can easily control the graphics. He can manually pick up the arm anytime during the production of graphics and place it on any position on the paper to alter the position of graphics to his choice.

The disadvantage here is that flatbed plotters occupy a large amount of space.

Drum Plotters

Drum Plotters use a drum revolver to move the paper during printing (as shown in Figure 6.5(b)). The arm carrying a pen moves only in one direction, perpendicular to the direction of the motion of the paper. Thus in drum plotters the pen is moved in a single axis track and the paper itself moves on a cylindrical drum to add the other axis or dimension. The combination of the pen and paper movement creates the graphics.

The size of the graph is therefore limited only by the width of the drum and can be of any length.

Drum plotters are very compact and lightweight as compared to flatbed plotters. This is one of the advantages of such plotters.

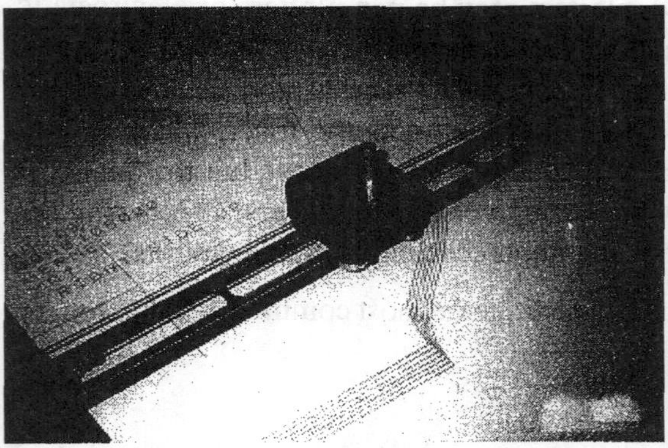

Figure 6.5(a) Top view of a flatbed plotter

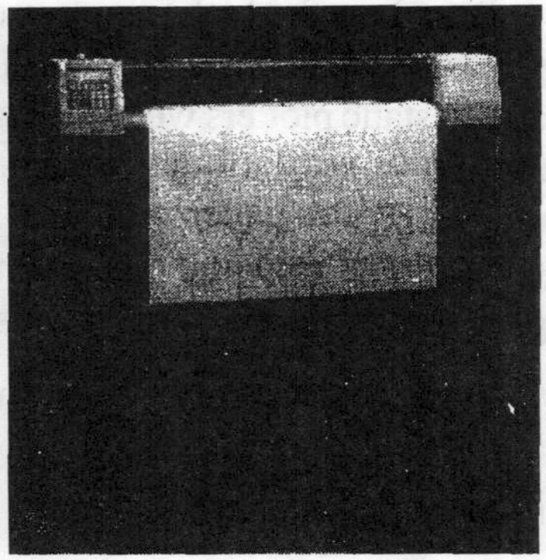

Figure 6.5(b) Drum plotter

The disadvantage, however, is that the user cannot freely control the graphics when they are being created.

Plotters are more expensive when compared to printers. Typical application areas for plotters include: CAE (computer-aided engineering) applications like CAD (computer-aided design) and CAM (computer-aided manufacturing), architectural drawing, map drawing etc.

COMPUTER OUTPUT MICROFILM (COM)

COM is a process characterised by copying/printing data from media located on PCs, mini or mainframe computers onto a microfilm. It consists of a high-speed recorder, which transfers digital data onto a microfilm using laser technology, and a processor that develops the microfilm once exposed to the light source.

A computer output microfilm device translates information normally held on magnetic tape into miniature images on a microfilm (also called microfiche–'fiche' pronounced as 'fish'). The device displays information as characters on a CRT screen and then using photographic methods records the display onto the film. Drawings and images can also be displayed along with narrative text.

A special reader/printer can subsequently be used to view the processed film. The reader operates on a 'back projection' principle displaying one frame at a time on a translucent screen, typically about A4 size. The printer can then be used selectively to produce a hard copy of what is presented on screen.

The figure below identifies the various steps in COM production.

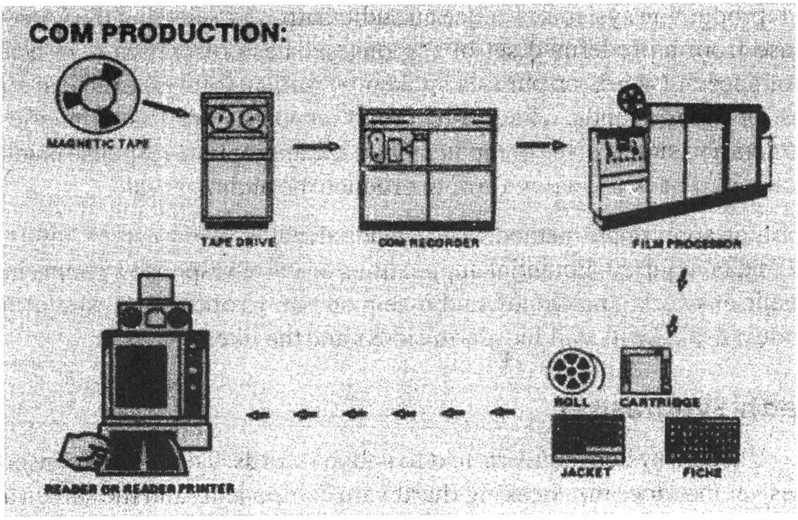

Figure 6.6 Steps in a COM production

A COM system provides an easy and compact way of recording and storing information, and subsequently retrieving desired pieces of information. It offers various advantages like reduction of paper, reduction in cost (since it is cheaper than most electronic media), improved quality (COM technology provides superior image quality), and electronic record retention/archiving.

COM is ideal for data that requires long-term storage, because microfilm is less volatile than magnetic media such as disks and tapes. It stores data in a very compact format; up to 270 pages can be contained in a single 4 × 6 inch fiche.

Converting magnetic tapes to microfilm is quite inexpensive for closed files. However, if the data is highly active, or requires regular updating, microfilm may be less efficient than retaining the information online. It is therefore useful for data that must be archived for long periods of time and referenced only occasionally, e.g., information that must be archived to comply with legal regulations, information maintained by insurance companies, banks, government agencies, and various of organisations of this type.

VOICE RESPONSE SYSTEMS

Voice response systems enable the computer to talk to its users. It consists of an audio-response device that produces the audio output.

Voice response systems are typically of two types: voice reproduction system and speech synthesiser.

Voice Reproduction System

Voice reproduction systems produce an audio output by selecting the appropriate response from a predefined set of responses. These responses may be in the form of speech (words or phrases spoken by human beings), musical sounds, alarms, or other sounds. The pre-recorded responses are first converted into digital data and stored in the computer. Once the appropriate response is selected, it is converted back to analog form to produce the audio output.

This is an appropriate method where standard replies to requests for information are all that is required. Potential applications of voice response systems include automatic answering machines, audio help on how to operate a system, enquiry on product availability, talking alarm clocks and the like.

Speech Synthesiser

A speech access system converts text to spoken words. The system consists of a synthesiser that does the speaking (hardware component) and the screen access program that directs the synthesiser (software component). Some synthesisers and speech access programs are linked and sold as a package, while others are sold independently.

The screen access software allows the user to access commercial software applications and to convert the text or display into verbal output. Users can hear their keystrokes spoken aloud and can read the display on command.

The building blocks of speech output are phonemes. The phoneme is the smallest segment of sound such that if one phoneme in a word is substituted with another, the meaning itself will change. For example, substituting the first phoneme in the word 'coffee' can change the word to 'toffee'. Because the definition is somewhat subjective, it is not possible to say precisely how many phonemes there are in the English language, but it is generally agreed that there are around forty.

There are various applications of synthetic speech but in particular two areas of applications exist for people with disabilities: augmentative communication and computer access for the visually handicapped.

'Augmentative communication' refers to the use of technology (usually computer-based) to facilitate personal communication. In other words, someone who cannot speak for one reason or another may use a device through which he or she can specify utterances to be communicated to another person. The obvious medium of communication for such a device is (synthetic) speech, since it is the voice that is being replaced. Cosmologist Stephen Hawking uses one of these devices.

The other major application relies on the fact that text on a computer screen can be converted into speech. This is carried out by a 'screen reader,' which is a piece of software that runs alongside other programs, capturing whatever they display on the screen. The great advantage of a screen reader is that it will work with standard application software, so it is not necessary to develop (say) a talking word processor or a talking spreadsheet.

Like all computer technology, speech synthesisers have greatly reduced in price over recent years. As always, the main aim of research and development is to improve quality, and progress is being made. Already synthesisers exist, based on new technology, which produce voices that would be hard to distinguish from a recording of human speech. What they lack currently is the facility to convert from text to speech in real time. It is only a matter of time before the techniques and technology are developed to the point that this becomes feasible.

KEY POINTS

- An output device is an electromechanical device that accepts data from the computer and translates into a form that can be understood by the outside world.
- Output can be produced in two way–on a display unit/device, or on paper. Output produced on display unit or device is called softcopy output while that produced on paper is referred to as hardcopy output.
- Monitors are by far the most common output devices used to produce softcopy output. They resemble a television screen and use the cathode ray tube (CRT) to display information.
- The monitor is usually associated with a keyboard to input characters and these together are termed as the visual display unit (VDU). It serves both as an input and output device and is the commonest I/O device used with today's computers.
- A multimedia projector is an output device used to project information from the computer onto a large screen so that it can be viewed by a large group of people. These are becoming increasingly popular in seminars, presentations, classrooms etc.
- Terminals can be classified as dumb, smart, and intelligent based on their local processing capability. Dumb terminals do not possess any processing capability. Data entered is directly sent to a main computer. Smart terminals have a microprocessor and limited internal storage. Preliminary processing can be done before sending the data to the main computer. Intelligent terminals are small computers by themselves possessing extensive local data processing power. The user can also program its built-in microprocessor.
- X terminals are graphic terminals having rich set of commands to draw graphics and images along with display of characters.

- Printers are the commonly used output devices used to produce hardcopy output.
- Based on the printing technology used, they can be classified as impact or non-impact printers. Impact printers use a mechanism by which a hammer strikes the paper through an inked ribbon to create an image while non-impact printers do not touch the paper when creating an image. They use chemical, heat or electrical signals to etch symbols on paper.
- Based on the printing speed, printers may be classified as character printers (prints one character at a time), line printers (prints one line at a time), and page printers (prints the entire page at one time).
- Based on the printing quality, printers are classified as near-letter-quality (NLQ), letter-quality (LQ), near-typeset-quality (NTQ), or typeset-quality (TQ).
- Dot matrix printers are impact printers that create characters images using a pattern of dots.
- Inkjet printers fall under the category of non-impact printers and create characters and images by spraying minute drops of ink on the paper.
- Laser printers are page printers that produce very high quality output. They form characters and images using very tiny ink particles.
- Plotters are used to produce graphical output on paper. They are capable of producing charts, drawings, maps etc. Typical applications of plotters include CAD, CAM, architectural drawing, map drawing etc.
- Flatbed plotters have a flat base like a drawing board on which the paper is laid. The arm carrying the ink pen moves in two different directions over the paper to draw the image.
- Drum plotters use a drum revolver to move the paper during printing. Unlike flatbed plotters, the arm in drum plotters moves only in one direction over the paper to draw the image. The combination of pen and paper movement creates the image.
- Computer output microfilm (COM) is an output device that enables computer output to be recorded on a sheet or roll of microfilm as microscopic filmed images. The microfilm recorder is used to record the information on the microfiche while the microfilm reader is used to retrieve the same information. COM is ideal for applications that require large volume of information to be stored and subsequently selectively retrieved offline.
- Voice response systems enable the computer to talk to its users. It consists of an audio-response device that produces the audio output. Voice reproduction systems and speech synthesisers fall under the category of voice response systems.
- A voice reproduction system produces an audio output by selecting the appropriate response from a pre-defined set of responses.

- A speech synthesiser converts text to spoken words. Phonemes (the smallest slices of sound) are considered to be the building blocks of speech output.

REVIEW QUESTIONS

1. Choose the appropriate answer:

i. Which of the terms is not associated with display devices:

(a) CGA (b) TGA
(c) VGA (d) EGA

ii. Output printed through a printer is referred to as:

(a) Softcopy output (b) Hardcopy output
(c) Temporary output (d) Volatile output

iii. Plotters are very useful in applications such as:

(a) Financial accounting (b) Word processing
(c) Computer aided design (d) All of these

iv. High quality, high speed, high volume, and non-impact are terms associated with:

(a) Laser printers (b) Dot matrix printers
(c) Inkjet printers (d) Plotters

2. State whether True or False:

i. Keyboard, monitor and printers are essential for computers.
ii. Projection displays can be used for classroom teaching.
iii. Printer speed is measured in dpi.
iv. COM provides an easy and compact way to record and store large quanta of information.
v. Speech synthesisers enable users to speak to the computer.

3. Match the following:

X	Y
1. Selects appropriate response from pre-defined set of responses	(i) Phonemes
2. Building blocks of speech output	(ii) Drum plotters
3. Data archived to comply with legal regulations	(iii) Dot matrix printers
4. Impact technology	(iv) Voice reproduction system
5. Arm carrying a pen moves only in one direction	(v) COM

4. Fill in the blanks with the appropriate choices listed below:

(i) Inkjet (ii) Dot matrix (iii) COM (vi) Voice response (v) Flatbed

1. ______________ plotters have a flat base on which the paper is laid.
2. "Augmentative communication" is an application of ______________ system.
3. Characters produced by a ______________ printer are in a matrix format.
4. ______________ printer uses a series of nozzles to spray drops of ink directly on paper.
5 ______________ technology is associated with storing information in the form of images on a microfilm.

5. Differentiate between:

1. Impact and non-impact printers
2. Dot matrix and laser printers
3. Dumb and intelligent terminals

CHAPTER 7

Multimedia

DEFINITION

In simple words, multimedia means multi (many) and media refers to communication/transfer medium. Multimedia is any combination of text, graphic art, sound, animation and video elements delivered to you by your computer or any other electronic means. A computer's encyclopedia containing images, audio and video effects along with the content is a simple example of a multimedia application. Although the definition of multimedia is fairly simple, making it work can be quite complicated. You would need to understand the importance of each individual element and also have knowledge about the usage of multimedia tools and technologies, to weave the elements of multimedia in a meaningful manner.

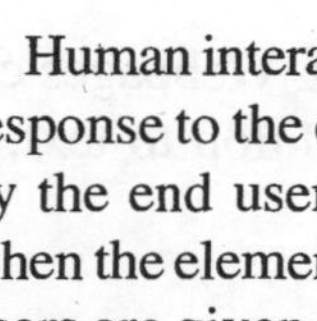

Text

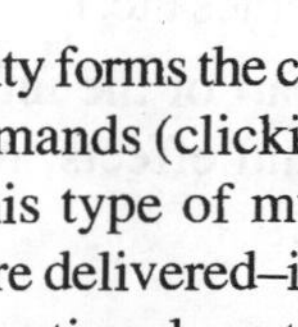

Graphic art

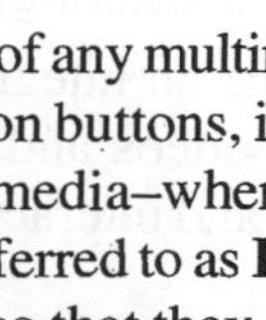

Sound

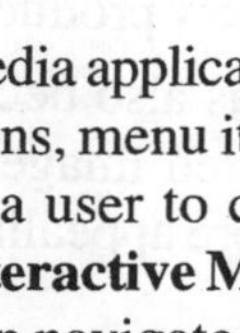

Animation

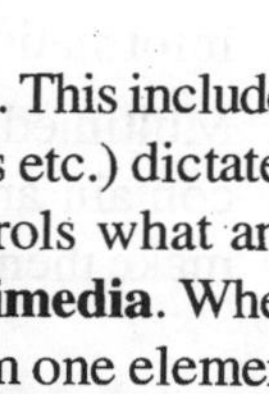

Video

Human interactivity forms the core of any multimedia application. This includes response to the commands (clicking on buttons, icons, menu items etc.) dictated by the end user. This type of multimedia–where a user to controls what and when the elements are delivered–is referred to as **Interactive Multimedia**. When users are given navigational control so that they can navigate from one element to another in a non-linear fashion, interactive multimedia becomes **Hypermedia**. The World Wide Web (www) is probably the most successful network information system in history. One of its advantages is certainly the ease of use of its interface. The concept of hypertext and hypermedia has gained familiarity after the introduction of www.

Kiosks and CD-ROM applications are excellent vehicles for presenting information with the dynamics of multimedia. Multimedia equipped PCs are used to host such applications. Such computers come equipped with a CD-ROM drive, a sound card with speakers, microphone and may also include a scanner and a digital camera (Figure 7.1). Multimedia applications also require large amounts of digital memory when stored in the users computer.

Figure 7.1 Typical multimedia computer

Importance of Multimedia

- Multimedia is characterised by an audio-visual interface, which provides an excellent medium for user interactivity.
- It improves information retention. (According to a research conducted by computer technology, people only retain 20% of what they see and 30% of what they hear. But they remember 50% of what they see and hear, and as much as 80% of what they see, hear, and do simultaneously.)
- Computer games are the most common applications of multimedia. Other widely used applications include educational CDs (CBT) and promotional information (new products, marketing schemes etc.).
- Multimedia has also become an integral part of the internet. Webpages can contain animated images, videos and sound effects, in addition to text, to make them more appealing and interactive.

MULTIMEDIA TOOLS

Authoring Tools

The key to successful multimedia production is a seamless integration of multimedia elements for graphic design, content management, production and packaging. The whole process of developing a multimedia package is called **Authoring**. An authoring system is a collection of software tools that help in various aspects of multimedia production. Multimedia elements are woven together using authoring tools. These tools are designed to manage individual multimedia elements and provide user interaction. Multimedia authoring software can be used to make:

- Video productions
- Animations
- Games
- Presentations
- Interactive kiosk applications
- Interactive training
- Simulations, prototypes and technical visualisations

Steps in Multimedia Production

1. ***Media capture:*** Multimedia authoring systems streamline data capture by providing interfaces to a range of image and data capture devices.
2. ***Media conversion:*** Images, audio clips, animation, sequences and video clips exist in a variety of formats. A well-equipped multimedia authoring system will include a set of utilities for converting between many of the commonly used formats.
3. ***Media editing:*** After data has been captured and converted to the native format of the authoring system, it may need some polishing before it is suitable for presentation. For instance, 'noise' can be removed from audio clips, images can be touched up, etc. Multimedia authoring systems provide media – specific editors for these operations.
4. ***Media composition:*** The core of a multimedia authoring system includes a tool for combining media and specifying their spatial (one image being juxtaposed or placed side-by-side within a second) and temporal (when an audio track is added to a visual sequence) relationships.

ELEMENTS OF MULTIMEDIA

Text

Text, containing words and symbols, is the most common form of communication. It is one of the popularly used mediums of appearance that is used to deliver information accurately and in detail. Usually text provides the core structure to the package. Words are vital elements of multimedia that can appear in the titles, menus, navigation aids and in the content of a multimedia application or project. It is most essential to use words that have the most precise and powerful meanings to express what you need to convey.

A major drawback of using text is that it is not user friendly as compared to the other elements of multimedia. For example: it is harder to read from a screen for long, as it tires the eyes more than reading it in its print version.

Designing with text: From a design perspective, the choice of font size, style and other text attributes needs to be related both to the complexity of the message and to its venue.

Some useful tips for designing the text in your multimedia application:

- use legible fonts that can be easily read.
- vary the font size and style according to the importance of your message.

- indent your paragraphs wherever required.
- explore the effects of different colours and shadows to add depth to your application.
- use menus for easy navigation and meaningful words for menu items.
- use buttons, icons or symbols for user interaction.

- you can also use stylish fonts for displaying attention-grabbing results.

Hyperlinks: Hypertext is the organisation of information units into connected associations that a user can choose to make. An instance of such an association is called a **Hyperlink.** When a user clicks on such a link, more information on the particular topic is displayed. It, therefore, provides the user an option of reading as much information as required. Hyperlinks can contain cross-linking of words not only

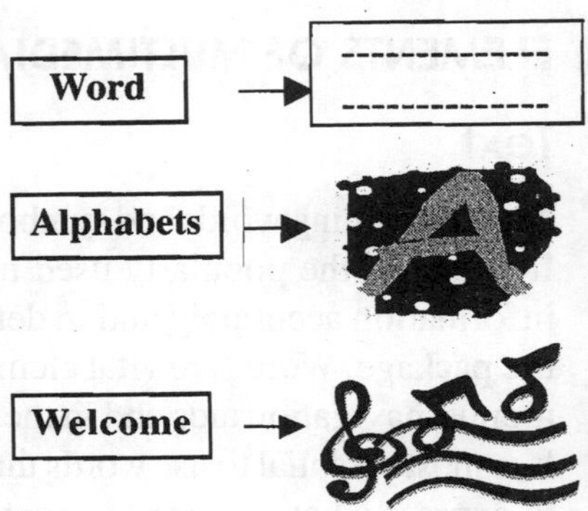

to words but also to images, videos or sound files. Hyperlinks are used for non-linear navigation, which is not an option available in a sequentially organised book.

Graphics

Pictures/graphics enhance the overall look of a multimedia package. Pictures express more than normal text and are generally considered as the most important element of a multimedia application.

It is often noticed that a webpage containing numerous images takes longer to download than a simple text based webpage. Image files are therefore compressed to save memory and disk space of your computer. **GIF** (Graphics Interchange Format), **JPEG** (Joint Photographic Experts Group) and **PNG** (Portable Network Graphics) are examples of compressed image file formats.

Pictures can be created using any of the following ways:

- You can use drawing tools like MS paint to create simple pictures. paint allows to create or assemble pictures by drawing straight, wavy or curved lines, using shapes like squares, circles and polygons, or simply by freehand drawing.

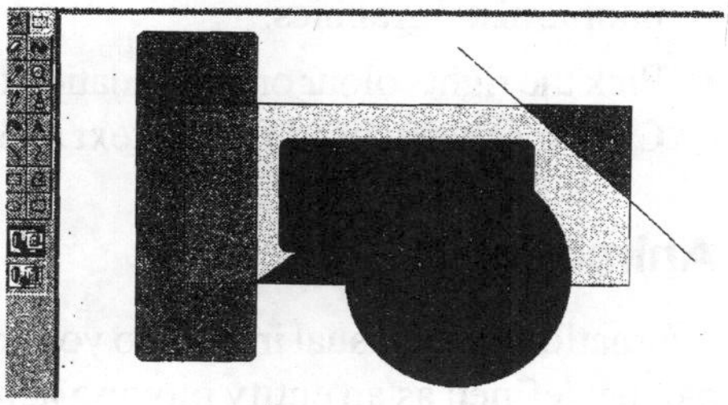

- You can insert images from the clipart gallery. A clipart collection typically contains a series of images for different categories. Clip art is available through CD-ROMs or from the internet.

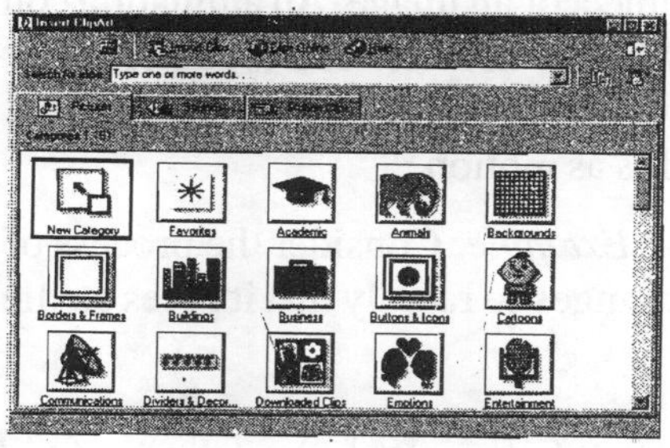

- You can use scanner or digital camera to capture original pictures in digitised form. You can also scan images, created using traditional methods like watercolours, crayons etc.

Digital camera

Scanner

- If you are still not satisfied with scanned pictures or images downloaded from the clipart gallery, you can use image-editing tools to manipulate images according to your taste. Picture properties that can be manipulated using these tools include brightness, contrast, color, depth, hue and size. Apart from correcting the blemishes in your image, you can add additional effects like filters, shadows, patterns, 3D-effects and many more. Image editing tools are indispensable for excellent multimedia production. Adobe Photoshop, Microsoft Photo draw are some examples of image-editing tools.

Some useful tips for adding images in your multimedia application:

- Do not overload your application with too many images. This would not only make your application look clumsy, but it would also consume excessive computer resources.
- Do not include heavy (oversized) graphics.
- Use context – sensitive images.
- To the extent possible, use compressed image file formats. Avoid using unoptimised graphics.
- Pick the right colour or combination of colours for your multimedia application. Colour scheme used for the text should blend well with the images.

Animation

Animation gives visual impact to your multimedia application. In simple terms, it can be defined as an entity moving across the screen. This entity could be a text object or an image. An animation consists of a series of rapidly changing objects, which when blended together gives an illusion of movement. The speed with which each object is replaced by the next one is so rapid that the eye perceives this as motion.

Example: Consider the process of rotating a wheel, the position of the arrow changes so rapidly that it gives an illusion of spinning.

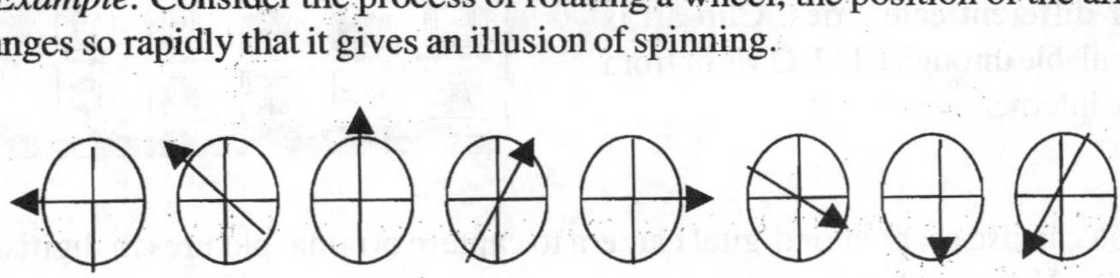

Animation tools: MS powerpoint is a tool used for creating primitive animations. Visual effects like wipes, dissolves, fades and zooms can be added to any object. For example: you can make a text to fly from top or left. Such effects are available with almost all authoring packages. You can create complex animations using tools like Director, 3D Studio Max, CompuServe and Shockwave. Such animations can be ported across platforms and applications by making use of suitable translators.

Some useful tips for adding animations in your multimedia application:

- before you create an animation, organise its execution into a series of logical steps. First choose the objects in your presentation that you wish to animate, and then decide upon the sequence of animation. In case of complicated presentations, writing a detailed script of the list of activities that will prove useful.
- you can animate one or all objects of an application. As mentioned earlier, applications intended for the web should not contain too many animations as it would affect the download time.
- add user interactivity wherever essential to the application.
- you can combine animations with lively sounds for grabbing the user's attention.

Sound

Sound is used to set the rhythm or a mood in a package. Speech gives an effect of a language (pronunciation) for instance. Proper usage of sound can make all the difference between an ordinary multimedia presentation and a professional one.

Sound types: Musical Instrument Digital Interface (**MIDI**) is a communication standard developed in early 1980's for electronic musical instruments and computers. A MIDI file consists of a list of commands that represent the recordings of musical actions. When these commands are sent to a MIDI Playback device, a sound is produced. The main disadvantage of MIDI data is that it is not digitised. In contrast, **Digital Audio** is a recording that depends on the capabilities of your sound system. Digital audio data are the actual representations of sound data and are stored in the form of thousands of individual numbers known as **Samples**. Digital sound is used for music CDs.

Creating sound: Sound can be recorded using a microphone, a synthesiser, or any other medium like tape or cassette player and then be digitised using audio digitising software. Therefore, sound may be digitised from any source – natural or pre-recorded. Digitised sounds are stored as wave (.WAV) files (Windows Platform). These can then be played using Windows Media player.

Some useful tips for adding sounds to your multimedia application:

- a distorted recording sounds terrible, so before a sound file is added it must be tested for clarity. If required, it must be edited using Audio-Editing tools like Wave Studio Sound or Macromedia's Sound Edit 16-2. It may be worth noting that higher the sound quality, the larger would be the file size.
- decide the kind of sound you need (such as background music, special sound effects or spoken dialogue).

- test the sound, to ensure they are synchronised properly with images and or animations.

Video

If pictures can paint a thousand words, then motion pictures can paint a million. Digital video is the most engaging of multimedia venues and is a powerful tool for bringing users close to the real world.

NTSE (National Television Standards Committee), PAL (Phase Alteration Line), SECAM (Sequential Colour and Memory), HDTV (High Definition Television) are commonly used broadcast and video standards across the globe.

Current television is based on analog technology and fixed international standards for the broadcast and display of images. Computer video, on the other hand is based on digital technology and other standards for displaying images. Digital Video is produced using analog video as a base. The conversion of analog video into its digital equivalent requires a special hardware called **Video Capture Card.**

Video data is also compressed using different compression techniques. MPEG (Motion Pictures Expert Group), JPEG (Joint Photographic Experts Group), P*64, real video are examples of commonly used compressed video formats.

Some useful tips for adding video clips to your multimedia application:

- video clippings which are not appropriately designed can degrade your presentation rather than add value to it. Carefully planned, well-executed clips can make a dramatic difference in a multimedia presentation.
- titles used in video clips should be plain enough to be easily read.
- avoid making busy title screens; use more screen if required.
- again, any multimedia element that is added to an application intended for Web should be compressed to support quick and easy download.

APPLICATIONS OF MULTIMEDIA

Multimedia in Education

As compared to traditional '**Stand and Deliver**' teaching methodology, training imparted using animated, interactive and instructional multimedia applications has proven to be more useful. Apart from making the subject interesting, it increases information retention and learning capacity of the users. The potential for students of all ages to author as part of a creative educational programme that focuses on achievement of goals and competencies rather than time served, will help educators to shift from teacher to facilitator and mentor. Some applications of multimedia in education, are stated below:

- Computer encyclopedias have gained considerable popularity in recent years as they allow the user a non-linear navigation of text; user can quickly access the desired topic.
- The web can be thought of as a global digital multimedia library. The concept of e-learning or online learning using interactive communication tools has grown tremendously with the popularity of www. It is accessible to a large number of people, can be accessed from any where and everywhere and promotes the quality of learning experiences and outcomes.
- Schools are perhaps the most best users for multimedia. Many school reform models propose a shift from a teacher-centered didactic model to a learner-centered model to enable students to learn the subject area faster, and in a much greater depth. Multimedia presentation tools can be used to design, develop, publish, and present course-curriculum concepts to audiences inside and outside the classroom.
- Multimedia based presentations and tutorials provide an easy-to-learn environment for the young generations. Reading and retention skills grow when concepts are explained using animated pictures. It can be a used as a homework helper or serve as a literature guide.
- Multimedia can prove to be tremendously useful in the medical field. It gives an opportunity of indepth, clear and interactive learning of new clinical advancements.
- Multimedia can be used for stimulating different types of environments used for training purposes. For example: flight attendants can be trained to manage terrorism and security by artificially simulating such an environment.
- Libraries, arts and cultural centres, and learner support systems are already using interactive communication tools. Multimedia documents can also be designed to receive information from the reader and subsequently process it to provide individualised solutions. This has added a new dimension to the reading/writing process and the skills involved can be reinforced.

Multimedia in Entertainment

With the arrival of the CD-ROM and the Internet, the entertainment industry made a huge leap into a new era with a winning card–multimedia. Armed with animated images, sounds, full-motion video and interactive capability, multimedia became a dominant factor in today's information age. The fast but steady growth of electronic technology allowed multimedia to gain popularity within a short span of time. Some applications of multimedia in the entertainment field are stated below:

- Games are the first thing that come to mind when we talk about multimedia. Multimedia capabilities are used to develop interactive games with sophisticated animations, 3D and sound effects. These games can be played on the computer, mobile devices or on the Internet. Live internet pay-for-play gaming with multiple players has attained significant popularity.
- Movies and cartoons unleashing full effects of multimedia, which were only available on VHS tapes, are now stored on CD-ROM (VCD) to allow the users to watch on their computer screen. Multi-layered digital versatile disk with more storage capacity and even higher processing speed, is making its way into the market and slowly replacing the CD-ROM. It can be used to view movies and play audio files. Multimedia can be used in voice mail, chatting and video conferencing as well. You can also do real time video conferencing with your colleagues spread across the globe.
- Another common application of multimedia is the advent of animated e-greeting cards for different occasions.
- Wedding albums and family histories can be created on the World Wide Web using the power of multimedia.
- Multimedia has also found its application in hotels, pubs, shopping malls, museums, cinema halls, where stand-alone terminals or kiosks are made available for guiding users. Printers are also usually attached so that users can walk way with a printed copy of the desired information.

Multimedia in Marketing

Advertising has become very prevalent in our daily surroundings, so for a product to stand apart, it is very essential to present it in a dynamic, visually stimulating manner to grab the attention of consumers. The business world is slowly rejecting run of the mill traditional methods (like placing ads in yellow pages, distributing pamphlets, etc.) and adopting solutions from the electronic era. Only companies with a nerve to radically change their marketing strategies for the new millennium will survive and be able to cater to the ever-changing customer's mindset. Applications of multimedia in the marketing field include:

- Presentations–for launching the products of a company. Reaching the target audience with necessary technical services or products requires clear communication, stating the benefits and features, outlining its applications and any other product related details, all presented in a well-designed and interactive manner so that the users familiarise faster. Multimedia presentations are an excellent way to motivate, inform, and captivate a wide range of audiences via PC's, laptops, plasma screens, or kiosks delivered via CD-ROM or the internet.
- Multimedia–to create interactive product catalogues, training tutorials, buyer guides, and information directories with adequate search and navigation facilities

to guide the user to easily trace the desired information. A buyer guide can list the nearby dealers, a comparison of the top brands, maps of the city and other helpful guest services.

- E-mail advertising or placing banner ads on the Internet–an extremely cost effective method of launching a product, promoting an event or selling services. Effective use of multimedia in advertising can make potential clients sit up and make notice.
- Interactive applications–a great way to build brand loyalty and drive inquiries or sales. Sales may be increased by allowing users to view product options real-time. Brand loyalty can be built by giving users a custom application that entertains, informs or assists them.
- Motion, graphical elements, animation, audio and video can be used to more effectively deliver sales, instructional, or marketing messages to differentiate your firm from competitors.

KEY POINTS

- Multimedia is any combination of text, graphic art, sound, animation and video elements delivered to you by your computer or any other electronic means. A computer encyclopaedia containing various images, audio and video effects along with the content is a simple example of a multimedia application.
- The type of multimedia where you allow the user to control what and when the elements are delivered is referred to as interactive multimedia. When users are given navigational control so that they can navigate from one element to another in a non-linear fashion, interactive multimedia becomes hypermedia.
- Kiosks and CD-ROM applications are excellent vehicles for presenting information with the dynamics of multimedia. Multimedia applications require large amounts of digital memory when stored on the computer.
- Multimedia provides excellent audio-visual interface between the user and information. It has also become an integral part of the internet.
- The whole process of developing a multimedia package is called authoring. An authoring system is a collection of software tools that help in various aspects of multimedia production.
- The main steps in multimedia production include media capture, media conversion, media editing and media composition.
- Text, containing words and symbols, is the most common form of communication. It is one of the most popularly used media of appearance, used to deliver information accurately and in detail. From a design perspective, your choice of font size, style and other text attributes should be related both to the complexity of your message and to its venue. A major drawback of

using text is that it is not user – friendly compared to the other elements of multimedia. Hypertext is the organisation of information units into connected associations that a user can choose to make. An instance of such an association is called a hyperlink. When a user clicks on such a link, more information on the particular topic is displayed.

- Pictures/graphics enhance the overall look of a multimedia package. Pictures express more than normal text and are generally considered the most important element of a multimedia application. Typically, image files are compressed to save memory and disk space of a computer. GIF, JPEG and PNG are examples of compressed image file formats. Pictures can be created using drawing tools like MS Paint, inserted from the clipart gallery or can be scanned using scanner or any other suitable device. Image-editing tools like Adobe Photoshop, MS Photodraw can be used to manipulate images according to your taste.
- Animation in simple terms can be defined as an entity moving across the screen. This entity could be a text object or an image. It gives visual impact to your multimedia application. An animation consists of a series of rapidly changing objects, which when blended together conveys an illusion of movement. Simple animations can be created using powerpoint; however, you can create complex ones using many of the animation tools available, like Director, 3D Studio Max, CompuServe and Shockwave.
- As compared to traditional 'Stand and Deliver' teaching methodology, training imparted using animated, interactive and instructional multimedia applications can be very useful. Apart from making the subject interesting, it increases information retention and learning capacity of the users. Encyclopedias, schools, libraries, www, learning centers all make use of Multimedia in some form or the other.
- Armed with animated images, sound, full-motion video and interactive capability, multimedia has became a dominant factor in today's information age. Games, Movies, E-greeting cards are some applications of multimedia in the entertainment field.
- Multimedia presentations are an excellent way to motivate, inform, and captivate a wide range of audiences via PC, laptop, plasma screen, or kiosk delivered via CD-ROM or Internet. You can use multimedia to launch/promote your product, advertise, and to create buyer guides, training tutorials, interactive catalogs and many more.
- Sound is used to set the rhythm or a mood in a package. A MIDI file consists of a list of commands that represent the recordings of musical actions and when these commands are sent to a MIDI Playback device, a sound is produced. The main disadvantage of MIDI data is that it is not digitised. In contrast, Digital Audio is a recording that depends on the capabilities of your sound system. Sound can be recorded using a microphone, a synthesiser, or any other medium like tape or cassette player.

- Digital video is the most engaging of multimedia venues, and is a powerful tool for bringing users close to the real world. NTSE (National Television Standards Committee), PAL (Phase Alteration Line), SECAM (Sequential Color and Memory), HDTV (High Definition Television) are commonly used broadcast and video standards across the globe. Current television is based on analog technology and fixed international standards for the broadcast and display of images. Computer video is based on digital technology and other standards for displaying images. The conversion of analog video into its digital equivalent requires a special hardware called **Video Capture Card.** MPEG, JPEG, P*64, Real Video are all examples of commonly used compressed video formats.

REVIEW QUESTIONS

1. Choose the most appropriate answer:

i. Point the odd one out:

(a) Sound	(b) Animation
(c) Graphics	(d) www

ii. Which of the following cannot be considered an element of multimedia computer?

(a) CD ROM	(b) Speakers
(c) Microphone	(d) Network Card

2. State whether True or False:

(a) Multimedia applications require large amounts of digital memory when stored in a user's computer.

(b) It is not possible to hyperlink words to images or sound files.

(c) You can manipulate a scanned image using an image-editing tool.

3. Match the following:

X	Y
A. Vehicle for presenting information with the dynamics of multimedia.	a. User Interactivity
B. Combining media and specifying their spatial and temporal relationships.	b. GIF
C. Icons, buttons and symbols.	c. CD-ROM and DVD
D. Compressed image file format.	d. MPEG
E. Compressed video file format.	e. Media Composition

4. Fill in the blanks with the appropriate choices listed below:

(i) MIDI (ii) Animation (iii) Digital audio (iv) Packaging (v) Hypermedia (vi) Authoring (vii) Hyperlink

1. In ______________, users are given navigational control so that they can navigate from one element to another in a non-linear fashion.
2. The whole process of developing a multimedia package is called __________.
3. When a user clicks on a ______________, more information on the particular topic is displayed.
4. An ______________ consists of a series of rapidly changing objects, which when blended together gives an illusion of movement.
5. A ______________ file consists of a list of commands that represent the recordings of musical actions.

5. Explain in brief the various elements of multimedia.

6. Write a short note on applications of multimedia in the field of education.

CHAPTER 8 Computer Software

Today's computers are highly versatile tools across a myriad disciplines and usages. They can perform varied tasks, from correspondence to maintaining inventory information to creating drawings and illustrations and many more. The list is almost never-ending. The important thing to understand is that the computer hardware itself cannot perform these tasks. It requires instructions (also known as programs or software) to successfully carry out these tasks. In fact computer hardware is useless without programs or software. Let us therefore distinguish between these two commonly used terms, Hardware and Software.

Relationship between Hardware and Software

Hardware constitutes the electronic circuits used in building the computer. The electronic, magnetic, and the mechanical devices together are referred to as computer hardware. Software, on the other hand, is the name given to the set of instructions, or programs to be executed by the computer. It is the hardware that executes the software. To take an analogy, a television set bought from the shop is hardware and the various entertainment programs it receives, is its software. Thus, while hardware is necessary, software is vital. An important point that is brought out from this analogy is that hardware is a one-time expense while software is an ongoing expense.

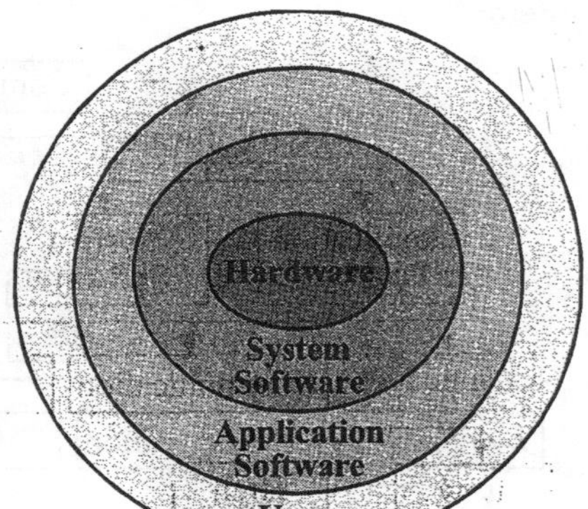

Figure 8.1 Relationship between hardware, software, and end users

Computer software can be classified into two broad categories; system software and application software.

System Software

System software includes general programs written for the system that provide the environment to facilitate the writing of application software. System software is therefore the stuff that makes your computer work. The computer's basic operating system, whether it is Windows 2000 on the PC or Unix on an HP server, all form a part of system software. The term usually encompasses any software used to manage the computer and network, which includes diagnostic software and software used to tune the computer's performance. Novell Netware and other network management packages, utilities like Editor, Monitor, and Debugger also fall under this category.

Application Software

Application software or programs are programs designed to perform specific functions directly for the user or, in some cases, for another application program. Examples of application programs include word processors, database programs, Web browsers, development tools, drawing, paint, and image editing programs, and communication programs. Application programs use the services of the computer's operating system and other supporting programs.

System software therefore runs your computer while application software runs your business.

The figure below explains the basic classifications of software in a computer system:

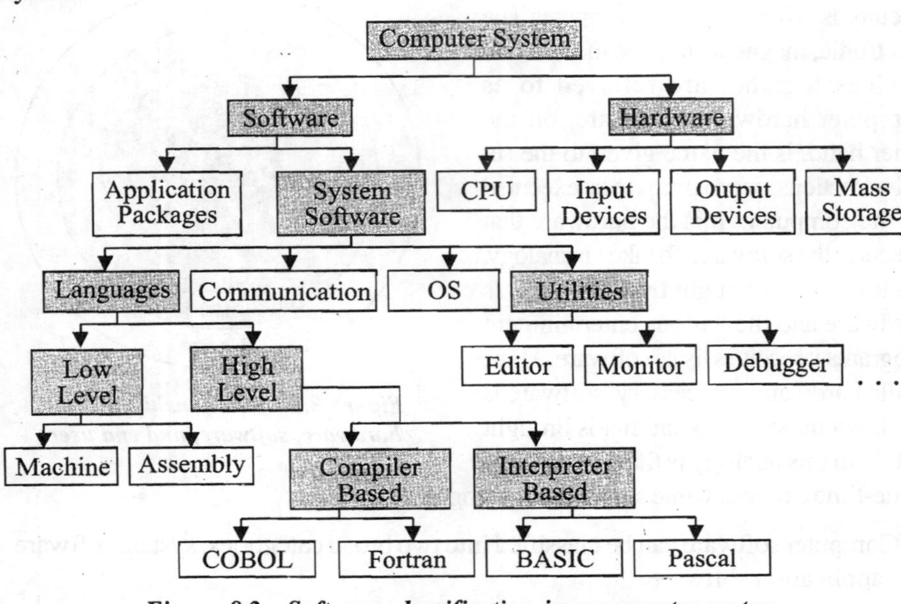

Figure 8.2 Software classification in a computer system

Computer Languages

A computer language is a language that can be understood by the computer. It is the computer's native language. Computer languages serve the same purpose as human languages. They are a means of communication. Let us understand the similarity and differences between computer languages and human languages.

A natural or human language is the language that people like us speak daily, like English, Hindi, French, German etc. It is made up of words and rules known as lexicon and syntax respectively. These words are joined to make meaningful phrases according to the rules of the syntax. A computer language also consists of lexicon and syntax, i.e., characters, symbols, and rules of usage that allow the user to communicate with the computer.

The main difference between a natural language and computer language is that natural languages have a large set of words (vocabulary) to choose from while computer languages have a limited or restricted set of words. Thus, fewer words but more rules characterise a computer language.

Each and every problem to be solved by the computer needs to be broken down into discrete logical steps before the computer can execute it. The process of writing such instructions in a computer or programming language is called programming or coding.

Just as computer hardware has improved over the years, programming languages have also moved from machine-oriented languages (that used strings of binary 0s and 1s) to problem-oriented languages (that use common English terms). All computer languages can, however, be classified under the following categories:

- Machine Language (First Generation Language)
- Assembly Language (Second Generation Language)
- High-Level Language (Third Generation Language)

The characteristics of these are explained in the sections that follow.

Machine Language

The computer can understand only binary-based language. As already discussed, this is a combination of 0s and 1s. Instructions written using sequences of 0s and 1s are known as machine language. First generation computers used programs written in machine language.

Machine language is very cumbersome to use and is tedious and time consuming for the programmer. It requires thousands of machine language instructions to perform even simple jobs like keeping track of a few addresses for mailing lists.

Every instruction in machine language is composed of two parts – The command itself, also known as the 'operation code' or opcode (like add, multiply, move etc.), and the 'operand' which is the address of the data that has to be acted upon. For example, a typical machine language instruction may be represented as follows:

OP Code	Operand
001	010001110

The number of operands varies with each computer and is therefore computer dependent.

It is evident from the above that to program in machine language, the programmer needs information about the internal structure of the computer. He will also need to remember a number of operation codes and will also need to keep track of the addresses of all the data items (i.e., which storage location has which data item). Programming in machine language can be very tedious, time consuming and still highly prone to errors. Further, locating such errors and effecting modifications is also a mammoth task. Quite understandably, programmers felt a need for moving away from machine language.

Assembly Language

Assembly language was the first step in the evolution of programming languages. It used mnemonics (symbolic codes) to represent operation codes and strings of characters to represent addresses. Instructions in assembly language may look like this:

Opration	Opration address
READ	M
ADD	L

Assembly language was designed to replace each machine code by an understandable mnemonic and each address with a simple alphanumeric string. It was matched to the processor structure of a particular computer and is therefore (once again) machine dependent. This meant that programs written for a particular computer model could be executed on another one. In other words, an assembly language program lacked portability.

A program written in assembly language needs to be translated into machine language before the computer can execute it. This is done by a special program called 'Assembler' which takes every assembly language program and translates into its equivalent machine code. The assembly language program is called the source program, while the equivalent machine language program is called the object program. It may be useful to know that the assembler is a system program supplied by the computer manufacturer.

Second generation computers used Assembly language.

High-level Language

The lack of portability of programs (written using machine or assembly languages) between different computers led to the development of high-level languages, so called because they permitted a programmer to ignore many low-level details of the computer's hardware. Also it is apparent that the closer the syntax, rules and mnemonics of the programming language could be to 'natural language' the easier it would be for the programmer to program and lesser would be the possibility of introducing errors (or 'bugs') into the program. Hence, third generation languages came into being in the mid-1950s.

These algorithmic, or procedural, languages are designed for solving a particular type of problem. They contain commands that are particularly suited to one type of application. For example, a number of languages have been designed to process scientific or mathematical problems. Others emphasise on commercial applications and so on.

Unlike machine or symbolic languages, they vary little between computers. But they must be translated into machine code by a program called a compiler or interpreter. Once again, the high-level program is called the source code while its equivalent machine language program is referred to as the object code.

Easy to learn and program, machine independence, easier maintenance, and portability contribute towards the popularity of high-level languages. Slow program execution is the main disadvantage since programs need to be converted into machine language (by an interpreter or a compiler) before they can be executed.

Interpreter vs Compiler

Programs written in high-level languages need to be converted into machine language before the computer can execute them. 'Interpreters' and 'Compilers' are translation or conversion programs that produce the machine code from high-level languages.

The original program is called a source program and after it is translated by the interpreter or compiler, it is called an object program.

The interpreter and compiler perform the same function but in fundamentally different ways. An interpreter translates the instructions of the program one statement at a time. This translated code is first executed before the interpreter begins work on the next line. Thus instructions are translated and executed simultaneously. Object code is not stored in the computer's memory for future use. The next time the instruction is to be used, it needs to be freshly translated by the interpreter. For example, during repetitive processing of instructions in a loop, every instruction in the loop will need to be translated every time the loop is executed.

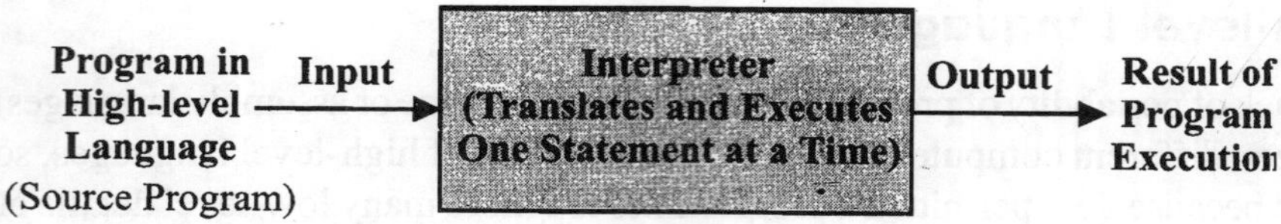

Figure 8.3 Translation process using an interpreter

Compiler on the other hand, takes an entire high-level language program and produces a machine code version out of it. This version is then run as a single program.

Typically, a programmer writes language statements in a language such as COBOL or C using an editor. The file that is created contains what are called the source statements. The programmer then runs the appropriate language compiler, specifying the name of the file that contains the source statements. These statements are converted into their corresponding machine code, which can then be executed by the computer.

The object code can be stored in the computer's memory for executing in future. A compiler does not need to translate the source program every time it needs to be executed thereby saving execution time.

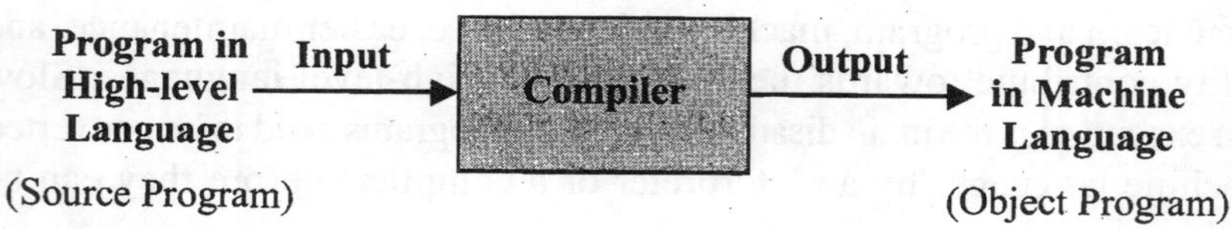

Figure 8.4 Translation process using a compiler

To summarise, an interpreter allows the programmer to have online interaction with the computer, i.e., the program can be corrected/modified while it is running which means that it is possible to debug the program as it is being executed. This however results in slower execution speed. On the contrary, a compiler permits offline interaction, i.e., it is not possible to make changes while the program is running. The source program will need to be modified offline and compiled every time a change is made, however minor the change may be. This can be quite frustrating for new programmers but is good for those needing fast execution speed.

Some High Level Languages

FORTRAN Early computers were almost exclusively used by scientists. The first high-level language, FORTRAN (FORmula TRANslation) was developed about 1956 by John Backus at IBM. This language was designed to solve scientific and engineering problems and is still one of the most popular languages for such applications.

FORTRAN has a number of versions with FORTRAN IV being one of the earlier popular versions. In 1977 the American National Standards Institute (ANSI) published standards for FORTRAN with the view to standardising the form of the language used by manufacturers. This standardised version is called FORTRAN 77.

COBOL COBOL (COmmon Business Oriented Language), the first language intended for commercial applications, was developed by a committee of computer manufacturers and users under the leadership of Grace Hopper, a US Navy programmer, in 1959. The maintenance and further growth of the language was handed over to a group called CODASYL (COnference on DAta SYstems Languages).

It is written using statements that resemlde simple English and can be understood easily. For example, to add two numbers (stored in variables A and B) a simple statement in COBOL would be: ADD A TO B GIVING C.

COBOL was standardised by ANSI in 1968 and in 1974. COBOL became the most widely used programming language for business and data processing applications.

BASIC BASIC (Beginner's All-purpose Symbolic Instruction Code) was developed by two Dartmouth College professors, John Kemeny and Thomas Kurtz, as a teaching tool for undergraduates in 1966. This language was primarily designed for beginners and is very easy to learn. It was immediately picked up for most business and general-purpose applications, particularly on small computers. BASIC subsequently became the primary language of the personal computer revolution.

A minimum version of BASIC was standardised by ANSI and is so simple that it has been incorporated in every subsequent version of BASIC. Some versions of BASIC include MBASIC (Microsoft BASIC), and CBASIC (Compiler based BASIC).

One of the newer versions of BASIC commonly known as visual basic has also evolved from the original BASIC language. It contains various statements and functions that can be used to create applications for a Windows or GUI environment.

PASCAL PASCAL was designed by a Nicholas Wirth, a Swiss professor, in 1971. He developed a more structured language for teaching that he named Pascal (after the French mathematician Blaise Pascal, who built the first successful mechanical calculator). His primary aim was to provide a language that supported beginners learning good program solving and programming techniques.

In addition to manipulation of numbers, PASCAL supports manipulation of vectors, matrices, strings of characters, records, files and lists thereby supporting non-numeric programming. Hence it is proved to be an attractive language for professional computer scientists.

PASCAL has been standardised by ISO (International Standards Organization) and ANSI.

ADA PL/1 (Programming Language 1), developed in the late 1960s by IBM, and ADA (named after Ada Augusta, countess of Lovelace, biographer of Charles Babbage), developed in 1981 by the US Dept. of Defense, were designed for both business and scientific use.

LISP LISP (LISt Processing) was developed by John McCarthy at the Massachusetts Institute of Technology in the early 1950s. It was implemented in 1959, and was a program that handled recursive algorithms better. It has become the standard language for the artificial intelligence community.

C and C ++ In order to implement the UNIX operating system, Dennis Ritchie of Bell Laboratories produced a language that he called C. Bjarne Stroustrup of Bell Laboratories developed extension of C, called C++. C++ is also used to write procedural programs like C but the reason for its increased popularity is perhaps because of its ability to deal with the rigours of object-oriented programming. C and C++ are the most widely used general-purpose languages among professional programmers.

JAVA JAVA is an object-oriented language similar to C++ but simplified to eliminate features that are prone to programming errors. It was developed specifically as a network-oriented language, for writing programs that can be safely downloaded through the Internet and run without fear of computer viruses. Using small Java programs called applets, World Wide Web pages can be developed that include a full range of multimedia functions.

JAVA is a 'secure to use over' the internet and platform independent language.

Fourth Generation Languages

Fourth generation languages are non-procedural. This means that they specify what needs to be accomplished without describing how to do it. Fourth generation languages are characterised by simple English-like instructions and a quick and easy learning process. They are so user-friendly that with little training and practice an individual can write his/her own programs and generate the desired reports. It does not require the services of a professional programmer to do the same.

The first fourth generation language called FORTH was developed in 1970 by an American astronomer named Charles Moore. FORTH is used in scientific and industrial control applications. FOCUS is another commonly known fourth generation language.

Most fourth generation languages are written for specific purposes.

Fifth Generation Languages

Fifth generation languages are an outgrowth of research in the area of artificial intelligence. They are however, still in their infancy. PROLOG (PROgramming LOGic), developed by French computer scientist Alain Colmerauer and logician Philippe Roussel in the early 1970s, is useful for programming logical processes and making deductions automatically.

Many other languages have been designed to meet specialised needs. Some of the more popular ones include GPSS (General Purpose System Simulator) used for modeling physical and environmental events, SNOBOL (String-Oriented Symbolic Language) designed for pattern matching and list processing. LOGO, a version of LISP, developed in the 1960s to help children learn about computers, and PILOT (Programmed Instruction Learning, Or Testing) used in writing instructional software.

Free Domain Software

To understand this let us distinguish between these commonly used terms – Freeware, and Free Domain software.

The term 'freeware' has no clear accepted definition, but is commonly used for packages that permit redistribution but not modification. This means that their source code is not available.

Free Domain software is software that comes with permission for anyone to use, copy, and distribute, either verbatim or with modifications, either gratis or for a fee. In particular, this means that the source code must be available. Free Domain software can be freely used, modified, and redistributed but with one restriction: the redistributed software must be distributed with the original terms of free use, modification and distribution. This is known as 'copyleft'.

Free software is a matter of freedom, not price. Free software may be packaged and distributed for a fee. The 'Free' here refers to the ability of reusing it – modified or unmodified, as a part of another software package.

The concept of free software is the brainchild of Richard Stallman, head of the GNU project. The best known example of free software is Linux, an operating system that is proposed as an alternative to Windows or other proprietary operating systems. Debian is an example of a distributor of a Linux package.

Free software should therefore not be confused with freeware, which is a term used for describing software that can be freely downloaded and used but which may contain restrictions for modification and reuse.

KEY POINTS

- Hardware refers to the electronic circuitry used in building the computer. The physical components of a computer like electronic, magnetic and mechanical devices are all a part of computer hardware.
- Software is a term given to the set of instructions or programs to be executed by the computer.
- The set of programs that provide an environment to write application programs is known as system software. Windows 2000 and Unix are examples of system software.
- Programs or software designed to perform specific functions directly for the user, or other programs, are called application software. Database programs, web browsers, image editing programs and the like are examples of application software.
- Computer language refers to a language that can be understood by the computer. Writing instructions in such a language is called programming or coding.
- Computer languages can be broadly classified as machine language, assembly language, and high-level languages.
- Programs written using combination of binary symbols 0s and 1s are called machine language. They are machine dependent and do not require a translation program. They are, however, very tedious to program in machine language.
- Assembly language uses mnemonics to represent operation codes and strings of characters to represent addresses. A program written in assembly language needs to be converted into machine code using a translator program called assembler. Assembly language has one-to-one correspondence with the machine language of the computer and is therefore machine dependent.
- High-level languages were developed to allow application programs to run on a variety of computers. They are procedural in nature and are designed to solve a particular type of problem. High-level languages are machine independent.
- Programs written in high-level languages need to be converted into machine language using translator programs. Interpreters and Compilers are the two types of translators used for this activity. A single high-level language statement may be translated into many statements in its machine language equivalent.
- An Interpreter is a translator program that converts a high-level language program into its corresponding machine code one statement at a time.
- A Compiler takes the entire high-level program and produces machine code version out of it. It is then run as a single program.
- Most commonly used high-level languages include FORTRAN, COBOL, BASIC, PASCAL, ADA, LISP, C and C ++, and JAVA.

- Fourth generation languages are characterised by simple English instructions that are easy to learn. These are non-procedural in nature which means that they only specify what is to be accomplished without describing how to do it.
- Fifth generation languages are still in their infancy. These have been designed to meet specialised needs. PROLOG, SNOBOL, LOGO are examples of fifth generation languages.
- Free domain software refers to software that comes with permission for anyone to use, copy, and distribute, either as it is or with modifications, either for a fee or free.
- Freeware refers to packages that permit redistribution but no modification. Source code is therefore not available.

REVIEW QUESTIONS

1. Choose the appropriate answer:

i. Which of the following cannot be classified as system software?

(a) Linux　(b) Windows 2000

(c) MS DOS　(d) Oracle

ii. Which of the following checks the syntactic correctness of a source program?

(a) Interpreter　(b) Compiler

(c) Interpreter and Compiler　(d) None of the above

iii. High-level languages are characterised by:

(a) English-like statements　(b) Translator for machine code

(c) Portability of programs　(d) All of the above

iv. Which of these cannot be classified as a third generation language?

(a) COBOL　(b) PROLOG

(c) FORTRAN　(d) LISP

2. State whether True or False:

i. A programmer is likely to choose COBOL or FORTRAN equally to program a given problem.

ii. 'Procedural' is a term associated with assembly language.

iii. Programs written using combination of 0s and 1s are called assembly language programs.

iv. Fourth generation languages specify 'how' a problem's solution is to be accomplished.

v. Translating and executing a program one statement at a time is the function of an interpreter.

3. Match the following:

X		Y
1. Machine independent	a.	High-level languages
2. Translates instructions of a program one statement at a time	b.	Interpreter
3. Machine dependent	c.	Machine language
4. Programs written using combination of 0s and 1s	d.	Compiler
5. Translates the entire program to produce the machine code version	e.	Assembly language

4. Fill in the blanks with the appropriate choices listed below:

(i) Hardware (ii) System (iii) Application (iv) Programs (v) Software

1. _______________ are instructions written to solve a particular problem.
2. Set of instructions to be executed by the computer is termed as _______________.
3. Editor is an example of _______________ software.
4. Development tools are examples of _______________ software.
5. _______________ constitutes the physical components of the computer.

5. Differentiate between:

a. Hardware and software
b. System and Application software
c. Low-level and high-level languages.
d. Compiler and Interpreter
e. Freeware and Free domain software

CHAPTER 9

Disk Operating System (DOS)

An Operating system (OS) is the main control program of a computer that manages all other programs in a computer. The other programs commonly referred to as 'Application Programs', use the services provided by OS through a well-defined Application Program Interface (API). Every computer necessarily requires some type of operating system that tells the computer how to operate and utilise other programs installed on the computer. The role of an operating system in a computer is similar to the role of a principal in a college who is responsible for the overall management of the college.

e.g. DOS, Windows 95/98, Windows NT, Unix, Linux etc.

Any computer system can be broadly classified in terms of four component dimensions:

1. Hardware
2. Operating system
3. Application programs (like MS Word, Games, Calculator etc.)
4. Users (people who work on the computer)

Below is an abstract view showing these components of the computer system.

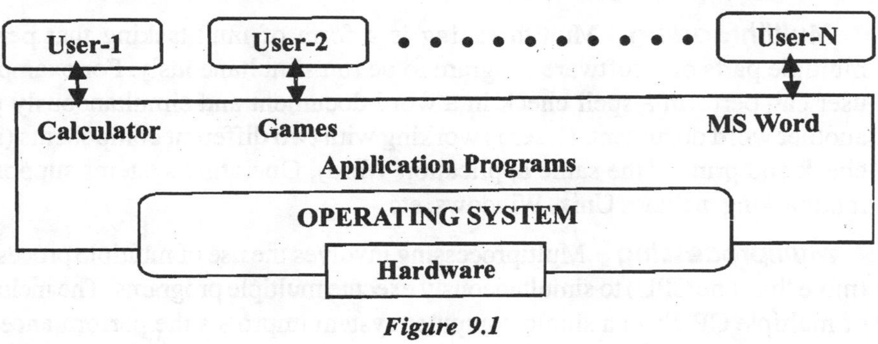

Figure 9.1

Main Functions of an Operating System

Resource management Computer resources include main memory (RAM), Storage Devices (Floppy Disk & Hard Disk Drives), input and output devices (keyboard, mouse, monitor, printer etc.) etc. The OS is responsible for:

i. Allocating and deallocating memory space as needed by various application programs.
ii. Secondary storage management. All application programs, compilers, loaders are stored in the secondary storage (hard disk).
iii. Handling input and output to and from attached hardware devices, such as hard disks, printers, scanners, modem etc.

File management OS is responsible for the creation and deletion of files/ directories and the mapping of these files/directories onto the secondary storage.

Security management OS is responsible for protecting the resources and information of a computer system from destruction and misuse.

Operating system services OS is responsible for providing a set of services to programs and users of those programs. Main services include:

i. Program execution–It loads the program requested by the user into the memory.
ii. Error detection–It generates messages to each application or users about the status of the operations that have been performed. It constantly detects and corrects errors generated by the system.
iii. It ensures efficient utilisation of the computer resources.

Common Terminology

Multitasking This type of OS permits multiple programs to be run simultaneously by the same computer. For example, a user of the computer can simultaneously play games while a Word document is being printed. (User is simultaneously working with two different applications (Word and Games)). Operating systems supporting multitasking includes – Unix, Windows 95/98.

Multithreading Multithreading is a form of multitasking that permits multiple parts of a software program to be run simultaneously. For example, a user can perform a spell check in a word document and simultaneously print another word document. (User is working with two different components (spell check and print of the same application Word). Operating systems supporting multitasking includes Unix, Windows, etc.

Multiprocessing Multiprocessing involves the use of multiple processors (more than one CPU) to simultaneously execute multiple programs. The inclusion of multiple CPU's in a single computer system improves the performance to a large extent. Multiprocessing involves simultaneous processing by a computer system having multiple CPU's whereas multitasking involves simultaneous processing by a computer system with single CPU. Operating systems supporting multiprocessing include Unix, Windows NT, etc.

Single user This type of OS does not permit multiple users to use the computer and run programs at the same time. This assumes that at any given time only one user uses the system and runs only one program, i.e., it does not allow two users to concurrently work on the same program, e.g., MS-DOS.

Multiuser This type of OS permits multiple users to use the computer and run programs at the same time, e.g., Unix, Linux, Windows NT.

MS-DOS

Microsoft Disk Operating System (MS-DOS) is a single user, single tasking operating system. DOS has a command-line, text-based/non-graphical user-interface commonly referred to as Character Based User Interface (CUI). When the computer is switched on, a small program checks all internal devices, electronic memory and peripherals. Once this process is completed, MS-DOS is loaded.

The Prompt

The DOS prompt known as the command prompt looks like C:\> or D:\> where 'C','D' represent the hard drives of the computer system. All commands are typed at the DOS prompt. Enter key is pressed to view the output of the typed command. If the command is correctly typed desired output would be displayed. Otherwise an error message (bad command or filename/Invalid parameter) is displayed on the screen.

Limitations of MS-DOS

1. It has a text based user interface where the commands have to be typed for each operation that the user wants to perform. The user is expected to remember the commands as well as their syntax.
2. It is a single user, single tasking operating system and is limited to working with one megabyte of memory, 640 kilobytes of which is usable for the application program.
3. It does not allow using long file names. The user is restricted to eight-character file names with three-character extensions.

Below is the list of commonly used DOS commands. All DOS commands are case-insensitive (i.e., there is no difference whether you type COPY, copy or coPY). The same is true for the attributes, parameters and filenames. To view the complete description of each command type HELP followed by the command name, e.g., HELP COPY. Alternatively help can also be displayed using <command>/? (COPY/?).

Simple DOS Commands

Command	*Syntax*	*Explanation*	*Example*	*Notes*
COMMAND	COMMAND	Starts a new instance of the DOS command interpreter.	C:\>Command	Starts a new instance of the DOS command interpreter.
EXIT	EXIT	Quits the COMMAND.COM program (command interpreter).	C:\>EXIT	Quits the command interpreter.
CLS	CLS	Clears the screen display completely leaving only the DOS prompt.	C:\>CLS	Clears the screen and displays C: Prompt at the top of the screen.
DATE	DATE	Displays the system's current date and prompts to enter the new date.	C:\>DATE	Current date is Fri 05-09-2003 Enter new date <mm-dd-yy>:
TIME	TIME	Displays the current time and prompts the user to enter the new time.	C:\>TIME	Current time is 12:55:25.34p Enter new time.
VER	VER	Displays the windows version.	C:\>VER	Displays the Windows version installed on your computer.
HELP	HELP <Command Name> or Command Name/?	Provides complete, interactive help information for MS-DOS commands.	C:\>DATE/?	Complete information about the DATE command is displayed.
DOSKEY	DOSKEY	Edits command lines, recalls MS-DOS commands, and creates macros.	C:\>DOSKEY	Once the Doskey is installed then Up and Down arrow keys can be used in the subsequent commands to recall the previous commands.

Command	*Syntax*	*Explanation*	*Example*	*Notes*
PROMPT	PROMPT [Text]	Changes the MS-DOS command prompt to the specified text. If the command is typed without any parameters then the default prompt setting is restored.	D:\>PROMPT	Changes the prompt to the default setting.
PRINT	PRINT <Filename>	Prints a text file while you are using other MS-DOS commands.	C:\DATA>PRINT TEMP.TXT	Prints 'TEMP.TXT' stored in the 'DATA' folder of the C: drive.
LABEL	LABEL	Creates, changes, or deletes the volume label of a disk.	C:\>LABEL	Displays the current volume label and volume serial number. Also prompts to enter a new label.
MEM	MEM	Displays the amount of used and free memory in your system.	C:\>MEM	Displays the total amount of memory, amount of used and free memory in the system.
MORE	MORE <Filename>	Displays output one screen at a time for the text files. Useful in cases where the content of text file does not fit in a single screen.	C:\DATA> MORE TEMP.TXT	Breaks the contents of 'TEMP.TXT' in multiple screens. Subsequent screens can be viewed by pressing the 'enter' key.
ECHO	ECHO	Displays messages, or turns command echoing on or off.	C:\>ECHO	Displays the current echo setting. ('OFF' or 'ON')
EDIT	EDIT	Starts MS-DOS editor, which creates and changes ASCII files.	C:\>EDIT	Opens the MS-DOS editor.
SET	SET	Displays, sets, or removes MS-DOS environment variables.	C:\>SET	Displays the settings for the current environment variables.

Command	*Syntax*	*Explanation*	*Example*	*Notes*
CHKDISK	CHKDISK <Drive-Name>	Checks a disk and gives the information like how many bytes have been used and how many are free and if any bad sectors are there on the disk.	C:\>CHKDSK A:	Checks A: drive and gives information about the disk.
SCANDISK	SCANDISK <Drive-Name>	Checks a drive for errors and repairs any problems it encounters.	C:\>SCANDISK A:	Scans the A: drive and repairs the disk if any problem is there, like damaged area or virus etc.
DISKCOPY	DISKCOPY	Copies the content of one floppy disk to another floppy disk.	C:\>DISKCOPY A:	Copies the entire content of one floppy to another.
FORMAT	FORMAT <Drive-Name>	Formats the specified drive.	C:\>Format A:	Floppy inserted in the A: drive will be formatted. Any information in the floppy A: will be erased.

Simple File Operations

Command	*Syntax*	*Explanation*	*Example*	*Notes*
MOVE	MOVE <Source> <Destination>	Moves the file from one source to the specified destination. File will exist only at the specified destination.	C:\DATA>MOVE TEST.TXT \LETTER	Moves the file 'TEXT.TXT' from 'DATA' folder in the C: drive to the 'LATTER' folder in the C: drive.
COPY	COPY <Source> <Destination>	Creates a copy of the specified file and places it in the specified location. file will exist at the specified location as well as the source location.	C:\DATA> MOVE HELLO.TXT \LETTER	Creates a copy of HELLO.TXT in the LETTER folder of the C: drive.

Command	*Syntax*	*Explanation*	*Example*	*Notes*
REN	REN <Path> <Oldfile> <Newfile>	Renames the old file name by the specified new file name.	C:\DATA>REN HELLO.TXT Hi.TXT	Renames 'HELLO.TXT' as 'Hi.TXT'
DEL/ERASE	DEL <Path><Filename>	Deletes the specified file present in the specified path/location from the hard disk.	C:\DATA>DEL Hi.TXT	Deletes the file 'Hi.TXT' located in the 'DATA' folder of the C: drive.
TYPE	TYPE <Filename>	Displays the contents of a text file.	C:\DATA>TYPE TMP.TXT	Displays the contents of TMP.TXT.
ATTRIB	ATTRIB [+A | –A] [+R | –R] [+H | –H] [+S | –S] <filename> + Sets an attribute + Clears an attribute A-Archive attribute R-Read only attribute H-Hidden file attribute S-System file attribute	Displays or changes file attributes.	C:\>ATTRIB+H +R FIRST.TXT	Sets the attributes of 'FIRST.TXT' as Read only and hidden.
FC	FC <File1> <File2>	Compares two files or sets of files, and displays the differences between them. Generally used to compare files with same names located in different directories.	C:\>DATA\ ONE.TXT INFO\ ONE.TXT	Compares the file 'ONE.TXT' located in DATA folder with 'ONE.TXT' located in INFO folder and displays the differences between them.

Command	*Syntax*	*Explanation*	*Example*	*Notes*
XCOPY	XCOPY <Source> <destination>	Copies files and subdirectories to the specified location.	C:\>XCOPY C:\DATA C:\INFO	Copies the entire contents of the 'DATA' folder to 'INFO' folder. If the 'DATA' folder contains 'anu' subdirectories then they will also be copied to the 'INFO' folder.
BACKUP	BACKUP <Source> <Destination>	Copies the files onto diskettes or to other source.	C:\>BACKUP C:\DATA\TEMP.TXT C:\INFO	Copies 'TEMP.TXT' file in the 'DATA' folder into the 'INFO' folder,
RESTORE	RESTORE<Source> <Destination>	Restores files that were backed up by using the BACK UP command.	C:\>RESTORE C:\DATA\TEMP.TXT C:\INFO	Restores 'TEMP.TXT' file in the 'DATA' folder into the 'INFO' folder.

Wild Cards

Wild card characters can be used in specifying filenames in DOS. There are two types of wild cards (?,*):

? It is used to represent any single character in the file name.

SYNTAX: C:\ DIR BA?.TXT

Displays all the text files in the C: drive starting with 'BA' and ending with any single character.

Examples: BAT.TXT, BAG.TXT, BAR.TXT, BAD.TXT etc.

* It is used to represent one or more characters in a file name.

SYNTAX: C:\ DIR CON*.TXT

Displays all the text files in the C: drive starting with 'CON'.

Examples: CONCEPT.TXT, CONCATENATE.TXT, CONTEMPT.TXT, CONSOLE.TXT etc.

Directory Related Commands

Command	*Syntax*	*Explanation*	*Example*	*Notes*
DIR	DIR <Drive / Directory - Name Name>	Displays all the sub-directories and files of the specified drive/directory. It also shows the size of the files and the date and time they were last modified.	C:\> DIR D:	Displays all the contents (files and directories) of the D: drive.
DIR/P	DIR <Drive/ Directory-Name>/P	Displays the contents of directory one screen at a time and pauses until any other key is pressed to continue the display.	C:\> DIR DATA/P	Displays the contents of the 'DATA' directory by pausing the screen.
DIR/W	DIR <Drive/ Directory>/W	Displays the contents of the directory width-wise. It omits file size, date and time of creation of file so that more files can be displayed at one time on the screen.	C:\> DIR DATA/W	Displays the contents of the 'DATA' directory width-wise.
DIR/W/P	DIR <Drive/ Directory>/W/P	The Wide and Pause display option can be combined.	C:\> DIR DATA/W/P	Displays the contents of the 'DATA' directory width-wise and by pausing the screen.
CD	CD<Directory-Name> CD\ - Directly takes to the root directory.	Displays the name of the current directory if no parameter is specified with the command. Changes the current directory to the specified directory.	C:\>CD DATA\SUBDATA	Changes the current directory to 'DATA\SUBDATA'.
MD	MD <Drive/ Directory-Name>	Creates a new directory in the specified location.	C:\>MD 'HELLO'	Creates a directory named 'HELLO' in the C: Drive.

Command	*Syntax*	*Explanation*	*Example*	*Notes*
RD	RD <Directory-Name>	Removes the specified directory.	C:\>RDHELLO	To remove a directory first you should come to one level above the current directory and then remove command should be given. This command will delete the 'HELLO' directory from the C:drive.
DELTREE	DELTREE <Directory-Name>	Deletes a directory and all the sub-directories and files in it.	C:\>DELTREE TEMP	Prompts the user for confirmation. If user selects 'Y' (Yes) then the directory 'TEMP' and all its sub-directories will be deleted.

REVIEW QUESTIONS

1. Choose the appropriate answer:

i. OS that permits multiple programs to be run simultaneously using a single processor is referred to as:

(a) Multitasking (b) Multithreading
(c) Multiuser (d) Multiprocessing

ii. DOS command that is used to quit the command interpreter:

(a) EXIT (b) CLOSE
(c) QUIT (d) None of the above

iii. DOS-Command that is used to Copy the contents of one floppy to another floppy:

(a) MOVE (b) DISKCOPY
(c) TRANSFER (d) None of the above

iv. DOS-Command that is used to rename a file:

(a) MOVE (b) REN
(c) ERASE (d) RD

2. Enter True or False:

i. An operating system loads the program requested by the user into the memory.

ii. DOS is a multi-user operating system.

iii. DOS commands are case sensitive, i.e., 'DATE' and 'date' carry different meaning in MS-DOS.

iv. 'MAKE' is used to create a new directory in MS-DOS.

v. 'DISPLAY' is used to display the contents of a text file.

vi. CHKDSK formats the specified drive.

vii. RD removes the specified directory from the disk.

viii. /W and /P switches of the DIR0 command can be combined together.

ix. MOVE is used to copy one file from one destination to another.

x. SCANDISK is used to display the amount of used and available memory.

3. Match the following:

X	Y
1. Starts a new instance of the DOS command interpreter.	(a) Operating system
2. Recalls MS-DOS commands	(b) DOSKEY
3. Creates, changes, or deletes the volume label of a disk.	(c) COMMAND

4. Main control program of a computer that manages all other programs in a computer.	(d) MD
5. Creates a new directory.	(e) LABEL
6. Displays all the files and subdirectories.	(f) Multiuser operating system
7. Compares two files and displays the differences among them if any.	(g) DELTREE
8. Permits multiple users to use the computer and run programs at the same time.	(h) DIR
9. Deletes a directory and all the sub-directories and files in it.	(i) FC

4. Fill in the blanks with the appropriate choices listed below:

(i) DIR/W (ii) Multi user (iii) CD (iv) ATTRIB -R (v) DIR/P (vi) VER (vii) TYPE (viii) ATTRIB +R (xi) CLEAR (x) ? and * (xi) CLS (xii) Single user (xiii) Graphical (xiv) DE? (xv) Text Based (xvi) DE?

1. DOS is ________________ type of operating system.
2. ________________ are termed as wild cards in DOS.
3. ________________ is used to clear the contents of screen.
4. DOS has a ________________ interface.
5. ________________ is used to display the windows version information.
6. ________________ is used to set the read file attribute.
7. ________________ is used to display the contents of a text file.
8. ________________ is used to display the contents of a directory by one screen at a time.
9. ________________ is used to change from the current working directory.
10. ________________ will display all the files starting with 'DE' and ending with any single character.

5. What is an operating system? Explain its major functions.

6. Explain the use of wild cards in MS-DOS.

7. Write briefly about the following DOS commands:

(i) ATTRIB (ii) XCOPY (iii) DIR (iv) SCANDISK (v) ERASE

CHAPTER 10

Microsoft Windows

INTRODUCTION TO WINDOWS

Until a couple of years ago, Windows predecessor MS DOS (Microsoft Disk Operating System) used to rule the roost. Because of its numerous drawbacks (as discussed in the previous chapter), a new class of system software emerged. Windows, which was a product of this class, was based on a radically different approach called Graphical User Interface (GUI). With a Graphical User Interface, the various commands and options are represented on the screen in the form of small images called Icons. The user is not expected to remember or type any command, all he is required to do is to click on the appropriate picture (icon) with the help of a small hand-held device called a mouse. Since using a mouse is considerably easier than using a keyboard- and clicking on an icon is much easier than having to type out commands through a keyboard—GUI-based interfaces are much more user friendly. And since GUI based interfaces work on WYSIWYG (What You See Is What You Get) technology, the work of the user is made that much more easy.

With Windows, Microsoft has successfully addressed all the limitations of MS DOS in addition to new user-friendly features. Incidentally, Windows is so called because it allows users to work on several Windows at the same time. There are many operating systems in the market, but MS Windows (with its various versions like Windows 3.1, Windows 3.11, Windows 95, Windows 98, Windows NT, Windows 2000, Windows XP etc.) are the most widely used and have a phenomenal and near monopolistic market share.

Overview of Different Versions of Windows

Windows 1.0: Microsoft released the first version of Windows way back in 1985. It marked a major breakthrough in as much as it allowed users to switch from character based (CUI)/non-graphical MS DOS to the GUI based operating system. The product included a set of desktop applications, including the MS-DOS file management program, and value additions such as a calendar, card file, notepad, calculator, clock, and telecommunications programs. It allowed users to work with multiple applications at the same time (multitasking).

Windows 2.0: Microsoft released its second version of Windows in 1987. It allowed users to overlap windows, control screen layout, and use various keyboard combinations (shortcut keys or keyboard shortcuts) to move rapidly through Windows operations. It included support for inter-application communication using Dynamic Data Exchange (DDE). DDE is the basic foundation for inter-process communication between applications.

Windows 3.0: Microsoft released this version of Windows in 1990. Some of its main features were:

- 32 bit operating system with support for advanced graphics.
- Inclusion of Program Manager, File Manager, and Print Manager.
- A completely rewritten application development environment with new capabilities and native support for applications running in extended memory, and fully pre-emptive MS-DOS multitasking. (In pre-emptive multitasking, once a task is assigned to CPU, it can be taken away from the CPU during its execution. This would ensure optimum utilisation of CPU resources.)
- Inclusion of Windows software development kit (SDK), which helped software developers focus more on writing applications and less on writing device drivers.
- An improved set of Windows icons.

Windows 3.1/3.11: Microsoft released this version of Windows in 1993. It provided several additional utilities like sending a fax (Microsoft Fax), hooking up computers in a network (network), linking up to an outside information service (terminal) etc.

Windows NT 3.1: Microsoft released this version of Windows on July 27, 1993. This OS marked an important milestone for microsoft. Some of its main features were:

- it was the first Windows operating system to combine support for high-end client/server business applications.
- it included new features for security, operating system power, performance, desktop scalability, and reliability.
- it included support for multiprocessor (more than one CPU) architecture.
- Windows NT was geared towards business users and had a rich Application Programming Interface (API), which made it easier to run high-end engineering and scientific applications.

Windows 95: Microsoft released this version of Windows in 1995. Some of its main features were:

- true 32 bit operating system with built in Internet-support.
- facilitated easy installation of hardware peripherals and software applications through plug and play capabilities.
- enhanced multimedia capabilities, more powerful features for mobile computing, and integrated networking.

Windows NT 4.0: Microsoft released this version of Windows in 1996. It was an upgrade to Microsoft's business desktop operating system with increased ease of use and simplified management. It used the Windows 95 interface and included improved networking support, easy access to the Internet and corporate intranets.

Windows 98: Microsoft released this version of Windows in 1998. It is often described as an operating system that "Works Better, Plays Better". Some of its main features were:

- New features were added to enable easy access to Internet related information.
- Multiple display support – allowed using several Visual Display Units (VDU) simultaneously to increase the capacity of the desktop and to allow running of different programs on separate monitors.
- USB Support – the Universal Serial Bus made a computer easier to use, with advanced plug-and-play capabilities. It allowed adding devices to your computer without having to restart each time a device is added to the computer.
- Accessibility wizard – made it easier for people with disabilities to operate a computer without installing any special software.
- Help – an extensive and easy-to-use self-help system was provided.

Windows Millennium Edition (ME): Microsoft released this version of Windows in 2000. It was the last Microsoft operating system to be based on the Windows 95 technology. Windows ME offered consumers numerous music, video, and home networking enhancements and reliability improvements.

Windows 2000 professional: Microsoft released this version of Windows in 2000. It was an upgrade to Windows NT 4.0. It was designed with the aim to replace Windows 95, Windows 98, and Windows NT 4.0 on all business desktops and laptops. It added major improvements in reliability, ease of use, Internet compatibility, and support for mobile computing. It made hardware installation much easier by adding support for a wide variety of new Plug and Play hardware, including advanced networking and wireless products, USB devices and infrared devices.

Windows XP: Microsoft released this version of Windows in 2001. It was a major breakthrough for desktop operating systems. Two main versions of Windows XP were released, viz., Windows XP Home Edition and Windows XP Professional Edition.

Windows XP home edition: Windows XP Home Edition offers a clean, simplified visual design that makes frequently accessed features more accessible. The product offers many enhancements aimed at home users such as the Network Setup Wizard, Microsoft Windows Media Player (allowed users to easily find, organise, and play digital media), Windows Movie Maker (provided users with the tools to digitally edit, save, and share home videos), and enhanced digital photo capabilities.

Windows XP Professional

- Benefits from the long track record of Microsoft Windows NT technology: superior operating system performance including preemptive multitasking, fault tolerance, and system memory protection.
- A redesigned interface that includes features for business and advanced home computing. It included support for Remote Desktop, file, system restore and advanced networking features (Wireless Networking Support). System Restore is a very useful feature that allows users to roll back their PC software configuration to a date or time before a problem occurred.

Basic Elements of Windows

Once Windows is loaded into the memory of the computer, the focus is placed on the desktop. The desktop is designed to act just like an actual desktop. The desktop is a window that covers your entire computer screen. It is the interface through which all of the programs are accessed. All other programs run on the top of the Windows desktop. A typical Windows 98 desktop contains a series of labeled pictures referred to as 'Icons'. These icons represent the applications loaded onto your computer and clicking on the icon launches the associated application. The desktop can contain icons, files and folders. Desktop can be customised according to the users requirements by adding or deleting icons, inserting background picture or by changing color schemes. Therefore, the number of icons displayed on the desktop could vary from computer to computer, depending on users' choices.

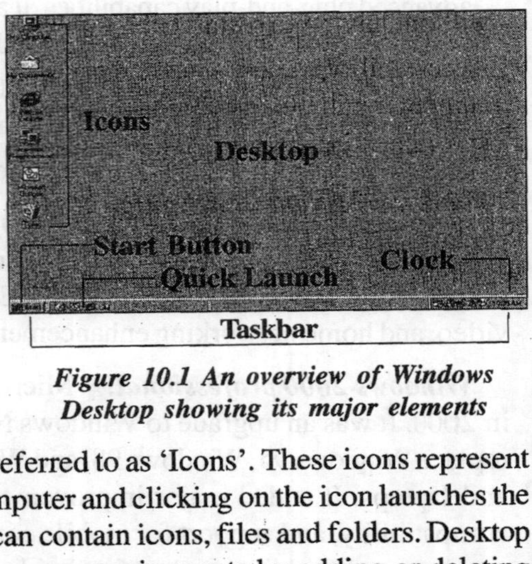

Figure 10.1 An overview of Windows Desktop showing its major elements

Key Elements of the Windows Desktop

While there may be more or less options enabled on a particular display, we would discuss the basic elements. The Windows desktop is comprised of three key elements:

1. Icons
2. Start Menu
3. Taskbar

Icons Icons can be further classified into five categories:

i. ***Folder Icons:*** When a folder icon is double clicked, a folder window is opened displaying the contents of the folder (folders are explained later in this section).

ii. ***Program Icons:*** When a Program icon is double clicked, the corresponding program is loaded into the memory of the computer and the application starts running in a Window.

iii. ***Document Icons:*** When a document icon is double clicked, the document itself is opened. Windows starts the application (Word processing program, spreadsheet, database, or whatever) in which the document was created, and then opens the document (data file) itself.

iv. ***Shortcut Icons:*** Shortcut icons provide an alternate way to open programs, documents, and folders. Shortcut icons are indicated by a little curved arrow in a box in the lower left hand corner of the icon and their labels generally begin with "Shortcut to." Deleting a shortcut icon does not delete the program or file; only the shortcut that leads to it is deleted.

v. ***System Icons:*** System icons are mandatory programs or files that are located on your desktop. User is not allowed to delete the system icon, since deleting the system icon would mean deleting the actual program from the hard drive of the computer. Examples of System Icons are Recycle Bin, MyComputer, Network Neighborhood etc.

a. *Recycle Bin:* Any file that is deleted from the hard disk of the computer is moved to a separate folder called Recycle Bin. The files stored in the bin can be restored to their original location by using the 'Restore' option of Recycle Bin. 'Restore' option can be accessed by right clicking on Recycle Bin icon. This feature is useful if any of the files/folders/shortcuts are accidentally deleted. The file remains in the Recycle Bin, until the bin is emptied explicitly. To empty the Recycle Bin, simply right click on this icon and select 'Empty Recycle Bin' option. To permanently delete files from the hard disk without moving them to the bin, use a combination of the shift and del keys while deleting the files (deletion of files explained later in this section.) Any files that are deleted from a floppy are not stored in the Recycle Bin.

b. *My Computer:* Double-clicking on the "My Computer" icon will open a window that displays the contents of the computer. All the files and folders available in the computer can be viewed here. It also allows you to display the system and hardware information.

c. *Network Neighborhood:* If your computer is connected to a network, then the "Network Neighborhood" icon will be displayed on the desktop. Double-clicking this icon will open a Window that displays other computers and resources, like printers, connected to the network.

Start Menu Clicking on the Start button gives access to the 'Start Menu'. All the applications and tools available in the computer can be accessed from this menu. The menu choices may vary for different versions of Windows. The standard options are discussed below:

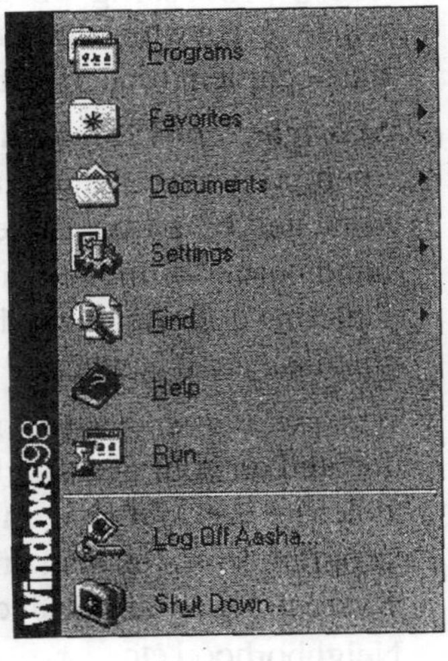

i. ***Programs:*** Opens a series of menus for starting the programs and applications installed on the computer. Programs can be added/deleted from this menu. A link is added to this menu for any new application that is installed on the computer.

ii. ***Favorites:*** Opens the web pages that have been marked as favorites. While surfing the Internet, it is possible to record the addresses of frequently visited websites using 'Favorites' option of the browser.

iii. ***Documents:*** Opens a menu containing the shortcuts to the most recent documents or data files. The list of files displayed in the Documents menu can also be cleared. To delete a file from this menu simply right click on the file name and press the 'Del' key from the keyboard.

iv. ***Settings:*** Opens a menu for customising Windows, the Taskbar, the Start menu and the printers. It gives access to 'Control Panel'. Control Panel contains utilities for customising the Windows interface, adding/removing installed components, changing number, date, time and currency formats, assigning sounds to program events and many more.

v. ***Find:*** Opens a dialogue box that allows users to search for files, folders located anywhere within the computer or within the network. (If the computer is connected to network). Files can be searched by name, location, date, type, content etc.

vi. ***Help:*** Opens the Windows Help topics. An extensive and easy to use Help system with informative screens and tools is provided for navigating and finding the required information. A table of contents displaying all the topics as well as a search facility is provided for quick access to the desired information.

vii. ***Run:*** Opens a dialogue box that allows you to run programs and commands directly by typing in the name of the command/program rather than clicking an icon or shortcut.

viii. ***Shut down:*** Opens a dialogue box that permits you to shut down, restart, or log off/on the computer.

Taskbar The Windows taskbar is the grey bar located at the bottom of the desktop. The taskbar usually stays on the screen all the time. It is comprised of several elements. Start button is also an element of the taskbar. The other elements of Taskbar are Quick Launch Toolbar and System Tray.

Quick Launch may or may not be available in all computers. The Quick Launch allows for immediate access to a variety of elements through a mouse click. On clicking the icon the associated program or Windows tool will be launched. Icons for different programs can be added to the quick launch toolbar.

The System Tray contains icons for applications that are running in the background of the computer. Programs such as anti-virus, task scheduler, etc., may be running in the System Tray. It also includes a clock that displays the current date and time as set by the user.

In addition to these elements, the taskbar also contains buttons for each application that is actively running on the computer. For example, if the user is working on a document in Microsoft Word, then there will be a corresponding button on the taskbar for Microsoft Word.

ANATOMY OF AN APPLICATION WINDOW

Most programs designed to run on Windows look and behave similarly. Application windows, folder windows and files windows have several common features. A brief summary of the common features is discussed below:

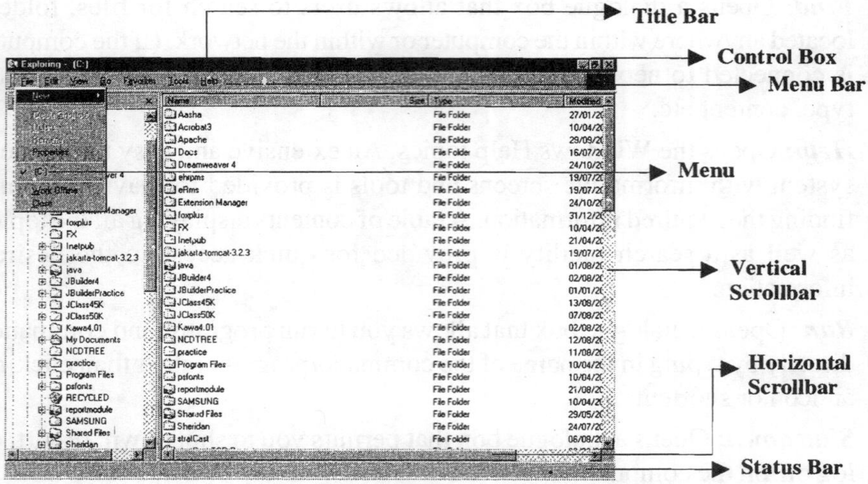

Figure 10.2 Overview of a Windows Explorer Window

(Windows Explorer explained later in the section)

Title Bar The Windows Title bar is displayed at the top of the window. It usually tells something about the contents of the window. For application programs name of the document along with the program name is displayed in the title bar.

Control Box

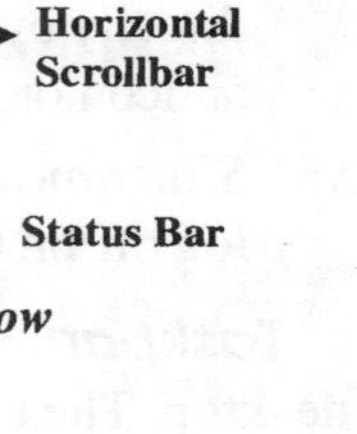

i. *Minimize window:* When the minimize button is clicked, the window disappears and is replaced by a button in the Taskbar. Clicking on this button again will restore the Window to its previous size. Minimising a Window does not close an application, it simply removes it from the user's view.

ii. *Maximize/Restore Window:* When the maximize button is clicked, the window is expanded to fill the screen. Once a Window is maximized, the restore button replaces this icon. Clicking on the restore button will restore the window to its previous size.

iii. *Close Window:* When the close button is clicked, the window/application is closed.

Menu Bar It is located just below the title bar. The menu bar generally comprises a set of words, such as File, Edit, View, and Help, laid out horizontally starting at the left edge of the screen. All Window applications utilise menus in some form or the other. In the picture shown above (Windows Explorer) 'File',

'Edit', 'View' etc. are referred to as menus and the items within each menu are referred to as menu items. 'New', 'Open', 'Save', 'Exit', etc., form the menu items for the 'File' menu. Menu items can be invoked by clicking on the desired menu item. Menu items within a menu can be navigated using 'Up' and 'Down' arrow keys.

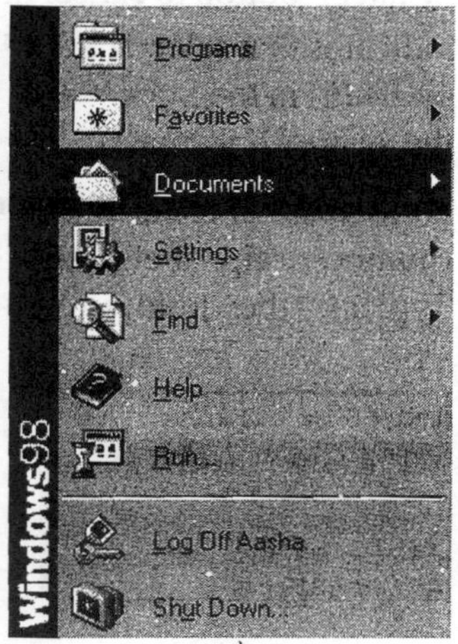

Shortcut keys: If a menu item has a letter in it that is underlined, the item may be selected by holding down the Alt key on the computer and pressing the underlined key whenever the menu is visible. For example, pressing 'Alt' and the 'D' key can open 'Documents' shown in the Screen Shot below. This combination is usually written as 'Alt+D'.

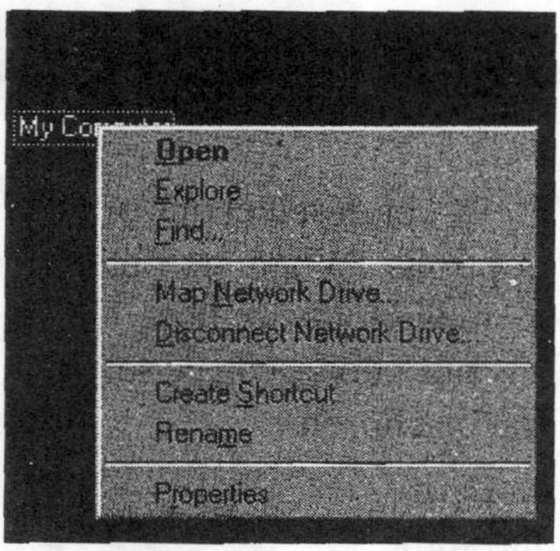

Sub-menu: A little arrow after a menu item, like the one after the "Settings" item, indicates that this option has several sub-options. Menu options that lead to sub-menus typically have arrows to their right. Items on that second menu can be linked to yet another menu. Nesting of menus extending to several layers is possible, and often encountered.

Context menu: If an object is right clicked, a menu is displayed, this menu is referred to as context or shortcut menu. The menu displays a list of options for that objects, the contents of the list could vary depending upon the object. For example, if you right click on the 'My Computer' icon, a menu is displayed showing options related to 'My Computer'.

Dialog boxes: Dialog boxes are small windows that appear when a program needs more information before it can complete an operation. A dialog box is used to capture user preferences and when the user has entered his preferences he can put his

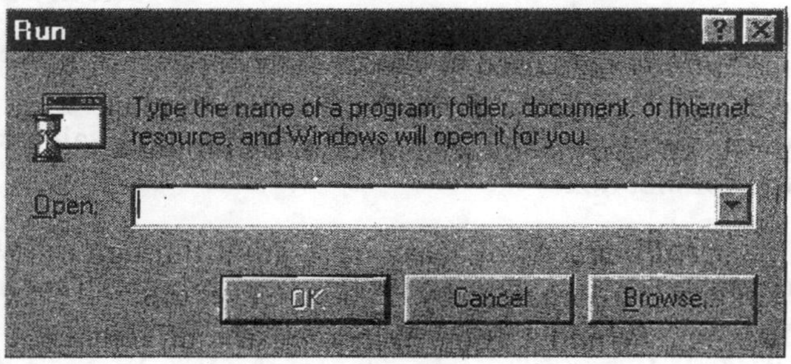

preferences into effect by clicking on the 'OK' button. The user can click on the 'Cancel' button to cancel the operation. If a menu item has ellipses (...) after it, it indicates that selecting the item will open a dialogue box. For example, clicking on 'Run' in the Start Menu will display a dialog box prompting the user to enter the desired information.

Textbox is used to enter any information (numbers, alphabets, special characters etc). Typically they hold a single line of text.

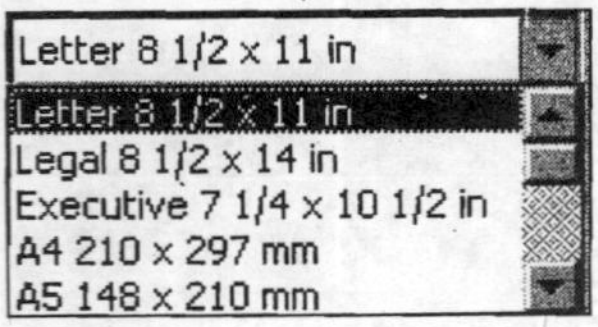

Drop down box/list box is used to make a selection from a list of options. Displays a set of options when the down arrow key is clicked. The list box has a scroll bar (discussed later in the section), if there are more options than the list has room to show.

Option button is used to select one option among several options. Also called as a radio button. It appears as a small circle that, when selected, has a smaller, filled circle inside it.

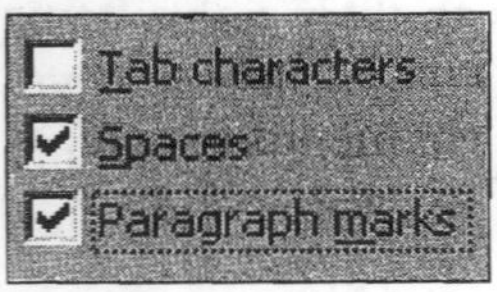

Checkbox is used to select or deselect one or more options from a set of options. When an option is selected, a check mark appears in the box. Unlike option buttons where only one choice can be selected, here multiple options can be chosen.

Command button is used to carry out some action. Clicking on the command button will carry out some action.

Folios or tabs are used to move from one sheet/window to another sheet/window. They are analogous to a set of dividers in a notebook.

Spinners are used to choose from a range of numeric values by 'spinning' through the values by clicking the up or down arrows on the spinner or by typing a value into the spinner box.

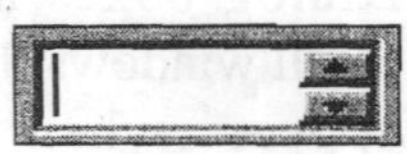

Scrollbars Allow easy navigation through a long list of items or a large amount of information by enabling a user to scroll either horizontally or vertically within a Window. If the Window isn't tall enough, a vertical scrollbar will be displayed along the right edge of the Window and if it's not wide enough, a horizontal one will be displayed.

Status Bar: usually located at the bottom of an application Window. It is used to display various kinds of status data on the current environment; it can contain text or pictures.

Customising Windows

Creating Shortcuts Shortcuts are icons that provide a quick way to start a program or open a file or folder without having to go to its permanent location in Windows Explorer. Windows Explorer can be accessed using Start ® Programs ® Windows Explorer. (Explained in detail later in this section). Shortcuts are useful for programs, files, and folders that are used frequently.

Creating a shortcut for file/folder/program

i. Select the file/folder/program from the Windows Explorer. For programs the '.exe' (Executable) file has to be selected from the Windows Explorer, in order to create a shortcut.

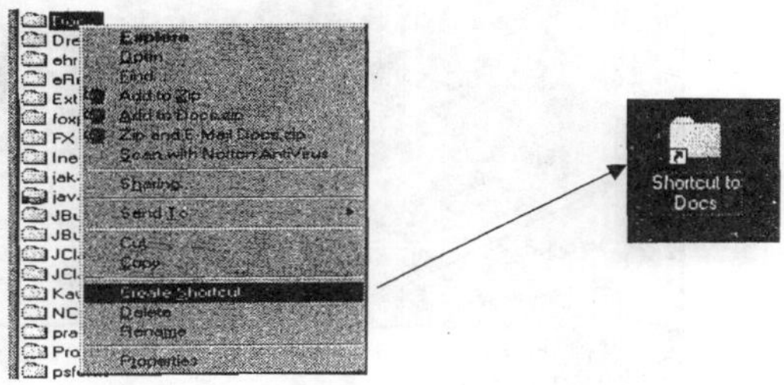

ii. Right click on the file/folder/program and select 'Create Shortcut' from the context menu. This would create the shortcut in the same folder as that of file/folder/program.

iii. Drag the newly created shortcut to the desired place. You can drag the shortcut to the Desktop also.

Deleting a shortcut: Deleting a shortcut will not delete the actual file/folder/program from the computer. When a shortcut is deleted, the set of directions pointing towards the file/folder/program is deleted; the actual file/folder/program stays in its usual location. Follow the steps below to delete a shortcut:

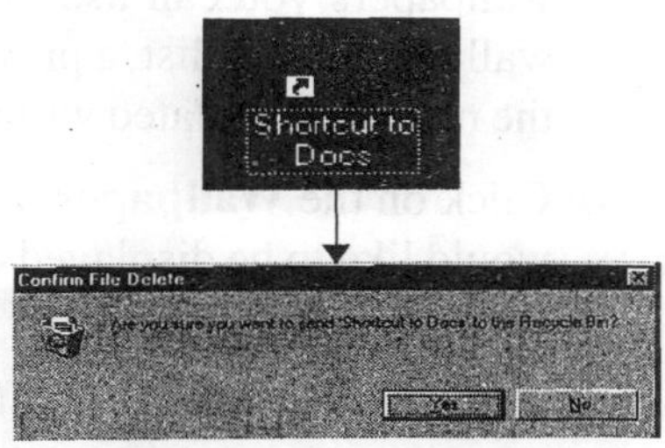

i. select the shortcut by clicking on it.

ii. press 'Del' key from the keyboard.

iii. a dialog box is displayed asking for confirmation for deleting this shortcut.

iv. click on the 'Yes' button to confirm deletion.

Inserting background picture: Desktop Wallpapers do exactly what your room wall paper does–decorates your surroundings and adds colour and fun to your life. Use this option to modify and apply different pictures and images as your desktop wallpapers. You can also use repetitive designs called Patterns to get a woven fabric or block printed look on your desktop.

Right click on the Windows desktop, select Properties option from the Context menu, the following screen will be displayed:

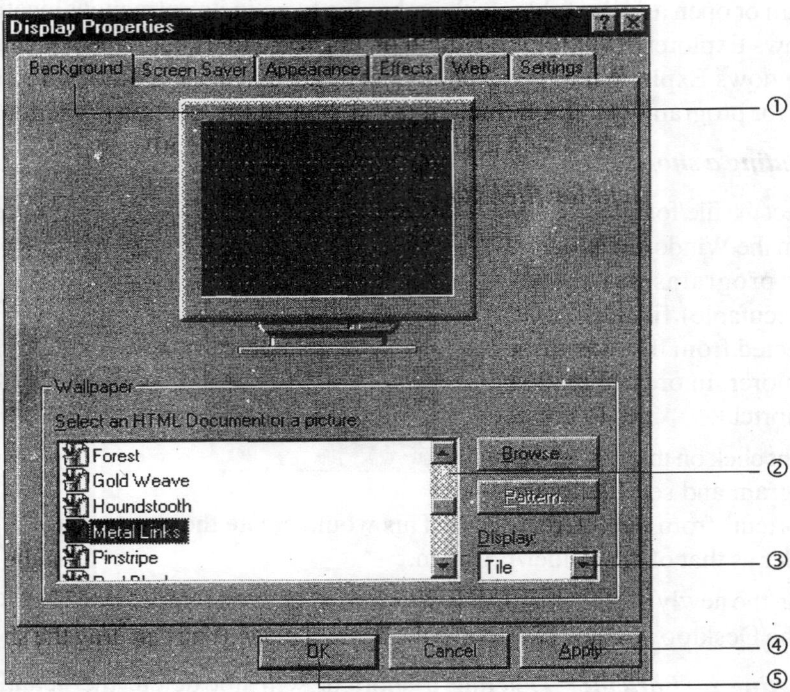

① Click once on **Background folio/tab**. Background lists the available wallpapers you can use to decorate your desktop. When you click on a wallpaper in this list, a preview of how the wallpaper will look appears on the monitor simulated within the box.

② Click on the **Wallpaper** or HTML document from the list given that you would like to be displayed on your desktop.

③ Click on the **Display** box to choose how you want the wallpaper to be displayed–whether tiled, stretched or centered.

④ Click on **Apply** button to apply the settings that you have changed.

⑤ Click on **OK** button to continue.

Screen saver A screen saver is a moving image or pattern that appears on your monitor when you have left your computer idle for a specified limit. Screen saver serves four main functions:

a. Most of them are interesting and provide fun and entertainment.

b. When the same static image stays on a screen for a long period of time it can burn the delicate phosphors on the inside surface of the picture of your monitor. This can leave a permanent ghost of the image on the screen, thereby damaging your monitor.

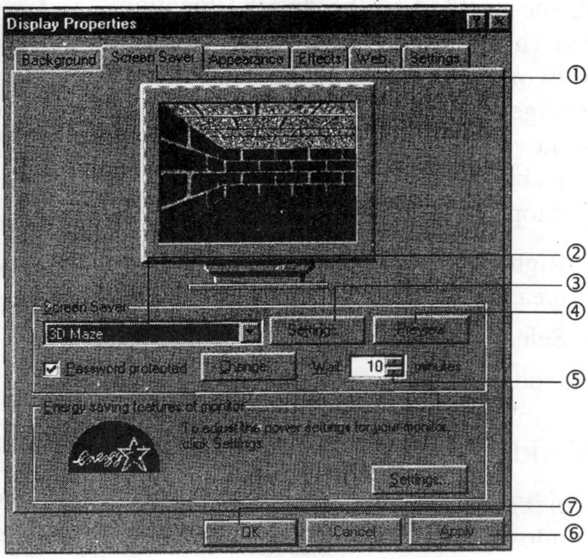

c. Many newer computers have inbuilt power saving option built into them (e.g. EPA energy star, VESA etc.) which powers down the monitor as soon as the screen saver comes into effect, thereby saving on your electricity bills.

d. The screen saver also has an optional security feature. Through this option you can define a password. Once the screen saver is activated it requires the user to type in the correct password before he can resume working. This makes sure nobody peeps into and or messes around with someone's computer file while she is away from her desk.

Right click on the Windows desktop the following screen will be displayed:

① Click on **Screen Saver** folio/tab. The Screensaver lists the available screen savers.

② Click on the **Screen saver** roll-down list and choose the screen saver that you want to apply.

③ Click on the **Settings** button to change the settings.

④ Click on **Preview** button to preview the screen saver before applying it.

⑤ Click here to increase or decrease the time after which the screen saver would appear.

⑥ Click on **Apply** button to apply the changes made.

⑦ Click on **OK** button to continue.

Arranging icons on the desktop: Windows allows you to organize the icons placed on the desktop. Icons can be arranged by name, type, date and

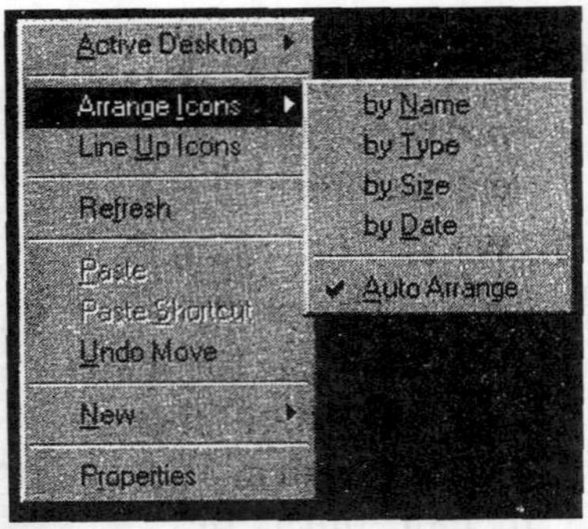

size. Windows allows dragging of icons on the desktop to the desired location. But the system icons (Recycle Bin, Network Neighborhood etc.) can only be arranged within the desktop. They cannot be moved onto other locations. Follow the steps below to arrange the icons on your desktop:

i. Right click on the desktop in the empty area, the context menu will be displayed.
ii. Select 'Arrange Icons' ® Name.
iii. Icons will be arranged accordingly.

Working with Windows

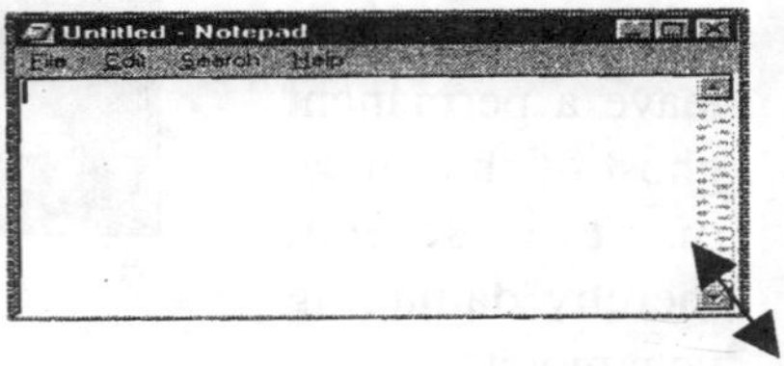

Moving Windows: You can move a window on the screen (if it is not maximized) by left clicking on and dragging its title bar with the mouse.

Resizing Windows Start by slowly moving the mouse pointer across the border until the pointer changes into a double-headed arrow. Then press the left mouse button and hold it down as you drag the border of the Window. When the window is the desired size, release the mouse button.

Switching between multiple Windows: Most Window applications allow opening of multiple document Windows, but only one among them can be active at a time. The active Window is said to have the focus. Follow the steps below to switch between muıtiple documents:

i. Press 'Alt +Tab' from the keyboard. Icons representing each program you're running are displayed at the center of the screen.
ii. Hold down Alt and continue to press Tab, Windows cycles through the programs, enclosing one after another within a box, and listing its name at the bottom of the window.
iii. Release both the keys when the desired program receives focus.

Minimizing all Windows: When multiple document Windows are opened, all of them can be minimised using a single command rather than clicking on the minimise button for each window that is opened. Follow the steps given below to minimise all Windows at one go:

i. Click on the task bar in the empty area.

ii. Select 'Minimise all Windows' from the context menu.

iii. All the open Windows will be minimised. The windows can be restored to their original positions by selecting 'Undo Minimise All' from the context menu.

Arranging Windows: Windows provides three options for displaying all the open Windows namely Cascade, Tile Horizontally and Tile Vertically. Follow the given below steps to display all open Windows:

i. Click on the task bar in the empty area.

ii. Select 'Cascade' or 'Tile Horizontally' or 'Tile Vertically' from the context menu.

iii. All the open Windows will be arranged according to the selected option. The Windows can be restored to their original positions by selecting 'Undo Cascade' or 'Undo Tile' from the context menu.

Exploring Control Panel

Control panel contains utilities for customising the Windows interface. Through Control Panel you can define what colour scheme would be used by Windows (Colour), what fonts would be available (Fonts), what currency format would you be using (International), which events would generate which sound (Sounds), how fast or slow your mouse would work (Mouse), what is the current date and time (Date/Time) etc.

Some of the utilities contained in the Control panel are explained below. Control Panel can be accessed from:

Start ⟶ **Settings** ⟶ **Control Panel**

Installing or Removing Programs

A Select Add/Remove Programs option by double clicking on it. The following screen (**'B'**) would be displayed:

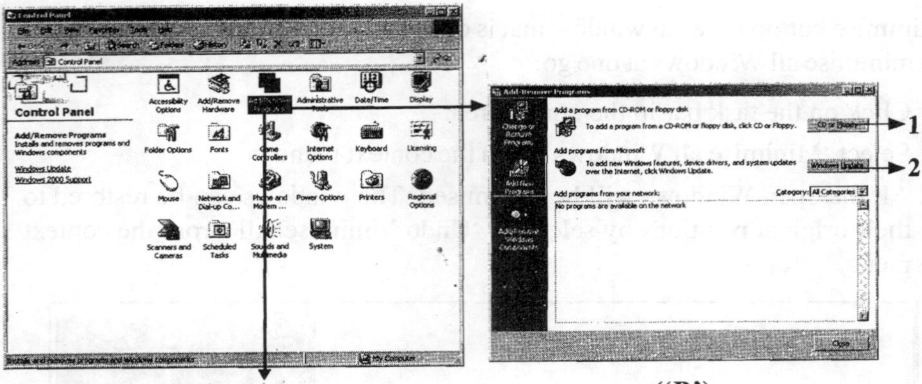

A ('B?')

A Install/Uninstall: Select this option if you want to install/uninstall any programs into/from your computer.

1. **CD or Floppy:** Select this option if you want to install any program into your computer. A new program can be installed using either a CD or a floppy.
2. **Update:** You can choose Windows Update to add new Windows features or system updates over the Internet.

B Windows Setup: Select this option for installing/uninstalling specific components or sub-components of Windows.

1. Displays the list of currently installed components of Windows in your computer.

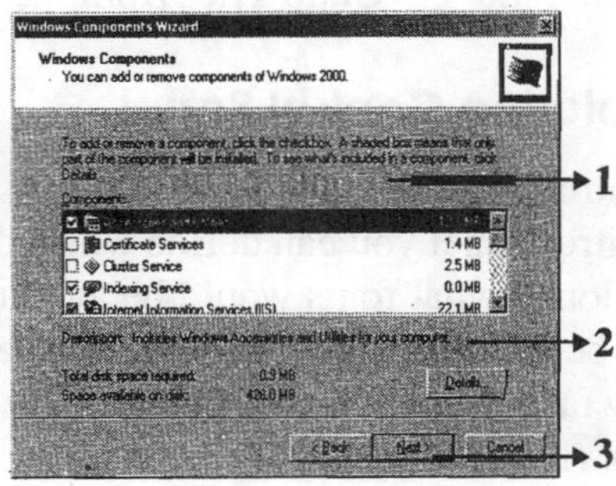

2. **Details:** It gives the details of the selected component. You can add or remove individual sub-components contained in the selected component group.
3. **Have Disk:** Click on 'Next' button to install the component.

Date and Time

Inside your computer there is a small component called a Real Time Clock (RTC). This RTC and CMOS set up powered by a battery cell ensures that the basic settings of your computer are not lost when you switch off your computer. RTC stores the current date and time in your computer and passes on this information to put a date and time stamp on all file operations. The date and time option lets you adjust the system's date and time to correct settings. It is important that your computer works on the correct clock and calendar timings, so that your computer uses current date and time information to create and update your files.

A Select 'Date/Time' from the control panel.

① Click once on the Date & Time folio/tab.

② Click on the month roll-down list to change the month.

③ Click on this button to change the year.

④ Click on any of the dates to change the date.

⑤ Click on this Window to change the time.

⑥ Click on Apply button to apply the changes you have made.

⑦ Click on OK button to continue.

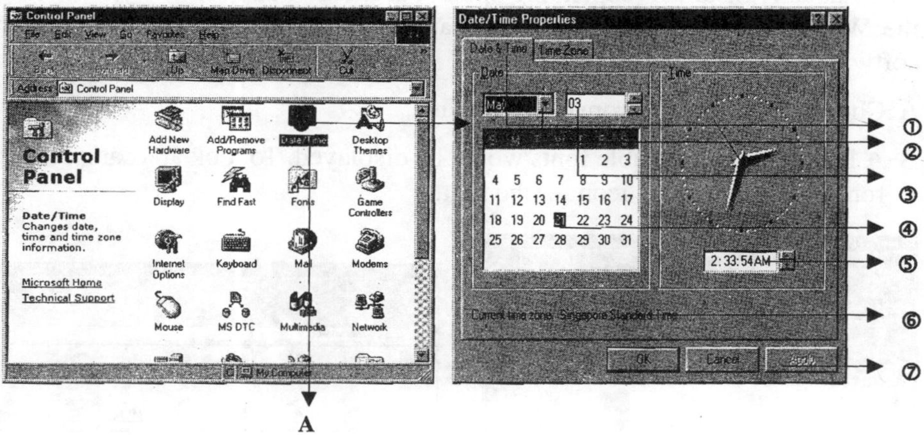

Time Zone

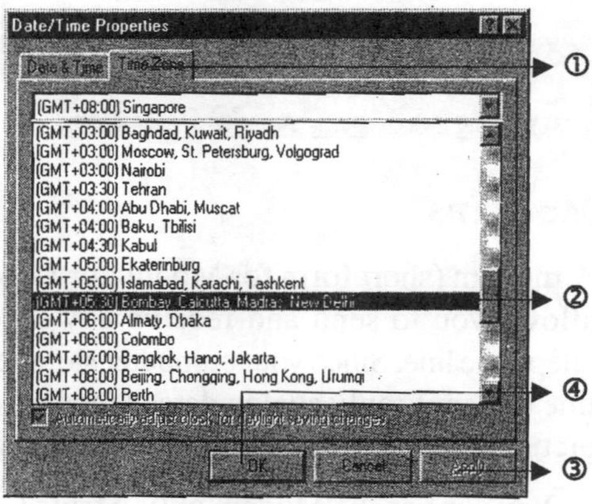

This option determines which time zone you are in. Especially for Laptop users who zip across many countries (and time zones) frequently, this is a great boon and helps them maintain the computer date and time as per the local settings. For India the time zone is GMT+ 05:30 Mumbai, Calcutta, Chennai, New Delhi.

① Click once on **Time Zone** folio/tab.

② Choose the time zone you want to change to by scrolling up or down in the list displayed here.

③ Click on **Apply** button to apply the changes you have made.

④ Click on **OK** button to continue.

Fonts

Fonts are like having different handwritings available on your computer. Fonts are type faces that you can use to pep up your work and change the appearance of characters on your screen and on the printed paper. Fonts help you to express your message more clearly and emphatically. Broadly, there are two types of fonts Serif and Sanserif. A serif is a short stroke at the end of, or at an angle to, the letter form. An example of Serif is Times New Roman font and Sanserif is Arial font. Windows comes bundled with a large number of fonts, which are automatically installed (depending upon your monitor and printer type) during the Windows setup installation. You can install additional fonts from other softwares, as and when required.

A Choose Fonts option from Control Panel.

B A list of all the available fonts would be displayed. To look at a sample of a font, double-click the icon for the font.

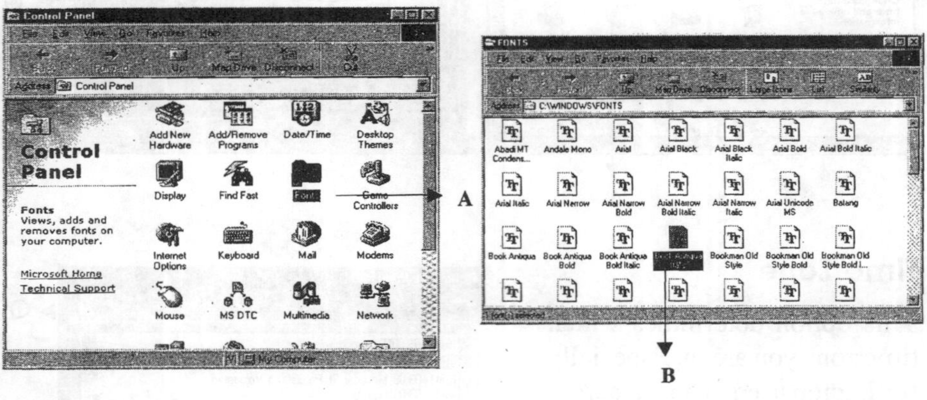

Modems

A modem (short form for Modulator DeModulator) is an electronic device that allows you to send and receive any kind of digital data through the normal telephone line. Since your computer stores data in digital format and your telephone line transmits only analog data, a modem converts any kind of digital data (text, pictures, sound, movies etc.) into analog data and vice versa.

You can use the Modem option from Control Panel to install new modems or to check the performance and settings of pre installed modems.

A Choose **Modem** from **Control Panel**.

① Click on the **Modems** folio/tab.

② Click on the modem to highlight it.

③ Click on the **Add** or **Remove** button to add or remove the modem.

④ Click on the **Properties** button to configure the modem.

⑤ Click on the **Apply** button to apply the changes made.

⑥ Click on **OK** button to continue.

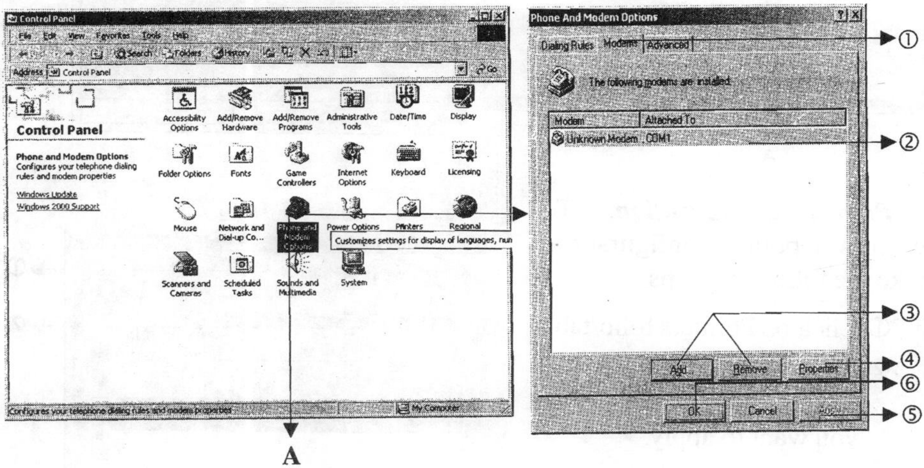

Mouse

As explained earlier, a mouse is a small hand held device through which you can quickly and easily navigate the different parts of the screen. You can customise the various aspects of mouse to make them work the way you prefer. You can control the mouse pointer speed, shape, button configuration, double click speed etc. You can even swap the left and right buttons. If you frequently lose track of where your mouse pointer is, you can choose to have a mouse trail effect, which will make the mouse pointer more visible.

A Choose Mouse option from Control Panel.

Button configuration: To customise button configuration, take the following steps:

① Click on the **Buttons** folio/tab.

② Click on **Right handed** radio button of the **Button configuration** option to convert your left mouse button into right button, and vice versa.

③ Drag this button to increase or decrease the clicking speed of the mouse.

④ Click on **Apply** button to apply the changes that you have made.

⑤ Click on **OK** button to continue.

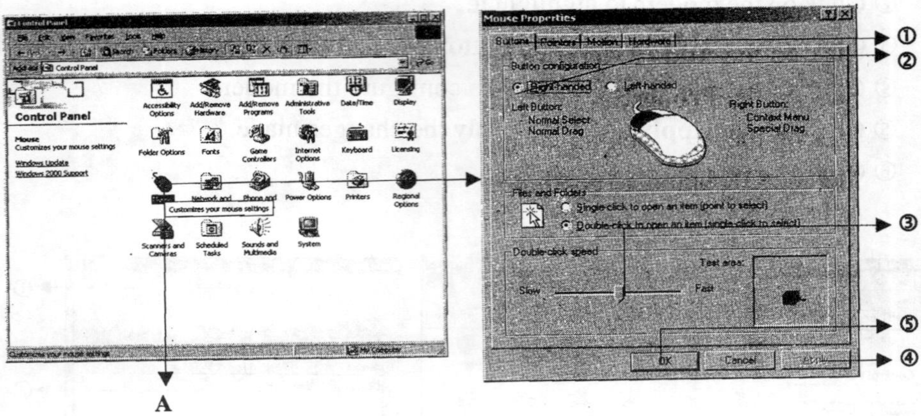

Pointers configuration: To customise pointer configuration, take the following steps:

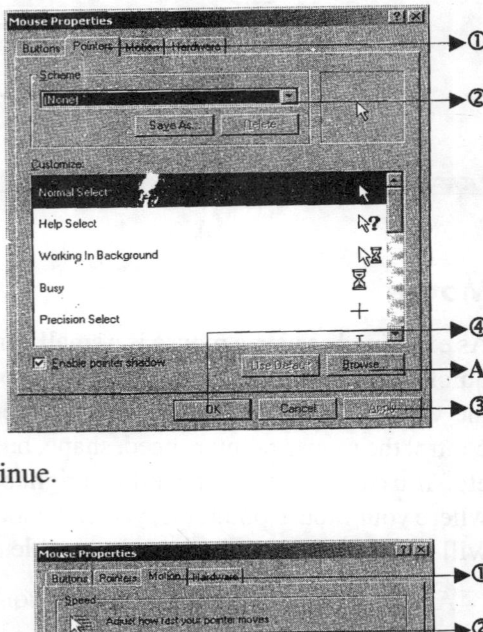

① Click on Pointers folio/tab.

② Click on the pull-down list to choose the scheme that you want to apply.

A You can choose a scheme from another location by clicking on the Browse button.

③ Click on Apply button to apply the chosen scheme.

④ Click on the OK button to continue.

Motion configuration: To customise motion configuration, take the following steps:

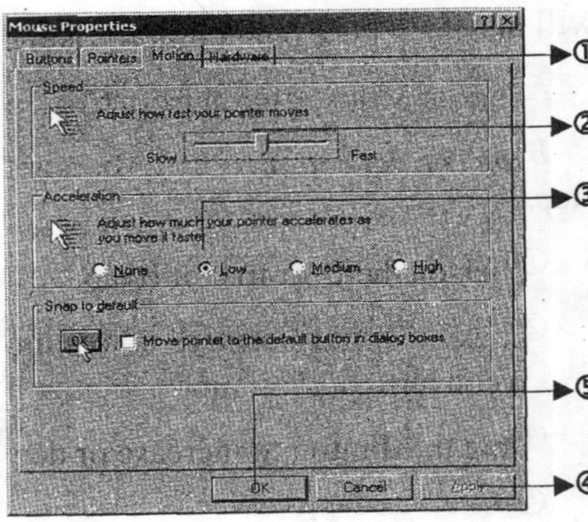

① Click on the Motion folio/tab.

② Click on this button to increase or decrease the pointer speed.

③ You can also click on the pointer trails radio buttons to make them look long or short.

④ Click on Apply button to apply the changes you have made.

⑤ Click on the OK button to continue.

Mouse pointers At this stage, it is important to understand the various mouse pointers that would be shown to you at different times. In short, the mouse pointer gives you a clue about the work that Windows is either doing, or expecting you to do. Let us see these pointers one by one:

Vertical Resize: Whenever you move the cursor on the top or bottom boundary of a Window/object, your Mouse Pointer would turn into this shape.

Horizontal Resize: Whenever you move the cursor on the left or right boundary of a Window/object, your mouse pointer would turn into this shape.

Diagonal Resize 1: Whenever you move the cursor on the upper left or lower right diagonal corner of a window/object, your mouse pointer would turn into this shape.

Diagonal Resize 2: Whenever you move the cursor on the upper right or lower left diagonal corner of a window/object, your mouse pointer would turn into this shape.

Move: Whenever you have selected an object for moving, your mouse pointer would turn into this shape.

Normal Select: Whenever you normally point the mouse pointer at any object or icon, scroll bar or menu, the mouse pointer would turn into this shape.

Help Select: Whenever you press the Help Icon to get help on a specific topic, the mouse pointer would turn into this shape. Once you get this mouse pointer, simply click on the icon for which you want help and Windows will show you the help text.

Working: Whenever you have executed a command which takes a couple of moments, Windows would display this mouse pointer. This means that Windows is processing your request in the background.

Busy: Whenever Windows is trying to load some information into the computer memory or is busy trying to open or save a file, this mouse pointer would be displayed. At this stage, you would not to be able to execute any other command.

Text Select: Whenever and wherever you can work on some text matter or some typed input is required from the user (usually in a Word processor like Note Pad or MS Word), this mouse pointer would be displayed.

Printers

Use this option to install new printers. You would need Windows 2000 CD or the Printer Installation CD to run this option. Windows 2000 installation CD includes many printer drivers from various well-known printer manufacturers. However, if your printer or it's exact model is not listed in the driver's list provided by Windows 2000, you don't need to worry. Simply insert CD or floppy (which must have come along with the printer) and complete the printer installation procedure.

A Select **Printers** option from **Control Panel.**

B Double click on the **Add Printer** button and follow the steps explained in the wizard to install a new printer.

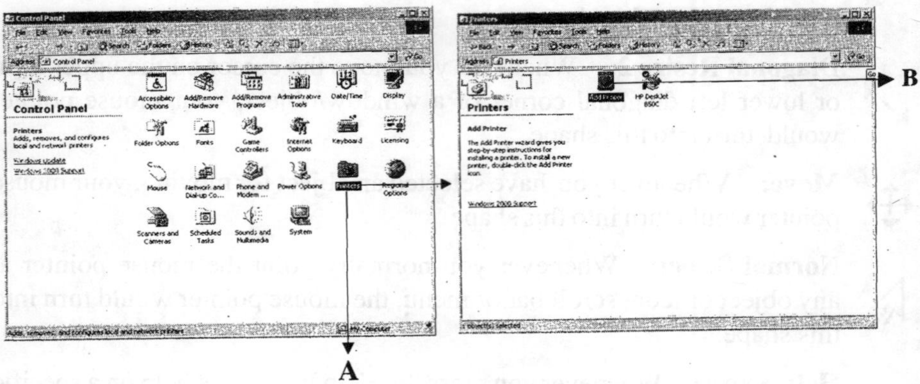

Regional Settings

If you are using Windows 2000 in any country other than USA or are using any language other than American English, you need to go to this option to define the various regional settings like language, number formatting, currency, date and time format.

A Select **Regional Settings** option from **Control Panel**.

① Click on the **General** folio/tab.

② Click on this roll-down list to choose the regional settings. Choosing a regional setting automatically changes settings on the Number, Currency, Time and Date tabs.

③ Click on **Apply** button to apply the changes you have made.

④ Click on the **OK** button to continue.

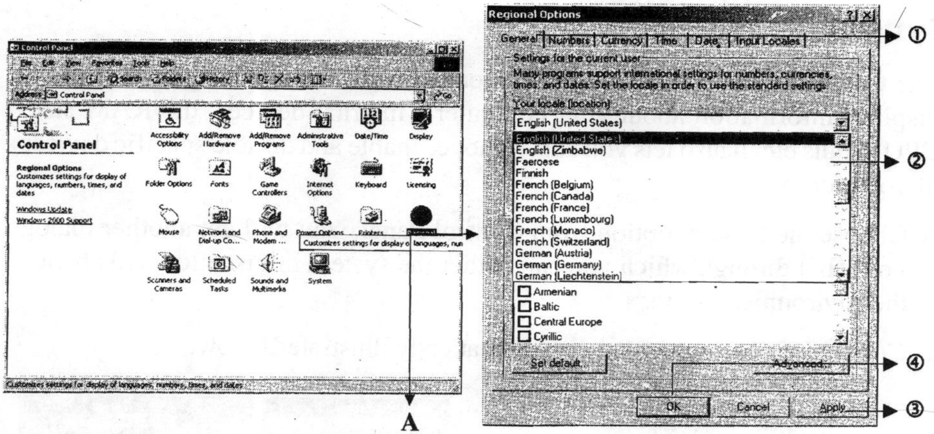

Sounds

You can use this option for assigning different sounds to various system events such as error messages, warning dialog boxes, starting and exiting Windows etc. Needless to say, this option will work only if you have a Sound Card and Speakers installed.

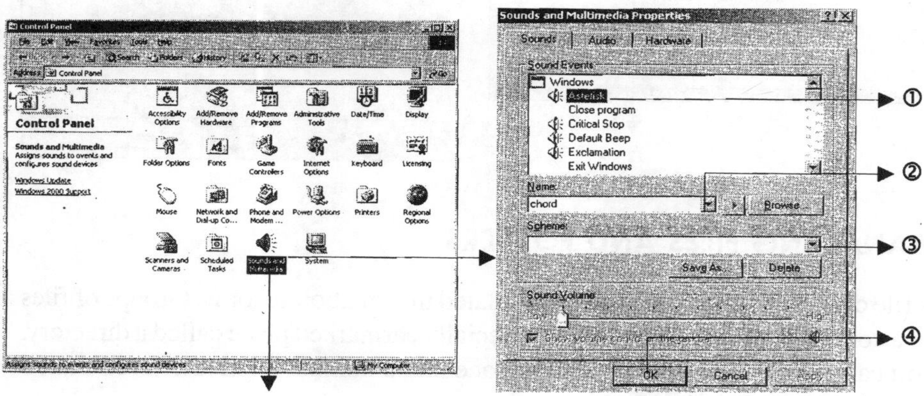

A Choose **Sounds and Multimedia** option from **Control Panel**.

① Choose the sound type.

② Click on the **Name** roll-down list to choose from the various instruments from which you can assign sounds.

③ Click on the Schemes roll-down list to choose a scheme. This list displays schemes that you can use to simultaneously change the sounds assigned to many system events.

④ Click on OK button.

System

The Control Panel's System applet is loaded with features for power users. It displays information about your computer's internal devices, the RAM size, CPU details etc. It also lets you add, remove, enable and disable specific devices of your computer.

A Choose the System option from Control Panel. You will get another dialog box **('B')** through which you can gather the system information and change the environment settings.

Concept of files and folders is systematically illustrated below:

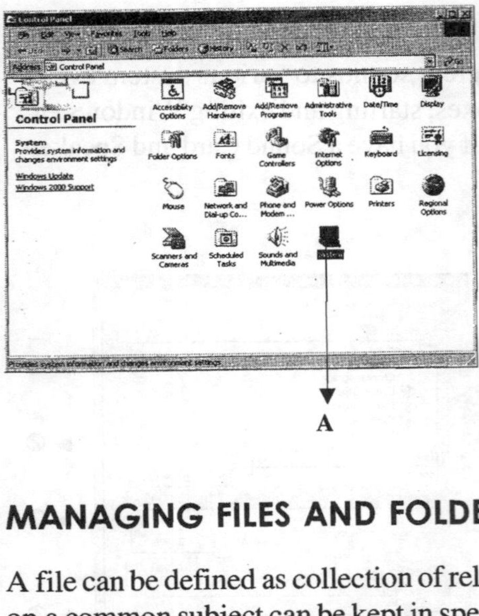

A

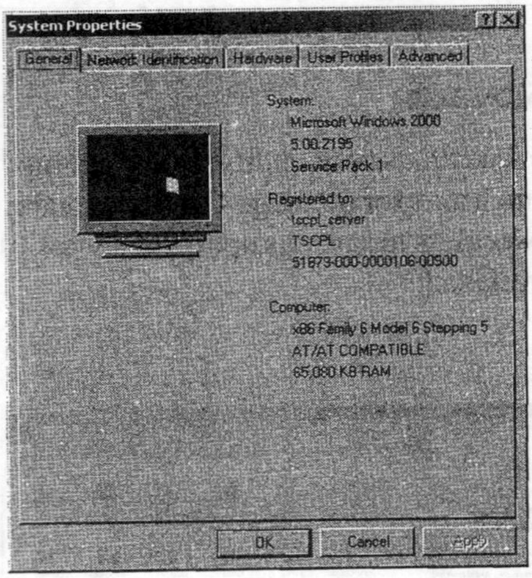

MANAGING FILES AND FOLDERS

A file can be defined as collection of related information/records. Groups of files on a common subject can be kept in specially earmarked place called a directory. You can divide your total hard disk space into a number of smaller units called Directories and Sub-directories.

Basically all the files are maintained on your hard disk in the form of an inverted tree like structure. At the top is the root directory under which there are sub-directories and sub-sub-directories. Each of these directories or sub-directories may contain one or many files. Microsoft decided that Folders is a more helpful word than directories and therefore they are called **Folders and Sub-folders**. A folder can consist of files as well as sub-folders. It is also possible to have an empty folder. The number of files in a folder or sub-folder is limited only by your hard disk capacity. File names should convey some sense of their contents (for instance you would not like to call your love letter that you wrote to your girlfriend/boyfriend - **The National Charter of Demands!!!)**

Whenever the user creates a new file, an extension is automatically appended to it. The extension of file tells about the type of the file and the program(s) through which the file can be opened and viewed.

For example, Hello.txt ('Hello' is the file name and .txt is the extension, which indicates that 'Hello' is a text file).

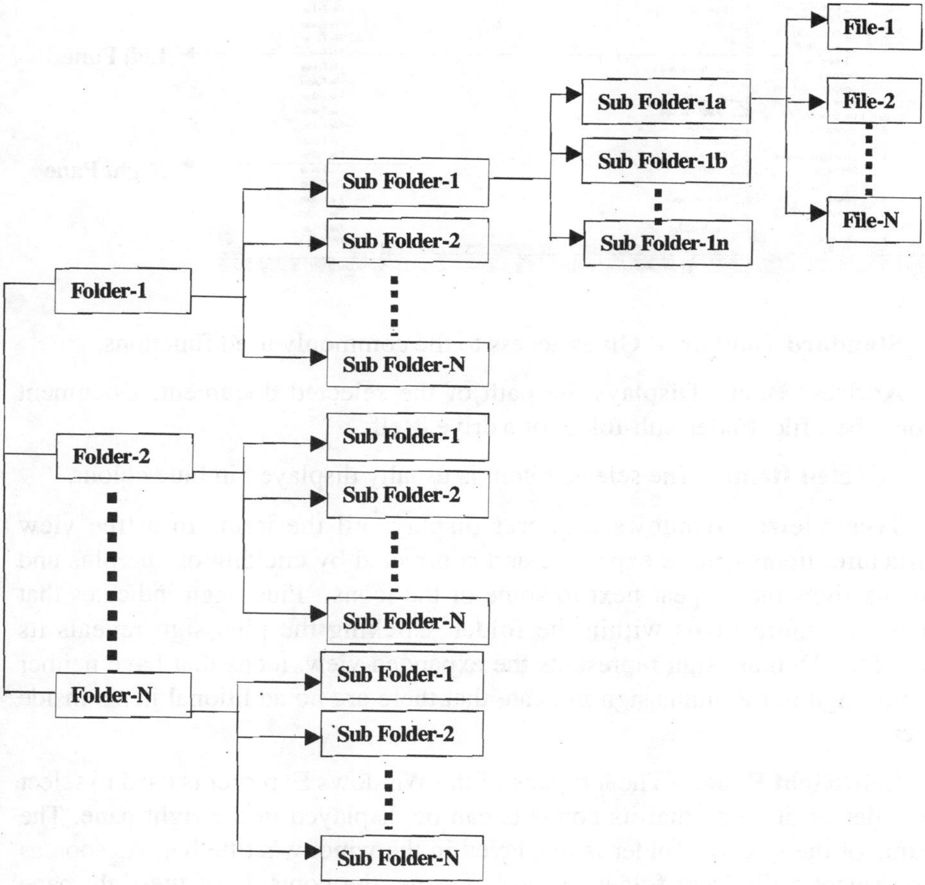

Overview of Windows Explorer

Windows Explorer is a utility that represents the contents of your computer in a graphical form. It allows you to do various file and disk management tasks like copy, rename, move and delete file(s) and create folder(s) and sub-folder(s), format floppies etc. It is the quickest way to get a complete view of the contents of your computer. You can take its help to quickly determine which files are available and where it. Windows Explorer can be accessed:

Start → Programs → Windows

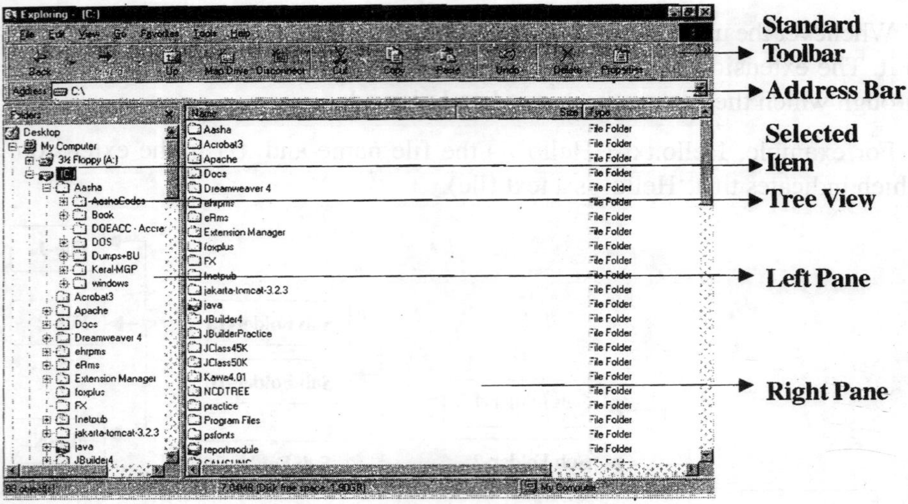

Standard Toolbar: Gives access to the commonly used functions.

Address Bar: Displays the path of the selected document. Document could be a file, folder, sub-folder or a drive itself.

Selected Item: The selected item is usually displayed in blue colour.

Tree View: Windows Explorer displays all the items in a tree view structure. Items can be expanded and contracted by clicking on the plus and minus signs that appear next to some of the icons. 'Plus' sign indicates that there are more items within the folder. Clicking the plus sign reveals its contents. 'Minus' sign represents the expanded view. Icons that have neither a plus sign nor a minus sign indicate that there are no additional items inside them.

Left/Right Pane: The left pane of the Windows Explorer is used to select a folder or drive so that its contents can be displayed in the right pane. The name of the selected folder is displayed in the window's title bar. As soon as you select a different folder in the left pane, the contents of the right pane change to reflect that folder's contents.

Creating Folders

Follow the steps below to create a new folder:

1. Select the drive ('C' or 'D' or 'A' etc.) in Windows Explorer where you want to create the new folder. A drive can be selected by clicking on its name. If desired, desktop can also be selected for creating a new folder. The selected drive will be displayed on the Address bar of the Windows Explorer.

2. On the **File** menu, point to **New**, and click on **Folder**. The new folder appears with a temporary name in the same location as that of the selected drive/folder.
3. Type a name for the new folder, and then press ENTER.

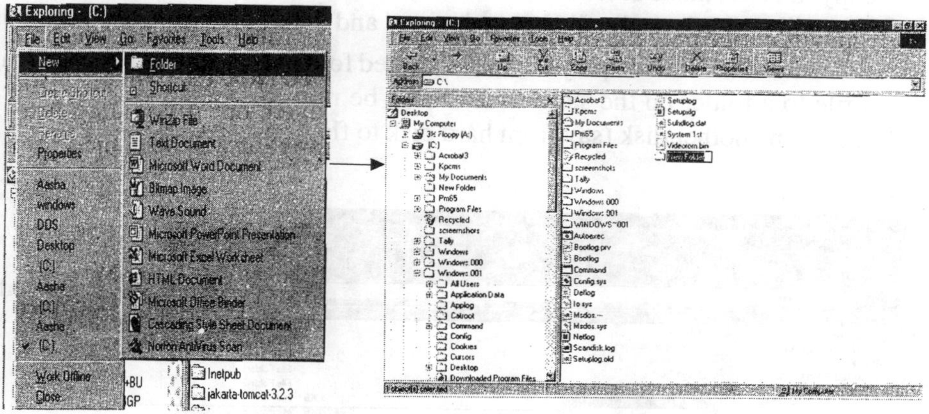

Note A file name can contain up to 255 characters, including spaces. It cannot contain the following characters:’ \’,’ /’,’:’,’ *’ ‘? ‘,’”’,’ <>’,’ | ‘. Since it may be difficult for you to remember which symbols are allowed and which are not, it is best to avoid all symbols while giving any folder and file names.

Creating Sub-folders Follow the steps below to create a sub-folder:

1. Select the folder within which you want to create a sub-folder.
2. Repeat Steps ‘2 ‘ and ‘3’ explained in ‘Creating Folders’.

Opening folders Follow the steps below to view the contents of a folder:

1. In the left pane, select the drive in which the folder is located.
2. Click on the folder name to view its contents. The contents of the folder will be displayed in the right pane.

Opening files As a general rule a file can be opened only through the application program through which it was created. The extension name of a file indicates the program through which it was created. There are exceptions to this rule also – for instance, files created in one type of word processor (say Word Perfect) can be opened in another word processor (say MS Word) provided necessary conversion tools are installed.

Follow the steps given below to open a file:

1. Select the desired file from the Windows Explorer. If the file is stored within a folder then open that folder using the steps explained above.
2. Double click on the file name.
3. The desired file will be opened using the associated program.

Copying Files in Explorer by Click & Drag Method

① Click on the file that you want to move to another folder. Keep the mouse button pressed on the highlighted file, drag it to the folder where you want to copy it. Here, make sure that the folder you want to drag the file to is visible. You will notice here the file being dragged and the folder being highlighted.

② You will see the file displayed in the required folder. Note that when you drag a file to a folder on the same disk, it will be moved, but if you drag it to a folder on another disk (say from hard disk to floppy), it will be copied.

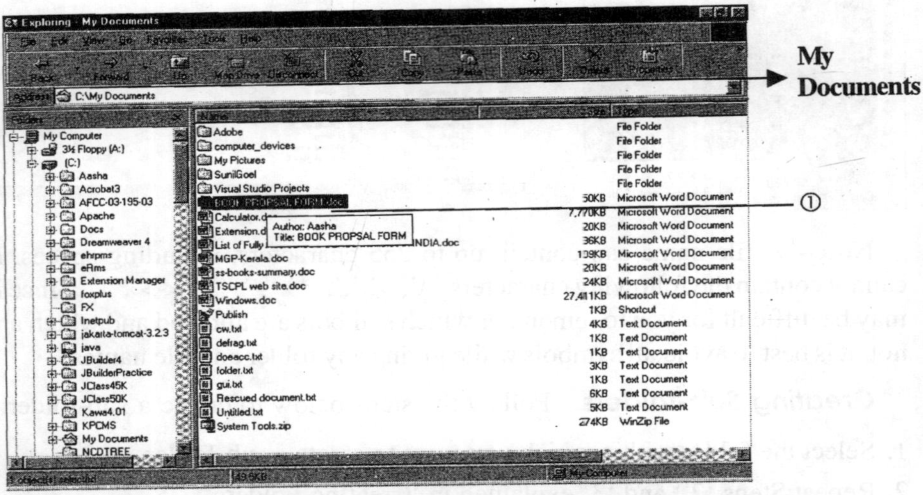

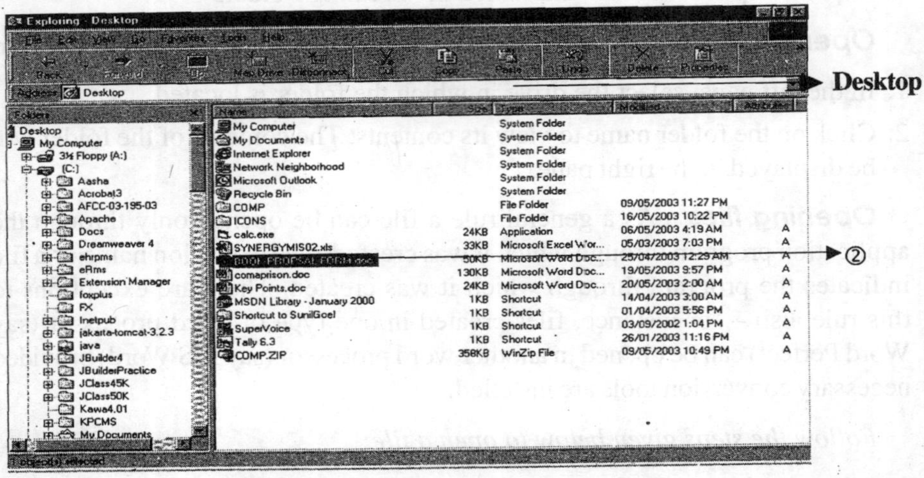

Notes:

1. When a file is copied from one location to another then the file is available in the original location and a copy of it is saved at the destination. But when a

file is moved from one location to another location then the file is available only at the destination.

2. To copy a file using Click and Drag method from one folder to another (both located in the same disk), select the desired file, drag the file using the right mouse button and when you reach the destination, simply right click and select 'Copy here' option.

Copying Files Discontinuously

① Click on a file that you want to copy and press the CTRL key.

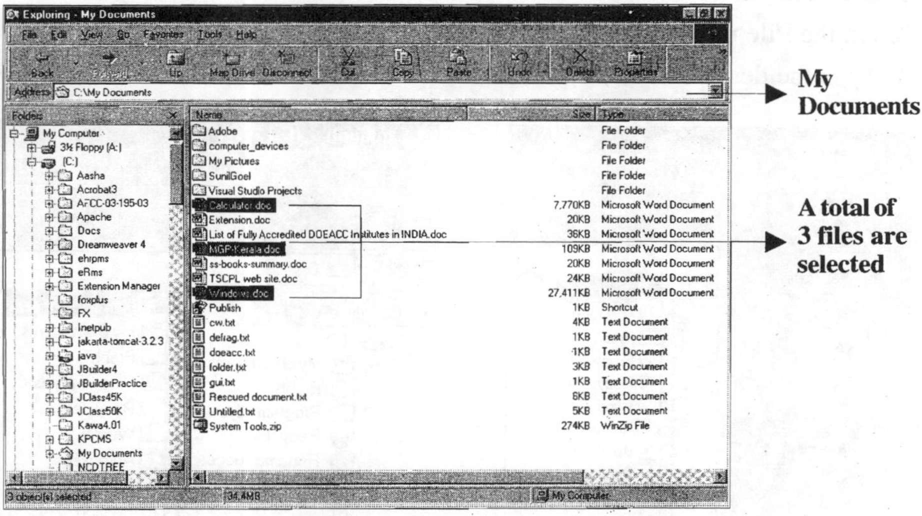

② Keeping the CTRL key pressed, click on another file. After that simply follow the steps that you take to copy a file to another folder. This is easier in the sense that you do not have to copy the required files one by one.

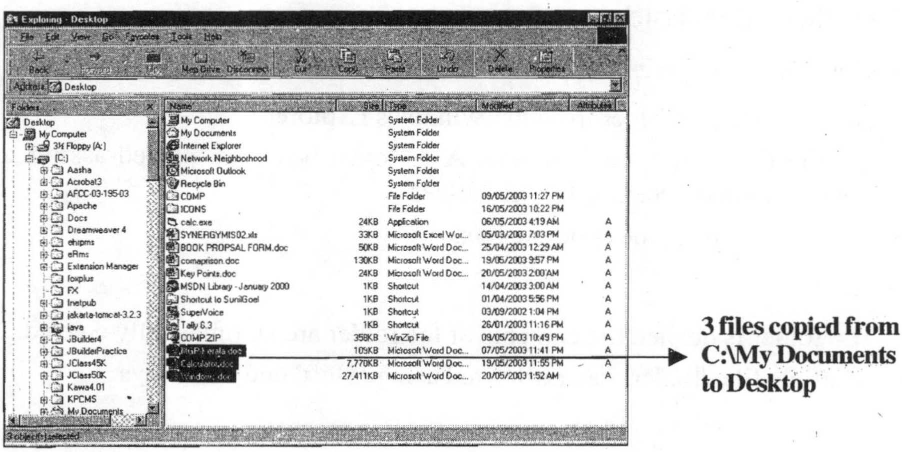

Copying a Continuous Range of Files

You can also select a continuous range of files by using the SHIFT key. Click on the first file, press and hold the SHIFT key and click on the last file of the range to highlight a range of files. After that you can Cut or Copy them in any other folder.

Renaming Files/Folders

Follow the steps given below to rename a file/folder:

1. Select the file or folder from the Windows Explorer.
2. On the File menu, click **Rename**.
3. Type the desired name, and then press ENTER.

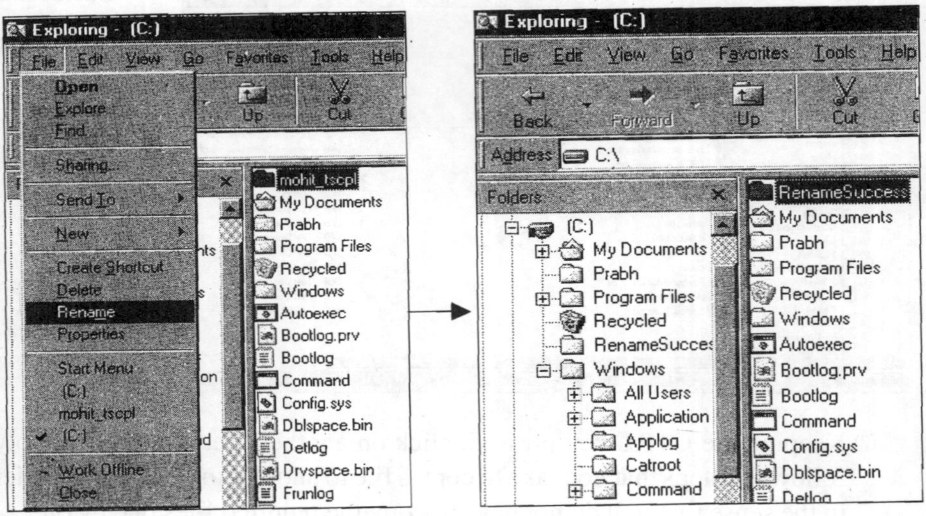

Deleting Files/Folders

Follow the steps given below to delete a file/folder:

1. Select the file or folder from the Windows Explorer.
2. On the File menu, click **Delete**. A dialogue box is displayed asking for confirmation for deleting this file/folder.
3. Select 'Yes' from the dialogue box.

Notes:

- If a folder is deleted the contents of the folder are automatically deleted.
- Multiple files/folders can be deleted using 'Shift' and 'Alt' keys.

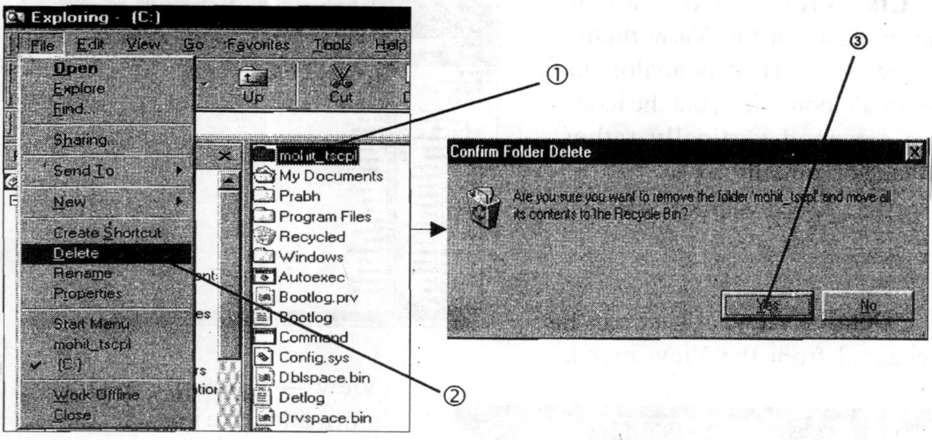

Notes: Copy, Rename, Delete command can also be accessed by right clicking on the file name.

Changing the Folder Views

The folders in the Windows Explorer can be displayed in several views. Below is a brief description of these views:

Large Icons View: This can be accessed from the View menu. (View — Large Icons). In this view each drive, folder, or file is shown as a large icon with a name or description underneath.

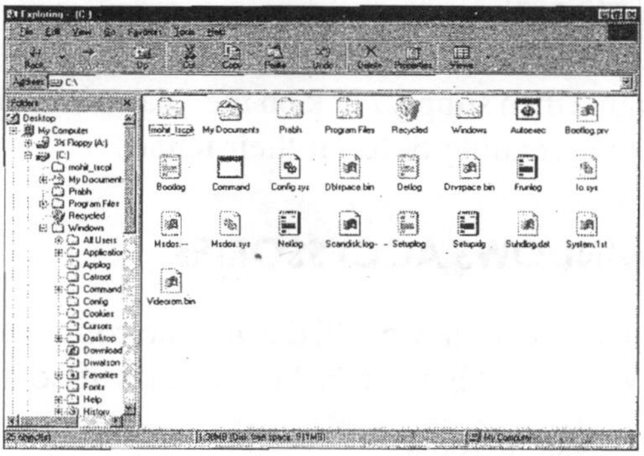

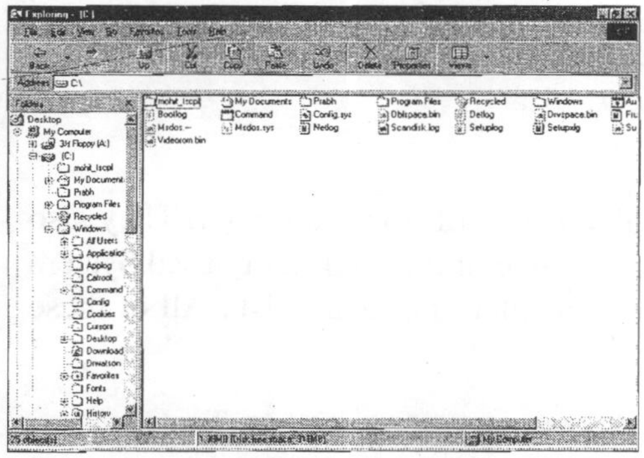

Small Icons View: This can be accessed from the View menu. (View — Small Icons). In this view each drive, folder, or file is shown as a small icon with a name or description to its right. The items are arranged horizontally in this view.

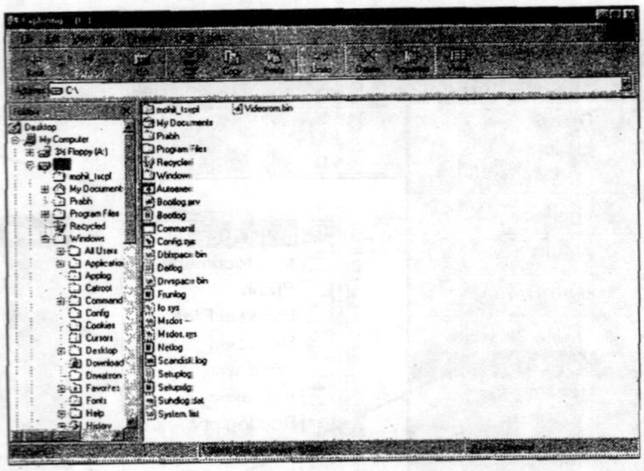

List View: This can be accessed from the View menu. (View — List). It is analogous to Small Icons view, but the icons are arranged vertically rather than horizontally.

Details View: This can be accessed from the View menu. (View — Details). It displays information like item name, size, type (folder or file type), and the date the item was last modified. Dragging the borders between the column headings will change column widths in the details view. To sort the items by Name or Size or Type or Modified simply click on the corresponding column heading. For example, if you want to sort the items by name then simply click on the 'Name' column. All the items will be displayed in the ascending order of their names.

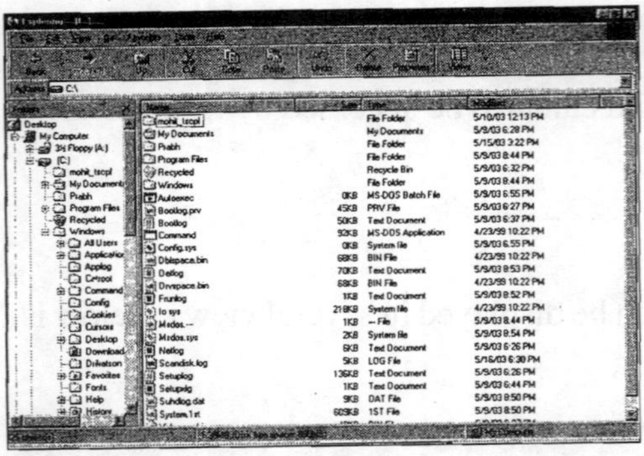

WINDOWS ACCESSORIES

In this section, we will discuss the commonly used accessories that are built into Windows. They can be broadly classified into the following categories:

1. System Tools
2. Entertainment Utilities
3. Miscellaneous Accessories

System Tools

These built-in tools aid in the easy maintenance of your computer. They also help you to troubleshoot minor problems. Some of the commonly used System Tools include Disk Cleanup, Disk Defragmenter and Scan Disk. All of these utilities can be accessed from:

Start ⟶ **Programs** ⟶ **Accessories** ⟶ **System Tools**

Disk Cleanup This utility helps to free up space on your hard disk. It first searches the entire hard disk and then lists temporary files, Internet cache files, downloadable program files (These are ActiveX controls and other Java Applets that are automatically downloaded from the Internet and stored onto the hard disk of your computer.), contents of Recycle Bin and unnecessary program files that can be safely deleted. Disk cleanup should be periodically used to free up the space in the hard disk. It cannot be used for CD-ROM's or Network Drives. It can be accessed from:

Start ⟶ Programs ⟶ Accessories ⟶ System Tools ⟶ Disk Cleanup

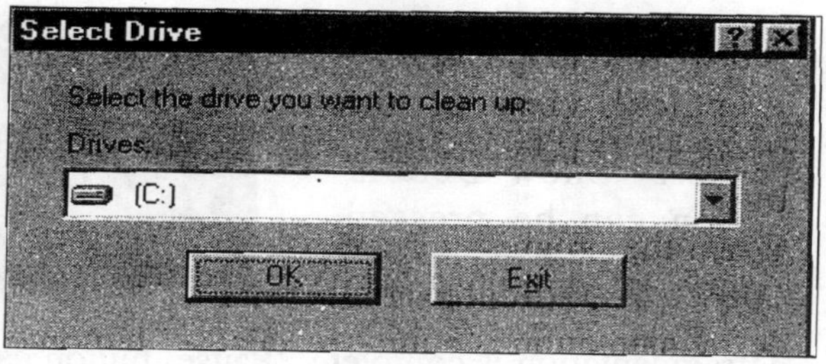

a. The following screen will be displayed. All the hard drives of the computer will be displayed in the drop down box. The desired drive can be selected and then 'OK' button should be pressed to start the disk clean up.

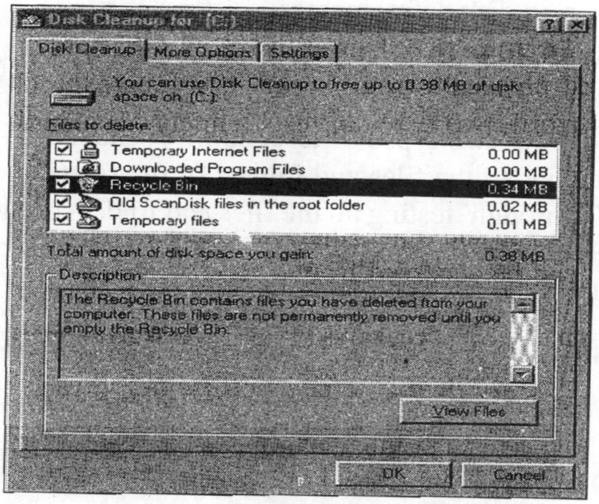

b. Process of disk clean up will be displayed to the user and in the end a dialog box is prompted to the user asking for confirmation for deleting the list of unnecessary files. If desired the user can view the list of files that would be deleted. It will also display the amount of space that will be freed.

Disk defragmenter This utility helps to rearrange files and unused hard disk space to enable programs run faster. Large files that cannot be accommodated in a single location on the hard disk are usually fragmented and are stored at the nearest available free space on the hard disk. System takes more time to access fragmented files. This utility rearranges all such free spaces on the hard disk; as a result, files become quickly accessible. The defragmenter arranges them in adjacent units and consolidates all the free spaces recovered from various locations of the hard disk. It is always advisable to close other programs while the disk is being defragmented, because defragmenter restarts each time whenever other programs write to the disk. It can be accessed from:

Start ⟶ Programs ⟶ Accessories ⟶ System Tools ⟶ Disk Defragmenter

a. The following screen will be displayed. All the hard drives of the computer will be displayed in the drop down box. The desired drive can be selected and then 'OK' button should be pressed to start the process of defragmentation.

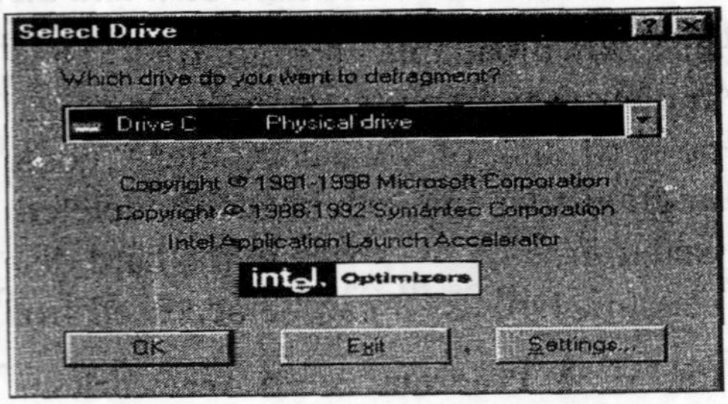

b. Progress of defragmentation is displayed to the user. For graphical view of this process 'Show Details' button can be pressed. When the progress reaches 100%, it indicates that defragmentation is complete. 'Pause' button can be pressed to temporarily stop disk defragmenter.

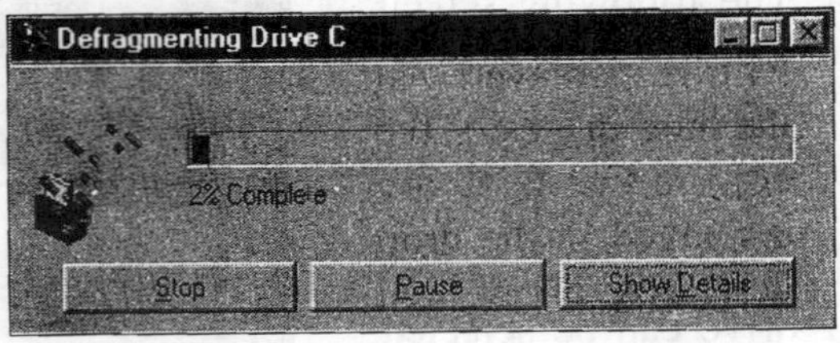

Scan Disk This utility checks the hard disk and removable disk for logical and physical errors. It can then repair the damaged areas. It can be used to perform two types of tests namely 'Standard' and 'Thorough'. In 'Standard' testing all the files and folders of the selected drive are checked for errors. In 'Thorough' testing all the files and folders of the selected drive are checked for errors. In addition to that it also checks the physical integrity of the disk's surface. It can be accessed from:

Start ⟶ Programs ⟶ Accessories ⟶ System Tools ⟶ Scan Disk

The following screen will be displayed:

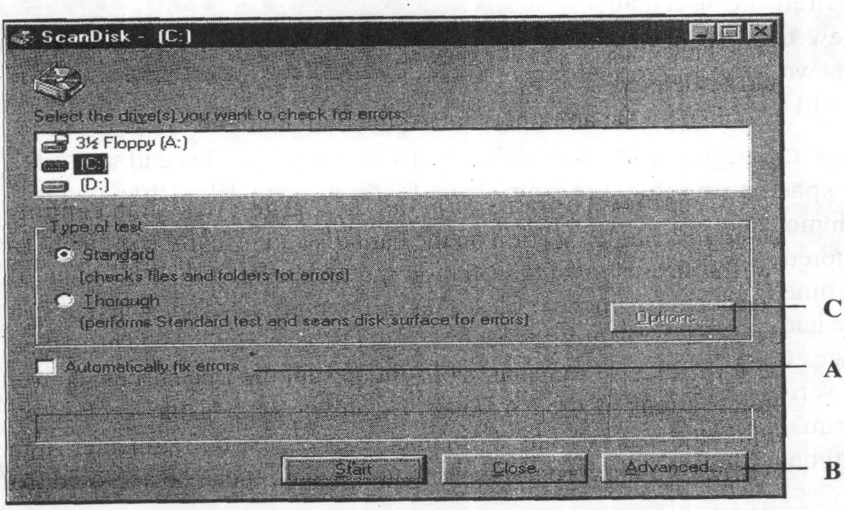

A If this option is selected then scan disk will automatically repair the errors using pre-defined settings (Settings can be changed by clicking on the 'Advanced' button). Otherwise the scan disk would prompt the user to specify how the errors should be corrected.

B This button is used to change the settings the scan will use while checking the drives for errors.

C This button will be enabled only for 'Thorough' testing. It allows you to specify the settings the scan disk will use while checking the disk surface for errors.

The scanning process will start as soon as the 'Start' button is clicked. After the scanning is completed, a summary report detailing total disk space, disk space occupied by bad sectors, files, and folders will be displayed. The summary report is displayed only if 'Display Summary' is enabled in settings.

Entertainment Utilities

Some of the commonly used Entertainment Tools include CD Player, Sound Recorder, Volume Control and Windows Media Player. All of these utilities can be accessed from:

Start ⟶ Programs ⟶ Accessories ⟶ Entertainment

CD player It can be used to play audio compact discs on a CD-ROM drive connected to your computer. CD player can be used to play multiple CDs provided your computer has a multidisk player. You can listen to a CD over your speaker system provided your computer has a sound card. It can be accessed from:

Start ⟶ Programs ⟶ Accessories ⟶ Entertainment ⟶ CD Player

The following screen will be displayed:

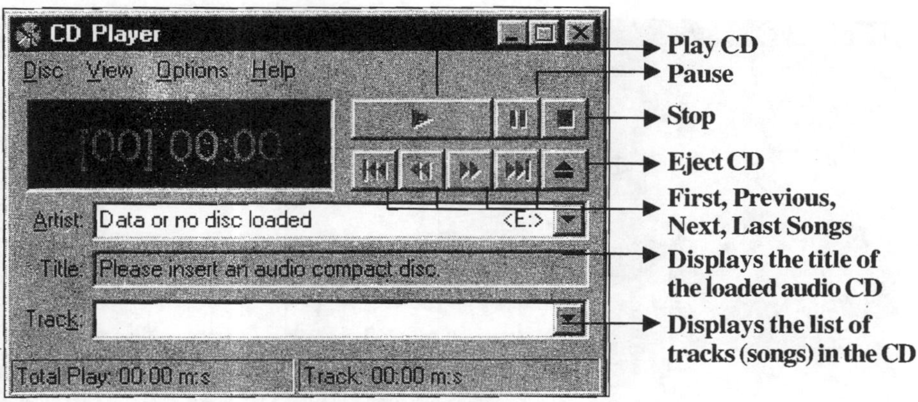

Sound recorder It can be used to record, edit and play ound files. The computer must have a microphone for recording and a sound card and speakers for listening to sound files. It can be accessed from:

Start ⟶ Programs ⟶ Accessories ⟶ Entertainment ⟶ Sound Recorder

The following screen will be displayed:

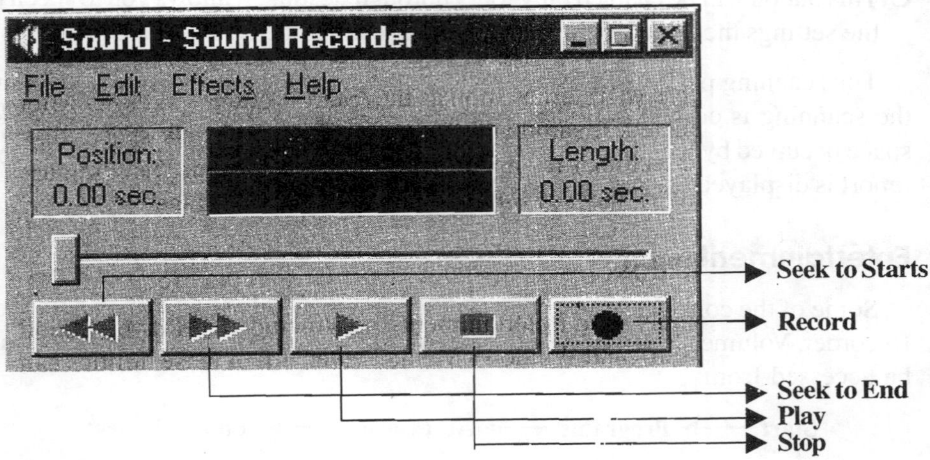

Volume control It can be used to adjust the volume when playing audio files. It can be used to adjust the recording volume as well as the playback volume. It has a facility that allows muting of all or some volumes. It can be accessed from:

Start ⟶ Programs ⟶ Accessories ⟶ Entertainment ⟶ Volume Control

The following screen will be displayed:

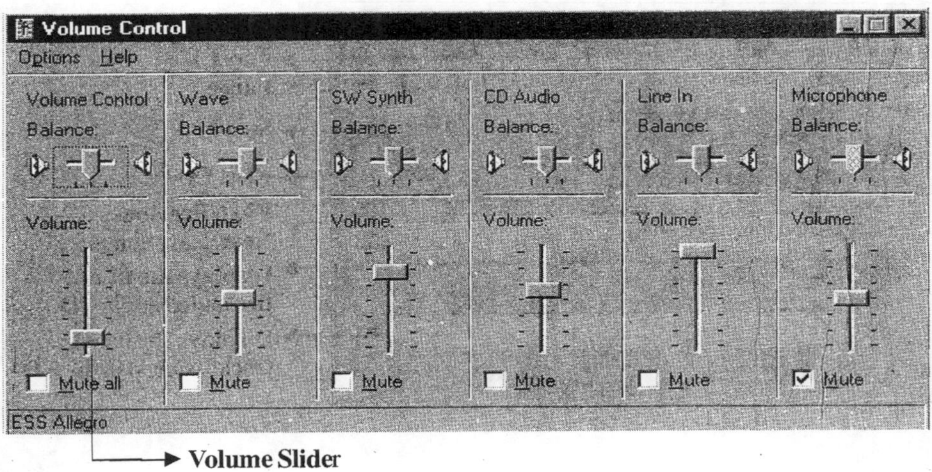

Windows media player It is an efficient and simple media player that can be used to play audio, video or animation files. It allows playing of streaming media files from the Internet in addition to the media files stored on your computer. It supports multiple media formats (.mp3, .mpeg, .wav, .avi etc.). It is flexible enough and can be customised according to your preferences. You can quickly change the size of the video window and even enlarge it to full-screen size. It provides continuous viewing even when playing a file that consists of multiple media types. In addition, it supports intelligent streaming, which monitors network conditions and automatically makes adjustments to ensure the best reception and playback. It can be accessed from:

Start ⟶ Programs ⟶ Accessories ⟶ Entertainment ⟶ Media Player

The following screen will be displayed:

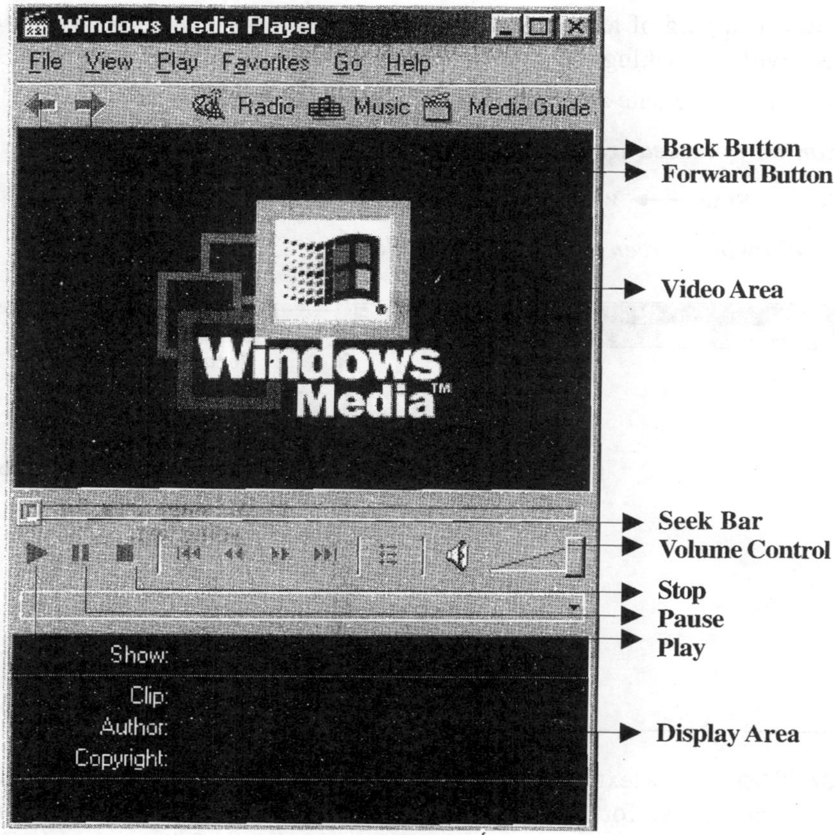

Miscellaneous Accessories

Some of the commonly used Windows accessories include Notepad, Wordpad, Calculator, Imaging, Paint and Games.

Notepad It is a simple text based editor that can be used for creating and editing text files that do not require any special formatting. Files larger than 64 KB cannot be created or edited in Notepad. Some of the features of Notepad are as follows:

- It opens and saves text in ASCII (text-only) format only.
- A simple search facility is built into the editor that allows searching for words in the current document.
- Supports cut, copy and paste operations. Text can be copied from one location and can be pasted to another location. This is accomplished with the help of Windows clipboard. (A clipboard is a temporary storage location for the information you cut or copy). It is always comes into play whenever you cut, copy or paste information. Information moved to the clipboard remains there until it is replaced with another piece of information, or the computer is switched off.
- Allows wrapping of text so that the complete text can be displayed on the screen without making use of horizontal scrollbars.
- Allows inserting date and time into the current document.

It can be accessed from:

Start → Programs → Accessories → Notepad

The following screen will be displayed:

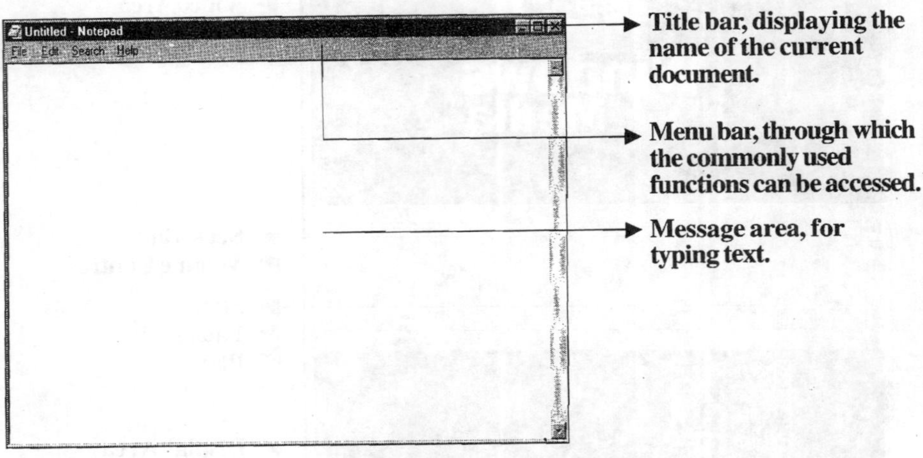

WordPad It is a text based editor that supports more features than Notepad. Wordpad can be used for files larger than 64 KB. It supports all the features of Notepad. Some of the features specific to Wordpad are as follows:

- Allows formatting of text using different font styles, colours and bullets.
- Different alignment options (Left, Right, Center) are provided for the paragraphs.

- Allows to set page margins and a preview of the page can be seen of how document would appear in print.
- Toolbars are provided that provide quick access to commonly used functions. User has the option to view/hide the toolbars.
- Allows to embed/link an object into a WordPad document from another file.

It can be accessed from:

Start ⟶ Programs ⟶ Accessories ⟶ Wordpad

The following screen will be displayed:

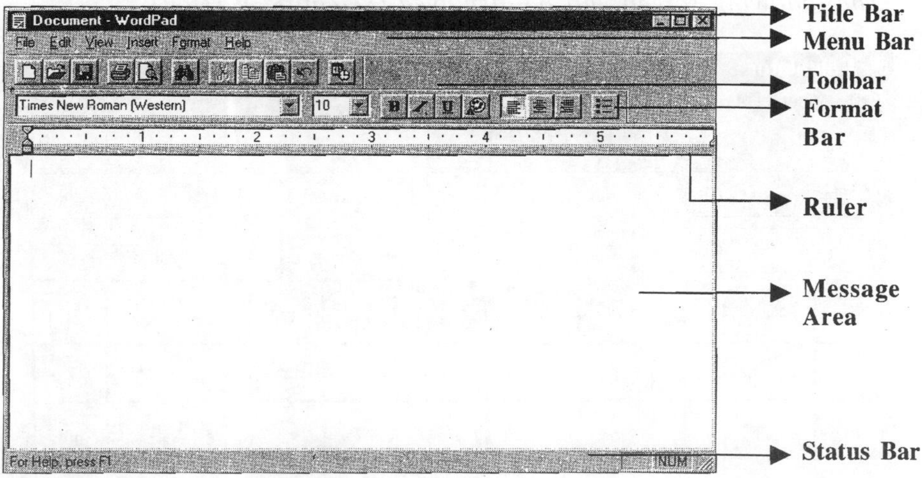

Imaging It allows you to view, annotate, and perform basic tasks with image documents, including fax documents and scanned images. It can be used for scanning documents, defining image resolution and supports image compression. It can be accessed from:

Start ⟶ Programs ⟶ Accessories ⟶ Imaging

The following screen will be displayed:

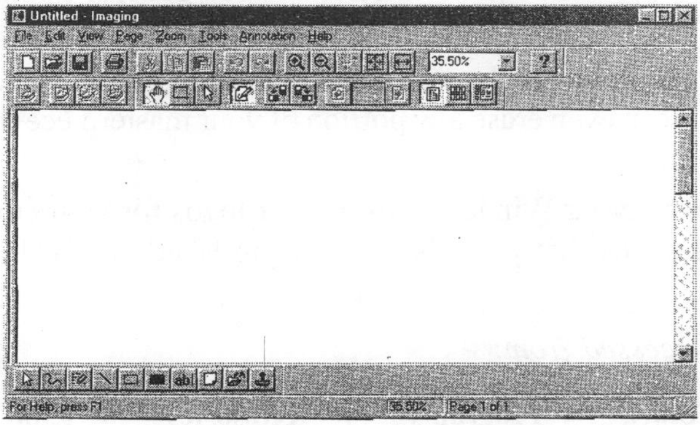

Calculator A full-fledged calculator is provided through which you can perform various calculations. You have the option of using the scientific (With Cos, Sin, Tan, log, Square-Root, Cube-Root functions etc.) or the standard calculator having basic mathematical functions. You can use either the keyboard or the mouse to enter numbers and operators into the calculator. In case you need the result of your calculations somewhere in your document, you can use the copy command provided along with the calculator to copy the result at the desired place. It can be accessed from:

Start ⟶ Programs ⟶ Accessories ⟶ Calculator

The following screen will be displayed (Scientific Version):

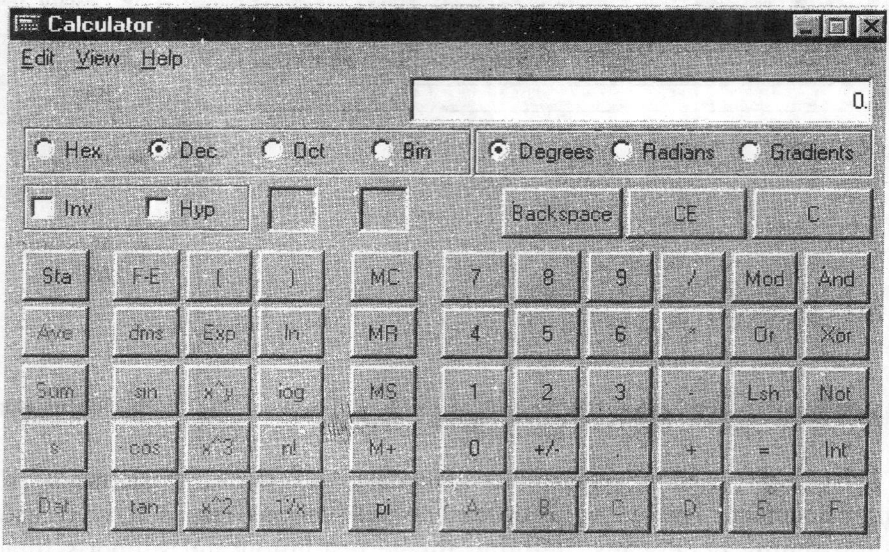

Paint Allows you to create, edit and view pictures. Some of the features of Paint are as follows:

- Allows to create or "assemble" pictures by drawing straight, wavy or curved lines, using shapes like squares, circles and polygons, or by simply free hand drawing.
- A colour box is provided that can be used for filling different colors into your document. It can even erase any portion of your masterpiece that you are not satisfied with.
- Wall papers for your Windows desktop, or logos for your company, or any free hand drawing that you wish to insert in Word or Excel can be created using paint.

It can be accessed from:

Start ⟶ Programs ⟶ Accessories ⟶ Paint

The following window will be displayed:

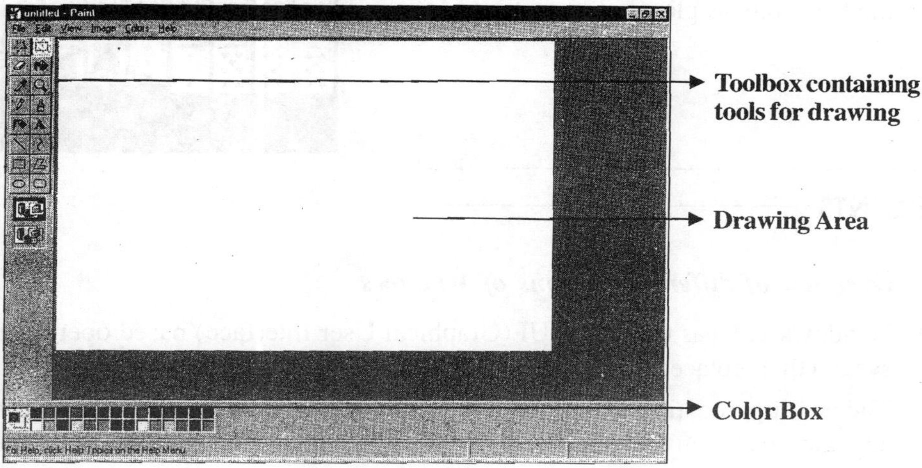

Games Windows contains some standard games – Solitaire, Minesweeper, Hearts and FreeCell. Games can be accessed from:

Start ⟶ Programs ⟶ Accessories ⟶ Games

i. **Solitaire** The object of this game is to use all the cards in the deck to build up the four suit stacks from ace to king.

ii. **Minesweeper** The object of this game is to find all the mines on the playing field as quickly as possible without uncovering any of them.

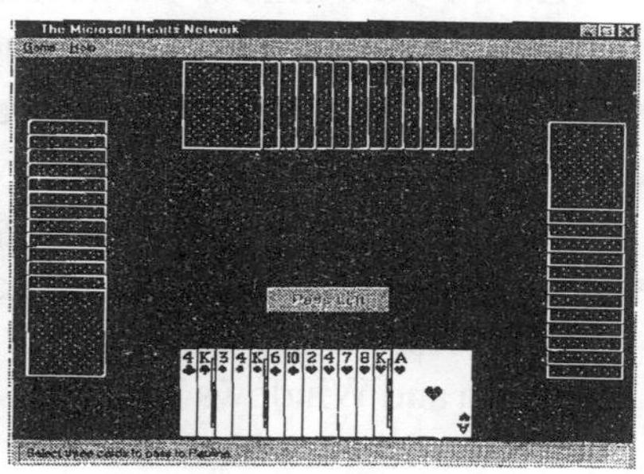

iii. **Hearts** The object of Hearts is to have the lowest score at the end of the game.

iv. **FreeCell** The object of FreeCell is to move all the cards to the home cells, using the free cells as placeholders.

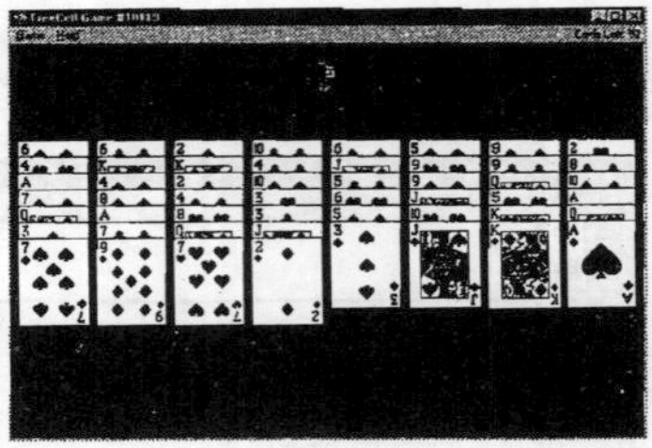

KEY POINTS

Overview of different versions of Windows

- Windows 1.0 was the first GUI (Graphical User Interface) based operating system that replaced the aging patriarch MS-DOS.
- The next upgradation was Windows 2.0 which included features like inter-application communication, use of keyboard shortcuts for switching between windows etc.
- Windows 3.0 was a 32 bit operating system that included Program Manager, File Manager, Printer Manager, improved set of icons and a powerful application development environment.
- Window 3.1/3.11 did many miscellaneous operations like sending a fax (Microsoft Fax, hooking up to a network (Network), linking up to an outside information service company (Terminal) etc.
- Windows NT 3.1 was geared towards business users and it included support for Client/Server applications and multi-processor architectures.
- Windows 95 was a truly 32 bit operating system with built in Internet-support and plug and play capabilities.
- Windows NT 4.0 was an upgrade to Microsoft's business desktop operating system with increased ease of use and simplified management.
- Windows 98 is often described as an operating system that "Works Better, Plays Better". Its main features were multiple display support, USB support, an Accessibility wizard and a comprehensive help system.
- Windows ME was the last OS to be based on Windows 95 technology. It offered consumers numerous music, video, and home networking enhancements and reliability improvements.
- Windows 2000 Professional was an upgrade to Windows NT 4.0. It added major improvements in reliability, plug and play hardware, ease of use, Internet compatibility, support for mobile computing.
- Windows XP was a major breakthrough for desktop operating systems. Two main versions of Windows XP were released namely Windows XP Home Edition and Windows XP Professional Edition.

Basic Window Elements

- Once Windows is loaded into the memory of the computer, the user works on the Windows Desktop. Desktop comprises of icons that represent various applications loaded onto your computer. Icons are further classified into five categories namely Folder Icons, Document Icons, Program Icons, Shortcut Icons and System Icons.
- System Icons are actual programs or files that are located on your desktop. Examples of System Icons – Recycle Bin, My Computer, Network Neighborhood etc.
- Other elements of Desktop are Start button and Taskbar. Standard items included in the Start menu are 'Programs', 'Favorites', 'Documents', 'Settings', 'Find', 'Help', 'Run' and 'Shut Down'. Start button is also an element of the Taskbar.
- The other elements of taskbar are Quick Launch Toolbar and System Tray. The Quick Launch allows for immediate access to a variety of elements through a mouse click. The System Tray contains icons for applications that are running in the background of the computer.
- A typical Application Window in Windows contains the following elements - Title Bar, Menu Bar, Control box (Minimize button, Maximize/Restore button and Close button), Scroll bars and a Status bar.
- Menus can be classified into Sub-Menus and Context Menus. Clicking on some menu items may lead to a Dialogue box. Dialog boxes are small Windows that appear when a program needs more information before it can complete an operation.
- Some frequently used controls in Windows are Textbox, Drop down box, Option button, Check box, Command button, Tab and Spinners.
- Windows can be customised according to user preferences. Shortcuts can be created/deleted, Background pictures and Screen Savers can be added.
- Control panel contains utilities for customising the Windows interface, adding/removing installed components, changing number, date, time and currency formats, changing desktop display, configuring modems, customising mouse, defining regional settings, assigning sounds to program events and many more.

File Management

- The contents of a hard disk can be organised in different folders. Each of the folders can contain any number of sub-folders or files. The number of files in a folder or sub folder is limited only by your hard disk capacity.
- Windows Explorer is a utility that represents the contents of your computer in a graphical form. It allows you to do various file and disk management tasks

like copy, rename, move and delete file(s) and create folder(s) and sub-folder(s), format floppies etc.

- Windows Explorer contains various functions that can be used to create, rename and delete files as well as folders in the hard disk.
- Multiple files from one folder can be copied to different locations at one go using 'Ctrl' and 'Shift' keys of the keyboard.
- Files/Folders once created can be renamed or deleted. Deleting a folder will automatically delete all its contents.
- Files/Folders can be displayed using different views in Windows Explorer – Small Icons View, Large Icons View, List View and Details View.

Windows Accessories

- Windows has many built in accessories. Some of the commonly used accessories can be classified into three categories, viz., System Tools, Entertainment and miscellaneous utilities.
- Some of the commonly used System Tools include Disk Cleanup, Disk Defragmenter and Scan Disk. Disk Cleanup frees up space on your hard disk by deleting all temporary cache files. Defragmenter rearranges files and unused hard disk space to enable programs run faster. Scan Disk checks the hard disk and removable disk for logical and physical errors.
- Entertainment Tools include CD Player, Sound Recorder, Volume Control and Windows Media Player. CD Player is used to play audio compact discs on a CD-ROM drive connected to your computer. Sound Recorder is used to record, edit and play sound files. Volume Control is used to adjust the volume when playing audio files. Media player can be used to play audio, video or animation files.
- Some of the commonly used Windows accessories include Notepad, Wordpad, Calculator, Imaging, Paint, and Games. Notepad is a simple text-based editor with limited features. Wordpad is a text-based editor that supports text formatting using different fonts and styles. Calculator can be used for performing mathematical as well as scientific calculations. Paint is used to create, edit and view pictures. Windows contains some standard games – Solitaire, Minesweeper, Hearts and FreeCell.

REVIEW QUESTIONS

1. Choose the appropriate answer:

i. Microsoft Windows 2000 is an up gradation of

(a) Windows 98 (b) Windows NT

(c) Windows ME (d) None of the above

ii. Which type of icons cannot be deleted from the desktop?

(a) Folder Icons (b) System Icons

(c) Program Icons (d) Document Icons

iii. Which of the following is a system icon?

(a) MS Word (b) Windows Explorer

(c) My Computer (d) None of the above

iv. Which control is used by Windows for viewing text beyond the screen?

(a) Status Bar (b) Task Bar

(c) Title Bar (d) Scroll Bar

v. The menu that displays a list of options when a particular item is right clicked is referred to as:

(a) Main Menu (b) Sub Menu

(c) Context Menu (d) None of the above

vi. Which of the following utilities displays the contents of your computer in graphical form?

(a) Start Menu (b) Desktop

(c) Internet Explorer (d) Windows Explorer

vii. Which of the following combination of keys can be used to delete a continuous range of files that are stored in the same folder?

(a) 'Alt+Del' (b) 'Shift+Del'

(c) 'Ctrl+Del' (d) None of the above

viii. Which type of folder view displays complete information about a folder?

(a) List View (b) Large Icons View

(c) Details View (d) None of the above

ix. This utility rearranges discontiguous files and free space on your computer so that your files are stored in contiguous units and free space is consolidated in one contiguous block.

(a) Disk Cleanup (b) Patch

(c) Logical addressing (d) Defragmenter

x. Find the odd one out:

(a) Scan Disk (b) CD Player

(c) Volume Control (d) Media Player

2. Enter True or False:

i. Windows is a single task operating system.

ii. Desktop consists of a series of icons and a taskbar placed at the bottom of the screen.

iii. All files that are deleted from the computer are stored in Recycle Bin.

iv. Windows Explorer contains utilities for customising the Windows interface, adding/removing installed components, changing number, date, time and currency formats, assigning sounds to program events and many more.

v. Dialog boxes are small windows that appear when a program needs more information before it can complete an operation.

vi. In a GUI a list box can be used for displaying a list of values.

vii. Deleting a shortcut for a folder would actually delete the folder itself.

viii. A folder can consist of any number of sub-folders.

ix. Address bar of the Windows explorer is used to display the path of the selected document.

x. Scan disk is used to delete temporary cache files from your computer.

3. Match the following:

	X	Y
1.	For application programs name of the document along with the program name is displayed here.	(a) Start Button
2.	Quick Launch Toolbar and System Tray	(b) Folder
3.	Provides a quick way to start a program or open a file or folder without having to go to its permanent location in Windows Explorer.	(c) Windows 98
4.	Switching between multiple Windows Saver.	(d) Screen
5.	Gives access to a series of menus like 'Programs', 'Documents', 'Settings', 'Shut Down' etc.	(e) Elements of Task Bar..
6.	A collection of files.	(f) Title Bar
7.	A text based editor.	(g) Wordpad
8.	A moving page or a pattern that appears on your monitor when you have left your computer idle for a specified limit.	(h) 'Alt + Tab'
9.	A GUI based multitasking operating system.	(i) Scan Disk
10.	Checks hard disk for logical and physical errors and then repairs the damaged areas.	(j) Shortcuts

4. Fill in the blanks with the appropriate choices listed below

(i) Start Button (ii) Search (iii) Shift +Del (iv) Shortcut (v) Icons (vi) Windows Explorer (vii) Taskbar (viii) Calculator (xi) Alt + Del (x) CD Player (xi) Pictures (xii) Find (xiii) Media Player (xiv) Details View (xv) Scan Disk

1. Desktop contains a series of labeled pictures referred to as ____________.
2. To permanently delete files from the hard disk without moving them to the bin use ____________ while deleting the files.
3. All the applications and tools available in the computer can be accessed from ____________.
4. ____________ allows searching for files, folders located anywhere within the computer or within the network.
5. Buttons are placed on the ____________ for each application that is actively running on the computer.
6. If a menu item has a letter in it that is underlined, the item may be selected by holding down the Alt key on the computer and pressing the underlined key whenever the menu is visible. This type of keys are referred to as ____________ keys.
7. ____________ allows you to do various file and disk management tasks like copy, rename, move and delete file(s) and create folder(s) and sub-folder(s), format floppies etc.
8. ____________ for folders displays information like item name, size, type (folder or file type), and the date the item was last modified.
9. ____________ can be used for performing mathematical calculations.
10. ____________ can be used to play audio and video files of multiple formats.

5. Give a brief overview of different versions of Windows.

6. Write short notes on Windows Explorer.

7. Explain briefly the basic elements of Windows Desktop.

8. Write short notes on

(a) Disk Defragmenter (b) Scan Disk

9. Write short notes on

(a) CD Player (b) Windows Media Player

10. Discuss in brief the main features of Word Pad.

CHAPTER 11

Linux

OVERVIEW OF LINUX

Linux is a UNIX like operating system originally developed by Linus Torvalds, a student of University of Helsinki. It has its roots in Minix, an educational version of UNIX developed by Andrew Tannenbaum. Few people today have heard of Minix today, far less than have heard about Linux. It was Torvalds and a group of programmers who combined their talents and created an operating system called Linux.

Linux was developed by thousands of developers and is available for free on the Internet. In fact, one can download the complete source code for Linux from the Internet. Since the complete source code for Linux is open and available to everyone, it is referred to as **Open Source** or **Free Software**. The user has the freedom to copy the program, change the program or give it away to friends and co-workers. Linux is written and distributed under the GNU General Public License, which means that its source code is freely distributed and available to the general public.

Technically Linux is strictly an OS kernel (Kernel is the core of an Operating System.) The first Linux kernel was released to the public in the year 1991. It had no networking, ran only on 80386-compatible Intel processors and PC hardware, and had very limited device-driver support. But later versions of Linux come with a collection of software including desktop, server programs, networking suites, compilers, and many more utilities making it a complete operating system. For example, the recent version of Linux includes the XFree86 version of the X Window System, the GNU C compiler GCC, and code from quite a lot of other sources. Typically organisations integrate the versions of all these programs with the Linux kernel, test that everything works together, and then release what is called a **Distribution** of Linux. The Red Hat distribution is the most popular commercial distribution for Linux. Linux Mandrake, SuSE,

Connectiva, Caldera and Red Flag are other main distributions of Linux. These commercial versions make money by selling their implementation, installation, maintenance and other services. Linux is also distributed by Debian, a non-profit organisation.

Linux is the number one growing version of UNIX, and an ever-growing competitor for Windows. It is being used by a number of companies, primarily as a server, and by countless individuals, often as a home UNIX system. It owes its empowering popularity to features like stability and reliability (as tested by major corporations like IBM).

FEATURES OF LINUX

Multi-tasking Linux is a multi-tasking system, allowing multiple users to run multiple programs on the same system at the same time.

Multi-user It is multi-user operating system, allowing multiple users to use the computer and run programs at the same time.

Hardware support Runs on a variety of computer architectures, including ARM, SPARC, Alpha, PowerPC, M68k, MIPS and Intel.

Reliable Highly reliable and stable operating system, it can run for months, even years, without having to be rebooted.

Multiple processor support Supports the use of multiple processors. More processors can be added without disturbing the existing hardware set up.

Software dependencies Implements shared libraries. For example, if Program A and Program B share a common piece of code then the common code is placed in a separate file so that any program requiring this common routine can refer to this file rather than including the code in each program. This saves a large amount of space on your system.

GUI Linux provides the freedom to use any user interface programming library you choose. KDE (K Desktop Environment, K does not have an expansion) and GNOME are the two main graphical user interfaces aiming to make Linux easy for computer users to operate. They are free softwares coming under the GNU General Public License.

KDE is a powerful Open Source graphical desktop environment that combines ease of use, contemporary functionality and outstanding graphical design. KDE desktop is very similar to the Windows 98/NT environment. It provides a complete desktop environment by including:

- Standardised menus and toolbars, key bindings, colour-schemes and many more.
- Dialog driven desktop configuration.

- File Manager for easy management of files and directories.
- KDEPrint for administration of various printing engines and management of enterprise networked printing systems.
- An integrated help system allowing for convenient, consistent access to help on the use of the KDE desktop and its applications.
- Browser Support including support for Java Script and DHTML.
- Innumerable utilities and applications like:
  - KDE-Network: KMail, KNode, Knewsticker etc.
  - KDE-Graphics: Graphics applications such as KDVI, KGhostview, KPaint, Kfax
  - KDE-Utilities: KEdit, KCalc, KHexEdit, KNotes
  - KDE-Edu: Edutainment related programs
  - KDE-Games: KAsteroids, KPat, KTetris
  - KDE-Admin: Various tools to aid system administration
  - KOffice: Integrated office suite

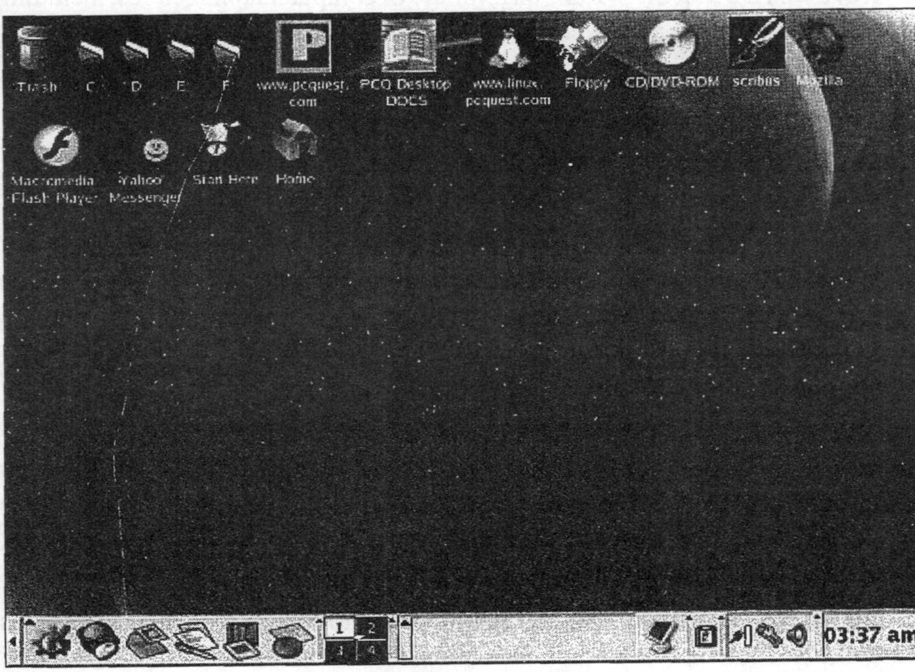

Figure 11.1 KDE Desktop of Red Hat Linux 8.0

TCP/IP networking support Linux supports most Internet protocols. TCP/IP (Transmission Control Protocol/Internet Protocol) is built into the kernel itself. TCP/IP is the communication protocol that binds the Internet.

High level security It has many built in security features to protect your system from unauthorised users. It stores the passwords in encrypted form which cannot be decrypted.

Web server It can be used to run web servers like Apache, serving various application protocols such as HTTP, FTP, SMTP and many more. It can also be used as an email server or a file server.

Database support All major brands like Sybase, Informix and Oracle run well on Linux.

Programming support It provides programming support for various languages like Fortan, Pascal, C, C++ and many web technologies.

Free It can be downloaded for free from the Internet and its source code is freely available to everyone. Since the source code is open, bugs can be fixed easily without having to wait for proprietary vendors to fix the encountered problems.

GNU software support Linux supports a wide range of free software written by the GNU Project, including utilities such as the GNU C and C++ compiler, and so on. Many of the essential system utilities used by Linux are GNU software.

The X Window system X Windows is the *de facto* industry standard graphics system for UNIX machines. A free version of The X Window System, known as 'Xfree86' is available for Linux. The X Window System is a very powerful graphics interface that allows multiple login sessions in different windows on the screen at the same time.

STRUCTURE OF LINUX

The Linux operating system is categorised into three major components namely **Kernel**, **Shell** and **Utilities & Application Programs** (Figure 11.2).

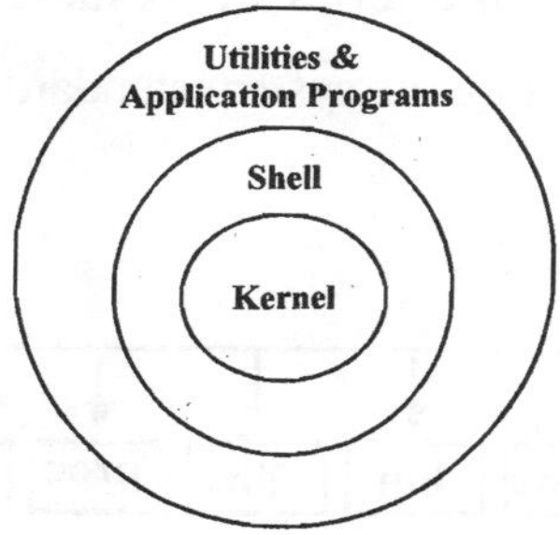

Figure 11.2

Kernel

- Core of an operating system.
- Performs the critical tasks that are required to maintain the Linux environment.
- Runs all the programs.
- Master program that controls all the resources of the computer.
- Keeps track of the peripheral devices attached to the computer.
- Automatically starts an interactive program called **'Shell'** for each user whenever they log into the system.

Shell

- Acts as an interface between the user and the kernel, accepts requests from the user, passes them to kernel, which then processes them and submits requests to the hardware. Shell is often referred to as the **Command Interpreter** as it interprets the commands given by the user. In Linux, the commands can be either typed in through the command line or contained in a file called **Shell Script**.
- There are a number of different types of shells. Bourne shell, C shell and Korn shell were the most important ones that originated from UNIX. These Unix shell interfaces are available to Linux as well. Originally Linux-based and most widely used shell, is the Bourne-Again shell (bash). It is based on the original Bourne shell and has extensions similar to the Korn shell, coupled with its own further extensions. Linux also offers a Windows-based shell interface, commonly known as X-Windows or simply X.

Utilities and Application Programs

- Utilities are the software tools included with the Linux operating system.
- Application Programs include Word Processors, Spreadsheets, Presentation Packages and many more.

FILE SYSTEM IN LINUX

Linux uses a hierarchical file structure, i.e., directories are linked in the form of a family tree. All the hardware devices (I/O devices, storage devices) are also treated as files. In Linux, the root directory ('/') is the main directory and all other directories are its sub-directories.

Linux file system standard is represented below:

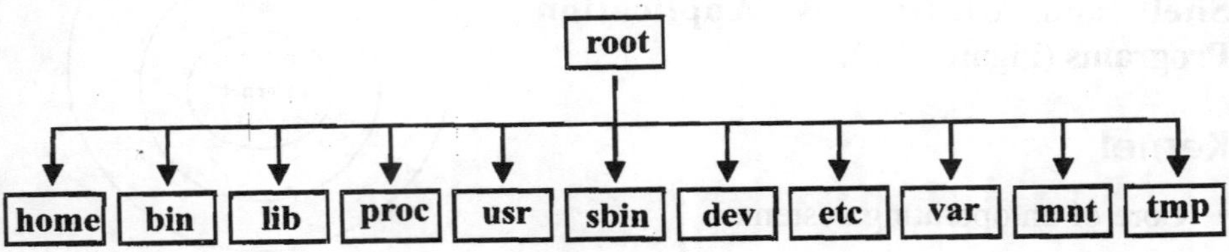

Directory Description

home Is the user area for maintaining all user related files.

bin Contains all the executable files. It essentially contains commands needed during booting. Other commands required by the regular user are also maintained in this directory.

lib Contains shared libraries and routines needed by different programs. These shared libraries are particularly important for booting the system and executing commands within the root file system.

proc Contains special files that either extract information from or send information to the kernel.

usr Contains Linux utilities and libraries. In earlier versions of Linux, it was used to store user's home directories.

sbin Contains system admin commands intended for the root user of a system.

dev Contains special device files pertaining to the peripheral devices attached to the system.

etc Contains all the configuration files that are local to the machine.

var Contains variable data files including printers log files, transient and temporary files.

mnt Reserved for temporarily mounted file systems, such as CD-ROMs and floppy disks. Contains the sub-directories named 'floppy' and 'cdrom', which displays the contents of CD or floppy when mounted.

tmp Contains temporary files; files that are not required after a program has been completed.

File Types in Linux

Normal files Used for storing data, such as text information and programs.

Directory files Stores information about a directory, its relationship with other directories, files and sub-directories under it and related access permissions. This type of file is updated every time any alteration is made to the directory, its related directories or files and sub-directories that reside under it.

Special files Represents various routines in the kernel. For example: Block and character special files represent device drivers by which terminals, printers, disk drives and other peripherals are controlled.

Symbolic link files Contains the location/full pathname of actual files to which they point.

Pipe files Used as pipeline channels of information to be passed from one process to another. They hold their contents only till the receiving file has not read that information.

FILE HANDLING IN LINUX

Naming Conventions for Files

It is usually a good practice to give descriptive file names, so that by looking at the name itself, it is possible to identify the contents of a file. File naming in Linux follows the convention below:

1. A name can be up to 256 characters.
2. A name cannot contain spaces.
3. Although special characters are allowed, it is suggested that only the following are used:
   - Lowercase letters (a-z)
   - Uppercase letters (A-Z)
   - Numbers (0-9)
   - Underscore (_), period (.) and comma (,)

Note: Linux is highly case sensitive, i.e. lowercase and uppercase letters are **not** treated alike. This holds good for the Linux commands as well.

Pathname

A file or directory in Linux may be referred to as follows:

Full Pathname Lists each directory, starting from '/' (root), down to the file itself. Each directory and the filename must be separated by a '/'.

Example: Suppose you are working in a directory named 'MyDir' stored under the 'home' directory then you can refer to a file named 'first.c' (An extension or the suffix '.c' indicates that it is a 'C' language source file) contained in 'MyDir' using: **/home/MyDir/first.c** (This suggests that 'home' is the parent directory for 'MyDir' and 'root' is the parent directory for 'home').

Partial pathname If the file is in the working directory or in a sub-directory below the working directory, the names of higher directories may be omitted.

Example: If your working directory is /home/MyDir, then file 'first.c' in that directory may be referred simply by: first.c.

Relative pathname If the file is in a directory near the working directory, a relative path may be used. It gives the location of a directory/file, relative to the current working directory. To do this, the following conventions are used:

1. . (Single dot) Current Working Directory
2. .. (Double dots) Parent Directory

Example: If your working directory is /home/MyDir, the file second.c under the directory/home/Demo may be referred to by: ../Demo/second.c.

Simple File and Directory Handling Commands

The commands are typed at the shell prompt ($ or #) and the **Enter** key is pressed to view the output of the typed command. Prompt is a symbol that appears at the start of a command line. The first word following the prompt is the command and the characters following the hypen ('-') represent the arguments of the command. These arguments are however optional. In a GUI based Linux (Linux 8.0), this prompt can be got by choosing **Terminal** from the **Start** menu.

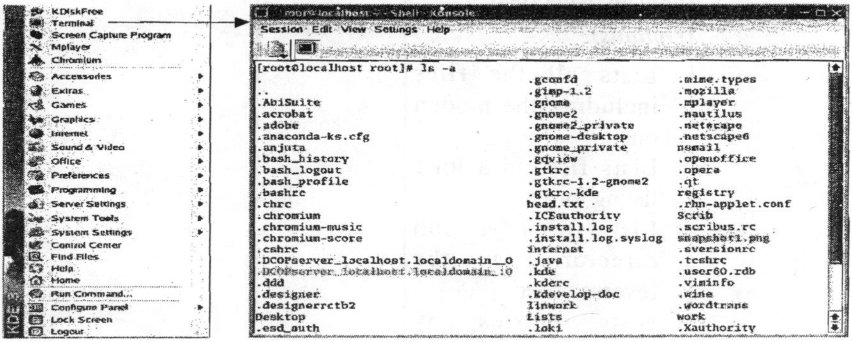

Command	*Function*	*Example*	*Effect*
1. cat	Displays the contents of a file	cat File.txt	Displays the contents of File.txt.
		cat > Test	'>' symbol can be used to create a file named Test. You would be prompted to enter the contents for the file after you press the **Enter** key. Type the desired data and press 'Ctrl+D' to terminate the command line.
2. cd	Changes the current working directory to another directory. You can always navigate to directories hierarchi cally above or below (Similar to CD command of MS-DOS).	cd ..	Changes the directory to the parent of the current directory. For example: if you are initially working in /usr/mydir then you would be moved to /usr.
		cd usr/games	Changes the current working directory to /usr/games.

Command	Function	Example	Effect
3. pwd	Prints the full path of the current directory on the command line.	pwd	Prints the full path of the current working directory.
4. ls	Lists the files in the current directory. The names are sorted in alphabetical order. ***Options:*** a Lists all the files including the hidden ones. l Lists files in a long listing format. r Lists files & sub directories in the reverse order. C Lists entries by columns t Lists all the files according to order of time.	ls - a	Lists all the files (including hidden files) in the directory.
5. mkdir	Creates a directory.	mkdir mydir	Creates a directory 'mydir' in the current working directory.
		mkdir mydir/sub1	Creates a sub-directory 'sub1' under the directory mydir.
6. mv	Moves or renames a given file or directory. ***Options:*** f Moves or Renames without prompting the uer. i Prompts the user before overwriting. u Moves only when the source file is newer than the destination file or when the destination file is missing.	mv myfile ourfile mv test./	Renames 'myfile' to 'ourfile'. Moves the file named 'test' to an existing directory named 'newdir' (Existing under the current directory).

Command	Function	Example	Effect
7. rmdir	Deletes the directory provided it is empty. An error message is displayed, if the specified directory contains files or sub-directories. *Options:* p Removes the parent along with all its sub directories. v Outputs a diagnostic for every directory that is processed.	newdir rmdir mydir rmdir/ mydir/sub1/ sub2 -p	Removes the directory 'mydir'. Removes sub2, sub1, mydir i.e. all the sub-directories are deleted along with the parent directory.
8. rm	Deletes the specified file(s). *Options:* f Ignores nonexistent files and does not prompt the user before deletion. i Prompts the user before actually deleting the file. r or – R Removes the contents of directories recursively. v Explains what is being done.	rm File.txt rm file1.txt file2.txt	Removes the file named 'File.txt'. Removes 'file1.txt' and 'file2.txt'. You can delete multiple files by separating the file names using the Space character.
9. grep	Searches for the specified pattern in each file or standard input. *Options:* f Obtains pattern from the specified file. i Ignores case distinctions. w Forces the pattern to match only the pattern to match only whole words. x Forces whole lines.	grep-i 'hello world' menu.h main.c grep-f * newfile	Searches the string 'hello world' in the files 'menu.h' and 'main.c'. Searches the string contained in 'myfile' in

Command	Function	Example	Effect
10. head	Prints the first 10 lines of each FILE to standard output.	head myfile.txt	'newfile'. Shows the first 10 lines of 'myfile.txt'.
11. tail	Prints the last 10 lines of each FILE to standard output.	tail myfile.txt	Shows the last 10 lines of 'myfile.txt'.
12. cp	Creates a copy of the file supplied to it.	cp my file.txt ../	Copies the file myfile.txt from the current directory to the parent directory.

Notes:

1. All the Linux commands must be typed in lowercase letters.
2. For most commands you can obtain the help and version information using the following options: —help and —version.

   For example, to access the available options for 'cp' command, you can type cp —help at the command prompt.

KDE FILE MANAGER

KDE File Manager (KFM) is quite similar to Windows Explorer. (For details on working with Windows Explorer, refer to the chapter on Windows.) The KDE File manager (also called as Konqueror) of the KDE desktop environment helps in the management of files and directories by providing an easy to use graphical interface. KFM can be accessed by choosing **Home** from the **Start** menu.

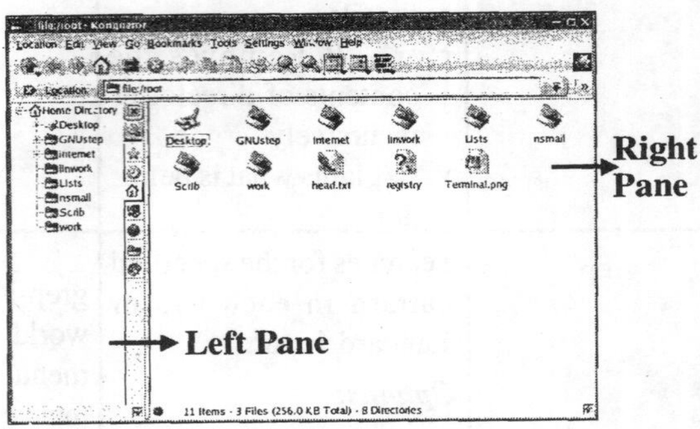

Figure 11.3 KDE file manager

Creating a Directory

1. Select the parent directory under which you wish to create your directory by clicking once on the icon of the directory in the left pane.

2. Right click in the right pane and choose **Directory** under the Create New option from the pop up menu.

3. Type a desired name for your directory in the dialogue box and click the **Ok** button to conclude.

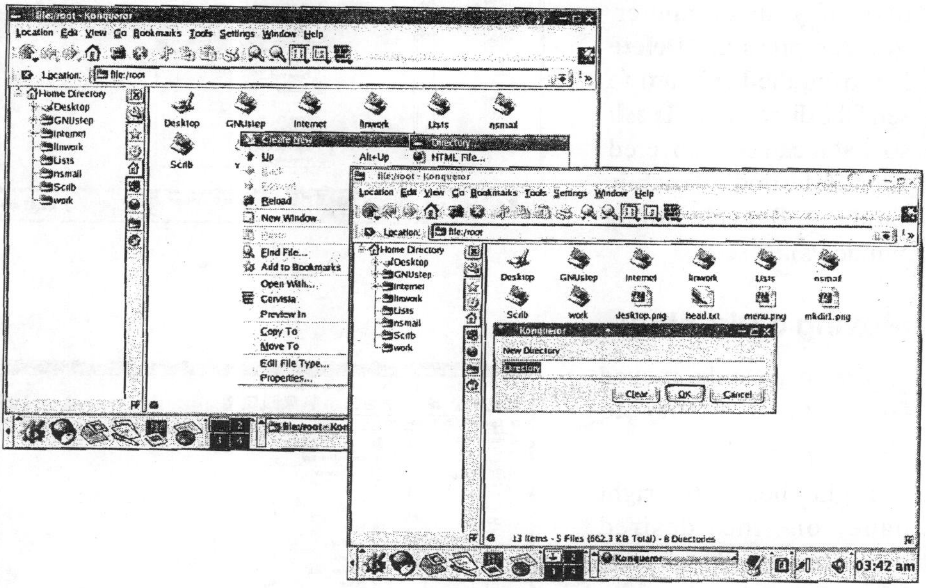

Renaming a Directory

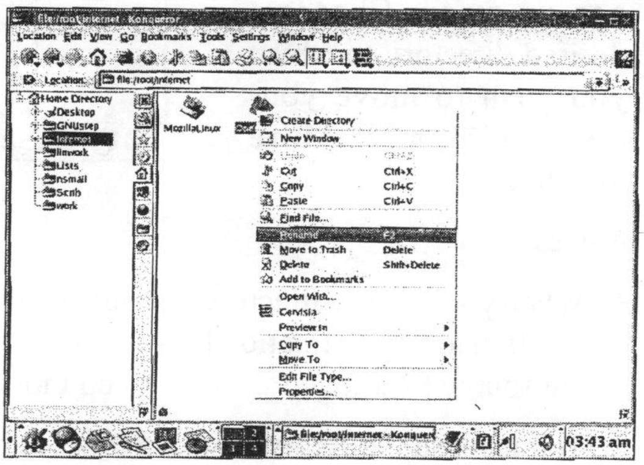

1. Right click in the right pane on the desired directory and choose **Rename** option from the pop up menu.

2. Type the desired name and press the **Enter** key to conclude.

Deleting a Directory

1. Right click in the right pane on the desired directory and choose **Delete** option from the pop up menu.

2. A dialogue box is displayed to the user for confirming the deletion of the directory. Click **Yes** to delete the directory.

Note: When you delete a directory using the steps mentioned above, the directory would be deleted permanently from the hard disk of your computer. You can press the **Delete** key from the keyboard to send the directory to **Trash** so that it can be recovered later, if desired. (**Trash** is similar to **Recycle Bin** of Windows).

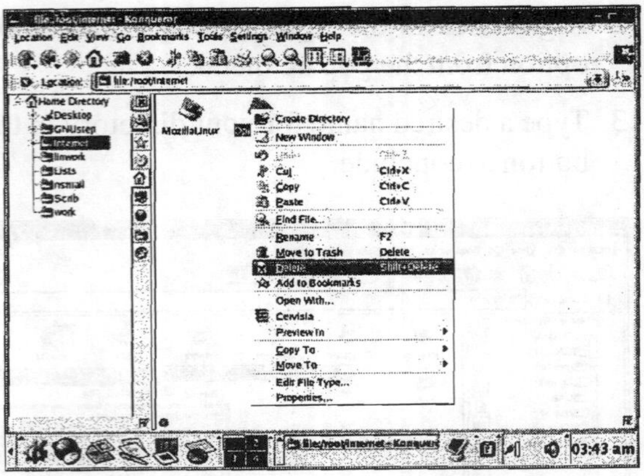

Moving a Directory

A directory can be moved from one directory to another directory.

Right click in the right pane on the desired directory and choose **Move To** option from the pop up menu. Choose a desired directory to which you wish to move your directory from the **Move To** option.

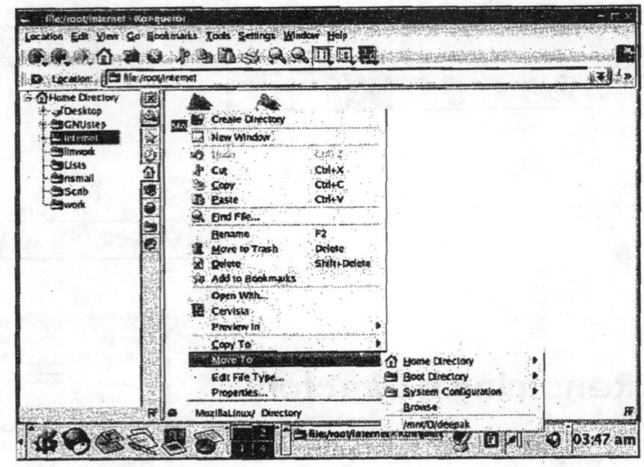

Notes:

1. When you move a directory, the directory is moved from the source (original) location to the destination location, i.e., no copy of the directory will exist in the source location after it has been moved to the new location.
2. You can use the **Browse** option to select your destination directory.

Copying a Directory

1. Right click in the right pane on the desired source directory that you wish to copy to another location and choose **Copy** from the pop up menu.
2. Select the destination directory where you wish to create a copy of the selected directory.
3. Right click in the right pane on the destination directory and choose **Paste** from the pop up menu.

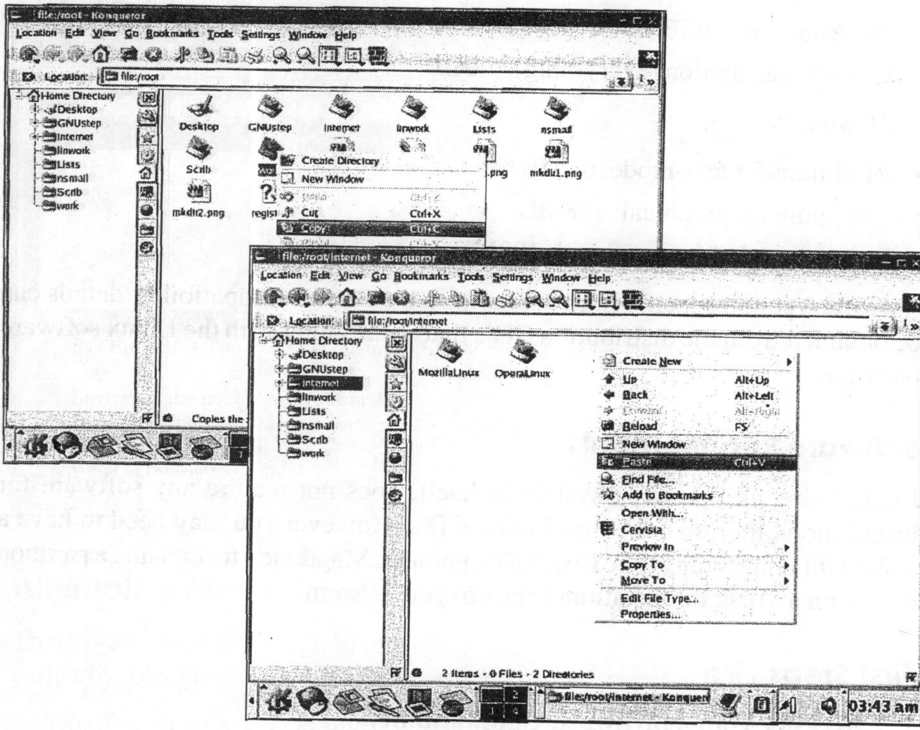

Note: When a file is copied from one location to another, the file is available in the original location and a copy of it is saved at the destination.

INSTALLATION OF LINUX

Detailed below are the hardware and software requirements for a typical Linux installation. These are followed by the installation steps required for installing Linux. To explain the above **RED HAT LINUX 8.0** has been chosen.

Minimum Hardware Requirements

CPU

- Minimum: Pentium-class
- Recommended for text-mode: 200 MHz Pentium-class or better
- Recommended for graphical: 400 MHz Pentium II or better

Hard Disk Space (**Note**: Additional space will be required for user data):

- Custom Installation (minimum): 475MB
- Server (minimum): 850MB
- Personal Desktop: 1.7GB

- Workstation: 2.1GB
- Custom Installation (everything): 5.0GB

Memory

- Minimum for text-mode: 64MB
- Minimum for graphical: 128MB
- Recommended for graphical: 192MB

Note: Version specific hardware requirements and compatibility details can be obtained from the distribution CD's that come along with the Linux software package.

Software Requirements

Linux being an operating system in itself, does not require any software for installation other than the installation CD's. However you may need to have a disk-partitioning utility (like BootIt NG, Partition Magic etc.) for creating a partition on your hard disk for installing Linux in your system.

First Steps First

1. Checking your Hardware Compatibility

All Linux Distributions are compatible with most computer systems that were factory built within the last two years. However, with hardware specifications changing and improving almost daily, it would be difficult to guarantee complete hardware compatibility. The hardware compatibility details can be obtained from the Linux software package CD's.

2. Checking your Disk Space

Installing Linux may require disk (hard disk) partitions (Details about disk partitions have been explained in the next section).

Case 1 If Linux is the only operating system on your system, you would need to ensure that you have enough available disk space on your hard drive(s) for this installation.

Case 2 If Linux has to be installed on a system that already has an operating system like Windows or OS2 then you must separate your hard disk space for individual operating systems. This is accomplished by dedicating one or more partitions to your new Linux installation.

Before you begin with the installation process, one of the following conditions must be met:

- Your computer must have enough **unpartitioned** disk space available to install Red Hat Linux.

- Your computer must have one or more partitions that may be cleaned or cleared, thereby freeing up enough disk space to install Linux.

3. Choosing an Installation Option

You must decide which type of installation best fits your needs. Possible options include:

CD-ROM: If you have purchased a Linux boxed set (or have a Linux CD-ROM), you would require a boot disk or a bootable CD-ROM.

Hard drive: If you have copied the Linux files to a local hard drive, you would require a boot disk.

HTTP: If you plan to install directly from an HTTP Web server, you would require a network boot disk.

4. Choosing a Boot Media

Depending on the installation method you chose in Step 3, you would need to decide as to how you would start the installation process, i.e., which boot media you would use.

Bootable CD-ROM: If your system will allow you to boot from your CD-ROM drive, you can use the Bootable Linux CD-ROM to perform a local CD-ROM installation.

Local Media Boot Disk: If you had purchased an Official Linux boxed set, i.e., a licensed copy, you may find a local boot disk in the box. This diskette can be used for CD-ROM installations for which your CD-ROM drive is not bootable, or for a hard drive installation.

Network Boot Disk: If you are performing an installation via HTTP then you must create your own network boot disk. (The network boot disk image file is bootnet.img, and is located in the images directory on your Red Hat Linux/ Intel CD in the case of Red Hat Linux).

Making Installation Diskettes

It is sometimes necessary to create a diskette from an image file; an image file contains an exact copy (or image) of a diskette's contents. Since a diskette contains file system information in addition to the data contained in files, the image file would not be usable until it has been written to a diskette.

To start with, you will need a blank, formatted, high-density (1.44MB), 3.5-inch diskette. You will also need access to a computer with a 3.5-inch diskette drive, and capable of running an MS-DOS program, or the **dd** utility found on most Linux-like operating systems.

Making a Diskette under MS-DOS

We can use the **rawrite** utility included on the Red Hat Linux CD in the 'dosutils' directory to create a diskette. Firstly, label a blank, formatted 3.5-inch diskette appropriately (such as 'Boot Disk'). Then, insert it into the diskette drive. Now, use the following commands (assuming your CD drive is drive D:):

C:\> d:
D:\> cd \dosutils
D:\dosutils> rawrite
Enter disk image source file name as: ..\images\boot.img
Enter target diskette drive as: a:
The following message would be displayed on the screen:

Please insert a formatted diskette into drive A:

Insert a floppy in the floppy drive to create your bootable installation disk. This disk can then be used to install your Linux operating system.

First, rawrite prompts you for the filename of a diskette image; enter the directory and name of the image you wish to write (for example,..\images\boot.img). Then rawrite asks for a diskette drive to write the image to; enter a:. Finally, rawrite asks for a confirmation that a formatted diskette is in the drive you've selected. After pressing Enter to confirm, rawrite copies the image file onto the diskette.

Making a Diskette under a Linux-like OS

To make a diskette under Linux (or any other Linux-like operating system), you must have permission to write to the device representing a 3.5-inch diskette drive (known as /dev/fd0 under Linux).

First, label a blank, formatted diskette appropriately (such as 'Boot Disk'). Insert it into the diskette drive. After mounting the Red Hat Linux CD, change directory to the directory containing the desired image file, and use the following command

 # dd if=boot.img of=/dev/fd0 bs=1440k, this would copy the input file('if') 'boot.img' onto the output file('of') '/dev/fdo', i.e., the floppy disk.

5. Choosing an Installation Type

Linux vendors offer several customised installation options. Options available with Red Hat Linux include:

Workstation: A workstation-class installation is most appropriate if you are new to the world of Linux and would like to give it a try.

Server: A server-class installation is most appropriate for you if you'd like your system to function as a Linux-based server, and you do not wish to substantially customise your system configuration.

Custom: A custom-class installation provides the greatest flexibility during your installation. It allows to choose your partitioning scheme, packages you wish to install etc. Custom-class installations are most appropriate for users who are already familiar with Red Hat Linux installations.

Upgrade: If you already have an existing version of Red Hat Linux running on your system and wish to update it to the latest version, the upgrade installation option can be used.

SPECIFICS ON HARD DRIVE REPARTITIONING

Partitions

Partitions can be defined as 'parts' of your hard drive. They are logical divisions of a hard disk, which can be treated as physically distinct drives by the operating system.

Advantages

- Allows you to organise your data and applications in more efficient ways and make better use of. space. For example, you can create a separate 'data' partition to maintain your personal documents. It becomes a lot easier to take a backup of just that partition than an entire drive.
- The need for partitions arises because of the computer's dependence on 'clusters' or blocks of information. A disk of huge capacity implies a huge cluster. The file occupies a whole number of clusters when it is stored on the disk. Partitioning reduces disk size, thereby reducing fixed cluster size, thereby saving space.
- You can partition the hard disk of your computer to contain multiple operating systems so that their files are separate and will not conflict with each other.

Drive Names

Windows uses the notation A:, B:, C: to represent the drives of a computer. Linux adopts a different methodology; a drive in Linux is called a device and is treated like a file. Therefore reading data from a drive or writing onto it is similar to reading from or writing to a file. Hard drive partitions in Linux are referred in the form:

/dev/<IDE-device-name><partition number>

Disk Deice	Linux Name
Primary Master	hda
Primary Slave	hdb
Secondary Master	hdc
Secondary Slave	hdd

Linux differentiates between physical hard drives and logical partitions within physical drives. The <IDE-device-name> is as follows:

In Windows	In Linux
C:	/dev/hda1
D:	/dev/hda5
E:	/dev/hda6
F:	/dev/hda7

The following table shows how **Windows** partitions are referred to in **Linux**.

Linux can support up to four Primary partitions and thus the Secondary partitions in Linux start from '/dev/hda5'. Floppy drives, A: and B: in Windows are referred to as /dev/fd0 and /dev/fd1 respectively in Linux.

Partition Scheme

Partitioning scheme typically includes decisions on whether or not more than one operating systems should co-exist on the system, and if so, what should be the space allocation for each, also which should be the default operating system at the boot time. If the choice is to have more than one operating system co-existing, you would need to set up separate partitions for each operating system. Linux includes a boot loader (called LILO on Intel-based systems) which allows you to specify which operating system you want to boot at power on, with a time-out default boot of your favourite operating system.

For partition space requirements, the following approximation of space works pretty effectively. However, these are guidelines which can be manipulated according to your need.

Given:

A given disk of X MB/GB (e.g. 2 GB)

Calculate:

(swap) about double main RAM (e.g. 64 MB system gets 128 MB swap)

/(root) about 10% of available (e.g. 200 MB)

/home about 20% of available (e.g. 400 MB)

/usr any remaining space (e.g. 1272 MB)

Note: (swap) - Linux works on the concept of "virtual memory" by which it makes available larger amount of memory to users than the actual physical RAM installed on your system. The swap partition along with the main RAM is used by Linux to accomplish this. As a thumb rule, your swap partition should be at least double the size of physical RAM installed on your system.

Mount Points

Before you use a partition, a directory must be assigned to it. This process is referred to as **Mounting** (Similar to assigning drive letters to partitions in Windows). Once mounted, the corresponding directory called the **Mount Point** will contain all the directory and files on that partition. When you create a Linux partition, you specify a mount point for it like '/'.

'I/mnt/floppy' and '/mnt/cdrom' represent mount points for Floppy and CDROM respectively.

Unmounting (the opposite of mount) is sometimes required, for instance when you want to eject a mounted CD-ROM. To unmount (release), right click on the device icon and choose **Unmount**.

Preparing your Hard Disk for Linux

Before you can install Linux, you will need to prepare your hard disk for the installation.

Preparing your hard disk may involve any one of the following scenarios.

Scenario 1

You have a new system with a new hard disk with no partitions and you wish to use the entire hard disk space for Linux. You can have a perfectly functioning Linux system even on a single partitioned system.

Scenario 2

You have two partitions. In the primary partition you have installed Windows. Now you want to use the second logical partition on the extended partition for Linux. For this, first boot in full DOS mode if you have Windows 95 or 98 or boot from a bootable floppy in case of Win ME or 2000 (For Windows 95/98, you can create a bootable floppy by choosing Add/Remove programs option from the control panel). After booting run the fdisk utility. Delete the logical partition by selecting the third option. This will give you unpartitioned free space for Linux.

Note that we have only freed disk space for Linux Partitions. The partitions for Linux will be created as a part of the Linux installation (using a utility called Disk Druid).

Installation Steps for Red Hat Linux 8.0

1. Insert the Linux install CD into the CD-ROM drive and reboot your system. The computer will automatically boot from the CD and a text-based menu will be displayed.

2. You will then need to choose an installation environment. The default is the graphical installation (GUI). If you prefer a text-based install, type "text" at the prompt and hit the Enter key (The text-based install is faster on machines with comparatively less resources).
3. The installer will then prompt for a language for the installation program. All text will be displayed in the language selected. English is the preferred language.
4. Select your keyboard layout. Accepting the default [US (English)] should work in most cases.
5. If you are using the GUI installation, you will be asked about your mouse. You can select your mouse type from the list or select any one generic mouse (if your mouse has a scroll-wheel, select Microsoft Intellimouse).
6. Select the type of installation (Workstation /Server/ Custom). If you have a previous installation, the option of updating it will also be provided.
7. You would now need to create appropriate partitions to install Linux. Choose Disk Druid or fdisk. Partition sizes and numbers may vary with your set up, but as a bare minimum, you will need to create a '/' (root) and a swap partition. It is recommended to create /boot, /home, /, and a swap partition. In case you decide to reinstall, you can safely reuse the /home partition with all your user data intact. Save the partitioning scheme and proceed to the next step.
8. Enter the details of configuration of your network interfaces.
9. The firewall configuration screen offers a choice of firewall configurations. Choose 'Medium Firewall' for the time being without worrying too much as this stage about the concept of a firewall.
10. For time zone selection for India, choose "Asia/Calcutta". You can also set the UTC to +5.
11. Enter a root password when prompted. Do not forget it. You should create a user account here, which you will be using to work on your machine. It is not advisable to work as root at all times.
12. Select the packages that you want to install. You get to choose from installing KDE, GNOME and a collection of other utilities.
13. Select the video card that you have, the installer would try to auto detect the card for you, failing which you can select it manually.
14. If you are doing a graphical install, you'll be prompted for some additional information that starts with the type of monitor that you have. If your monitor type is not listed, select custom and enter your monitor specifications manually. Select the colour depth and the screen resolution that you wish to run the X Window system in, after installation. Choose your default desktop environment and whether you want a graphical or a text-based login. You can test the X

Window configuration after installation and then switch to graphics based login.

15. The installer will now format the Linux partitions and will install the required packages. You can watch the progress of the formatting by switching to the virtual terminals using Alt+1 to Alt+5 (if you are doing a text based install) or by using Ctrl+Alt+2 to Ctrl+Alt+5 (for graphics based install).
16. After some time you would be prompted to insert other CD's one-by-one. Insert these as prompted by the installation.
17. Once all the packages are installed, you will be given the opportunity to create a boot disk. It is strongly recommended that you create one at this stage.

At this point, the installation is complete. Remove the CD-ROM from the drive and reboot using the Linux system that you have just installed.

BOOTING A LINUX SYSTEM

Booting

Starting a computer by loading the kernel is known as **Booting/Bootstrapping** of a system. Booting from any device requires a boot-loader. (It is small piece of program stored in the Read Only Memory (ROM) of a system.) Boot-Loader initialises all aspects of the system such as CPU registers, device controllers and contents of the main memory and then loads the operating system from the Hard Disk. Computer bootstrapping is a long and complicated task because when the computer is switched on all the hardware devices are in an unpredictable state the RAM is inactive and in a random state. Typically, the booting procedure accomplishes these steps:

1. Checks the various devices (RAM, CPU, Hard Disk, Keyboard, Floppy dive, CD-ROM drive etc.) of your computer.
2. Determines the boot sequence coded in the BIOS (Basic Input-Output System).
3. Loads the boot-loader. [The Master Boot Record (MBR) loads the boot-loader.]

Note: Restarting a computer when it is already running, is called **rebooting** the system.

Linux Booting Options

We shall look at various methods that can be used to simplify the process of booting into the Linux system. But before we proceed any further, let's take a brief look in the different ways a system can be booted:

- Booting Linux from a Floppy disk
- Booting Linux from a Hard disk

Booting Linux from a floppy disk When booting from a floppy disk, the instructions stored in the first sector of the floppy disk is loaded in RAM and executed. These instructions then copy all the remaining sectors containing the Kernel image into RAM.

Booting Linux from a hard disk When booting from the hard disk, the booting procedure is different. The first sector of the hard disk, called the Master Boot Record (MBR) includes the partition table and a small program. This program loads the first sector of the partition containing the operating system to be started. Linux is a highly flexible and sophisticated piece of software, thus it replaces this small program in the MBR with a sophisticated program called LILO (Linux boot Loader). LILO allows users to select the operating system to be booted.

The LILO is a boot loader program that can boot the Linux kernel and other OSs. What makes LILO excellent as compared to other boot loaders is that it can accept command line arguments/options and holds a choice of 16 different images to boot from: Windows, OS/2, SCO Unix, PC-Dos, Linux, to name a few.

LILO can be installed in the Master Boot Record (MBR) or on the first sector of the root partition. After installation, the computer boots up to display a GUI screen with the OS options. Different options can be selected with the up and down arrow keys. By default, LILO waits for five seconds for the user to select a choice. If there is no response from the user, LILO boots the default boot image. In case the user wants to pass special arguments while booting, he can press 'Ctrl + X' to get a boot prompt. You can hit the 'Tab' key to see the boot options that can be passed here.

Note: To obtain more information on LILO arguments, type 'man lilo' in a terminal window after booting into Linux.

Using 'loadlin'

You can use 'loadlin' to boot into Linux. You will find 'loadlin' with every major Linux distribution in the 'dosutils' folder. Here is how to do it.

During Linux installation, opt to write LILO on the first sector of the Linux partition. Now boot into Linux using the boot floppy and copy the file 'vmlinuz' from the /boot directory to a blank floppy using the command:

```
mcopy vmlinuz a:\
```

Reboot the computer and boot into the DOS (Windows) partition. Copy the vmlinuz file from the floppy to your Windows root partition (normally C:\). Now copy 'loadlin.exe' file from the Linux distribution CD to C:\ and type the command:

loadlin vmlinuz root="/dev/hdxy" - where 'xy' is your Linux boot partition (e.g. hda2)

This will boot your computer into Linux.

Third-party Boot Loaders

Other boot loaders like XOSL (Extended Operating System Loader) GRUB, etc. can be used to boot into Linux. However, make sure that you have boot floppies for all your OSs before you go on to install them on your MBR.

KEY POINTS

Introduction

- Linux is a free UNIX – like operating system originally developed by Linus Torvalds, a student of University of Helsinki. The first Linux kernel was released to the public in the year 1991. It had no networking, ran on only 80386-compatible Intel processors and PC hardware, and had very limited device-driver support. Currently Linux comes with a collection of software including desktop, server programs, networking suites, compilers and many more utilities making it a complete operating system.
- Linux is written and distributed under the GNU General Public License, which means that its source code is freely-distributed and available to the general public.
- Unlike Windows, Linux is available from many different companies. A number of organisations integrate the versions of all these programs with the Linux kernel, test that everything works together, and then release what is called a **Distribution** of Linux. The Red Hat distribution is the most popular commercial distribution for Linux. Linux Mandrake, SuSE, Connectiva, Caldera and Red Flag are other main distributions of Linux.
- Some of the features of Linux include Multi-tasking, Multi-user, Multi-processor support, implementation of shared libraries, support for TCI/IP networking, databases and programming languages etc.
- The X Window system is the de facto industry standard graphics system for UNIX machines. A free version of the X Window System, known as 'Xfree86' is available for Linux. KDE and GNOME are the two main graphical user interfaces aiming to make Linux easy for computer users to operate. KDE is a powerful open source graphical desktop environment that combines ease of use, contemporary functionality and outstanding graphical design. KDE desktop is very much similar to the Windows 98/NT environment.
- The Linux operating system is categorised into three major components namely Kernel, Shell and Utilities and Application Programs.

- Kernel performs the critical tasks that are required to maintain the Linux environment. It is like a Master program that controls all the resources of the computer.
- Shell acts as an interface between the user and the kernel, accepts requests from the user, passes them to kernel, which then processes and submits them to the hardware. Shell is often referred to as **Command Interpreter**.
- Bourne shell, C shell and Korn shell were the most important shells that originated from UNIX and are available in Linux as well. The most widely used, originally Linux-based shell is the **Bourne-Again shell** (bash). Bash is based on the original Bourne shell, it includes extensions to Korn shell, coupled with its own extensions.
- Utilities are the software tools included with the Linux operating system. Application Programs include Word Processors, Spreadsheets, Presentation Packages and many more.

File Structure and File Handling

- Linux uses a hierarchical file structure. That is, directories are linked in the form of a family tree. The root directory ('/') is the main directory and all other directories are its sub-directories. 'home' directory contains all the user data.
- Files in Linux can be broadly classified into five types namely Normal, Directory, Special, Symbolic Link and Pipe files. Normal files are used for storing data, such as text information and programs. Directory files are used for storing information about a directory, its relationship with other directories, information about what sub-directories are stored in it and access permissions. Special files represent various routines in the kernel. Symbolic link files are used for storing the location/full pathname to the actual files they are pointing to. Pipe files are used as channels of information to be passed from one process to another.
- Linux is highly case sensitive, i.e., lowercase and uppercase letters are not treated as the same. This holds good for the file names, directory names and Linux commands.
- A file or directory in Linux may be referred to by either it's full path, partial path or relative path. Full path name lists each directory, starting from '/' (root), down to the file itself. If the file is in the working directory or in a sub-directory below the working directory, the names of higher directories can be omitted when using partial path name. If the file is in a directory near the working directory, a relative path may be used. It gives the location of a directory/file, relative to the current working directory.
- In Linux, a single dot(.) represents the current working directory and double dots(..) represent the parent directory.

- Linux comes with several file and directory handling commands for managing files and directories. These commands can either be typed at the shell prompt ($ or #) or can be executed using the KDE File manager to manage the files and directories through a windows-based graphical interface.

Installation of Linux

- Minimum hardware requirements for installation of Red Hat Linux 8.0 include Pentium class CPU, hard disk space - 475 MB (Custom installation), 850 MB (Server), 1.7GB (Personal Desktop) and 2.1 GB (Workstation) and 128 MB RAM.
- Linux being an operating system in itself, does not require any software for installation other than the installation CD's. However you may need to have a disk-partitioning utility (like BootIt NG, Partition Magic etc.) for creating a partition on your hard disk for installing Linux in your system.
- Preliminary steps installing Linux in your system include checking your hardware compatibility, checking your disk space, choosing an installation option, choosing a boot media and choosing an installation type.
- It is sometimes necessary to create a diskette from an image file; an image file contains an exact copy (or image) of a diskette's contents. Since a diskette contains file system information in addition to the data contained in files, the image file would not be usable until it has been written to a diskette.
- Installation diskette can be created under MSDOS or by using a dd utility available under most Linux distributions.
- Partitions can be defined as 'parts' of your hard drive. That is, they are logical divisions of a hard disk, accessible by the operating system as physically distinct hard drives.
- A drive in Linux is called a device and is treated as if it is a file. Hard drive partitions in Linux are referred in the form: /dev/<IDE-device-name><partition number>
- Floppy drives, A: and B: in Windows, are referred to as /dev/fd0 and /dev/fd1 (respectively) in Linux.
- To use a partition you must assign a directory to it. This process is referred to as **Mounting** (Similar to assigning drive letters to partitions in Windows). Once mounted, the corresponding directory called the **Mount Point** will contain all the directory and files on the partition.
- '/mnt/floppy' and '/mnt/cdrom' represent mount points for floppy and CDROM respectively.
- The procedure of starting a computer by loading the kernel is known as booting of a system. Booting on any device needs a boot-loader. (It is small piece of code typically stored in the Read Only Memory (ROM) of a system.)

Boot-loader first initialises all aspects of the system from CPU registers to device controllers and the contents of the main memory and then loads the operating system.

- Generally the booting procedure involves the following steps: Checking various devices (RAM, CPU, Hard Disk, Keyboard, Floppy dive, CD-Rom drive etc.) of your computer, determining the boot sequence given in the BIOS (Basic Input-Output System), loading the boot-loader. (The Master Boot Record or MBR loads the boot-loader.)
- The LILO is a boot loader program that can boot the Linux kernel and other OS' s. LILO can be can accept command line arguments/options and holds a choice of 16 different images to boot from: Windows, OS/2, SCO Unix, PC-Dos, Linux, to name a few.
- You can use 'loadlin' to boot into Linux. You will find 'loadlin' with every major Linux distributions along with the manual in the 'dosutils' folder.
- Other boot loaders like XOSL (Extended Operating System Loader) GRUB, etc. can also be used to boot into Linux.

REVIEW QUESTIONS

1. Choose the appropriate answer:

i. Linux has strong similarities to:

(a) Windows NT (b) Unix
(c) Windows ME (d) None of the above

ii. LILO is a:

(a) Loader (b) Disk Partitioning utility
(c) Command Interpreter (d) None of the above

iii. KDE utilities and applications include:

(a) KDE-Edu (b) KDE-Games
(c) K-Office (d) All of the above

iv. Contains all the configuration files that are local to your machine:

(a) usr (b) var
(c) etc (d) config

v. This can be used to create an installation diskette for installing Linux:

(a) dd utility (b) fdisk
(c) Disk Defrag (d) None of the above

2. State whether True or False:

i. Linux is a single user and single tasking operating system.

ii. Special files represent various routines in the kernel.

iii. Linux is a free, open source operating system owned by Microsoft.

iv. You can use the rawrite utility included on the Red Hat Linux CD in the 'dosutils' directory to create a diskette.

v. Shell is referred to as command interpreter.

vi. Mounting in Linux is similar to assigning drive letters to partitions in Windows.

vii. Linux commands can be written in either upper or lower case.

3. Match the following:

	X		Y
1.	Graphical Interfaces of Linux.	a.	Partition
2.	Components of Linux.	b.	GNOME and KDE
3.	You can use this option to alter the boot equence.	c.	ls
4.	Lists the files in the current directory. The names are sorted in alphabetical order.	d.	Booting
5.	Logical division of a hard disk, which show up to the operating system as if they were physically distinct hard drives.	e.	BIOS
6.	The procedure of starting a computer by loading the kernel.	f.	Kernel, Shell, Utilities and Applications

4. Fill in the blanks with the appropriate choices listed below

(i) Hierarchical (ii) Version (iii) Konqueror (iv) Lower (v) Distribution (vi) Kernel (vii) sbin (viii) bin (ix) Linked (x) Upper

1. ________________ is the core of an operating system.

2. Red hat can be referred to as a Linux ________________.

3. Linux uses a ________________ file structure.

4. ________________ helps in the management of files and directories by providing an easy to use graphical interface.

5. ________________ contains system admin commands intended for the root user of a system.

6. Linux commands can be written only in ________________ case.

5. **Discuss briefly the features of Linux.**
6. **Write briefly about the following DOS commands:**

   (a) cp (b) head
   (c) ls (d) rm
   (e) mkdir

7. **Briefly explain the preliminary steps that are needed before installing Linux.**
8. **What are the minimum hardware and software requirements for installing Linux?**

CHAPTER 12

Word Processing

WORD BASICS

Microsoft Word is a full-featured word processing program which can be used for any work involving creating and managing text. You can use it for the simplest to the most complex word processing applications. Using Word, you can write letters and reports, prepare bills and invoices, prepare office stationery–letter heads, envelopes and forms, design brochures, pamphlets, newsletters, magazines, etc.

In short, you would find it extremely difficult to think of a word processing feature not available in Microsoft Word. For most tasks, Word offers several ways of doing the same thing. It is up to the user to find which method is more preferable to him. Since covering all the different methods for doing the same task would require a book running into a thousand pages, I have taken the liberty of illustrating the method(s) I considered most user-friendly. As you gain more proficiency in using Word, you will yourself discovering other methods of doing your tasks, some of them perhaps more personally preferable to you than the ones I have selected.

STARTING WORD

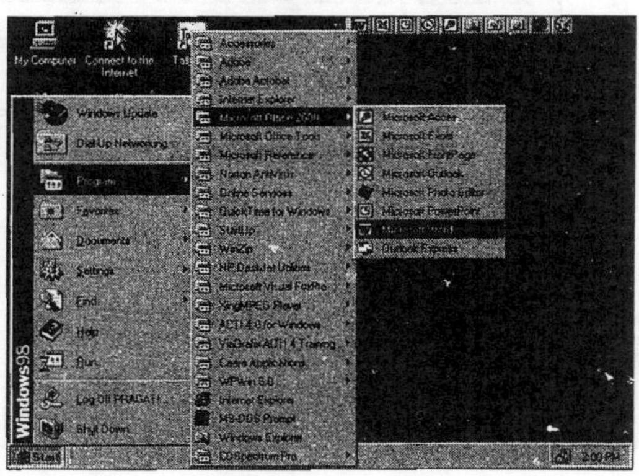

To start **Word** click once on the **Start** button, choose **Programs** and click once on **Microsoft Office** and then once on **Microsoft Word.**

On starting Word you would see a Word main screen with the Tip of the Day. These tips

are Word's way of teaching you new tricks and techniques while you work. Most of these tips are quite informative and some are even entertaining.

Read the tip, if you have the time and the inclination, then click once on Close OK button in the dialogue box to start working on the document.

Word always starts by opening an untitled "normal" document so that you can begin from scratch. This "normal" document is based upon all the default values (another name for pre-defined settings) provided by Word, i.e., standard page size, standard margins, font type and size etc. These settings can also be changed, details of which have been covered later in the book.

Different Views of Word

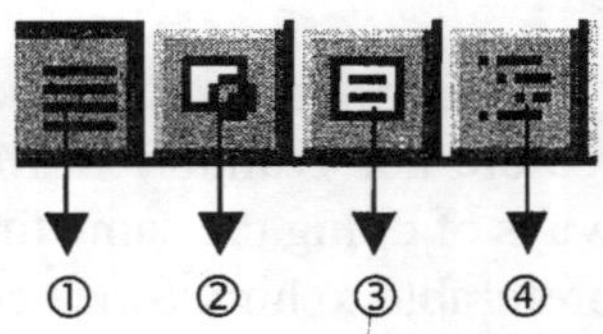

Any Word document can be viewed in four different types of views namely **Normal** View, **Web Layout** View, **Print Layout** View and **Outline** View. You can switch from one view to another by simply clicking on the corresponding icon.

① **Normal View:** This is the default view.

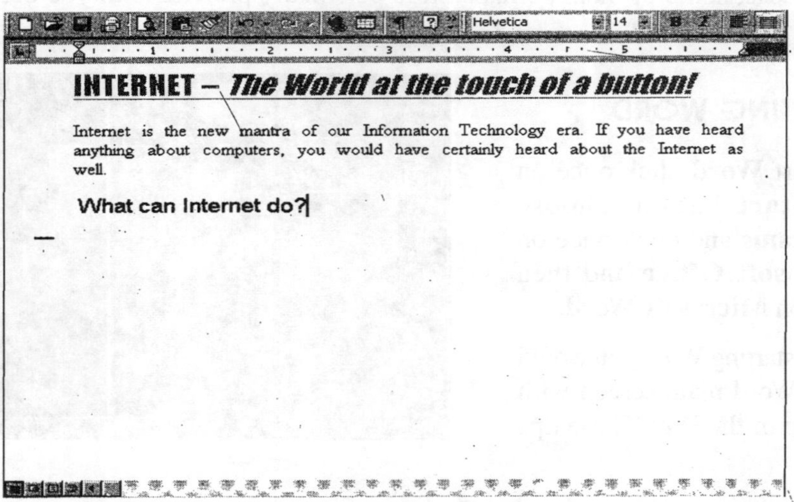

② **Web Layout View**: In this view you can preview your page, as it will appear in a web browser.

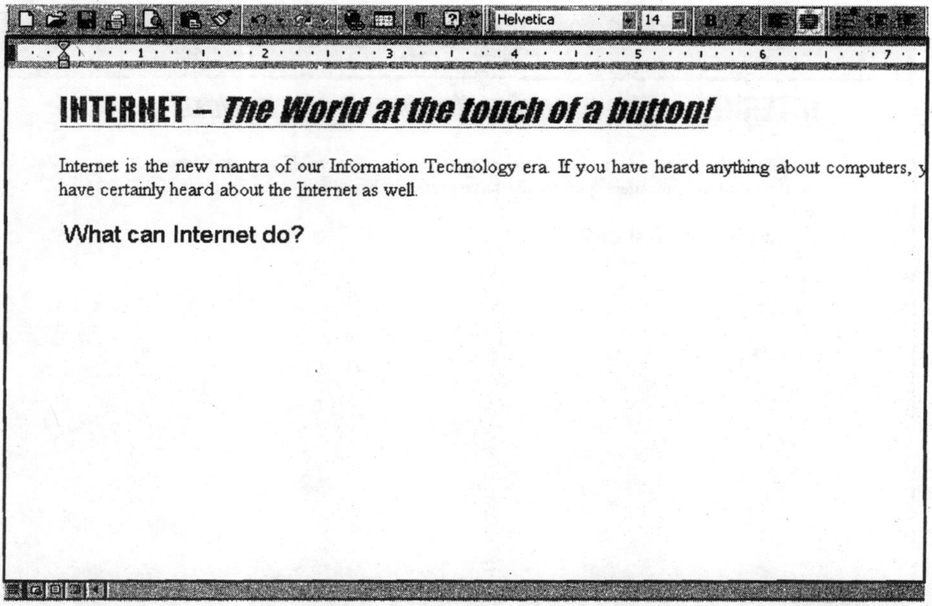

③ **Print Layout View:** In this view you can preview your page, as it will appear when printed. You can see the page margins and borders.

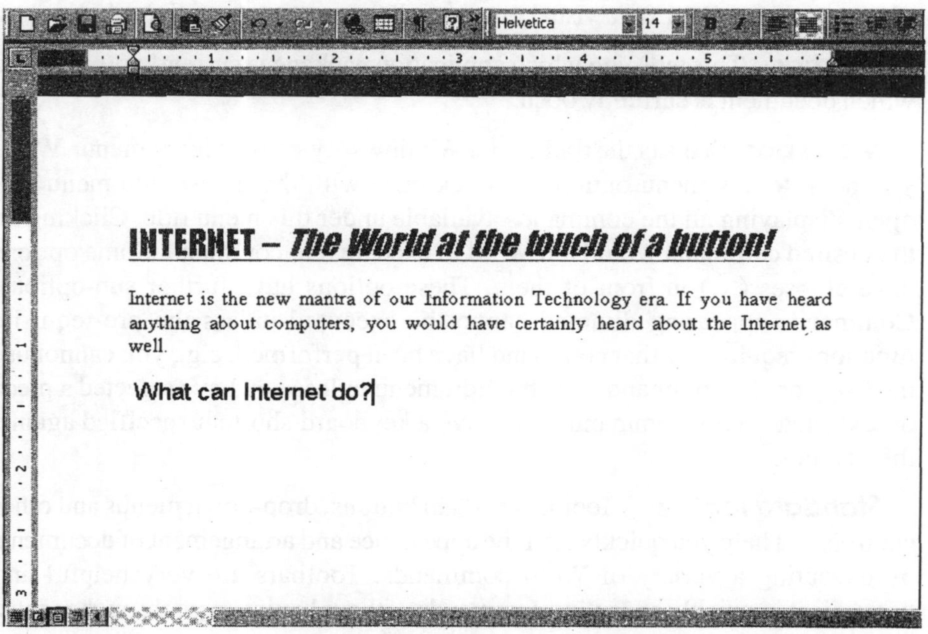

④ **Outline View:** In this view you can specify upto seven levels of headings. You can rearrange both the headings as well as its content to revise the structure of the document.

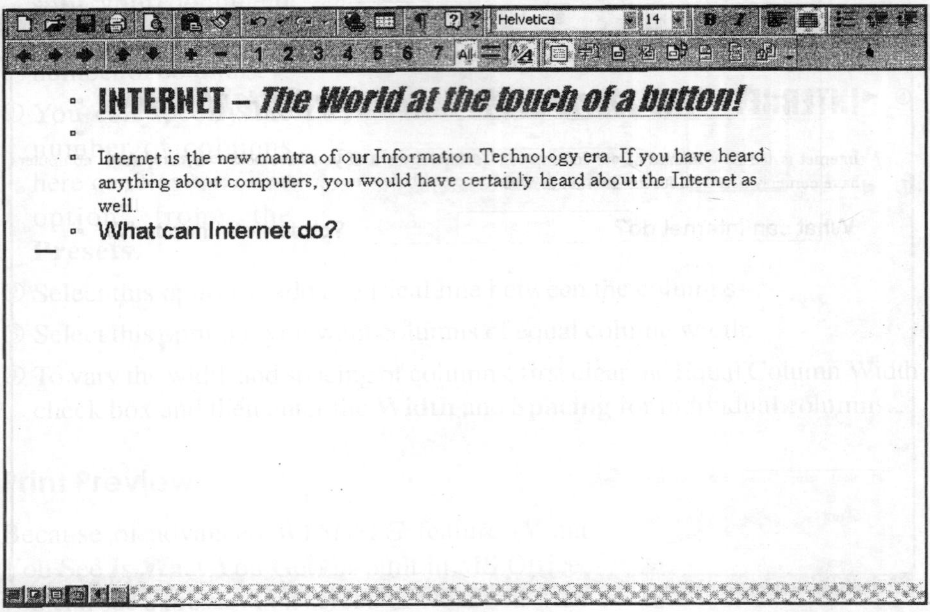

PARTS OF WORD WINDOW

Please see Figure 12.1 for a visual image of all these parts. An active window has:

Title bar This tells you which application package is currently running and which document is currently open.

Menu bar This is the traditional Windows style drop-down menu. When you point to any menu option and click once with the mouse, the menu will open, displaying all the commands available under this menu title. Clicking on the desired command would tell Word to execute that command. Some options have ellipses (…) in front of them. These options have further sub-options. Commands appearing dimmed cannot be executed unless the pre-requisite functions required by that command have been performed, e.g., you cannot use the Copy or Cut command from the Edit menu unless you have selected a piece of text first. Many commands also have a keyboard shortcut specified against their names.

Standard toolbar Toolbars contain buttons, drop-down menus and other controls that help you quickly alter the appearance and arrangement of documents by executing a variety of Word commands. Toolbars are very helpful and convenient in quickly executing commands without having to go through menus.

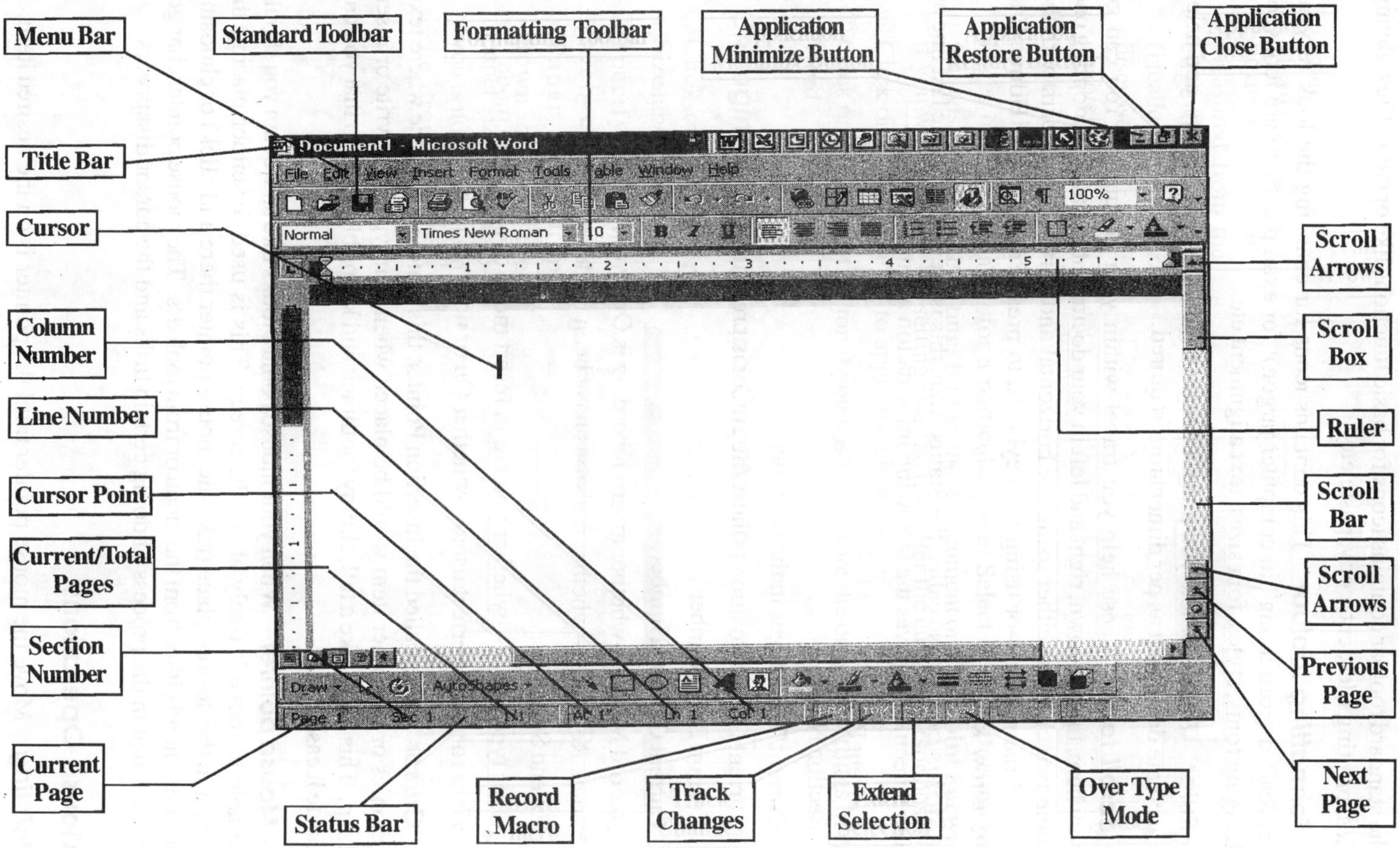

Figure 12.1 Parts of a Word Window

The standard toolbar contains icons for basic functions like opening files, saving files, printing files, cut, copy, paste etc.

Formatting toolbar This contains icons for changing the look of your text (called "formatting" in computer jargon); for example, there are icons for changing fonts, styles, font sizes, text alignment etc.

Ruler The Ruler lets you make changes to margins and indents, and helps you create document as per dimensions required.

Scroll tools These help you travel within your document. You can go anywhere, up and down, right and left in your document mainly by adopting one of the two choices: either using the horizontal and vertical scroll bars with the help of the mouse—or using the keyboard to press PgUp, PgDn, Home, End and arrow keys.

Status bar Also called the Status Area, this is the normally the last line on your screen. This gives the following information about your work—

- Current Page
- Section Number
- Current/Total pages in the document
- Current Cursor Position (where the cursor is presently located)
- Current Line Number
- Current Column Number
- Record Macro—whether macro recording is On or not
- Track Revision—whether revisions have been made or not
- Extend Selection
- Over type Mode—whether you are in Insert mode or overwrite mode
- Help for WordPerfect users—whether On or not.

Cursor Also called the Insertion Pointer, this denotes the place where text, graphics or any other item would be placed when you type, overwrite or insert them. This looks like a tall, skinny toothpick and keeps blinking so that you can locate it easily.

Mouse pointer When your mouse pointer looks like an I-beam you should be able to move it freely about the screen. This is used for either placing the cursor at the desired place (take the mouse pointer there and click) or choosing any command either from the menu or from toolbars. The mouse pointer changes shape when in the process of doing certain tasks and the cursor disappears.

Mouse Operations

Pointing Move the mouse pointer until the pointer is on the desired item.

Clicking Move the mouse pointer to the position you want, then press the mouse left button once.

Double-clicking Move the mouse pointer to the position you want, then press the mouse left button twice in rapid succession. Alternatively, if your mouse has been so installed, you can also click the middle button once, instead of pressing the left button twice.

Right-clicking In some cases like changing the properties of an object, or for correcting a mis-spelt word, or even for cut, copy and paste—the mouse right button can be used. In such cases, simply select the object and click once on the mouse right button.

Dragging Move the mouse pointer to the right place, highlight the desired text by clicking once in the beginning and releasing the left button at the end, then click once again in the highlighted block, keep the mouse left button pressed and roll the mouse to move the block to a new location by releasing the left button at the desired location.

At first, using the mouse may be difficult (particularly double-clicking and dragging). However, learning to use it is worth the trouble because many of the advanced tools in modern programs are only operated with the mouse. In any case most operations are much simpler and faster to execute through the mouse rather than through the keyboard.

Keyboard Operations

Typing keys The part of the keyboard which is used to type letters, numbers and other characters. The alphabets layout resembles a standard typewriter keyboard exactly. However there are some extra keys for entering commands, e.g., *Ctrl* key, *Alt* key, *Shift* key, *Enter* key etc. On most keyboards, these extra keys are grey in colour whereas the alphabet, number, symbol and punctuation keys are white in colour. The *Ctrl*, *Alt* and *Shift* key is always used in conjunction with some other key.

Shift and Caps Lock key The *Shift* key is used to type capital letters, i.e., if you want to type the letter "F", you have to press the *Shift* key, keep it pressed with one finger and press "f" key with the other. However, if you want to type an entire word or a sentence in capital letters, use the *Caps Lock* key instead. Unlike the *Shift* key, *Caps Lock* key is a toggle key and does not need to be pressed continuously. Press it once and it becomes *On* (you will see the Caps Lock indicator on the keyboard lighting up when you do this) and thereafter whatever you type would be in capital letters; press it again and it becomes *Off*.

Function keys The row of 10–12 keys—*F1* to *F12* above the typing keys are called the Function keys and are used to execute special commands or as shortcut keys. The use of these keys varies from program to program, however within MS Office some degree of standardisation has been achieved. In Word, the function keys are used alone or together with the *Shift, Alt* and *Ctrl* keys to give commands.

Cursor control keys A group of special keys used to control and navigate the cursor - arrow keys (Up -, Down ¯, Left ¬ , Right ®). *Home* and *End* are used to quickly place the cursor in the beginning or end of a line. To delete an alphabet to the left of the cursor press the *Backspace* key ¬ (normally above the *Enter* key), to delete an alphabet to the right of the cursor press the *Del* key.

Numeric keypad The keys on the extreme right of the keyboard (resembling a calculator's keyboard), which can be used both to enter numbers (when the *Num Lock* is *On*) as well as to move the cursor (when the *Num Lock* is *Off*). The *Num Lock* key is located above the number 7 (Home) key on the Numeric keypad and its *On* or *Off* status is displayed by the *Num Lock* indicator light on your keyboard. Since *Num Lock* is also a toggle key, pressing it once makes it *On* and pressing it again makes it *Off*.

Note: Press the keys briefly with a light pressure, unless you want repeated characters.

The Most Important Keys

Alt and Ctrl The command keys are used in combination with another key or with the mouse. For example, the Alt+F4 key combination (press down the Alt key, hold it down and press the F4 function key briefly and then release both) closes the program.

Shift Like Alt and Ctrl, the Shift key is also used in commands in combination with other keys. In typing, it is used in the same way as on a typewriter – to produce capital letters.

Enter When typing text, press Enter when you want to produce a forced line feed (e.g., at the end of a paragraph and to create blank lines). Enter is also used in combination with other keys to execute a few commands. On some keyboards, this key is named Return instead of Enter.

Esc The Esc key is located to the left of the function keys, in the upper left corner of the keyboard. It can be used to Cancel selection in a menu.

Backspace Pressing this key deletes the character to the left of the cursor.

Del (Delete) This key deletes the character to the right of the cursor.

How to type in Word Once Word has been started, you can immediately start typing. When you press character keys on the keyboard, you can see the corresponding characters appear in the Word window. Use the Spacebar when you want to separate characters and words from each other. Use the Tab key when you want to move the cursor or text from one Tab stop to another, and also when you want to create a blank longer than one space between words. Use 'Enter' key when you want to start a new paragraph.

Insert and Overtype modes Word normally uses the insert mode. In this mode, Word does not overtype the existing text but pushes it forward. By pressing the Ins key, you can switch to overtype mode. In this mode, the new text replaces the old text after the cursor. To switch between Overtype/Insert modes press the *Insert* key. In the Insert mode, when you place the cursor in the middle of two words and start typing, the new text is inserted between the two words and all the text below this line is automatically adjusted. In the Overtype mode, when you place the cursor in the middle of two words and start typing, the new text overwrites the previous text.

SOME 'DON'TS'

- Don't use the Spacebar to indent paragraphs. Instead, use the Tab key for the indent control in Word's ruler (the top handle on the left hand side)
- Don't use Spacebar to centre or otherwise position text. Use the Left, Right and Center alignment buttons from Formatting bar instead.
- Don't use Spacebar to create columns. Use Word's Table or Column command instead.
- Don't hit Enter key repeatedly for starting the matter on new page. Use Insert Page break command instead.

MENUS, COMMANDS, TOOLBARS AND THEIR ICONS

Till some years ago, users used to type long string of code words, called **Commands**, for making the computer do anything. The user had to remember these coded commands for each step that he wished to execute. Each command had an appropriate grammar, called **Syntax**. This meant that even if you made the slightest mistake in typing the command, it would not work.

Fortunately things have changed dramatically now. Users are not expected to be trained parrots that can reproduce phrases or sentences verbatim! Now, all Windows based software have a Graphical User Interface, consisting of icons and menus. Simply click on the desired icon through your mouse and presto – the command would be executed. To make sure that icons look different from each other, they have small pictures on them, e.g., the icon which prints your documents has a picture of a printer on it, the icon which saves your work has a picture of floppy on it, and so on. This makes it very easy to recognise and remember the individual use of these icons. To make things still simpler, whenever you leave your mouse pointer on the top of any icon, for a couple of seconds, the icon's name is shown below it, so that you know what this particular icon does for you.This text is reffered to as **Tool Tip** text.

In MS Word, groups of icons, which perform related tasks, are placed together in a ribbon, called a *Toolbar*. There are many toolbars available in Word—Standard toolbar, Formatting toolbar, Drawing toolbar, Tables and Borders toolbars etc. Each of these contain an assortment of related icons, specific to that toolbar. For executing most tasks, the user has three options:

1. Choose the desired command from the Menu options provided by either using the mouse or using cursor movement keys, or
2. Press the appropriate shortcut keys combination from the keyboard, or
3. Click once on the relevant icon from the displayed toolbars.

Although there is no wrong or right approach, most users find the third option simplest and fastest.

The present section deals in detail with toolbars and icons. It deals with all the Word toolbar–the names of icons within each toolbar, it's purpose and usage, it's menu equivalent option and it's keyboard shortcut, if any.

You are advised to just go through the pages in this section once. Do not worry if you do not understand everything and, most importantly —do not try to memorise anything. Mugging up is no substitute for actual practice. In the next section, when we do exercises based upon these menu options and icons, these would automatically become second nature to you. Later, this section may be used by you to refer to any specific command or icon's usage.

TOOLBARS AND THEIR ICONS

Word Standard Toolbar

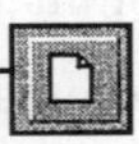

New

Creates a new document based on normal template.
Alternative: File→New
Shortcut→Ctrl+N

Open

Opens an existing document or template.
Alternative: File→Open
Shortcut→Ctrl+O

Save

Saves the active document or template
Alternative: File→ Save
Shortcut→Ctrl+S

E-Mail

It sends the contents of the document as the body of the e-mail message.
Alternative: File→ Send To→ Mail

Print
Prints the active document using current defaults.
Alternative: File→ Print
Shortcut→Ctrl+P

Print Preview
Displays full page as they are printed.
Alternative: File→ Print Preview
Shortcut→Ctrl+F2

Spelling
Checks the spelling in the active document
Alternative: Tools→Spelling and Grammar
Shortcut→F7

Cut
Cuts the selection and puts it on the Clipboard.
Alternative: Edit→Cut
Shortcut→Ctrl+X

Copy
Copies the selection and puts it on the clipboard.
Alternative: Edit→Copy
Shortcut→Ctrl+C

Paste
Inserts the clipboard contents at the insertion point.
Alternative: Edit→Paste
Shortcut→Ctrl+V

Format Painter
Copies the formatting of the selection to a specified location.
Shortcut→Ctrl+Shift+C

Undo
Reverses certain commands.
Alternative: Edit→Undo
Shortcut→Ctrl+Z

Redo
Reverses the action of the Undo command.
Alternative: Edit→Repeat
Shortcut→Ctrl+Y

Insert Hyperlink
Displays the destination object, document or page.
Alternative: Edit→Repeat
Shortcut→Ctrl+K

Insert Table
Inserts a table
Alternative: Table→Insert Table

Tables and Borders
Displays the tables and borders toolbar.
Alternative: View→Toolbars→Tables and Borders

Insert Excel Worksheet
Inserts Microsoft Excel Worksheet.
Alternative: Insert→File

Columns
Changes the column format of the selected sections.
Alternative: Format→Columns

Drawing
Shows or hides the Drawing Toolbar.
Alternative: View→ Toolbars →Drawing

Document Map
Shows an outline of a document heading and helps to quickly navigate around the document.
Alternative: View→Document Map

Show/Hide

Shows/hides non-printing characters.
Shortcut→ Ctrl+*

Zoom Control

Scales the editing view (Zoom).
Alternative: View→Zoom

Office Assistant

Provides help topics and tips to accomplish your task.
Alternative: Help→ Microsoft Word Help
Shortcut →F1

Word Formatting Toolbar

Style

Applies a style or records a style by example.
Alternative: Format→Style
Shortcut→ Ctrl+Shift+S

Font

Changes the font of the selection.
Alternative: Format→Font
Shortcut→ Ctrl+Shift+F

Font Size

Changes the font size of the selection.
Alternative: Format→Font→Size
Shortcut→ Ctrl+Shift+P

Bold

Makes the selection Bold.
Alternative: Format→Font→Font style
Shortcut→ Ctrl+B

Italic

Makes the selection Italics.
*Alternative:*Format→Font→Font style
Shortcut→ Ctrl+I

Underline

Formats the selection with continuous underline.
Alternative:
Format→Font→effects
Shortcut→ Ctrl+U

Align Left

Aligns the paragraph at left indent.
Alternative:
Format→Paragraph→Alignment
Shortcut→ Ctrl+L

Centre

Centres the paragraphs between the indents.
Alternative :
Format→Paragraph→Alignment
Shortcut→ Ctrl+E

Align Right
Aligns the paragraph at right indent.
Alternative:
Format→Paragraph→Alignment
Shortcut→Ctrl+R

Justify
Aligns the paragraph at both right and left indent.
Alternative:
Format→Paragraph→Alignment
Shortcut→Ctrl+J

Numbering
Creates a numbered list based on the current defaults.
Alternative:
Format→Bullets and Numbering

Bullets
Creates a bulleted list based on the current defaults.
Alternative:
Format→Bullets and Numbering

Decrease Indent
Decreases or promotes the selection one level.
Alternative:
Format→Paragraph→Indentation

Increase Indent
Increases indent or demotes the selection one level.
Alternative:
Format→Paragraph→Indentation

Borders
Shows or hides the border toolbar.
Alternative:
Format→Borders and Shading

Highlight
Highlights a selected piece of text in the chosen color.

Font Color
Selects and applies Font Color.
Alternative:
Format→Font→Color

Word Tables and Borders Toolbar

Draw Table
Inserts a table where you drag in the document. After you drag to insert the table, drag inside the table to add cells, columns, or rows.

Eraser
Removes a table cell line and merges the contents of the adjacent cells. If the cell has a border, Word removes the border but does not merge the cells. Click Eraser, and then drag the eraser pointer over the table cell lines or borders you don't want.

Line Width
Click the width you want for the border on the selected object.

Border Color
Click on the border color you want.

Fill Color
Adds, modifies, or removes the fill color or fill effect from the selected object. Fill effects include gradient, texture, pattern, and picture fills.

Merge Cells
It combines the contents of the selected adjacent cells into a single cell.

Align Top Left
Aligns horizontally oriented text with the top of the table cell. Similarly you can choose from the various options to align the text differently.

Distribute Columns Evenly
Changes the selected columns or cells to equal column width.

Change Text Direction
Orients selected text in a text box, cell, or frame horizontally, left to right.

Sort Descending
Sorts the selected items in order from the end of the alphabet, the highest number, or the latest date, using the column that contains the insertion point. If you previously set other sorting options, those options are still in effect.

Border Style
Click the style and thickness you want for the selected line.

Outside Border
Adds or removes a border around the selected text, paragraphs, cells, pictures, or other object.

Insert Table
Inserts a table in the document with the number of columns and rows you specify.

Split Cells
It splits the selected cells into the number of rows and columns you enter.

Distribute Rows Evenly
Changes the selected rows or cells to equal row height.

Table AutoFormat
It automatically applies formats, including predefined borders and shading, to a table. Automatically resizes a table to fit the contents of the table cells.

Sort Ascending
Sorts the selected items in order from the beginning of the alphabet, the lowest number, or the earliest date, using the column that contains the insertion point. If you previously set other sorting options, those options are still in effect.

AutoSum
Inserts a = (Formula) field that calculates and displays the sum of the values in table cells above or to the left of the cell containing the insertion point.

Word Drawing Toolbar

Draw
Activates the Draw Menu

Free Rotate
Rotates the selected object to any degree. Select the object, click on the icon and then drag a corner of the object in the direction you want to rotate it.

Line
Draws a straight line where you click or drag in the active Window. To constrain the line to draw at 15-degree angle from its starting point, hold down SHIFT as you drag.

Rectangle
Draws an rectangle where you click or drag in the active Window. To draw a square, press SHIFT and drag.

Text Box
Draws a text box where you click or drag in the active Window. Use a text box to add a text—such as captions or callouts—to your pictures or graphics.
Alternative: Insert→TextBox

Clip Art
Opens the Clip Gallery where you can select the clip art image you want to insert in your file or update your clip art collection.
Alternative: Insert→Picture →Clip Art

Select Objects
Changes the pointer to a selection arrow so that you can select objects in the active window. To select a single object, click the object with the arrow. To select one or more objects, drag the arrow over the objects you want to select.

Auto Shapes
Activates the AutoShapes menu.

Arrow
Inserts a line with an arrowhead where you click or drag in the active Window. To constrain the line to draw at the 15-degree angle from its starting point, hold down SHIFT as you drag.

Oval
Draws an oval where you click or drag in the active Window. To draw a circle, press SHIFT and drag.

Word Art
Creates text effects by inserting a Microsoft Office drawing object.

Alternative: Insert→Picture →Word Art

Fill Color
Adds, modifies, or removes the fill color or fill effect from the selected object. Fill effects include gradient, texture, pattern and picture fills.

Font Color
Formats the selected text with the color you click.

Line Color

Adds, modifies, or removes the line color ftom the selected object.

Line Style

Click the width you want for the selected line.

Dash Style

Click the dashed line or dashed-dot line style you want for the selected shape or border. Click the solid line if you don't want the dotted line.

Arrow Style

Click the arrowhead style you want for the selected line.

3-D

Click the 3-D style you want for the selected object.

Shadow

Click the shadow style you want for the selected object.

Note: Although by default the Standard and Formatting toolbars are normally displayed below the Menubar, it is the user who decides which toolbars he wants to be displayed while working. To display or remove any toolbar from the users view, click on the **View** menu, choose **Toolbars** and click on the desired toolbar.

The following exercise (Word Exercise - 1) explains the basic Word processing concepts.

- Creating a New Document
- Saving a Document
- Closing a Document
- Opening an Existing Document
- Selecting Text
- Editing Text
- Finding and Replacing Text
- Formatting Features
- Page Design and Layout
- Printing a Document

WORD EXERCISE 1

INTERNET – *The World at the touch of a button!*

Internet is the new mantra of our Information Technology era. If you have heard anything about computers, you would have certainly heard about the Internet as well.

What is Internet after All?

The Internet is a world - wide network of computer networks. Imagine a network of five computers in your office that are linked up together in such a manner that you can exchange data, correspondence (mail) and even software between these computers. Now imagine that you have a business associates or friends who also have several computers in their homes or offices organised pretty much like yours. Now imagine all these computers spread over different locations linked up in manner so that they (meaning you!) can communicate between each other. This is what Internet is all about. Internet is a global network linking millions of computers and people cutting across all barriers and boundaries of countries, race, class or sex. Internet can also be described as a collection of government, academic, commercial and individual's sites.

What can Internet do?

- E-Mail
- E-Commerce
- E-Chat
- Central Repository of Data
- Advertisement Billboard
- Distance learning
- Shareware Software
- Wide Area Networks and much more.

1. **E-Mail** Through E-mail (Electronic Mail), mail messages can be sent to or received from anywhere in the world, in a matter of minutes and even fewer rupees!
2. **E-Commerce** Through Internet you can shop for various products and pay through your credit card, ask your bank to transfer money from account of yours to another; all this without leaving your desk!
3. **E-Chat** Nowadays you can even make national and international telephone calls through the Internet at practically the cost of a local call.
4. **Central Repository of Data** The Internet is like a huge central ware house of data that can be accessed and queried by people from all over the world.

5. **Advertisement Billboard** You can launch your own site on the Internet or put up banner ads on other people's sites.
6. **Distance Learning** Several distance learning courses are available on the Internet through which you can study and complete courses on different subjects.
7. **Shareware Software** Internet is also a great place from where you can download shareware (free) software, games and utilities.
8. **Wide Area Networks** Using the Internet, organisations can collect and compile information from their offices spread over a huge geographical area.

CREATING A NEW DOCUMENT

① Choose **New** command from the **File Menu.** You can activate the menu in two ways:

1. Press ALT-F Key (or any Key underlined in Menu line to activate that menu list) and use the Keyboard to move up and down within the various options under the file menu and press Enter to select an option.
2. Use a mouse. Move the mouse pointer to File and click, this will open the menu list. Use the mouse to choose between various options and click once on the desired option.

② Click on the **General** folio.

③ Click here to choose **Blank Document**.

④ Click once on the **OK** button.

Entering Text

The blank white area is the place where you would be typing your matter. Notice the toothpick cursor at the beginning of first line, when you start typing, your text would appear from this point onwards. So let's begin. Start typing the text given in Sample Exercise 1. Type only till "Wide Area Networks, and much more" as shown below:

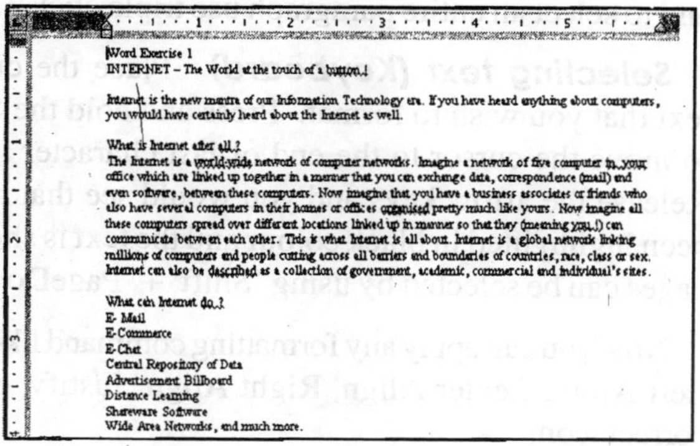

While typing do not bother about how your text looks, simply go ahead and type in continuity. One of the basic features of Word is Word-Wrap. This feature allows you to type in continuity without bothering about your line running out of right margin of your page. While you are typing as soon as you approach the end of a line (right side of your paper), Word automatically figures out whether the last word that you have typed can fit within the current line. If it will, fine, otherwise Word automatically picks up the whole word and places it in the next line.

When you reach the end of a paragraph or a paragraph heading (like – What is Internet after all?) press **Enter** to place your cursor in the next line. If you need a blank line then press **Enter** once more to create some blank space between two paragraphs. This point is so important that I am going to repeat it once again. Never press Enter after every line, but only at the end of a paragraph or a paragraph heading.

Paragraph Marks ¶

If this option is turned on then the paragraph symbol is displayed at the end of each paragraph. It helps in undestanding the formatting of your document. However this is a non-printable character, which means that when you print a document this symbol does not get printed. To turn off this option, click again on this symbol.

Selecting Text

All the formatting features offered by Word require pre-selection of a piece of text. This piece of text, also called a 'Block' or a 'Range'in computer speak, could be a single word, a phrase, a sentence, a paragraph, a page or the entire document. For applying various formatting commands this Block has to be specified first before choosing the desired formatting command.

Selecting text (Mouse) Place the mouse pointer at the beginning of the text that you wish to format. Click once, keep the left mouse button pressed and drag till the end of the Block. Release the mouse button and you would see that the Block selected by you has been highlighted in black colour and the text is shown in white colour. To select a word in a document simply double click on it and to select an entire paragraph use triple click.

Selecting text (Keyboard) Place the cursor at the beginning of the text that you wish to format. Press and hold the Shift key then use arrow keys to move the cursor to the end of last character in the text you wish to select. Release the arrow keys and you would see that the Block selected by you has been highlighted in black colour and the text is shown in white colour. Multiple pages can be selected by using 'Shift' + 'PageDown' keys.

Now you can apply any formatting command like Bold faced, Italics, Underline, Left Align, Center Align, Right Align, Justify, etc. by simply clicking on the correct icon.

Editing Text

If you make any mistakes while typing, use the **Backspace** and **Del** key to delete the incorrect text. **Backspace** key deletes a character to the left of the current cursor position whereas **Del** key deletes a character to the right of the current cursor position.

Finding Text

This utility can be used for searching for a word or a phrase in a document. Choose **Find** from the **Edit** Menu to access this utility.

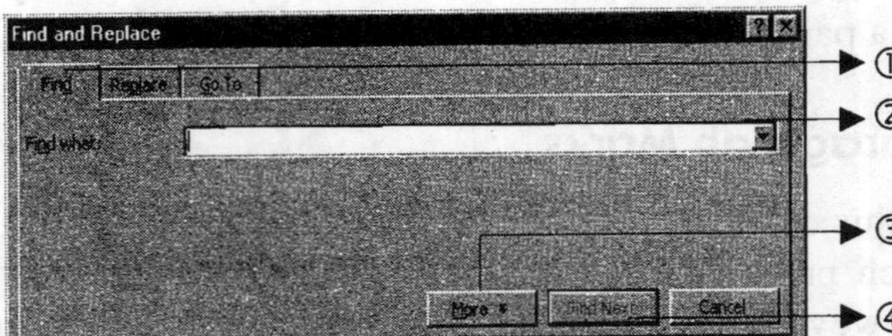

① Click on the **Find** tab/folio (or Ctrl + F keys).

② Enter the word/phrase that you want to search for in the document.

③ Click on this option if you want to specify more advanced options for performing the search.

④ Click here to locate the typed word in the document.

Replacing Text

This utility helps to replace a single or all instances of any word/phrase with another word/phrase. For example, you can replace all occurrences of 'Word97' in a document with 'Word2000' at one click using this feature.

① Click on the **Replace** tab/folio.

② Enter the word/phrase that you want to search in the document.

③ Enter the replacement word/phrase.

④ Click on this option if you want more advanced options.

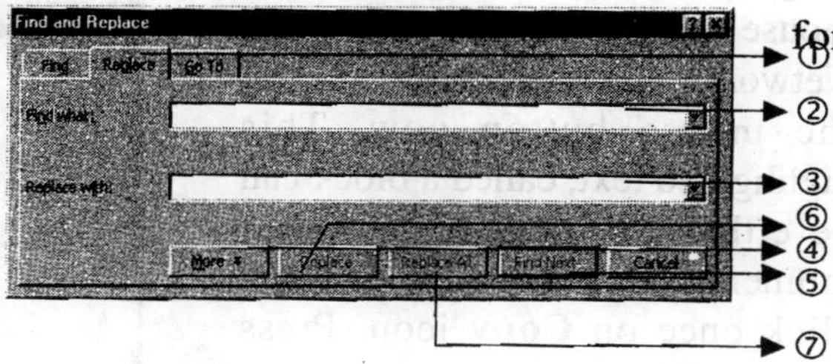

⑤ Click here to locate the typed word in the document.

⑥ Click here to replace the found text or click on Find Next to skip to the next occurrence.

⑦ Click here to replace all occurrences of found text in the entire document.

Undo Mistakes

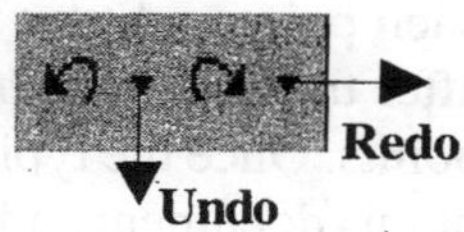

Undo command can be used to undo the effect of recent commands or actions taken by the user. Redo command can be used to redo something that the user has undone. Redo undoes an Undo.

Undo and Redo command can be accessed from the Standard toolbar.

Note: Click the arrow button next to Undo button to view the list of recent actions that the user has undone.

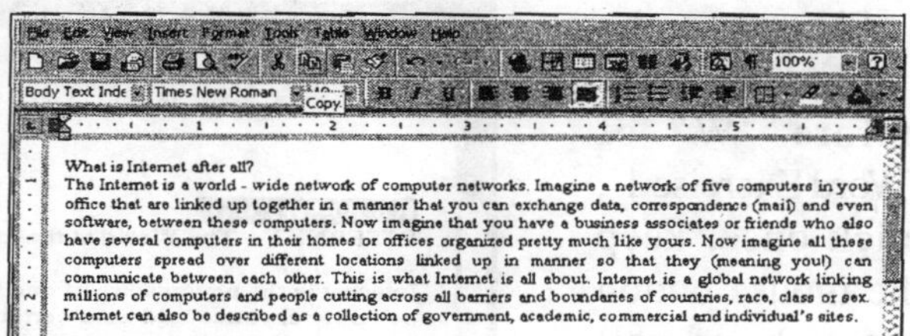

Coming back to our exercise, you will notice that the remaining text is a repetition of the same points about Internet, which have been briefly explained in the next section. This brings us to an interesting and very useful group of commands - Cut, Copy and Paste. Through **Cut** command you can move a block of text from one place to another. Through **Copy** command you can copy a block of text from one place to another such that the text appears at both the places. **Paste** command is used to insert the block of text, which has been either Cut or Copied. In the present example we will use the Copy and Paste command to copy the Internet features. Highlight all the Internet points by placing the cursor before "E-Mail",

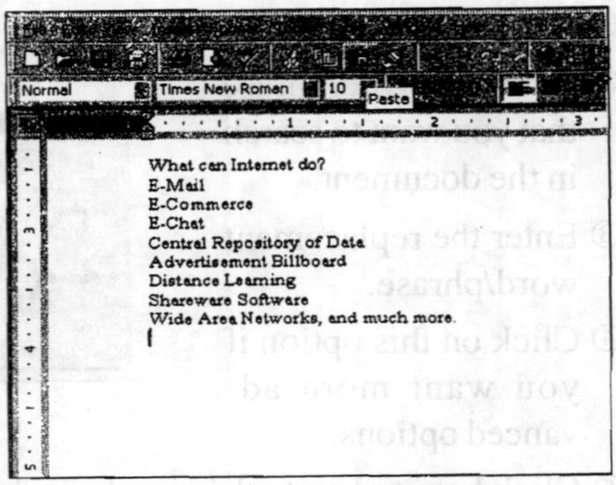

clicking on the mouse's left button, keeping it pressed and rolling the mouse till the end of "Wide Area Networks, and much more" release the mouse button now. This highlighted text, called a block can be either cut or copied. At the moment, since we want to copy, click once on **Copy** icon. Press Enter twice to come to a new paragraph and click once on **Paste** icon to get the same block of text here. Any block of text that is copied or cut is stored in a temporary location called **Clipboard** and whenever a paste command is issued the copied block of text is pasted into the selected location from the clipboard.

Now that you have a second block of text, you can place the cursor after each point and type a brief explanation about it. Take care not to press Enter after the end of each point, otherwise a blank line would be inserted between points. Once the typing work is completed, we can start on improving the look of this document and making it look exactly like the sample exercise page. This process involving changing the font type, font size, alignment of text, applying shades and colours etc. is called **Formatting**. So let us now start from the top of the document and move our way down.

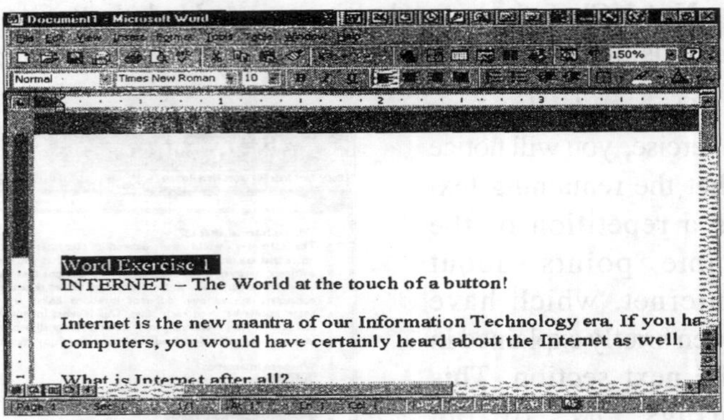

Place the mouse pointer before 'W' of 'Word Exercise 1', click once, keep the mouse button pressed and roll the mouse to highlight this block of text, release the mouse button after reaching the end of the text (after '1'). You will see that the text (called block) is highlighted in black and the text appears in white colour.

Now we have to make this text bigger, thicker and aligned to the right side. This would be done by three commands

- Increasing the font size,
- Applying Bold font style, and
- Right Aligning, respectively.

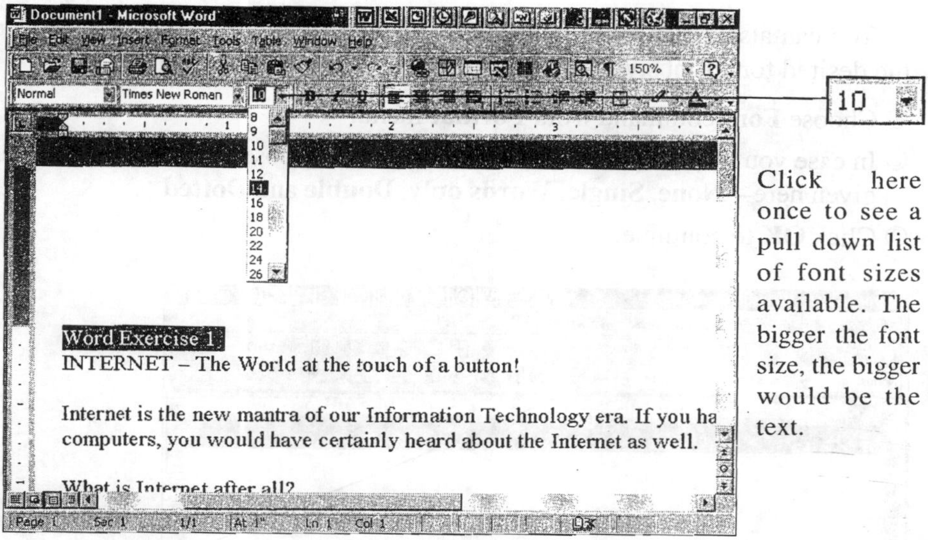

Click here once to see a pull down list of font sizes available. The bigger the font size, the bigger would be the text.

Alternative Method

There is an alternative method to change the font. Highlight the text as explained earlier by 'blocking'. Choose **Font** from the **Format** menu. A window will appear.

This is a very compact and feature rich dialog box. Through this you can change not only the fonts and point size, but also the styles like **Bold**, *Italics*, ***Bold Italics***, Regular etc.

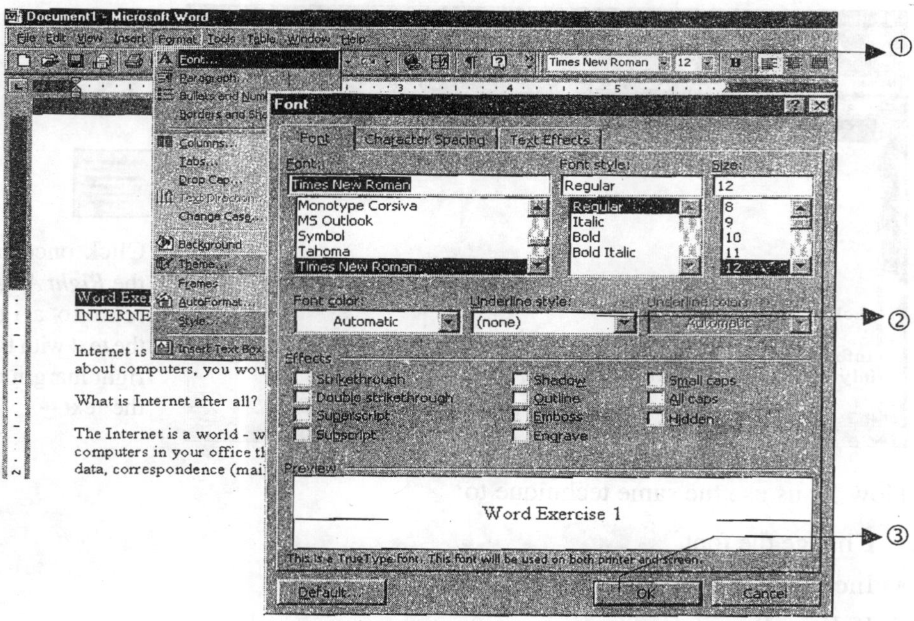

You can also apply other effects like strike through, underline etc. Choose the desired font, font style and size and click **OK** button to continue.

① Choose **Font** command from **Format** menu.

② In case you wish to underline the selected text, choose from the alternatives given here—**None**, **Single**, **Words only**, **Double** and **Dotted**.

③ Click **OK** to continue.

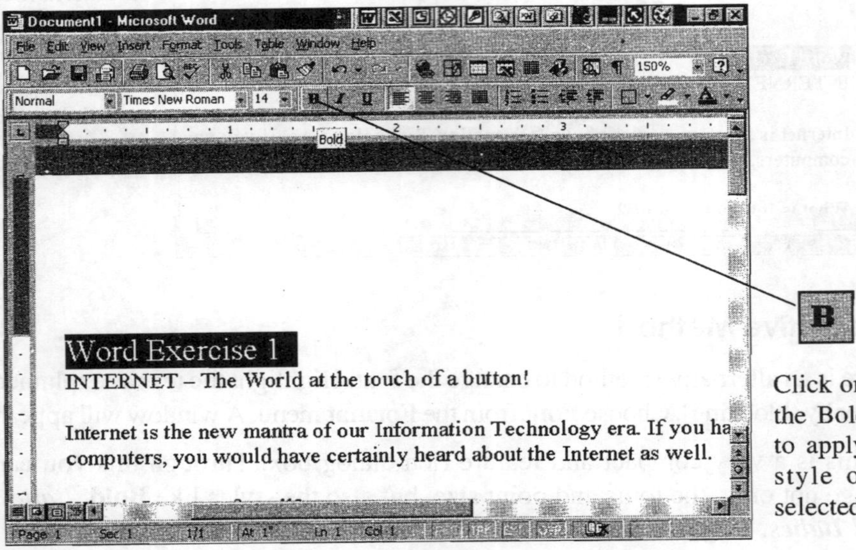

Click once on the Bold icon to apply bold style on the selected text.

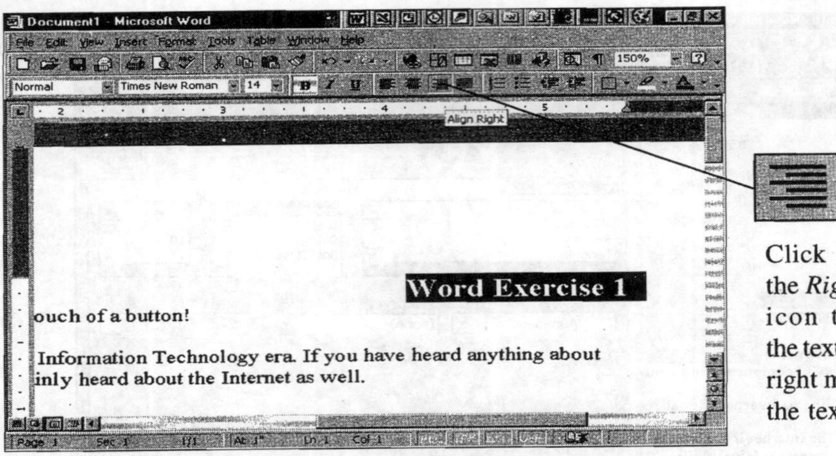

Click once on the *Right Align* icon to align the text with the right margin of the text.

Now let us use the same technique to:

- Change the font,
- Increase the font size,
- Italicise the selected text,

- Underline the selected text, and
- Centre the heading horizontally between the pages.

Fonts are like different handwriting scripts available to you. Just as different people write the same alphabets differently, similarly using the font facility of MS Word, you can choose the way in which your alphabet script is displayed and printed. You can have the same font for the entire document or you could apply different fonts for different pieces of text to make your document appear more interesting and appealing.

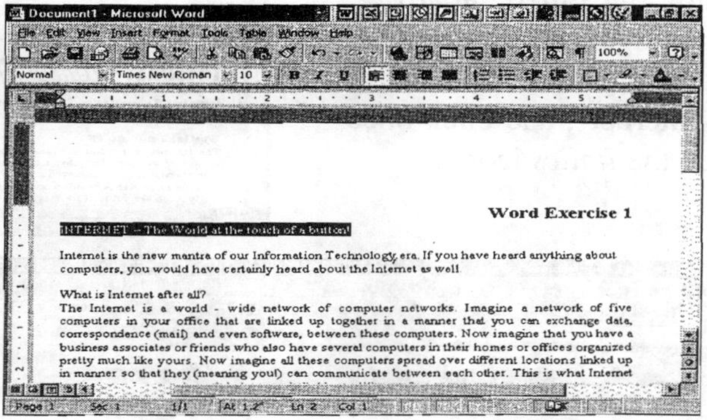

Highlight the document heading "Internet – The world at the touch of a button!" using the technique explained earlier to mark a block.

Click here once to get a pull down list of all the fonts available to you. Choose the *Impact* font by clicking on it.

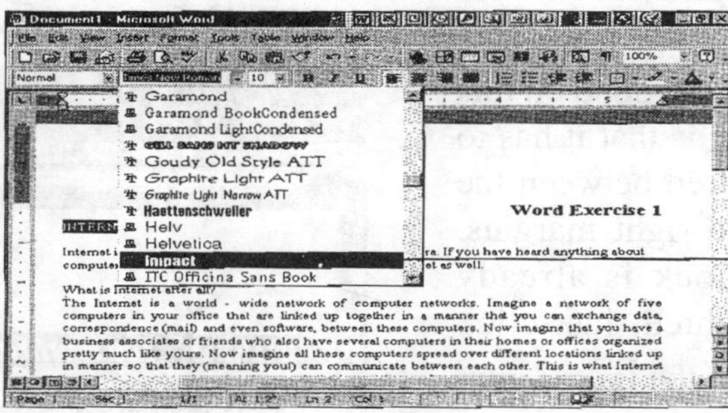

A

A Notice that each font is displayed in its own unique font style, so before you apply the font you can get to see what it looks like.

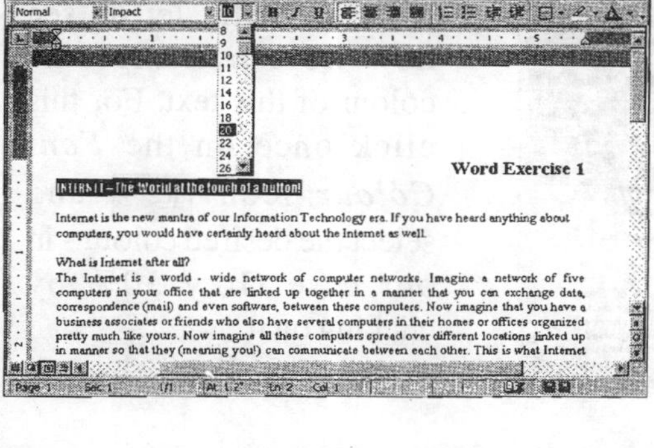

Click here once to increase the font size to 20.

Now since we want to Italicise only "The world at the touch of a button!" and not the entire heading, highlight only this portion, leaving out the word "Internet", and click once on the *Italics* icon.

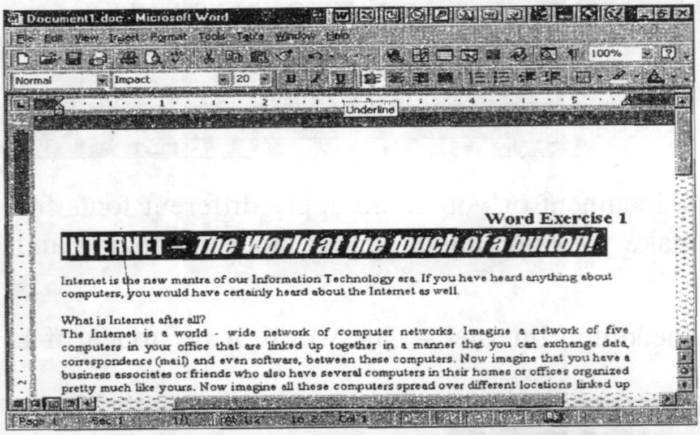

Now highlight the entire heading once again and click once on the *Underline* icon to apply underline style.

The next thing to be done on this heading is that it has to be centred between the left and right margins. The block is already highlighted, just click once on the *Centre Align* icon.

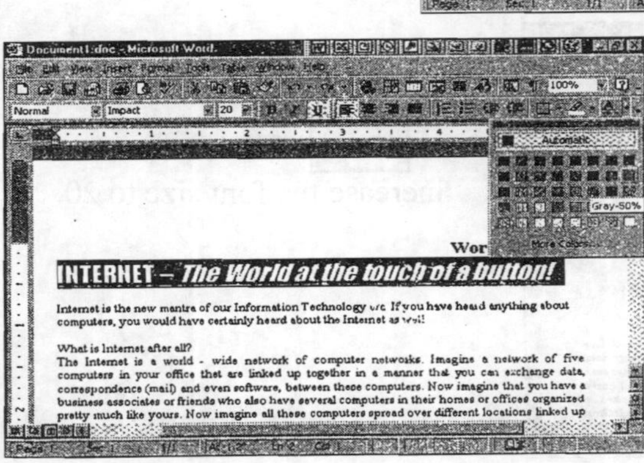

Now finally let us see how we can change the colour of this text. For this click once on the *Font Colour* icon and select the desired colour - in our case Grey 50% by clicking on it.

Now let us move ahead. You would have noticed that typically the first line of a paragraph is slightly indented, i.e., it begins not from the extreme left but slightly ahead. For doing this, place the cursor at the beginning of the first paragraph and press Tab key. You will see that the first line has got indented. Take care not to use the Space Bar to create this space, since this is not only more tedious and time consuming but may also result in different paragraphs having different indent spaces.

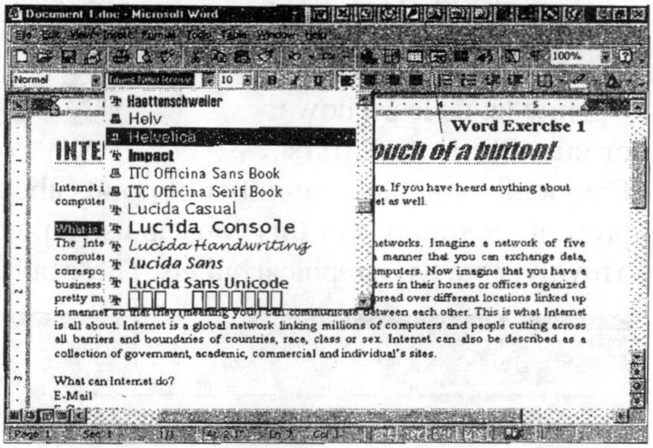

Let us now highlight the paragraph heading "What is Internet after all?" Click here once, [Times New Roman] use the scroll bar to scroll down to the font "Helvetica", click on it to apply it to the selected block.

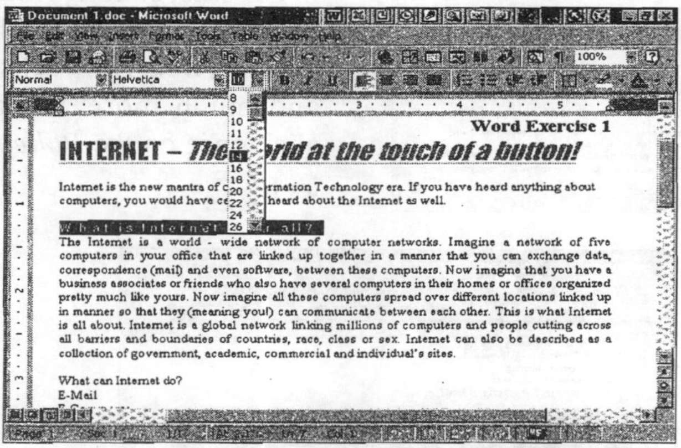

Click here once to get the font size pull down list and select point **14** by clicking on it once. Notice, the text would become bigger.

To give a highlight effect to any block of text, highlight the text and click here once and select the desired highlight by clicking on it.

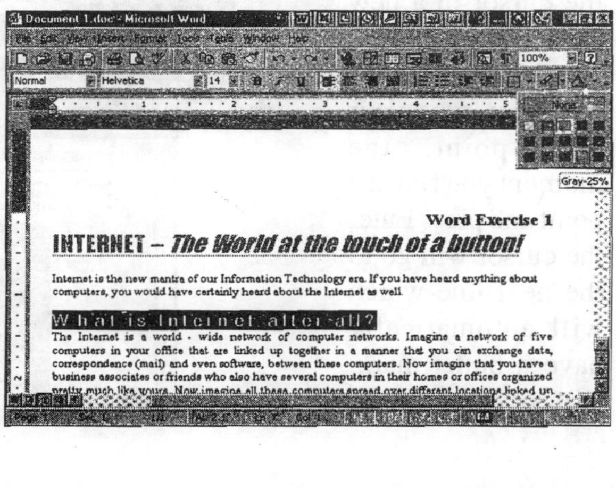

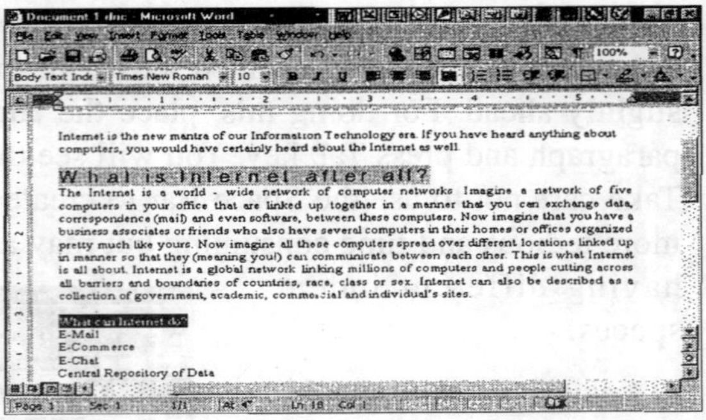

Now move to the next paragraph heading "What can Internet do?" and use the same techniques just learnt to increase the font size, change the font and apply the highlight effect on this text as well.

Now let us learn how to create "bulleted lists". Frequently you have a number of points about a specific topic that you want to present separately. For this you can use bullets. No, not the ones that you put in a revolver but typographical bullets. These bullets are small marks at the beginning of each new point.

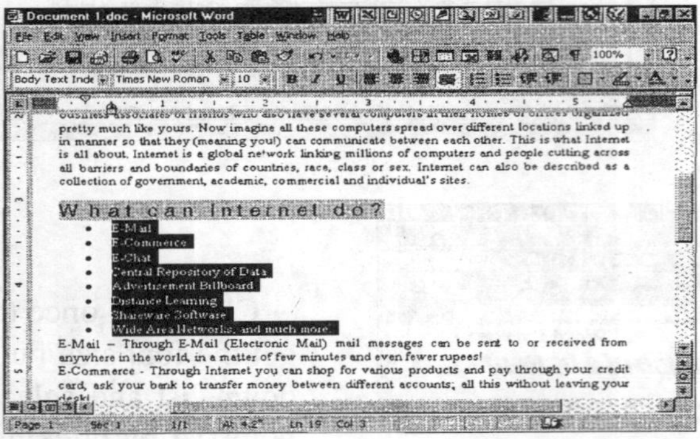

For applying bullets to points that already exist, highlight all the points (like in our case, starting from "E-Mail" and ending with "Wide Area Networks, and much more") and click once on the *Bullets* icon 

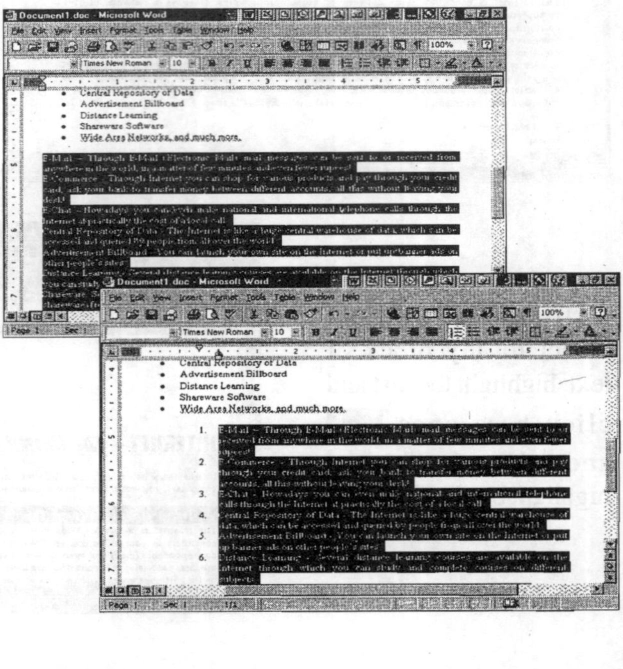

Alternatively you can also have bullet marks appear automatically when you begin a new point. For this, place the cursor in a new blank line and click once on the bulleted list. Now type your first point, the moment you finish a point and press Enter the cursor will go to the next line which will automatically have a bullet mark. When you have finished typing your last point, press Enter to go to a next line and click once again on the *Bullets* icon to turn the bullet list off. *Bullet* icon like most other icons on the *Formatting Tool* bar is a "toggle switch", which means that if you click on it once, it becomes *On* and if you click again on it becomes *Off*.

Similar to the bulleted list is the numbered list. In case of a numbered list each point starts with a point number (1, 2, 3... or A, B, C... I, II, III... etc.) instead of a bullet mark. The procedure for this is similar to that of bullet list. Highlight all the points and click once on the *Numbered List* icon .

Note: Bullets/Numbering can be customised by clicking **Bullets** and **Numbering** from the **Format** menu.

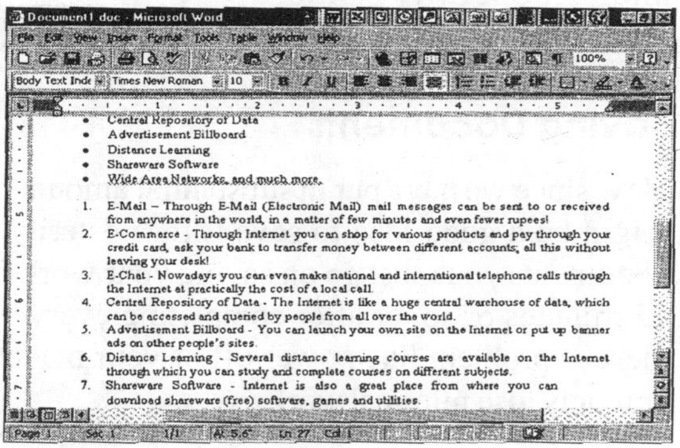

As we can see here that Word is taking the next matter as a part of the above matter, therefore, it is showing the numbered list as sub-points of the above bulleted list. To correct this you indent these points to the left, click once on the *Left Indent* icon . You will notice that all the points have moved to the left by one tab position. In case you want to further indent click on the *Left Indent* icon again. If not satisfied with the results you can always use the *Right Indent* icon to bring back the text by one tab position at a time.

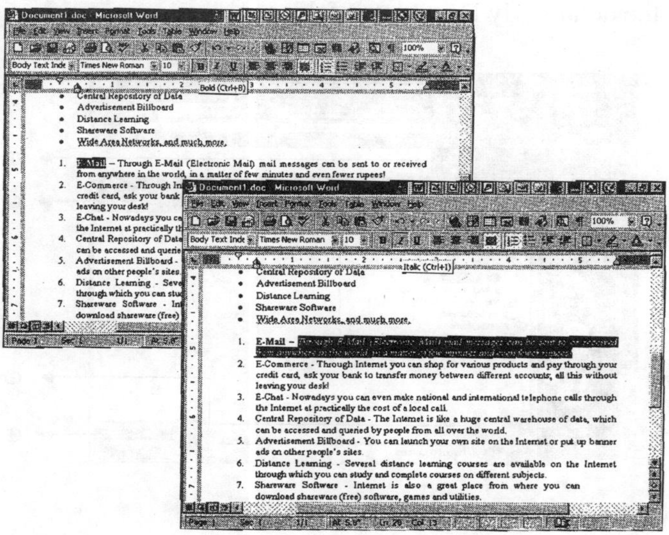

Notice all the points have a running number against them and the matter starts from a neatly aligned straight line. Try doing this manually by typing the numbers and using spacebar to create perfectly aligned text and it might take you more than fifteen minutes to achieve this perfectly, whereas through *Numbered List* icon it is a matter of seconds. Remember computers are all about saving time!

Now take a look at the Exercise 1 format given and apply *Bold* and *Italics* formatting on all the points.

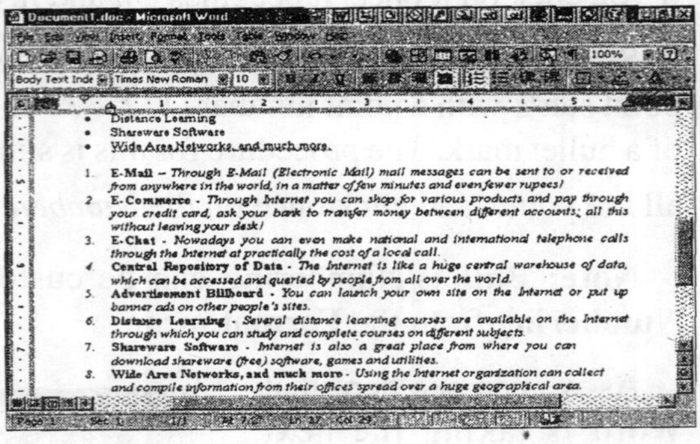

Congratulations! With this step you have completed your first exercise in MS Word. It may have taken you a bit of time to do it the first time but with practice you would become much faster, efficient and hopefully more innovative.

Saving Documents

Now since we have put in substantial amount of work creating this document, it might be a good idea to save it for posterity! In fact, for all your subsequent documents you must go on saving your work from time to time, let us say every 15 minutes or so, or after completing every section. Doing this ensures that if there is problem like power off or your machine has gone into hung state, etc. you only lose minimal work.

① Choose **Save** command from **File** menu or click the Save command icon in the Standard toolbar.

② Type the file name by which you wish to save your file.

③ Specify where you want to save your document. By default MS Word saves your documents in the default My Documents folder.

④ Click on the **Save** button.

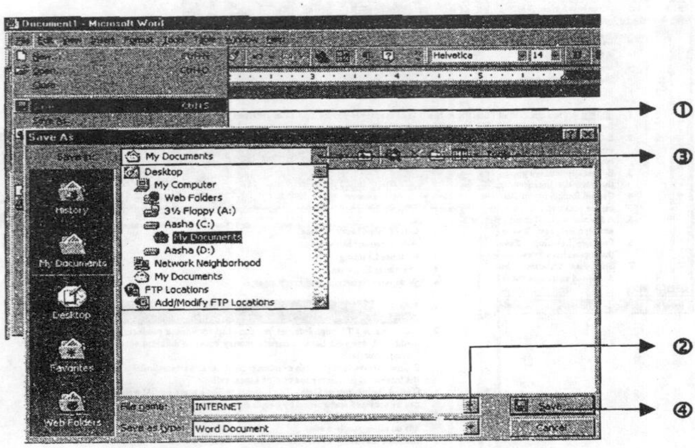

Note: In the **Save As** dialog box specify the name of your document. Although this name can be anything, but it would make a lot of sense to give a meaningful name to your documents, so that just by reading the name you can have the idea of its contents.

Closing the Document

Once your work is completed and you do not wish to continue working with a particular document then you can close that file.

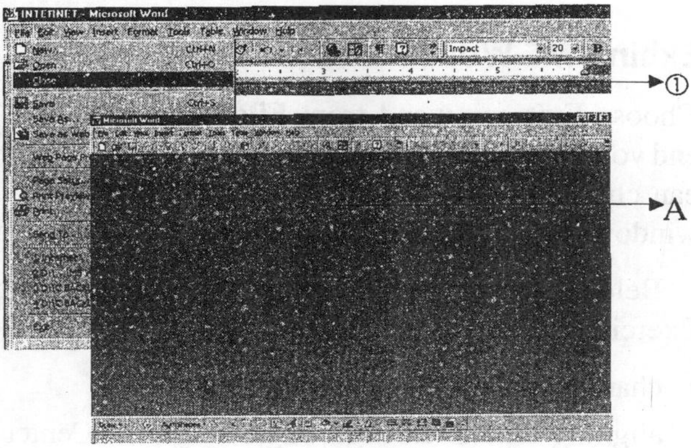

① Choose **Close** command from **File** menu.

A You will notice the exit screen of **MS Word**. If you wish to work on any other file, follow the steps explained later for opening files.

Opening the Document

Once a file is saved and closed, it can be again reopened and used at any time using the open command.

① Choose **Open** command from **File** menu or click the Open command icon in the Standard toolbar.

② Select the correct directory path where your file is stored.

③ Choose the desired file by clicking it once with the mouse.

④ Click once on **Open** button to open the chosen file. You can also double click on the file in rapid succession to open it.

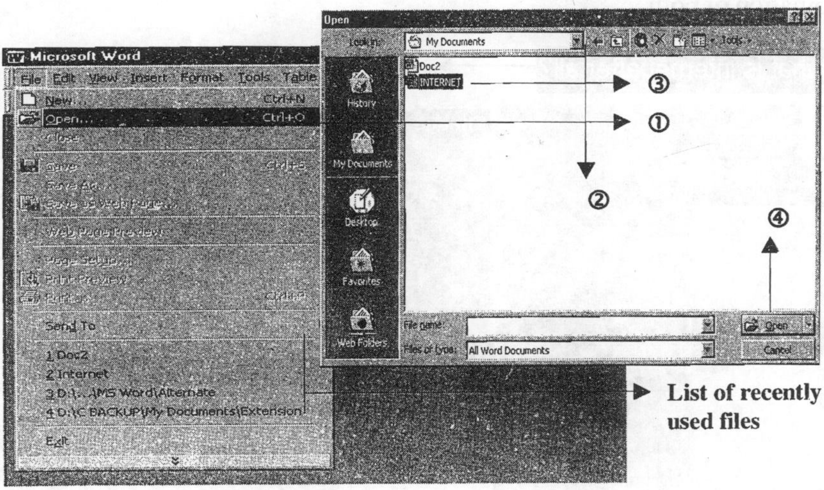

Note: If the file you wish to open is one of the last four files used by you, then that file will be displayed in the list of recent documents at the bottom of the File menu. You can simply click that file to open it.

Exiting MS Word

Click here to quit MS Word

Choose **Exit** command from **File** menu to end your MS Word session. Alternatively you can click on the Close button of the Word window. And you are back to where you started from.

Below is a brief summary of the formatting commands covered in Word Exercise 1:

- changing Font Style and Font Size
- aligning Text (Left Align, Right Align and Center Align)
- justifying Text
- boldfacing, Italicising and Underlining
- indenting paragraphs using the Tab key and 'Increase Indent' and 'Decrease Indent' icons located on the Formatting toolbar
- creating Bulleted Lists
- numbering Lists
- changing the text colour
- highlighting the text

Some additional formatting commands of MS Word are explained below:

Changing Text Case After having typed a particular piece of text, Word allows you to change the text case to lower case, upper case or a combination of both.

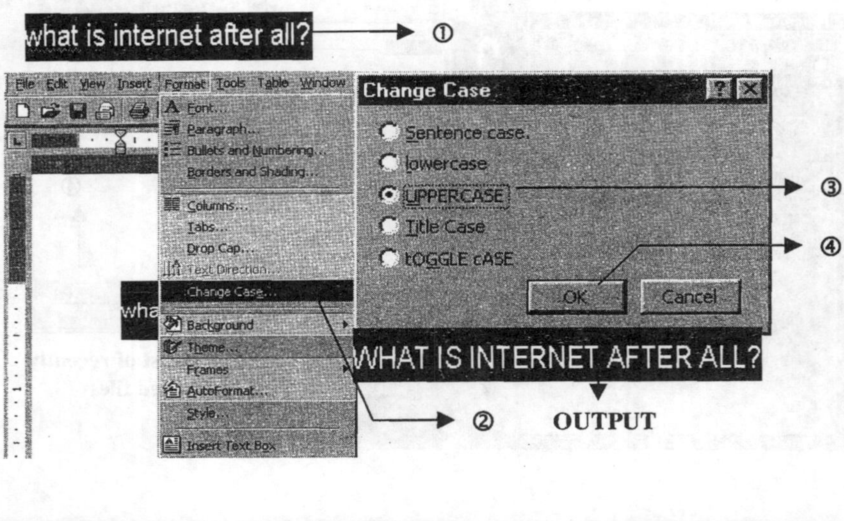

① Select the desired text.

② Select **Change Case** from the **Format** menu. A dialogue box will be displayed to the user.

③ Select an appropriate choice from the dialogue box.

④ Click on the **OK** button to apply the changes.

Paragraph spacing By default paragraphs are single spaced. This spacing can be customised according to the users preference. Paragraph spacing is used to create spaces between paragraphs. It is also possible to create additional spacing between lines of a paragraph. This is called as **Line Spacing**. As discussed earlier, formatting a block of text requires pre-selection of that block. So do not forget to select a block of text before you apply any formatting features.

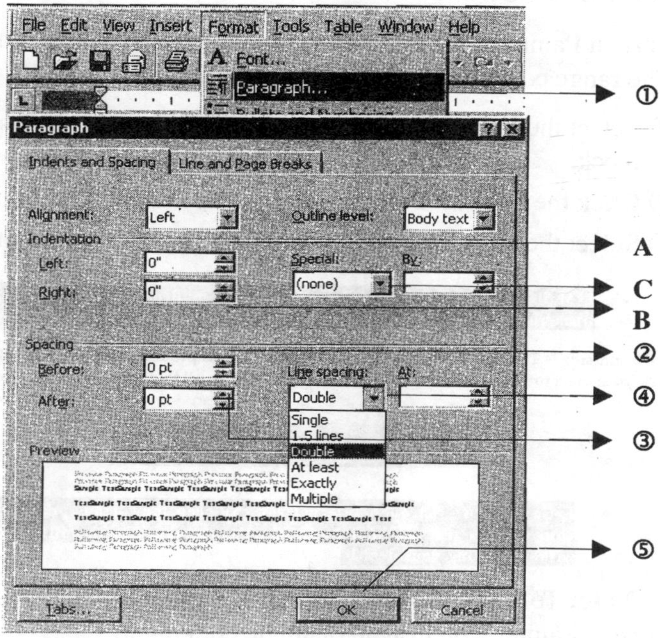

① Select **Paragraph** from the **Format** menu, a dialogue box will be displayed.

② Specify the amount of space you wish to leave before the start of a paragraph by clicking on the spinner or by directly typing a value.

③ Specify the amount of space you want to leave after the end of a paragraph by clicking on the spinner or by directly typing a value.

④ From the line spacing drop down box select the desired spacing. You can also choose 'Multiple' line spacing by selecting 'Multiple' from the drop down box and specifying the desired number of lines in the adjacent box (**'At'**).

⑤ Click on the **OK** button to apply the changes.

Indenting using paragraph dialogue box Paragraphs can be indented by specifying the desired indent measurements in the paragraph dialogue box. (Please refer the screenshot)

A Specify the left indentation by clicking on the spinner or by directly typing a value.

B Specify the right indentation by clicking on the spinner or by directly typing a value.

C If you want a first line or hanging indent then select this option using the **Special** drop down box. You can then set the amount of the desired indent in the adjacent box (**By**).

Format Painter

Format Painter is used to transfer formatting from one range of text to another. The range could be a word, a line, a paragraph or a table.

① Select the range containing the formatting that you wish to apply to another block.

② Click the **Format Painter** icon on the Standard toolbar.

③ Select the range on which you wish to apply the formatting.

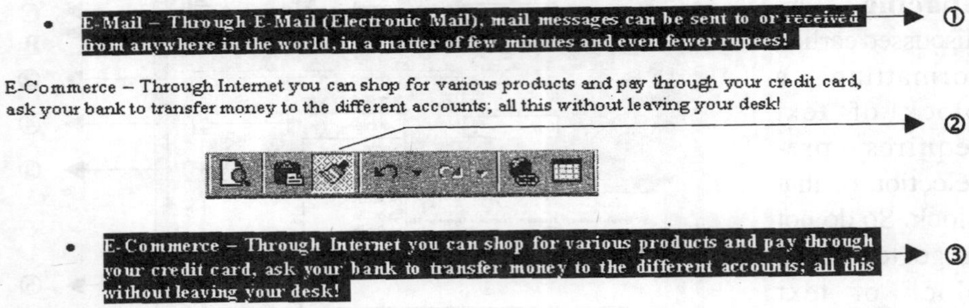

Note: To apply the same formatting to multiple locations, double click the Format Painter icon instead of single clicking it.

Formatting Pages

Page formatting involves setting the page margins, page size, page orientation etc. It is usually a good practice to specify the page settings before you start working on your document. MS Word adjusts the text in your document to fit in the specified page margins. By default whenever you create a new document, the document is created with predefined page settings. **Page Setup** can be accessed from the **File** menu.

Changing Page Margins

① Click on the **Margins** tab/folio.

② Specify the **Top**, **Bottom**, **Left** and **Right** margins, to specify how much blank space you wish to leave on the sides, top and bottom of each page.

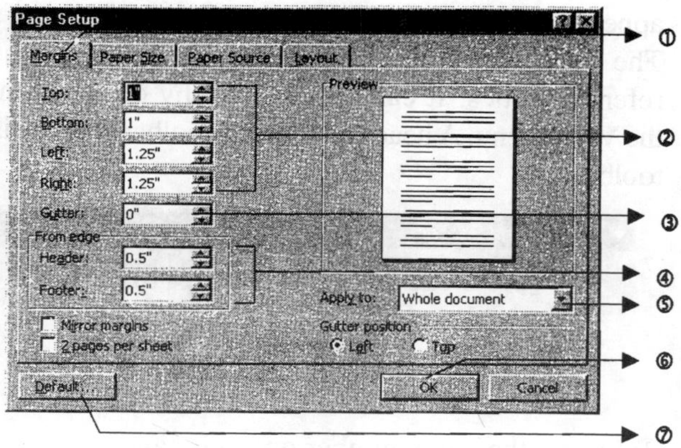

③ Specify the **Gutter** margin.

④ Specify the **Header** and **Footer** positions. They are measured from the edge of the page (Header and Footer discussed later in the chapter).

⑤ Settings can be applied for all the pages in a document or for a particular page. Select **Whole Document** if you wish to apply the settings for the entire document or **This Point Forward** if you wish to apply the settings for the text after the current cursor position.

⑥ Click on the **OK** button to apply the changes.

⑦ Click on the **Default** button if you wish to restore the original settings of MS Word.

Changing Page Size and Orientation

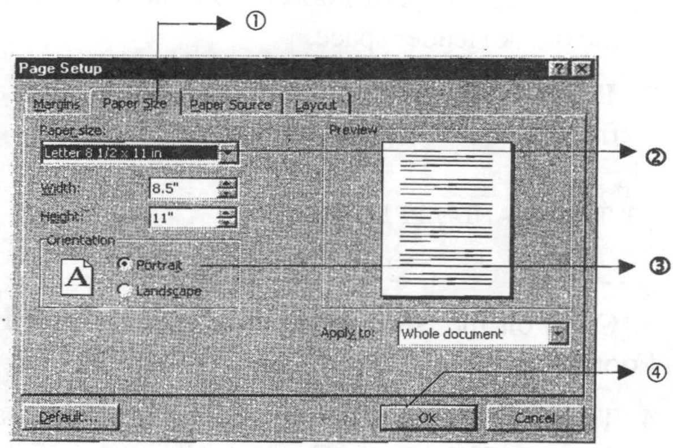

① Click on the **Paper Size** tab/folio.

② Specify the paper size by clicking on the **Paper Size** drop down box. If the paper size desired by you is not available in the drop down box then you can define the desired paper size dimensions by selecting **Customize** from the drop down box. After selecting customize from the drop down box, enter the width and height of the paper in the **Width** and **Height** boxes.

③ Select the page orientation - **Portrait** for Vertical or **Landscape** for Horizontal.

④ Click on the **OK** button to apply the changes.

Setting up Header and Footer Another helpful feature of Word is Header and Footer. Using this features you can print a standard piece of text and /or an image at the top or end of each page of your document. Headers appear at the top of each page and footers appear at the bottom of each page. The most common use of Headers and Footers is to print page numbers and reference titles. It can be accessed by clicking on **Header and Footer** from the **View** menu. A header and footer toolbar will be displayed below the formatting toolbar.

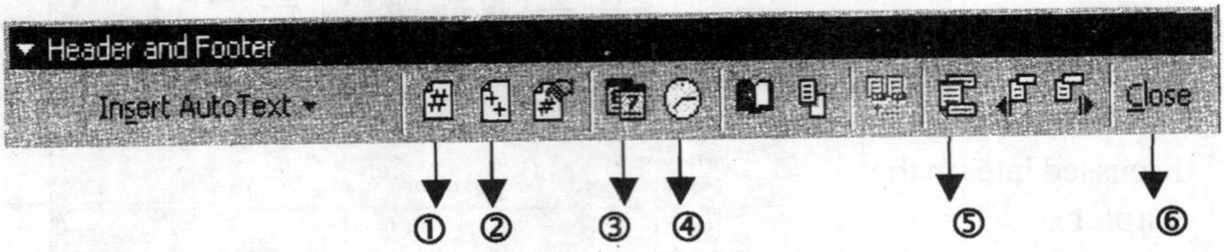

① Inserts the page number on each page.

② Inserts the number of pages in the document.

③ Inserts the current date.

④ Inserts the current time.

⑤ Allows the user to switch between Header and Footer.

⑥ Closes the Header and Footer toolbar.

To set up a Header and Footer

1. Select **Header and Footer** from the **View** menu. Word places the cursor in the blank Header space.
2. Type the desired text into the Header or insert any of the standard functions from the Header and Footer toolbar.

Header

IT TOOLS AND APPLICATIONS

3. Click on the **Switch between Header and Footer** icon to switch to the Footer.
4. Type the desired text into the Footer or insert any of the standard functions from the Header and Footer toolbar.

Footer

1 of 1   31/05/2003   3:10 AM

5. Click on the **Close** icon of the Header and Footer toolbar to close the toolbar.

Inserting Page Numbers Page Numbers can be inserted by making use of Headers and Footers. Alternatively page numbers can be inserted directly by selecting **Page Numbers** from the **Insert** menu. A dialogue box is displayed as shown below:

① Select the **Position** where you want the page number to app,,ear (Top or Bottom).

② Specify the **Alignment** of the page number in the selected position (Left, Right or Center).

③ Click on this button for formatting the appearance of page number in the document.

④ Click on the **OK** button to apply the changes.

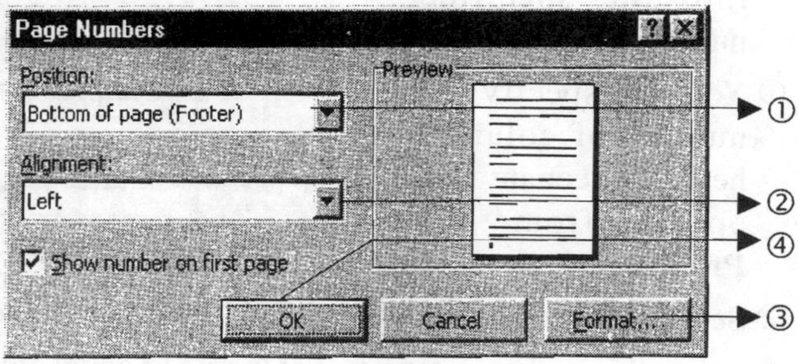

Creating multiple sections By default a new document contains only one section. (If no section break has been inserted explicitly.) Word allows inserting multiple sections into the same document. This feature allows the user to apply different formatting styles within the same document. Follow the steps below to insert a new section:

1. Place the cursor at which you wish to start a new section.
2. Select **Break** from the **Insert** menu.
3. Select one of the section break options from the dialogue box.

① Starts a section at the top of the next page.

② Starts a section without moving the following text to the next page.

③ Starts a section on the next even numbered page. If required it leaves a blank odd page.

④ Starts a section on the next odd numbered page. If required it leaves a blank even page.

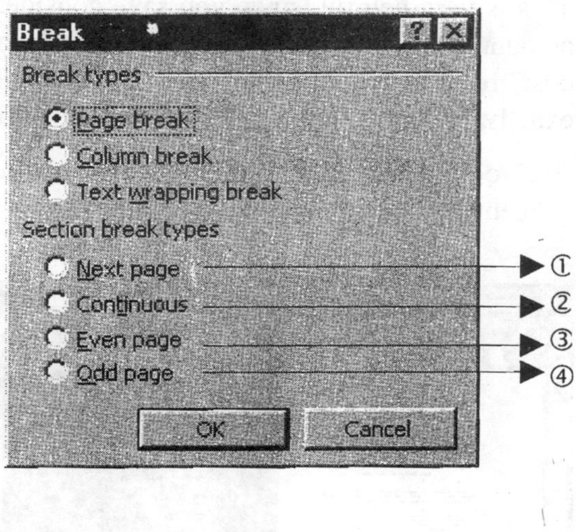

Setting up Multiple Columns

Word allows you to arrange your text in newspaper like columns. To set the number of columns for your document, follow the steps below:

1. Choose **Columns** from the **Format** menu.

2. Select the number of columns and then click on the **OK** button to split your document into the specified number of columns.

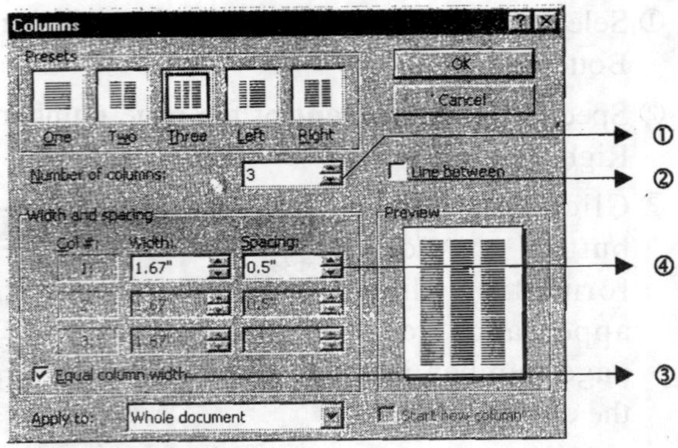

① You can specify the number of columns here or select any one option from the **Presets**.

② Select this option to add a vertical line between the columns.

③ Select this option if you want columns of equal column width.

④ To vary the width and spacing of columns, first clear the Equal Column Width check box and then enter the **Width** and **Spacing** for individual columns.

Print Preview

Because of advanced *WYSIWYG* feature (**W**hat **Y**ou **S**ee **I**s **W**hat **Y**ou **G**et) in-built in MS Office, you can see a preview, on screen of what you wish to print. In most cases, this preview would give you an exact replica of what your printer would print. This is very helpful, since you save considerable amount of time and money (in printing and stationery cost) by making sure that your document looks exactly the way it should, before you finally print it.

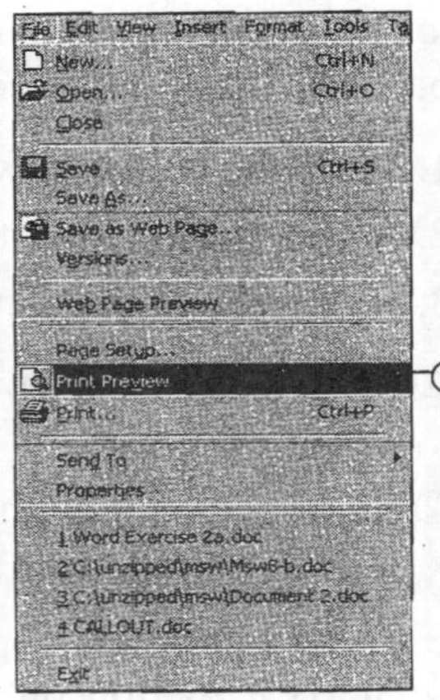

① Choose **Print Preview** command from **File** menu.

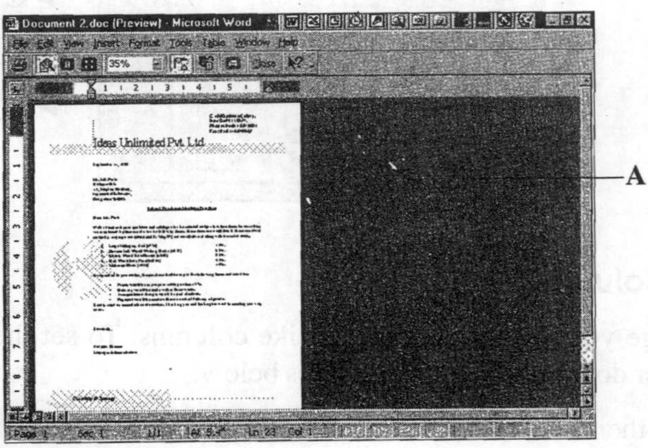

A This is what appears on the screen. An exact copy of the page, which your printer would print. If you are happy with what you see, go ahead and print the document. If not, go back to the main screen by clicking on **Close** button and make necessary changes.

Icons for Printing Toolbar

Print
Prints out the displayed document according to the default settings.

Magnifier
Using this button you can change the Print Preview function mode. When the mouse pointer looks like a magnifying glass, you are in view mode, and when the mouse pointer is normal, you are in edit mode.

One Page
Clicking this button causes Word to display one page at a time.

Multiple Pages
Using this button you can have Word display several pages at a time.

Zoom Control
The selected zoom level can be seen in the text box. By clicking the arrow button you can select another one of the available zoom alternatives.

View Ruler
Click this button to hide ruler. Clicking the button again causes the ruler to reappear.

Shrink to Fit
By choosing this button you can have Word shrink the document.

Full Screen
Hides everything except the document and the toolbar. Clicking again restores normal view.

Help
Changes the mouse pointer into a question mark, whereupon you can select a command to get information about it.

Close
Closes Print Preview mode.

Printing Documents

Print command can be accessed from the **File** menu. Alternatively you can click on the Print icon from the Standard toolbar. A Print dialogue box is displayed to the user where different print options can be set.

① Select your printer from this list. In most of the cases default printer would be the right one. All the printers attached to your computer will be displayed in the drop down box.

② Prints all the pages in the document.

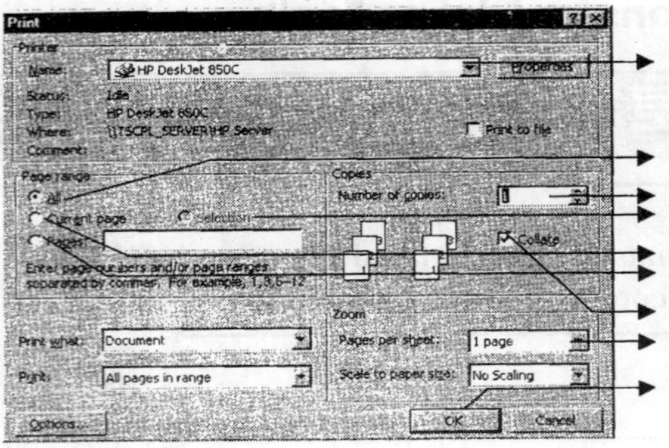

③ Prints only the current page; current page is the page where the cursor is currently placed.

④ Prints a range of pages in your document. Multiple page-ranges can also be specified by separating each range with a comma. For Example, 10-13,50-55,70-81 would print pages from 10 to 13 then 50 to 55 and then 70 to 81.

⑤ Prints a selected portion of a page.

⑥ Prints the specified number of copies. By default only one copy is printed whenever a print command is executed.

⑦ Collate option is very useful when printing multiple sets of a document. If this option is selected then the first set is printed completely and then it would proceed to the next set. If this option is not selected then Word would print the specified number of copies for the first page and then the second page and so on till the completion of the document. In this case the user has to rearrange the individual sets.

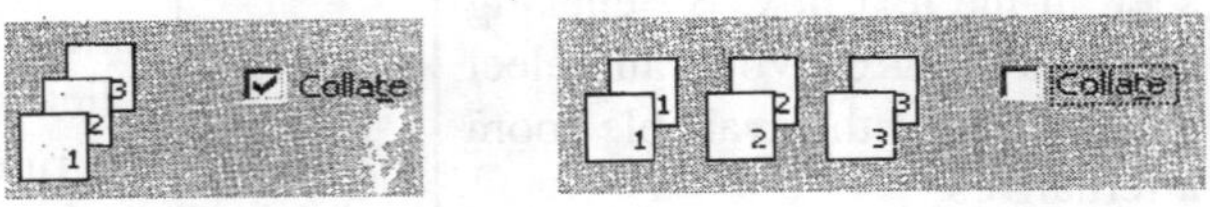

⑧ Prints the specified number of pages in a single sheet. If you wish to print 4 pages in one sheet then select 4 pages from the drop down box.

⑨ Click on the **OK** button to print your document(s).

Editing and Proofing Tools

Spelling and Grammar is one of the coolest features of Word and frees you from the bother of concentrating on the spelling and grammar of your text. Spell checker compares the words in your document with those in its main dictionary (inbuilt in MS Word). The main dictionary contains most common words, but it might not include proper names, technical terms, acronyms, and so on.

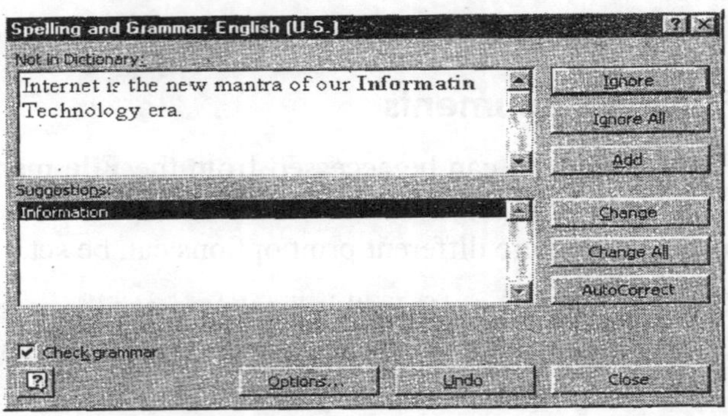

Spelling and Grammar can be accessed by choosing **Spelling and Grammar** from the **Tools** menu. A dialogue box will be displayed to the user.

Explanations for some of the options in the spell-check program are given below:

Suggestions	Based upon the misspelt word, Word would try to think of all possible suggestions for the correct word. You may either choose from the words suggested or simply type the correct word and click once on the change button.
Ignore	Though this word is not found in the dictionary, leave it unchanged.
Ignore all	Ignore this word for all subsequent occurrences.
Change	Change this word with the suggestion specified.
Change all	Change this word for all subsequent occurrences, with the suggestion specified.
Add	Add this word to the dictionary.
Auto-Correct	Add the suggested correction to Auto-Correct. AutoCorrect feature allows to automatically detect and correct typos, misspelled words, grammatical errors, and incorrect capitalisation. For example, if you type **teh** plus a space, then AutoCorrect replaces what you have typed with "the."
Options	For changing Spell Check's default settings.
Undo Last	Cancel one of the previous replacements.
Cancel	Terminate Spell Check and return to the document.

Spell Check's Default Settings

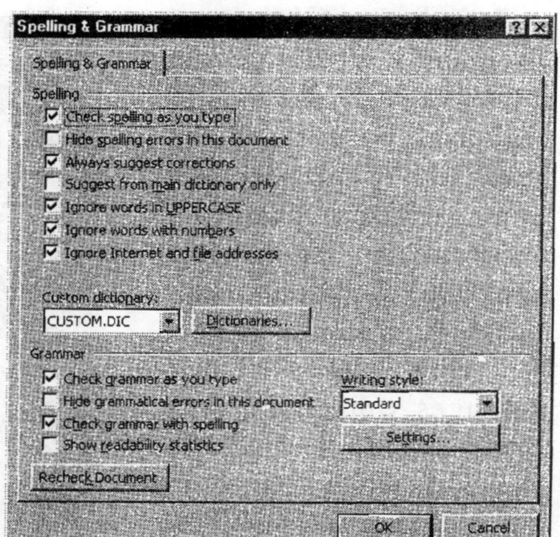

These can be accessed by clicking on the options button in the Spell Check dialogue box or by choosing **Options** from the **Tools** menu. By default the spelling and grammar checks are enabled. This is the reason we often find red and green wavy underlines in our word document. A red wavy underline indicates a spelling mistake where as a green one indicates a grammatical mistake. Various settings for Spelling and

Grammar are displayed in the given below screenshot. However, they can be customised according to the users requirement.

AutoText MS Word displays a Tool tip text when you type the first few characters of a date or an AutoText entry, at which point you can insert the entry by pressing the Enter key or continue typing. You can define your own entries and then add them to the AutoText entry list. This would help in minimising typing as well as typing errors. This feature can be accessed by choosing **Autotext** from the **Insert** menu.

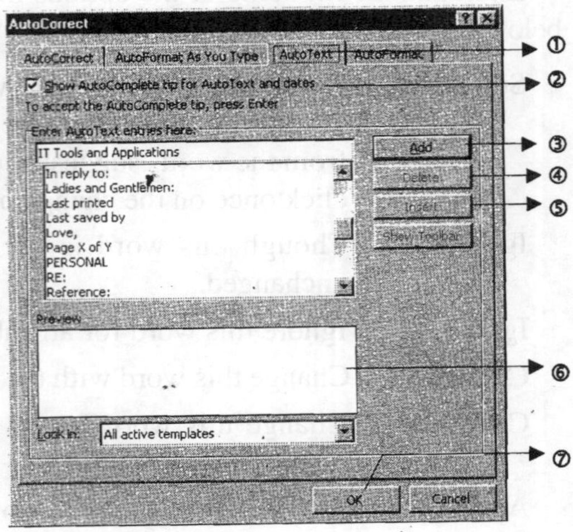

① Click on the **AutoText** tab/folio.

② Select this feature if you wish the tooltip text to be displayed when you type the first few characters of an AutoText entry.

③ Click on this button to add the entry typed in the textbox to the AutoText list.

④ Click on this button to delete the selected autotext entry from the drop down box.

⑤ Click on this button to insert the selected autotext entry into your document.

⑥ Displays the content of the selected autotext entry.

⑦ Click on the **OK** button to apply the changes.

Track Changes Frequently several people collaborate to finalise a single document. For instance, you may have prepared a contract agreement and then want to finalise it after seeking comments and advice from several people. In such cases Track Changes option is very useful to keep track of who has made which changes to the document. Once enabled,

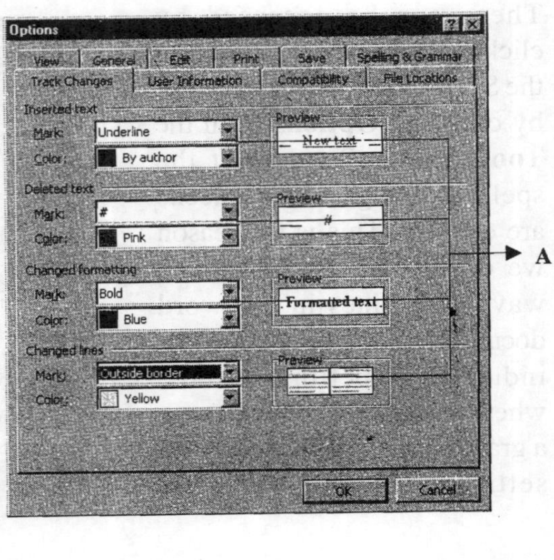

Word tracks all the changes made to your document. Changes could include insertion/deletion of text, formatting or moving text from one place to another in the document. Word makes use of revision marks to show the tracked changes to the user. A revision mark shows where an insertion, deletion or any other editing change has been made in the document. Word allows you to specify how the inserted or deleted text should appear in your document. These settings can be customised by clicking on the **Track Changes** tab/folio in the **Options** dialogue box from the **Tools** menu.

A You can specify the revision marks as well as the colour for various changes (Inserted text, Deleted text, Changed Formatting and Changed Lines). Clicking on **OK** button will then apply the specified settings.

Steps for Tracking changes in a document:

1. Open the desired file.
2. Click on the **Track Changes** icon from the Reviewing toolbar. If the Reviewing toolbar is not visible then select the **Reviewing** toolbar by choosing **Toolbars** from the **View** menu.
3. Make the changes you want by inserting, deleting, or moving text or graphics.

Tracked changes would appear as follows:

Internet is the new mantra of our I# Technology era. If you have heard anything about computers, you would have # as well. IT TOOLS AND APPLICATION

The following exercise makes use of two new features of Word:

WORD EXERCISE 2

Antique Arts

13 Mayfair Building, Jayamahal Extension, Bangalore 560046

Invoice / Bill

Customer Name		Bill. No.	
Customer Address		Bill. Date.	
Kind Attention		Ref. No.	

SL.NO	DETAILS	RATE	QTY	AMOUNT

Taxes	
Delivery Status	
Warranty Period	
Payment Period	

For Customer

Name

Designation

Company Seal

For AntiqueArts

Name

Designation

Company Seal

Creating Tables A table is made up of a grid of cells that you can fill with text and graphics. Horizontal grid of cells is called a Row and vertical grid of cells is called a column. Tables are often used to organise and present information, but they have a variety of other uses as well. Word allows you to create tables and format tables.

Inserting Graphics There are two basic types of graphics that you can use to enhance your MS Word documents – Drawing Objects and Pictures. Drawing objects include textboxes, curves, lines, and other objects. These objects can be accessed from the Drawing toolbar. Pictures are graphics that have been created using any graphics software. They include bitmaps, scanned pictures and photographs, and MS Word's inbuilt Clipart gallery. You enhance these objects with colors, patterns, borders, and other effects.

Creating Tables

① Type the name of the Company, Address and Document heading. Place the cursor after the line 'Invoice / Bill'.

② Keep the table icon pressed and a grid line box would appear. Drag the mouse. Highlight the number of rows and columns that you wish to have. In our example, 3 rows and 4 columns are selected. A table with the required number of rows and columns with dotted lines would appear.

③ In case the table goes beyond the right margin line, place the mouse on the right most column edge and drag it so that the last column fits within the right margin of the page.

④ Repeat step ③ for fitting the table within the page left margin.

⑤ Type the column titles.

Notes :

1 Use the same technique explained in step ③ to size individual columns width.

2 You can move from one cell to another by pressing Tab key or arrow keys from the keyboard.

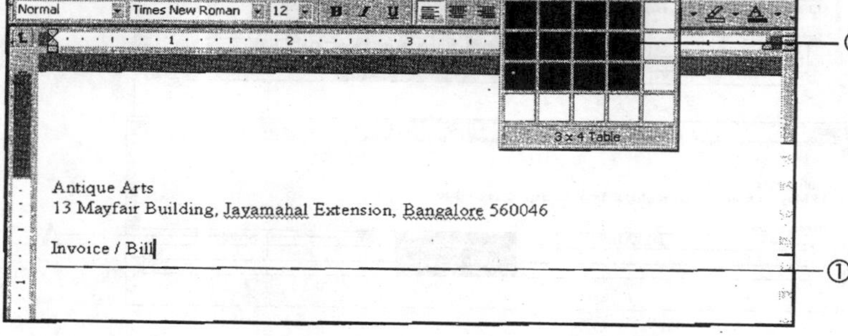

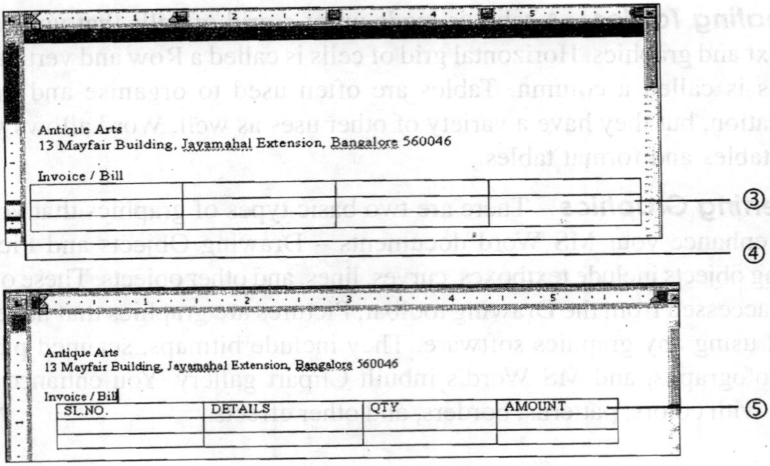

Inserting Columns

① In case you wish to insert another column called 'Rate' before the 'Qty' column; you can highlight an entire column by simply placing the cursor at the top of the column so that it looks like a thick arrowhead. Clicking once would automatically highlight the entire column. Alternatively, you can place the cursor inside any row in the desired columns (the column before which you wish to insert another column) and choose the option **Select column** from the **Table** menu. The selected area is shown in dark background.

② Choose **Columns to the left** from **Insert Command** from the **Table** menu.

A Another blank column would automatically be inserted before the 'Qty' column. Type the column heading 'Rate'.

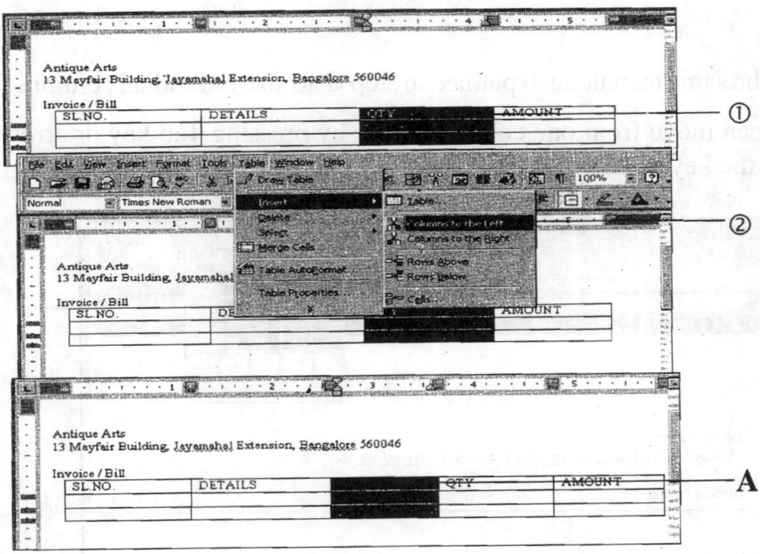

Inserting Rows

Now we would need more rows for typing the details in the bill.

① Highlight any blank row by choosing the option **Select Row** from **Table** menu.

② Click on this icon repeatedly or choose **Insert Row** from **Table menu** to insert as many rows you want.

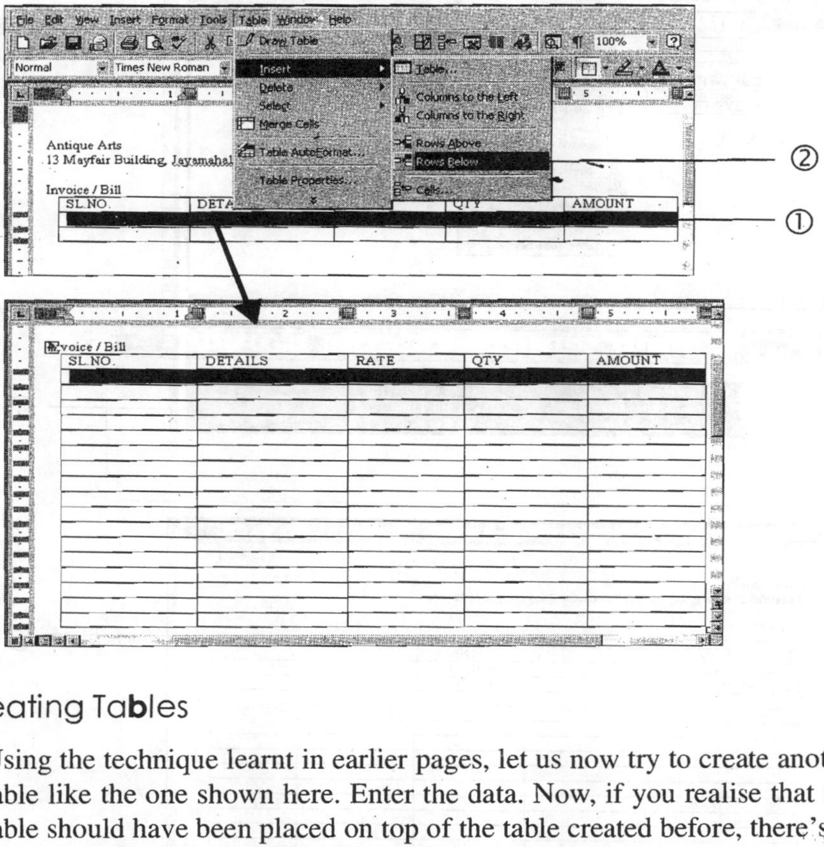

Creating Tables

① Using the technique learnt in earlier pages, let us now try to create another table like the one shown here. Enter the data. Now, if you realise that this table should have been placed on top of the table created before, there's no problem. Follow the following steps to move it to its right place.

② Place the cursor anywhere inside the new table.

③ Choose **Table** command from **Select** option from **Table** menu. The entire matter would be highlighted.

④ Click on **Cut** icon from Standard Toolbar to cut the table or alternatively choose the **Cut** command from the **Edit** menu. The customer details table would no longer be visible here.

⑤ Place the cursor above the table on top of which you wish to have the latter one and click on **Paste** icon or choose **Paste** command from **Edit** menu. The customer details table would now appear here.

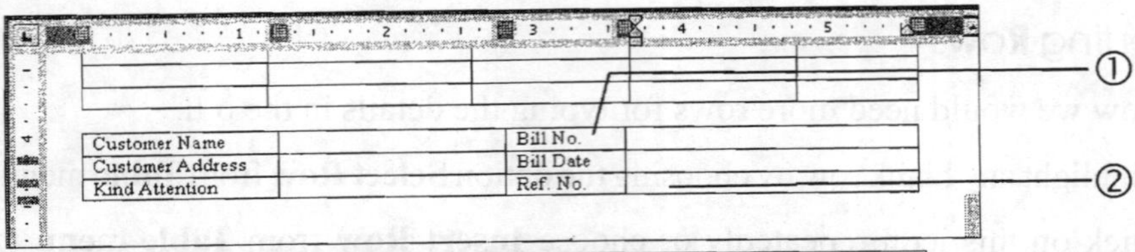

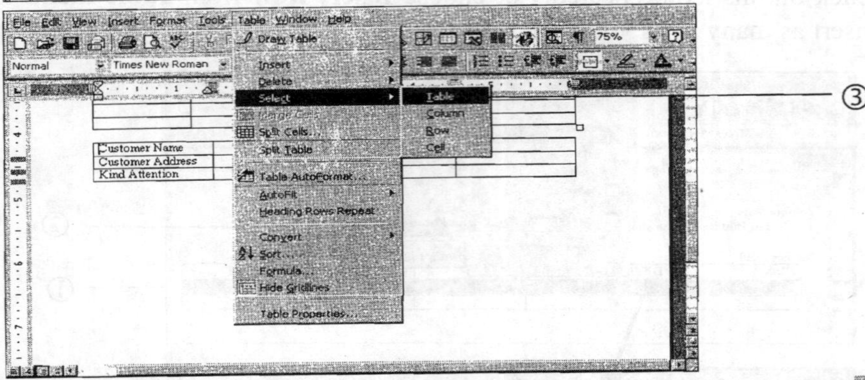

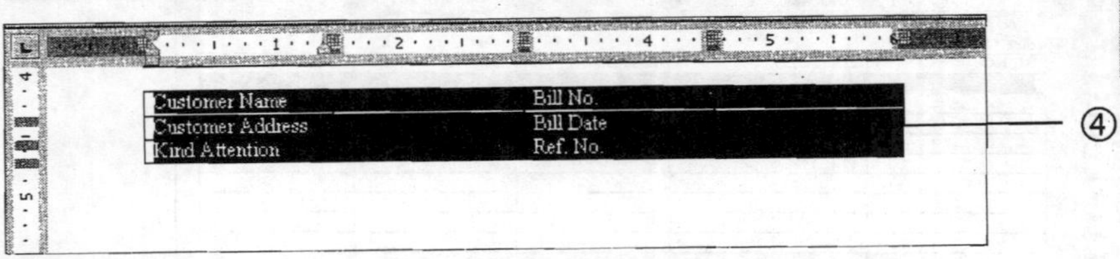

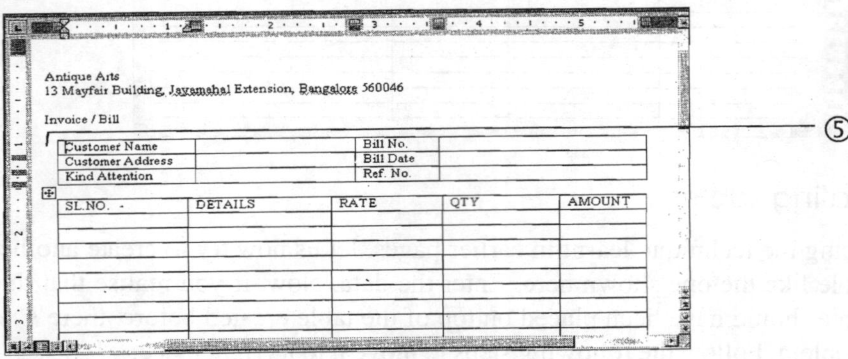

Creating More Tables

① Let's create the last table required in our example. Move the cursor to the place where you want the new table.

② Choose **Insert Table** from **Table** menu.

③ Specify the number of rows and columns required by you, say 2 columns and 4 rows for our example, and click on **OK** button.

④ Change the column width as per your requirement.

⑤ Type the required data as shown in the screen shot below:

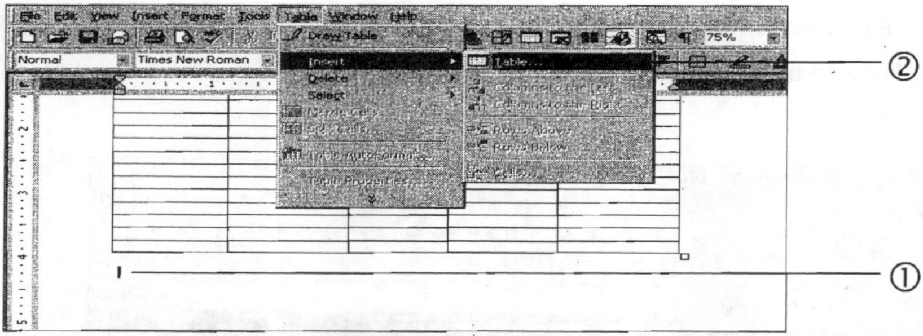

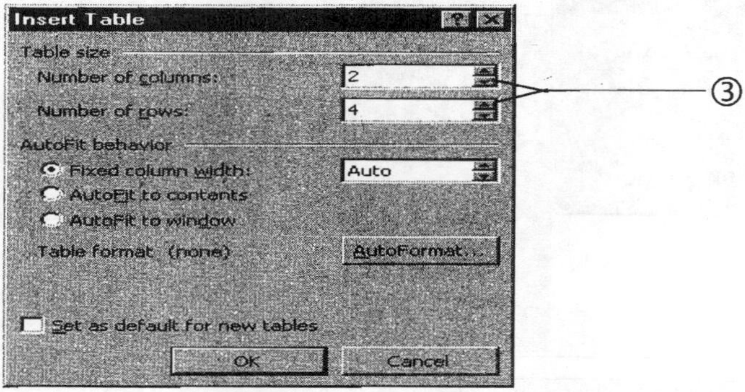

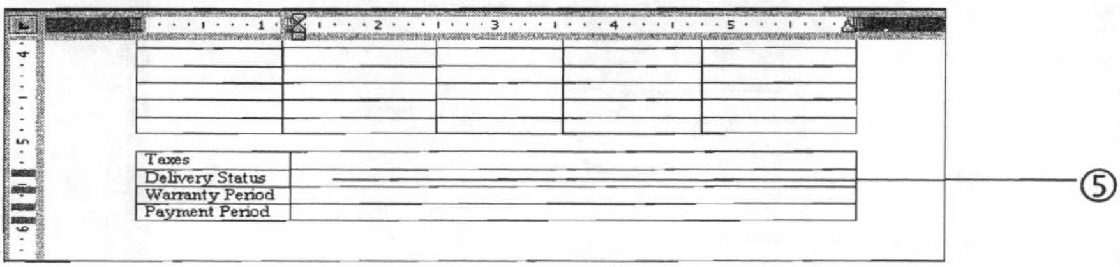

Since the structure of the table is now ready, you can simply type the required matter and do the necessary text formatting.

Borders

Now, let us start formatting. In order to start formatting our table we would need the Borders Toolbar.

① Choose **Tables and Borders** command from the **Toolbar** options from the **View** menu.

② Place the cursor in the first table. Choose **Select Table** from **Table** menu.

③ Select the line style that you like.

④ Click here to open borders frame.

⑤ Click here to apply style to '**All**' border frame.

A Final Result!

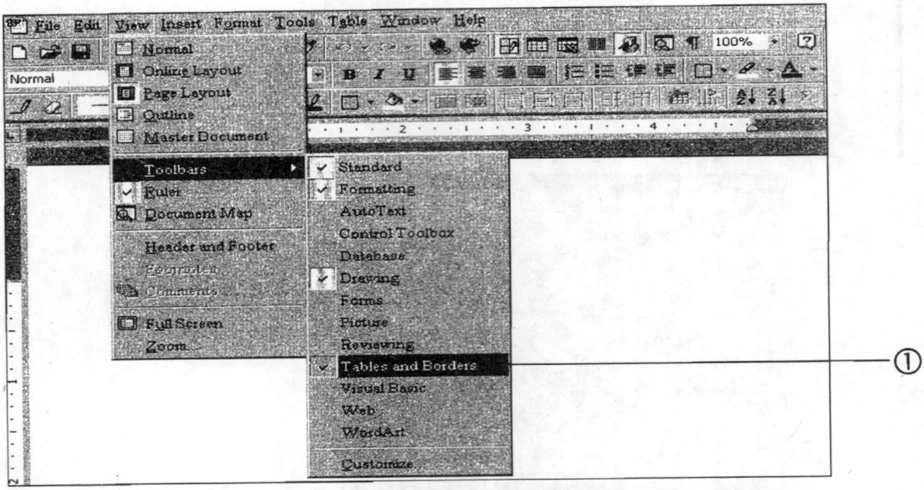

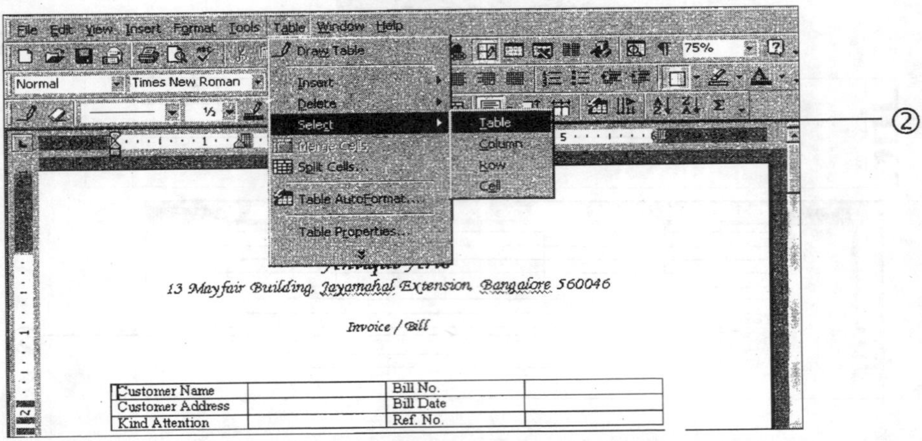

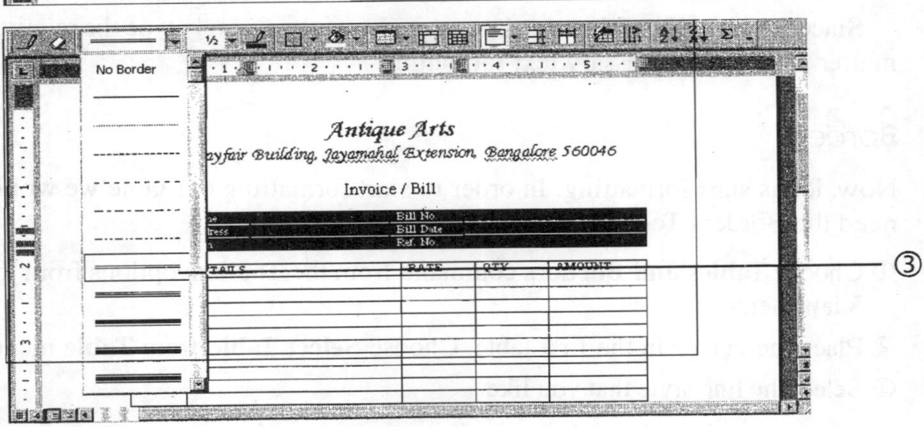

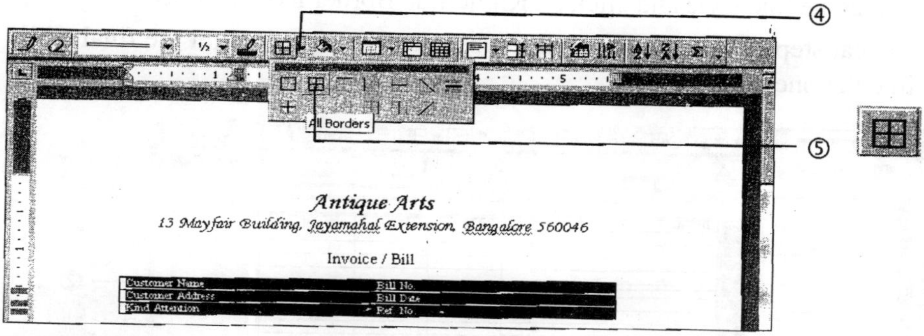

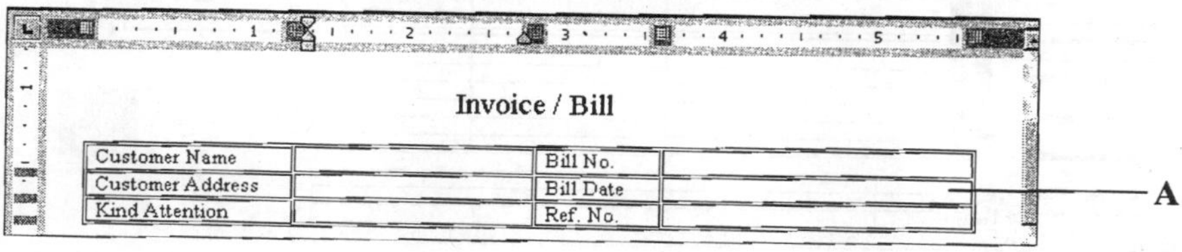

More Borders

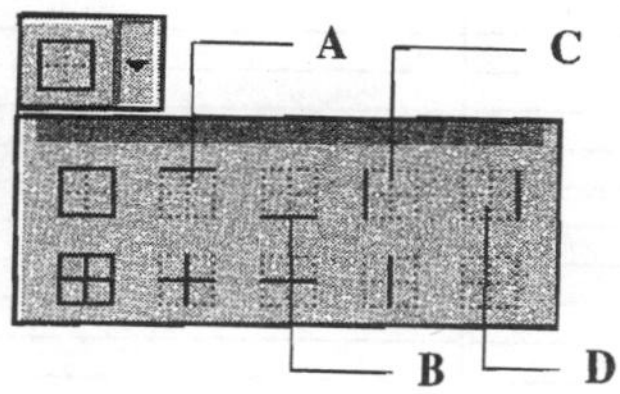

For Qty, Rate and Amount Table, we wish to apply only column border and not the row border. Therefore, border command would have to be applied individually to each column.

① Choose the Table by clicking **Select Table** from **Table** menu. Click this icon to apply the outside border.

A Applies top line border for the selected range.

B Applies bottom border.

C Applies left side.

D Applies right side.

② Select the first column.

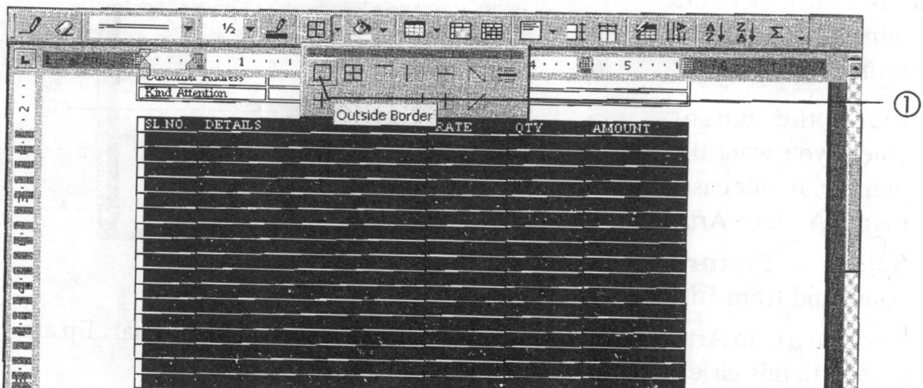

③ Select the line style and click on Right Side Border icon to apply.

④ Repeat steps ② and ③ for all the subsequent columns to get the final table like the one here.

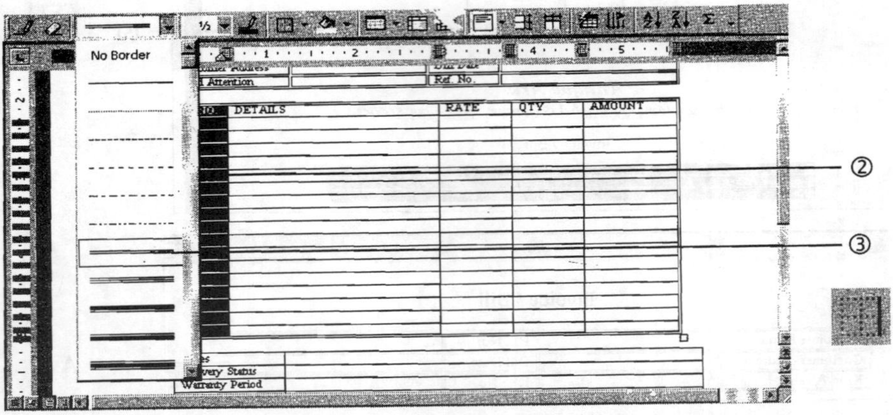

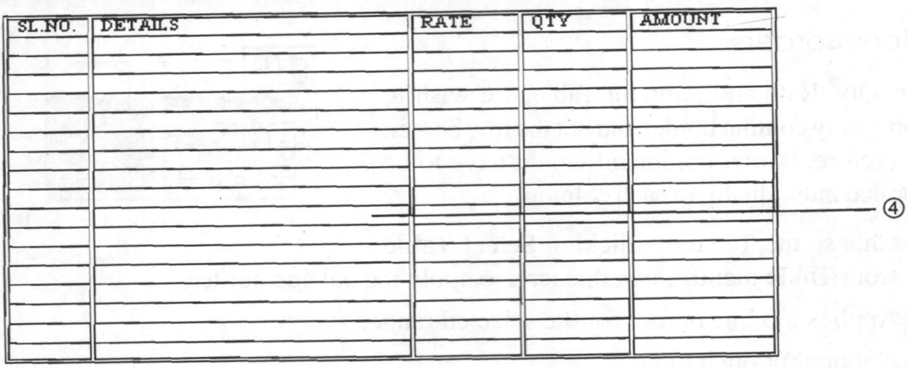

Insert Picture

Now let us try to improve the look of the document still further by inserting a graphic.

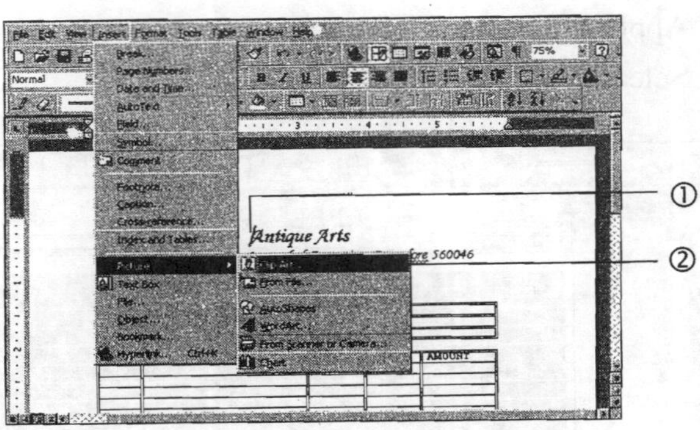

① Place the cursor where you want the graphic. In our case, before Antique Arts.

② Select **Picture** command from **Insert** menu.

③ Click on a Clip Art category from which you can select an individual clip art image. In this case click on Government category.

④ Click on the picture that you want to insert.

⑤ Choose **Insert Clip** command from the options given.

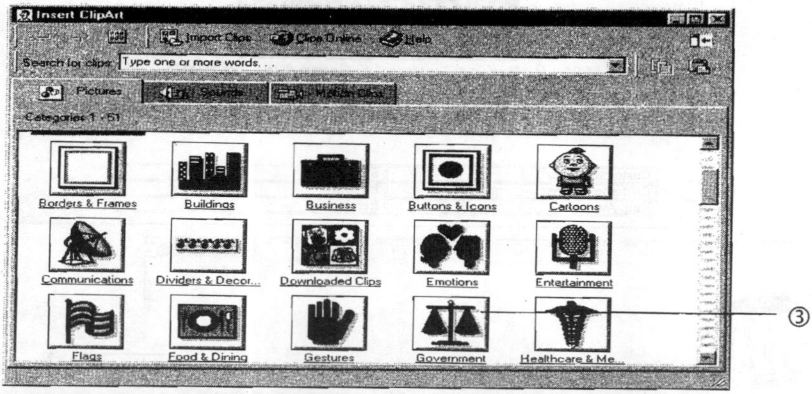

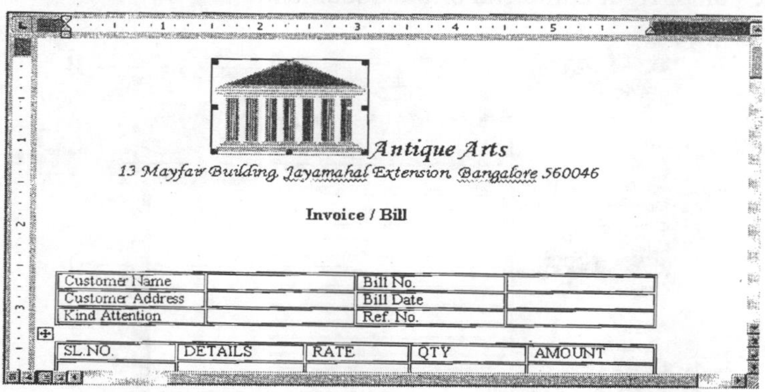

Aligning the Picture

① Highlight the graphic (or both the graphic and text as well, if desired) and click on the **Left Align** icon.

A Final result!

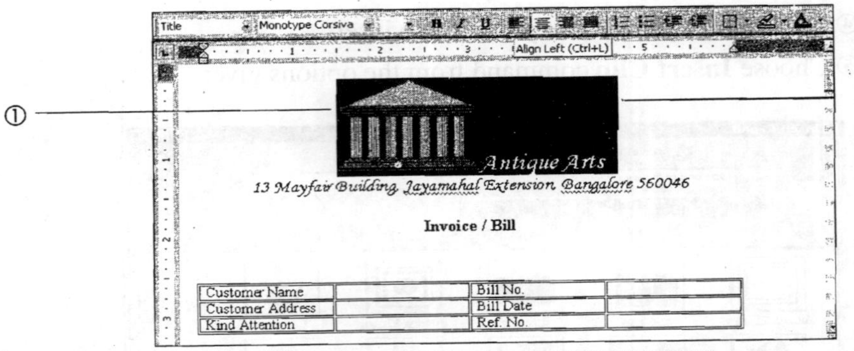

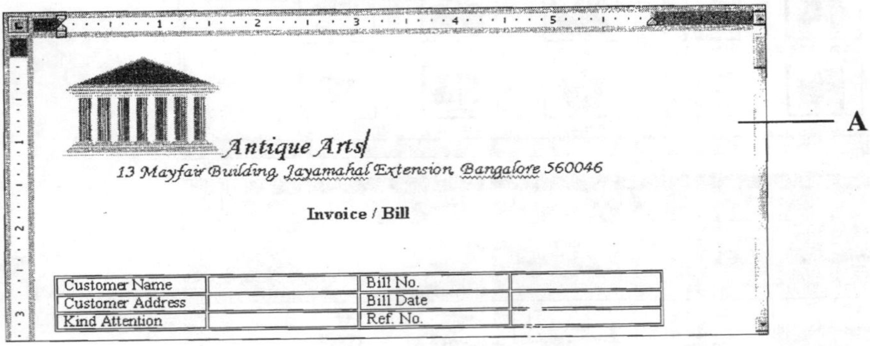

Text Box

Now let us try to create two text boxes below the tables, as shown in the sample exercise.

A First, place the cursor right at the end of the document.

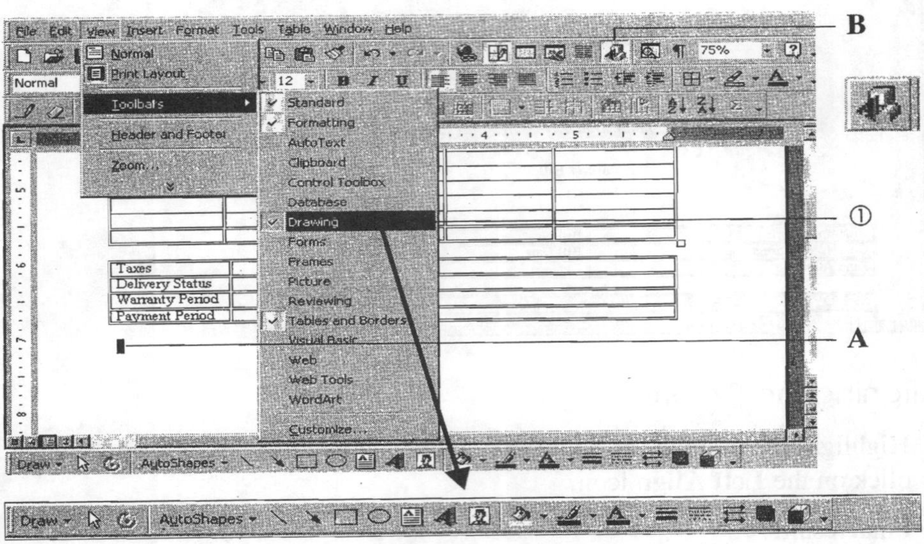

① Activate the Drawing Toolbar by choosing **Drawing** command from **Toolbar** option of **View** menu.

B Alternatively, you could activate **Drawing** Toolbar by directly clicking on this icon.

② Click here to create text box. Size it according to your requirement by dragging the mouse. Type the matter and format. You can also set the line thickness; line color and box fill colours.

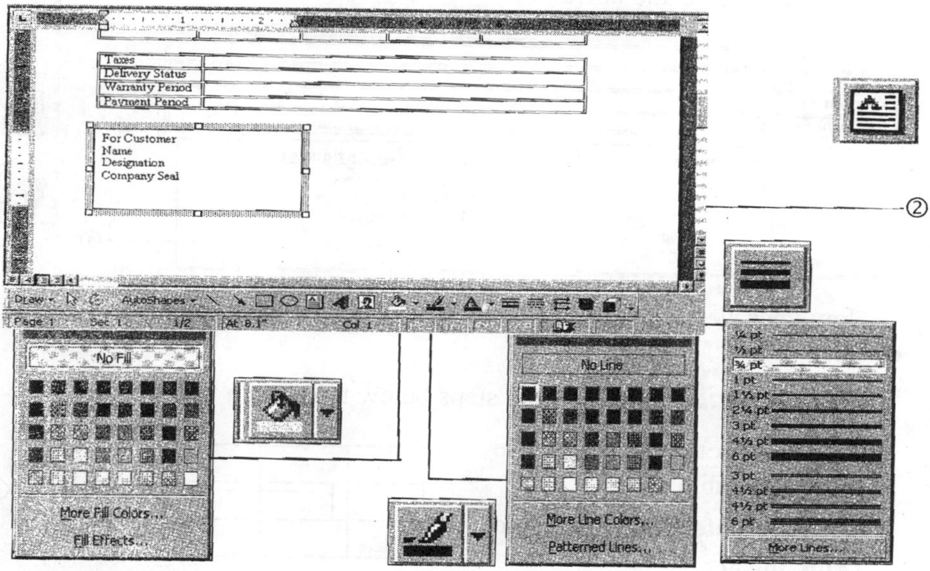

Box Fill Color   Line Color   Line Style and Thickness

Formatting

Now, let us start formatting the text box.

① Highlight the first line and click on this icon to centre the text.

② Highlight the rest of the matter in the box, click the **Left Align** icon to left align the text. Also click on the **Italics** icon to italicise the text.

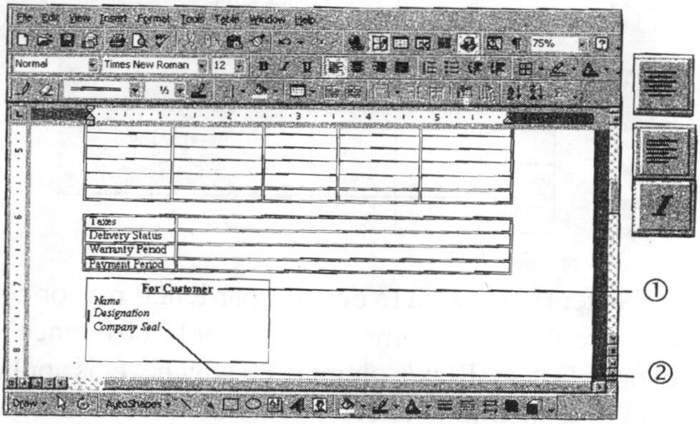

③ Click on the border of the text box so that the box is selected, click on the icon shown to copy this box.

④ Place the cursor outside the first text box, click on **Paste** icon to paste the box here. This action will overlap the new text box on the first text box. Drag the text box to the new location. You may now change the text contents of this box.

Note: Using **Copy** and **Paste** commands ensures that both the boxes will have the same size and attributes.

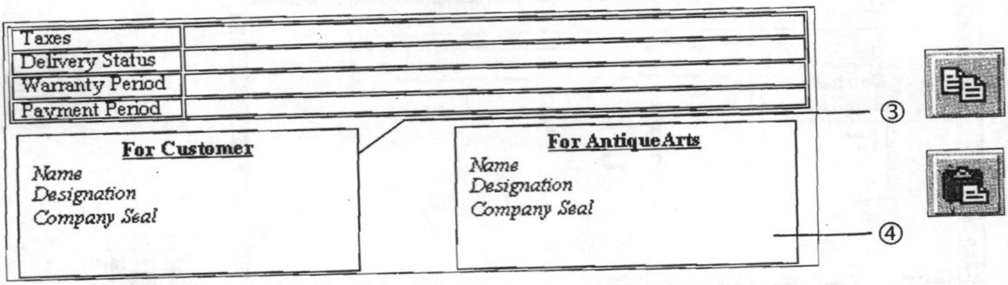

Now since we have completed our exercise, let us discuss some more features of Word Tables:

Deleting Table Follow the steps below to delete a table:

① Place the cursor anywhere within the Table.

② Choose **Delete (Table)** from the **Table** menu.

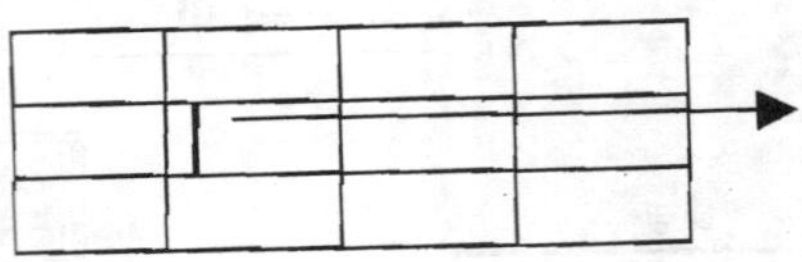

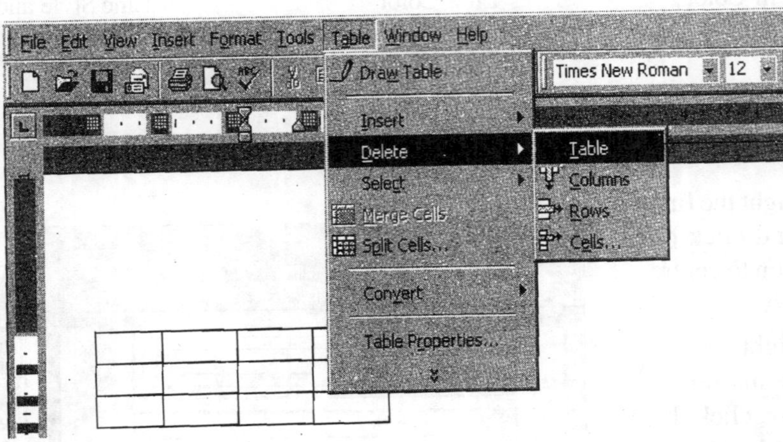

Note: If you wish to delete a particular row or column or cell of a table, you can use the same command. The only difference would be you will have to choose Delete (Row/Column/Cell whichever is applicable) from the Table menu. The row or column or cell having the focus will be deleted.

Merging Cells Word allows you to combine two or more cells in the same row or column into a single cell. For example, you can merge several cells horizontally to create a table heading that spans several columns.

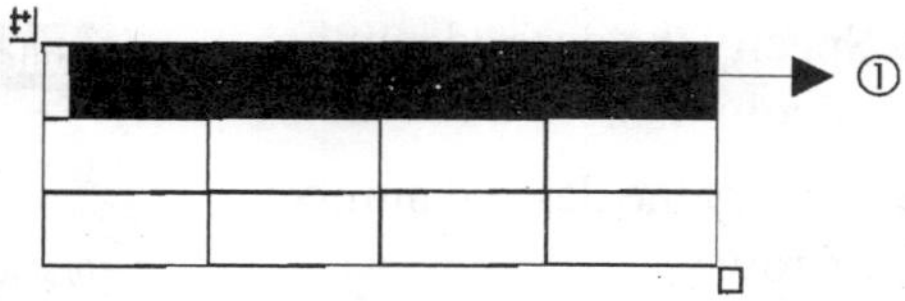

Follow the steps below to merge the cells of a table:

① Select all cells in a row or a column that you wish to merge.

② Choose **Merge Cells** from the **Table** menu.

A Merged Cells

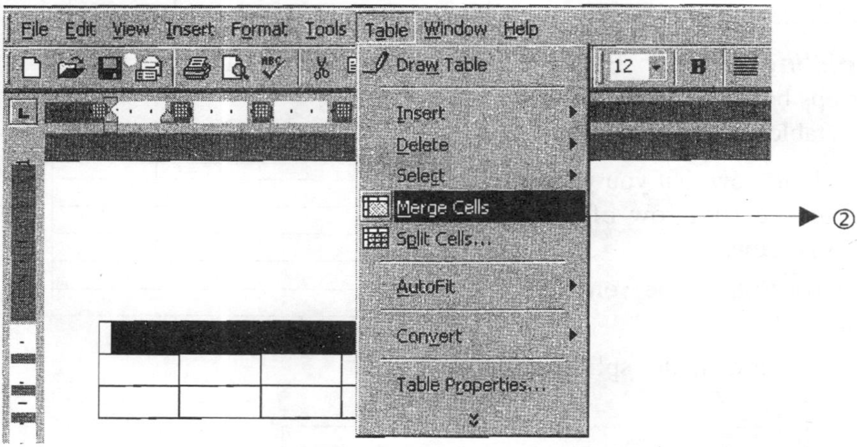

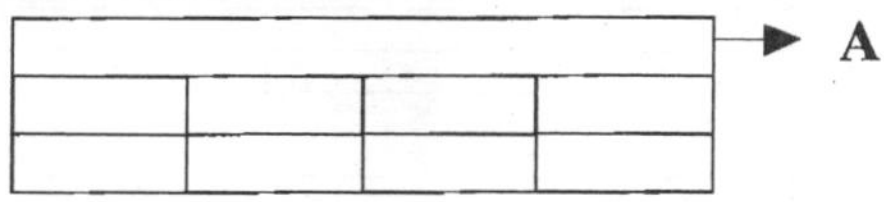

Splitting Cells Word allows splitting a cell of a table into multiple cells.

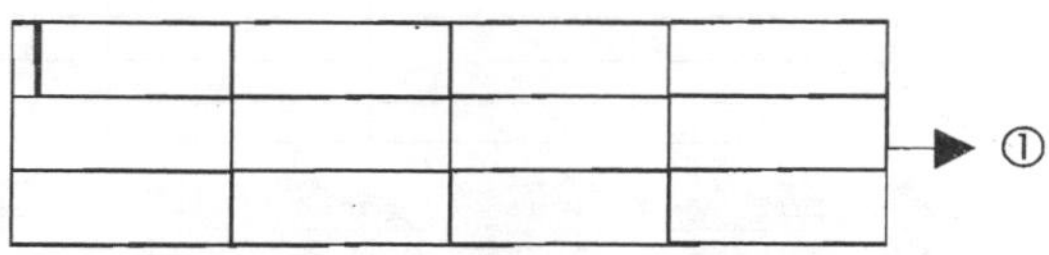

Follow the steps below to split the cells of a table:

① Place the cursor inside the desired cell of the table.

② Choose **Split Cells** from the **Table** menu. A dialogue box will be displayed.

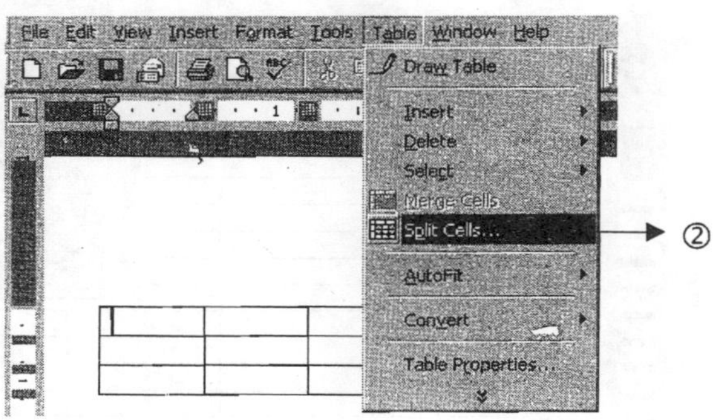

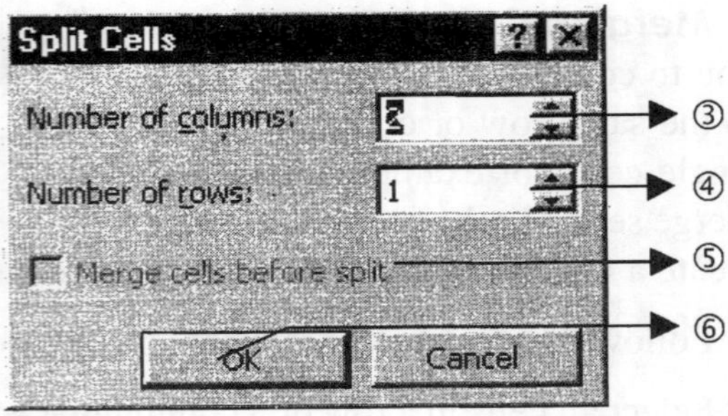

③ Specify the desired number of columns.

④ Specify the desired number of rows.

⑤ Applicable when splitting multiple cells of a table. Select this option if you want to merge cells before splitting them.

⑥ Click on the OK button to apply the specified settings.

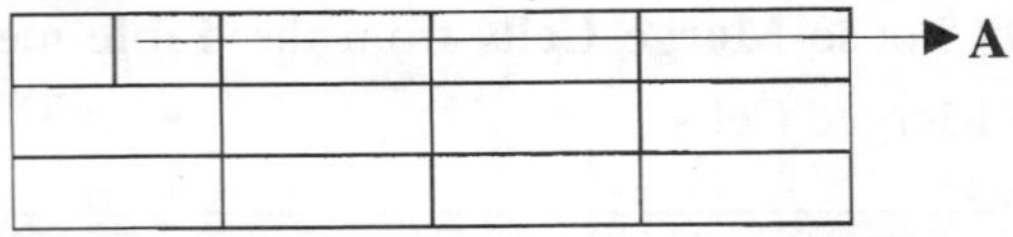

A One cell split into two.

Splitting Tables Follow the steps below to split a table in two tables:

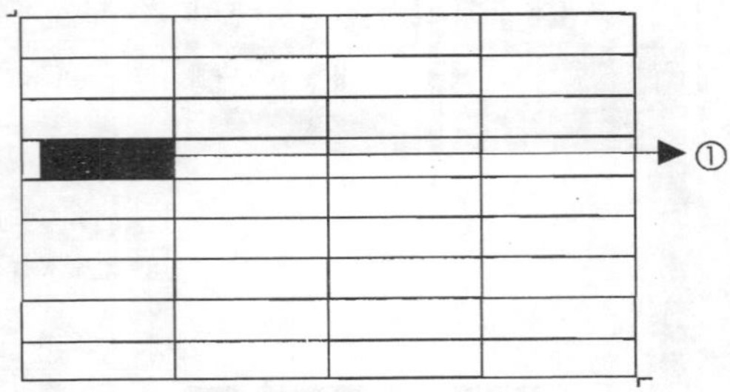

① Click the row that you want to be the first row of the second table.

② Choose **Split Table** from the **Table** menu.

A Two separate tables split from one.

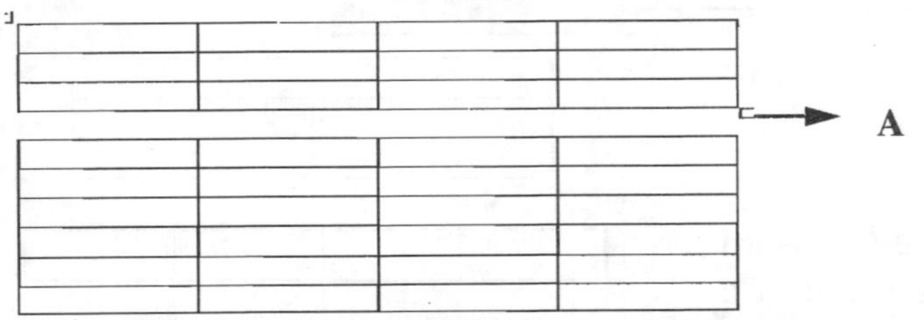

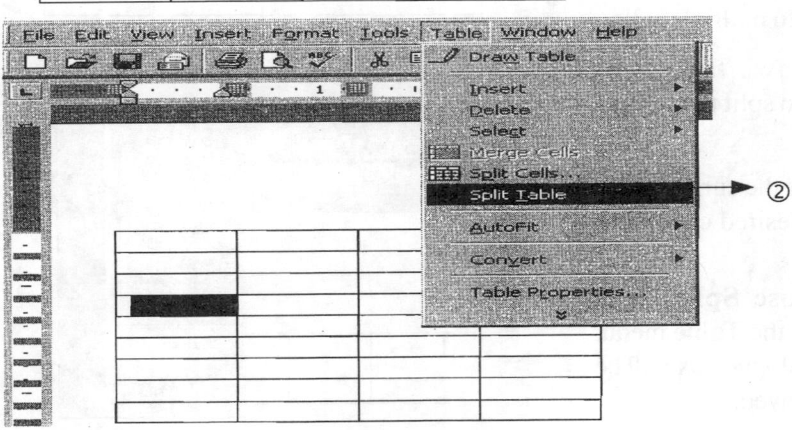

MAIL MERGE

Mail Merge does what it says - merges mail! To explain further, let me give you some examples. Sometime or other you must have had the need to send the same document to a large number of people. This document could be a pleasant one, like a mailer informing people of new products and services, or informing people about change of your address or phone numbers, or informing people that they do not have to pay their rent any longer (I wish I received one like that!) etc. It could even be an unpleasant one, like asking people to pay up their dues promptly (I'm sure some of us have already received lots of these!) or, informing people about some bad news (withdrawal of a faulty product, or death of a person) etc.

Now, what is common in all these letters is that the SAME matter has to be sent to a number of people. In the days of typewriters (for some of you - presently) what you did was something like this–you typed the main body of the letter on your typewriter, leaving out space for the name and address of the recipients, ran your office boy to the nearest photostat shop asking him to get 100 copies made. Then you picked up each of these copies and either manually wrote the recipient's name and address (which is more common) or if you are more meticulous, asked your secretary (in some cases yourself!) to type out the recipient's name and address separately on each of these photocopies.

This works fine, except for two things. One, the end product (your letter) doesn't exactly look beautiful (the recipient can make out exactly what you have done) and two, next time you have to send another (similar) letter to these people, the entire exercise has to be done again.

Fortunately, Mail Merge overcomes both these problems. Because of skills learnt through the preceding exercises, producing beautiful looking letters can't exactly be called difficult. Secondly, with Mail Merge facility you can create a database of your contacts (including friends, relatives, acquaintances etc.) and automatically merge the main body of letters, this database in such a manner that many personalised letters would be generated. Each of these letters would be addressed individually to different people and all the recipients would feel as if you have personally written the letter to him or her.

The file that contains the form letter is called the *main document* and the file containing the database (names, addresses and other information) is called the *data source*. Each entry in the database file (data source) containing details about one person is called a *record* and each item of detail in this record (like name, phone number, subscription number etc.) is called a *field.* So, put simply, many related fields put together form a record and many records put together is called a database.

Enough of theory. Let's get down to actually doing mail merge. As I said earlier, for mail merge we have to create two files – main document and data source. Let's begin with the main document first (although there is no hard and fast rule for this). Before you begin, take a look at the sample letter shown on the next page. In our present exercise we shall use the Mail Merge option to prepare personalised letters like this and see how, with very little additional work, we can create 20 or 200 or even 2000 such letters.

Another great advantage in using the mail merge is that the next time you want to send the same or another letter to the same group of people, all you need to do is to create the main letter and merge it with the existing database, which already contains the names and addresses of the recipients.

WORD EXERCISE 3

Synergy Solutions

142A Greater Kailash I,
New Delhi 110048
Ph: 6482922 Fax: 6228363
E Mail: sanjeev@synergy.com

Dr. Mike Rodell,
Financial Consultant,
IHS,
Suite No. 202, Hotel Southern Star,
Mysore, Karnataka

Customer ID : 124779

Subject : <u>Renewal of your subscription for Cyber Mate - Internet Help Line for 2000</u>

Dear Mr. Rodell,

Warmest greetings for the year! I hope the New year brings you less problems than the one gone by (but not so less that you do need our Cyber Mate Help Line!). With a view to improve the quality and extent of services provided to you, we are pleased to launch a new release of our Internet based Help line Software, (you guessed it right!) called Cyber Mate 2000.

Cyber Mate 2000 has the following new features:

☺ Totally new and extremely user-friendly graphics User Interface.

☺ Provision for sending and receiving Emails - **Free** !

☺ Provision for participating in E-Chats, on latest trends and products in IT - **Free !**

☺ And several other features which make it even simpler (and you thought it couldn't be done!) to ask Cyber Mate 2000 about any technical questions about computers.

And of course all this at no extra cost!

So don't miss out. Please fill up the enclosed form and send it across with your subscription no. (which we remember as) latest by 15th July 2000.

And by the way, **the first hundred subscribers would get free tickets to The Michael Jackson Show to be held in Delhi on the 15th of August 2000.**

So hoping to see you at the MJ show. Happy surfing and Happy New Year.

Please feel free to ring me up for any clarifications.

Yours sincerely　　　　　　　　　　　　　　　　　　　　30th June 2000

Monica Dhaul
Director - Customer Relations

Creating the Main Document

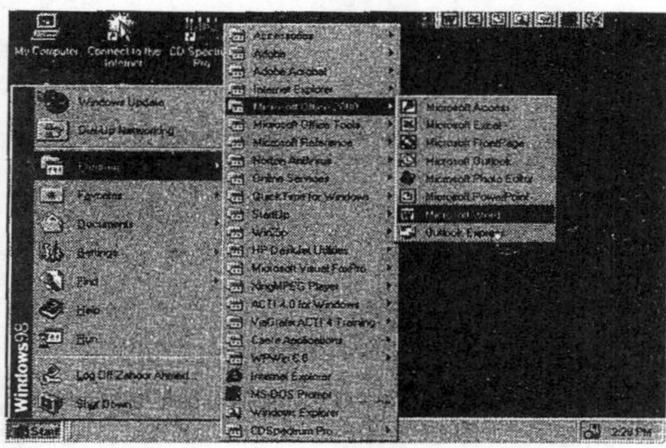

①

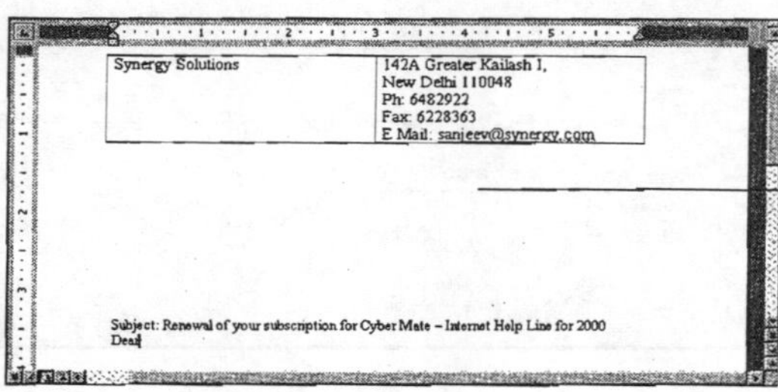

②

① Start Word by choosing **Microsoft Word** from **Programs** option.

② Type the complete body of the letter first. It is always preferable to type the body of the letter first and then apply the formatting styles later. This results in great savings in time.

Create the letterhead with a single row, two-column table.

Also ensure that sufficient space is left in the beginning of the letter for names, addresses and other details of the recipients.

③ Once having typed the entire matter, apply the fonts, point sizes, alignment, and other attributes to the text, based upon sample provided.

Now that you have put in some bit of work, let us save the file with any name. Since the steps involved in saving a file have already been explained to you, I'm going to move ahead to the next steps.

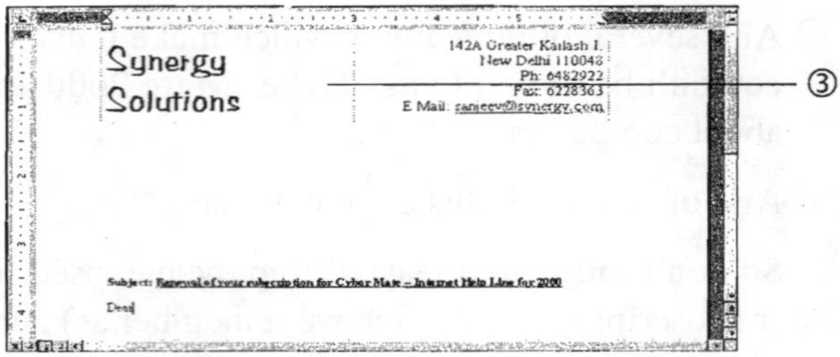

Now let us start Mail Merging.

Creating Data Source

① Choose **Mail Merge** from **Tools** menu. The following Window will be displayed.

② Click on **Create** button.

③ Choose **Form letters** option.

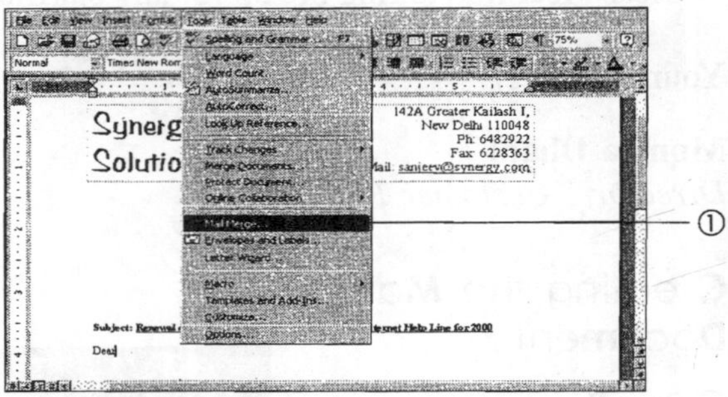

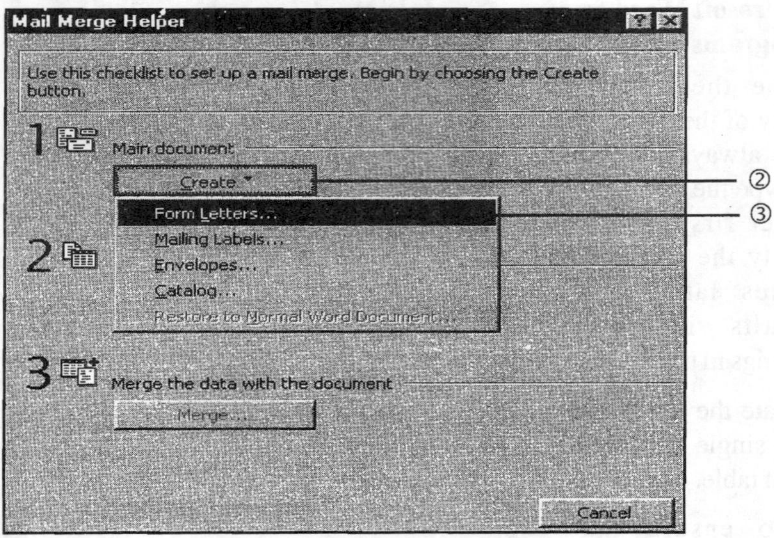

The following Window would be displayed.

④ Click here to choose the currently active document (in which you typed the main text of the letter).

A This option may be chosen in case a new document (i. e. other than the one that is currently open) has to be used for mail merging.

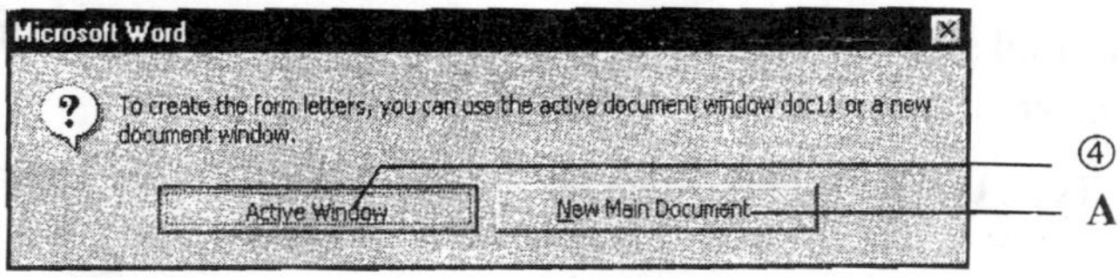

⑤ Click on **Get Data.**

⑥ Choose **Create Data Source** option.

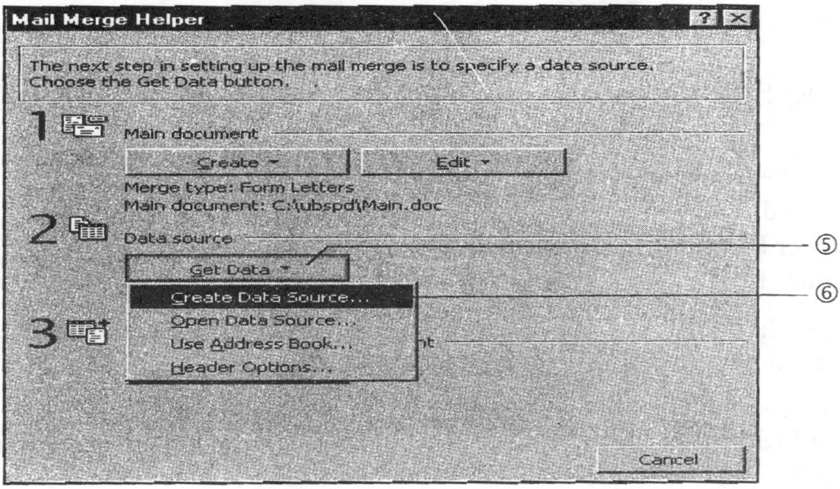

A Window for customising the Database Structure (header row) appears, as shown below.

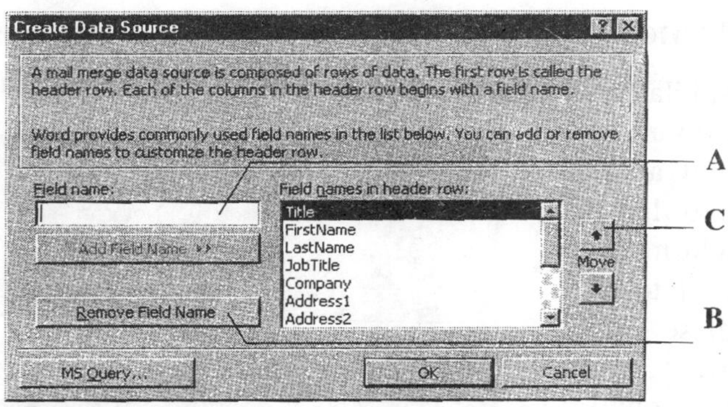

Now is the time to do some serious thinking! At this stage you have to decide about what all information you wish to store in the data file. Typically this file contains the names, address details, contact numbers, etc., of people that you wish to send letters to. (Though the phone and fax numbers are only required for sending the letters through courier, nonetheless it is helpful to store them here so that your contact database is complete). You may also add any other specific fields that you may require, like the customer identification number etc. Word would automatically create a data file with whatever fields you finally select from here. Do not bother if you do not have any data for any field for some or all records. You can decide upon the final shape of this file now and can always fill up the missing information as and when it becomes available to you.

A Type the desired field name and click on **Add Field Name** button to add any additional field(s) that is not already provided.

B Highlight the field name from the next Window and click on **Remove Field Name** button to remove any fields that are not required.

C To re-arrange the order of any field(s) click on the respective field name and click on up arrow or down arrow buttons to place this field at the desired place.

Adding Fields

For the present exercise, let us add a new field called **Customer ID** to this predefined list.

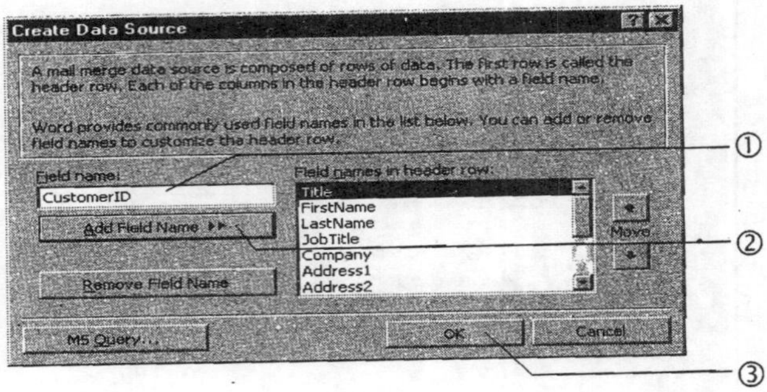

① Type **Customer ID** here.

② Click once on the **Add Field Name** button.

③ Click once on **OK** button.

Removing Fields

Similarly, let us now remove a field called **Country** from this predefined list (assuming that all the people to whom we wish to send these letters are from India only).

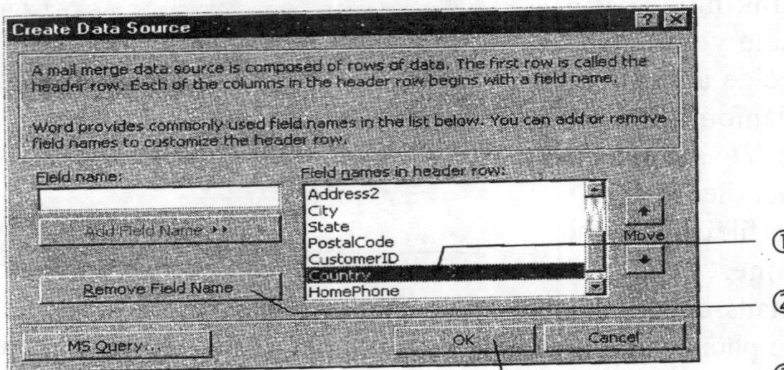

① Highlight **Country** clicking once on it.

② Click once on **Remove Filed Name** button.

③ Click on **OK** button to finalize the list of fields.

The following window will be displayed.

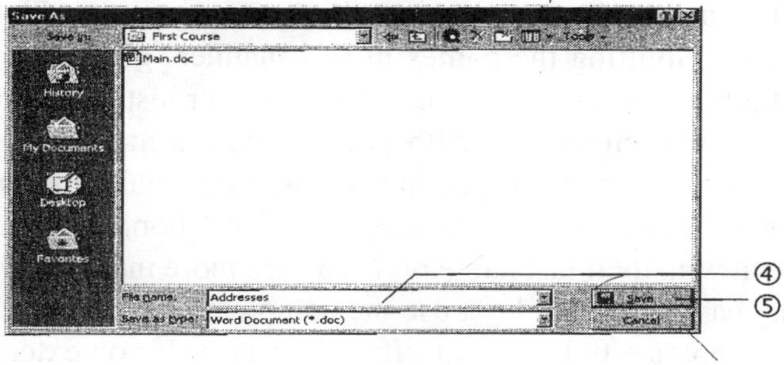

④ Type **Addresses** as the file in which you wish to save the customer details

⑤ Click on **Save** button.

The following Window would be displayed.

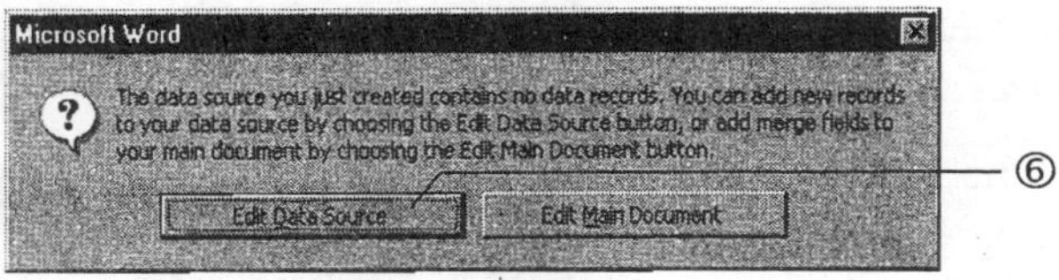

⑥ Click once on **Edit Data Source** to start typing the name and addresses to people to whom this letter has to be sent. The following Window will be displayed.

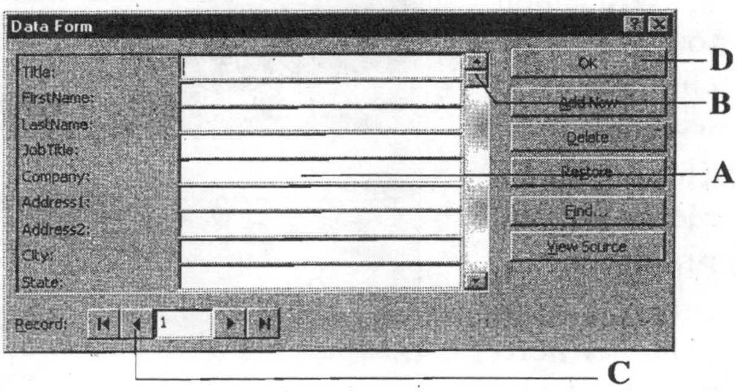

A Notice that the various items of information chosen or specified by you earlier appear here as field names.

B You can see all the fields by scrolling down with the help of scroll bars shown here.

C Through these buttons you can travel through the different records in the database. Clicking once on left arrow button you can go to the previous record and by clicking on the right arrow button it would take you to the next record.

D Also notice that **Add**, **Delete**, **Restore**, **Find** and **View** options are available here. Through these options you can create and modify your database file.

Now type the details for ten people to whom this letter has to be sent. After typing details about one person (one record), click once on the **Add New** button to add the next record. Take care to fill up the information in the right fields, e.g., the field 'Title' has been created so that you can type salutations for different people like Mr., Mrs., Dr, Major General, etc. Similarly, all first names must go to the First Name field and all last names to Last Name. You might be wondering why have I split the name into three different parts - Title, First Name and Last Name. Splitting the names in this manner gives you complete control over which part of the name you use where. For instance, you are sending this letter to all you customers with whom you maintain a cordial and professional relationship (hopefully!). In that case you would normally address the letter to them as Dear Mr. Bhatnagar, Dear Dr. Chopra etc., i.e., you would address them with their last name or, if you are more intimate - with their first name. In any case you would not use the complete name. Therefore, it is important that two separate fields are specified for name. If you extend the logic further, you would also understand the need for splitting the complete address into Address 1, Address 2, City, State etc.

We have finished typing the names and addresses. Let us now see how we can merge the two files - **Main**, *the main document* and **Addresses**, *the data source*, to produce personalised letters.

The following dialog box would be displayed.

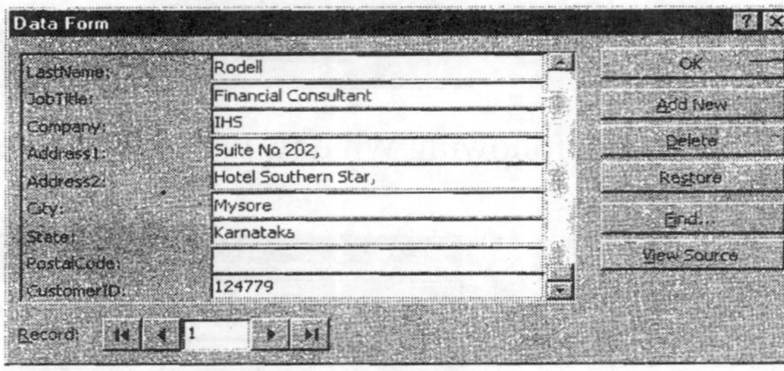

① Click once on the **OK** button to finish entering the records.

② This is the Mail Merge Toolbar.

③ Place the cursor at the place where you wish to insert the names.

④ Click once on **Insert Merge Field** button. A drop down list displaying all the fields that you created would be shown. Now by highlighting the desired field and clicking on it once, we can insert the field into the main document. Choose **Title** and click on it once.

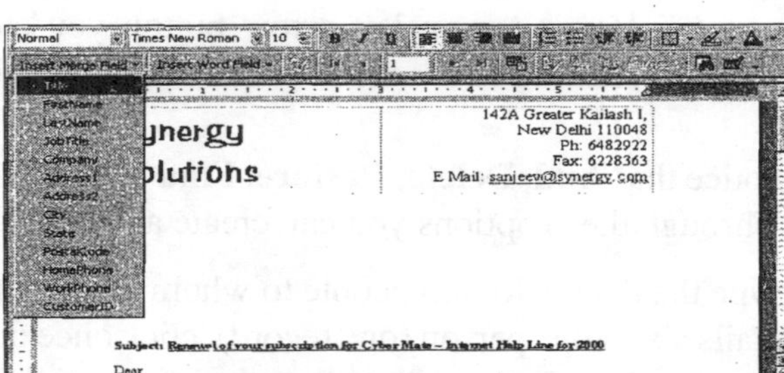

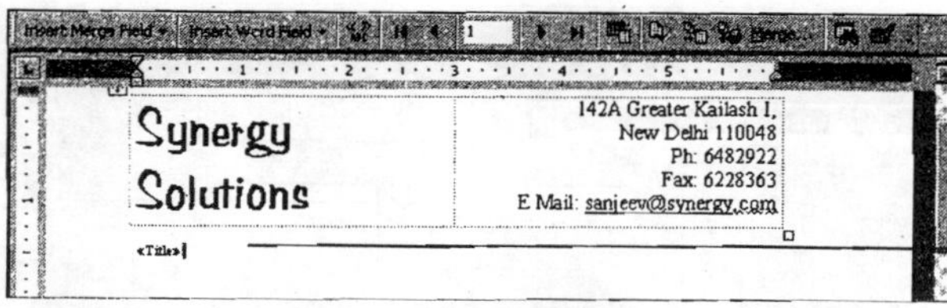

A

A Notice that the Title field has been inserted here. The effect of this would be that when you give the mail merge command, the field contents of the field 'title' (i.e., Dr. or Mr. or Ms. etc.) would get substituted at this place. Therefore, it is important that before you insert a field you must place your cursor at the right place, i.e., at the place you wish the field contents to be inserted.

Now use the same technique to insert all other fields as shown below.

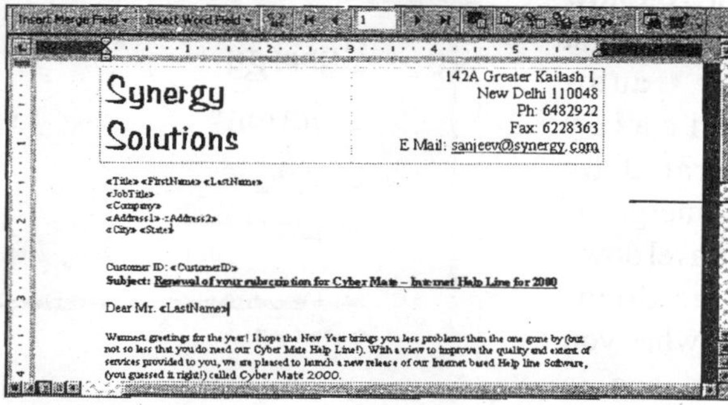

B

B Please note that wherever required, blank spaces, commas and hyphen marks have been typed while inserting different fields. For instance, if you do not give a space between Title, First name and Last name the actual output (after merging) would be something like this: *Mr.MikeRodell.*

Obviously this would not be acceptable. Therefore just visualise the output first and then insert the fields.

⑤ Now to begin mail-merging, click once on the **Mail Merge** Icon.

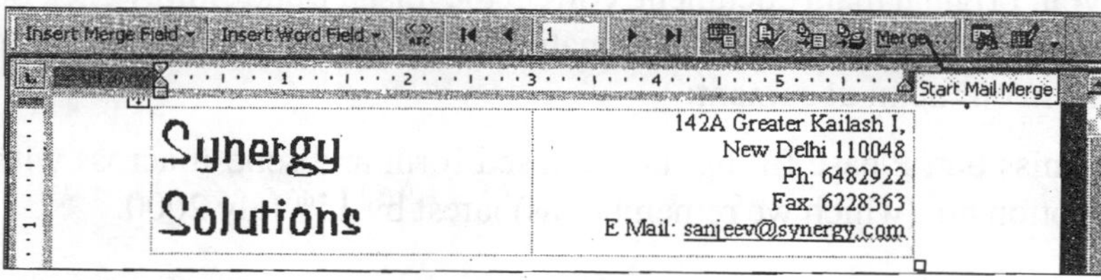

⑤

The following window would be displayed.

⑥ Simply click once on the **Merge** button to generate letters for all the records in your data source file.

A You may specify a range of records here, in case you wish to generate letters only for some selected people.

B Click here in case you do not wish to leave blank lines for those fields that are empty.

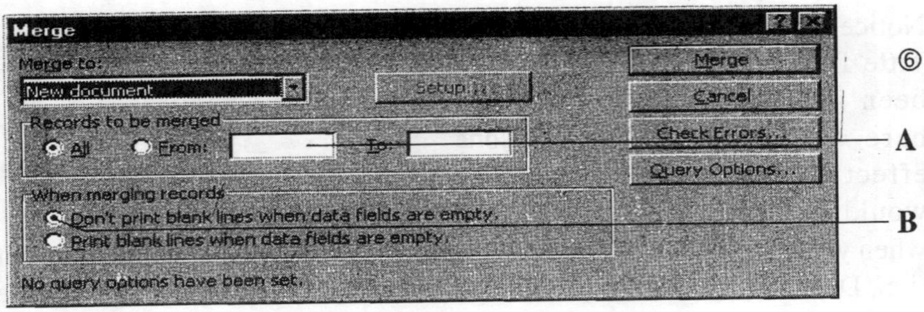

The following results would be displayed.

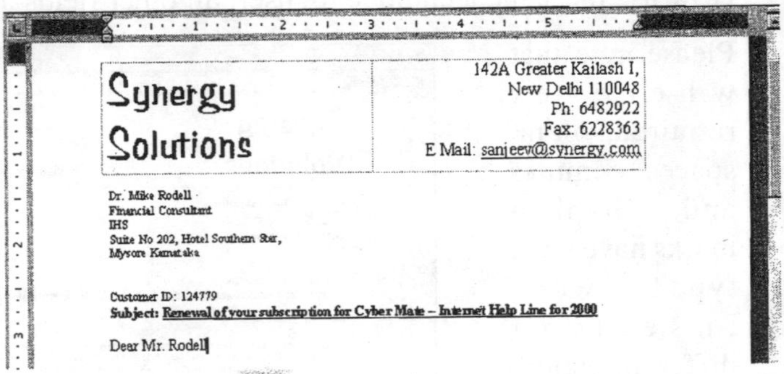

Bravo! What you now see is the first letter automatically generated by mail merge. If you travel down in this document what you would see is that there are ten pages – one for each person who had a record in your data source file. This new document is either saved under any file name specified by you or can simply be printed and closed without saving. Since we would be saving our original main document, this new document containing the letters can always be generated again by a click at Mail Merge Icon.

If you find any mistake in these letters, simply close this file without saving, go back to your original main document; correct the mistake and simply click on the Mail Merge icon to generate these personalised letters once again. For instance, we had a line in our main document:

So don't miss out. Please fill up the enclosed form and send it across with your subscription no. (which we remember as) latest by 15th July 2000.

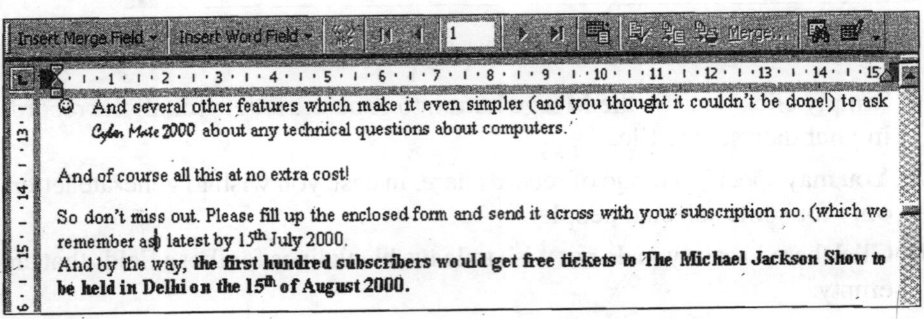

Here we want to insert the CustomerID inside the parentheses, simply place the cursor after 'as' and insert the field **CustomerID.** You may then apply the Bold attribute to this number to make the number more prominent.

So don't miss out. Please fill up the enclosed form and send it across with your subscription no. (which we remember as_**«CustomerID»**) latest by 15th July 2004.

You will notice that after mail merging, again this number would be inserted and shown as below:

So don't miss out. Please fill up the enclosed form and send it across with your subscription no. (which we remember as **124779**) latest by 15th July 2000.

So hurry now, dig out all the visiting cards of all the people you know and surprise them by sending them a mail-merged greeting/letter!

MACROS

Now that you've done a fair bit of work in Microsoft Word, let's now move on to do something more advanced. By now you have learnt to execute many commands and get the desired result one by one. It's a bit like having to explain to your servant all the steps on how to make a cup of tea - over and over again. Possible, but a bit tedious! Sooner or later you're bound to get frustrated and wish that your servant was a bit smarter and could learn from experience. In simple words, you would want that having once explained in simple and precise steps to him the process of making a cup of tea, he should be able to follow the explained steps and make a perfect cup of tea every time you ask him to.

If you like to do things the right way, better write down all the steps involved in it. This process of writing down many commands together in a logical and sequential manner is called Programming in computer jargon. Programming enables you to group many commands together and execute them at a press of a button. In Microsoft Word you can create your programs which automate any repetitive tasks involving several steps. These programs are called **Macros.**

A macro is a small software program. A program is a series of instructions written in a computer language to execute a specific task or tasks. It enables the execution of a series of sequential and logical commands without having to give those commands one by one.

A macro is a series of Word commands which have been grouped together as a single command. Any repetitive operation which involves executing a number of sequential steps can be automated by creating a macro for it. In other words, if you perform any operation repetitively, involving many commands and / or steps, you can group these together into a single command, such that by giving one command all these grouped commands / steps are executed automatically.

It is a bit like having a very faithful and obedient servant – just show him how to do anything once and he will faultlessly do it again whenever asked to do so. In short, Macros can save you considerable time and effort by automating your repetitive tasks.

There are two stages in using macros:

- Creating Macros, and
- Running Macros

While creating a macro, you require two things:

- The actual commands/steps which are to be grouped together to run as one, and
- Assigning the macro. 'Assigning' means specifying to the computer how you would prefer to run this macro.

You can create the macros in two ways:

- Record a series of steps / actions using the keyboard and mouse, or
- Type a macro directly into a macro editing Window using Visual Basic programming language.

Needless to say, the first option is easier, while the second is more powerful and flexible. For creating complex and sophisticated macros you can combine the two approaches – record as much as you can, and then edit the result using Visual Basic editor.

You can assign a macro as follows:

- An option in any menu, or
- As an icon in a toolbar, or
- To a button, or
- To a shortcut key (like function keys), or
- To a key combination.

Given below are the steps involved in recording a macro.

① Choose **Record New Macro** command from **Macro** option, in the **Tools** menu.

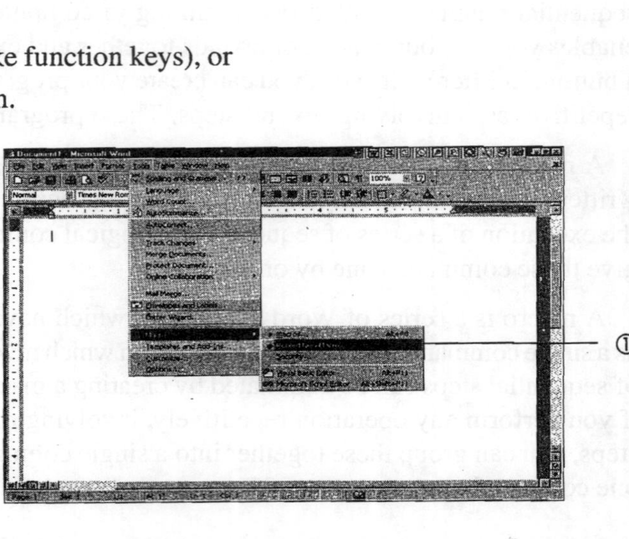

The following dialog box would be displayed.

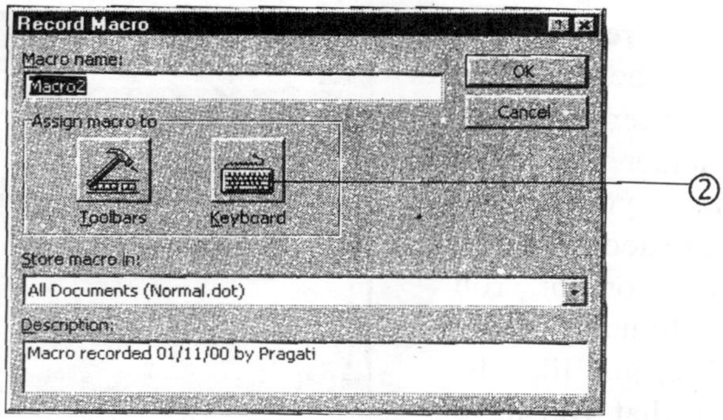

② Click on the **Keyboard** button to define the macro from the keyboard. The following dialog box would be displayed.

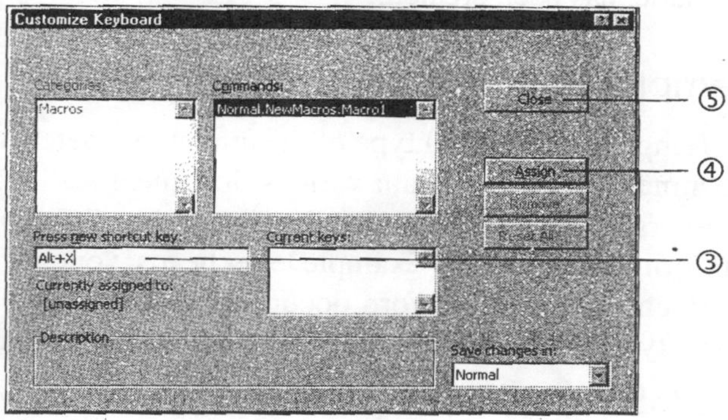

③ Click in this box and press **Alt** and **X** keys from the keyboard together. This is now the macro shortcut.

④ Click on **Assign** button to assign the macro to these two keys.

⑤ Click on **Close** button to close this dialog box.

You would notice the small macro box on the left side.

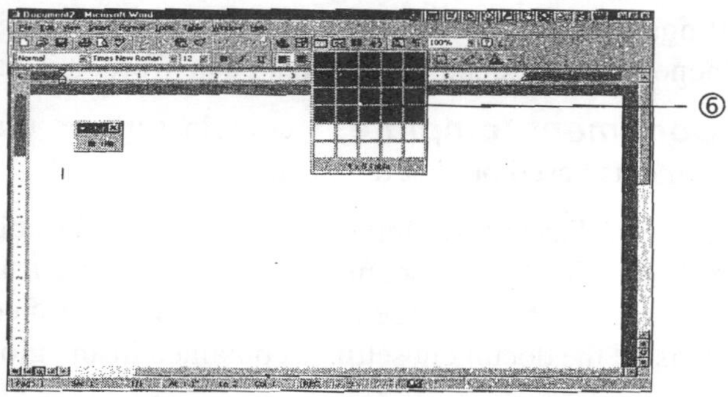

⑥ Choose a table with the dimension of **4 rows and 5 columns** from **Insert Table** icon on the Standard Toolbar.

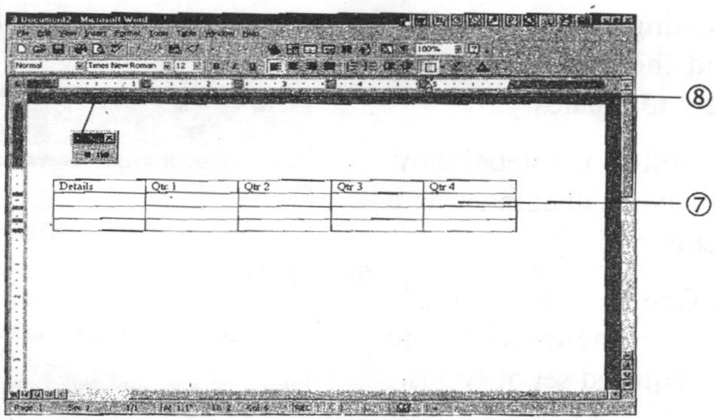

⑦ Fill in the details of the columns as shown below.

⑧ Click on the **Stop Recording** button to stop recording the macro.

A Now press Alt+X from the keyboard together to see whether the macro that you have recorded actually works or not. You would notice that a table, just like the one that you have made, has been created.

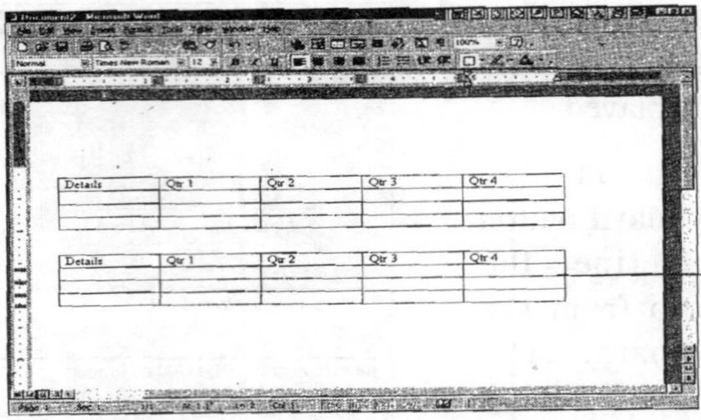

A

Templates

A Template is a special type of document that determines the basic layout of a document and can contain various document settings like fonts, page layout, toolbars, special formatting and styles. Using different templates is like having pre-printed stationery (Example letter heads, voucher forms, fax forms etc.) for different uses. Every Word document is based on a template. There are two basic types of templates – Global templates an '. Document templates.

Global templates contain settings that are available to all documents. The Normal template by design is always a Global template; this is because any settings added to the Normal template are always available to other documents. Whenever a new document is created in Word, it is based on Normal template.

Document templates contain settings that are available only to documents based on that template.

Letters, Faxes and Memos are some of the in-built document templates of MS Word. If a new document is created using a Letter template then that document will have all the document settings defined in the letter template as well as all the document settings contained in any global template.

Word provides a variety of document templates and allows you to modify the existing templates. It allows to save your own document design as a new template and then use it to create new templates.

Follow the steps below to save a document as a Template:

A Create a sample document with the required set of styles.

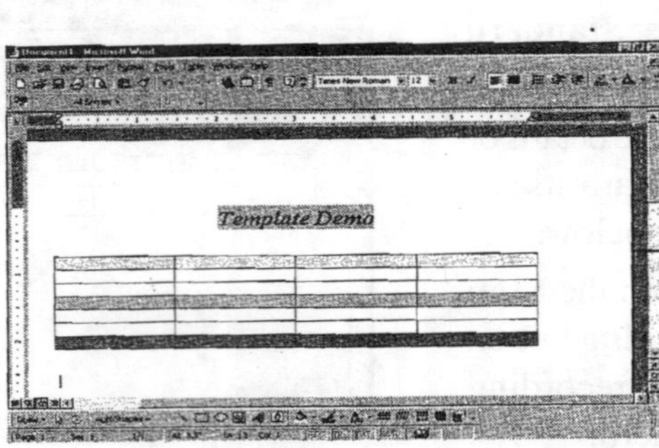

A

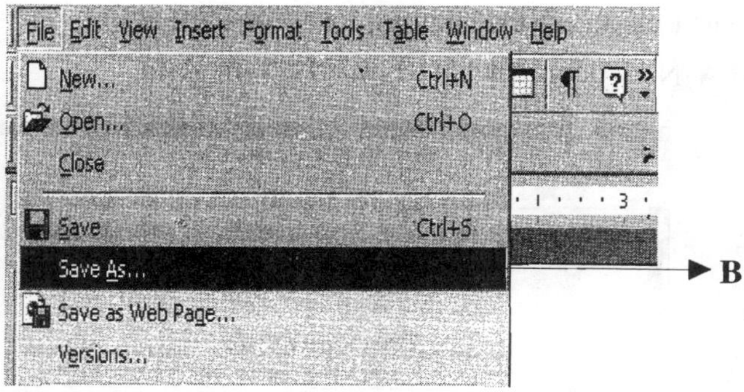

B Choose **Save as** from the **File** menu.

C In the Save drop down box choose **Document Template.** All templates have their extension name as .DOT unlike Word files that have .DOC as their extension name.

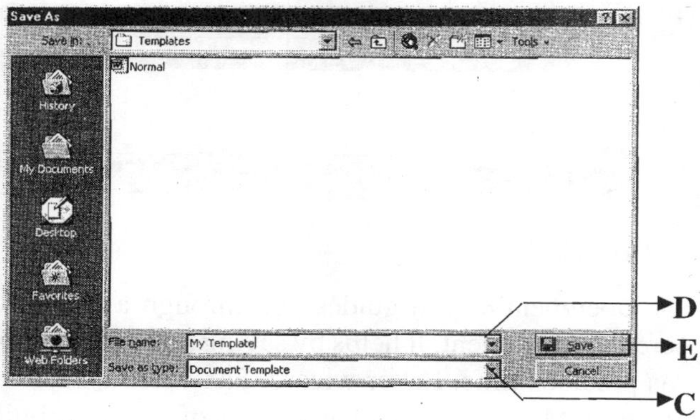

D Type a name for your template. All the templates must be stored in the **Template** directory so that they can be used as a base for creating new documents. In Windows 95 or 98, the **Templates** folder is located by default in either the C:\Windows_folder/Application Data/Microsoft folder or the C:\Windows_folder/Profiles/User_name/Application Data/ Microsoft folder.

E Click on the **Save** button to save your template.

Follow the steps below to create a new document based on.

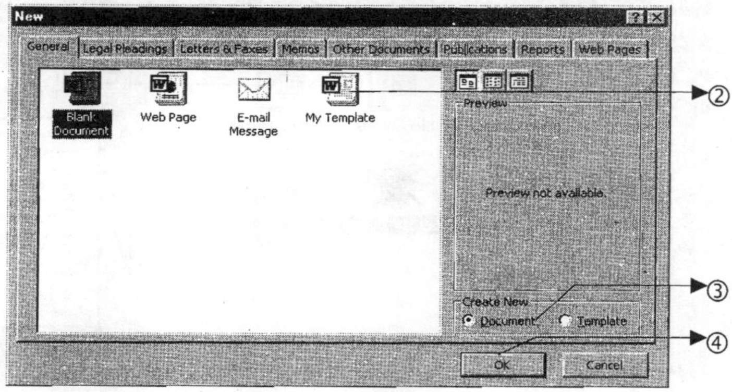

① Choose **New** command from **File** menu, a dialog box will be displayed to the user.

② Select **My Template**.

③ Click on **Document** to create document based on My Template.

④ Click on the **OK** button.

A New document based on **My Template**.

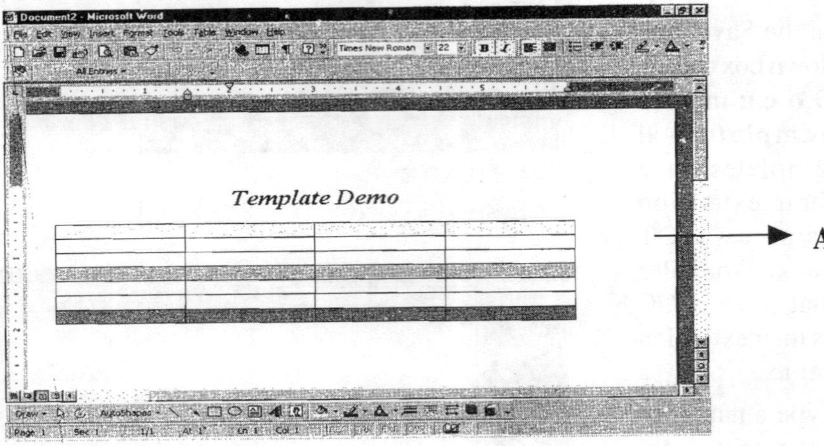

Wizards

A DocumentWizard guides you through a series of instructions to help you create a document. It helps by saving you considerable amount of effort as well as precious time. Letter wizard, Fax wizard, Mailing Label wizard, Envelope wizard, Memo wizard are examples of Word's inbuilt wizards. We will discuss the most commonly used wizard of Word:

Letter Wizard The Letter Wizard in Word can help you write letters quickly and easily. It provides frequently – used letter elements – such as date, reference lines, salutations, and closings – that you can select from lists. It also helps you structure your letters based on frequently – used letter styles.

Follow the steps below to create a letter using a Letter Wizard:

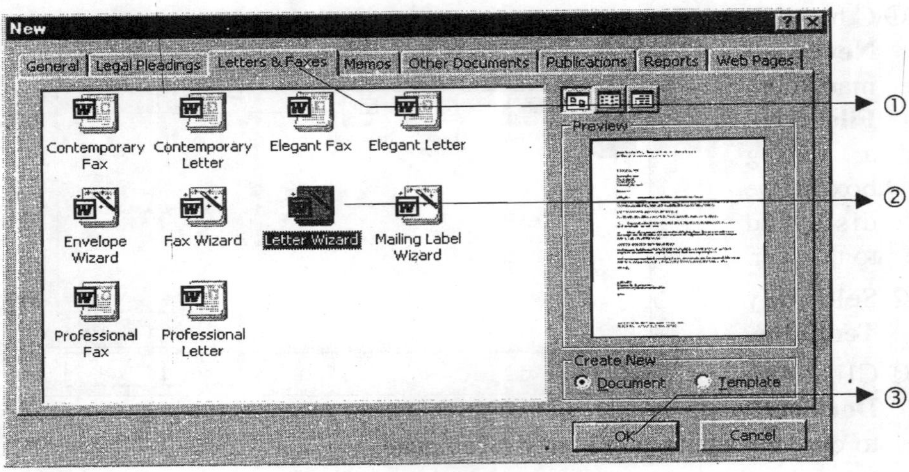

① Choose **New** from the **File** menu. Click on Letters and Faxes in the New file dialogue box.

② Choose Letter wizard.

③ Click on the **OK** button to open the Letter wizard.

Letter Wizard – Step 1

① Choose **Date Line** to insert date in the selected format as shown in the drop down box.

② Choose the type of letter you wish to create (Contemporary, Normal, Professional or Elegant). Preview of the selected type will be displayed.

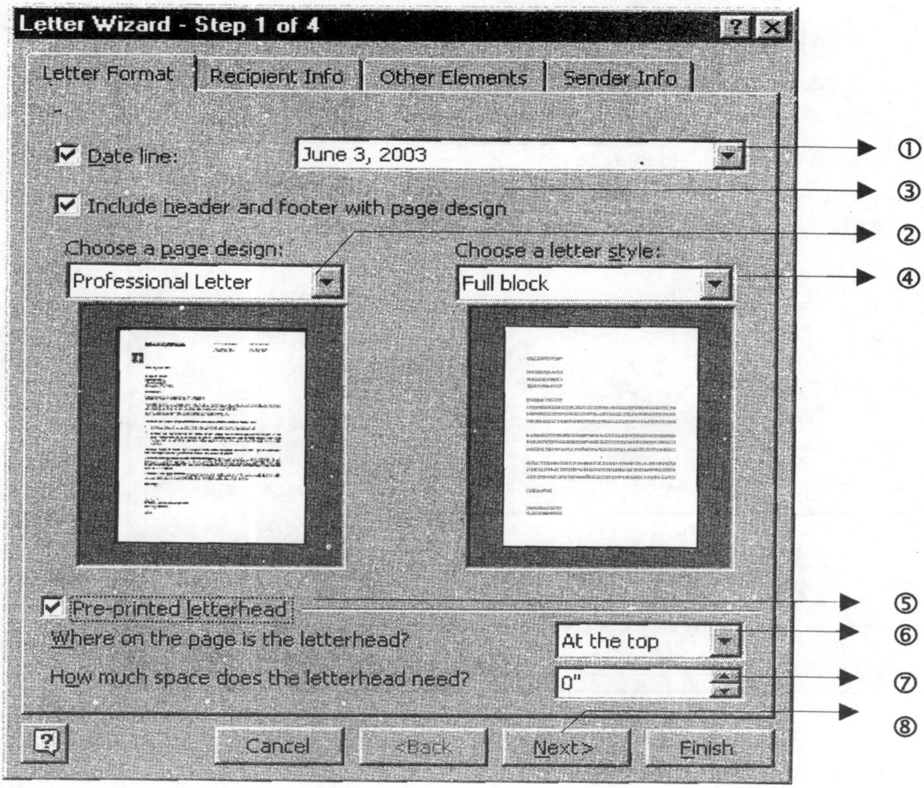

③ Choose **Include Header and Footer** if you wish to insert any header or footer to your letter.

④ Choose the **Letter Style** from the drop down box. Preview of the selected type will be displayed.

⑤ Choose **Preprinted letterhead** if you wish to leave space for your letter head.

⑥ Select the position of the letterhead (Top, Bottom, Left or Right) from the drop-down box.

⑦ Select the space required by the letterhead on the page.

⑧ Click on the **Next** button to continue. The following screen will be displayed:

Letter Wizard – Step 2

① Type the **Recipient's Name** or select from the drop down box.

② Type the **Delivery** address for this letter.

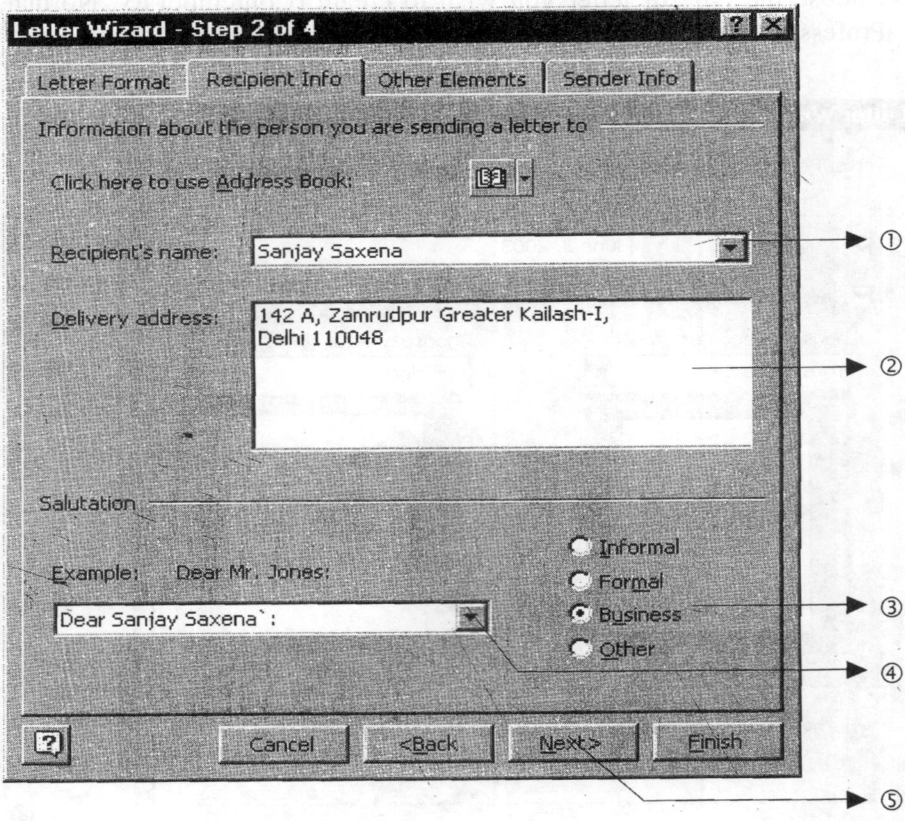

③ Choose the **Salutation Style**.

④ Choose a Salutation from the drop down box or type a value.

⑤ Click on the **Next** button to continue. The following screen will be displayed:

Letter Wizard – Step 3

① Click once on the check box to add **Reference Line.** It can be selected from the drop down menu or a value can be typed.

② Click once on the check box to add **Mailing Instructions**.

③ Click once on the check box to add **Attention** line.

④ Select the check box to add **Subject** line.

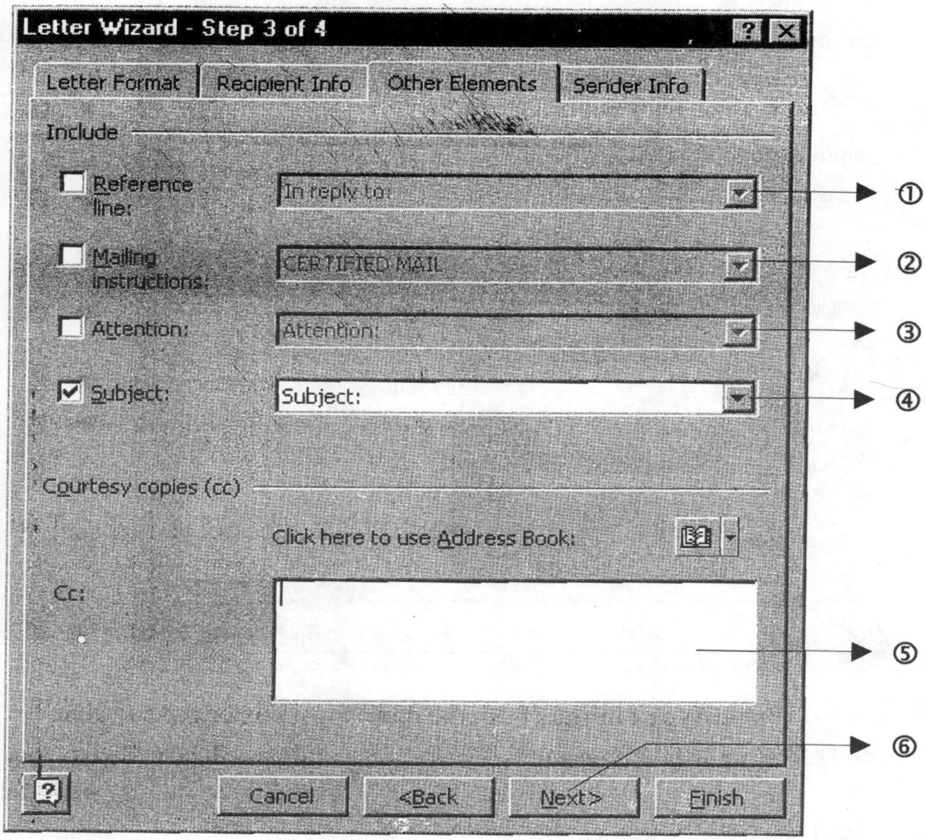

⑤ If you wish to send a courtesy copy of the letter then specify the recipient's name and address in the **cc** box.

⑥ Click on the **Next** button to continue. The following screen will be displayed:

Letter Wizard – Step 4

① Enter the **Sender's** name.

② Select **Omit** if you do not wish to specify the **Return** address. Clear Omit if you wish to specify the Return address.

③ Choose **Complementary Closing** from the drop down box.

④ Choose **Job Title** from the drop down box or type a value.

⑤ Choose **Company** from the drop down box or type a value.

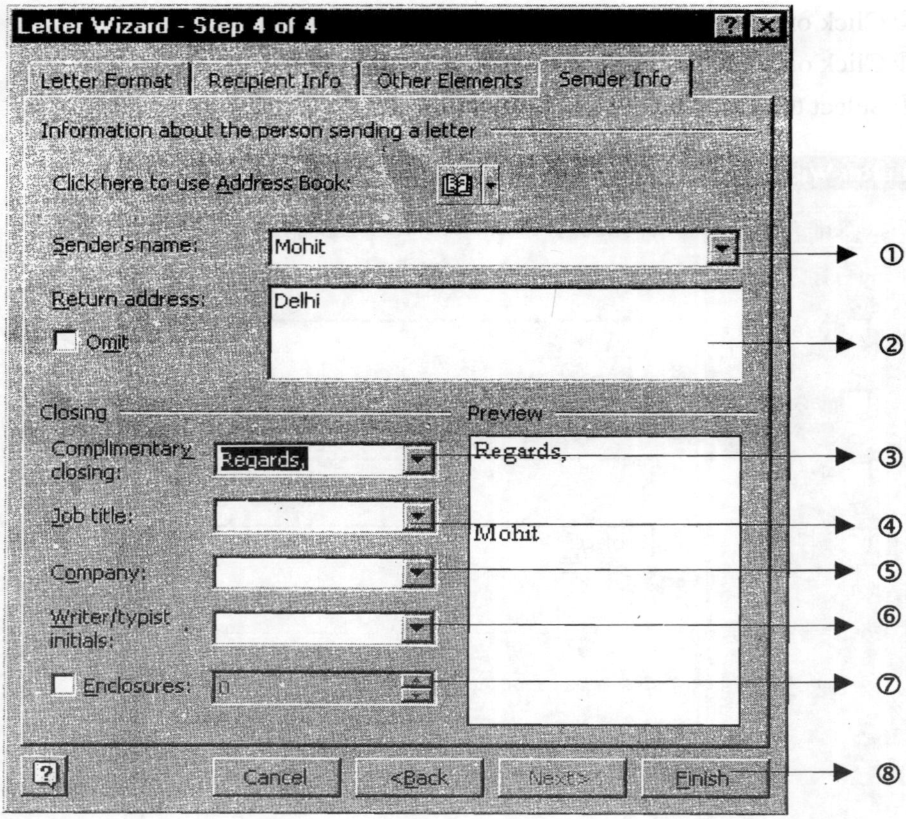

⑥ Choose **Writer/typist initials** from the drop down box or type a value.

⑦ Specify the number of enclosures. Enclosures notation will be added to your letter.

⑧ Click on the **Finish** button to finish your letter.

A The following output will be displayed to the user. User can edit existing information as well as add new information to the letter.

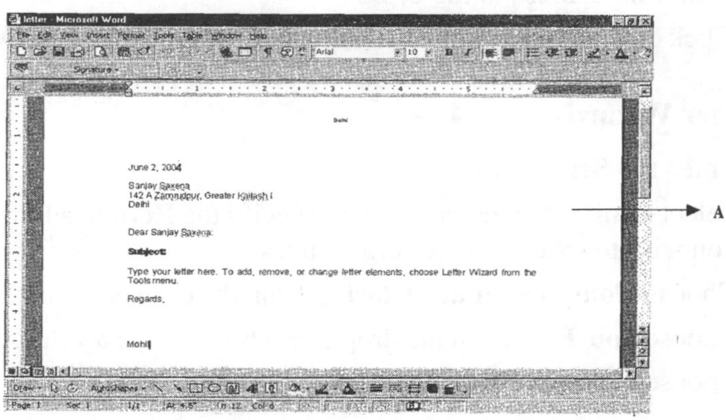

KEY POINTS

Word Basics and formatting features

- Microsoft Word is a full-featured word processing program that can be used to write letters and reports, prepare bills and invoices, prepare office stationery – letter heads, envelopes and forms, design brochures, pamphlets, newsletters, magazines and many more.
- Any Word document can be viewed in four different types of views viz., Normal View, Web Layout View, Print Layout View and Outline View. Normal view is the default view. In Web Layout View you can preview your page as it will appear in a web browser. In Print Layout view you can preview your page as it will appear when printed. In Outline view you can specify upto seven levels of headings. You can rearrange both the headings as well as its content to revise the structure of the document.
- Title bar, Menu bar, Standard toolbar, Formatting toolbar, Scroll bars and Status bar are the key elements of a Word Window. Standard toolbar contain icons that help you quickly alter the appearance and arrangement of documents by executing a variety of Word commands. Formatting toolbar contains icons for changing the formatting of your text. Status bar displays information like Current Page, Section Number, Current/Total pages in the document, Current Line Number etc.
- For executing most tasks in MS Word, the user has three options:
  1. Choose the desired command from the Menu options provided, by either using the mouse or using cursor movement keys, or
  2. Press the appropriate shortcut keys combination from the keyboard, or
  3. Click once on the relevant icon from the displayed toolbars.
- One of the basic features of Word is Word-Wrap. This feature allows you to type in continuity without bothering about your line running out of right margin of your page.
- The process of changing the appearance of text by changing the font type, font size, alignment of text, applying shades and colours etc. is called Formatting. All the formatting features offered by Word require pre-selection of a piece of text.
- Fonts are like different handwriting scripts available to you. Just as different people write the same alphabets differently, the font facility of MS Word enables you to choose the way in which your alphabet script is displayed and printed.
- The last four files that have been used recently are displayed in the list of recent documents at the bottom of the File menu. Simply click on that file name to open it.

- Paragraph spacing is used to create spaces between paragraphs. It is also possible to create additional spacing between the lines of a paragraph. This is known as Line Spacing.
- Page formatting involves setting the page margins, page size, page orientation etc. By default, whenever you create a new document, the document is created with predefined page settings.
- Header and Footer allow you to print a standard piece of text and/or an image at the top or end of each page of your document. Headers appear at the top of each page and footers appear at the bottom of each page.
- By default a new document contains only one section. (If no section break has been inserted explicitly.) Word allows inserting multiple sections into the same document. This feature allows the user to apply different formatting styles within the same document.
- Word allows to preview on screen what you wish to print. In most cases, this preview would give you an exact replica of what your printer would print.

Editing and Proofing Tools

- Spelling and Grammar is one of the coolest features of Word and frees you from the bother of concentrating on the spelling and grammar of your text. Word contains an inbuilt dictionary, but it does not always include proper names, technical terms and acronyms.
- AutoText – MS Word displays a Tool tip text when you type the first few characters of a date or an AutoText entry, at which point you can insert the entry by pressing the Enter key, or ignore it and continue typing.
- MS Word allows you to track the changes made to your document. Word makes use of revision marks to show the tracked changes to the user. A revision mark shows where an insertion, deletion or any other editing change has been made in the document.

Tables and Pictures

- Tables are often used to organise and present information, but they have a variety of other uses as well. Word allows you to create and format tables. The following operations can be performed for a Word table:

  i. Deletion of a Row, Column, Cells, Table.

  ii. Insertion of Rows, Columns, Cells.

  iii. Merging multiple rows or columns into a single row or column.

  iv. Splitting a cell into multiple rows and columns.

  v. Formatting a table – Changing the border colour, border width, border style, text colour, background colour and many more.

- There are two basic types of Graphics in MS Word – Drawing Objects and Pictures. Drawing objects include textboxes, curves, lines, and other objects. These objects can be accessed from the Drawing toolbar. Pictures are graphics that have been created using any graphics software. They include bitmaps, scanned pictures and photographs, and MS Word's inbuilt Clipart gallery. You can enhance these objects with colors, patterns, borders, and other effects.

Mail Merge, Macros and Templates

- Mail Merge does what it says – merges mail! It is useful for sending the same matter to a number of people, with each letter addressed individually.
- Mail Merge facility allows you to create a database of your contacts (including friends, relatives, customers, acquaintances etc.) and automatically merges the main body of letter, and this database to generate personalised letters.
- The file that contains the form letter is called the main document and the file containing the database (names, addresses and other information) is called the data source. Each entry in the database file (data source) containing details about one person is called a record and each item of detail in this record (like name, phone number, subscription number etc.) is called a field.
- A macro is a small software program that enables the execution of a series of sequential and logical commands without having to give those commands one-by-one.
- There are two stages in using macros – Creating Macros and Running Macros.
- You can create the macros in two ways:
  i. Record a series of steps/actions using the keyboard and mouse, or
  ii. Type a macro directly into a macro-editing window using Visual Basic programming language.
- A template is a special type of document that determines the basic layout of a document and can contain various document settings like fonts, page layout, toolbars, special formatting and styles. Using different templates is like having pre-printed stationery for different uses.
- There are two basic types of templates – Global templates and Document templates. Global templates contain settings that are available to all documents. Document templates contain settings that are available only to documents based on that template.
- A Document Wizard guides you through a series of instructions to help you create a document. It helps you in saving a considerable amount of your work as well as your precious time. Letter wizard, Fax wizard, Mailing Label wizard, Envelope wizard, Memo wizard are examples of Word's inbuilt wizards.
- A brief summary of all the Commands covered in this chapter are outlined below:

Action	Command	Icon
To create a new document	Choose **New** from the **File** menu.	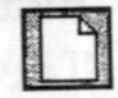
To open an existing document	Choose **Open** from the **File** menu.	
To Save a document	Choose **Save** from the **File** menu.	
To make a copy of the entire document	Choose **Save As** from the **File** menu.	
To set Page margins and Page size	Choose **Page Setup** from **File** menu.	
To print a document	Choose **Print** from **File** menu.	
To preview document before printing	Choose **Print Preview** from **File** menu.	
To close a document	Choose **Close** from the **File** menu.	
To close MS Word	Choose **Exit** from the **File** menu.	
To cancel your last action	Choose **Undo** from the **Edit** menu.	
To redo an undone action	Choose **Redo** from the **Edit** menu.	
To copy a block of text	Choose **Copy** from the **Edit** menu.	
To cut a block of text	Choose **Cut** from the **Edit** menu.	
To paste a block of copied/cut text	Choose **Paste** from the **Edit** menu.	
To search for a word or a phrase in a document	Choose **Find** from the **Edit** menu.	
To replace a single or all instances of any word/phrase with another word/phrase	Choose **Replace** from the **Edit** menu.	
To change the Font style, size and other formatting styles	Choose **Font** from the **Format** menu.	
To highlight the text	Click on the Highlight icon from the **Formatting** toolbar.	
To align (Left, Center, Right) the text/ paragraph	Click on the desired Alignment icon from the **Formatting** toolbar.	
To justify the text	Click on the Justify icon from the **Formatting** toolbar.	
To insert bullets/numbers	Choose **Bullets** and **Numbering** from the **Format** menu.	

Action	Command	Icon
To indent the text	Click on left and right indent icons from the **Formatting** toolbar.	
To change the text case (Capitals to Lower or vice versa)	Choose **Change Case** from the **Format** menu.	
To change paragraph and line spacing	Choose **Paragraph** from the **Format** menu.	
To create newspaper-like columns.	Choose **Columns** from **Format** menu.	
To transfer formatting from one range of text to another.	Click on the **Format Painter** icon from the **Formatting** toolbar.	
To insert header and footer	Choose **Header and Footer** from the **View** menu.	
To insert page numbers	Choose **Page Numbers** from the **Insert** menu.	
To view all the toolbars	Choose **Toolbars** from the **View** menu. Click on the desired toolbar that you wish to be displayed.	
To insert multiple sections into the same document	Choose **Break** from the **Insert** menu.	
To check spelling and grammar	Choose **Spelling** and **Grammar** from the **Tools** menu.	
To access Autotext	Choose **Auto Text** from the **Insert** menu.	
To track the changes in your document	Choose **Track Changes** in the Options dialogue box from the **Tools** menu.	
To insert table	Choose **Insert (Table)** from the **Table** menu.	
To delete table	Choose **Delete (Table)** from the **Table** menu.	
To Select table	Choose **Select (Table)** from the **Table** menu.	
To insert picture from the clipart gallery.	Choose **Picture (Clipart)** from the **Insert** menu.	
To insert picture from a file	Choose **Picture (From File)** from the **Insert** menu.	
To merge mail	Choose **Mail Merge** from the **Tools** menu.	
To create a macro	Choose **Record New Macro** command from **Macro** option from **Tools** menu.	

DO-IT-YOURSELF EXERCISES

Exercise - I

COMPUTER EDUCATION

Course Highlights

Hardware & Networking

1. Computer Assemble
2. Maintenance
3. Servicing
4. Operation System
5. LAN, WAN
6. MS Server 2000

Call Centre

- Business English
- Soft Skills
- Communications
- Telephony Skills
- Customer Behaviour
- MS Office 2000

100% FREE

Web Designing & Multimedia

- ✍ Flash
- ✍ Java Script
- ✍ Photoshop
- ✍ Sound Forge
- ✍ Director with Lingo
- ✍ Dream Weaver

Programming

- ✍ HTML, Java Script
- ✍ SAP. Net C++
- ✍ COM/DCOM
- ✍ MTS, MSMQ
- ✍ Java & Rational Rose
- ✍ SQL Server 2000

Why Free Training?

In fact, we finance your training, Instead of charging a big amount we just charge nominal amount towards lab maintenance etc., and a month's salary after you get employed in Industry.

1. Create a document which looks exactly like the Sample Exercise above. Save this file with the name **TestExercise1.doc** in the **My Documents** folder.
2. Perform Spell check for this document.
3. Insert "IT Tools and Applications" in the Header area and current date and time in the Footer area.
4. Print 2 copies of this document with the following settings:
   a. Left Margin = 1"
   b. Right Margin = 1"
   c. Top Margin = 2"
   d. Bottom Margin = 1"

Exercise - II

Send a greetings letter to all your friends and associates, wishing them a happy new year. A sample letter is shown below. The same letter has to be sent to ten different people. Angular brackets denote that data has to be substituted as applicable.

<Mr.> <Rahul><Verma>

Dear <Rahul>,

Wishing you a very **HAPPY AND PROSPEROUS NEW YEAR 2004**. May this new year bring joy and peace into your lives. Please convey my greetings to your wife <Simran> and kids <Divya> and <Damini>

Thanking You,

Yours truly,

Sandeep Sinha

Exercise - III

Define a macro for creating the table shown below. Assign a shortcut key 'Alt + T' to the macro.

Item Name	Nos.	Rate	Amount

Exercise - IV

Create the sample letter shown below using the Letter Wizard:

Total Synergy Consulting

142A, Zamrudpur, Opposite LSR College, Greater Kailash I, New Delhi 110048
TeleFax:01-11-6228363 / 6482922 / 6451337

Tuesday, July 15, 2004

Mr. Anand Singh

CMD- Mayo Industries Ltd.
Mayo House, 27 Surya Nagar,
Hydrabad, A.P.

Dear Mr. Singh,

Subject: BPR Study for Mayo Industries

With reference to our discussion regarding the above-mentioned subject, I am sending you extracts from the Business Today article on Total Cost Management (TCM). As has been mentioned in this article:

"…cost-management, wielded wisely, acts as a crucial bridge between strategy and operational efficiency-one that can channel the working of the entire organization towards the unified goal of achieving competitive advantage. Used thus, cost-management effortlessly transcends the daily drudgery of numbers-oriented cost-cutting and launches the corporation into an orbit of global competitiveness.

Here, a company capitalizes on continuous cost-reduction to ensure better prices.

Here, a company makes cost-management an organization-spanning issue to ensure total commitment…."

I am sure that you would find TCM concepts very useful and directly relevant to what you are trying to achieve in your organization.

Regards,

Rakesh Kumar

Exercise - V

Create the following template and save this in the templates folder. (C:\Windows_folder\Application Data\Microsoft\Templates for Windows 98).

XYZ BANK
Date ---- / ----/ 2004
Pay
RUPEES

REVIEW QUESTIONS

1. Choose the most appropriate answer:

i. Which of the following is a Word Processing program?

(a) MS Windows (b) MS Access
(c) MS Outlook (d) MS Word

ii. This toolbar contains icons for changing the look/style of your text:

(a) Reviewing Toolbar (b) Standard Toolbar
(c) Formatting Toolbar (d) None of these

iii. This command displays a preview on screen of what you wish to print:

(a) Preview (b) Print Preview
(c) Page Preview (d) Document Preview

iv. In mail merge the file that contains the form letter is referred to as:

(a) Data source (b) Record
(c) Field (d) Main document

v. A series of word commands that have been grouped together as a single command:

(a) Macro (b) Menu
(c) Function (d) None of these

vi. This tool can be used to print a standard piece of text at the top and bottom of each page:

(a) Title (b) Message Box
(c) Header & Footer (d) None of these

vii. This is a special type of document that determines the basic layout of a document and can contain various document settings like fonts, macros, page page layout, toolbars, special formatting and styles:

(a) Table (b) Page Layout

(c) Template (d) None of these

2. Enter True or False:

i Toolbars contain buttons and dropdown menus that can be used for quickly executing the commands without having to go through the menus.

ii. All the formatting features offered by Word require pre-selection of a piece of text.

iii. Whenever a copy command is issued, the copied text is placed in Windows clipboard.

iv. Paragraph symbol is a non-printable character.

v. Once bullets are added to a paragraph, they cannot be removed from that paragraph.

vi. Word allows opening the recent documents without having to go to the open command.

vii. Scanned pictures can be inserted inside a `Nord table.

viii. Data source in the mail merge contains the names and addresses of recipients.

ix. Every Word document is based on some template.

x. Document templates contain settings that are available to all documents.

3. Match the following:

X	Y
1. Proofing Tool.	a. Track Changes
2. Combining two or more cells in the same row or column into a single cell.	b. Mail Merge
3. Allows to change the page margins, orientation and paper size.	c. Spell Checker
4. This feature can be used to track the changes (insertion/deletion of text, formatting or moving text from one place to another in the document) in your document.	d. Merging cells
5. This feature can be used to send the same matter to multiple people	e. Page Set up

4. Fill in the blanks with the appropriate choices listed below:

(i) Format Painter (ii) Break (iii) Change (iv) Collate (v) Revision marks (vi) Undo (vii) Datasource (viii) Landscape (ix) Template (x) Format (xi) Replace (xii) Web Layout (xiii) Global (xiv) Redo.

1. In _________ view you can preview your page, as it will appear in a web browser.
2. A document can be printed in portrait or _______________ mode.
3. Changes in a document can be reverted by using the ______________ feature.
4. ____________ can be used to replace all occurrences of one word with another.
5. __________ can be used to transfer formatting from one object to another object.
6. ____________ command is used to create multiple sections within a document.
7. ________________ is a useful feature when printing multiple sets of a document.
8. Word makes use of _____________ to show the tracked changes to the user.
9. Mail merge requires two things; creating main document and creating ________________.
10. All the templates must be stored in _______________ directory so that they can be used as a base for creating new documents.

5. Explain the various uses of MS Word.

6. Write short notes on:

i. Tables ii. Macros

7. Discuss the different types of templates in MS Word, and their specific advantages.

8. Discuss the Editing and Proofing tools available in MS Word.

CHAPTER 13 Spreadsheet Package

EXCEL BASICS

If the job at hand requires lot of lists, tables, financial calculations, analysis and graphs, Excel is just the package for you.

Excel is great at organising all types of data, but it is the numerical data where Excel is on its home turf. If you not only need a tool for storing and managing data—and also analysing and querying it—Excel's powerful features help you do all this and more effortlessly. Excel, besides offering simple database capabilities, also allows you to create documents for the World Wide Web (WWW) also.

The menus, toolbars and icons of MS Excel are very similar (though not the same; after all, if they were the same, why would you need two different packages!) to MS Word. This is keeping in line with Microsoft's much hyped philosophy and strategy of offering users a totally integrated office suite pack. From the user point of view, this means less time spent in learning the second package, once you know the first, and almost effortless and seamless exchange of data between various components.

Excel—or for that matter any spreadsheet—essentially comprises of a grid of rows and columns. Intersection of a row and a column is called a cell. Typically, rows are numbered numerically, i.e., 1, 2, 3... and so on, and columns are labeled alphabetically, i.e., A, B, C... and so on. Of course columns do not end at Z, after Z they start as AA, AB, AC... and then BA, BB, BC... and so on.

A workbook is similar to a notebook, containing numerous individual pages. Each workbook is stored as a separate file in Excel. Each page/sheet in a workbook is called a worksheet. You can enter and edit data on several worksheets simultaneously, and perform calculations based on data from multiple worksheets. The names of the sheets appear on tabs at the bottom of the workbook window.

Each spreadsheet (also called a worksheet) contains 65536 rows and 256 columns. That makes 16,777,216 cells (65536 *256), each holding either text or numbers or formulas. And this is not all; each workbook can contain 16 or numerous such worksheets (limited only by your computer's memory and storage capacity)! Huge, isn't it?

So much for facts and figures. In spite of these impressive statistics, the real power of Excel—member-crunching apart—lies in it's cool graphical user interface and user friendliness, even while performing some very sophisticated tasks.

Starting Excel

To start MS Excel choose **MS Excel** from **Programs** option from **Start** button.

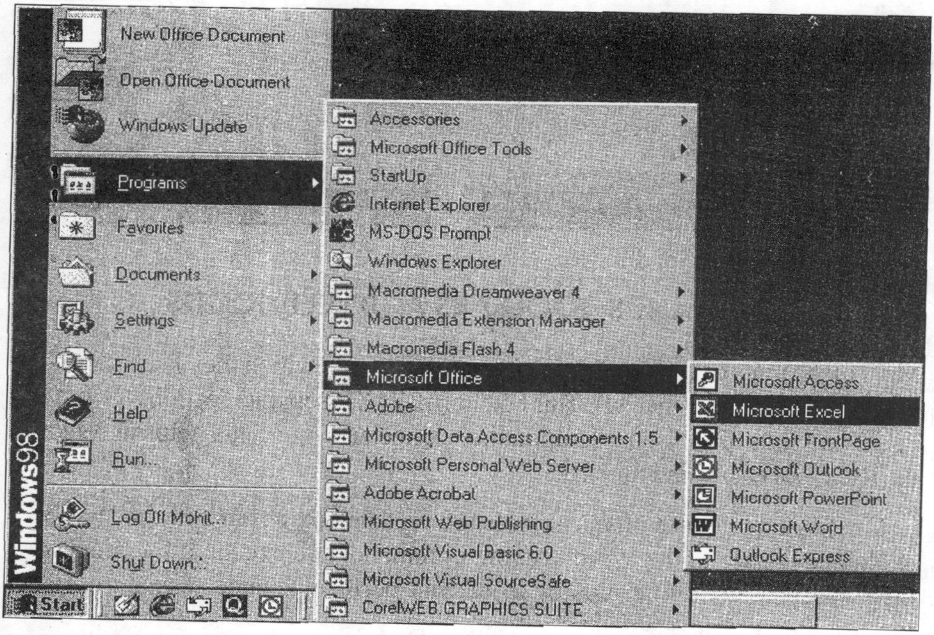

Elements of an Excel Window

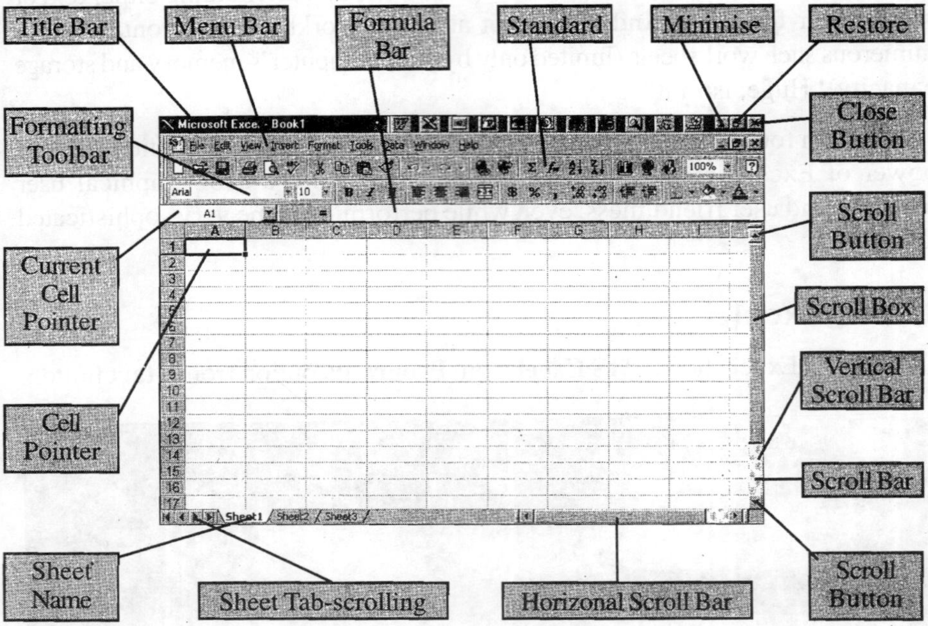

MENUS, COMMANDS, TOOLBARS AND THEIR ICONS

Most mechanics or technicians have a special box in which they keep their tools (working mechanics, that is!). This box normally has separate sections for keeping different kinds of tools, based upon their usage and size. This helps in selecting the right tool easily and quickly.

For MS Excel these physical tools are replaced by commands. As has been explained earlier in the Word section, commands are executed by clicking on their specific icons. Groups of icons that perform related tasks, are placed together in a ribbon, and called a Toolbar. There are many toolbars available in Excel – Standard toolbar, Formatting toolbar, Drawing toolbar etc. Each of these contains an assortment of related icons, specific to that toolbar. For executing most tasks, the user has three options:

1. Choose the desired command from the Menu options provided – either using the mouse or using keyboard cursor movement keys, or
2. Press the appropriate shortcut keys combination from the keyboard, or
3. Click once on the relevant icon from the displayed toolbars.

Although there is no wrong or right approach, most users find the third option simplest and fastest. Especially, for most commonly used commands, it is much simpler to use the Standard Toolbar and Formatting Toolbar icon, than using the menu options or keyboard shortcuts (which in any case are not available for all the commands).

The present section deals in detail with toolbars and icons. It discusses all the Excel Toolbars – the names of icons within each toolbars, their purpose and usage, their menu equivalents option and their keyboard shortcuts, if any.

You are advised to just go through the pages in this section once. Do not worry if you do not understand everything, and most importantly – do not try to memorise anything. Mugging up is no substitute for actual practice. In the next section when we do exercises based upon these menu options and icons, these would automatically become clear to you. Later, this section may be used by you as a ready reckoner to refer to any specific command or icon's usage.

TOOLBARS AND THEIR ICONS

Standard Toolbar

New
Creates a new blank file.
Alternative: File→New
Shortcut→Ctrl+N

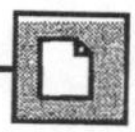

Open
Opens or finds a file.
Alternative: File→Open
Shortcut→Ctrl+O

Save
Saves the active file.
Alternative: File→ Save
Shortcut→Ctrl+S

E-mail
Sends contents of the current worksheet as body of the e-mail message.

Print Preview
Displays full page as they are printed.
Alternative: File→Print Preview
Shortcut→Ctrl+F2

Print
Prints the active file using current defaults.
Alternative: File→Print
Shortcut→Ctrl+P

Cut
Cuts the selection and puts it on the Clipboard.
Alternative: Edit→Cut
Shortcut→Ctrl+X

Spelling
Checks the spelling in the active file.
Alternative: Tools→Spelling
Shortcut→F7

Paste

Inserts the Clipboard contents at the insertion point.
Alternative: Edit→Paste
Shortcut→Ctrl+V

Copy

Copies the selection and puts it on the clipboard.
Alternative: Edit→Copy
Shortcut→Ctrl+C

Undo

Reverses certain last commands.
Alternative: Edit→Undo
Shortcut→Ctrl+Z

Format Painter

Copies the formatting of the selection to a specified location.
Shortcut→Ctrl+Shift+C

Insert Hyperlink

Displays the destination object, document or page.
Shortcut→Ctrl+K

Redo

Reverses the action of the Undo command.
Alternative: Edit→Repeat
Shortcut→Ctrl+Y

AutoSum

Adds numbers automatically with the SUM function. Excel suggests the range of cells to be added. If the suggested range is incorrect, drag through the range you want, and then press ENTER.

Paste Function

Displays a list of functions and their formats and allows you to set values for arguments.

Sort Ascending

Sorts the selected items in order from the beginning of the alphabet, the lowest number, or the earliest date, using the column that contains the insertion point. If you previously set other sorting options, those options are still in effect.
Alternative: Table→Sort →Ascending

Sort Descending

Sorts the selected items in the order from the end of the alphabet, the highest number, or the highest date, using the column that contains the insertion point. If you previously set other sorting options, those options are still in effect.
Alternative: Table→Sort→ Descending

Chart Wizard

Starts the Chart Wizard, which guides you through the steps for creating an embedded chart on a worksheet or modifying an existing chart.

Drawing

Shows or hides the Drawing Toolbar.
Alternative: View→Toolbars→Drawing

Zoom Control

Scales the editing view (Zoom).
Alternative: View→Zoom

Microsoft Excel Help

Provides help topics and tips to accomplish your task.
Alternative: Help→ Microsoft Word Help
Shortcut →F1

Formatting Toolbar

Font

Changes the font of the selection.
Alternative: Format→Font
Shortcut→Ctrl+Shift+F

Font Size

Changes the font size of the selection.
Alternative: Format→Font→Size
Shortcut→Ctrl+Shift+P

Bold

Makes the selection Bold.
Alternative: Format→Font→Font style
Shortcut→Ctrl+B

Italic

Makes the selection Italics.
Alternative: Format→Font→Font style *Shortcut*→Ctrl+I

Underline

Formats the selection with continuous underline.
*Alternative:*Format→Font→effects
Shortcut→Ctrl+U

Align Left

Aligns the paragraph at left indent.
Alternative:
Format→Paragraph→Alignment
Shortcut→Ctrl+L

Align Right

Aligns the paragraph at right indent.
Alternative:
Format→Paragraph→Alignment
Shortcut→Ctrl+R

Centre

Centres the paragraphs between the indents.
Alternative:
Format→Paragraph→Alignment
Shortcut→Ctrl+E

Merge and Centre

Combines two or more selected adjacent cells to create a single cell. The resulting merged cell contains only the upper left most data in the selection, which is centered within the cell. The cell reference for a merged cell is the upper left cell in the original selected range.

Currency

Applies on International currency style to the selected cells. Depending on the country selected in the **Windows Regional Settings** dialog box, the **International Currency Style** button might appear instead of the **currency style** button.

Percent Style

Applies the percent style to the selected cells. To change the Percent Style, use the **Style** command on the **Format** menu.

Comma Style

Applies the comma style to the selected cells. To change the comma style, use the **Style** command on the **Format** menu.

Increase Decimal

Increases the number of digits displayed after the decimal point in the selected cells.

Decrease Decimal

Decreases the number of digits displayed after the decimal point in the selected cells.

Decrease Indent

Decreases or promotes the selection one level.

Alternative:

Format→Paragraph→Indentation

Increase Indent

Increases indent or demotes the selection one level.

Alternative:

Format→Paragraph→Indentation

Borders

Shows or hides the border toolbar.

Alternative:

Format→Borders and Shading

Fill Color

Adds, modifies, or removes the fill color or fill effect from the selected object. Fill effects include gradient, texture, pattern or picture fills.

Font Color

Selects and applies Font Color.

Alternative: Format→Font →Color

Drawing Toolbar

Draw

Activates the Draw Menu.

Free Rotate

Rotates the selected object to any degree. Select the object, click on the icon and then drag a corner of the object in the direction you want to rotate it.

Line

Draws a straight line where you click or drag in the active Window. To constrain the line to draw at the 15-degree angles from its starting point, hold down SHIFT as you drag.

Select Objects

Changes the pointer to a selection arrow so you can select objects in the active Window. To select a single object, click the object with the arrow. To select one or more objects, drag the arrow over the objects you want to select.

AutoShapes

Activates the AutoShapes menu.

Arrow

Inserts a line with an arrowhead where you click or drag in the active Window. To constrain the line to draw at the 15-degree angles from its starting point, hold down SHIFT as you drag.

Rectangle
Draws an rectangle where you click or drag in the active Window. To draw a square, press SHIFT and drag.

Oval
Draws an oval where you click or drag in the active Window. To draw a circle, press SHIFT and drag.

Text Box
Draws a text box where you click or drag in the active Window. Use a text box to add a text – such as captions or callouts to your pictures or graphics.
Alternative: Insert→TextBox

WordArt
Creates text effects by inserting a Microsoft Office drawing object.

Insert Clip Art
Inserts existing picture into the file at the desired position from the picture gallery.
Alternative: Insert→Picture →ClipArt

Line Color
Adds, modifies, or removes the line colour from the selected objects.

Font Color
Formats the selected text with the colour you click.

Fill Color
Adds, modifies, or removes the fill colour or fill effect from the selected object. Fill effects include gradient, texture, pattern or picture fills.

Dash Style
Click the dashed line or dashed-dot line style you want for the selected shape or border. Click the solid line if you don't want the dotted line.

Line Style
Click the width you want for the selected line.

Shadow
Click the shadow style you want for the selected object.

Arrow Style
Click the arrowhead style you want for the selected line.

3-D
Click the 3-D style you want for the selected object.

Navigating

To move around the spreadsheets, either use the keyboard keys ↑ for going up, ↓ for going down, ← for going left, → for going right, Page Up for going one screen up, Page Down for going one screen down, and other related keys; or use mouse to traverse the different parts of the worksheet through scroll bars. You can also type the desired cell address directly in the Address name box to randomly go anywhere in the worksheet.

Selecting Cells

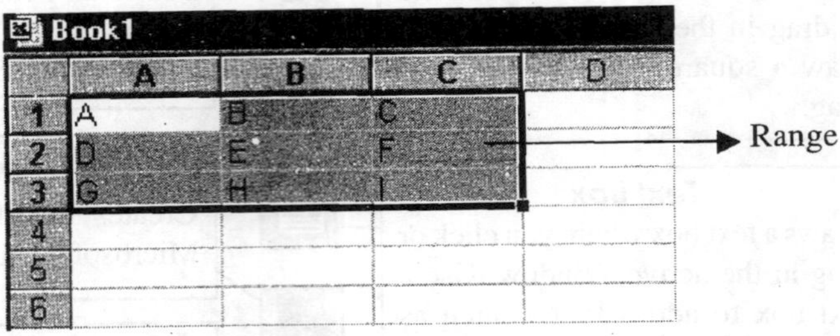

Before entering, editing or formatting cells, they need to be selected. You can select a single cell, or a group of continuous cells or even a discontinuous group of cells. This selection is called a range. A range is a rectangular group of cells that is referred to by its diagonal corners (top-left cell address and bottom-right cell address separated by a colon). Example A1:C3 implies a rectangle covering all the 9 cells from A1 to C3, i.e., A1, B1, C1, A2, B2, C2, A3, B3 and C3.

Selecting Cells with Mouse

1. To select a single cell, simply point and click on it to make it active.
2. Click on a row number to select the entire row.
3. Click on a column alphabet to select the entire column.
4. Click and drag to select a range of cells.
5. Click on the empty button at the intersection of the column and row numbers to select the entire worksheet.

Selecting Sheets

1. To select a single sheet, click on the desired sheet tab.
2. To select multiple adjacent sheets, select the first sheet by clicking on its tab, and then hold down the **Shift** key and click on the tab for the last sheet.
3. To select multiple non-adjacent sheets, select the first sheet by clicking on its tab, and then hold down the **Ctrl** key and click on the tabs for other sheets.

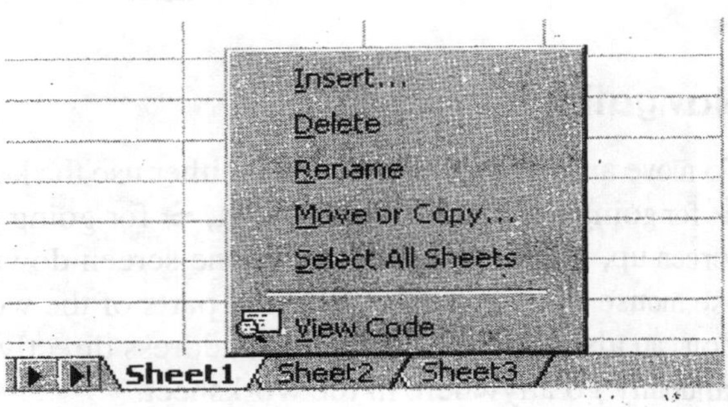

4. To select all the sheets in a workbook, right click on any sheet tab and choose **Select All Sheets** from the pop up menu.

Alignment

Any text that you type is always left aligned within the cell. Any number that you type is always right aligned within the cells. Like most other default settings, these alignments can be changed as per your requirements.

Entering Data into a Cell

There are two basic types of data that are used in a spreadsheet: Values and Formulas. Values include numbers and text, and Formulas are arithmetic calculations that change based on the input given to them. To enter values, simply select the desired cell and start typing. Press Enter key to conclude an entry. As you start typing, the text would appear in the active cell and in the formula bar. The data is not considered to be entered into your worksheet until the Enter key is pressed. When you press the Enter key, you may find that you are automatically moved one cell down on your worksheet.

If you wish to enter data into a range of cells, then it is advisable to select the entire range first and then use the Tab key to navigate within the selected range of cells.

Entering Formulas

The real power of Excel lies in it being able to store complex formulas. You can either build formulas using absolute numbers (like = 4+2) or use relative cell address (like = A1+B1). As a rule of thumb, you must always use relative cell referencing because in case the values change in future, the formulas based upon these values would automatically show the updated results. You place the formula in the cell in which you want to see the result. Start by activating the cell where you wish to place the formula, begin by typing either an equal sign (=) or plus sign (+) to tell Excel that you are about to start a formula. You can then either type the formula, one character at a time in the formula bar, or assemble it using mouse or keyboard. For instance, you could either type =A1-B1 in the cell C1 and press Enter, or place the mouse pointer in cell C1 and type = sign, point and click the cell A1, type -, point and click at cell B1 and press Enter. During this process when you point and click at cell A1, this cell would be surrounded by a dashed outline (some call it marching ants!) and simultaneously this address would appear in the formula bar. The same happens while pointing to cell B1. This process not only makes it unnecessary for you to type the cell addresses in the formula bar but also ensures that no mistakes are committed in specifying cell addresses.

Editing Data

Once you have entered a value or a formula into a cell, you may need to change it. If you make a mistake while typing and before pressing Enter, simply press

Backspace Key to erase the present contents and type the correct text. If you notice an error after finishing the entry, activate the relevant cell and press F2 Function Key. The current contents of the cell would be displayed in the formula bar, now you can correct the entry and press Enter to conclude. If you wish to replace the entire text, activate the relevant cell and simply type the new text. The new text would automatically replace the old text.

Editing a cell's contents is very similar to editing data in any Word document. You can use the arrow keys to navigate between the cells of a worksheet.

Creating a New Workbook

Workbooks are named consecutively, starting with Book1, Book2 and so on. By default a workbook contains three sheets. However, as many sheets can be added to the workbook as required.

Follow the steps below to create a workbook:

① Choose **New** from the **File** menu.

② Click on **Workbook** in the **New** dialogue box.

③ Click on **OK** button to create the workbook.

A Workbook

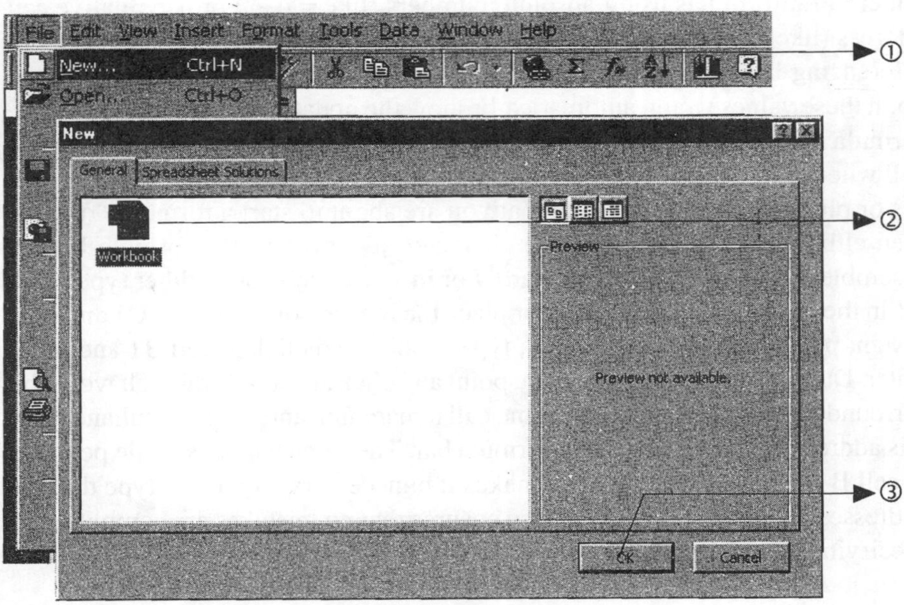

Note: You can also create new workbooks on existing templates. A template in Excel is a special type of workbook with pre-defined formats and controls that can be used as a base for creating other workbooks. To create a workbook based on an existing template, simply select the desired template from the Spreadsheet Solutions tab and click the **OK** button to create the desired template based workbook.

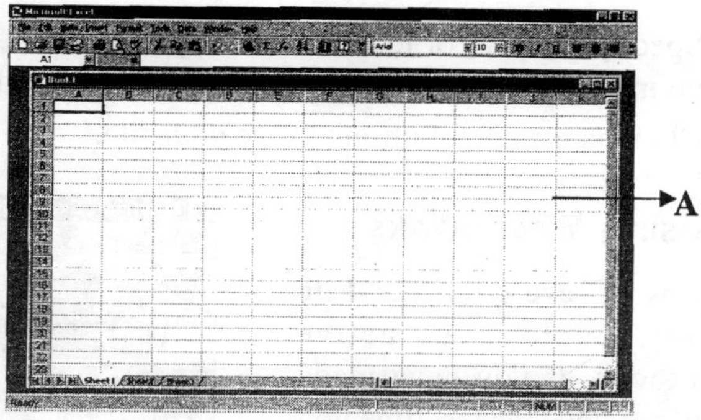

As explained earlier, a cell is an intersection of a vertical column identified by a column letter (A, B, C...) and a horizontal row identified by a row number (1, 2, 3...). This unique location (for each cell) is called the Cell Address (e.g., cell B3 means column B and third row, A27 means column A, row twenty-seven. The cell, which you are presently working on (where your cursor is presently placed), is called the Active or the Current cell.

Saving a Workbook

You must save your work so that it can be used again. It is usually a good practice to save your work frequently so that, in case of a power failure, you would loose only a minimal amount of work.

Excel file extensions

Extension	Description
.xls	Workbook
.xlw	Workspace
.xlt	Template
.xlk	Backup File

By default an Excel file is saved with .xls extension. Follow the steps below to save your work:

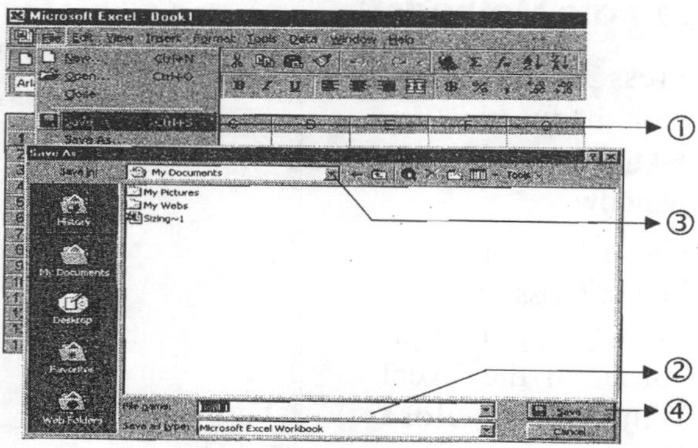

① Choose **Save** from the **File** menu.

② Type a file name, it is always advisable to give meaningful file names.

③ Specify the path or location where you wish to save your work. By default your workbook is saved in **My Documents** folder.

④ Click on the **Save** button to save your file.

Closing Workbooks

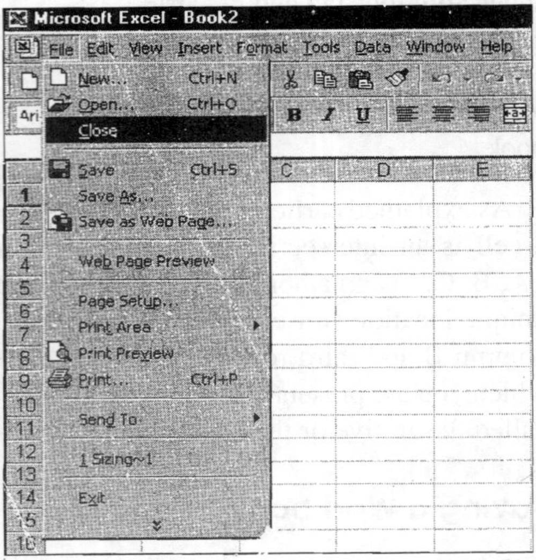

Choose **Close** from the **File** menu to close an active workbook. If you have made changes since the last time you saved your work then you will be prompted to save your changes. To close all open workbooks, hold down the Shift key before you click the File menu. The close command of the File menu changes to Close All. Click on this option if you wish to close all open workbooks at one go.

Closing Excel

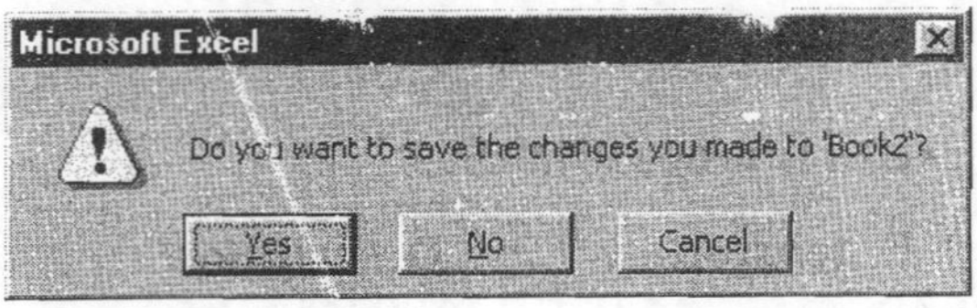

To quit Excel, Choose **Exit** from the **File** menu. If you have been working in a workbook that has not been saved then a dialogue box is displayed to the user, asking whether the user would like to save the changes.The user has three options – he can choose **Yes** to save the chang in the workbook, **No** to discard the changes or Cancel to return to working in Excel.

Alternate Methods

1. Press Alt key along with the function key F4 to close any active window.
2. **Close Button**: Click on the cross (X) mark in the upper right corner of the Excel Window to close Excel.

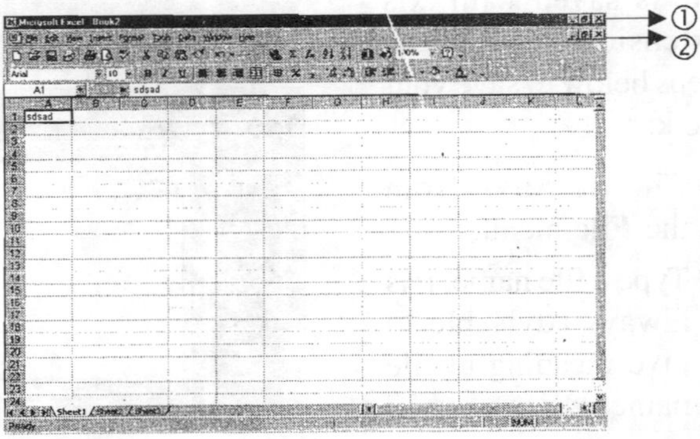

① Quits Excel.

② Closes the active workbook.

Working with Workbooks and Worksheets

Inserting Worksheets To add a new worksheet into your workbook, choose **Worksheet** from the **Insert** menu. Worksheet will be added to the left of active sheet.

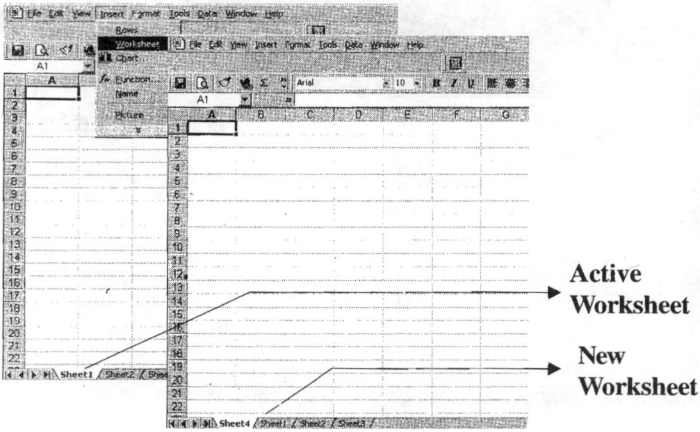

Note: To add multiple worksheets, hold down Shift key and click the number of worksheet tabs you want to add in the open workbook. Suppose you want to add three worksheets at one go then hold down shift key until you click on three worksheet tabs. Then choose Worksheet from the Insert menu.

Deleting Worksheets Select the sheet(s) you want to delete and choose **Delete Sheet** from the **Edit** menu. Choose **OK** from the dialog box to delete the selected sheet.

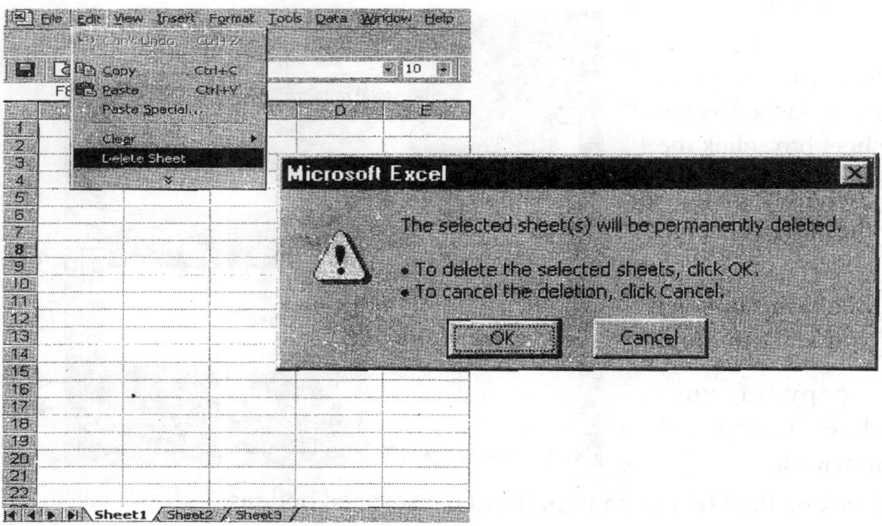

Renaming Worksheets You can Rename a worksheet to make it more user-friendly. To rename a worksheet, select the sheet and choose **Rename** from **Sheet** command from the **Format** menu. Alternatively, you can double click on the desired sheet tab and type the new worksheet name.

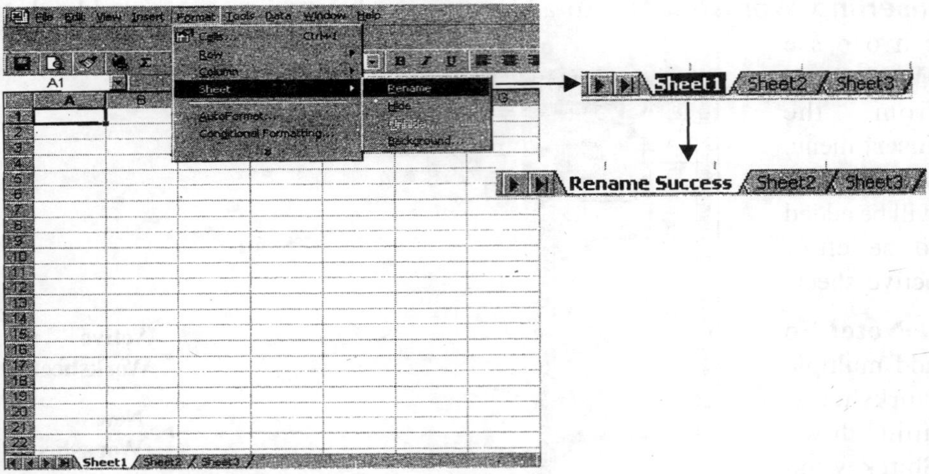

Moving Worksheets To move sheets within the current workbook, drag the desired sheet along the row of sheet tabs to the desired position. Alternatively, you can choose **Move or Copy Sheet** from the **Edit** menu. A dialog box as shown below is displayed to the user.

① The drop down box will contain the list of all open workbooks; the current workbook will be displayed at the first position. In case you wish to move the sheet to a different workbook, choose the desired workbook from the drop down box.

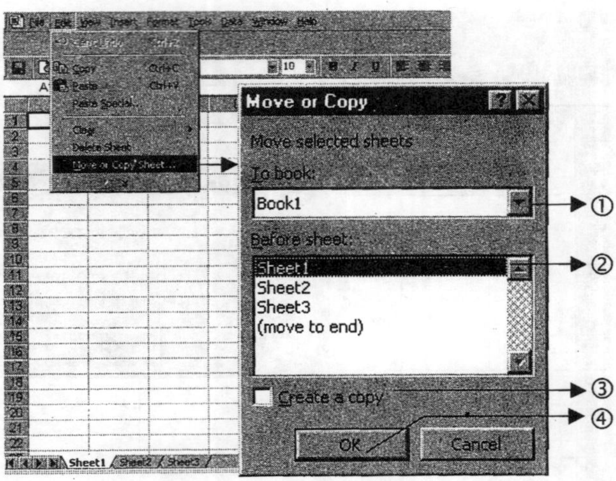

② Choose the new position of your sheet. In the **Before sheet** box, click the sheet before which you want to insert the moved or copied sheets.

③ Select this option if you want to create a copy of your sheet instead of moving it.

④ Click on the **OK** button to perform the selected options.

Hiding Workbooks/Worksheets A Workbook/Worksheet can be hidden from the user's view. Hiding a workbook/sheet does not delete its data. Hiding the worksheet(s) reduces the number of sheets on the screen. It is useful to hide the sheets that contain sensitive data to prevent unwanted changes.

Hiding Selected Rows and Columns of a Worksheet

① Selects the rows and columns you wish to hide in a worksheet.

② On the **Format** menu, choose either **Row** or **Column** and then click on **Hide.** To display the hidden rows/columns, choose **Unhide** from **Row** or **Column.**

A The selected rows would be hidden from the user's view.

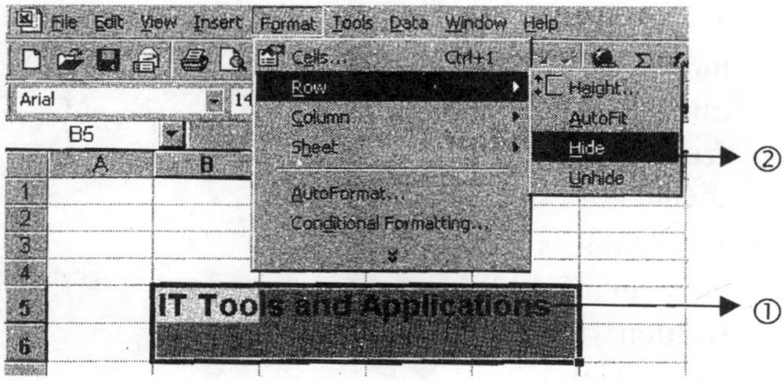

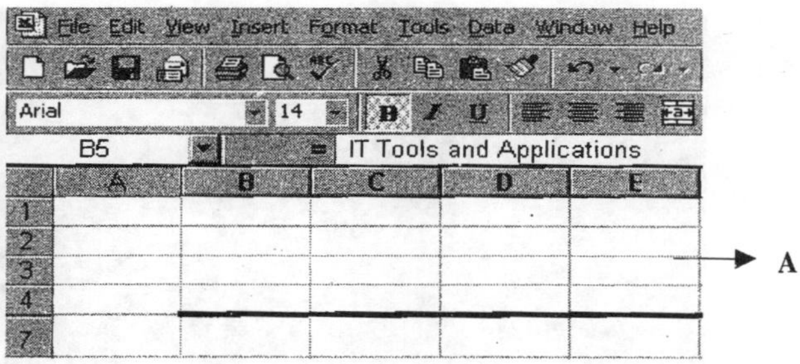

Hiding a Worksheet

① Selects the sheets you wish to hide by clicking on the sheet name.

② Choose **Hide** from the **Format** menu. To display the hidden sheets, choose **Unhide** from the **Format** menu.

A The selected rows would be hidden from the user's view.

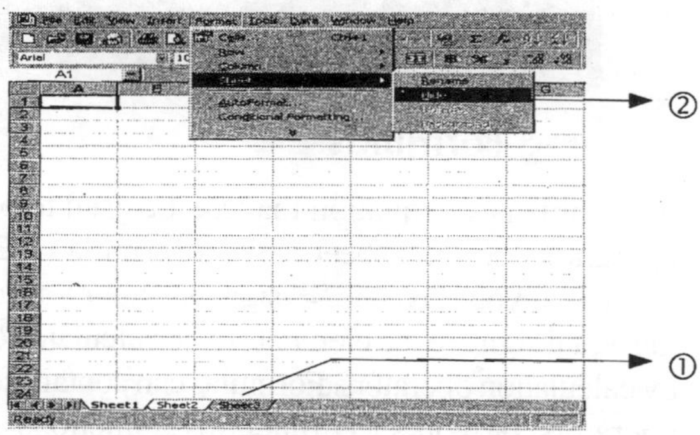

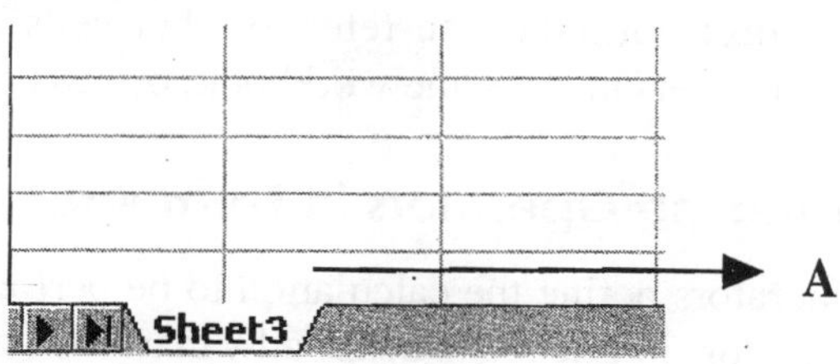

Hiding a Workbook

① Open the workbook(s) you wish to hide.

② Choose **Hide** from the **Window** menu. To display the hidden workbook(s), choose **Unhide** from the **Window** menu.

A Workbook(s) selected in ① will be hidden from the user's view.

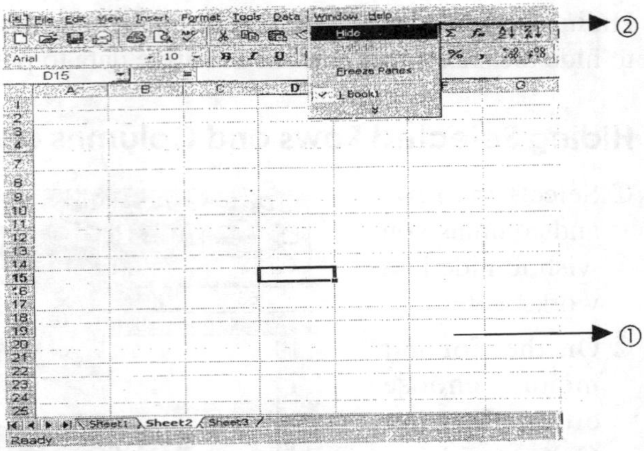

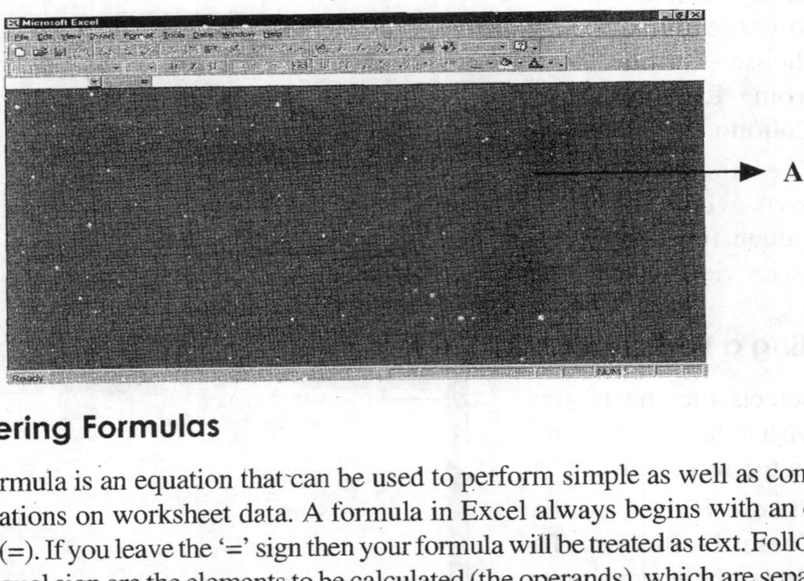

Entering Formulas

A formula is an equation that can be used to perform simple as well as complex operations on worksheet data. A formula in Excel always begins with an equal sign (=). If you leave the '=' sign then your formula will be treated as text. Following the equal sign are the elements to be calculated (the operands), which are separated by calculation operators. Formulas can contain constant values, valid cell references, operators, or worksheet functions (Functions are explained in the next section).

Note: Formulas can refer to other cells on the same worksheet, cells on other sheets in the same workbook, or cells on sheets in other workbooks.

Handling Operators in Formulae

Operators define the calculation to be performed by the formula. Calculation operators in Excel can be broadly classified into four categories:

1. **Arithmetic operators** – They are used to perform basic mathematical operations such as addition, subtraction, or multiplication or division. Examples: + (Addition), - (Subtraction), * (Multiplication), / (Division), ^ (Exponentiation) etc.
2. **Comparison operators** – They are used to compare two values and the result of comparison is a logical value (true or false). Examples: = (Equal To), > (Greater than), < (Less than), >= (Greater than or Equal to), <= (Less than or equal to), <> (Not Equal to)
3. **Text concatenation operator** (&) – They are used to join, or concatenate, one or more text strings to produce a single piece of text. Example: "Hello" & "World" = HelloWorld
4. **Reference operators** – They are used to combine ranges of cells for calculations with the following operators:

Range operator [: (colon)] – Used to produce one reference to all the cells between two references, including the two cell references. Example - A2:A20

Union operator [, (comma)] – Used to combine multiple cell references into a single reference. Example – Sum(A2:A4, B2:B4)

Intersection operator (space) – Used to refer to the cell at the intersection point of two ranges. Example – The cell D2 will be at the intersection of the ranges D2:D4 and C2:E2.

Order of precedence of operators – Calculates the formula as per the standard mathematical BODMAS (Brackets of Division, Multiplication, Addition and Subtraction) protocol, and in the following order:

Operator	Description
: (colon)	
(single space)	
, (comma)	Reference Operators
%	Percent
^	Exponentiation
/ and *	Division and Multiplication
+ and –	Addition and Subtraction
&	Concatenation Operator
= < > <= >= <>	Comparison Operators

Excel calculates the formula from left to right, according to a specific order for each operator in the formula. However, you can change the order of operations by using parentheses. Operations within parenthesis to take precedence in calculations. Example: the following two formulas are identical, with the exception of parenthesis.

2+(6/3) = 4 and (2+6)/3 = 2.7

Now let us learn how to create formulas in Excel using an example. The following example explains:

- How to define a formula
- Some of the commonly used formatting features in MS Excel
  - Changing Data alignment
  - Changing Font Style and Font Size
  - Changing Date, number and currency format.
- Previewing and Printing Worksheets.

Excel Exercise I

Ideas Unlimited Pvt. Ltd.

C-100 Defence Colony, New Delhi, India

Payroll for the month of January 1997

Figures in '000

Sl.No.	Employee Name	Joining Date	Basic	DA	HRA	CCA	PF	I.Tax	Net Salary
1	Bill Hates	1-Dec-92	5000.00	1666.50	999.98	597.99	742.97	826.45	6695.04
2	Binder Gujral	5-Feb-97	8500.00	2833.05	1699.96	1016.57	1263.06	1404.96	11381.57
3	J.R.D. Bata	30-Mar-87	7500.00	2499.75	1499.96	896.98	1114.46	1239.67	10042.56
4	Lorry Ellison	30-Jun-86	9000.00	2999.70	1799.96	1076.37	1337.35	1497.60	12051.07
5	Manwoman Singh	5-Nov-81	6500.00	2166.45	1299.97	777.38	965.87	1074.38	8703.55
6	Only Birla	19-Feb-76	6700.00	2233.11	1339.97	801.30	995.59	1107.44	8971.35
7	Scot Really	27-Jan-95	4500.00	1499.85	899.98	538.19	668.68	743.80	6025.54
8	Steve Knobs	30-Sep-86	9100.00	3033.03	1819.95	1088.33	1352.21	1504.13	12184.97
9	Tea Chidambaram	15-Oct-95	10000.00	3333.00	1999.95	1195.97	1485.95	1652.89	13390.08
10	Witch Kapoor	15-Jun-87	2900.00	966.57	579.99	346.83	430.93	479.34	3883.12
	Totals		69700.00	23231.01	13939.65	8335.91	10357.07	11520.66	93328.84

Instructions for filling up various columns:

Dearness Allowances (DA) is paid @ 33.33% of Basic Salary.

House Rent Allowance (HRA) is paid @ 15% of Basic Salary + DA combined together.

City Compensatory Allowance (CCA) is paid @ 7.8% of Basic Salary + DA + HRA combined together.

Provident Fund (PF) is deducted @ 8.99% of Basic Salary +DA + HRA + CCA combined together.

Income Tax (I.Tax) is deducted @ 10% of Basic Salary + DA + HRA + CCA combined together.

Net Salary is summation of Basic Salary + DA + HRA + CCA less PF and I.Tax.

ENTERING TEXT IN CELLS

① Create a new worksheet and start typing the text in this blank worksheet. You would find it slightly different than typing in Word. Here, each piece of text is typed in a different cell. Type only till what is shown here and for the time being don't bother about the way it looks. Notice that columns for Employee Name and Joining Date appear trimmed off, we will see later how we can rectify this.

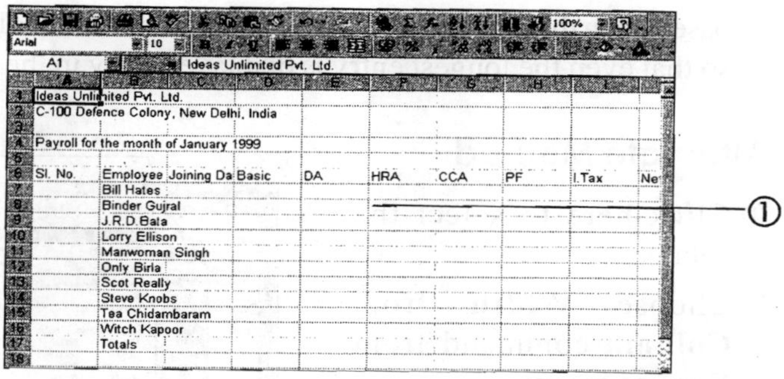

② Type the Joining Date of all the employees in American mm/dd/yy (month/date/year) format. Don't worry, we can always change this later to our Indian dd/mm/yy (date/month/year) format. Type the Basic Salaries in the next column.

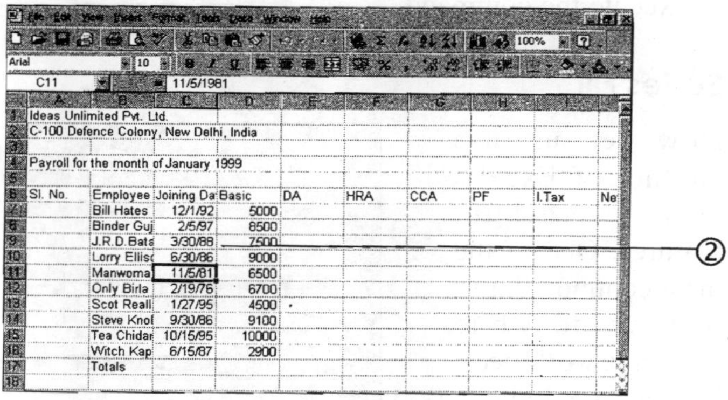

ColumnWidth

Now is the time to rectify the problems. To begin with, presently the employee names are not fitting within the current column width.

① Click once on the column label (B) to select the entire column.

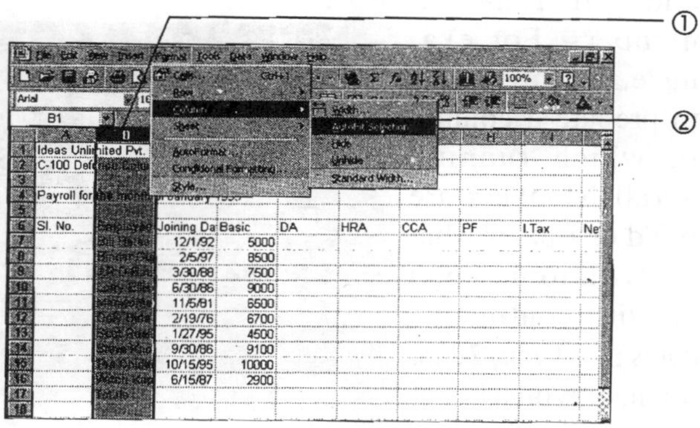

② Choose **AutoFit Selection** from **Column** command from **Format** menu. This command would check for the longest entry in the selected column and based upon that entry, would automatically adjust the column width accordingly, so that even the longest entry is displayed fully in the column width.

Alternate Method

① Click here to select the column.

② Choose **Width** from **Column** command from **Format menu**.

③ A dialogue box like this would pop-up. Specify the desired column width.

④ Click once on **OK** button to execute the command.

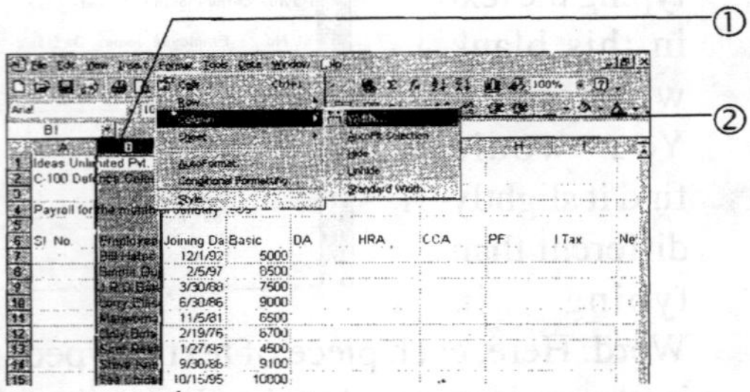

Series Fill

Now let us use another of Excel's many helpful features. One of the most common things that we do while preparing worksheets is that we have a range of cells in a column or a row, which we wish to fill up with consecutive and incremental numbers. For example, you might wish to prepare a column in which running Serial Numbers are filled up (that is what we wish to do now) or with continuous dates like 1 Jan, 2 Jan, 3 Jan, or with a list of

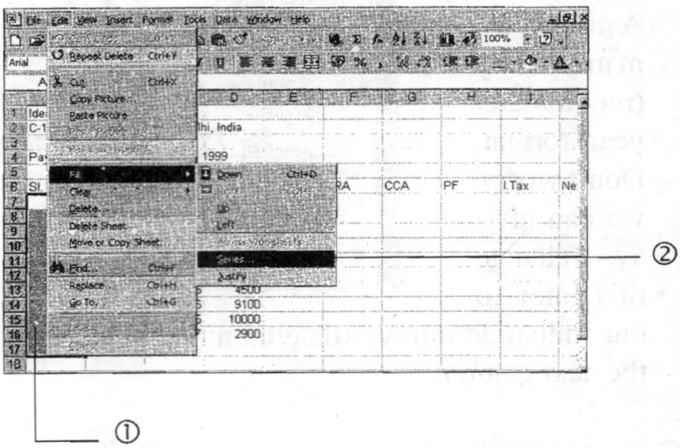

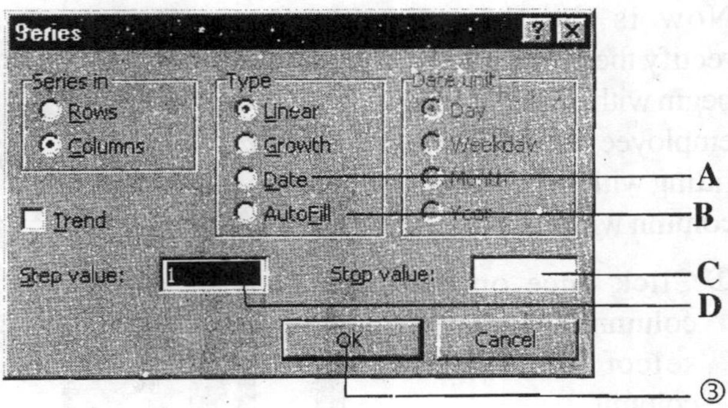

all Mondays in a year like 4 May, 11 May, 18 May,... and so on. For such cases, you need not waste your time in doing these things manually. You can ask Excel to do it for you. There is only one prerequisite, the common difference between any two consecutive numbers must be common throughout this series: 1, 1 and 7 in case of our three examples mentioned above, respectively.

① Type 1 in the place of first SL. No. Use the mouse and specify the whole range (including Sl. No. 1), which you wish to fill up with consecutive nos.

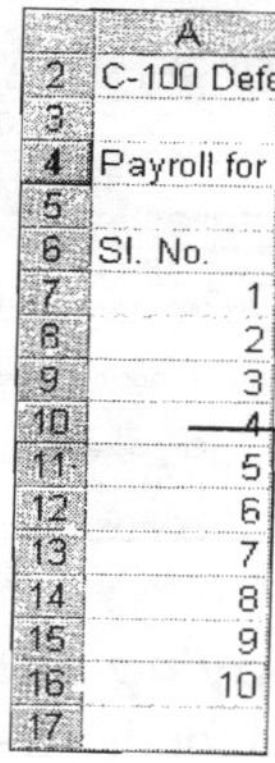

② Choose **Series** from **Fill** command from **Edit** menu.

③ Click once on **OK** button to continue.

A Click on this radio button for filling up for Dates.

B Through Auto Fill command, if you type Jan., Feb. in two cells and specifies a further range, Excel would automatically fill in March to December. Same for Sunday to Monday and so many more examples.

C Stop value need not be specified, since the length of range specified would automatically determine the last value.

D Common increment between two consequent numbers in the desired series.

E All serial numbers filled up automatically.

Entering Formulas

Now, as explained earlier, type or "assemble" the formulas for the subsequent columns for the first employee only.

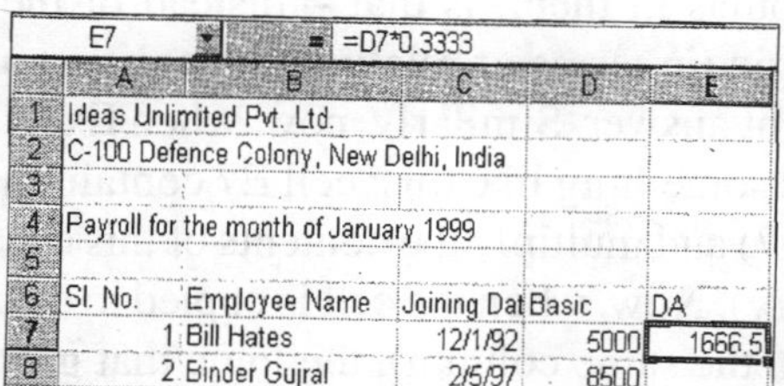

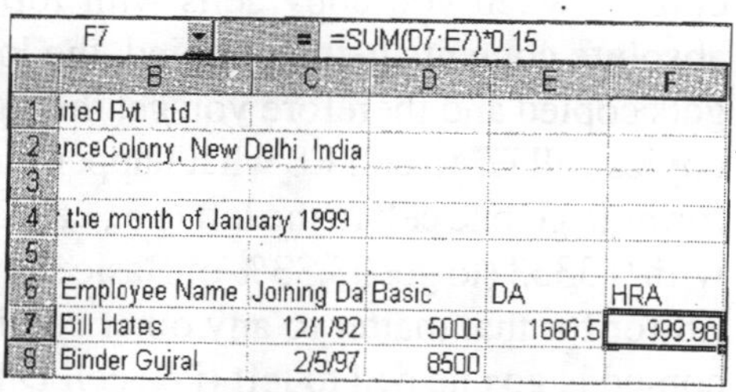

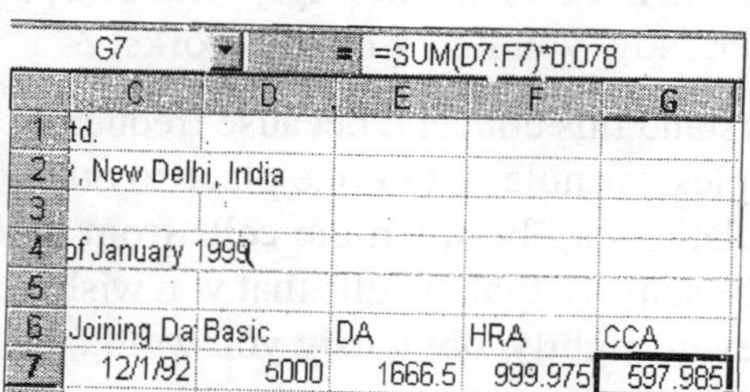

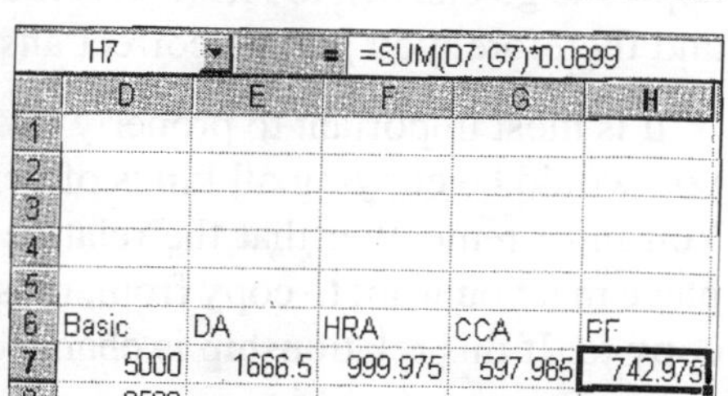

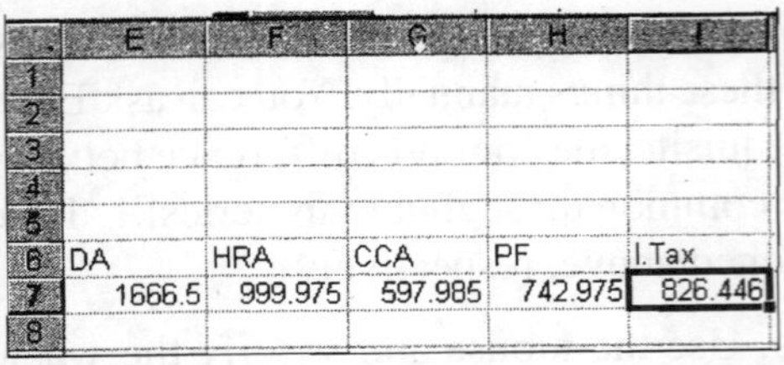

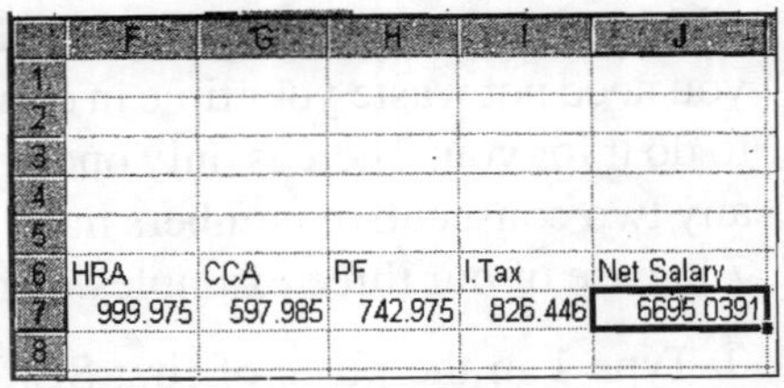

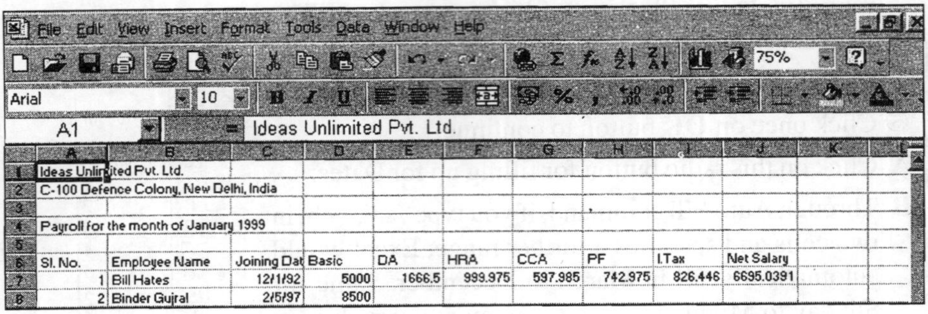

Copying and pasting the formula Once all the formulas have been created for the first employee, all you need to do now is copy these to the rest of the cells. That's right, simply copy! Excel does a very smart thing while copying formulas. It changes them based upon the relative positioning of cells. Let me explain this in more detail. When Excel builds a formula like =A1+B1 in cell C1, the computer does not understand A1, B1 or C1. What it does understand is "I'm in a cell called C1, go two cells to the left (i.e., A1) and go one cell to the left (i.e. B1), add up the contents of these two cells and show me the answer here (i.e. the cell C1)". The important thing here is the relative positions of cells A1, B1 and C1 to each other and the logic of the formula. What actually gets copied, when you copy cells with formulas in them, is that – instead of the absolute contents getting copied, the logic (in terms of relative cell positions) gets copied and therefore you get the right answer. Similarly, now, when Excel copies cell E7 to cell E8 what happens is something like this: cell E7 contains a formula go one cell to the left (i.e., cell D7) and multiply the contents of this cell with 0.3333 (to get 33.33% of Basic salary). Now, when the cell is copied to cell E8 (or for that matter to any other cell in the same column), the logic that gets copied is go one cell to left (i.e., cell D8, and not D7) and multiply with 0.3333 and therefore, you get the correct answer. Now you know how it works!

It is most important to properly understand this concept, because frequently you would be copying all kinds of complex formulas from one place to other. You must remember that the relative relationship between the cells from the place that you want to copy from, must be same as that of cells that you wish to copy to. If this relationship is changed even slightly, obviously you would get wrong answers.

① Place the cursor at cell E7. Choose **Copy** command from **Edit** menu.

② Highlight all the cells (E8 to E16) where you wish to copy the same formula and either press **Enter** or choose the **Paste** command from **Edit** menu or click once on **Paste** Icon.

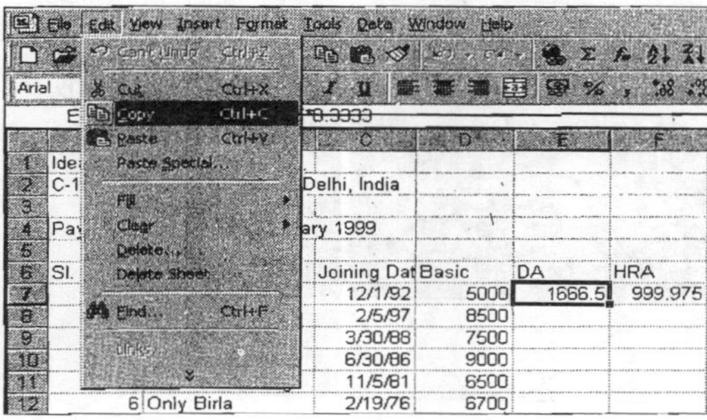

Basic	DA	HRA
5000	1666.5	999.975
8500	2833.05	
7500	2499.75	
9000	2999.7	
6500	2166.45	
6700	2233.11	
4500	1499.85	
9100	3033.03	
10000	3333	
2900	966.57	

②

Use the same technique to copy the formula into the rest of the cells. Do it column-by-column or better still, copy the entire row of formulas and specify all the subsequent rows to copy to, in a single command.

HRA	CCA	PF	I.Tax	Net Salary
999.975	597.985	742.975	826.446	########

HRA	CCA	PF	I.Tax	Net Salary
999.975	597.985	742.975	826.446	########
1699.958	1016.575	1263.057	1404.958	########
1499.963	896.978	1114.462	1239.669	########
1799.955	1076.373	1337.355	1487.603	########
1299.968	777.381	965.8674	1074.38	########
1339.967	801.300	995.5864	1107.438	########
899.978	538.187	668.6775	743.8014	########
1819.955	1088.333	1352.214	1504.132	########
1999.950	1195.970	1485.95	1652.892	########
579.986	346.831	430.9255	479.3387	########

A

A Notice that in some places instead of numbers you are getting hash symbols (#), it means that the current column width is not sufficient to display the entire contents.

③ Simply use the **AutoFit selection** command from the **Column** command from **Format** menu to adjust the column width of Net Salary.

Basic	DA	HRA	CCA	PF	I.Tax	Net Salary
5000	1666.5	999.975	597.985	742.975	826.446	6695.8391
8500	2833.05	1699.958	1016.575	1263.057	1404.958	11381.5664
7500	2499.75	1499.963	896.978	1114.462	1239.669	10042.5586
9000	2999.7	1799.955	1076.373	1337.355	1487.603	12051.0704
6500	2166.45	1299.968	777.381	965.8674	1074.38	8703.5508
6700	2233.11	1339.967	801.300	995.5864	1107.438	8971.3524
4500	1499.85	899.978	538.187	668.6775	743.8014	6025.5352
9100	3033.03	1819.955	1088.333	1352.214	1504.132	12184.9711
10000	3333	1999.950	1195.970	1485.95	1652.892	13390.0782
2900	966.57	579.986	346.831	430.9255	479.3387	3883.1227

③

Summation

Once all the values have been filled up for all the employees, let us now try and get the column sum, i.e. Total Basic, Total DA, Total HRA, Total CCA, Total PF, Total I.Tax and Total Net Salary paid by Ideas Unlimited Pvt. Ltd.

① Highlight all the Salary related columns, *excluding* the column heading row and *including* a blank row at the bottom, where you want the totals to appear.

② Click on **AutoSum** icon Σ to get an AutoSum of all columns total.

A Notice this row has automatically been filled in with the totals of all the salary items.

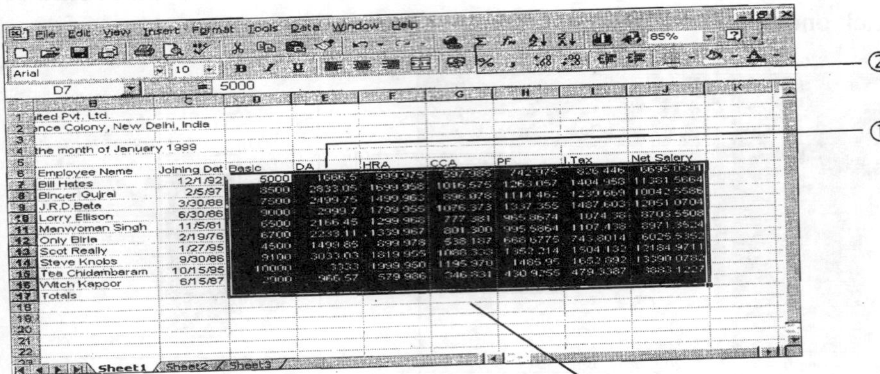

Basic	DA	HRA	CCA	PF	I.Tax	Net Salary
5000	1666.5	999.975	597.985	742.975	826.446	6695.0391
8500	2833.05	1699.958	1016.575	1263.06	1404.96	11381.5664
7500	2499.75	1499.963	896.978	1114.46	1239.67	10042.5586
9000	2999.7	1799.955	1076.373	1337.35	1487.6	12051.0704
6500	2166.45	1299.968	777.381	965.867	1074.38	8703.5508
6700	2233.11	1339.967	801.300	995.586	1107.44	8971.3524
4500	1499.85	899.978	538.187	668.677	743.801	6025.5352
9100	3033.03	1819.955	1088.333	1352.21	1504.13	12184.9711
10000	3333	1999.950	1195.970	1485.95	1652.89	13390.0782
2900	966.57	579.986	346.831	430.925	479.339	3883.1227
69700.00	23231.01	13939.652	8335.912	10357.07	11520.66	93328.8449

A

Formatting Cells

You might have noticed by now that some columns have decimal places and some do not. Also, it is not very easy to read long numbers without comma (,) marks. So to solve this problem, let us format the range.

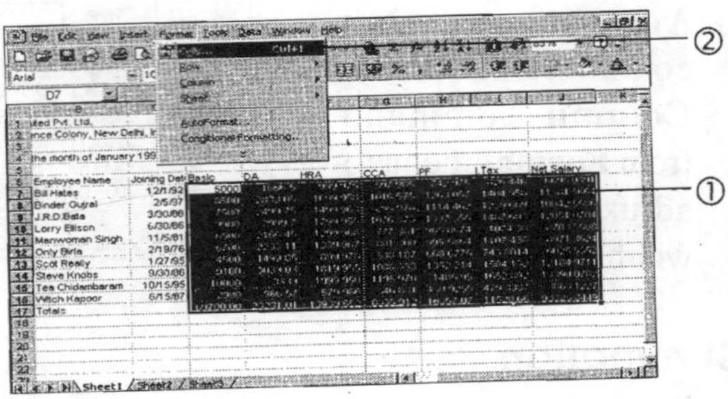

① Highlight all the columns containing numbers.

② Choose **Cells** command from **Format** menu.

③ Choose **Number** Folio.

④ Choose **Number** from **Category** list.

⑤ Specify 2 decimal places.

⑥ Click here to have (,) after every 3rd digit in each numbers

⑦ Click once on **OK** button to execute the command.

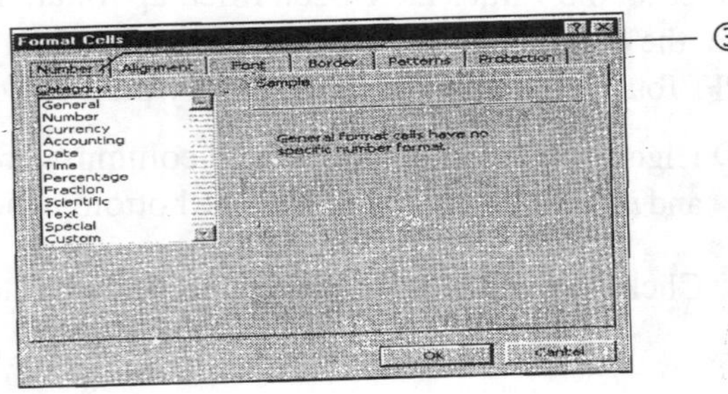

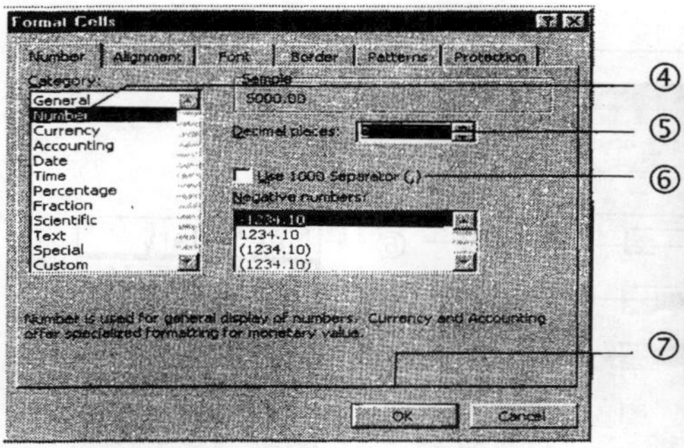

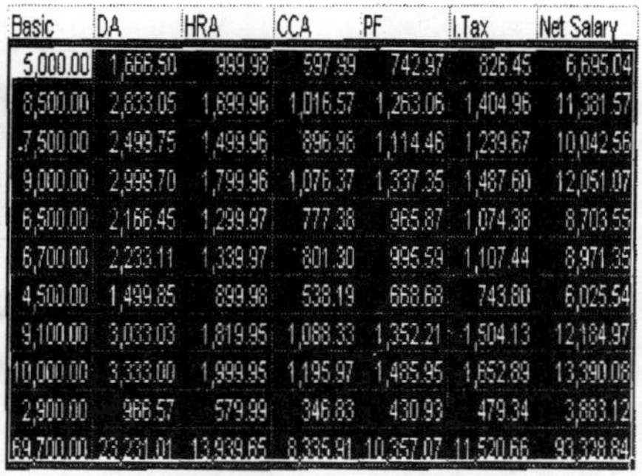

Currency Notation

Next, let us say, we want that the Net salary should display the currency symbol as a prefix for all the numbers. Here, we have derived this Net Salary as a formula, so it is treated as a number, however even if you had typed certain numbers (e.g., Basic Salary) and wanted these to be displayed in currency format, NEVER type the currency symbol before the numbers. This would cause Excel to understand these values as text and not as numbers and as a result, you would not be able to do any calculation on these values.

① Highlight the column range you wish to format.

② Select **Cells** command from **Format** menu.

③ Select **Number** from the Folios presented.

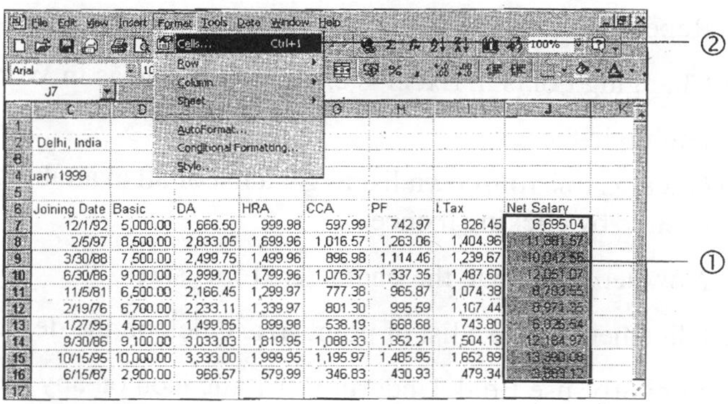

④ Select **Currency** from **Category** list.

⑤ Choose the symbol that you want.

⑥ Choose the number of decimal places.

⑦ Choose the way the negative numbers are to be displayed.

⑧ Click on **OK** button to execute the command.

Note: If you do not find the Rs. currency symbol in the available options, then choose Control Panel from the Microsoft Office shortcut toolbar. Double click on the Regional Settings, a dialog box would appear. Click on the Currency folio. Type Rs. symbol in the Currency Symbol Window and click on OK button.

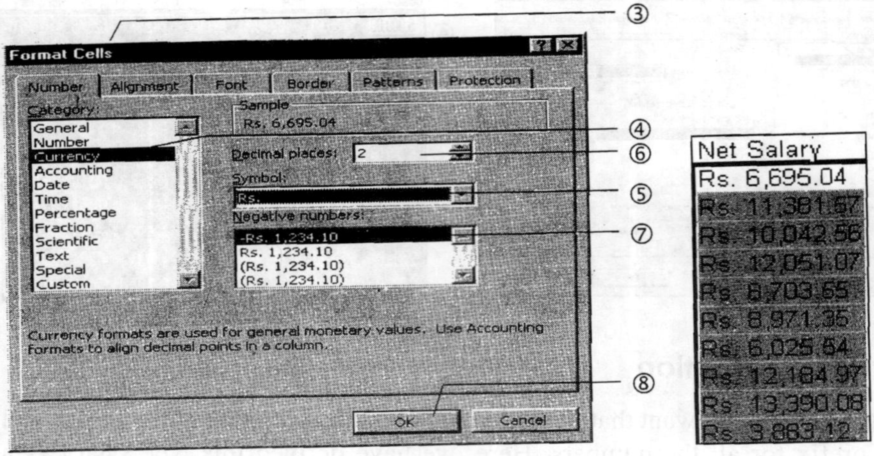

Centering Across Selection, Changing Font and Size

① Select the text as well as all the columns across which you wish to center this text.

② Click the **Center Across** icon to center text.

A Repeat the process 1 & 2 to center across other rows.

Changing Fonts in Excel is exactly the same as in Word.

③ Highlight the text.

④ Click on this roll-down list to get a list of all available fonts. Choose the one desired by clicking it once.

Now let us change the character (font) sizes.

⑤ Click here to see a list of point size. Click on the desired one.

Similarly, use Bold, Underline or Italic icon on any piece of worksheet. Do this by simply highlighting the desired area and click once on **B** *I* U

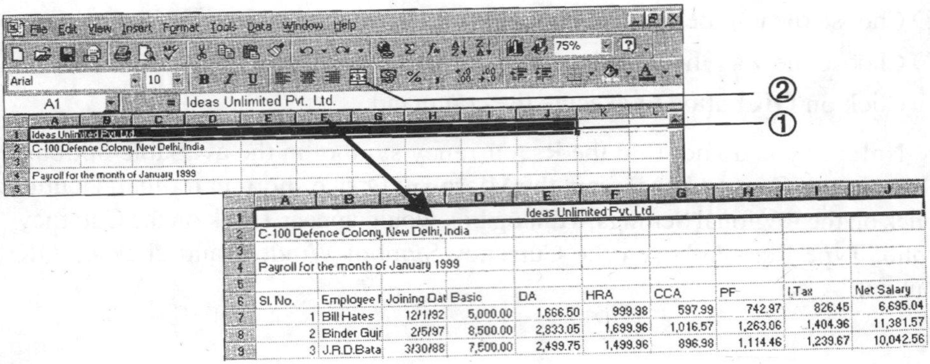

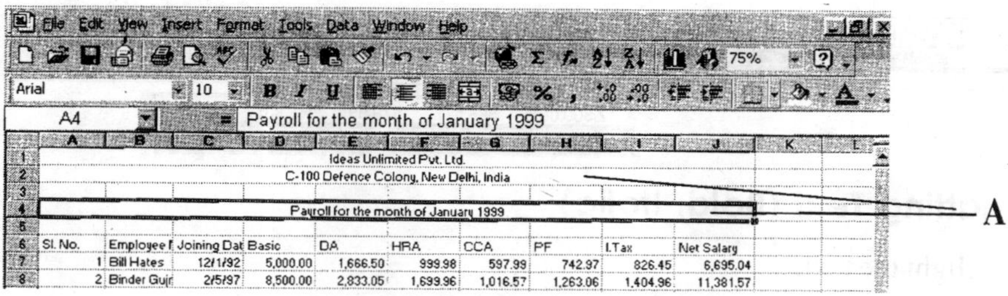

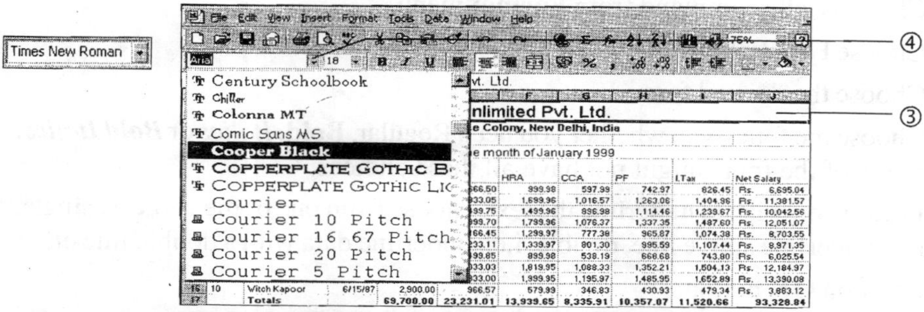

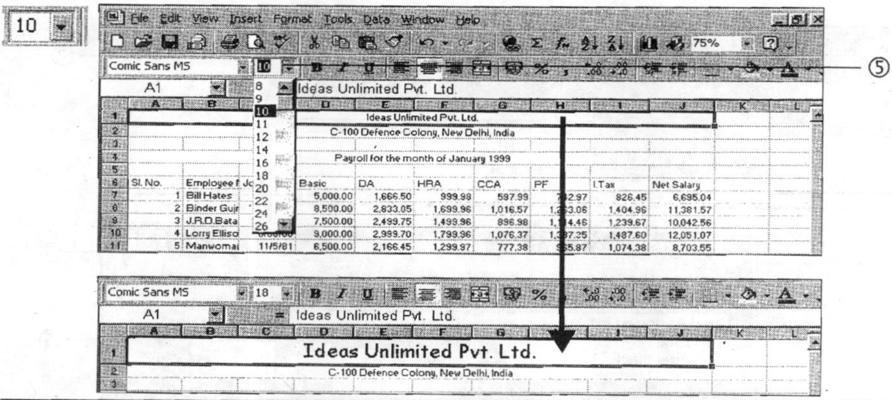

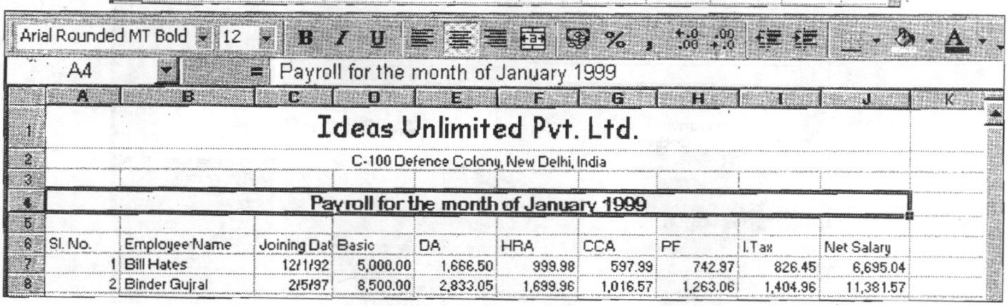

Column Autofit

In case you notice that in some places instead of numbers you are getting hash symbols (#), it means that the current column width is not sufficient to display the entire contents, i.e. numbers along with the applied format. Simply use the **Autofit** selection command from the **Column** command from **Format** menu.

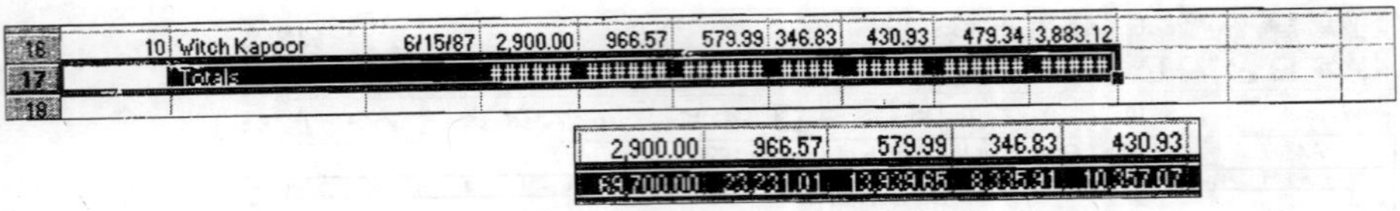

Formatting Text (Bold, Italic)

① Highlight the text.

② Choose **Cells** command from **Format** menu.

③ Choose Font Folio.

④ Choose the desired font.

⑤ Choose the font style, whether you need Regular, **Bold**, *Italics* or ***Bold Italics***. Some of the fonts might not have all these choices.

⑥ In case you wish to underline the text, choose from one of the choices, single, i.e., underline single line, double, i.e., underline data with a double line etc.

⑦ Click on **OK** button.

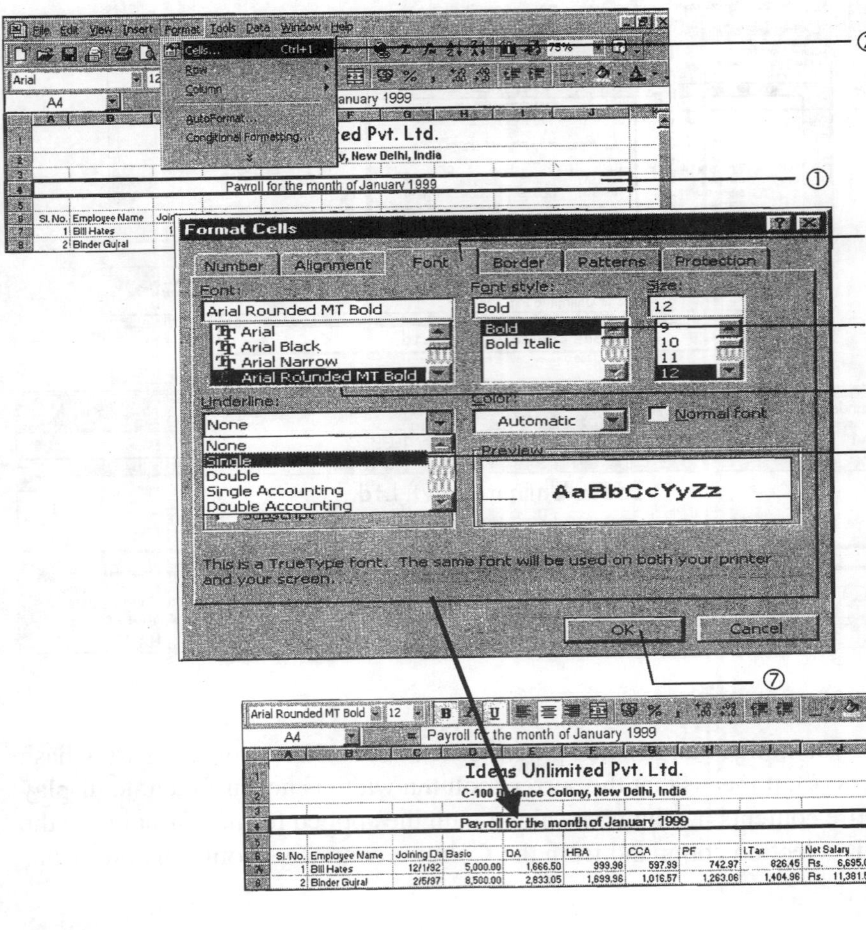

⑧ Enter text.

⑨ Highlight the text and the next cell also to centre the text across two cells.

⑩ Click here to italicise the text.

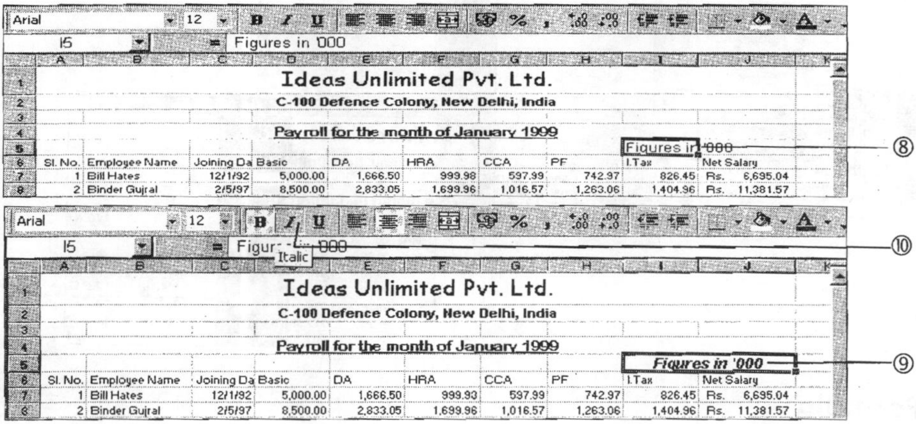

Inserting Rows

Sometimes, you might want to insert row(s) or column(s) in your data. This can be easily done. Let us say that you wish to insert a row above the line “Payroll for the month of January 1997” and you wish to insert a column called gross salary before the PF column.

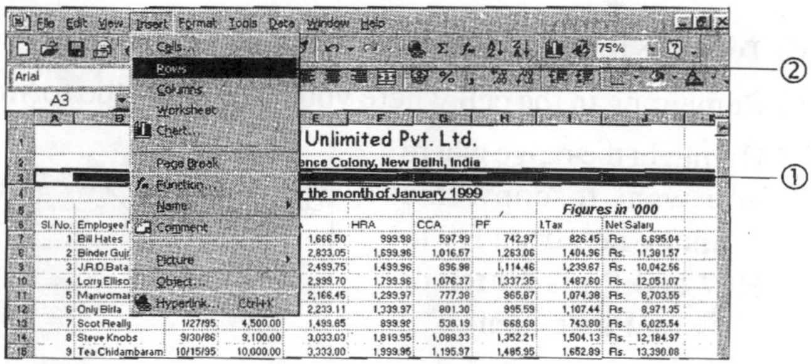

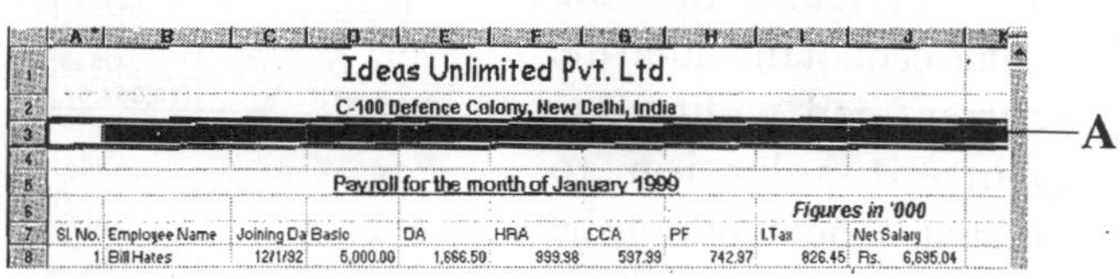

① Highlight the row where you wish to insert a row.

② Choose **Rows** command from **Insert** menu.

A You would see a blank row insterted here.

Inserting Columns

① Highlight the column where you wish to insert a column.

② Choose **Column** command from the **Insert** menu.

A A blank column is inserted here.

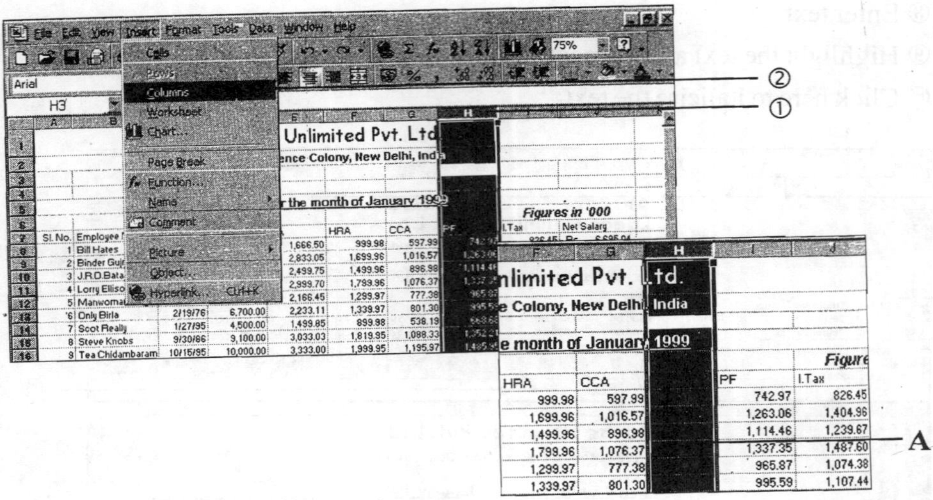

Formula

Now let us fill this column with Gross Salary, i.e., Summation of basic, DA, HRA and CCA. For this you may either use the AutoSum technique explained earlier in the exercise or alternatively, type =SUM (D8:G8) and press Enter in cell H8. In this formula, D8:G8 specifies that you wish to add all the value in the range starting from D8 and ending at G8.

① Type the formula and press Enter.

② Remaining in the cell where you have given the formula, click on **Copy** icon.

③ Highlight the range where you want to copy this formula, i.e., from H9 to H17 and Press **Enter** or click on **Paste** icon.

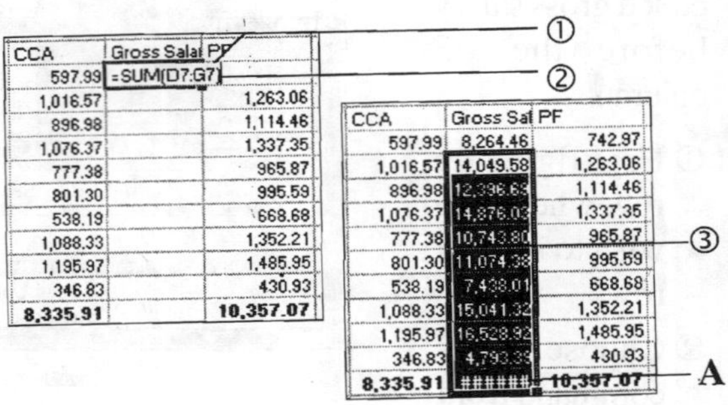

A This indicates that the value cannot fit within the current cell width. Use AutoFit selection to increase the width of the column.

Aligning the Data

As you would have noticed by now, all text entries are left aligned and all numeric entries are automatically right aligned within the cells. The default alignment can be changed in the following way.

① Highlight the range for which you wish to change the alignment.

② Choose **Cells** command from the **Format** menu

③ Choose **Alignment** Folio.

④ Click here to select left alignment.

⑤ Click on **OK** button to continue. Alternatively, simply follow step no.① click on the Left Align icon to left align data.

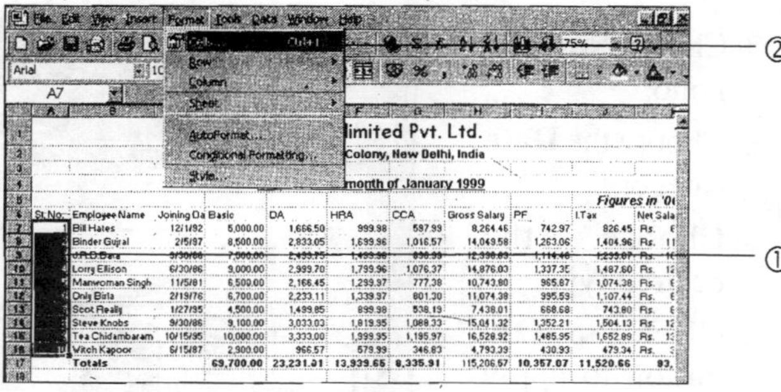

⑥ Highlight the new range and click here to center text. Alternatively, follow the step mentioned above and choose **Center Alignment** from **Alignment** Folio from **Cell** command from **Format** menu.

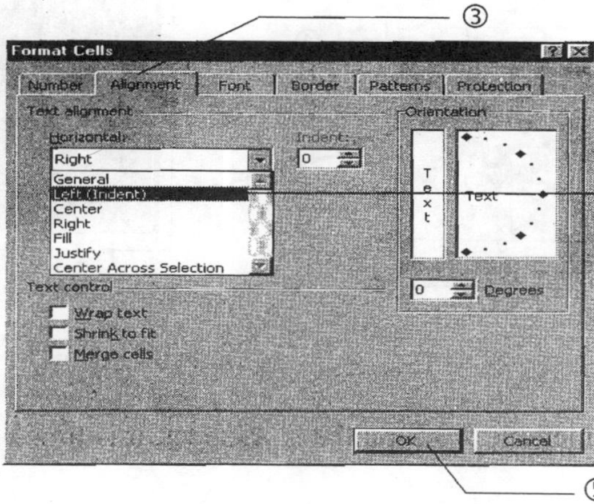

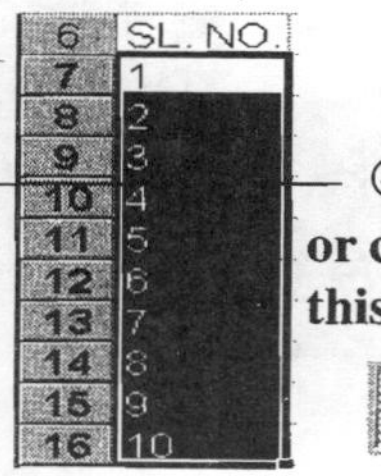

or click on this icon

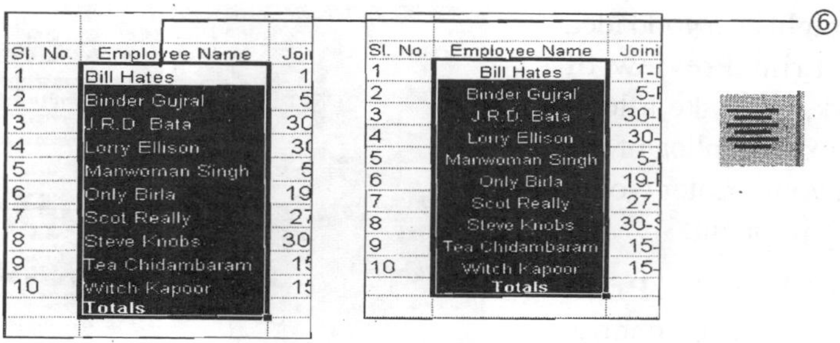

Formatting Date Range

① Highlight date range.

② Choose **Cells** command from **Format** menu.

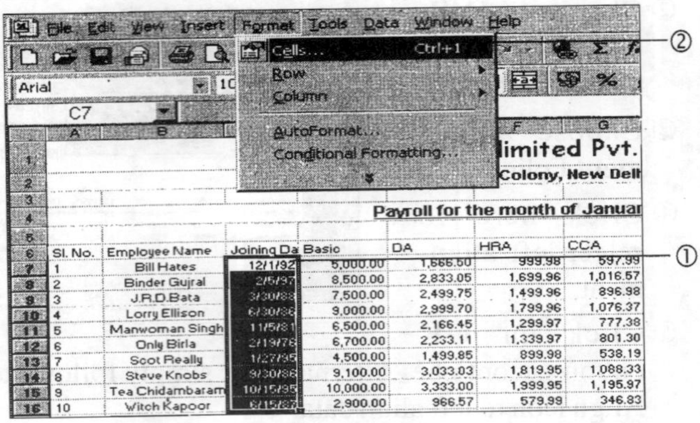

③ Choose **Number** Folio.

④ Choose the **Date** category.

⑤ Choose the desired type.

⑥ Click on **OK** button to apply the chosen Format.

A Final Result!

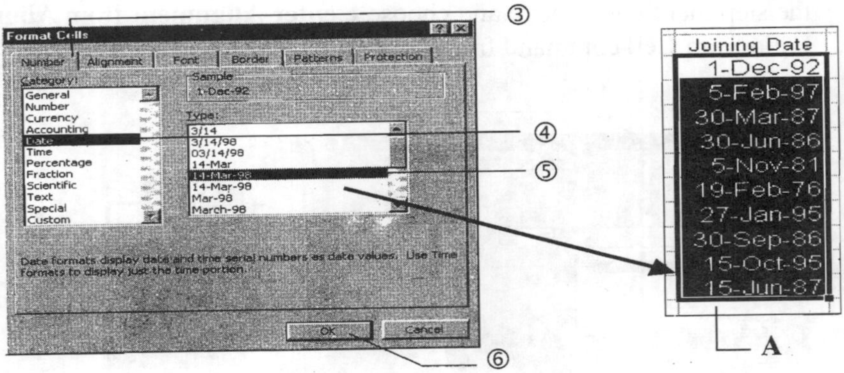

Preview

Now that you have done considerable work on the worksheet, it is time to sit back and take stock of your work. It might be a good idea to see a Print Preview of your work, i.e., take a look at a near exact replica of the Page that your printer would eventually print out.

① Either click the **Print Preview** icon or choose **Print Preview** command from the **File** menu.

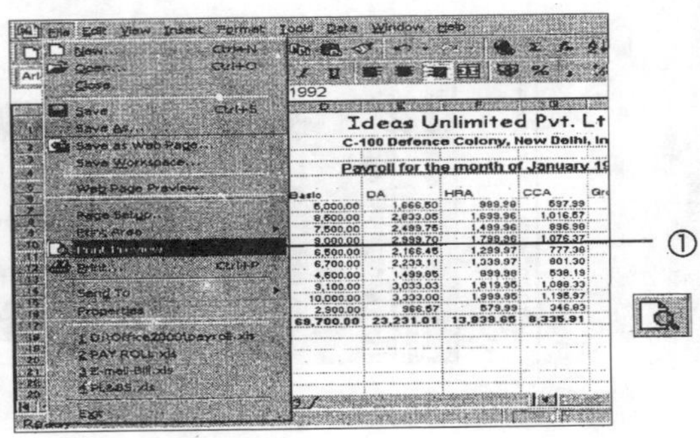

A This is what your screen would look like and also what your current page would look like, when printed.

① Click here to specify the print settings.

B Click here to close the Print Preview window without printing the document.

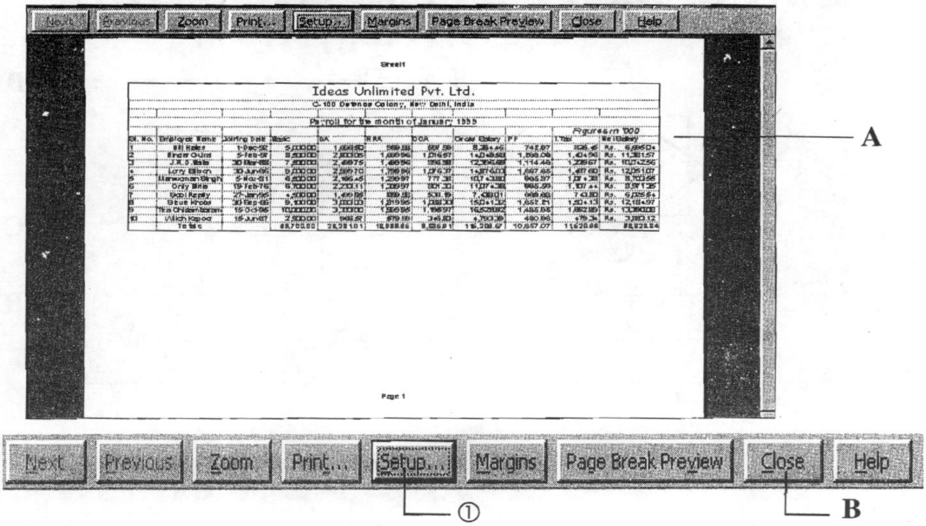

① Click here to Print lengthwise.

② Click here to Print widthwise.

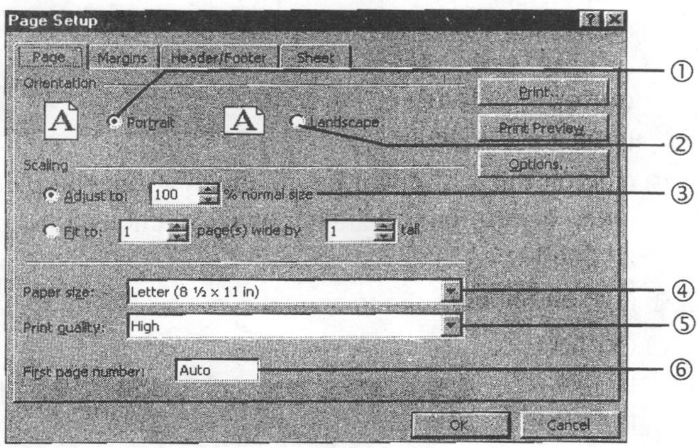

③ You can increase or decrease the size of the printed matter by specifying the scaling percentage.

④ Check whether the paper size selected here is the actual size of your Printer paper, otherwise choose the correct size.

⑤ Specify whether you want low, medium or high quality print.

⑥ Specify the first page number.

A Click on **Margins** folio to open this dialog box.

B Specify the header and footer margin.

C Specify the top, bottom, left and right margin.

D Specify whether you wish to center the data, horizontally or vertically or both, within the page.

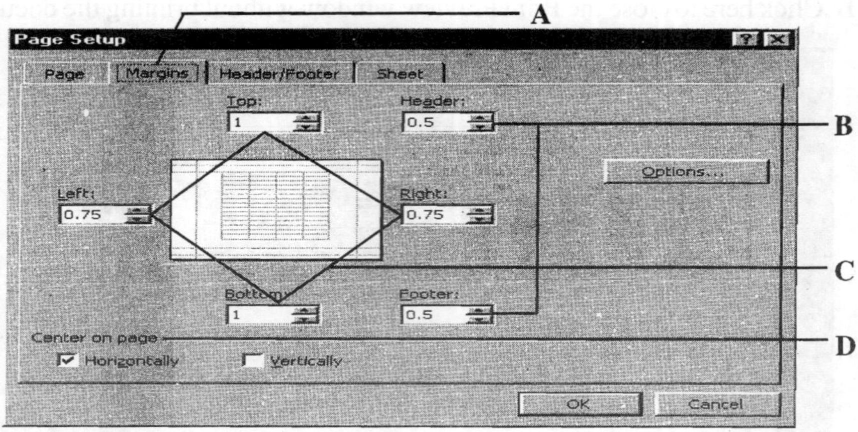

① Click on the **Header and Footer** folio to open this dialog box.

② Click on this roll-down list to choose from already given header matters, or you can create your own by clicking on the **Custom Header** button and define it.

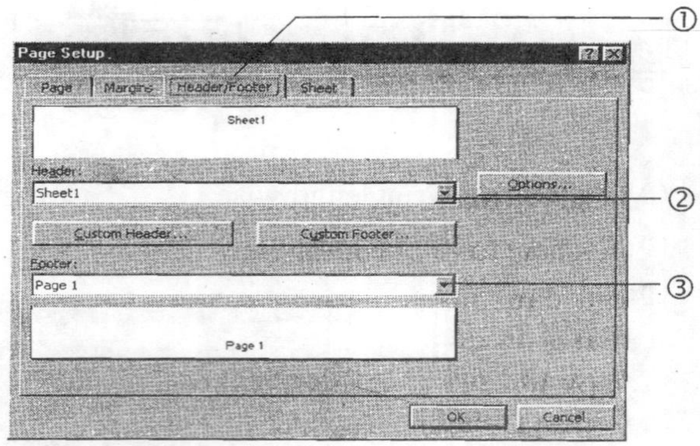

③ Click on this roll-down list to choose from samples footer of textual/other matter, or you can create your own by clicking on the **Custom Footer** button and define it.

① Click on **Sheet** folio to open this dialog box.

② Click here to print the grid lines along with the data.

③ Click on OK butt -on.

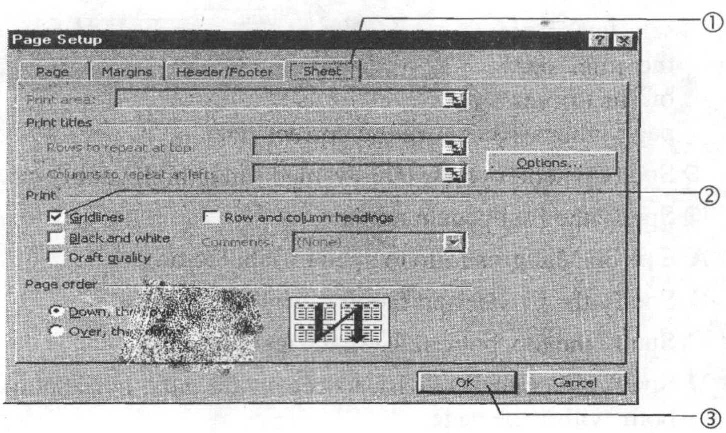

Print

Once you are fully satisfied with the print and page setting, you should go ahead with the actual printing of your worksheet.

① Click once on the **Print** icon or Choose **Print** command from **File** menu.

② Choose your Printer.

③ Specify whether you wish to print all pages or some particular pages. Since the present example has data on one page, both the options would give the same results.

④ Click on **OK** button to start printing.

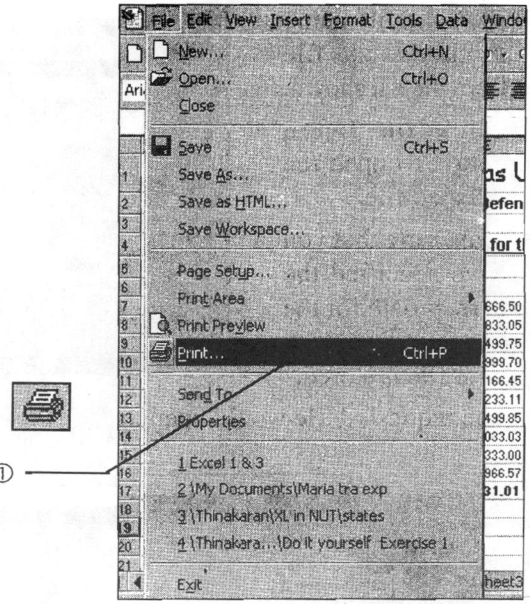

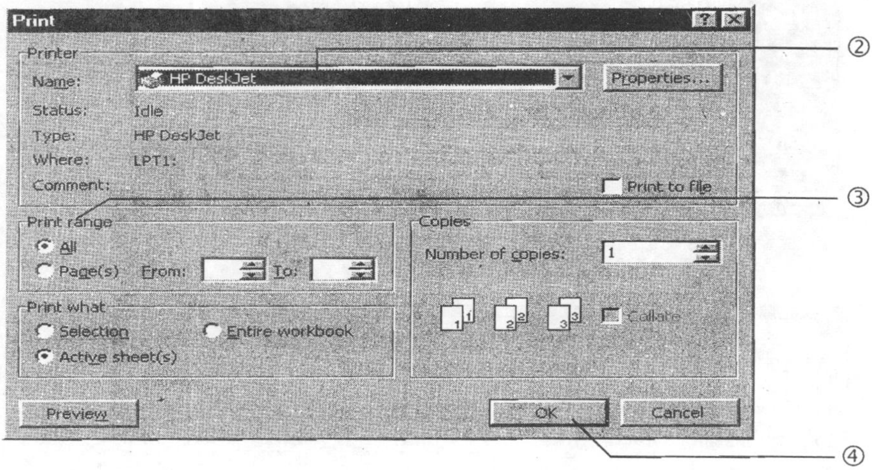

Saving File

Once you have finished your work, you can save it for your record (Saving a file has been explained in the beginning of the chapter).

Opening File

① Once you have saved a file, you can retrieve it any time. For this, choose **Open** Command from the **File** menu.

② Type the file name or choose the file from the list shown.

③ Click on **Open** button to open the selected file.

A Make sure that you have specified the correct path for the directory in which your file is stored.

B The requested file would open up.

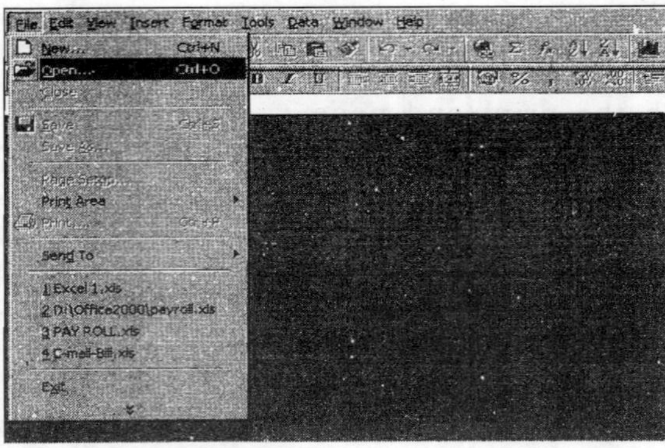

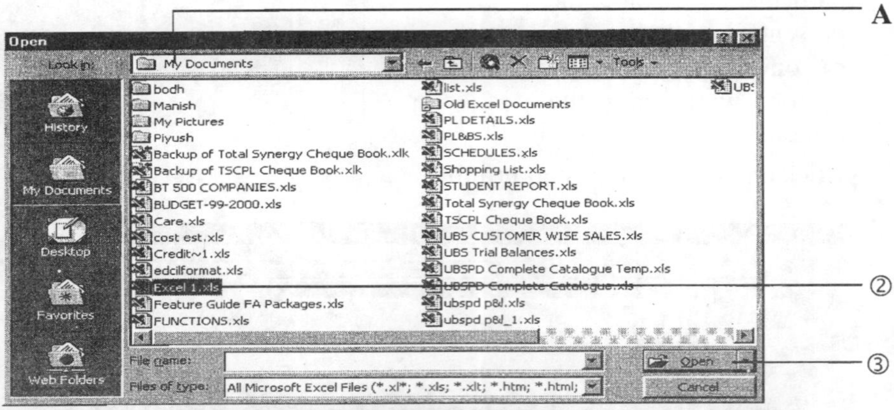

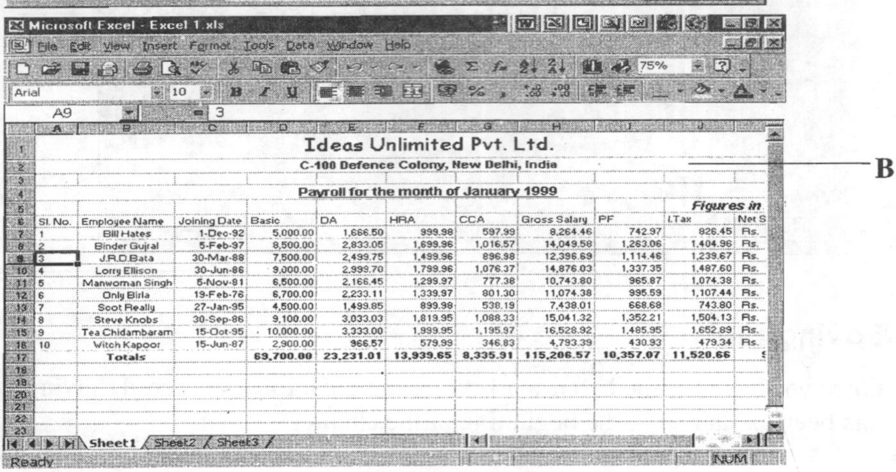

Excel offers a unique set of formatting features that can be used to effectively display your data. Now that we have completed our exercise, let us explore some more formatting features of Excel:

Format Painter This tool is common to all MS office packages. As discussed in Word, this can be used to copy formatting of one object into another. In Excel, this can be used to copy the formats from one cell (or a group of cells) to another cell or group of cells.

Text Wrap This feature can be used to display multiple lines of text within a single cell. To wrap the text:

① Type the desired text in the usual way.

② Choose **Cells** from the **Format** menu.

③ Under the **Alignment** tab, choose **Wrap Text** from the **Text Control.**

④ Click on the **OK** button to wrap the text.

A Output–text wrapped into a single cell.

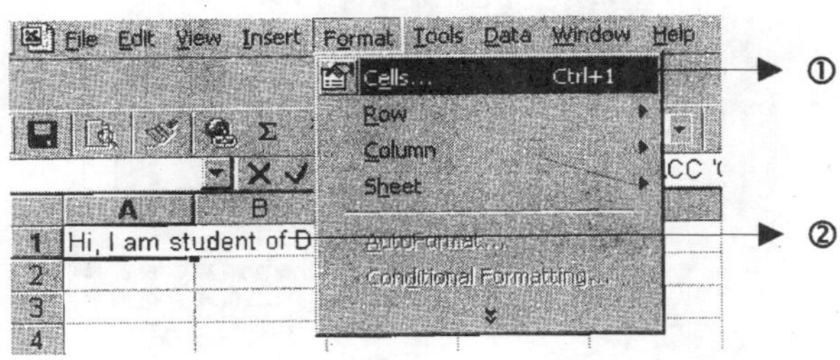

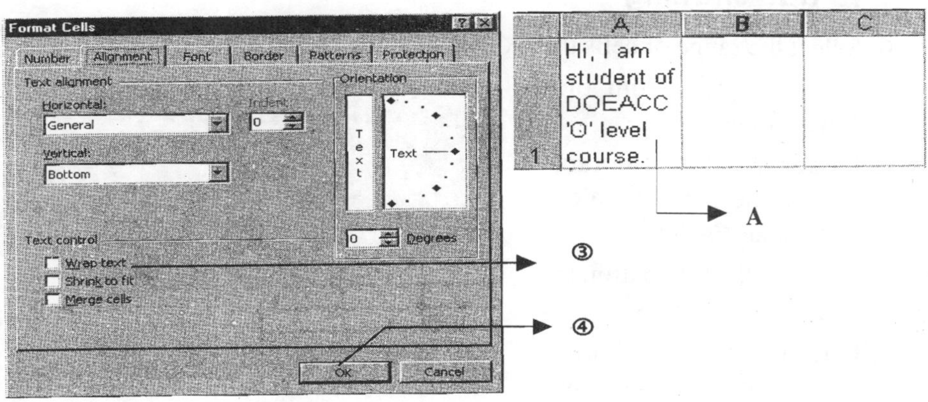

Borders and Shadings

Excel allows you to add borders to your worksheet cells to make them more visually appealing. You can also fill the cells with different colours and patterns.

To add borders

① Select the range of cells for which you wish to add border.

② Choose **Cells** from the **Format** menu.

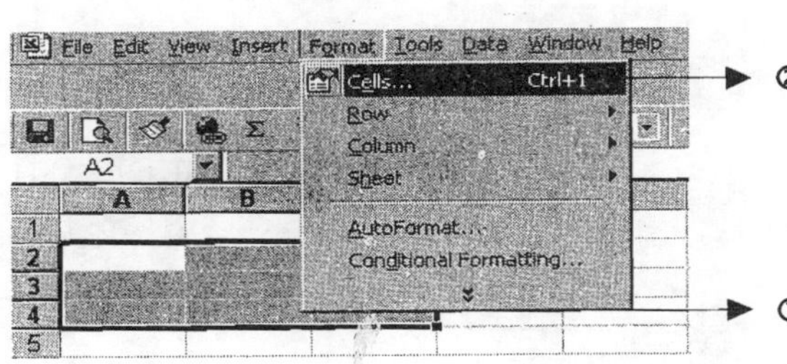

③ Under the **Border** tab, choose the desired **Border Style** from one of the presets. You can also choose a different **Line Style** and **Color** for your selected border style.

④ Click on the **OK** button to apply your changes

A Output—range of cells selected in ① with border.

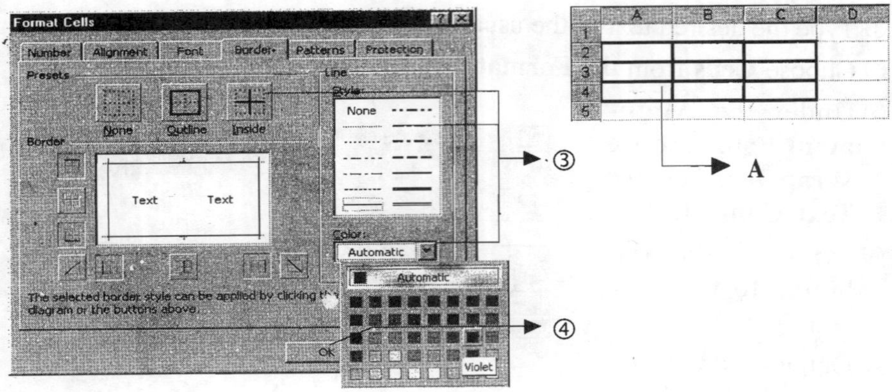

To add shading

① Select the range of cells that you wish to shade.

② Choose **Cells** from the **Format** menu.

③ Under the **Format** tab, choose the desired **Color** and shade **Pattern.**

④ Click on the **OK** button to apply your changes

A Output—range of cells selected in ① with shading.

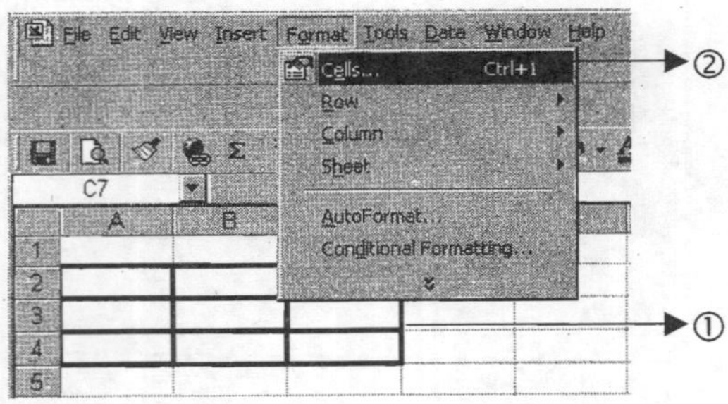

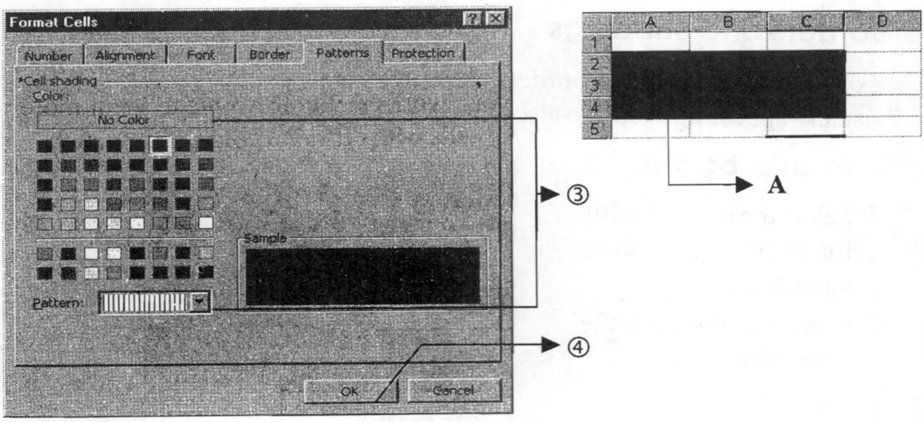

Editing Workbooks

1. **Undo** command can be used to undo the effect of recent commands or actions taken by the user. Redo command can be used to redo something that the user has undone. Redo undoes an Undo!

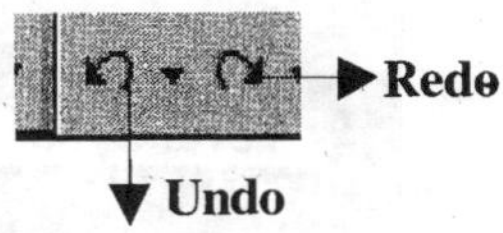

Undo and Redo command can be accessed from the standard toolbar.

Note: Click the arrow button next to Undo button to view the list of recent actions that the user can undo.

2. **Spelling and Grammar** – This feature—also included in Excel—frees you from the bother of concentrating on the spelling and grammar of your text.

3. **Finding or Replacing data** – This feature can be used to search for specific text or numbers that you want to review or edit, and you can automatically replace data you find.

All the three editing features explained above are common to MS word as well. For details, refer to the chapter on Word processing.

4. **Copying Text between Worksheets** – Copy & Paste commands can also be used to copy the entire contents of one worksheet into another sheet.

① Click here to select the entire worksheet.

② Click on **Copy** icon to copy the contents of the worksheet to the memory.

③ Click here to choose **Sheet 2** within the same workbook file.

④ Place the cursor at home position, i.e., at cell A1.

⑤ Click on **Paste** icon to copy the contents of the memory to worksheet.

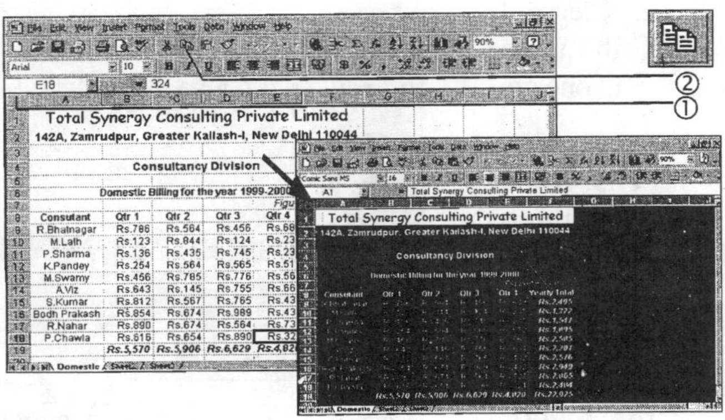

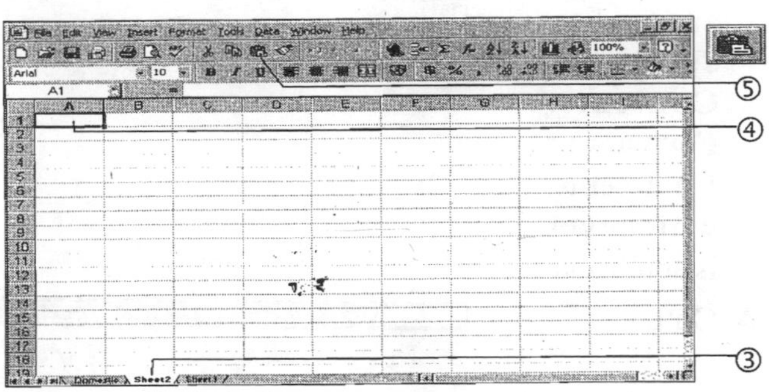

A You will see that the Domestic Billing sheet has been copied, below.

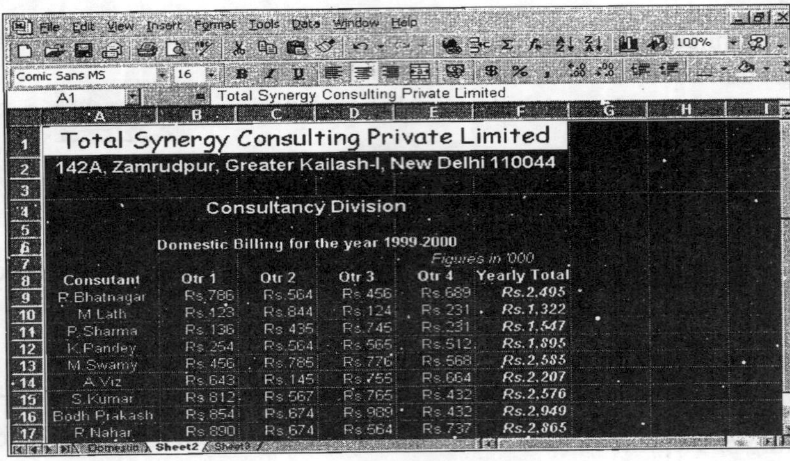

A

5. **Clear contents, formats, or comments from cells - Clear** command can be used to:

   a. Clear the cell formats,

   b. Clear the comments, or

   c. Clear the cell contents - When the contents of a cell are deleted, only its contents are removed but the cell formats, comments remain intact.

   d. Clear all the three at one go.

① Select the cells, rows, or columns you want to clear.

② On the **Edit** menu, point to **Clear**, and then click **All**, **Contents**, **Formats**, or **Comments**, whichever is applicable

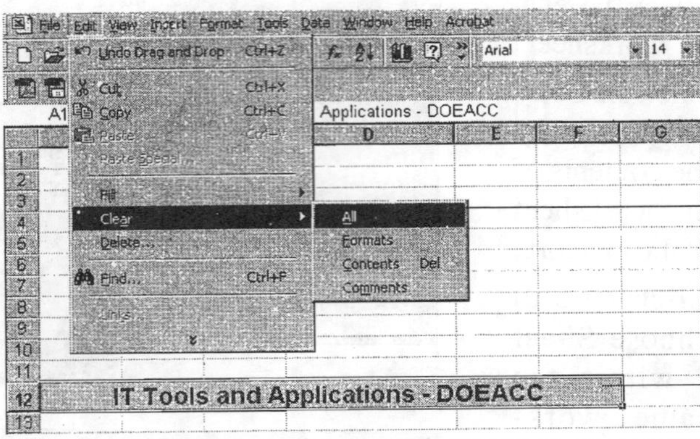

②

①

A Output

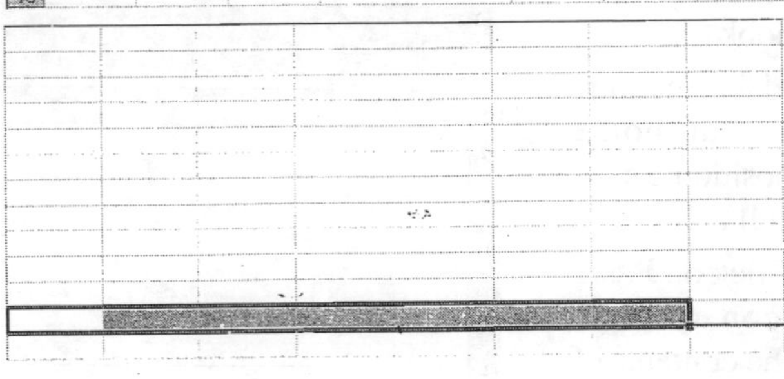

A

DATA SORT

Having once prepared the basic spreadsheet, let us now learn a few new commands. As you would notice, in the present spreadsheet, since the products and their details have not been entered in alphabetical order, in case you wish to look for specific product you have to read the entire list. In this case the list is not very large. Try imagining a real life scenario where the number of products could well run into hundreds, if not thousands. It would be simply maddening to hunt for any product!

Fortunately Excel has a simple solution (in fact, there are several solutions, but for the time being we shall confine ourselves to one) called **Data Sort.** Simply put, this command allows you to alphabetically rearrange any type of data, either in ascending (*A to Z or 1 to 10 or 1st January 1999 to 31st December 1999*) or descending (*Z to A or 10 to 1 or 31st December 1999 to 1st January 1999*) order. This frees you from the bother of having to arrange data while typing. Just enter the data in random order and apply Data Sort to rearrange it for you.

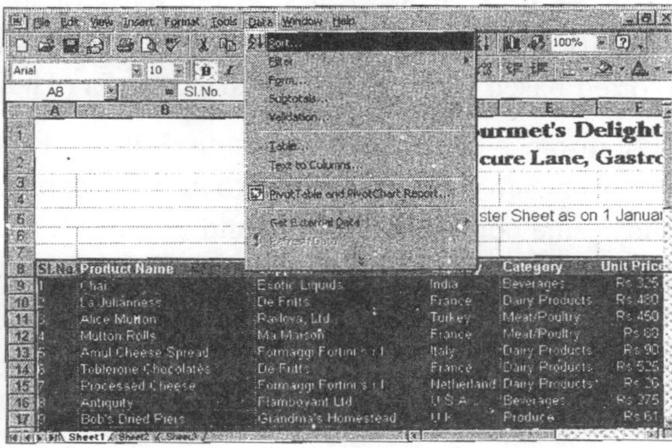

Note: While using Data Sort command the entire table, including the column headings, has to be selected for this command to work properly. Care should also be taken that the selected range does not contain any blank rows or columns or any other row other than the column headings and the data.

① Highlight the range starting from cell **A8** and ending at **J60.**

② Choose **Sort** command from **Data** menu.

The following Window would be displayed:

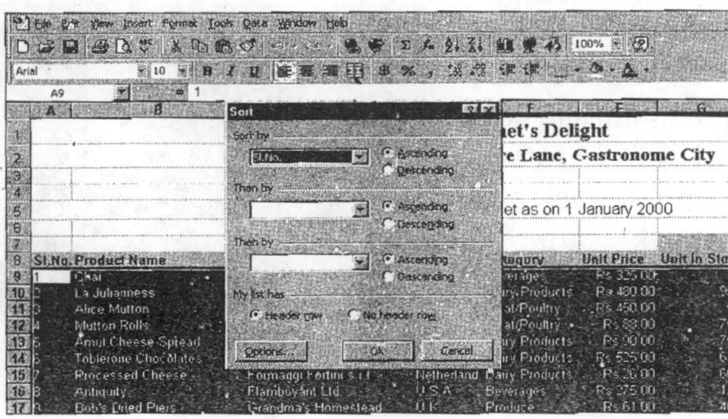

③ Click here to see a roll down list displaying all the column headings. Choose **Product Name**.

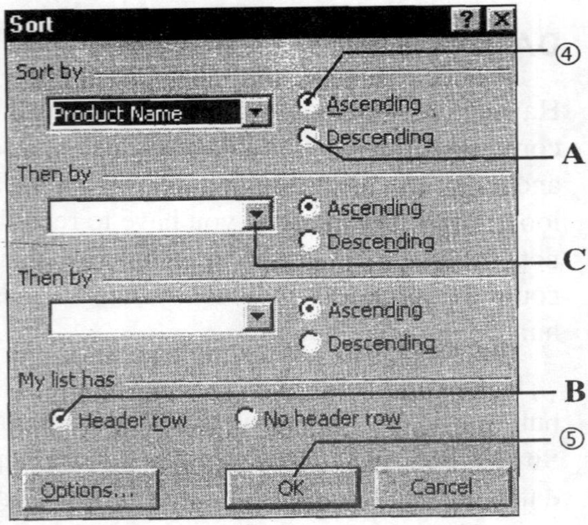

④ Click here once to choose the **Ascending Order** radio button.

⑤ Click on **OK** to execute the data sort command.

A If you want to do a reverse sort, i.e., on descending order, choose this option.

B While highlighting we had also included the column header row, therefore click here to choose the **My list has Header Row** radio button.

C If you wish to apply a sort within sort, choose this option. This means that the data would first be sorted on the basis of the primary column (Sort By) specified above, and only if there is a tie for that column, the data would sorted based upon the secondary column (Then By) chosen here.

For instance if the primary column chosen is Product Name and the secondary column chosen is country and if there are two products both called "Chocolate Candy" one coming from Italy and one coming from France, the one coming from France will be listed first (presuming that ascending order has been chosen for secondary column).

Once having clicked on OK button from the data sort Window the following results will be shown.

Using the same technique you can sort this table in ascending or descending order on the basis of any column.

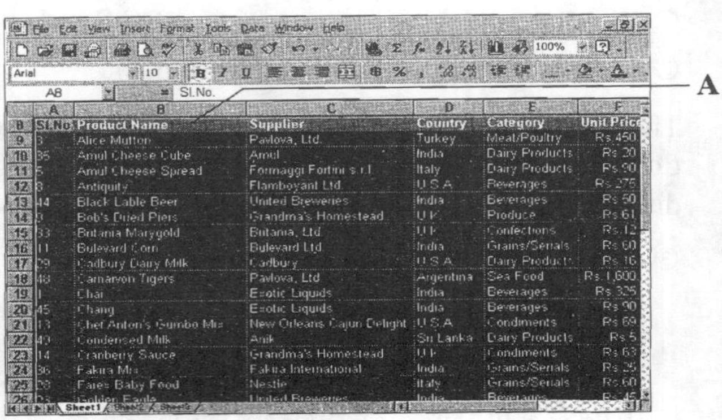

Sl.No.	Product Name	Supplier	Country	Category	Unit Price
3	Alice Mutton	Pavlova, Ltd.	Turkey	Meat/Poultry	Rs.450
35	Amul Cheese Cube	Amul	India	Dairy Products	Rs 20
5	Amul Cheese Spread	Formaggi Fortini s.r.l.	Italy	Dairy Products	Rs.90
8	Antiquity	Flamboyant Ltd.	U.S.A	Beverages	Rs 275
44	Black Lable Beer	United Breweries	India	Beverages	Rs 50
3	Bob's Dried Piers	Grandma's Homestead	U.K.	Produce	Rs 61
33	Britania Marygold	Britania, Ltd.	U.K.	Confections	Rs.12
11	Bulevard Corn	Bulevard Ltd.	India	Grains/Serials	Rs 60
29	Cadbury Dairy Milk	Cadbury	U.S.A	Dairy Products	Rs 16
48	Carnarvon Tigers	Pavlova, Ltd	Argentina	Sea Food	Rs 1,600
1	Chai	Exotic Liquids	India	Beverages	Rs 325
45	Chang	Exotic Liquids	India	Beverages	Rs 90
13	Chef Anton's Gumbo Mix	New Orleans Cajun Delight	U.S.A	Condiments	Rs 69
40	Condensed Milk	Anik	Sri Lanka	Dairy Products	Rs 5
14	Cranberry Sauce	Grandma's Homestead	U.K.	Condiments	Rs 63
36	Fakira Mix	Fakira International	India	Grains/Serials	Rs 25
28	Farex Baby Food	Nestle	Italy	Grains/Serials	Rs 60

A Notice that the entire table has been rearranged based upon the **Product Name** column and now it is obviously much easier to look up a specific item. In our present example, since serial numbers were also assigned initially in ascending order, this column hence also gets rearranged.

Data Filters

Sometimes you might want a listing of only those entries which meet certain criteria, e.g., suppose you want a list of products purchased from India filtering helps in viewing only those records that meet a specific condition.

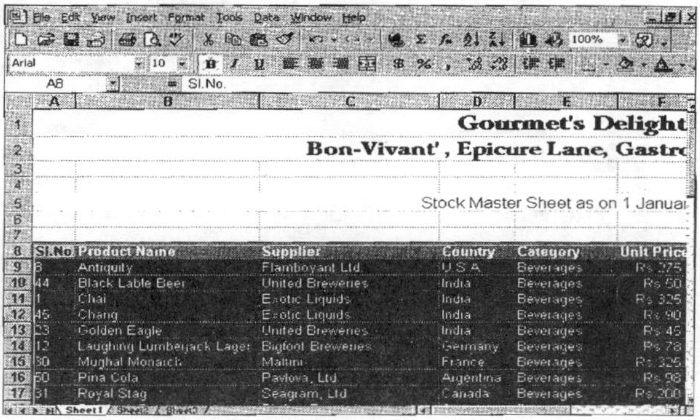

As usual, all commands are always preceded by selection of range. Highlight the entire table including the column headings and data rows.

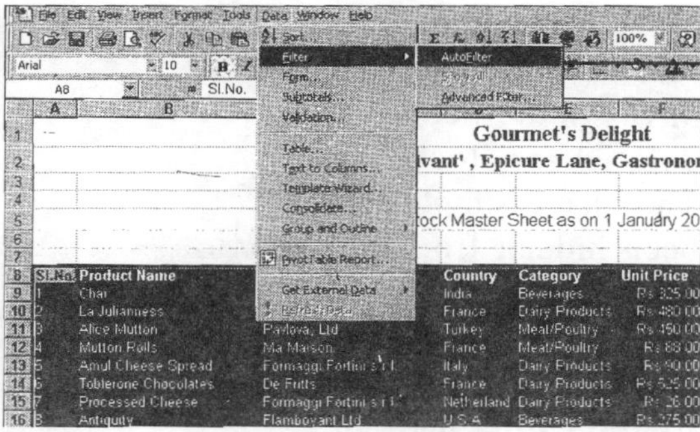

①

① Choose **Auto Filter** command from the **Filter** option from the **Data** menu.

A Notice that the drop-down list buttons begin shown against each column heading. Now with the help of these buttons you can apply various conditions and get the desired output.

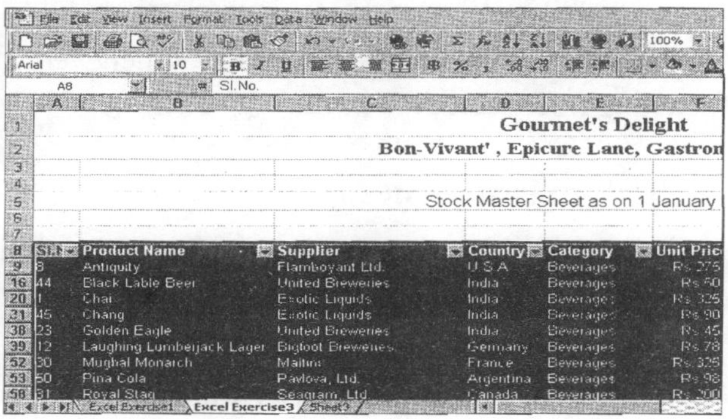

A

Sl.N	Product Name	Supplier	Country	Category	Unit Pric
8	Antiquity	Flamboyant Ltd.	U.S.A.	Beverages	Rs.275.
44	Black Lable Beer	United Breweries	India	Beverages	Rs.50.
1	Chai	Exotic Liquids	India	Beverages	Rs.325.

① Click here to see the list for country filter.

② Select U.S.A. [Use scroll bar (if provided) to travel in this list].

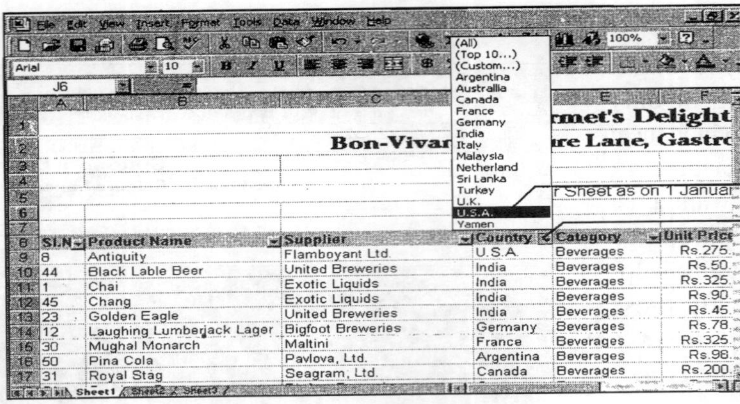

② ①

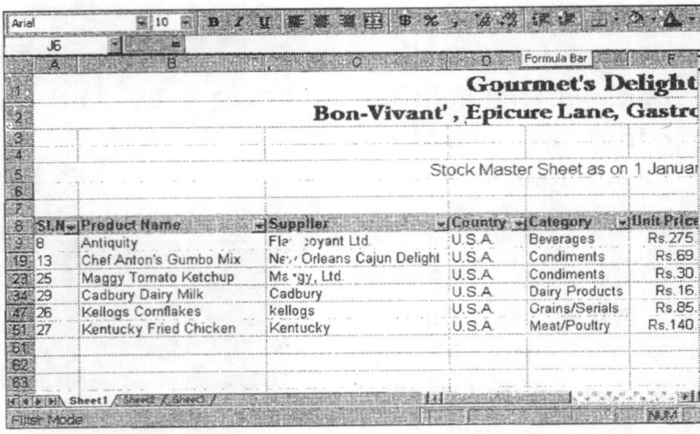

A Do not worry, the rest of the items have not been deleted or lost! They have simply been hidden from display and can be got back by simply clicking on the **Country filter** and selecting **All.**

Note: All is very helpful feature. Whenever you get stuck or have given a wrong filter selection, use this option to get back to the complete table.

Custom Data Filters

Filters can be used to pull out records based upon a mathematical criteria (condition). In our present example let us try to filter records for those products which have a unit price of more than Rs. 200.

① Click once on the **Unit Price** Filter and choose **Custom** option. Through this option you can specify various criteria which, if met, ought to yield the results sought.

A You will get this dialog box.

② Through this drop-down list, you can select the operator that you want to use for specifying your criteria.

③ Either you can make a selection from this drop-down list, which displays all possible entries existing in the current filter column; or you can type the desired figure straight away. In most cases, the second alternative is easier. Click on the "**is greater than or equal to**" option.

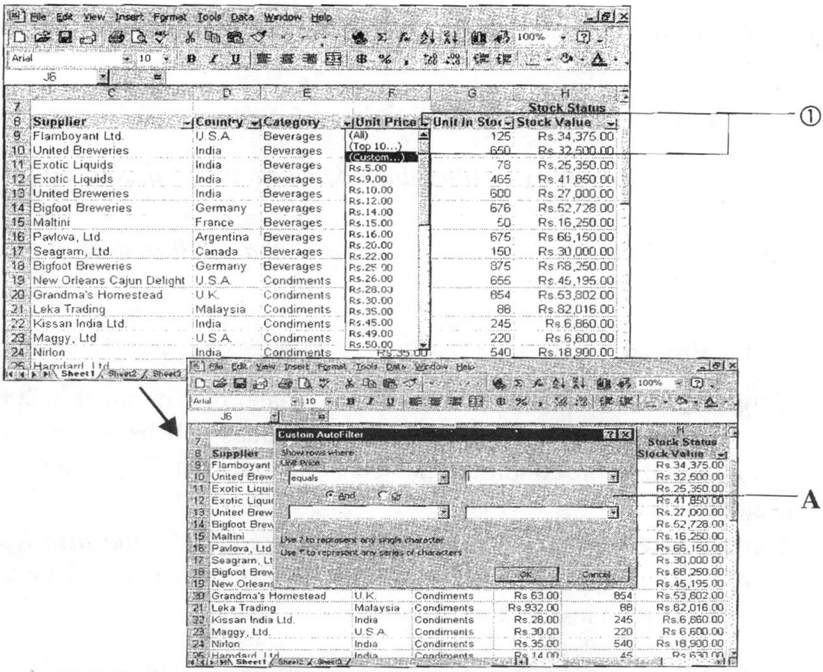

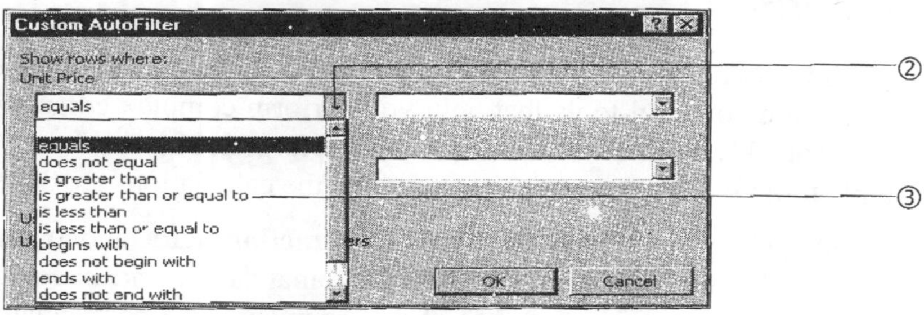

④ Click on the second window to type the Unit Price.

⑤ Click on **OK** button to view the desired result.

Using **And** between two conditions means *both the conditions must be satisfied by a record for it to be eligible for selection.* Using **Or** between two conditions means that *even if one of the two conditions is satisfied by a record, it would be eligible for selection.*

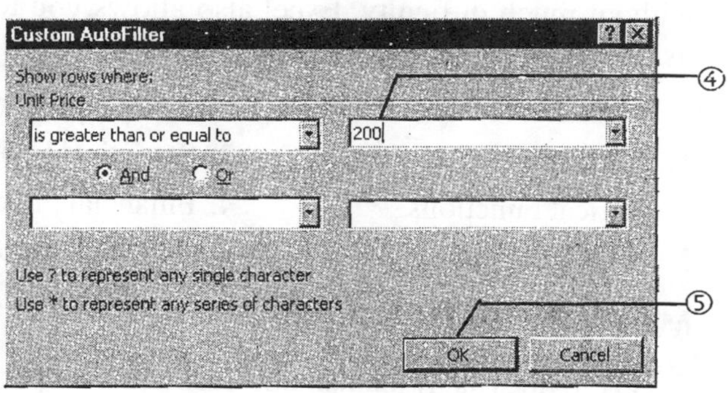

To make it still clearer, let us take a look at a few valid and invalid multiple criteria statements (conditions).

Valid Criteria

- '>=200' **And** '<=500', i.e., *all values between 200 and 500, both figures inclusive.*
- '>200' **Or** '<100', i.e., *all values greater than 200 and all values less than 100.*

Invalid Criteria

- '>=200' **Or** '<=500', i.e., all values either greater than or equal to 200 or all values less than or equal to 500. Since all values will be either >=200 or <=500 these multiple conditions have the effect of including all the values in our data range.
- '>200' **And** '<100' i.e. *all the values greater than 200 but also less than 100.* A value if greater than 200 cannot be less than 100 and vice versa, therefore this is an invalid criterion.

FUNCTIONS

Let us now move to yet another powerful feature of Excel, called Functions. **Functions** are powerful tools that help you perform complex computations–easily and quickly. Functions are like predefined formulas in which the user has to simply provide the values based upon which the calculations are done.

Typically, a function consists of two parts–**function name** and **arguments**. Arguments (or values) may in some cases be mandatory and in some cases optional. Even within a function, one of the arguments may be mandatory and another optional. Functions always return a result.

There are hundreds of worksheet functions that come along with your Excel package; we shall be restricting ourselves to only a few commonly used ones. Once you get the hang of it, you should be able to figure out the rest yourself without much difficulty. Excel also allows you to create your own functions using VBA (Visual Basic for Applications).

Worksheet functions in Excel can be broadly classified into:

1. Mathematical Functions
2. Statistical Functions
3. Logical Functions
4. Financial Functions
5. Text Functions
6. Date and Time Functions

Mathematical Functions

Excel provides many mathematical functions for performing different arithmetical operations. Some of the commonly used functions are explained below:

ROUND( ) The ROUND( ) function rounds off a number to the specified number of decimal places. In our present example, we have a number 3.786 which we want to round off to only two decimals. This can be done as shown.

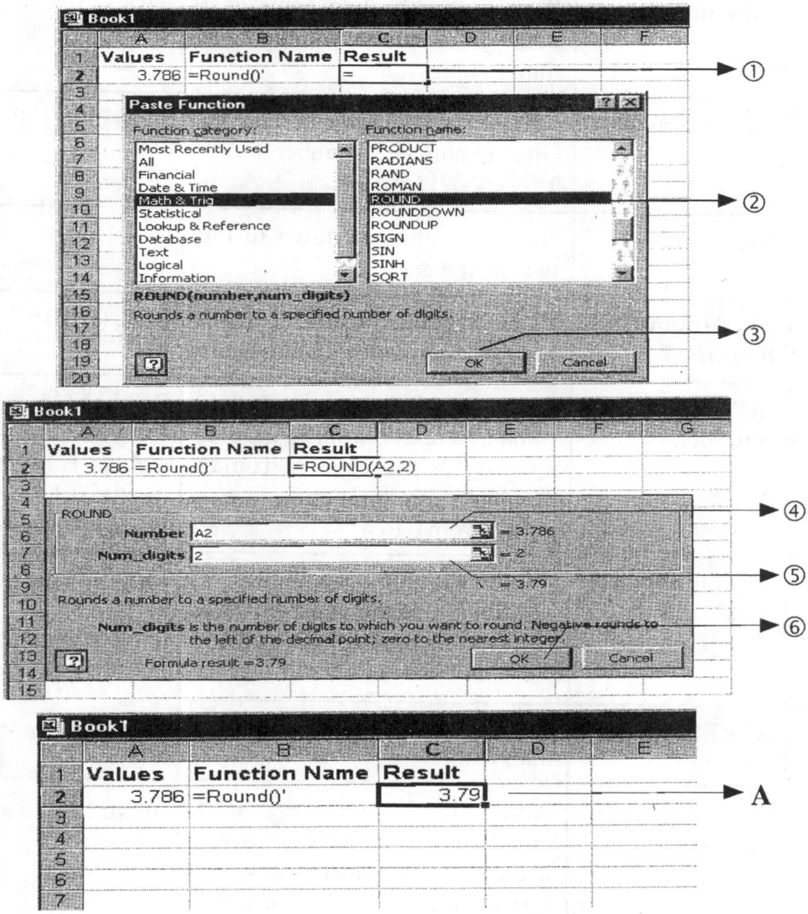

(1) Place the cursor where you want the function result to appear and choose **Function** from the **Insert menu.**

(2) Choose the **Math & Trigo** from the **functions Catagory** and **Round** from the **functions name.**

(3) Click once on the **OK** button.

(4) Type or point on the Cell number which has to be rounded off.

(5) Type the number of digits you want its round off.

(6) Click once on the **OK** button.

A The result would be displayed in the cell where you had initially placed the cursor.

Other Mathematical Functions

S.No.	Function	Description	Example
1.	ABS **(number)**	Returns the absolute value of a number, a number without plus or minus sign.	ABS(-45) = 45
2.	FACT **(number)**	Returns the factorial of a number, equal to number * number-1.... * 1.	FACT(5) = 120
3.	INT **(number)**	Rounds a number down to the nearest integer.	INT(4.9) = 4
4.	MOD **(number, divisor)**	Returns the remainder after a number is divided by a divisor.	MOD(10,3) = 1
5.	ROMAN **(number,** from)	Converts an arabic numeral to roman, as text. Form is a number specifying the type of roman numeral you want. Form can take values from 0 to 4.	ROMAN(4,0) = IV ROMAN(-4,0) = If number is negative, the #VALUE! error value is returned.
6.	SIGN **(number)**	Returns the sign of a number, 1 if positive, 0 if the number is zero, or -1 if the number is negative.	SIGN(-5) = -1
7.	SQRT **(number)**	Returns the square root of a number.	SQRT(9) = 3
8.	SUM **(number1,** number2.....)	Adds all the numbers in a range of cells. Number1, number2, ... are 1 to 30 arguments for which you want the total value or sum.	SUM(3,2,3) = 8
9.	SUMIF **(range, criteria,** sum_range)	Adds the cells specified by a given criteria. Sum_range are the actual cells to sum, if omitted the cells in range will be added.	Suppose A1:A4 contain 1,2,3,3 then SUMIF(A1:A4,">1") = 8
10.	TRUNC **(number,** num_digits)	Truncates a number to an integer by removing the fractional part of the number. Num_digits specify the position of truncation.	TRUNC(5.999,1) = 5.9

Notes:

1. An argument in bold letters indicates that it is mandatory; it must be supplied to view the output of a function.
2. Follow the steps explained for **ROUND( )** function to work with the above functions.

Statistical Functions

Excel provides many functions that can be used for analysing and summarising data.

AVERAGE ( ) The AVERAGE ( ) function calculates the average of a series of specified numbers. Let us see how this can be done:

① Place the cursor where you want the function result to appear and choose **Function** from the **Insert Menu.**

② Choose **Statistical** from the **Function Category** and **AVERAGE** from the Function Name. Click once on the OK button.

③ Either type the range or point to the cells (with the mouse) which contains the numbers for which average has to be calculated.

④ Click once on the OK button.

A The result would be displayed in the cell where you had initially placed the cursor.

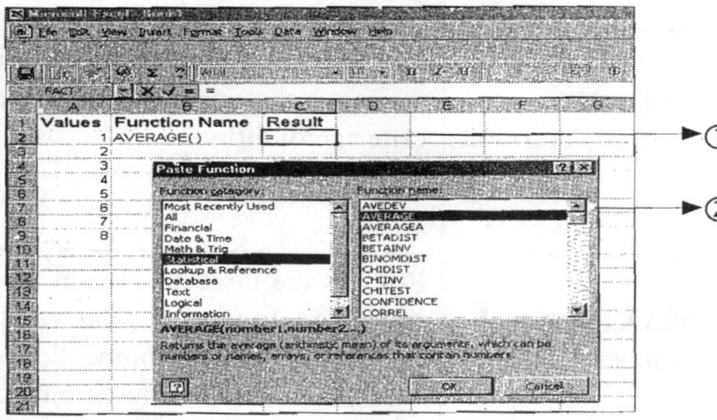

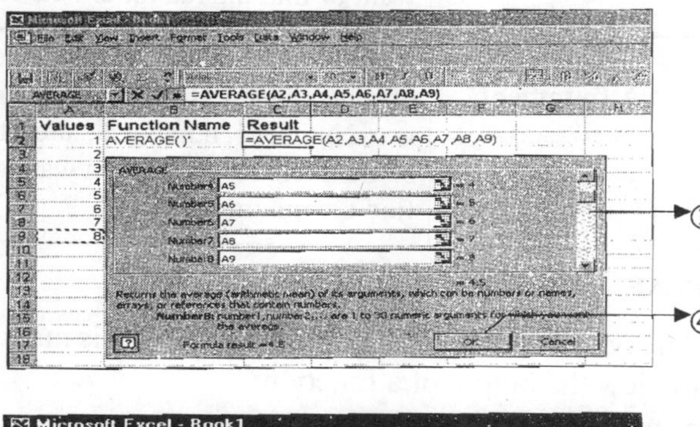

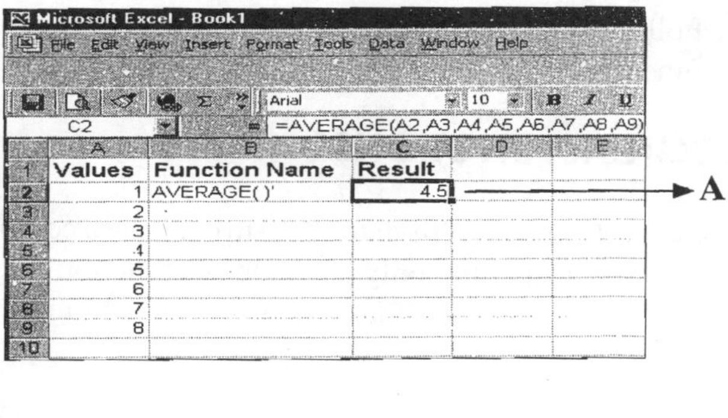

Other Statistical Functions

Function	Description	Example
1. COUNT **(value1,** value2....)	Returns the number of entries in a specified range. Value1, value2, are 1 to 30 arguments that can contain or refer to a variety of different types of data, but only numbers are counted.	Suppose A1 contains 'Hello', A2 contains 20 and A3 contains' 20-11-1978' then COUNT (A1:A3) = 3
2. COUNTBLANK **(range)**	Returns the number of empty cells within the specified range. Cells with zero values are not counted.	Suppose A1 contains 1, A2 = 0, A3 = "and A4 =" then COUNTBLANK (A1:A4) = 2
3. COUNTIF **(range, criteria)**	Returns the number of cells within the range that meets the specified criteria/condition.	Suppose A1 contains 1, A2 contains 20 and A3 contains 25 then COUNTIF (A1: A3,">20") = 2
4. MAX (**number1,** number2,.....)	Returns the largest value in a set of values. Ignores logical values and text. Number1, number 2,...are 1 to 30 numbers for which you want to find the maximum value.	IF A1:A5 contain 1, 2, 3, 4, 5, then MAX (A1:A5) = 5 MAX (A1:A5,75) = 75
5. MIN (**number1,** number2,.....)	Returns the smallest value in a set of values. Ignores logical values and text. Number 1, number 2,...are 1 to 30 numbers for which you want to find the minimum value.	If A1:A5 contain 1,2,3,4,5 then MIN (A1:A5) = 1 MIN (A1:A5,-1) = -1

Notes:

1. An argument in bold letters indicates that it is mandatory; it must be supplied to view the output of a function.
2. Follow the steps explained for AVERAGE( ) function to work with the above functions.

LOGICAL FUNCTIONS

They use True and False statements to evaluate a condition or return information. 'IF' is the most commonly used logical function. Excel also provides 'AND', 'OR', 'NOT' operators that can be used in conjunction with the 'IF' function.

IF ( ) The IF ( ) function is one of the most useful and powerful functions available in Excel. Through this function you can conduct conditional tests on values and formulas and execute some operation based upon the result of that text. If the specified criterion or condition is satisfied IF returns a value T (for True) otherwise F (for False). In our present example we have a number in cell A2. Based upon the number in this cell we want to write down 'Century' or 'Better Luck Next Time' in cell C2. Let us see how this can be done.

(1) Place the cursor where you want the function result to appear and choose **Function** from the **Insert** menu.

(2) Choose the **logical** from the **Function category** and **IF** from the **Function name.** Click once on the **OK** button.

(3) Type the 'logical-test' value.

(4) Type the 'Value-if-true'.

(5) Type the 'Value-if-false'.

(6) Click on the **OK** button.

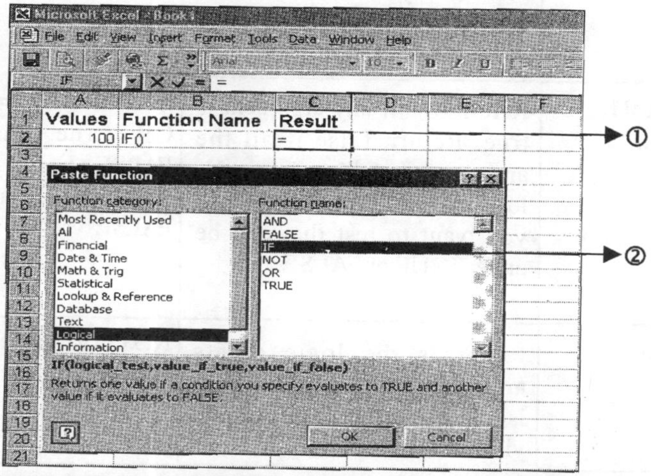

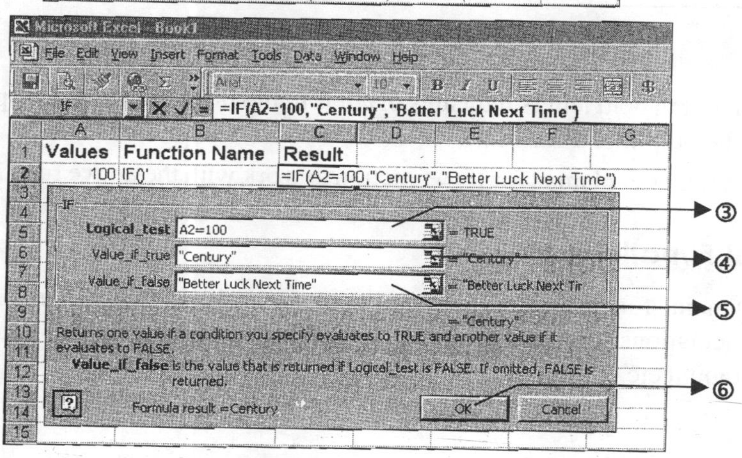

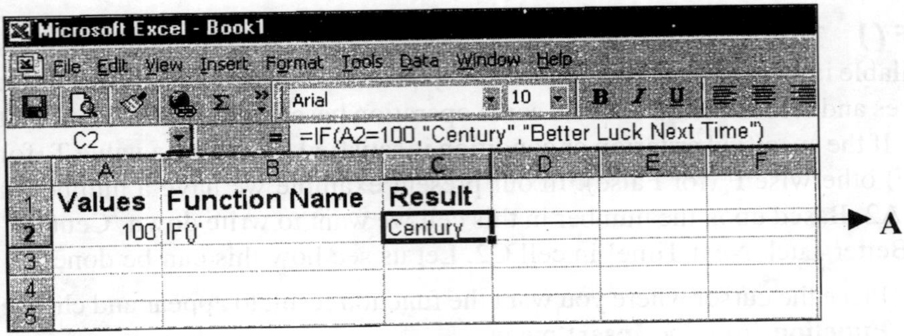

Other Logical Functions

S.No.	Function	Description	Example
1.	AND (**logical1, logical2,....**)	Return true if all the arguments are true. Returns false if any argument is false. Logical1, logical2, ... are 1 to 30 conditions you want to test that can be either TRUE or FALSE.	AND (true, true) = TRUE AND (true, false) = FALSE AND (false, false) = FALSE
2.	OR (**logical1, logical2,....**)	Return true if any argument is true. Return false if all the arguments are false. Logical1, lofical2,... are 1 to 30 conditions you want to test that can be either TRUE or FALSE.	OR (true, true) = TRUE OR (true, false) = FALSE OR (false, false) = FALSE
3.	NOT (**logical**)	Reverses the logic of its argument, i.e., if the argument is TRUE it returns FALSE and vice versa.	NOT (TRUE) = FALSE NOT (FALSE) = TRUE

Notes:

1. An argument in bold letters indicates that it is mandatory; it must be supplied to view the output of a function.
2. Follow the steps explained for IF( ) function to work with the above functions.

Financial Functions

Excel's financial functions can be used to perform the commonly required financial calculations. They can be used to calculate information such as interest, principal amount etc.

PMT(rate, nper, pv, fv, type) — Calculates the payment amount for the specified loan amount, interest rate and the number of payments to be made.

Rate	is the interest rate for the loan.
Nper	is the total number of payments for the loan.
Pv	is the present value, represents the amount being borrowed.
Fv	is the future value, or a cash balance you want to attain after the last payment is made. If omitted, it is taken as zero.
Type	It can be 0 (payments are due at the end of the year) or 1 (payments are due at the beginning of the year). If omitted, it is taken as zero.

Let us calculate the monthly payment on a loan of $3000 for 3 months at an annual interest of 10 per cent.

① Place the cursor where you want the function result to appear and choose **Function** from the Insert menu.

② Choose **Financial** from the function category and **PMT** from the function name. Click on the **OK** button.

③ Supply appropriate values for all the arguments.

④ Click once on the **OK** button.

A The result would be displayed in the cell where you had initially placed the cursor.

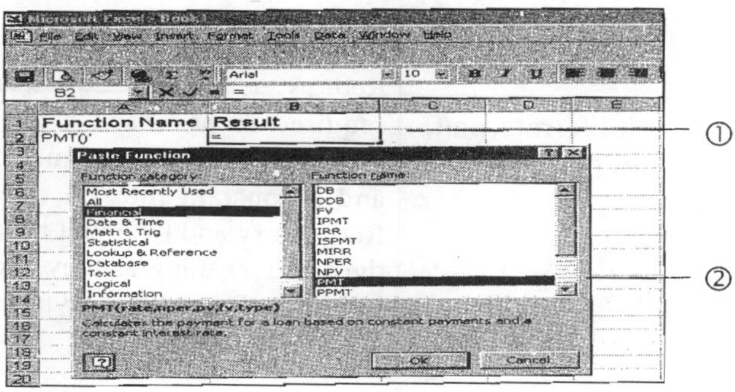

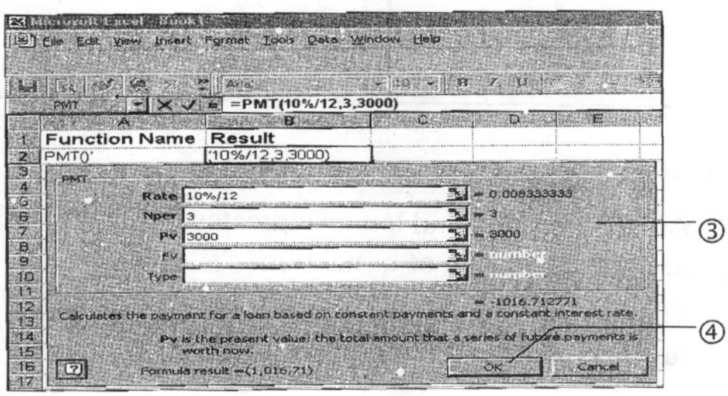

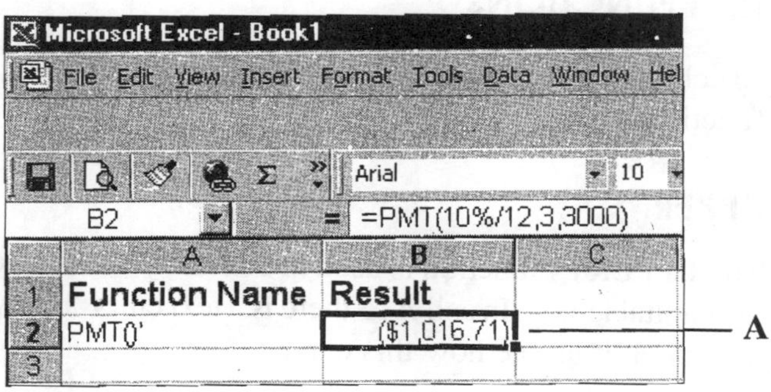

Other Financial Functions

S.No.	Function	Description	Example
1.	IPMT (**rate, per, nper, pv**, fv, type)	Returns the interest payment for a given period for an investment based on constant payments and a constant interest rate. Rate, nper, pv, fv and type will have the same meaning as they had in PMT(). Per is the period for which you want to find the interest and must be in the range 1 to nper.	To determine the interest due in the first month of a 3 month $3000 at 10% annual interest- IPMT (.1/12,1,3,3000) = $25
2.	NPER (**rate, pmt, pv**, fv, type)	Returns the number of periods required to pay back a loan assuming constant payments and a constant interest rate. Rate, pv, fv and type will have the same meaning as they had in PMT() Pmt is the payment made for each period.	NPER(.1/12,-50,3000) = 83.53 pmt is negative because the cash that you pay is taken as negative. This gives the number of periods needed to pay off a loan of $3000 when $50 are paid every month and the interest rate = 10% pa.

Notes:

1. An argument in bold letters indicates that it is mandatory; it must be supplied to view the output of a function.
2. Follow the steps explained for PMT() function to work with the above functions.

TEXT FUNCTIONS

Excel provides numerous for manipulating text strings. Some of the basic text functions are explained below:

UPPER( )

The UPPER ( ) function is used to convert your case text entry into upper case, i.e. capital letters. In cell A13 there is a text entry 'big' which has to be converted to caps. Let us see how this can be done.

① Place the cursor where you want the function result to appear and choose Function from the Insert menu.

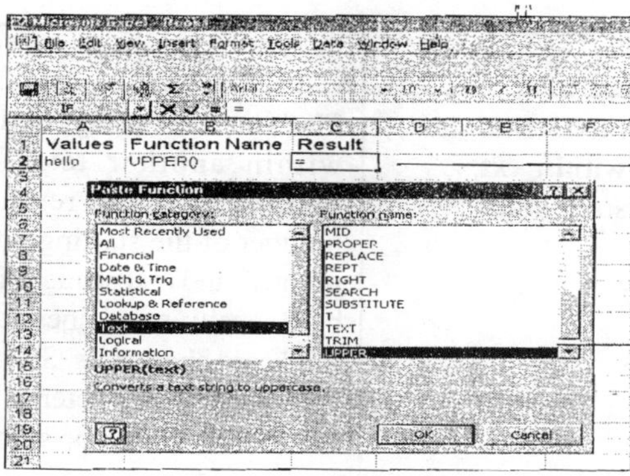

② Choose **Text** from the **Function Category** and **UPPER** from the **Function Name**. Click once on the **OK** button to continue.

③ Type or specify (through the mouse) the cell address in which the text to be converted is there, i.e., A2.

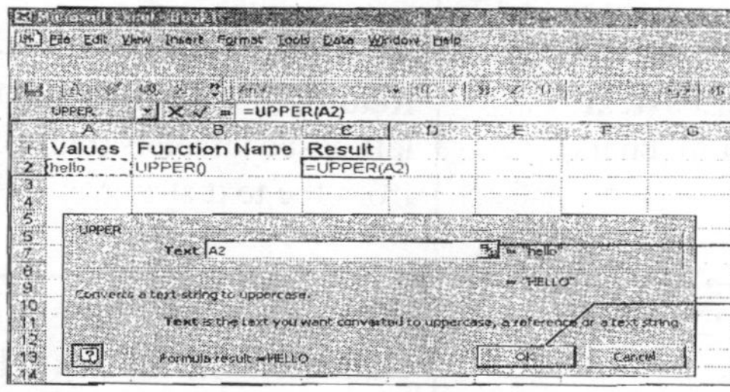

④ Click once on the **OK** button.

A Since the value in cell A2 was 'hello', the results would be displayed in the cell where you had initially placed the cursor.

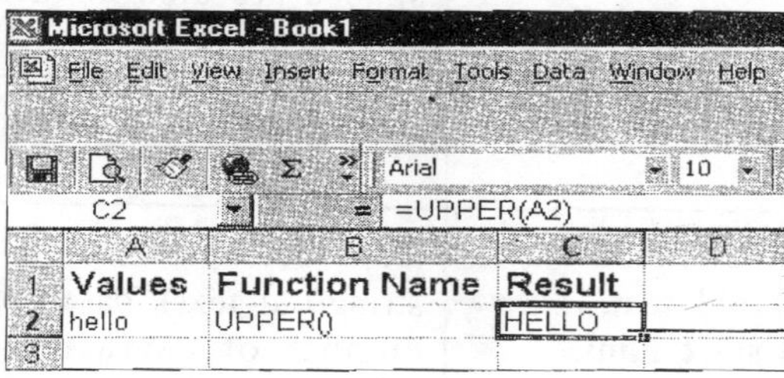

Other Text functions

S.No.	Function	Description	Example
1.	CHAR (**number**)	Returns the character for the specified code number from the character set used by your computer. Number is a number between 1 and 255 specifying which character you want.	CHAR(65) = A
2.	CODE (**text**)	Returns the code number for the first character in the specified text string, in the character set used by your computer.	CODE(A) = 65 CODE(AND) = 65

S.No.	Function	Description	Example
3.	FIND (**find_text, within_txt**, start_num)	Finds one text string (find_text) within another text string (within_text) and returns the number of the starting position of the found text string. FIND is case sensitive and doesn't allow wild card characters. Start_num specifies the character at which the search should be started.	FIND("e", "hello") = 2 FIND("e", "Elate") = 5
4.	LEFT(**text**, num_chars)	Returns the specified number of leftmost characters (num_chars) from the text string.	LEFT("HELLO",4) = HELL LEFT("HELLO") = H
5.	LEN (**text**)	Returns the number of characters in the text. Blank spaces are also counted as characters.	LEN ("HELLO WORLD") = 11
6.	LOWER (**text**)	Returns the text in lower case.	LOWER("HELLO) = hello
7.	REPLACE (**old_text, start_num, num_chars, new_text**)	Replaces part of a text string(old_text), based on the number of characters you specify, with a different text string(new_text). Start_num is the position of the character in old_text that you want to replace with new_text. Num_chars is the number of characters in old_text that you want REPLACE to replace with new_text.	REPLACE("2000",4, 1,"3") = 2003 REPLACE("A*D", 2,1,"BC") = ABCD
8.	RIGHT (**text**, num_chars)	Returns the specified number of rightmost characters (num_chars) from the text string.	RIGHT("HELLO", 4) = ELLO RIGHT("HELLO") = O
9.	SEARCH (**find_text, within_text**, start_num)	Similar to FIND() except that it allows using wildcards in the text string and is case in sensitive.	SEARCH("H", "HELLO") = 1

Notes:

1. An argument in bold letters indicates that it is mandatory; it must be supplied to view the output of a function.
2. Follow the steps explained for UPPER() function to work with the above functions.

DATE AND TIME FUNCTIONS

Date and time are internally stored as numbers in Excel. These numbers are called as Serial Numbers. Date and Time can be calculated from the serial number. Date can be calculated by counting the number of days passed since Jan. 1, 1900 and Time can be calculated as percentage of 24 hrs. Example–the serial number 37781.770833333 represents June 9, 2003 and 6.30 PM. Left portion of the decimal point indicates the date and the right portion indicates the time. Basic DATE and TIME functions are explained below:

Today ( )

The TODAY function is one of the few functions that do not require any user argument. It simply returns the current date. Let us see how this works.

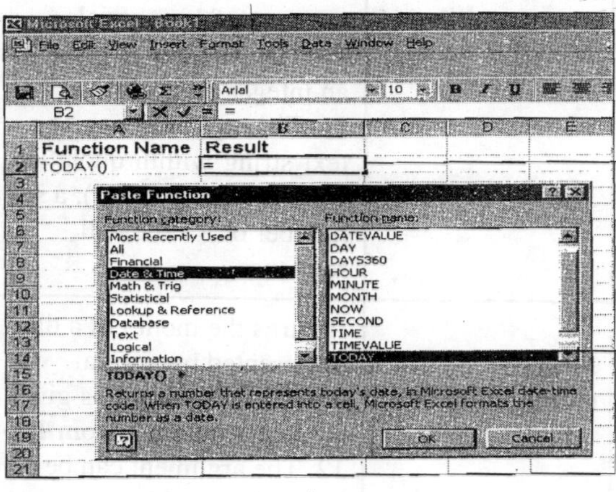

① Place the cursor where you want the function result to appear and choose Function from the Insert menu.

② Choose **Date & Time** from the **Function Category** and **TODAY** from the **Function Name**.

③ Click once on the **OK** button to continue.

A Output

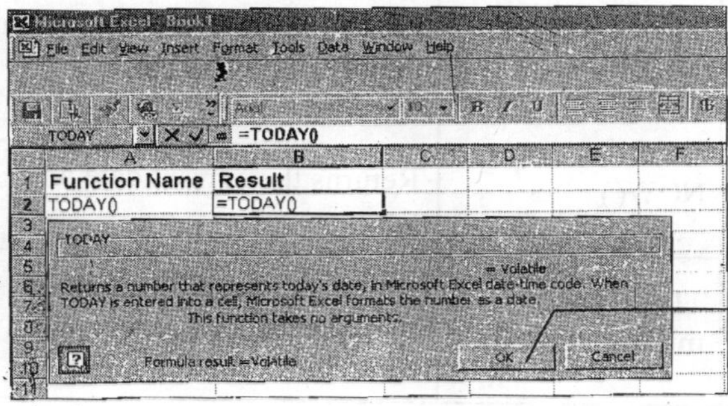

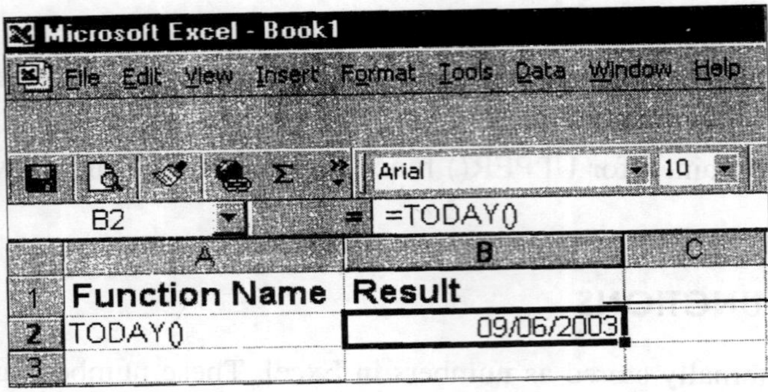

A

Other DATE and TIME Functions

S.No.	Function	Description	Example
1.	DATE **(year,month, day)**	Returns the serial number that represents a particular date. This serial number is immediately formatted as a standard date.	DATE(2003,5,5) returns 37746 which is automatically formatted by Excel as 05/05/2003
2.	DAY **(serial_number)**	Returns the day of a date, represented by a serial number. The day is given as an integer ranging from 1 to 31. The argument can be a text string within quotation marks ("20/11/1978"), a serial number or a valid cell reference.	DAY("15-Apr-2003") = 15
3.	MONTH **(serial_number)**	Returns the month of a date, represented by a serial number. The month is given as an integer ranging from 1 to 12. The argument can be a text string within quotation marks ("20/11/1978"), a serial number or a valid cell reference.	MONTH("15-Apr-2003") = 4
4.	NOW()	Returns the current date and time.	NOW() = 09/06/2003 18:30
5.	TIME **(hour, minute, second)**	Returns the decimal number that represents a particular time. This decimal number is	TIME(18,30,00) returns 770833333 which is automatically

S.No.	Function	Description	Example
		immediately formatted as a standard time. Hour is a number from 0 (zero) to 23 representing the hour. Minute is a number from 0 to 59 representing the minute. Second is a number from 0 to 59 representing the second.	formatted by Excel as 6.30 PM.
6.	YEAR **(serial_number)**	Returns the year of a date, represented by a serial number. The year is returned as an integer in the range 1900-9999. The argument can be a text string within quotation marks ("20/11/1978"), a serial number or a valid cell reference.	YEAR("15-Apr-1978") = 1978

Notes:

1. An argument in bold letters indicates that it is mandatory; it must be supplied to view the output of a function.
2. Follow the steps explained for TODAY() function to work with the above functions.

CREATING CHARTS AND GRAPHS

It is often easy to understand information that is presented graphically. Charts make it easy for users to see comparisons, patterns, and trends in data rapidly. Excel contains powerful charting wizards and tools that can be used to build effective and impressive charts. Excel comes with a wide variety of chart styles, including bar, pie, column, scatter, bubble and many more. Once a chart is created, you can customise it to suit your requirements. You can add, edit or delete titles, labels, legends and gridlines in a chart.

You can create a chart in its own chart sheet or as an embedded chart in a worksheet. A chart sheet is a separate sheet within your workbook that has its own sheet name. An embedded chart is a chart that is displayed directly in a worksheet. A chart is always linked to the worksheet data it's created from and any changes done on the worksheet data are automatically reflected in the chart.

By default Excel creates a Column type chart. However, the default chart type can be changed to some other chart type.

Creating a Chart using the default settings:

① Select the data you wish to include in the chart.

② Press the F11 key; a column type chart will be created.

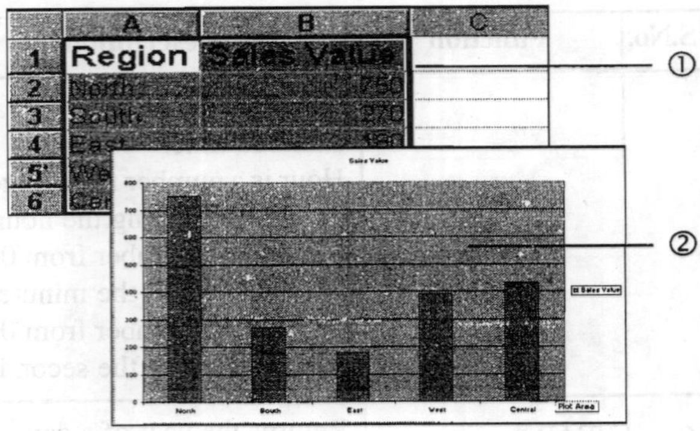

Changing the default Chart type:

① Right click on the chart and choose **Chart type** from the pop up menu.

② Select the desired chart type and click the **Set as Default Chart** button.

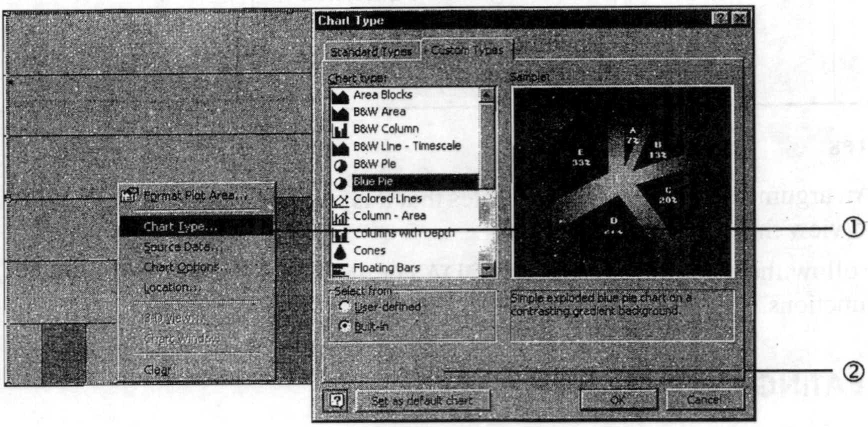

Chart Toolbar

To view the Chart toolbar Choose **Chart** from the **Toolbars** command under the **View** menu.

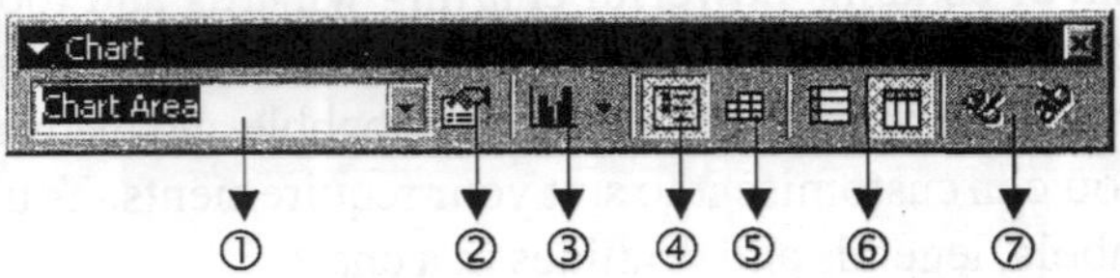

① Displays the various chart objects. A brief explanation of various chart elements/ objects is given below:

a. **Chart Area** It contains the entire chart and all of its elements. It is similar to a canvas.

b. **Plot Area** It contains the Axes, Gridlines and all Data Series. Usually values are plotted against the Y or the Vertical axis and categories

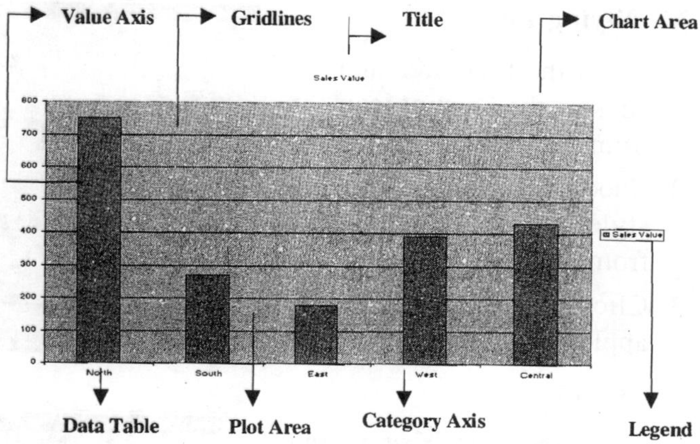

are plotted ag-ainst the X or Horizontal axis. Gridlines makes the data easier to view and evaluate. A chart can contain one or more data series.
A data series is made up of an array of values and names indicating what the series represent. Each data series has a unique pattern and is represented in the legend.

c. **Legend:** A box that identifies the colours/patterns assigned to various data series in the chart.

d. **Title:** A descriptive text that conveys the purpose of the chart.

e. **Data Table:** A grid that contains the numeric values used to create the chart. It is usually placed along the category (X) axis.

② **Format** – Allows formatting the selected chart object. An appropriate dialog box corresponding to the selected chart object is displayed to the user.

a. Modifying Chart Area

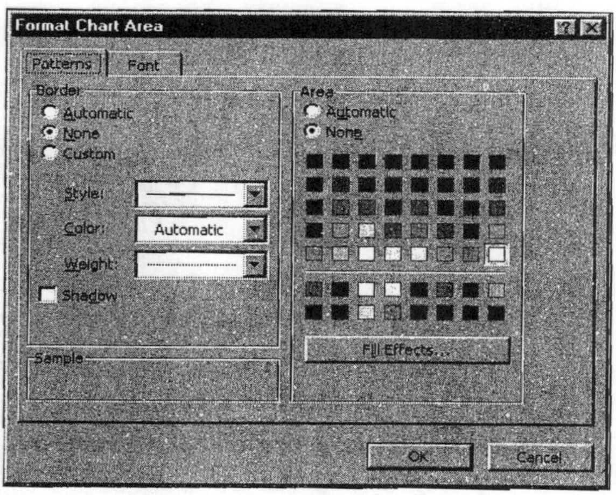

1. Select the Chart Area and click on the **Format** icon from the Chart toolbar.
2. Choose the desired border style, colour and weight from the **Patterns** tab.
3. Choose the desired font size, style and effects from the **Font** tab. The Chart will use the selected font styles.
4. Click on **OK** button to apply your changes.

b. Modifying Plot Area

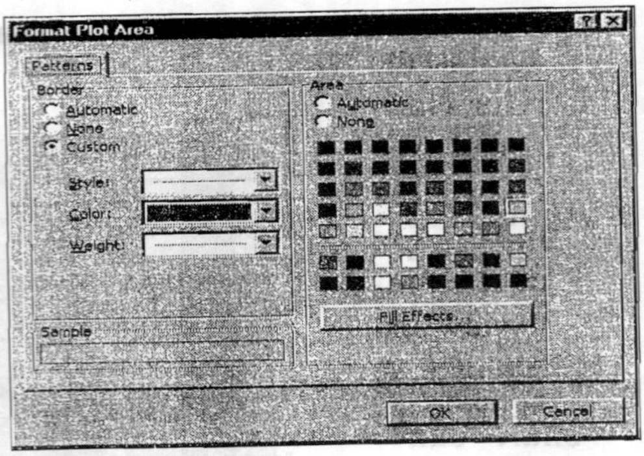

1. Select the Plot Area and click on the **Format** icon from the Chart toolbar.
2. Choose the desired border style, color and weight from the **Patterns** tab.
3. Click on **OK** button to apply your changes.

c. Modifying Axis

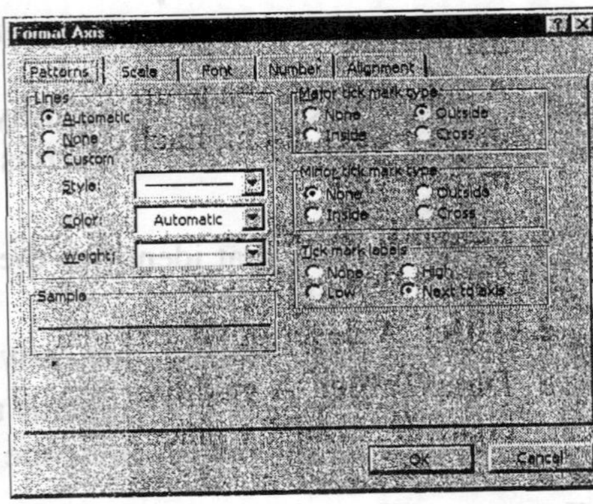

1. Select the Axis (X or Y) and click on the **Format** icon from the Chart toolbar.
2. Choose the desired line style, color and weight from the **Patterns** tab.
3. Specify the scale settings for Category and Value axis of your chart using the **Scale** tab.
4. Choose the desired font size, style and effects from the **Font** tab. The Axis will use the selected font styles.
5. Choose the desired number format for your axis labels from the **Number** tab.
6. Specify the alignment of axis labels using the Alignment tab.
7. Click on **OK** button to apply your changes.

d. Modifying Gridlines

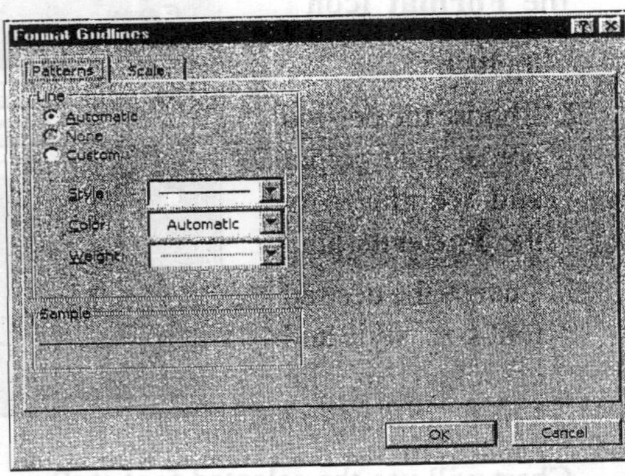

1. Select the Gridlines and click on the **Format** icon from the Chart toolbar.
2. Choose the desired line style, color and weight from the **Patterns** tab.
3. Specify the scale settings for Gridlines using the **Scale** tab.
4. Click on **OK** button to apply your changes.

e. Modifying Data Series

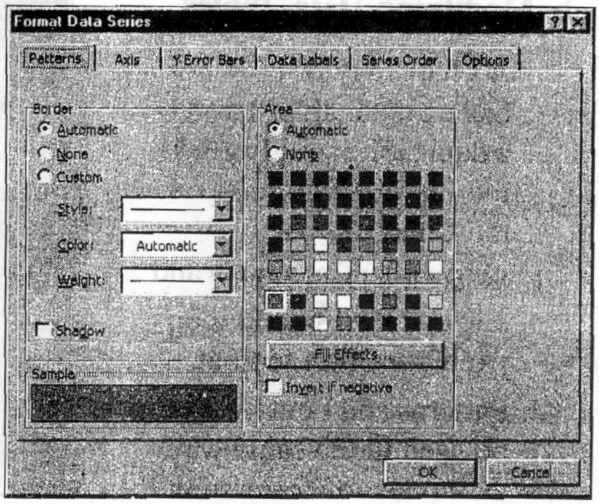

Each series in the chart can be formatted independently.

1. Select the Data Series and click on the **Format** icon from the Chart toolbar.
2. Choose label or value or per cent or both from the Data Labels tab.
3. Specify the order of data series using the **Series Order** tab. This holds good if your chart has multiple data series.
4. Specify the Overlap and Gap width using the **Options** tab.
5. Click on **OK** button to apply your changes.

f. Modifying Legend

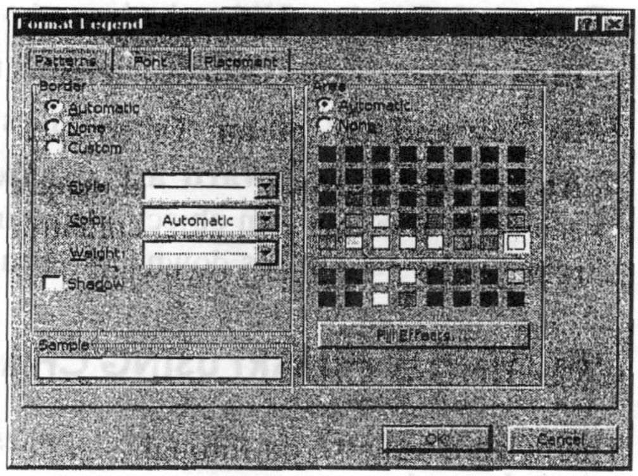

1. Select the Legend and click on the **Format** icon from the Chart toolbar.
2. Patterns and Font tab can be used in the same way as in case of formatting the Chart Area.
3. Choose the position (left/ right/ top/ bottom) of the legend in the chart.
4. Click on **OK** button to apply your changes.

g. Modifying Title

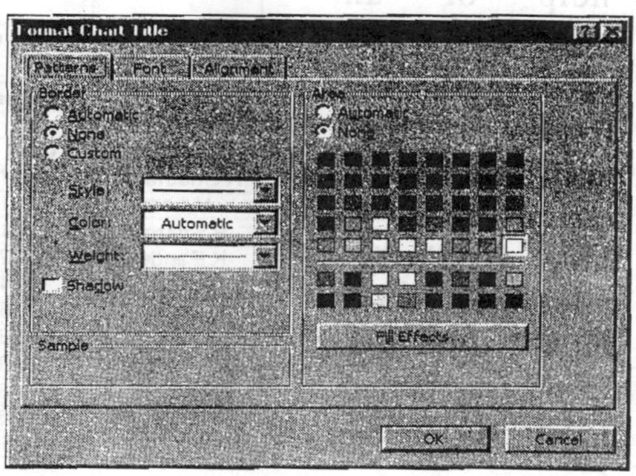

1. Select the Chart Title and click on the **Format** icon from the Chart toolbar.
2. Patterns, Font and Alignment tab can be used in the same way as in case of formatting the Axis.
3. Click on **OK** button to apply your changes.

h. Modifying Data Tables

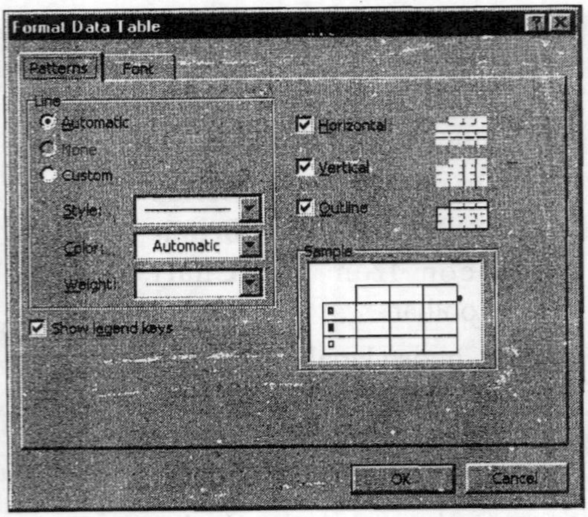

A chart may or may not have a data table. To add a data table, simply click the **Data Table** icon on the Chart toolbar.

1. Select the Data Table and click on the **Format** icon from the Chart toolbar.
2. Patterns and Font tab can be used in the same way as in case of formatting the Chart Area.
3. Click on **OK** button to apply your changes.

③ **Chart Type** Displays the available chart types in Excel. You can choose a type that that best suits your need.

④ **Legend** Displays/Hides the legend.

⑤ **Data Table** Displays/Hides the data table.

⑥ **By Row and By Column** Determines the chart's interpretation of your data.

⑦ **Angle Text Downward and Angle Text Upward** These buttons are enabled only when an object containing text is selected. They allow you to rotate text 45 degrees downward or upward.

CREATING A CHART USING CHART WIZARD

This wizard guides you through a series of steps that helps in creating your chart. Let us learn the usage of this wizard with the help of an example. The following example displays the quarterly billing of various consultants. You can calculate their annual total by defining an appropriate formula.

Total Synergy Consulting Private Limited					
142A, Zamrudpur, Greater Kailash-I, New Delhi 110044					
Consultancy Division					
Domestic Billing for the year 1999-2000					
				Figures in '000	
Consutant	**Qtr 1**	**Qtr 2**	**Qtr 3**	**Qtr 4**	**Yearly Total**
R.Bhatnagar	Rs.786	Rs.564	Rs.456	Rs.689	***Rs.2,495***
M.Lath	Rs.123	Rs.844	Rs.124	Rs.231	***Rs.1,322***
P.Sharma	Rs.136	Rs.435	Rs.745	Rs.231	***Rs.1,547***
K.Pandey	Rs.254	Rs.564	Rs.565	Rs.512	***Rs.1,895***
M.Swamy	Rs.456	Rs.785	Rs.776	Rs.568	***Rs.2,585***
A.Viz	Rs.643	Rs.145	Rs.755	Rs.664	***Rs.2,207***
S.Kumar	Rs.812	Rs.567	Rs.765	Rs.432	***Rs.2,576***
Bodh Prakash	Rs.854	Rs.674	Rs.989	Rs.432	***Rs.2,949***
R.Nahar	Rs.890	Rs.674	Rs.564	Rs.737	***Rs.2,865***
P.Chawla	Rs.616	Rs.654	Rs.890	Rs.324	***Rs.2,484***
	Rs.5,570	***Rs.5,906***	***Rs.6,629***	***Rs.4,820***	***Rs.22,925***

Annual total would be sum of the four quarters. We can determine the most productive consultant by creating a chart. Follow the steps below to create a start using this data:

① Highlight consultant names.

② Press **Control** (CTRL) key to specify another discontinuous range, and highlight Yearly Total figure also.

③ Click the **Chart Wizard** icon on the **Standard Toolbar** to start the Chart Wizard.

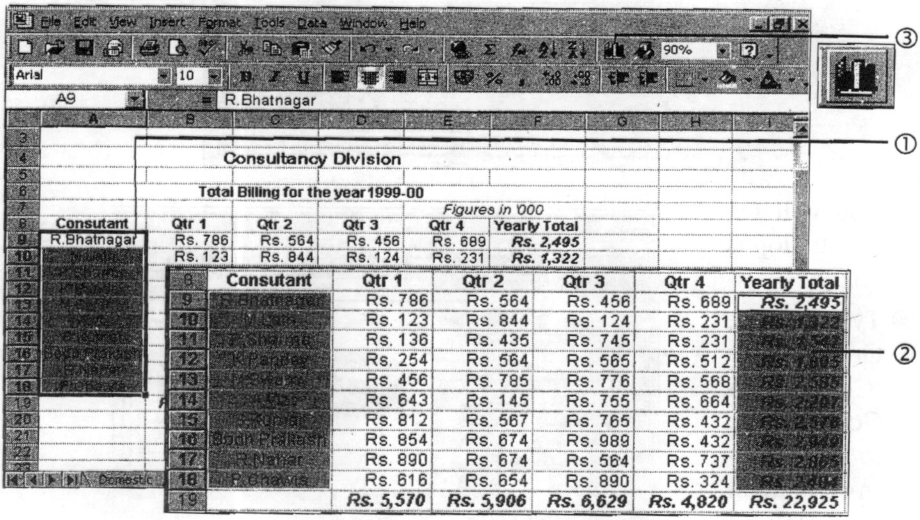

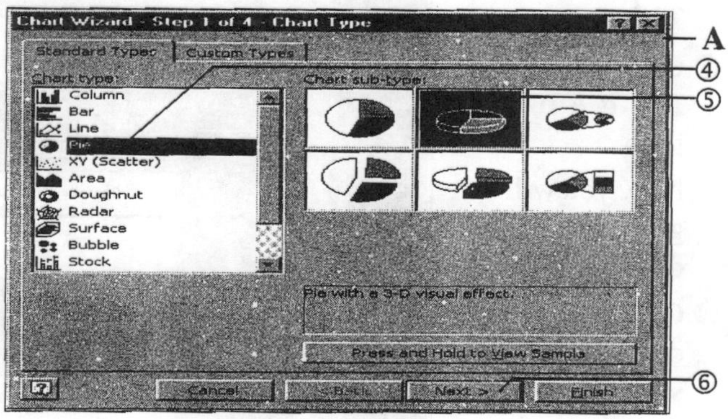

A You will get this dialog box.

④ Select the desired chart type.

⑤ Select the 3D Chart sub type.

⑥ Click on 'Next' tab to continue.

B You will get this dialog box.

C The range of cells, which you have highlighted earlier, would be selected here automatically.

D This signifies that your data series is in columns and not rows.

⑦ Click here to continue.

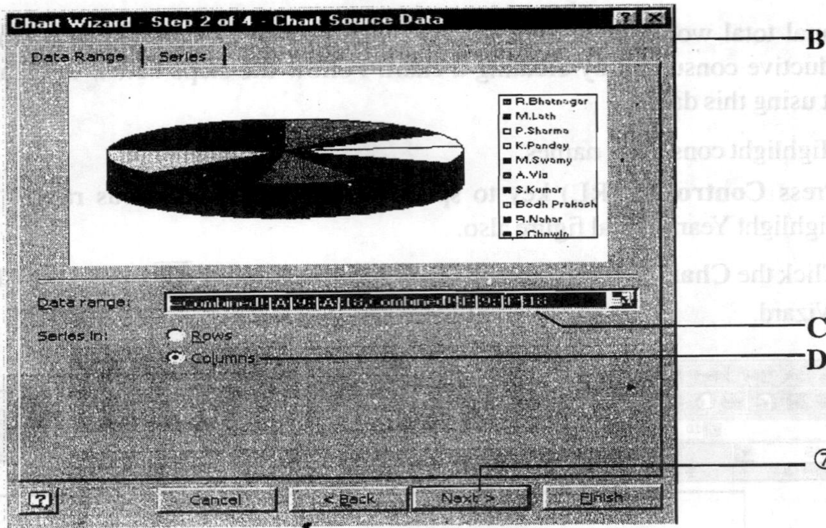

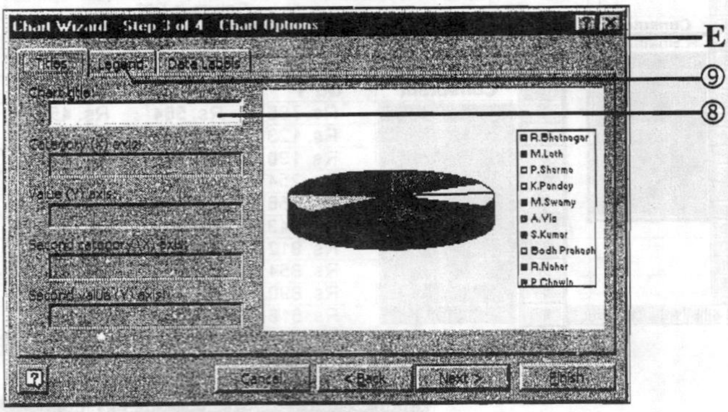

E You will get this dialogue box.

⑧ Type the Graph Title as 'Consultant's Contribution to Total Billing' after choosing **Title** folio.

⑨ Choose the **Legend** folio.

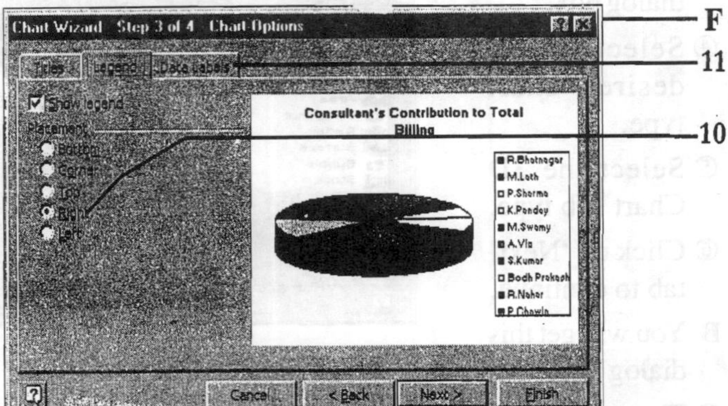

F Now you will get this dialogue box.

⑩ Click here once to specify the data legends to appear on any side of graph you desire (Here we let it remain on right side).

⑪ Choose **Data Labels** folio.

G You will get Data Labels dialog box.

⑫ Choose 'Show Percent' option to display the consultant's percentage contribution.

⑬ Click here to continue.

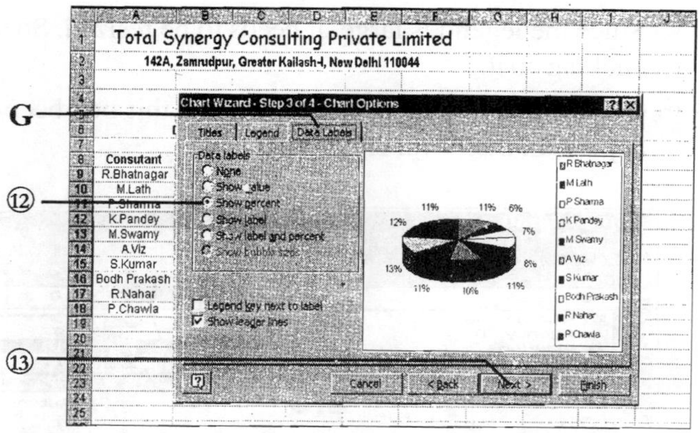

H You will get the last dialog box.

⑭ Choose **Combined** to place the graph as an object in this sheet.

⑮ Click on the **'Finish'** tab to see the graph.

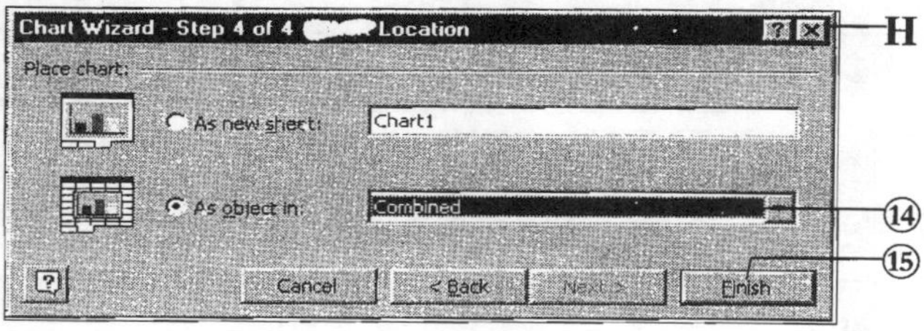

Modifying a Chart

① Now after getting the graph placed as an object in this sheet, first select the whole graph by clicking on it.

② Then right click and choose **Format Chart Area** from the option list. You will get another dialog box.

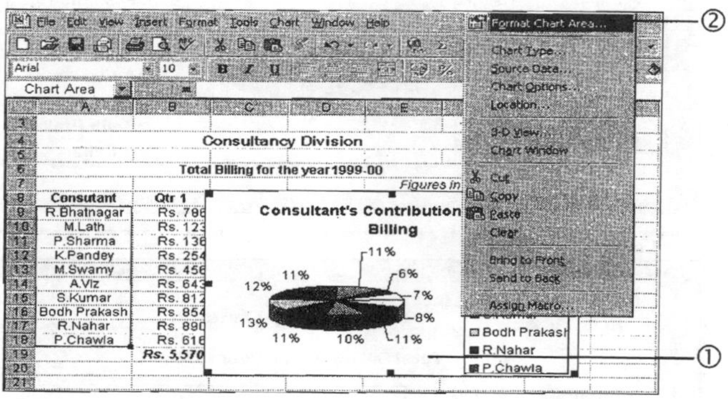

③ Choose the desired font.

④ Choose the font style.

⑤ Choose the font size.

⑥ Click on OK button to get the formatted graph.

⑦ Since the legend is large, it needs to be resized. So select only the legend by clicking on it.

⑧ Click here and drag the mouse so that this box becomes smaller. Now it will appear on the lower right corner.

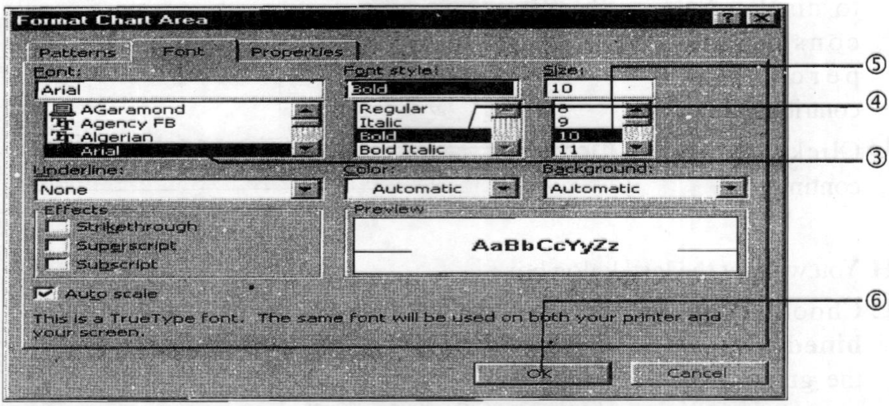

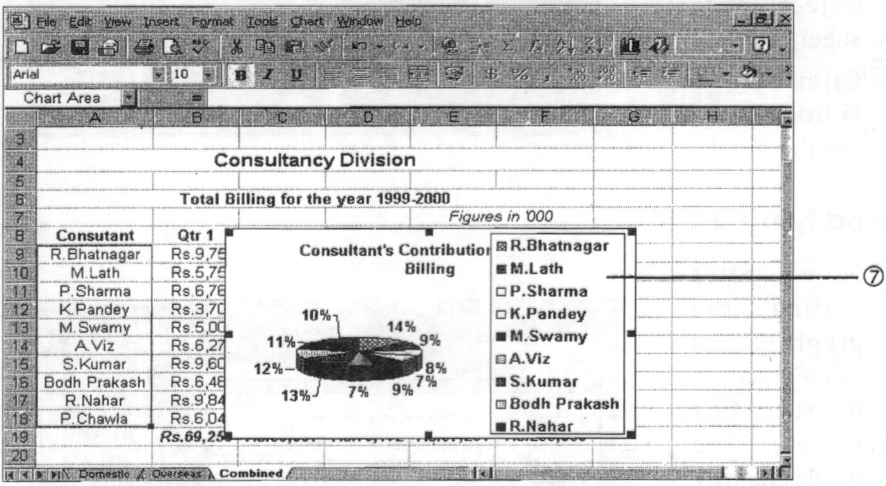

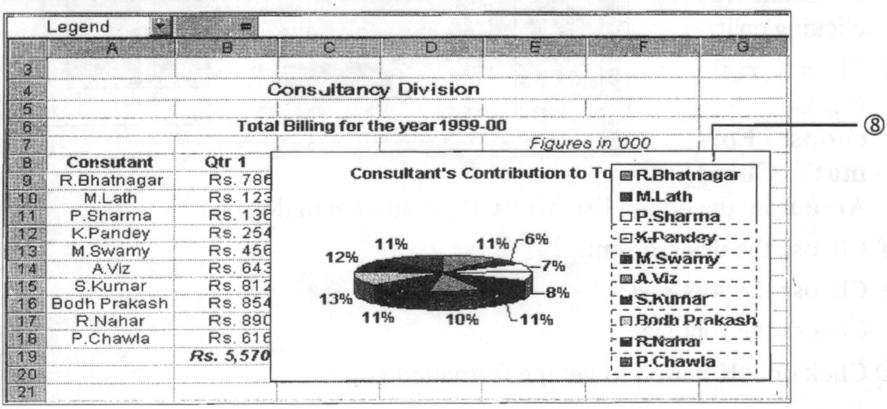

⑨ You would have noticed that the graph is placed over the text. To place it appropriately, click to select the whole graph and drag the mouse while keeping it pressed to place it below the text. Now you can see the final result.

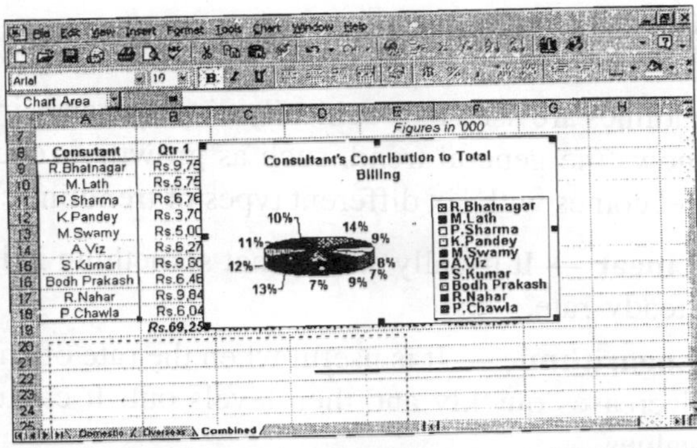

⑨

Note: Other Chart elements can be modified same manner as the Legend was modified.

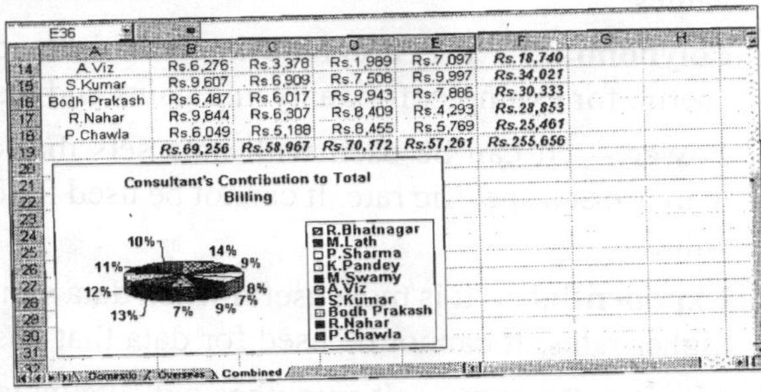

I

I Final Result!

Note: To get a three dimensional view of the chart, Choose **3D-View** from the **Chart** menu.

① Click here to increase/decrease the amount of elevation.

② Click here to increase/decrease the degree of rotation.

③ Click on the **OK** button to apply your settings.

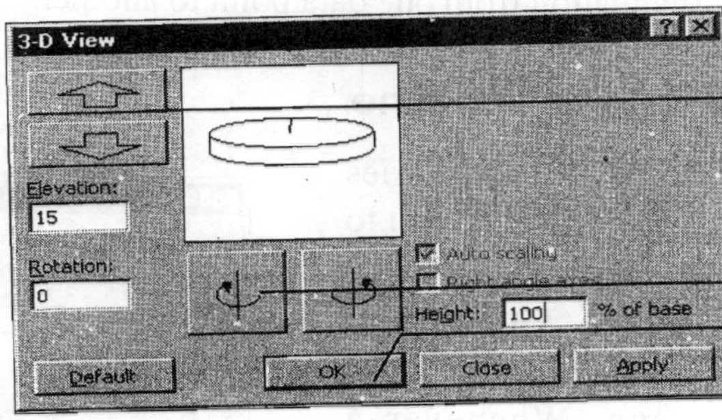

① ② ③

A Output

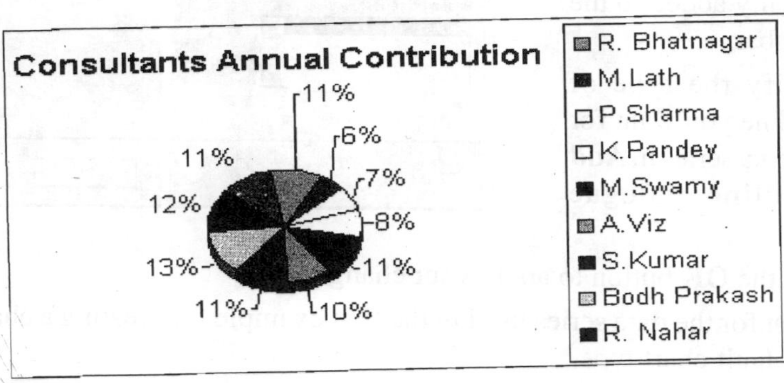

A

ADDING TRENDLINES

Trendlines are used to graphically display trends in data. As the name suggests, it shows the general trend, such as growth or decline that occurs in the data. Excel comes with six different types of trendlines:

1. **Linear** — It usually shows that something is increasing or decreasing at a steady rate.
2. **Logarithmic** — It is useful when the rate of change in the data increases or decreases quickly and then levels out. It can use negative and/or positive values.
3. **Polynomial** — It is a curved line that is used when data fluctuates. It is useful, for example, for analysing gains and losses over a large data set.
4. **Power** — It can be used with data sets that compare measurements that increase at a specific rate. It cannot be used for data that has zero or negative values.
5. **Exponential** — It is most useful when data values rise or fall at increasingly higher rates. It cannot be used for data that has zero or negative values.
6. **Moving Average** — It smoothes out fluctuations in data to show a pattern or trend more clearly. It uses a sequence of averages to reduce the effect of fluctuation from one data point to another.

To Add a Trendline

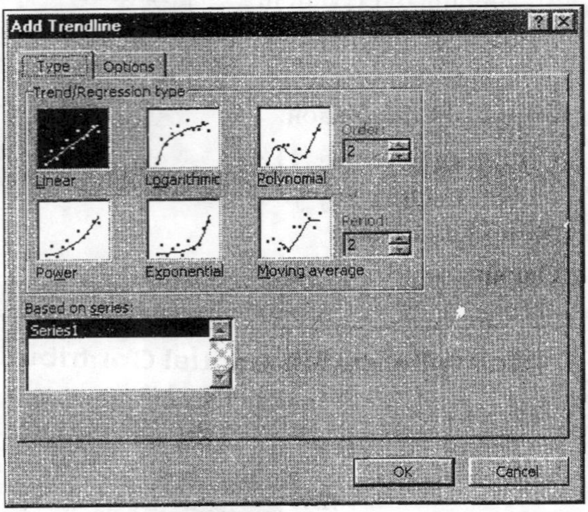

1. Select the data series for which you wish to add a trend line.
2. Choose **Add Trendline** from the **Chart** menu. Whenever a chart is created, the Chart menu is automatically added to the menu bar.
3. Specify the type of trendline you want for your data series in **Add Trendline** dialogue box.
4. Click the **OK** button to apply your changes.

A Output for the data series used in the first example for creating a chart using the default chart type.

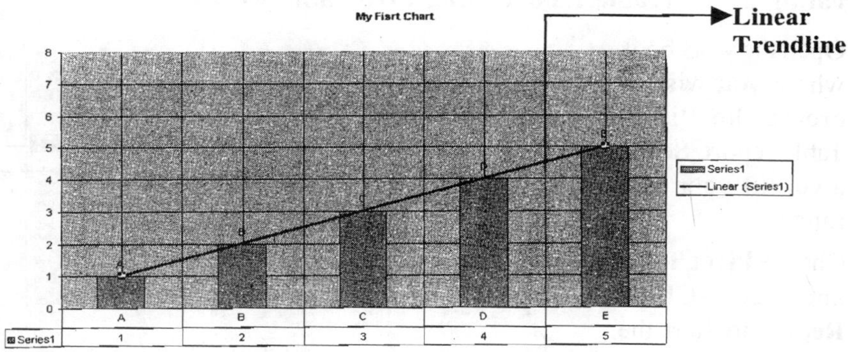

PivotTable Reports

These reports can be used in almost any environment to simplify data analysis but their real use is appreciated when dealing with large amounts of data. You can create a PivotTable report from an Excel worksheet or using an external source. An external source could be any source that exists outside MS Excel, such as a database (Access, Oracle or SQL Server), Text file or a source on the Internet. Some of the advantages of using PivotTable Reports are outlined below:

A PivotTable report can be used to:

- Summarise large amounts of data into a flexible format.
- Compare field/column values across multiple categories.
- Filter the data to display areas of concern.
- Compute the sub-totals and totals.

Once a PivotTable report is created:

- You can pivot the elements of the report to new positions within the table for a different view of the data.
- You can rotate its rows and columns to see different summaries of the source data without worrying about harming the original data source.
- You can dynamically add a new field of your choice or delete existing fields.

The product sales of various products of a Departmental Store are displayed in the following example. Let us understand the usefulness of a PivotTable report by taking this example:

	A	B	C	D	E	F
1						
2	Needs Departmental Store - Quarterly Sales (2003)					
3						
4	Product Name	Category	Month	Quantity	Unit Price	Sales (Rs.)
5	Pens	Stationary	April	50	25	1000
6	Pens	Stationary	May	55	25	1000
7	Pens	Stationary	June	40	25	875
8	Pencils	Stationary	April	100	12	720
9	Pencils	Stationary	May	96	12	960
10	Pencils	Stationary	June	86	12	960
11	SketchPens	Stationary	April	20	55	550
12	SketchPens	Stationary	May	18	55	550
13	SketchPens	Stationary	June	26	55	1100
14	Perfumes	Gift Items	April	35	190	3800
15	Perfumes	Gift Items	May	45	190	7600
16	Perfumes	Gift Items	June	52	190	7600
17	Wrist Watches	Gift Items	April	10	550	5500
18	Wrist Watches	Gift Items	May	8	550	2750
19	Wrist Watches	Gift Items	June	12	550	5500
20	Teddy Bears	Gift Items	April	5	300	1500
21	Teddy Bears	Gift Items	May	4	300	600
22	Teddy Bears	Gift Items	June	8	300	1500

Creating a PivotTable report using PivotTable wizard:

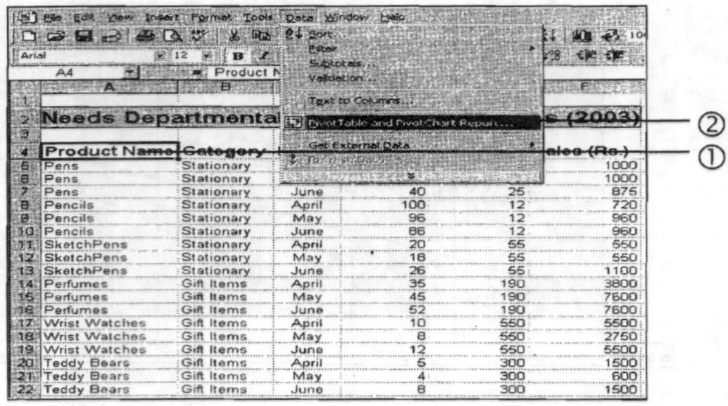

① Open the workbook where you wish to create the PivotTable report. Select a cell in your data range.

② Choose **Pivot Table** and **Pivot-Chart Report** to start the PivotTable wizard.

③ Choose **Microsoft Excel list** as your data source. If your data is stored in an Excel Workbook then you can choose this option. If your data is stored in a database then you can choose External Data Source option.

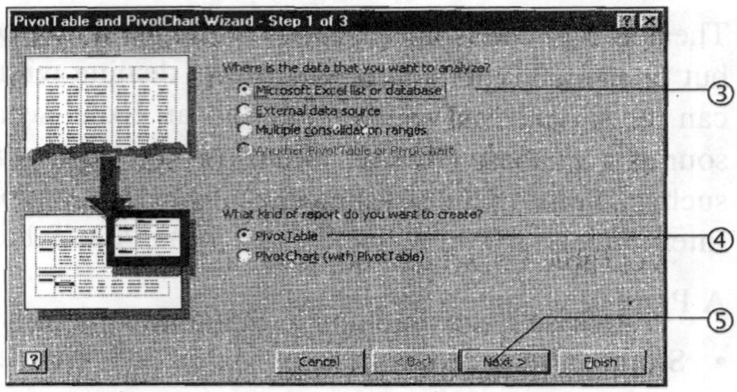

④ Specify the kind of report (PivotTable or PivotChart) you wish to create.

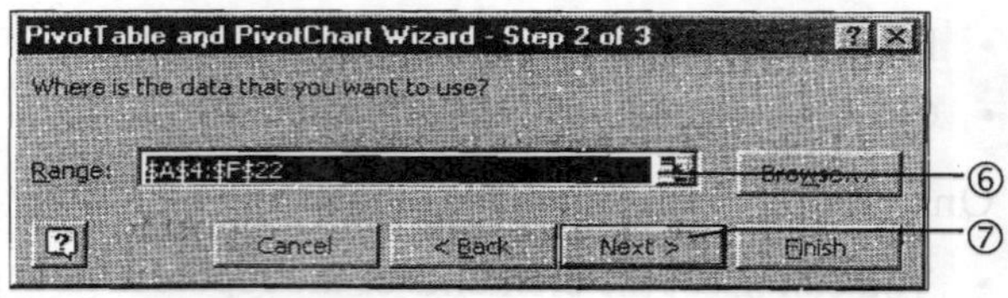

⑤ Click on the **Next** button to continue.

⑥ Indicate the location of the source data. If you have selected a cell in the data range prior to starting the wizard then Excel would automatically select the entire range, including the column headings.

⑦ Click on the **Next** button to continue.

⑧ Specify the location of the PivotTable report. You can choose to place the report in the existing workbook or a new workbook.

⑨ Click on the **Finish** button to create the PivotTable report.

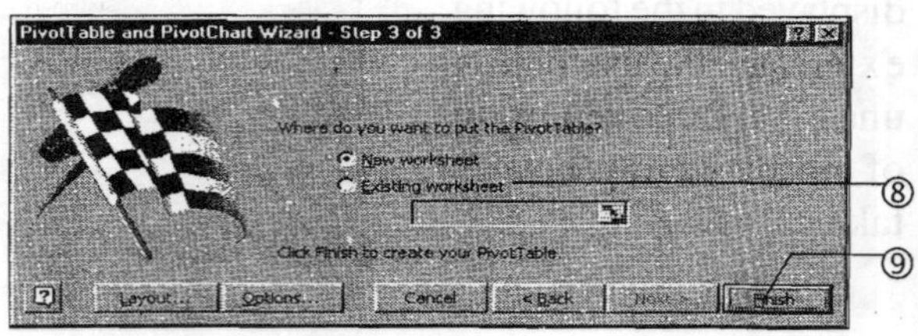

A Output–This kind of output is referred to as **OnScreen Layout**, which allows you to dynamically add fields directly onto the worksheet from the PivotTable toolbar. We can use this layout to build a report displaying the monthly sales of all/selected products for each category. Let us see how this can be done!

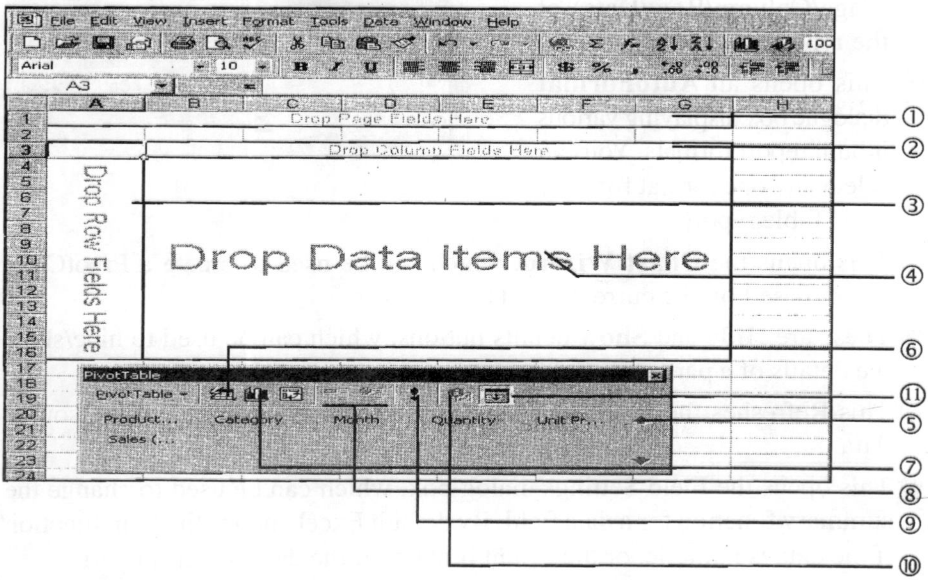

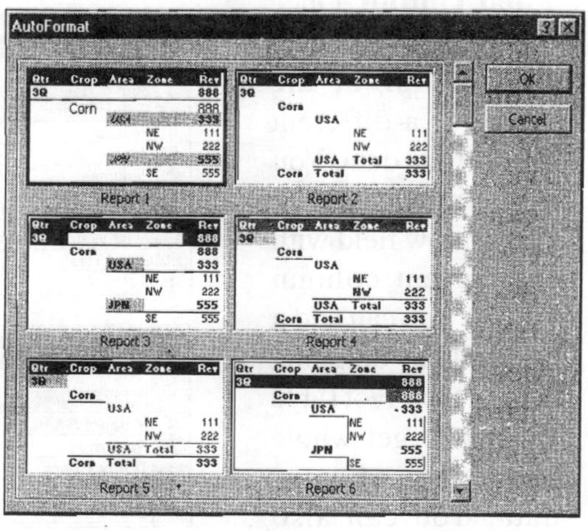

① Fields added here will be used to filter the view. When you select a value within a **Page Field**, the report changes to display records corresponding to the selected field. In our case we can add 'Category' field into this area to filter the records according to the product category.

② Fields added here will serve as column headings. In our case we can add 'Month' field.

③ Fields added here will serve as headings for the rows of information. In our case we can add 'Product Name' field.

④ Fields added here will give the actual data values used in the summary. In our case we can add 'Product Sales' field.

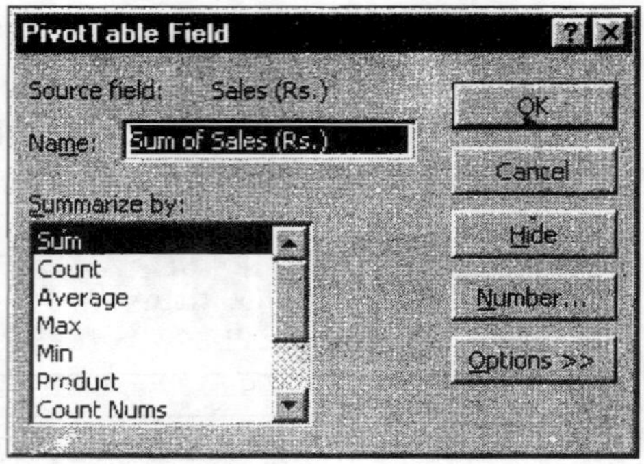

⑤ This is the **PivotTable Toolbar** displaying all the field headings used in the data source. You can drag the fields from here to various regions (Page/Column/Row/Data) of the report.

⑥ This opens an **AutoFormat** dialogue box displaying various inbuilt report formats. You can select any one format for your PivotTable report.

⑦ This opens the **Chart Wizard**, which can be used to create a PivotChart report based on the current PivotTable report.

⑧ These are **Hide** and **Show** details buttons, which can be used to hide/show the details of a particular field.

⑨ This Refreshes the PivotTable report to reflect any changes to the source data.

⑩ This opens the Field Settings dialog box, which can be used to change the summary function for a data field. By default Excel applies the Sum function if the data is numeric, or the Count function if the data is non-numeric.

⑪ This toggles the field heading area between hidden and visible.

A Final Output Once this report is created, you can pivot the table for a different view of the data. You can exchange the current row field with the current column field or you can add a new field by dragging it from the PivotTable toolbar to get whole new view of your data. You can also change the summary function with the help of Field Settings icon of the PivotTable toolbar.

	A	B	C	D	E	F	
1	Category	(All)					①
2							
3	Sum of Sales (Rs.)	Month					②
4	Product Name	April	May	June	Grand Total		③
5	Pencils	720	960	960	2640		
6	Pens	1000	1000	875	2875		
7	Perfumes	3800	7600	7600	19000		
8	SketchPens	550	550	1100	2200		
9	Teddy Bears	1500	600	1500	3600		
10	Wrist Watches	5500	2750	5500	13750		
11	Grand Total	13070	13460	17535	44065		
12							

	A	B	C	D	E
1	Category	Gift Items			
2					
3	Sum of Sales (Rs.)	Month			
4	Product Name	April	May	June	Grand Total
5	Perfumes	3800	7600	7600	19000
6	Teddy Bears	1500	600	1500	3600
7	Wrist Watches	5500	2750	5500	13750
8	Grand Total	10800	10950	14600	36350

① Click here to change your filter.

② Click here to change the Month

③ Click here to change the Product Name.

	A	B	C
1	Category	(All)	
2			
3	Sum of Sales (Rs.)	Month	
4	Product Name	June	Grand Total
5	Pencils	960	960
6	Pens	875	875
7	Perfumes	7600	7600
8	SketchPens	1100	1100
9	Teddy Bears	1500	1500
10	Wrist Watches	5500	5500
11	Grand Total	17535	17535

	A	B	C
1	Category	(All)	
2			
3	Sum of Sales (Rs.)	Month	
4	Product Name	June	Grand Total
5	Teddy Bears	1500	1500
6	Wrist Watches	5500	5500
7	Grand Total	7000	7000

PivotChart Report, created using the ChartWizard icon of the PivotTable toolbar. Different Chart objects can be modified (as explained earlier in this section) to suit the user's need.

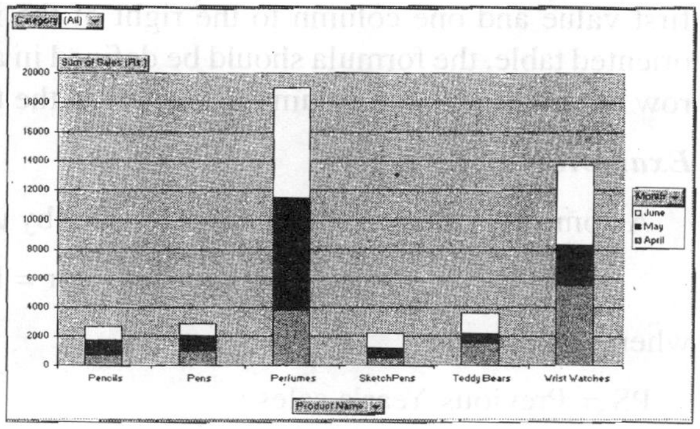

ANALYSING YOUR DATA

Excel provides a number of tools to formulate future performance and perform what-if analysis in your worksheets. What-if analysis, as the name suggests, is used to analyse your worksheet data to predict the future performance of your data by understanding its past behaviour, thereby assisting users in taking better decisions.

Ways to forecast values with what-if analysis:

1. Data Tables
2. Scenarios

Data Tables

A data table is a technique that can be used to view the variations in the formula result by substituting different input values in the formula. Variations can be substituted in the formula either down one column or across one row. If the variations are listed down a column, then it is known as Column-Oriented table. If the variations are listed down a row, then it is known as Row-Oriented table.

There are two types of Data Tables, viz., One-Variable Data Table and Two-Variable Data Table. A One-Variable Data table substitutes different values for one variable in the formula. A Two-variable data table substitutes different values for two variables in the same formula. For example: we can use a Two-Variable data table to determine how different interest rates and loan terms will affect a payment. Interest Rate and Loan terms would be the two variables.

Defining Formulas and Input Tables for the Data Tables For creating Data Tables, Excel needs an Input Cell. An Input cell is a blank cell lying outside the table range for holding calculations of the formula. Excel requires specific locations for the inputs and formulas used by data tables. For a column-oriented table, the formula should be defined in a cell, i.e., one cell above the first value and one column to the right of the input variable list. For a row-oriented table, the formula should be defined in a cell, i.e., is one cell below the row of values and one column to the left of the first value.

Example:

A company calculates the projected sales by using the following formula:

Project Sales for the year = PS + PS*R

where

PS = Previous Year's sales

R = Rate of growth in sales

You are given the following details:

Sales in 2001 (thousand Rs.)	:	1200
Rate of growth in sales	:	28%
Projected sales in 2002	:	1536

Let us have a better understanding of Data Tables by creating a Data Table for the above example. We shall be creating a One-Variable data table as this has only one variable namely 'R' for showing the projected sales if the growth rate is changed to 29%, 30%, 31%, 32%, 33% and 34%.

Creating a One-Variable Data Table

① Enter the data in your worksheet. Since we have entered the variables in a column, it is a column-oriented table.

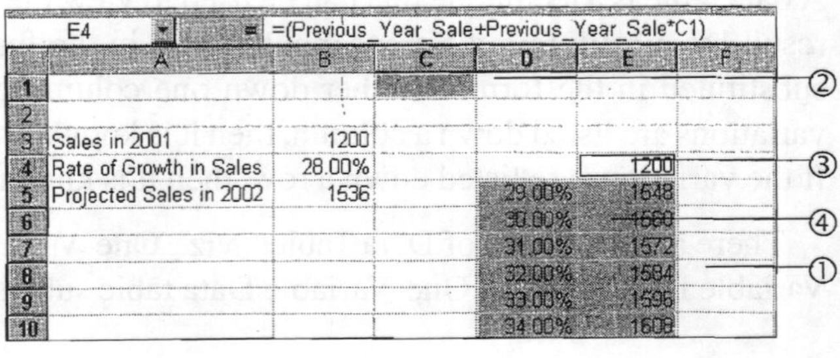

② Choose an input cell for holding the calculations, as the input cell will be over written many times during the creation of the Data Table, it should be blank. Let us choose 'C1' as our input cell.

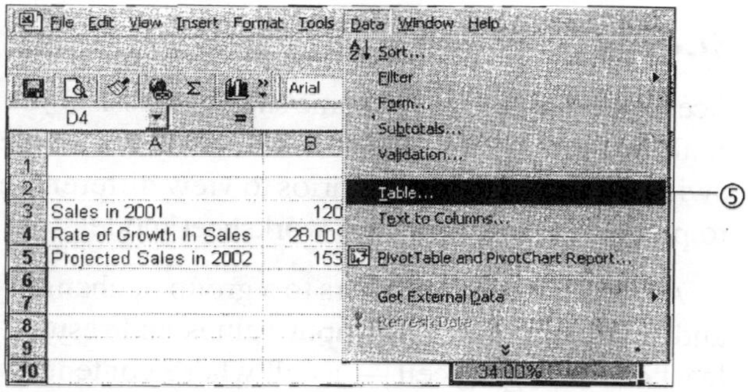

③ Enter the formula (PS+PS*C1 as C1 is our input cell). For a column-oriented table, the formula must be entered in a cell that is one row above and one column to the right of the top of the list of variations. In our case we will enter the formula in the cell E4.

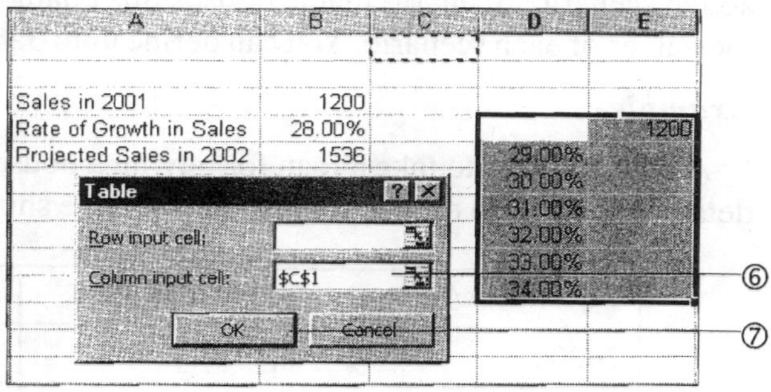

④ Select a minimum data range covering the input variables and the formula. D4:E10 would be our minimum data range.

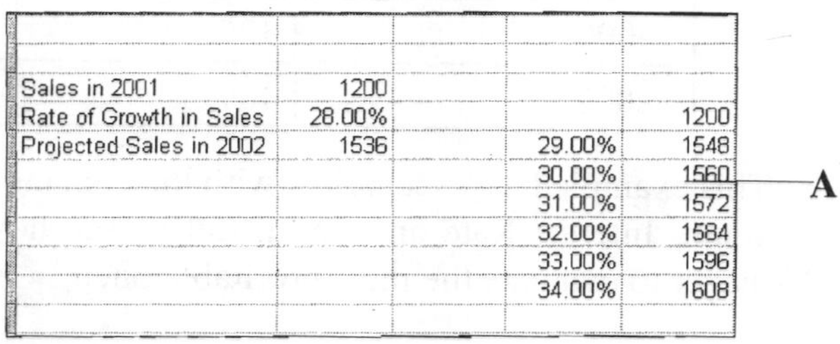

⑤ Choose **Table** from the **Data** menu.

⑥ Type the cell reference for the input cell in the **Column input cell** box. For row-oriented data table, the cell reference should be typed in the **Row input cell** box.

⑦ Click on the **OK** button.

A Output–displaying the projected sales for different values of 'R'.

Notes:

1. You can change the value of the input variable(s) and accordingly view the projected sales figure.
2. To clear a data table, select the entire data range and press **Del** key. You cannot delete individual entries, as they share a common formula.

Scenario Manager

Scenario Manager, as the name suggests, assists you in managing your scenarios. It allows you to view different scenarios in a single spreadsheet so that you can switch to any of these scenarios to view different results. You can use scenarios to predict the outcome of a worksheet model.

A scenario in Excel refers to a group of changing cells, where you can create and save various sets of input values and results. A scenario must contain at least one changing cell — a cell whose contents will vary depending upon the active scenario. Scenario manager uses this changing cell reference to display the values of each scenario. You can define upto 32 changing cells per scenario.

Example

A person wants to take a loan for buying a house. He visits a bank to get the details. He is given different options which are shown in the table below.

Investment Amount	Interest Rate	Term (Months)
20000	10%	60
20000	11%	48
14000	12%	84
12000	13%	60

This example has 4 scenarios, with three changing cells namely Investment Amount, Interest Rate and Term. Let us see how we can use the Scenario Manager to evaluate the most profitable one.

Creating Scenarios

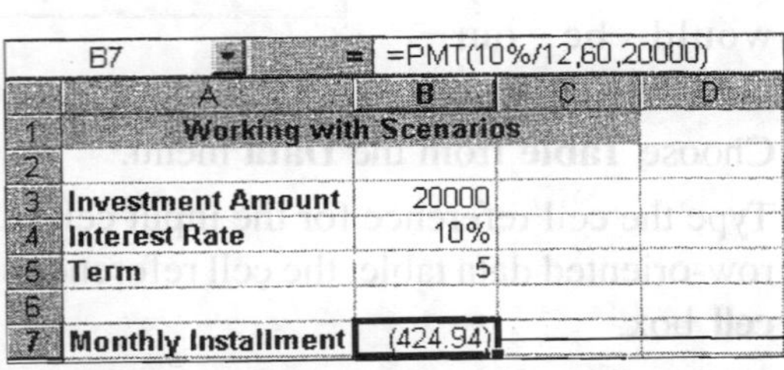

① Enter the data for the first scenario in a worksheet. And calculate the monthly payment amount. (Monthly Payment Amount = PMT (Interest Rate/12, Term, Investment Amount). (PMT function has been explained earlier in the chapter)

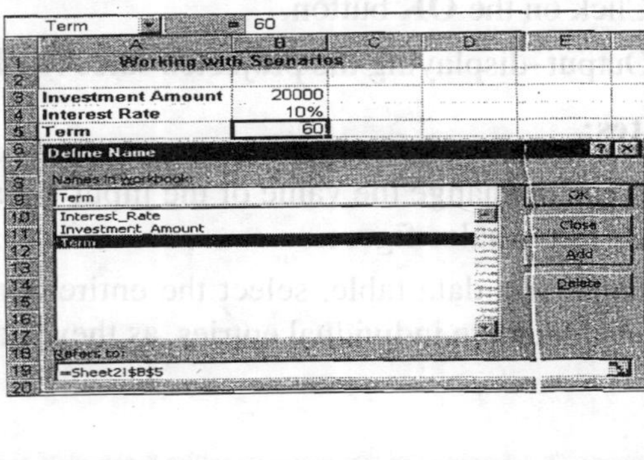

② **Naming the changing cells** — it would be

more meaningful if we assign a user-friendly name to each changing cell rather than referring the cell by its cell address. To assign a name, select the cell, choose **Define** under the **Name** option from the **Insert** menu and type the desired name in the **Name** box.

③ Choose **Scenarios** from the **Tools** menu. A **Scenario Manager** dialog box will be displayed.

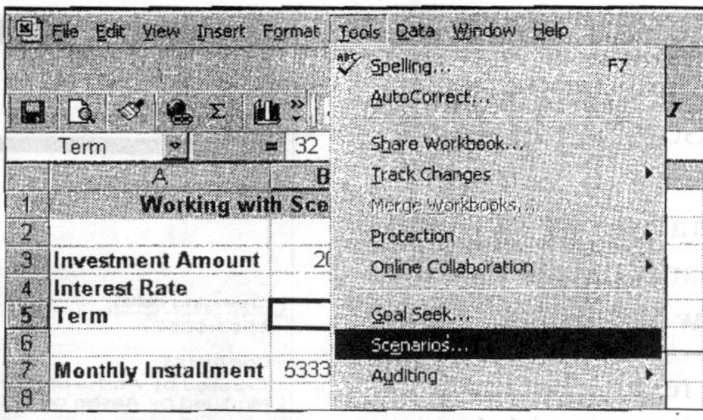

④ Click on the **Add** button from the **Scenario Manager** dialog box.

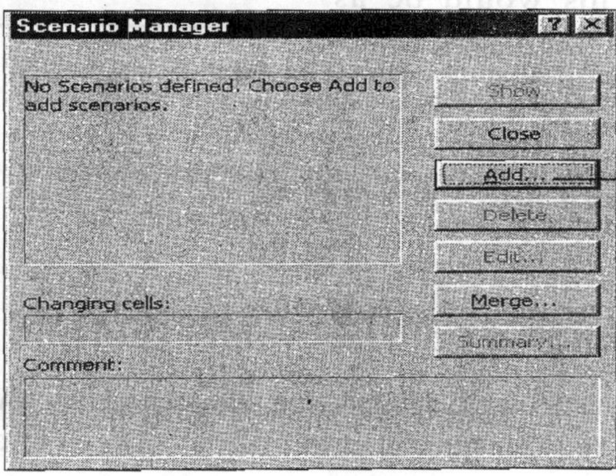

⑤ Type a name for your first scenario and specify the cell references of the changing cells (B3, B4 and B5). For specifying multiple cell references use **Ctrl** key. Click on the **OK** button to enter the scenario values.

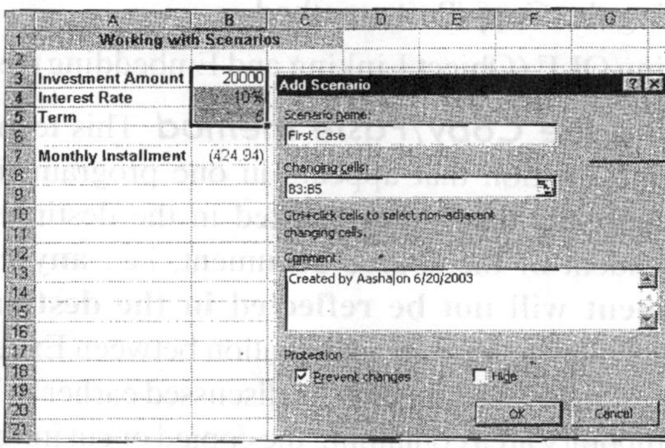

⑥ Enter the desired values for the Investment Amount, Interest Rate and Term in the Scenario Values dialog box. Click on the **OK** button to add the scenario to the Scenario Manager.

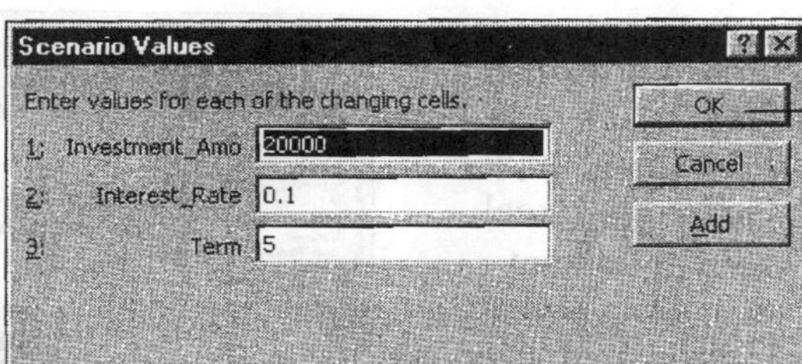

⑦ Similarly, add the remaining scenarios to the Scenario Manager. To view a particular scenario, select the scenario and click on the **Show** button.

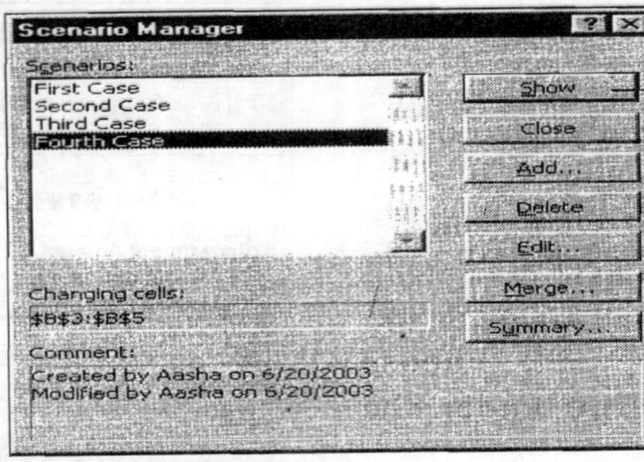

The results for the four scenarios would be as follows:

First Case	=	**424.94**
Second Case	=	**516.91**
Third Case	=	**247.14**
Fourth Case	=	**254.96**

Exchanging Data between Excel and Other Programs

You can exchange data between Excel and other MS office programs, and vice versa. You can transfer information between Excel and other applications in broadly two ways:

1. Using the Copy/Paste method.
2. Using OLE (Object Linking and Embedding) technology.

Using the Copy/Paste method This technique is used if you wish to copy information that appears in one program into another program. In this technique, the data that is pasted in the destination document is completely independent of the source document, i.e., **any changes done in the source document will not be reflected in the destination document.** The most common way to transfer information between Excel and Word or vice versa is to use the Windows clipboard. As discussed earlier in Windows chapter, a clipboard is a temporary area containing the copied or cut information and the paste function takes the information from the clipboard.

Example – Follow the steps below to copy a chart created in Excel into a Word document.

① Select the Excel chart and choose **Copy** from the **Edit** menu.

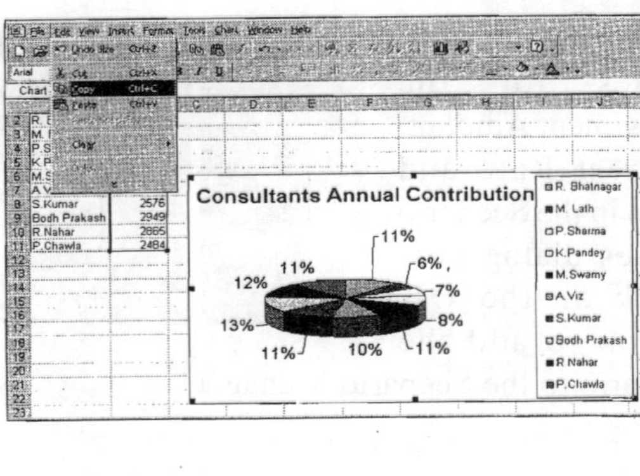

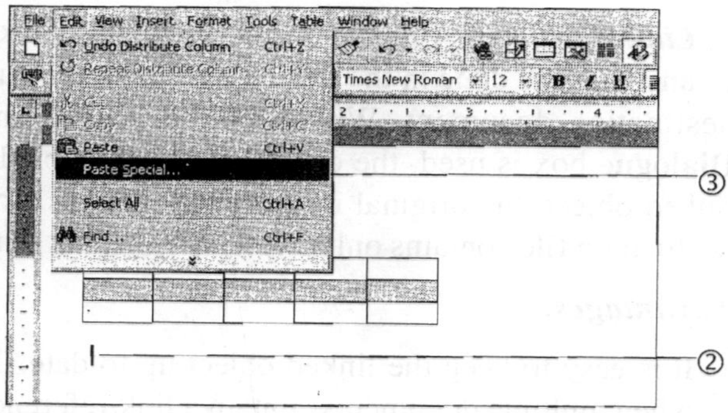

② Switch to your Word document and place the cursor where you wish to insert the chart.

③ Choose **Paste Special** from the **Edit** menu of MSWord.

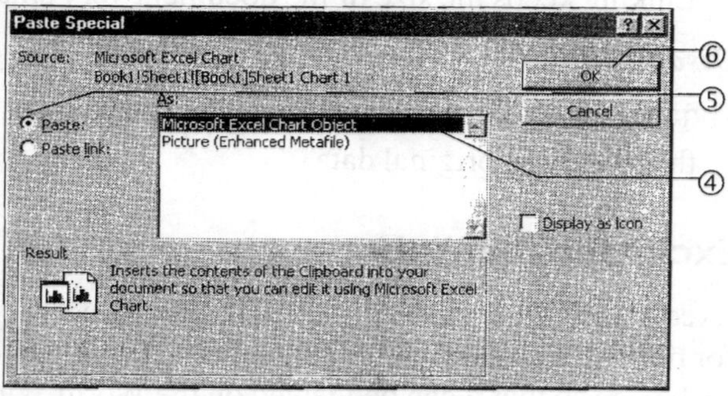

④ Choose **Microsoft Excel Chart Object** from the **Paste Special** dialog box.

⑤ Click on **Paste** as you wish to paste only the information reflected in the current chart.

⑥ Click on the **OK** button to paste the selected object.

Note: The same technique can be used to copy an object from a Word document into an Excel workbook.

Using OLE (Object Linking and Embedding) technology

Embedded Objects An embedded object has no link to the source document so any changes done in the source document will not be reflected in the destination document. Whenever the **Paste** option from the **Paste Dialog** box is used, the object is always copied as an embedded object. In the above example, the Excel chart is copied as an embedded object into the Word document. To change an embedded object, double-click the object to open it in its source program. Once the object is opened it can be edited using its source program. The source program (or another program capable of editing the object) must be installed on your computer.

Advantages:

- the document containing the embedded object is portable, i.e., you can transfer the document to a different computer without breaking a link.
- the embedded object can be edited without affecting the content of the source or the original document.

Disadvantages:

- embedding an object into a document increases its file size.

Linked Objects A linked object maintains a link with the source document, so any changes done in the source document are automatically reflected in the destination document. Whenever the **Paste Link** option from the **Paste Dialogue** box is used, the object is always copied as a linked object. With a linked object, the original information remains stored in the source file. The destination file contains only a reference or link to the source file.

Advantages:

- It is easy to keep the linked object up to date. This feature is very helpful when multiple documents contain a link/reference to a specific object.
- Linking keeps the size of the document very small.

Disadvantage:

- The source file must remain available on your computer or network to maintain the link to the original data.

Excel and the Web

Excel (As well as other MS office programs) incorporates unprecedented support for publishing information on the web. You can save your Excel workbook as a Web page so that it can be viewed on the World Wide Web (WWW). Once you have saved your Excel workbook in HTML format (Webpage), you can rearrange the items on the WebPage, add more text or graphics, or any additional features supported by HTML. (HTML–Hypertext Markup Language–is an encoding scheme that helps in creating web-pages.) Excel also allows reading web pages, i.e., you can open a webpage as an Excel worksheet.

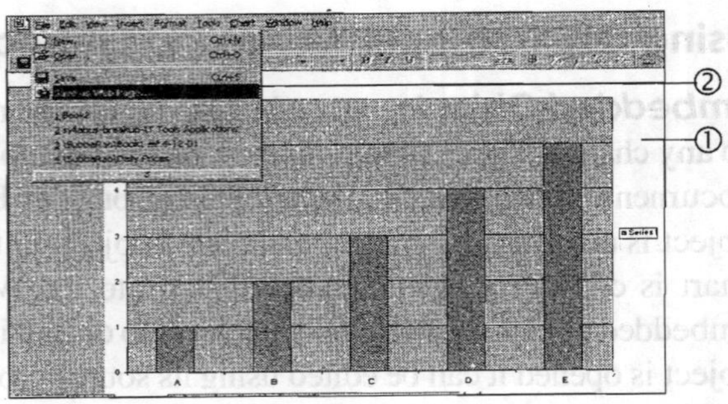

Saving an Excel Workbook as a Webpage:

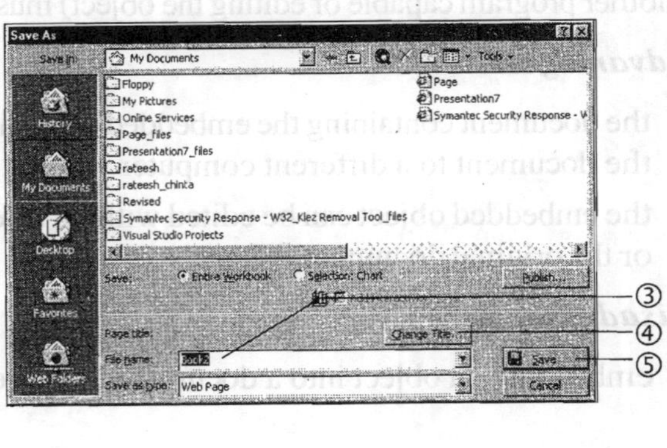

① Open the workbook that you wish to save as a Webpage.

② Choose **Save As Webpage** from the **File** menu.

③ Specify a file name in the **Save As** dialog box.

④ Click here to change the title of your webpage. This title will be displayed at the top of your browser window.

⑤ Click the **Save** button.

Notes:

1. Once a workbook is saved as a webpage, you can view it in any browser.
2. Whenever a workbook is saved as a webpage, a folder containing all the dependent files is automatically created in the same location. Example: If you saved your workbook as 'My Web Book' in C:\My Documents then a folder titled 'My Web Book_Files' will be created automatically in C:\My Documents.

Hyperlinks in Excel

Hyperlinks provide a simple way to navigate from one document to another. In Excel, a hyperlink can be used to navigate from one sheet to another within the same or a different worksheet. When you move the mouse pointer over a hyperlink, the pointer changes to a different symbol/image (usually a hand). Hyperlinked text is usually represented in blue colour.

Creating Hyperlinks

① Select the cell where you would like the hyperlink to be located.

② Click on **Insert Hyperlink** icon from the Standard toolbar.

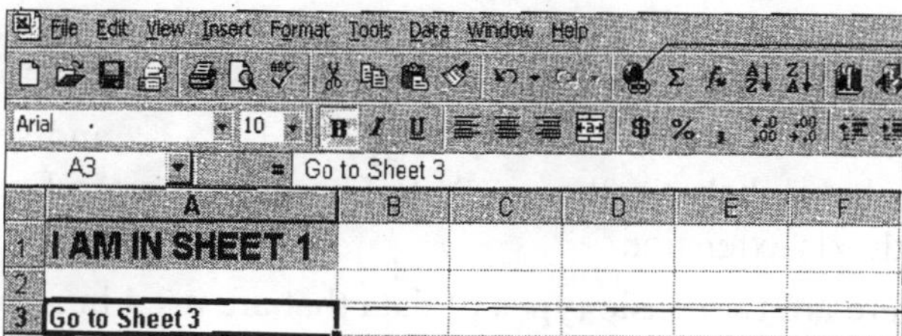

②

①

③ Type or choose the destination file from **Insert Hyperlink** dialog box. You can either type the location of the destination file or you can choose an alternative by clicking on the **File** button. If you wish to create a hyperlink within the same

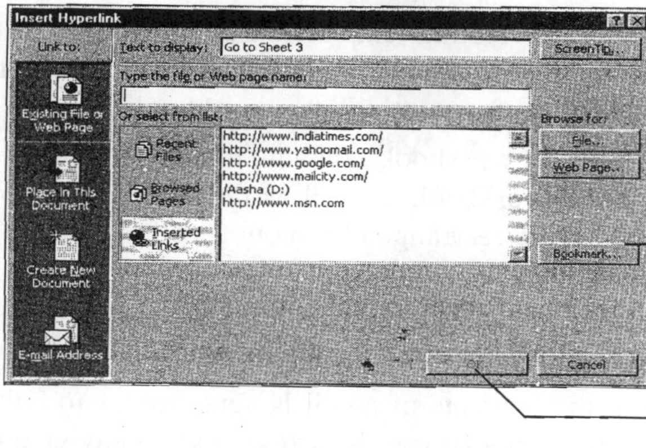

③

④

worksheet then click on the **Bookmark** button and select the desired sheet. Click on the **OK** button to close the Bookmark dialog box.

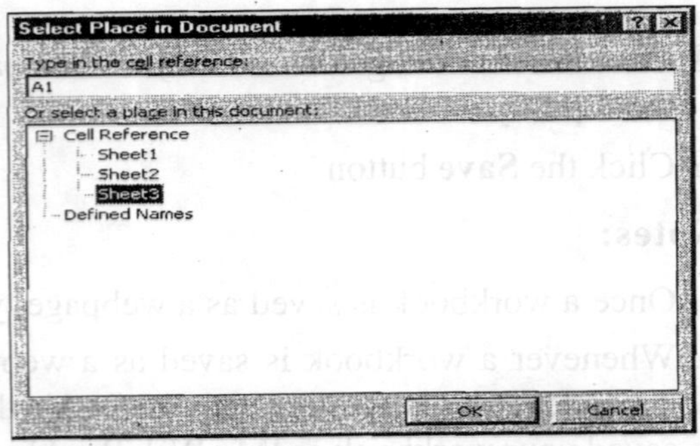

④ Click the **OK** button.

A Output – Clicking on the hyperlink would open the destination file.

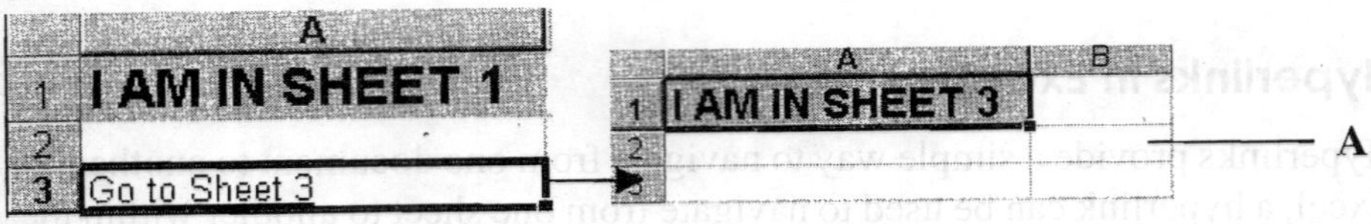

SUMMARY

Excel - Basics

- Excel is a spreadsheet package that can be used for financial calculations, analysis and creating graphs.
- Excel, or for that matter any spreadsheet, essentially comprises of a grid of rows and columns. Intersection of a row and a column is called a cell. Typically, rows are numbered numerically, i.e., 1, 2, 3... and so on, and columns are labeled alphabetically, i.e., A, B, C... and so on. An Excel file is always saved with .xls extension.
- There are two basic types of data that are used in a spreadsheet: Values and Formulas. Values include numbers and text and formulas are arithmetic calculations that change based on the input given to them.
- Excel allows creating template-based workbooks. A template in Excel is a special type of workbook with pre-defined formats and controls that can be used as a base for creating other workbooks.
- By default, a workbook contains three sheets. It is possible to add more sheets to a workbook as well as remove existing worksheets. Sheets can also be moved/rearranged from one location to another in a workbook. You can rename a sheet to make it more user friendly.
- Excel allows hiding a workbook/worksheet from the user's view. Hiding a workbook/sheet does not delete its data.
- Editing the contents of a cell is very similar to editing data in any Word document. You can use the arrow keys to navigate between the cells of a worksheet. To edit the contents of a cell in Excel, use the F2 function key.

- Undo command can be used to undo recent action(s)/errors done by the user. Redo command can be used to redo something that the user has undone.
- A spelling and grammar check can be performed on the data/text contained in an Excel workbook.
- Find and replace can be used to search for specific text or numbers that you want to review or edit, and you can automatically replace data you find.

Formulas and Functions

- A formula is an equation that performs operations on worksheet data. Formulas can perform mathematical operations, they can compare worksheet values or join text. Formulas can refer to other cells on the same worksheet, cells on other sheets in the same workbook, or cells on sheets in other workbooks.
- A formula in Excel always begins with an equal sign (=). Following the equal sign are the elements to be calculated (the operands), which are separated by calculation operators. Once a formula is defined for a particular row, it can be used for the rest of the rows by using a simple method of Copy and Paste.
- Operators define the calculation to be performed by the formula. Calculation operators in Excel can be broadly classified into four categories: **Arithmetic Operators** (+,-,*,/,^), **Comparison operators** (=,<>,>,<,>=,<=), **Text concatenation operator** (&) and **Reference operators** (Colon, Comma, Space).
- Excel calculates the formula from left to right, according to a specific order for each operator in the formula. You can change the order of operations by using parentheses.
- Excel contains many built-in formulas, which are known as functions. Functions are power tools that help you perform complex computations easily and quickly. Typically, a function consists of two parts–**function name** and **arguments**. Arguments (or values) may in some cases be mandatory and in some cases optional. Functions always return a result.
- Worksheet functions in Excel can be broadly classified into: Mathematical, Statistical, Logical, Financial, Text and Date and Time Functions. ABS(), FACT(), INT(), MOD(), and ROMAN() are some examples of Mathematical functions. AVERAGE(), COUNT(), COUNTIF(), MIN() and MAX() are some examples of Statistical functions. IF(), AND(), OR() and NOT() are some examples of Logical functions. PMT(), IPMT() and NPER() are some examples of Financial functions. CHAR(), CODE(), FIND(), LEFT(), RIGHT() and LEN() are some examples of Text functions. TODAY(), DATE(), TIME(), NOW() and DAY() are some examples of Date and Time functions.

Formatting Features

- Excel offers a unique set of formatting features that can be used to effectively display your data. Most of the formatting features can be accessed from the Format menu and the Formatting toolbar.
- You can format all of the text in a cell or only selected characters using different text formatting icons available in the Formatting toolbar.
- Text Wrap can be used to display multiple lines of text within a single cell.
- You can use merge and centre function to center the text across several columns.
- Autofit command can be used to adjust the column width according to its contents.
- You can format numbers by adding desired currency symbol, inserting percent symbol, increasing or decreasing the number of decimal places and much more.
- You can apply borders to a cell or range of cells. Excel allows customising the border style and colour.
- You can apply shading to a cell or range of cells. Excel allows customising the shading pattern and colour.
- Text is always left aligned within the cell and Numbers are always right aligned within the cells. These alignments can be changed as per your requirements.
- Excel allows using the existing headers and footers or you can create your own by defining custom header and custom footer.
- You can use Format Painter to copy formatting of one object into another.

Filters

- Data Sort feature can be used to alphabetically rearrange any type of data, either in ascending (A to Z or 1 to 10 or 1st January 1999 to 31st December 1999) or descending (Z to A or 10 to 1 or 31st December 1999 to 1st January 1999) order.
- While using Data Sort command, the entire table, including the column headings, has to be selected for this command to work properly. Care should also be taken that the selected range does not contain any blank rows or columns or any other row other than the column headings and the data.
- Filtering helps in viewing only those records that meet a specific condition.
- All is very helpful feature of Data Filters. Whenever you get stuck or have given a wrong filter selection, use this option to get back to the complete table.
- Excel allows defining custom data filters, which can be used to pull out records based upon a mathematical criterion (condition). You can use the 'And' and 'Or' operators for specifying the condition for filtering records.

Creating Charts and Graphs

- Charts make it easy for users to see comparisons, patterns, and trends in data rapidly. Excel contains powerful charting wizards and tools that can be used to build effective and impressive charts.
- Excel comes with a wide variety of chart styles, including bar, pie, column, scatter, bubble and many more. Once a chart is created, you can customise it to suit your requirements.
- You can create a chart in its own chart sheet or as an embedded chart in a worksheet. A chart sheet is a separate sheet within your workbook that has its own sheet name. An embedded chart is a chart that is displayed directly in a worksheet.
- By default, Excel creates a Column type chart. However the default chart type can be changed to some other chart type.
- Elements of a chart include Chart Area, Plot Area (Axes + Gridlines + Data Series), Legend, Title and Data table. All the elements of a chart can be modified using the Format icon from the Chart toolbar.
- Chart Wizard guides you through a series of steps that helps in creating a chart.
- Trendlines are used to graphically display trends in data. As the name suggests, it shows the general trend, such as growth or decline that occurs in the data.
- Excel comes with six different types of trendlines, Linear, Logarithmic, Polynomial, Power, Exponential and Moving average.
- PivotTable reports are summary reports, which can be used in almost any environment to simplify data analysis, but their real use is appreciated when dealing with large amounts of data.
- Once a PivotTable report is created, you can pivot the elements of the report to new positions within the table for a different view of the data; you can rotate its rows and columns to see different summaries of the source data without worrying about harming the original data source and you can dynamically add a new field of your choice or delete existing fields.

Analysing Your Data

- Excel provides a number of tools to formulate future performance and perform what-if analysis in your worksheets.
- A data table is a technique that can be used to view the variations in the formula result by substituting different input values in the formula. There are two types of Data Tables, viz., One-Variable Data Table and Two-Variable Data Table.

- For creating Data Tables, Excel needs an Input Cell. An Input cell is a blank cell lying outside the table range for holding calculations of the formula.
- Scenario Manager, as the name suggests, assists you in managing your scenarios. You can use scenarios to predict the outcome of a worksheet model.
- A scenario in Excel refers to a group of changing cells, where you can create and save various sets of input values and results.

Integrating Word Processor, Spreadsheets and Webpages

- You can exchange data between Excel and other MS office programs, and vice versa.
- You can use Copy/Paste technique to copy information that appears in one program into another program. When an object is copied using this technique, it is copied as an embedded object, i.e., any changes done in the source document will not be reflected in the destination document.
- A linked object maintains a link with the source document so any changes done in the source document are automatically reflected in the destination document.
- Excel (like other MS office programs) incorporates unprecedented support for publishing information on the web.
- You can save your Excel workbook as a Webpage so that it can be viewed on the World Wide Web (WWW). Excel also allows reading webpages, i.e., you can open a webpage as an Excel worksheet.
- Whenever a workbook is saved as a webpage, a folder containing all the dependent files is automatically created in the same location.
- Hyperlinks provide a simple way to navigate from one document to another. In Excel, a hyperlink can be used to navigate from one sheet to another within the same or a different worksheet.

REVIEW QUESTIONS

1. Choose the most appropriate answer:

i. Which one of the following is a spreadsheet package?

(a) MS Word (b) MS PowerPoint
(c) Windows (d) None of the above

ii. A workbook with predefined formats, controls and formulas that can be used as a base for creating other workbooks:

(a) Spreadsheet (b) Template
(c) Wizard (d) None of the above

iii. An equation that performs operations on worksheet data. It can refer to other cells on the same worksheet, cells on other sheets in the same workbook, or cells on sheets in other workbooks:

(a) Hyperlink (b) Formula
(c) Argument (d) None of the above

iv. This operator produces a single reference to all the cells between two references, including the two cell references:

(a) Range Operator (b) Union Operator
(c) Intersection Operator (d) None of the above

v. This function returns the interest payment for a given period for an investment based on constant payments and a constant interest rate:

(a) IPMT (b) NPER
(c) PMT (d) None of the above

vi. This feature can be used to alphabetically rearrange any type of data, either in ascending (A to Z or 1 to 10 or 1st January 1999 to 31st December 1999) or descending (Z to A or 10 to 1 or 31st December 1999 to 1st January 1999) order:

(a) Data Sort (b) Data Filter
(c) Arrange (d) None of the above

vii. This can be used to graphically represent the information. It can be used to view the comparisons, patterns, and trends in data rapidly.

(a) Chart (b) Table
(c) Macro (d) None of the above

viii. It contains the entire chart and all of its elements. It is similar to a canvas:

(a) Plot Area (b) Chart Area
(c) Data Table (d) None of the above

ix. This type of object maintains a link with the source document so that any changes done in the source document are automatically reflected in the destination document:

(a) Linked Object (b) Embedded Object
(c) Dependent Object (d) None of the above

x. It can be used to navigate from one sheet to another within the same or a different worksheet:

(a) Arrow Keys (b) Enter Key
(c) Hyperlink (d) None of the above

2. Enter True or False:

i. Sheets in a workbook cannot be moved/rearranged from one location to another.

ii. An Excel file is saved with .xls extension.

iii. Hiding a workbook will delete its data.

iv. Series fill can be used to fill up a range of cells with consecutive numbers.

v. All the formatting features offered by Excel require pre-selection of a piece of text.

vi. You can change the order of operations in a formula by using parentheses.

vii. An argument is compulsory for any type of function, i.e., it is not possible to have a function without any arguments.

viii. Date and Time are internally stored as serial numbers in Excel.

ix. In Excel values are plotted against the Y or the Vertical axis and categories are plotted against the X or Horizontal axis.

x. An Excel worksheet cannot be viewed on the Web.

3. Match the following:

X	Y
1. To edit the contents of a cell.	Legend
2. Rectangular group of cells that is referred to by its opposite corners.	Embedded Chart
3. This feature can be used to display multiple lines of text within a single cell.	Trendlines
4. This command can be used to adjust the column width according to its contents.	F2 key
5. Returns the code number for the first character in the specified text string, in the character set used by your computer.	ALL
6. This feature of Data filters can be used to get back to the complete table.	Input cell
7. This type of chart is displayed directly in a worksheet.	Autofit
8. A blank cell lying outside the table range for holding calculations of the formula.	Range
9. Displays the growth or decline that occurs in the data.	CODE()
10. A box that identifies the colours/patterns assigned to various data series in the chart.	Text Wrap

4. Fill in the blanks with the appropriate choices listed below

(i) FIND (ii) Scenario Manager (iii) Row-Oriented table (iv) Column-Oriented table (v) Function (vi) LEN (vii) CLEAR (viii) SEARCH (ix) Del (x) COUNT

i. _____________ can be used to find one text string (find_text) within another text string. It allows using wild card characters.

ii. _____________ is a built-in formula that can be used to perform complex computations - easily and quickly.

iii. _____________ is used to return the number of characters in the text.

iv. _____________ can be used to clear the contents, formats and comments in a cell.

v. _____________ can be used to view the list of scenarios.

vi. In a _____________, the variations of a data table are listed down a column.

5. Write short notes on:

i. Handling operators in Formulae.
ii. Relative Cell Referencing
iii. Data Filters
iv. What-if Analysis
v. Scenarios

6. Explain the needs of functions in a spreadsheet package with suitable examples.

7. How do Charts assist as a management tool?

14 Presentation Package

INTRODUCTION

PowerPoint is a presentation tool that helps you create eye-catching and effective presentations in a matter of minutes. A presentation comprises of individual slides arranged in a sequential manner. Normally, each slide would cover a brief topic. Once having prepared a presentation, you can ask PowerPoint to generate hand out material and speaker's notes also Similarly, you have the option of either printing out the slides—in case you want to use an overhead projector–or simply attach your computer to an LCD display panel that enlarges the picture several times and shows you the output on a screen.

When you create a new presentation, you have three options:

1. You can start by working with a wizard (called the AutoContent Wizard) that helps you determine the theme, contents and organisation of your presentation by using a predefined outline, or
2. You can also start by picking out a PowerPoint Design Template, which determines the presentation's color scheme, fonts, and other design features, or
3. You can also begin with a completely blank presentation with the colour scheme, fonts, and other design features set to default values.

Should you decide to choose the third option, PowerPoint designers have provided a wide assortment of predefined slide formats and Clip Art graphics libraries. Through these predefined slide formats, you can quickly create slides based upon standard layouts and attributes.

PowerPoint shares a common look and feel with other MS Office components, and once having mastered Word and Excel, learning PowerPoint is almost like playing a game. And of course it is easy to export data from Word and Excel directly into a PowerPoint presentation and vice versa.

The next page shows you the various parts of a PowerPoint screen (Figure 14.1). Also it is important to familiarise yourself with the PowerPoint toolbars. All these are presented in the following pages. Do not worry if everything does not make complete sense to you at this stage. Once you do the hands on exercise, you will understand these options much better.

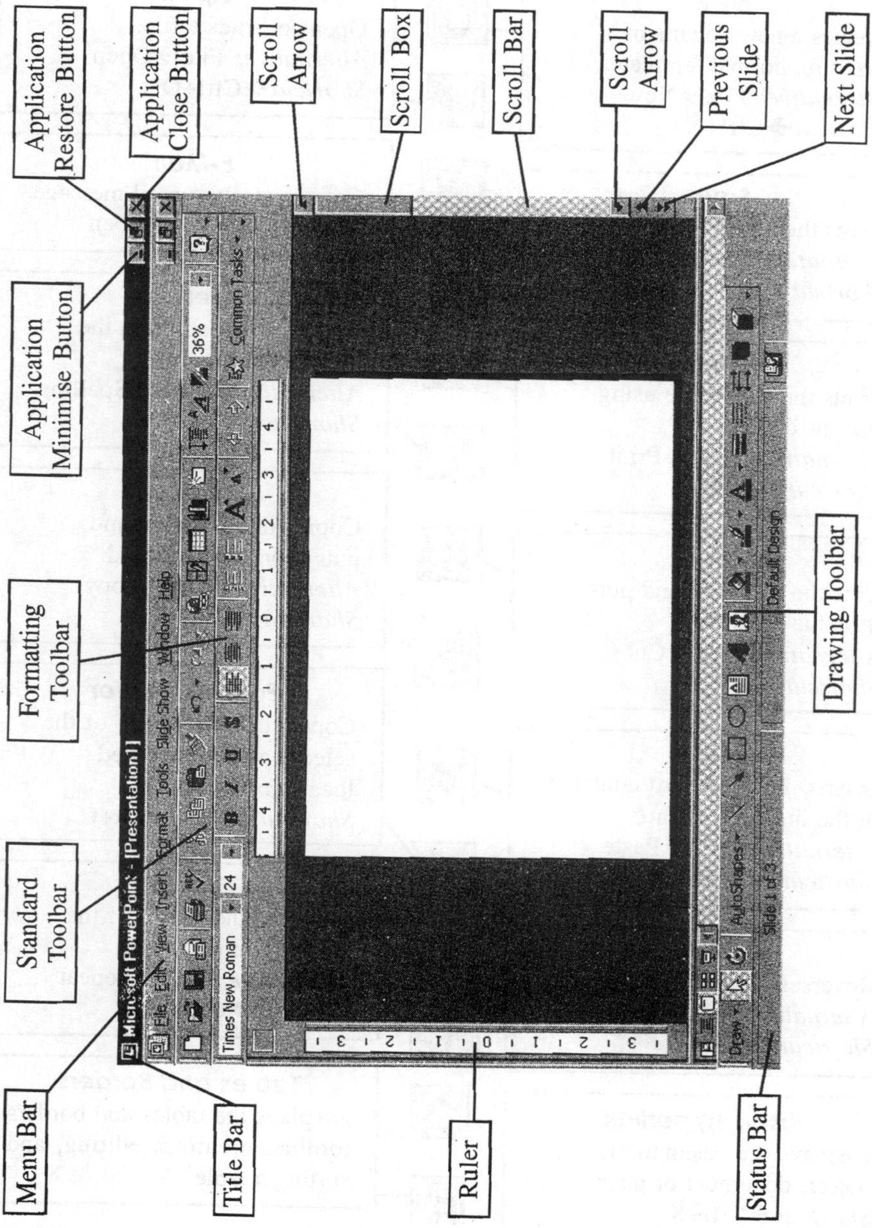

Figure 14.1 Parts of a PowerPoint Window

TOOLBAR, THEIR ICONS & COMMANDS

Standard Toolbar

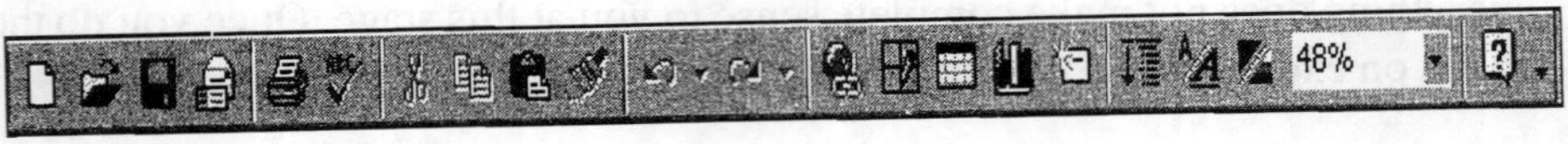

New

Creates a new document based on normal template.
Alternative: File→New
Shortcut→Ctrl+N

Open

Opens or finds a file.
Alternative: File→Open
Shortcut→Ctrl+O

Save

Saves the active file.
Alternative: File→ Save
Shortcut→Ctrl+S

E-Mail

Creates a new e-mail message.
Alternative: File→Open

Print

Prints the active file using current defaults.
Alternative: File→ Print
Shortcut→Ctrl+P

Spelling

Checks the spelling in the active document.
Alternative: Tools→Spelling
Shortcut→F7

Cut

Cuts the selection and puts it on the Clipboard.
Alternative: Edit→Cut
Shortcut→Ctrl+X

Copy

Copies the selection and puts it on the clipboard.
Alternative: Edit→Copy
Shortcut→Ctrl+C

Paste

Inserts the Clipboard contents at the insertion Point.
Alternative: Edit→Paste
Shortcut→Ctrl+V

Format Painter

Copies the formatting of the selection to a specified location.
Shortcut→Ctrl+Shift+C

Undo

Reverses certain commands.
Alternative: Edit→Undo
Shortcut→Ctrl+Z

Redo

Reverses the action of the Undo command.
Alternative: Edit→Repeat
Shortcut→Ctrl+Y

Insert Hyperlink

Displays the destination object, document or page.
Shortcut→Ctrl+K

Tables and Borders

Displays the tables and borders toolbar, creating, editing, and sorting a table.

Insert Table
Inserts a table in the document with the number of columns and rows you specify.

Insert Chart
Creates a chart by inserting Microsoft Graph object.
Alternative: Insert→Chart

New Slide
Prompts you to click a slide layout and then inserts a new slide after the active slide.

Expand All
Displays the titles and all the body text for each slide.

Show Formatting
Shows or hides character formatting (such as Bold & Italics) in normal view. In slide sorter view, switches between showing all text and graphics on each slide and displaying titles only.

Black and White
Displays the active presentation in black and white.

Office Assistant
Provides help topics and tips to accomplish your task.
Alternative: Help→Microsoft PowerPoint Help
Shortcut →F1

Zoom Control
Scales the editing view (Zoom).
Alternative: View→Zoom

Formatting Toolbar

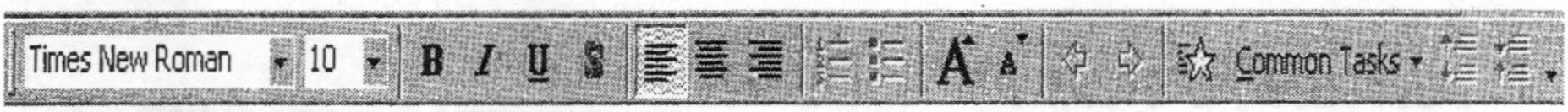

Font
Changes the font of the selection.
Alternative: Format→Font
Shortcut→ Ctrl+Shift+F

Font Size
Changes the font size of the selection.
Alternative: Format→Font→Size
Shortcut→ Ctrl+Shift+P

Bold
Makes the selection Bold.
Alternative: Format→Font→ Font style
Shortcut→ Ctrl+B

Italic
Makes the selection Italics.
*Alternative:*Format→Font→Font style
Shortcut→ Ctrl+I

Underline
Formats the selection with continuous underline.
Alternative: Format→Font→ effects
Shortcut→ Ctrl+U

Shadow
Adds or removes a shadow from selected text.

Align Left
Aligns the paragraph at left indent.
Alternative: Format→Alignment→Left
Shortcut→ Ctrl+L

Align Right
Aligns the paragraph at right indent.
Alternative: Format→Alignment→Right
Shortcut→ Ctrl+R

Bullets
Creates a bulleted list based on the current defaults.
Alternative: Format→Bullets

Decrease Font Size
Decreases the font size of the selected text to the next smaller size of the **font size** box.

Demote
Moves the selected paragraph to the next lower heading level (up one level, to the left).

Decrease Paragraph Spacing
Reduce space between selected paragraphs.

Centre
Centres the paragraphs between the indents.
Alternative: Format→Alignment→ Center
Shortcut→ Ctrl+E

Numbering
Creates a numbered list based on the current defaults.
Alternative:
Format→Bullets and Numbering

Increase Font Size
Increases the font size of the selected text to the next larger size of the **font size** box.

Promote
Moves the selected paragraph to the next higher heading level (up one level, to the left).

Animation Effects
Displays the Animation Effects toolbar.

Increase Paragraph Spacing
Adds more space between selected paragraphs.

Drawing Toolbar

Draw
Activates the Draw Menu.

Free Rotate
Rotates the selected object to any degree. Select the object, click on the icon and then drag a corner of the object in the direction you want to rotate it.

Select Objects
Changes the pointer to a selection arrow so you can select objects in the active window. To select a single object, click the object with the arrow. To select one or more, drag the mouse.

Line

Draws a straight line where you click or drag in the active window. To constrain the line to draw at the 15-degree angle from its starting point, hold down SHIFT as you drag.

Rectangle

Draws an rectangle where you click or drag in the active window. To draw a square, press SHIFT and drag.

Text Box

Draws a text box where you click or drag in the active window. Use a text box to add a text—such as captions or callouts—to your pictures or graphics.
Alternative: Insert→TextBox

Insert Clip Art

Opens the Clip Gallery where you can select the clip art image you want to insert in your file or update your clip art collection.
Alternative: Insert→Picture→Clip Art

Line Color

Adds, modifies, or removes the line color from the selected objects.

Dash Style

Click the dashed line or dashed-dot line style you want for the selected shape or border. Click the solid line if you don't want the dotted line.

Shadow

Click the shadow style which you want for the selected object.

Auto Shapes

Activates the AutoShape menu.

Arrow

Inserts a line with an arrowhead where you click or drag in the active window. To constrain the arrow to draw at the 15-degree angle from its starting point, hold down SHIFT as you drag.

Oval

Draws an oval where you click or drag in the active window. To draw a circle, press SHIFT and drag.

WordArt

Creates text effects by inserting Microsoft Office drawing objects.
Alternative: Insert→Picture→Word Art

Fill Color

Adds, modifies, or removes the fill color or fill effect from the selected object. Fill effects include gradient, texture, pattern or picture fills.

Font Color

Formats the selected text with the color you click.

Line Style

Click the width you want for the selected line.

Arrow Style

Click the arrowhead style which you want for the selected line.

3-D

Click the 3-D style which you want for the selected object.

NAVIGATING IN POWERPOINT

Now that you have a general idea of the various commands and toolbars, let us see how we can carry out simple operations like saving and opening files, creating and printing slides, etc. For this, follow the step-by-step instructions given below.

Creating a New Blank Presentation

① Choose **New** from the **File** menu.

② Choose **Blank Presentation** option from the **New Presentation** dialog box.

③ Click on the **OK** button to continue.

④ The following dialog box would be displayed. Click on the type of slide that you want.

⑤ Click on the **OK** button.

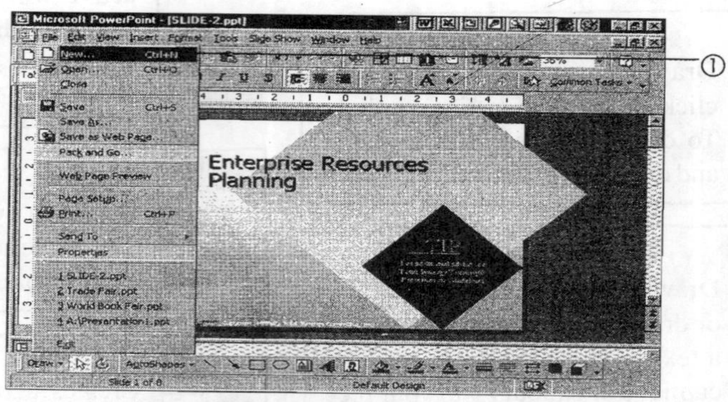

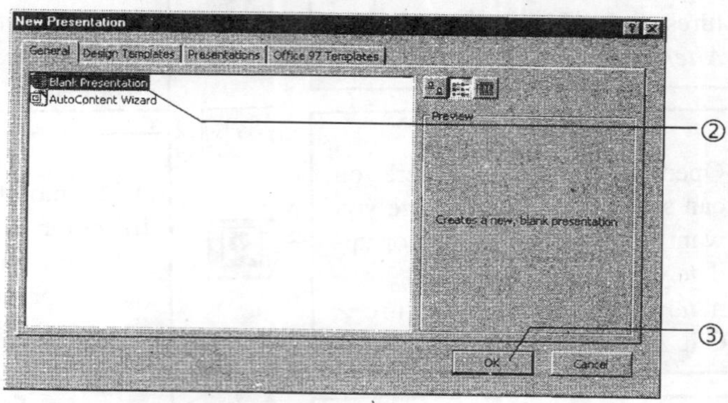

A The following blank presentation would be displayed.

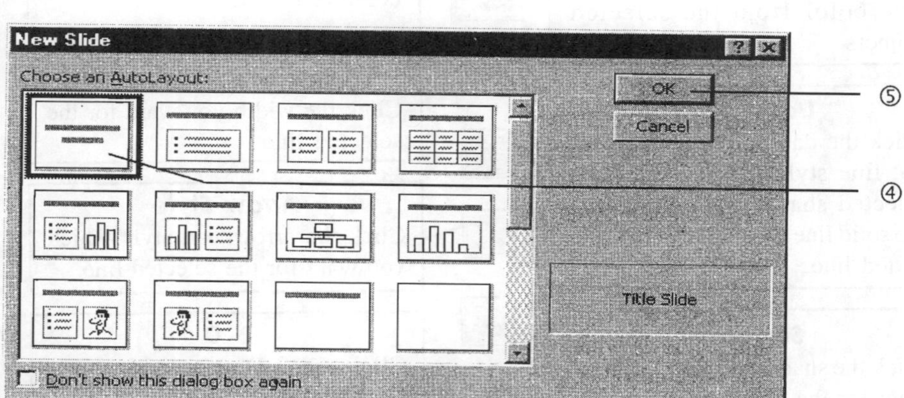

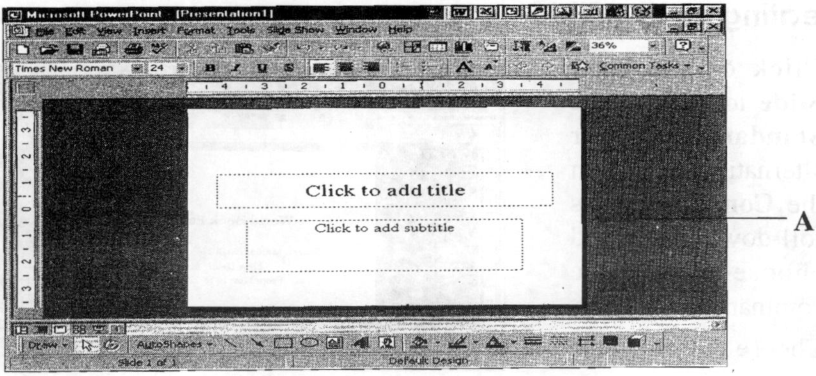

Opening a Presentation

Once a file is saved (saving a presentation has been explained later in the section) and closed, it can be opened again and used at any time using the **Open** command.

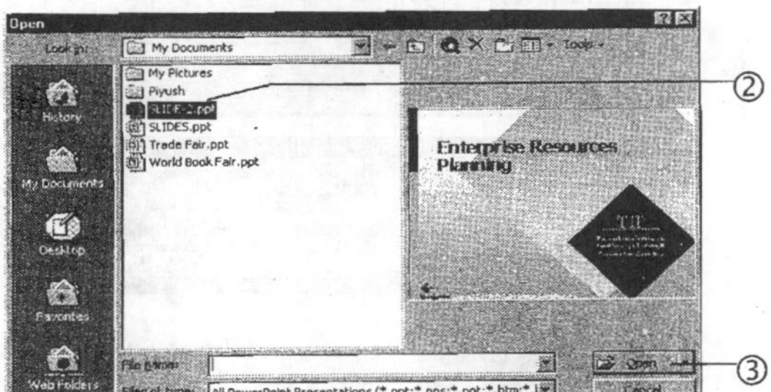

① Choose **Open** from the **File** menu.

② Choose the file that you want to open or type the name of the file in the "**File Name**" window.

③ Click on the **Open** button.

A The requested file would open up.

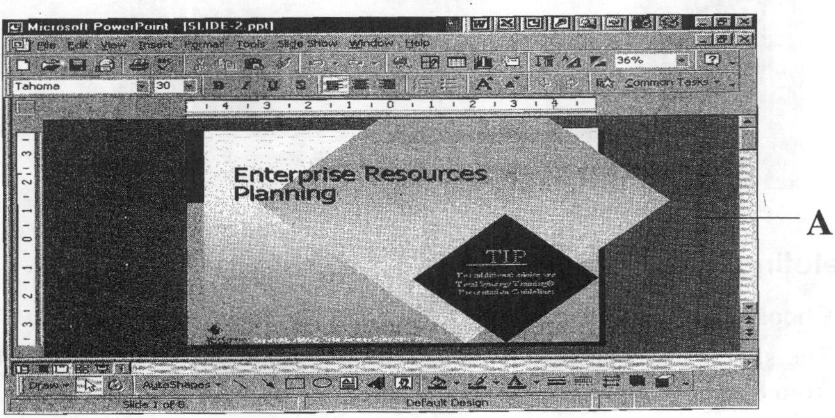

Creating a New Slide

① Click on the **New Slide** icon from the **Standard** toolbar or alternatively, click on the **Common Tasks** roll-down menu and choose **New Slide** command.

② Choose the slide type that you want.

③ Click on the **OK** button.

A A blank new slide would be inserted.

①

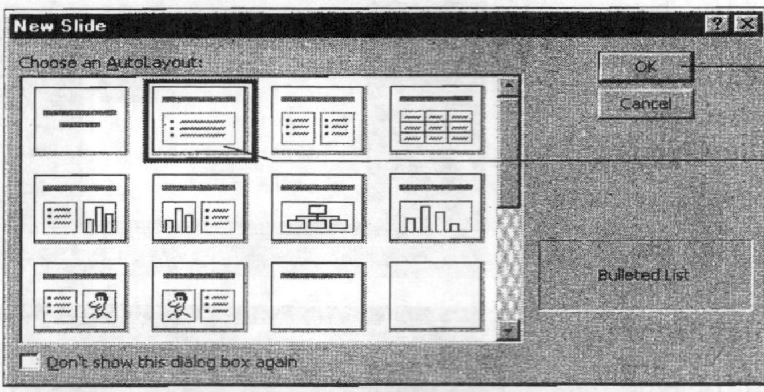

③

②

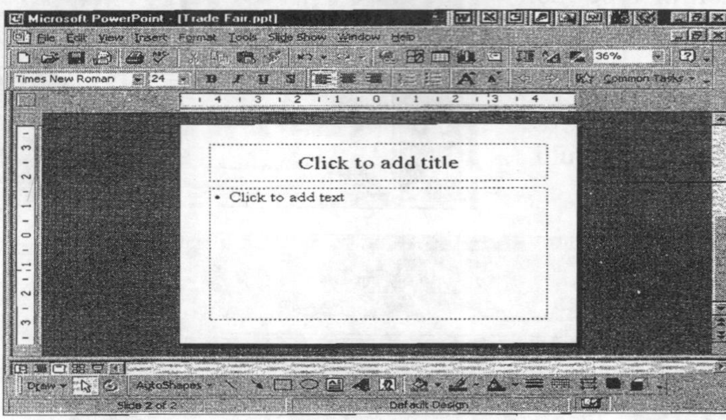

A

Deleting a Slide

① Choose **Delete Slide** from the **Edit** menu.

A The slide chosen has been deleted and the number of slides has changed from 8 to 7.

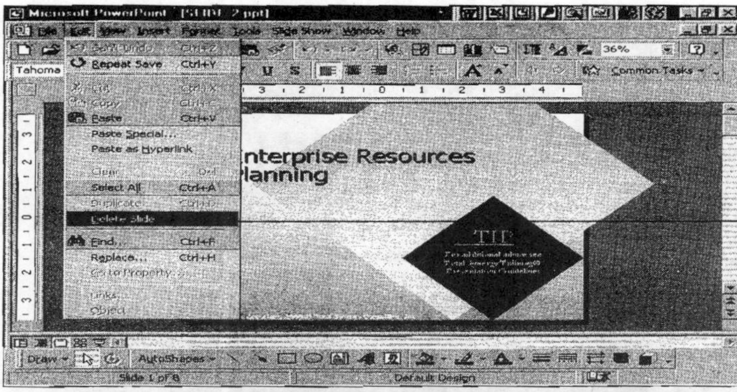

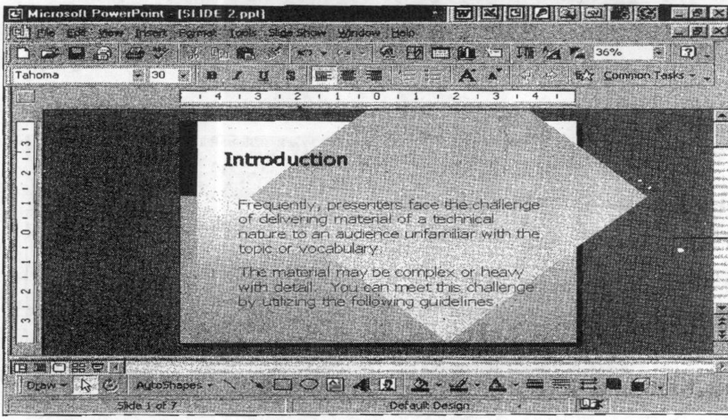

Copying a Slide

① Choose **Duplicate Slide** from the **Insert** menu.

A A duplicate slide has been inserted.

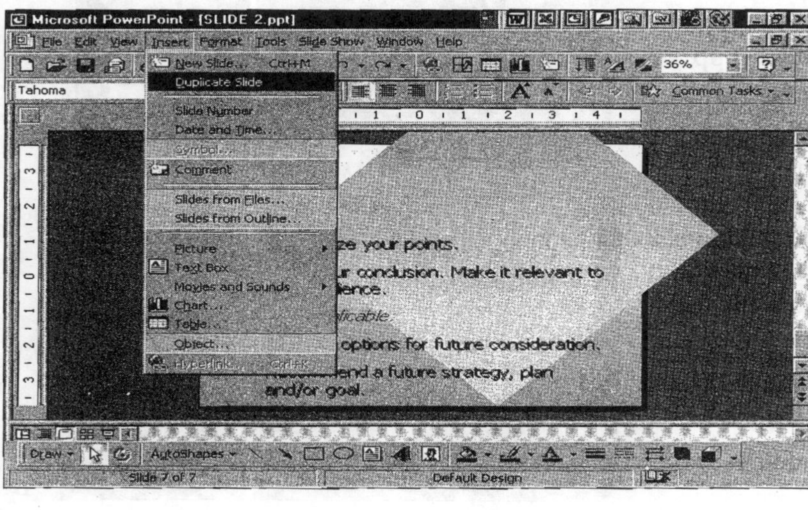

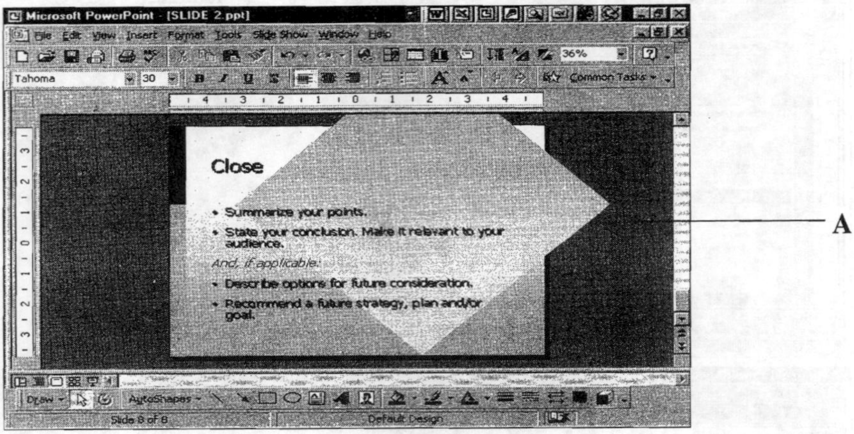

Slide Numbering

① Choose **Header and Footer** from the **View** menu.

② The following dialog box would be displayed. Click on the **Slide Number** check box.

③ Click once on **Apply to All** button to apply numbering to all the slides or click once on **Apply** button to apply numbering to the current slide only.

A You can also click on the Date and Time check box to apply the current date and time to the slides.

B You would notice numbering on all the slides.

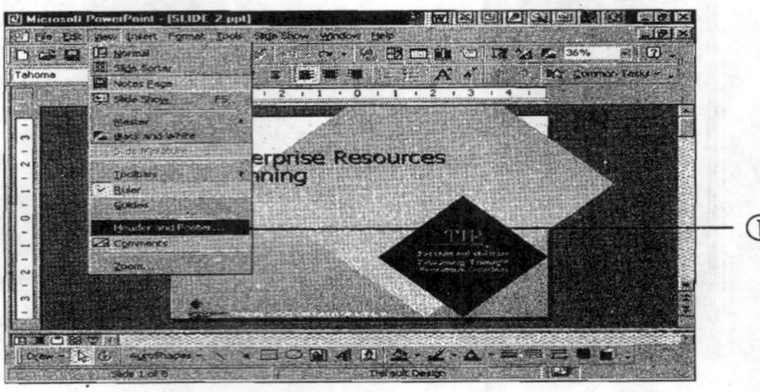

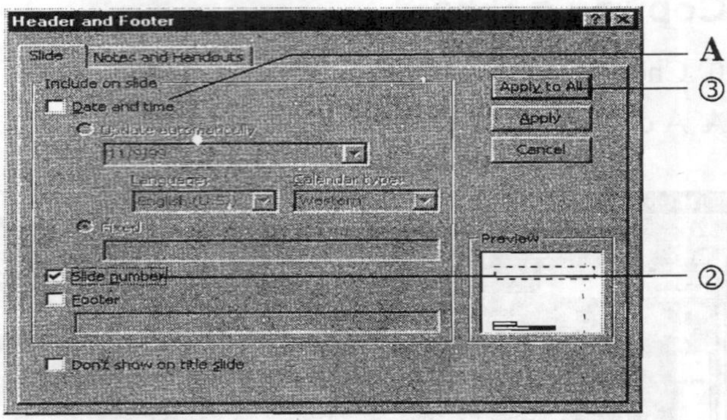

Saving a Presentation

By default a presentation is saved with .ppt extension.

① Choose **Save** from the **File** menu.

② The following dialog box would be displayed. Type the name of the presentation.

③ Click on the **Save** button.

A In case you wish to save the file into another directory, specify the correct path and directory here.

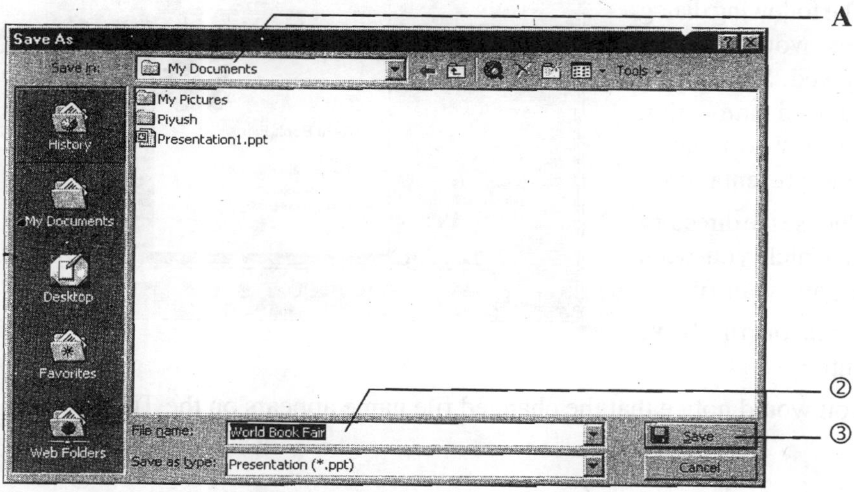

Closing a Presentation

① Choose **Close** from the **File** menu.

A You would see **PowerPoint**'s exit screen.

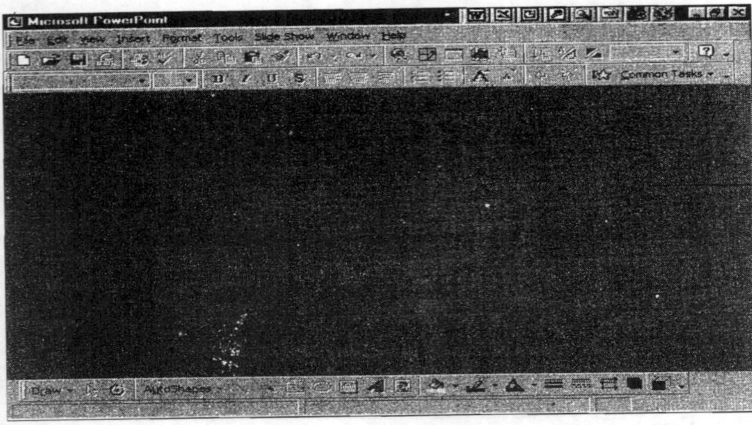

Saving a Presentation with a Different Name

① Choose **Save As** from the **File** menu.

② The following dialog box would be displayed. Specify the desired name that you wish to assign to your presentation.

③ Choose the directory in which you want to save your file.

④ Click on the **Save** button.

A You would notice that the changed file name appears on the Title bar.

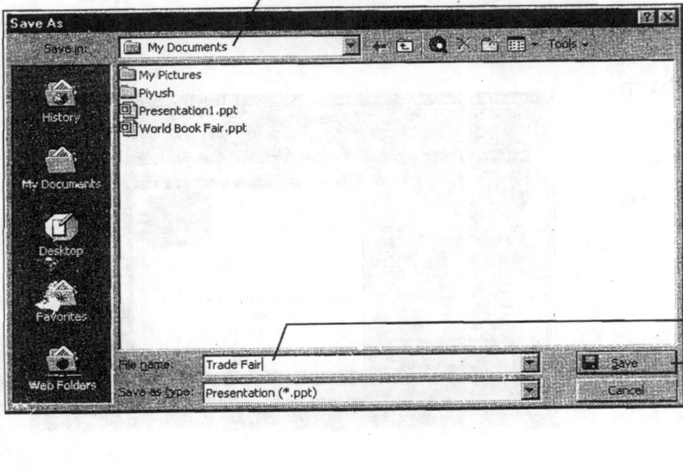

Changing the Default Directory

① Choose **Options** from the **Tools** menu.

② The following dialog box would be displayed. Click once on the **Save** folio/tab.

③ Type in the name of the Default directory.

④ Click on the **OK** button.

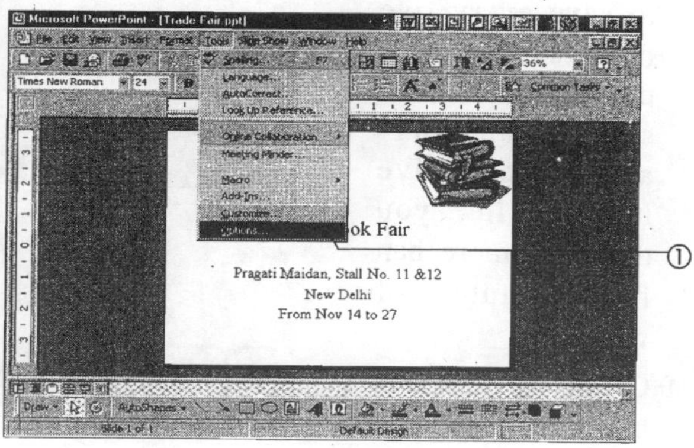

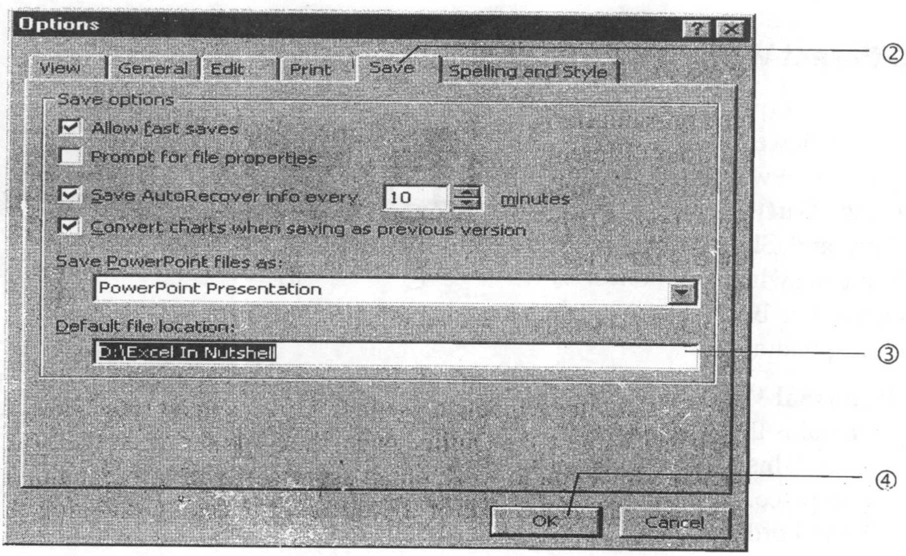

AutoSave

① Choose **Options** from the **Tools** menu.

② The following dialog box would be displayed. Click on the **Save** folio/tab.

③ Click on the spinner to increase or decrease the **AutoSave** recover time. For example, if AutoRecover is set to save every five minutes, your presentation will be saved automatically after every five minutes, i.e., you don't lose more than five minutes of work.

④ Click on the **OK** button to apply the specified settings.

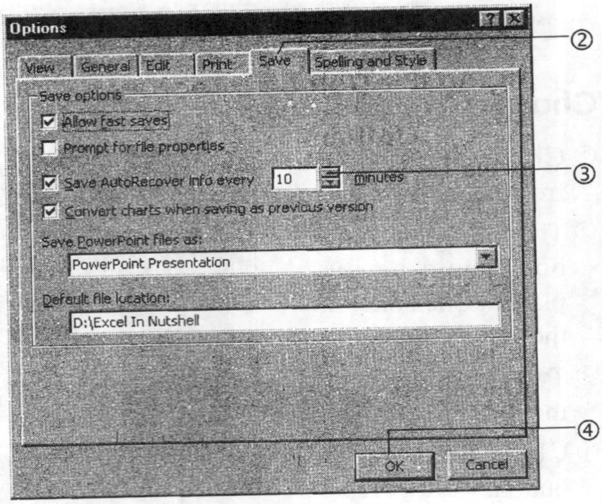

Different Views of Powerpoint

Any Powerpoint presentation can be viewed in four different types of views namely **Normal** View, **Outline** View, **Slide** View and **Slide Sorter** View. You can switch from one view to another by clicking on the corresponding icon.

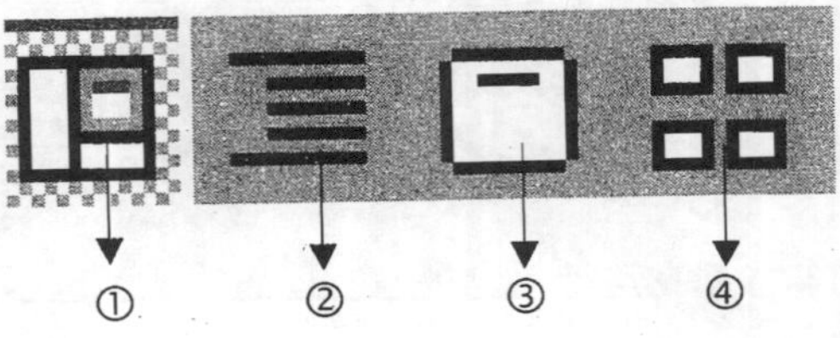

① **Normal View:** By default each new presentation opens in Normal View. It contains three panes namely the Outline pane, the Slide pane and the Notes pane. This view permits you to work on all aspects of your presentation at one place. You can adjust the size of the different panes by dragging the Pane borders.

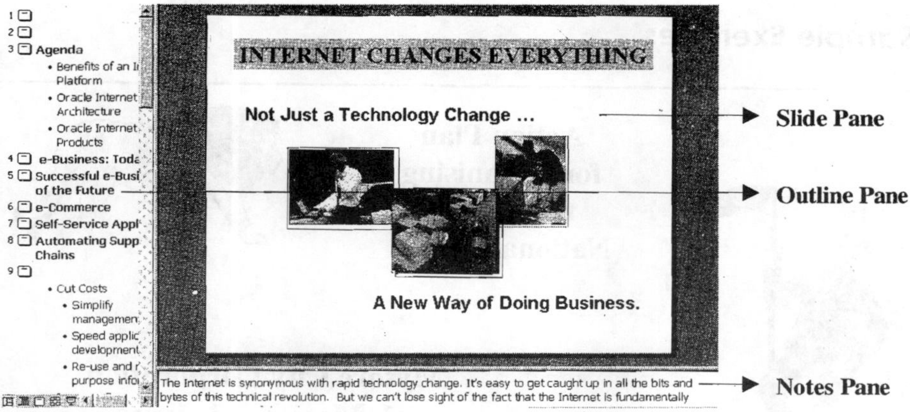

② **Outline Pane**: Displays a table of contents so that you can navigate through your presentation.

③ **Slide Pane**: Here you can easily view the contents of individual slides.

Notes Pane: Speaker notes or any information that you wish to be reminded of while delivering the presentation.

④ **Slide Sorter View:** Displays the thumbnail views of your presentation. You can rearrange the order of your slides, delete or duplicate slides in this view.

Designing Presentations

Now that you have got a general idea about PowerPoint, let us get down to brass tracks. We will create a presentation in PowerPoint to see how simple it really is.

You have already seen the various parts of the PowerPoint in the previous screen. Also, it is important to familiarise yourself with the PowerPoint standard toolbar, the formatting toolbar, the drawing toolbar, and the autoshapes toolbar. If you have skipped that section, please go back and read that section.

Let us start with a sample exercise (Ten Slides), given in the following pages, to familiarise ourselves with various features of Powerpoint. The following has been explained using this sample exercise:

- Starting Powerpoint
- Inserting new slides into your presentation
- Formatting text and paragraphs
- Resizing objects
- Inserting Clip Art
- Running Slide Shows.

Sample Exercises

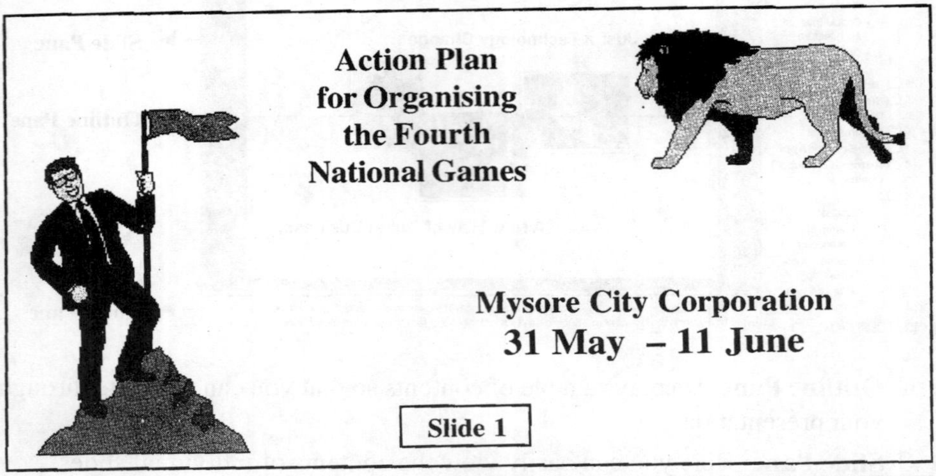

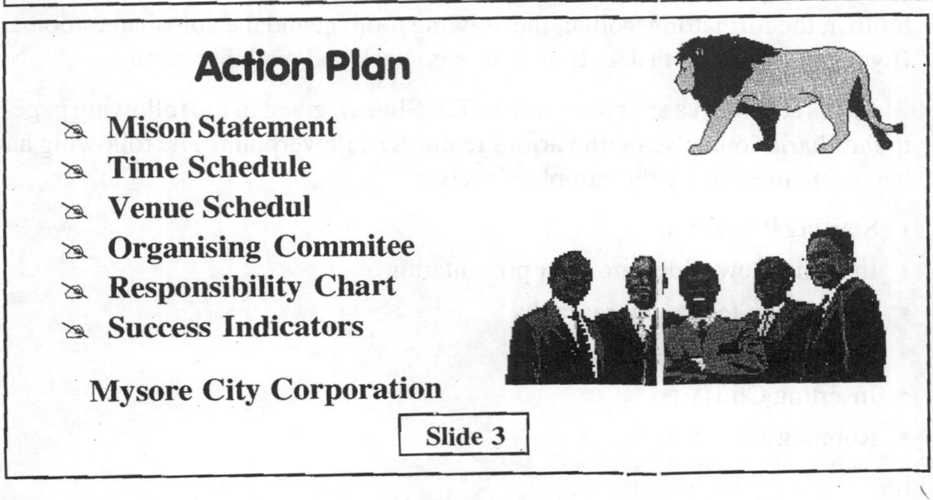

Mission Statement

Faster – Further - Higher

Not only for sportsmen, but also for organising officials!

We shall cross all hurdles !!!

Mysore City Corporation

Slide 4

Time Schedule

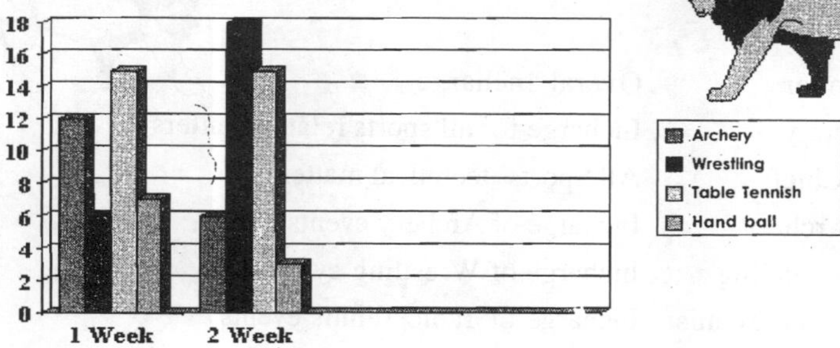

Mysore City Corporation

Slide 5

Venue Schedule

Archery	Chamundi Stadium
Wrestling	Chamundi Akhada
Table Tennis	Chamundi Stadium
Handball	Chamundi Stadium

Mysore City Corporation

Slide 6

Organising Committee

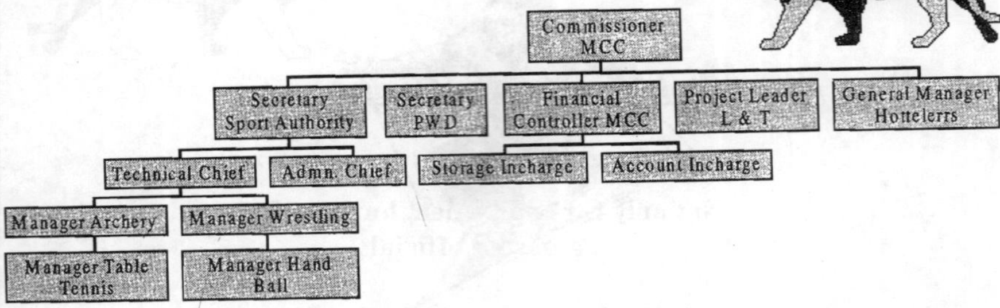

Mysore City Corporation

Slide 7

Responsibility Chart

Commissioner	Overal Incharge
Sport Secretary	Incharge for all sports related matters
Technical Chief	All Sports' technical matters
Manager–Archery	Incharge of Archery events
Manager–Wrestling	Incharge of Wrestling events
Manager–Table Tennis	Incharge of Table Tennis events
Manager–Handball	Incharge of Handball events

Mysore City Corporation

Slide 8

Success Indicators

- TIMELY START AND COMPLETION ALL EVENTS
- MAXIMISE SPECTORS
- PROPER CROWD CONTROL
- PROPER LAW AND ORDER
- PROPER HOSPITALITY TO ALL PARTICIPANTS
- PROPER MEDIA COVERAGE

Mysore City Corporation

Slide 9

Starting PowerPoint

① Choose **Microsoft PowerPoint** from **Microsoft Office 2000** from the **Programs** menu.

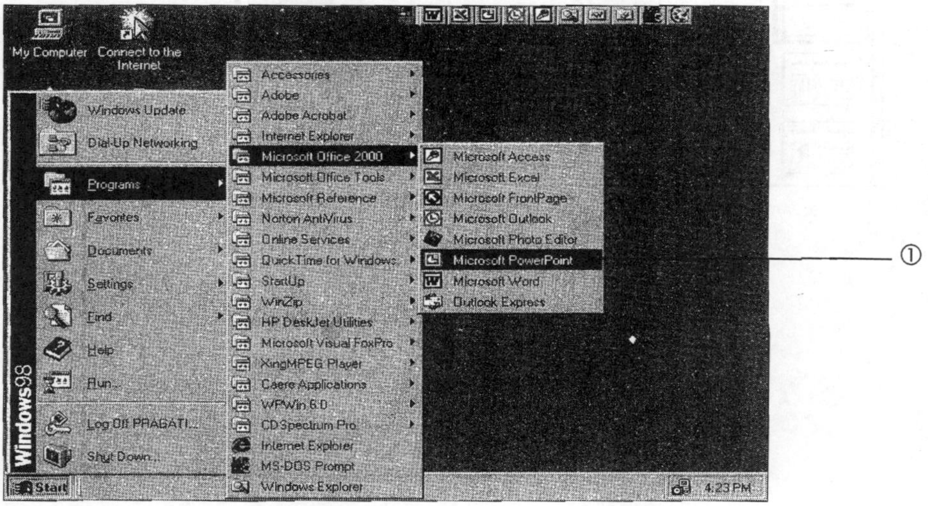

Creating the First Slide

This is the first screen that appears on starting PowerPoint. Let me briefly explain about the options here.

A This is the quickest way to create a presentation by choosing from predefined subjects and templates.

B In case you simply wish to use predefined templates containing colour schemes and background, etc. choose this option.

① To create a presentation from scratch, click here.

② Click on the **OK** button once to continue.

③ Choose **Title Slide** from the **Auto Layout** box.

④ Click on the **OK** button to continue.

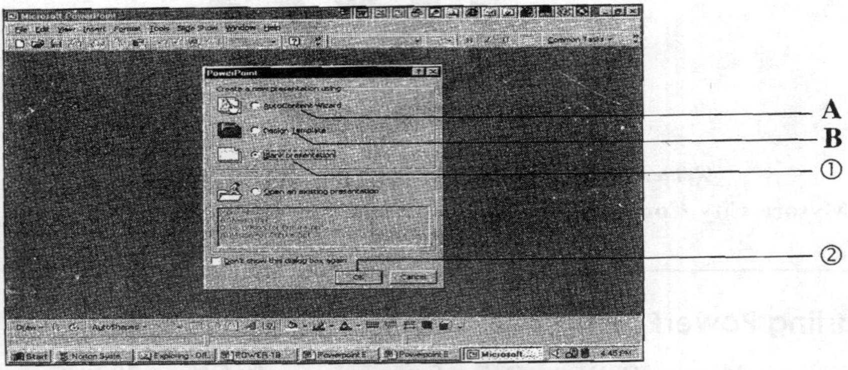

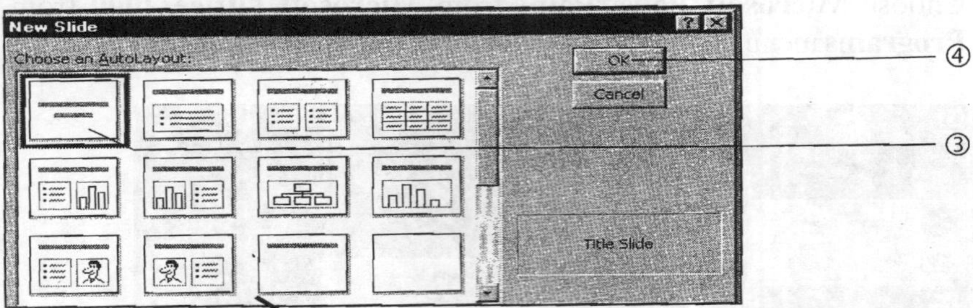

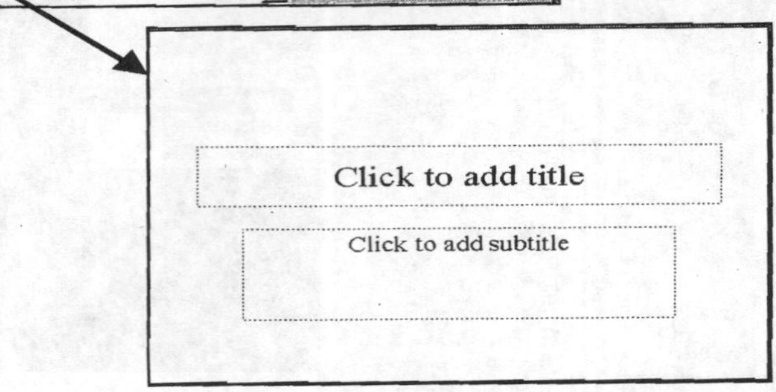

① Type the presentation title.

② Click on the text box boundary to select the entire text box.

③ Drag the box to the top of the slide and position it at the desired location. You can also resize this text box by dragging its size holder, that appears when the mouse pointer is placed on its corners.

④ Click here to continue.

⑤ Type the desired text.

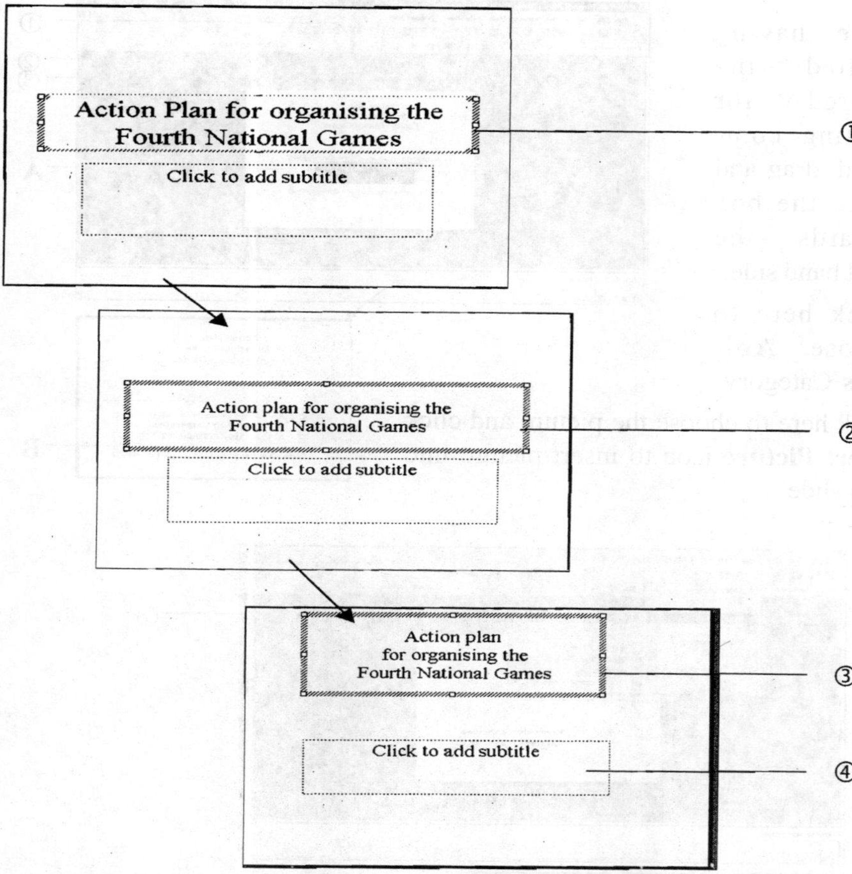

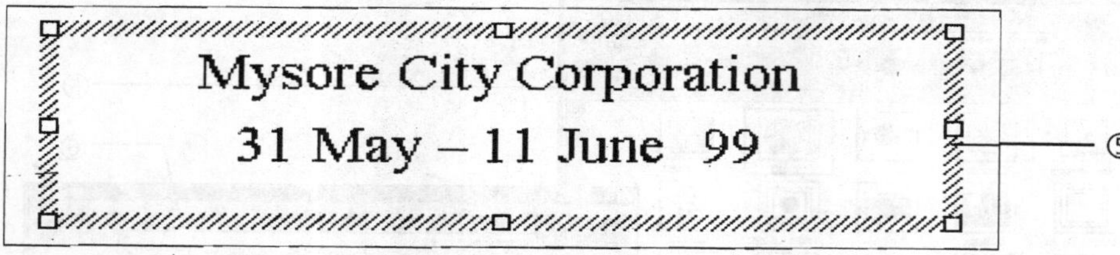

Inserting ClipArt

① Click here to increase **Font** size.

② Click here to decrease **Font** size.

③ Click here to apply shadow effect to the text.

④ Choose **ClipArt** command from **Picture** option of the **Insert** menu.

A Highlight the text and format the text to your liking. You can change the Font size, Font style and Alignment. You will notice that the formatting toolbar is very similar to Word or Excel.

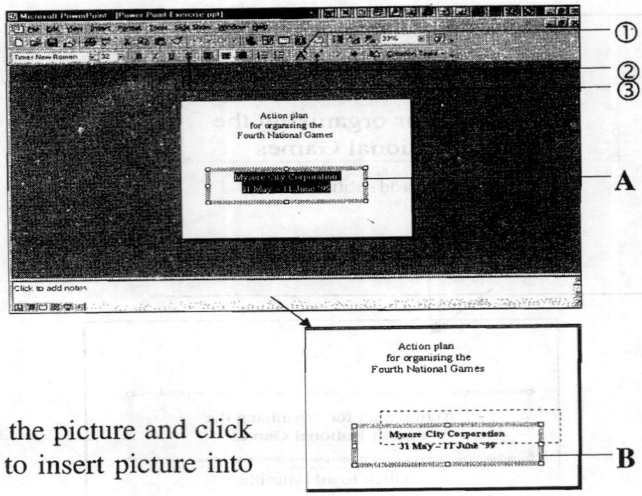

B Once having applied the desired formatting command, drag and move the box towards the right hand side.

⑤ Click here to choose **Animals** Category.

⑥ Click here to choose the picture and click **Insert Picture** icon to insert picture into your slide.

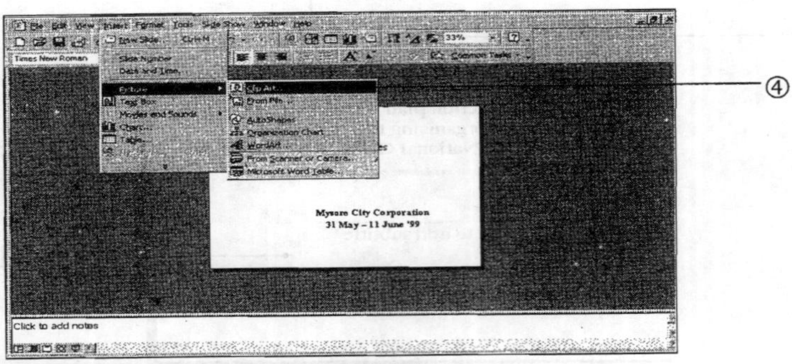

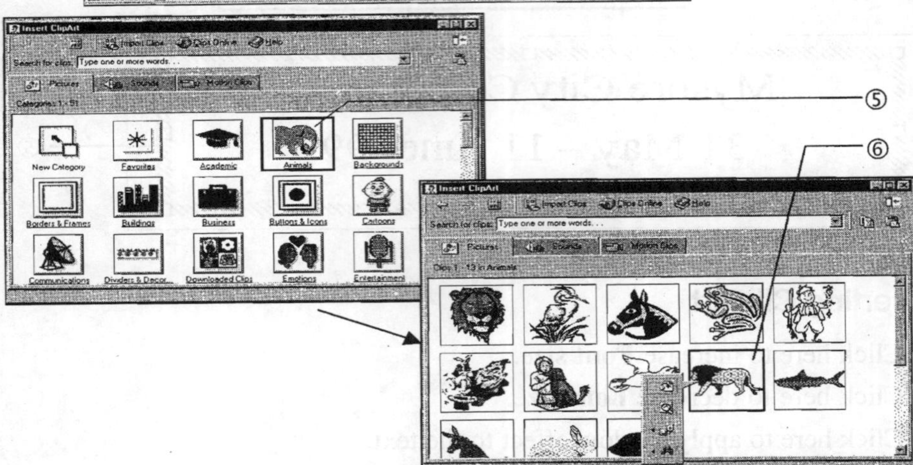

C You would see the picture inserted in your slide.

This dialogue box would be shown to you. Move up and down through various categories and pictures using scroll bars to see a preview of the pictures.

⑦ Drag and move the picture box to the new position.

⑧ Size the picture box to fit within the available space.

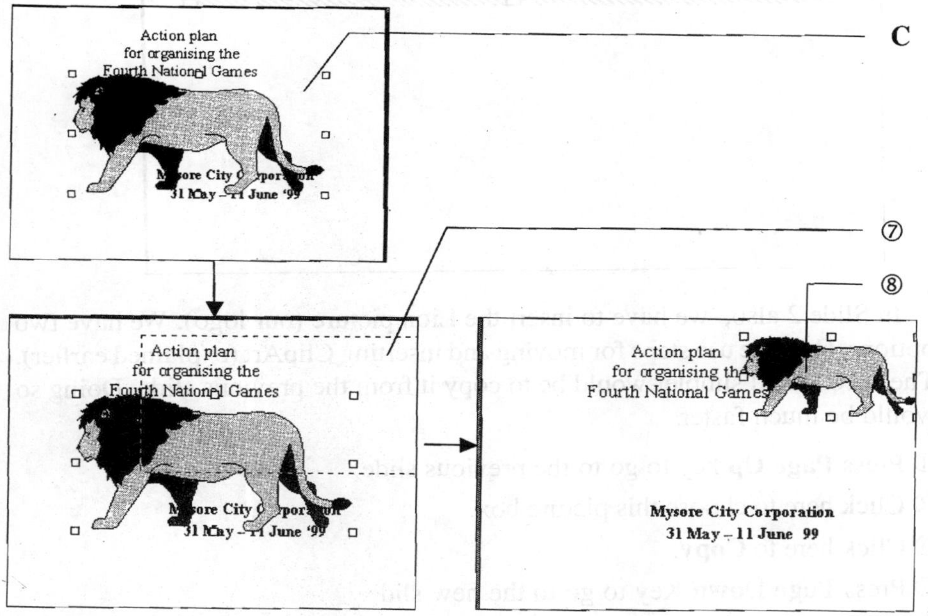

Now using the steps explained for inserting a picture, insert another picture from the clipart gallery and place it on the left side of your slide, this would complete your first slide. Let us proceed to create our second slide.

Inserting a New Slide

① Click here to create a new slide.

② Choose **'Title Only'** from the **Auto layout** box.

③ Click on the **OK** button once to continue.

④ Type the text and apply **Bold** attributes.

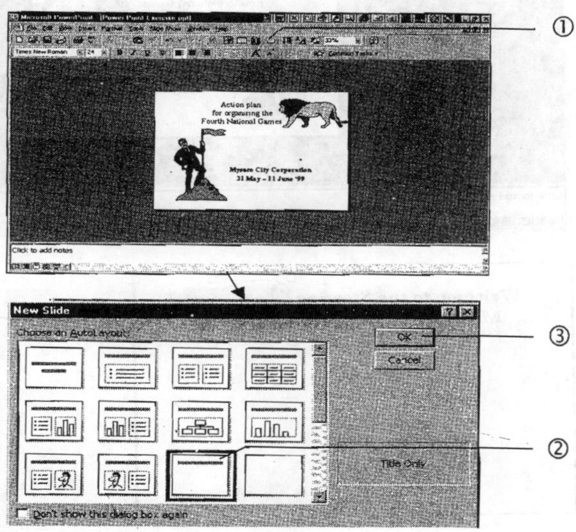

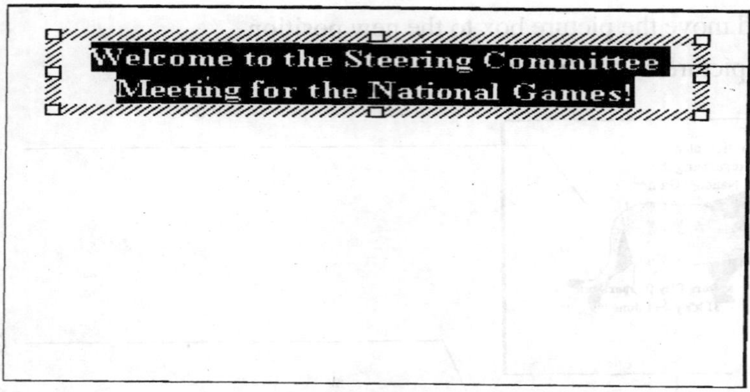

In Slide 2 also, we have to insert the Lion picture (our logo). We have two options. One, we use steps for moving and inserting ClipArt (explained earlier). The second and simpler would be to copy it from the previous slide. Doing so would be much faster.

① Press **Page Up** key to go to the previous slide.

② Click here to choose this picture box.

③ Click here to **Copy**.

④ Press **Page Down** Key to go to the new slide.

⑤ Click on the **Paste** icon to obtain the properly sized picture.

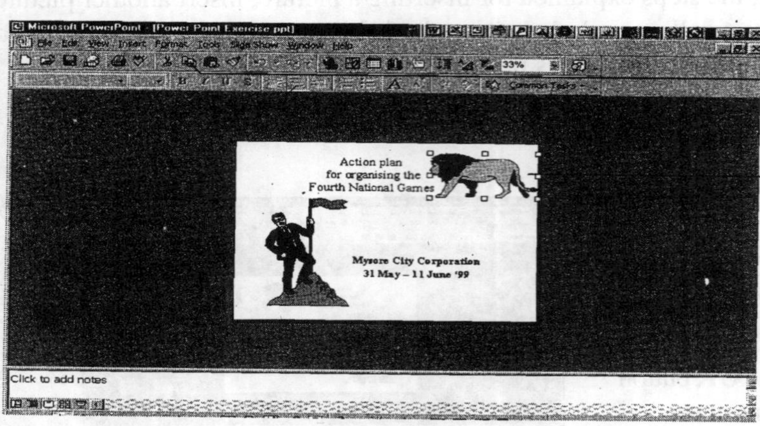

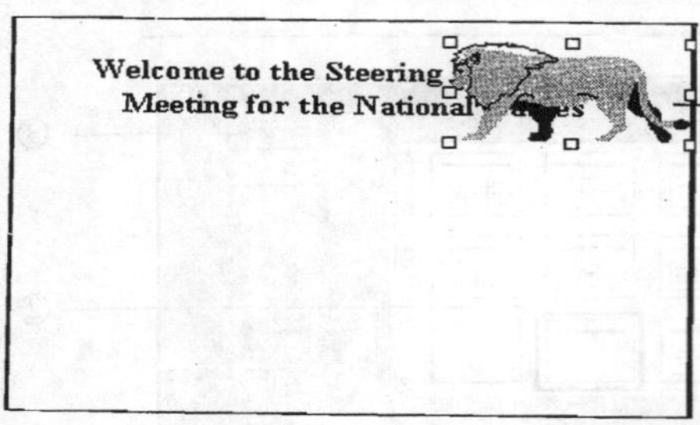

Moving the Text

Since the picture is overlapping on the text box, we will have to resize our text box.

Now using the steps explained earlier, simply insert different pictures from the clipart gallery so that your slide looks like this.

Inserting Text

① Click on this icon. Place the mouse pointer here by clicking it once. A small box with a cursor in it would appear.

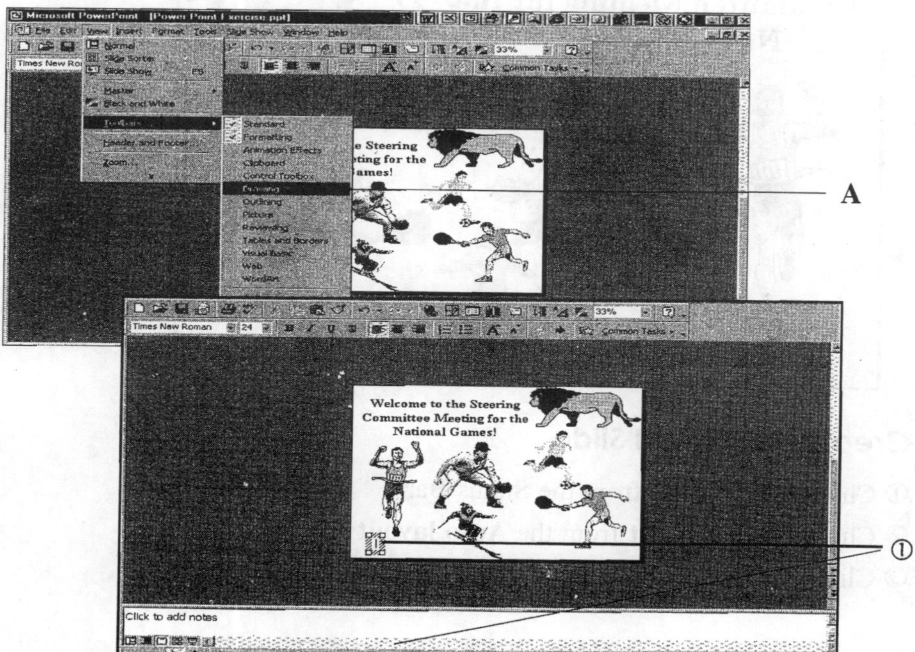

② Type 'Mysore City Corporation' and click anywhere outside this box to conclude.

A You can open the Drawing toolbar by clicking on the **Drawing** command under **Toolbars** option from the **View** menu.

B The second slide is complete.

②

B

Creating the Third Slide

① Choose **New Slide** from the Status Bar.

② Choose **bulleted list** from the **Auto layout** box.

③ Click on the **OK** to continue.

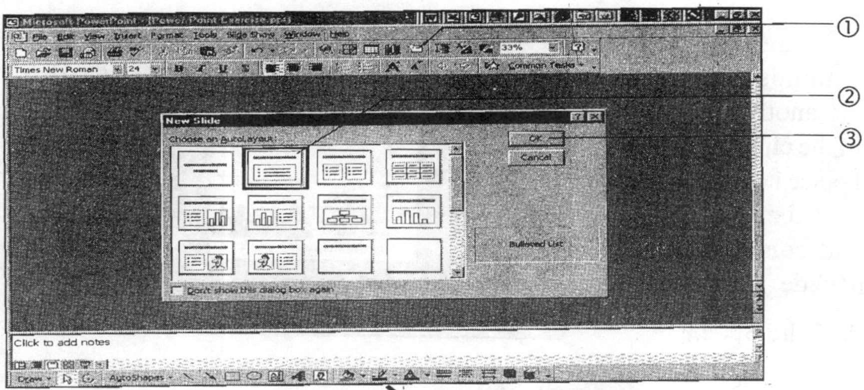

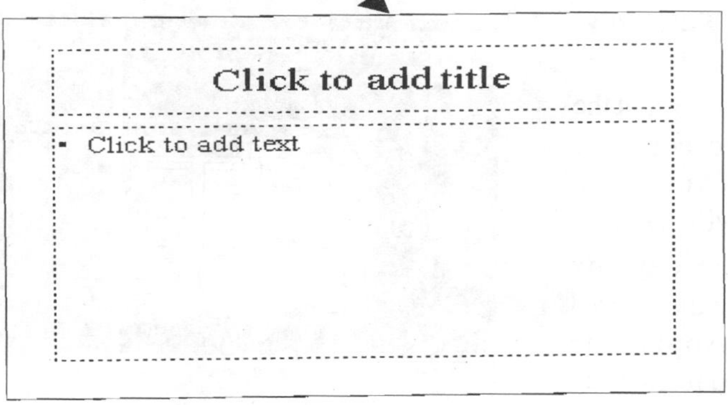

Changing the Font Size

① Type the title and highlight it.

② Click here to give a shadow effect.

③ Choose **'Comic Sans MS'** font.

④ Increase the size of the font.

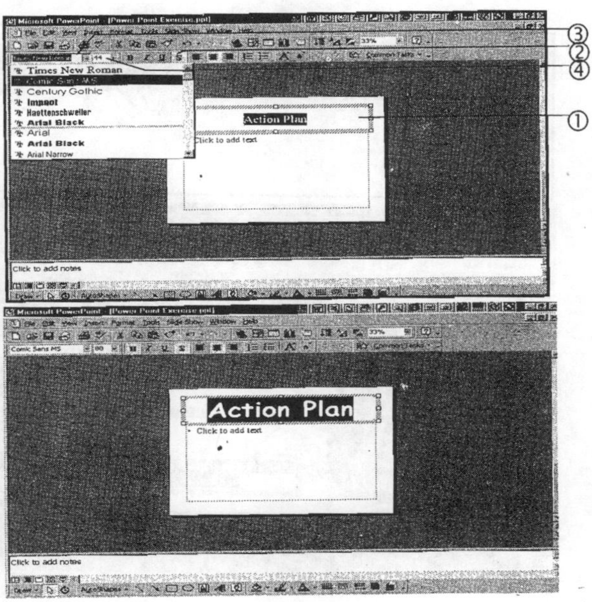

Now type the bulleted points and then resize the text box to the size of the text. You can copy the text 'Mysore City Corporation' from the previous slide by using copy and paste commands. Finally, insert another picture from the clipart gallery and place it on the right side of the slide. This would complete your third slide.

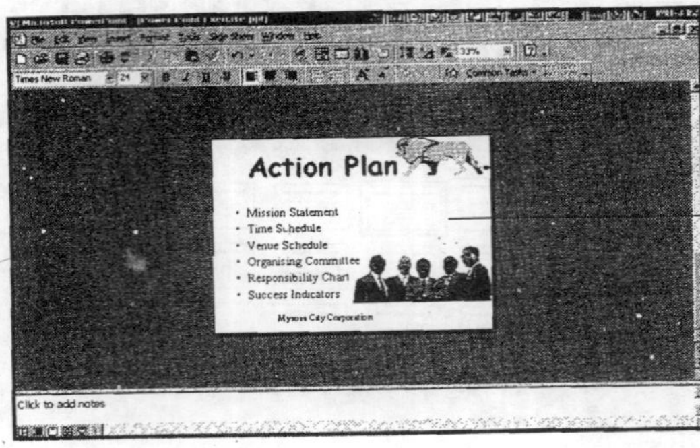

A

A Third Slide.

Creating the Fourth Slide

① Add a **'Title only'** slide.

② Type and format the text and copy the logo picture from the previous slide.

③ Insert a text box and type the desired text. Apply the required formatting attributes.

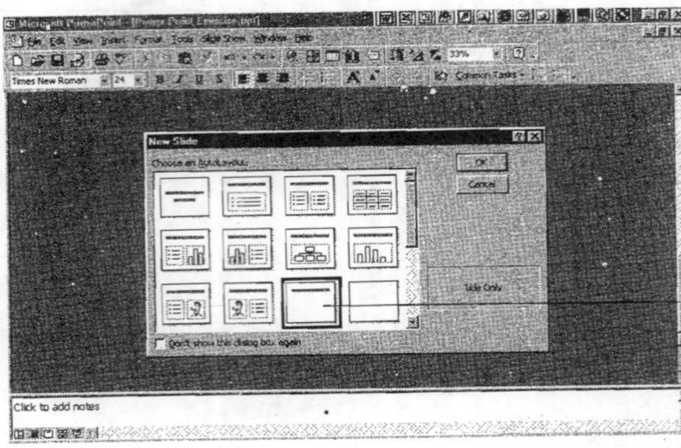

①

②

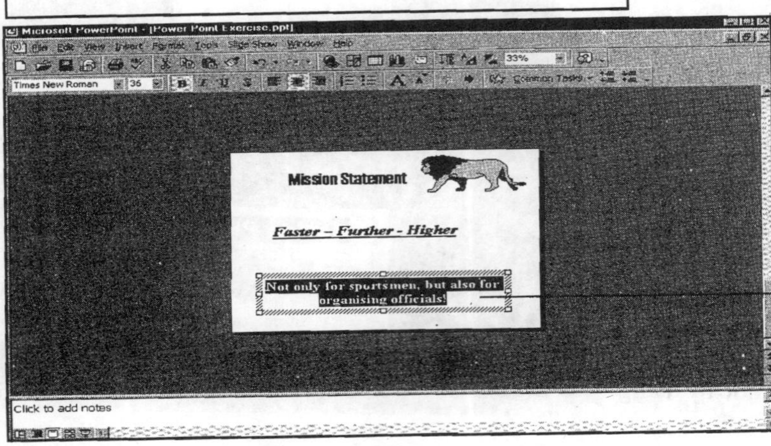

③

Now insert a picture and place it on the center of the slide. You would have noticed that the picture is overlapping on your text and therefore, the entire text is not legible. Let us see how we can use a special effect to send this picture in the background, so that instead of picture coming on top, the text comes on the top.

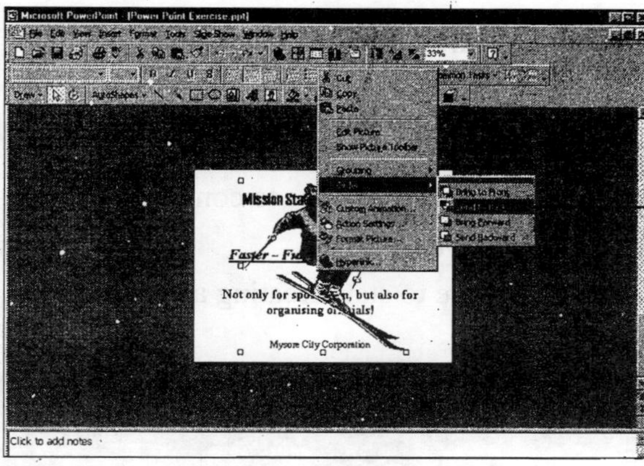

①

②

① Select the picture. Right click with the mouse on it. The following menu would appear. Select **Send to Back** command from the **Order** menu.

② Click on the text box once again to add something. Type the additional text and click outside the box to finish.

A Your fourth slide is complete!

A

Creating the Fifth Slide

① Insert a new slide.

② Choose **Graph** from the **Autolayout** box.

③ Click on the **OK** button once to continue.

④ Add the title and the logo.

⑤ Double click here to start creating a graph.

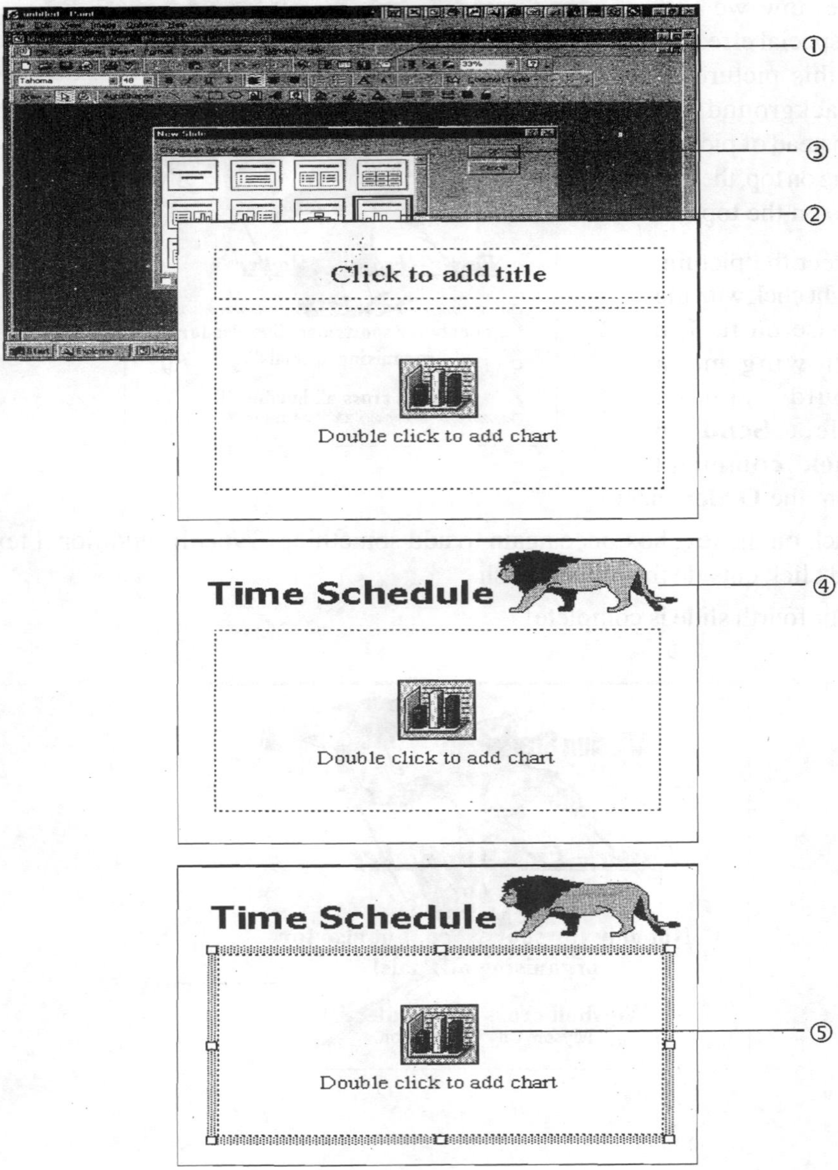

Entering Data to Graph

A This window would appear containing sample data.

① Overwrite the sample data with your data.

② Highlight and press **Del** to delete unwanted data.

③ Size this column so that the complete text is visible.

④ Click here to close the datasheet.

B You will see graph based upon provided data. You should insert the Footer after this and your fifth slide would be complete.

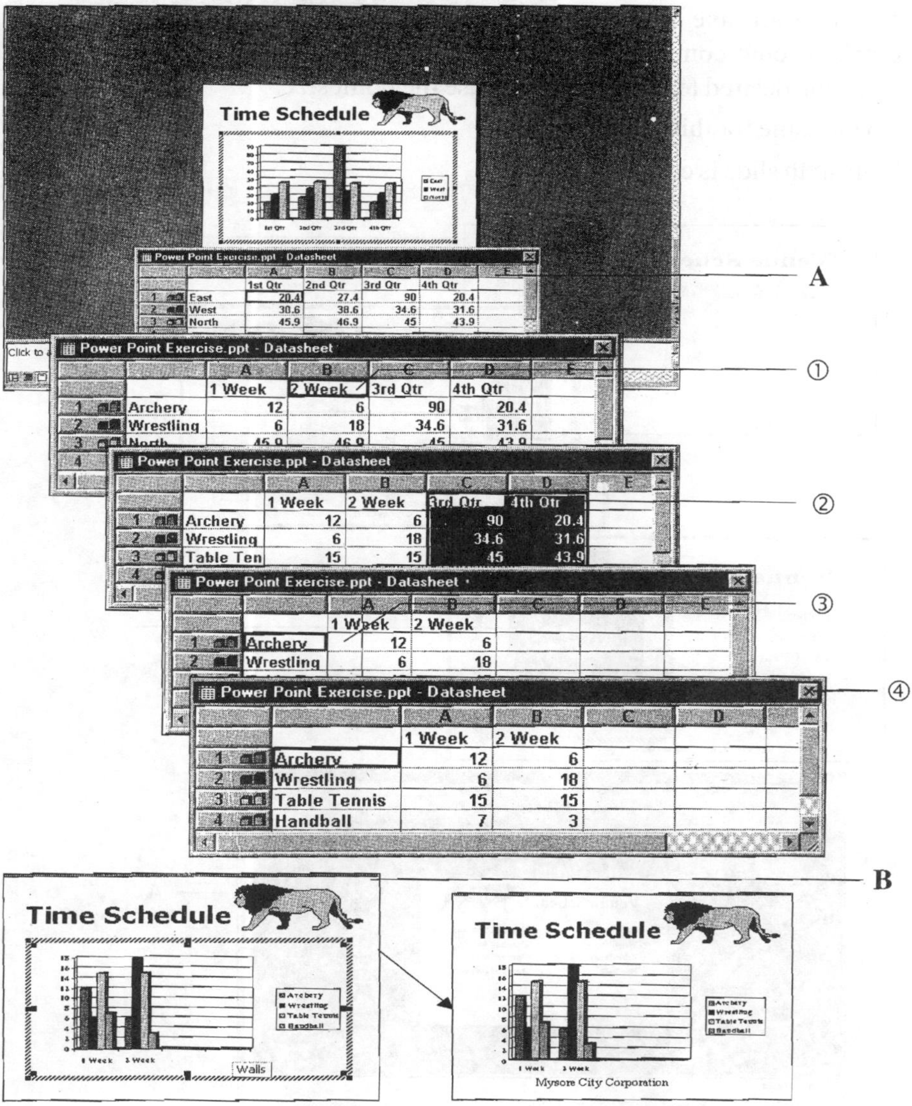

Creating the Sixth Slide

① Insert a new slide.

② Choose **2 column text** from the **Autolayout** box.

③ Click on the **OK** button once to continue.

④ Add the **title**, **logo** and **footer**.

⑤ Type the points and click on the Increase paragraph spacing command to get the desired text spacing. Increase the point size.

⑥ Do the same for this bulleted list.

A Your sixth slide is complete!

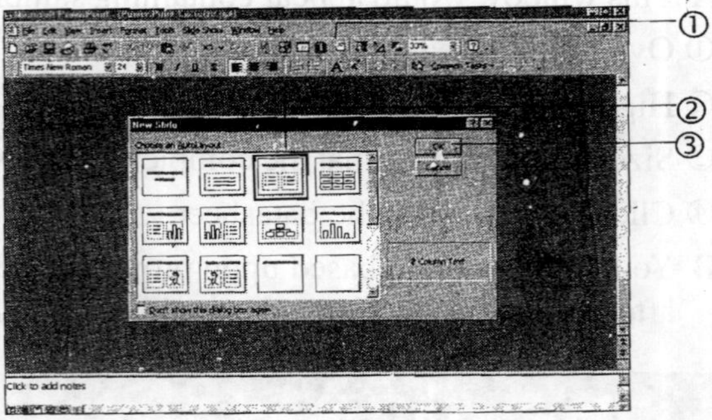

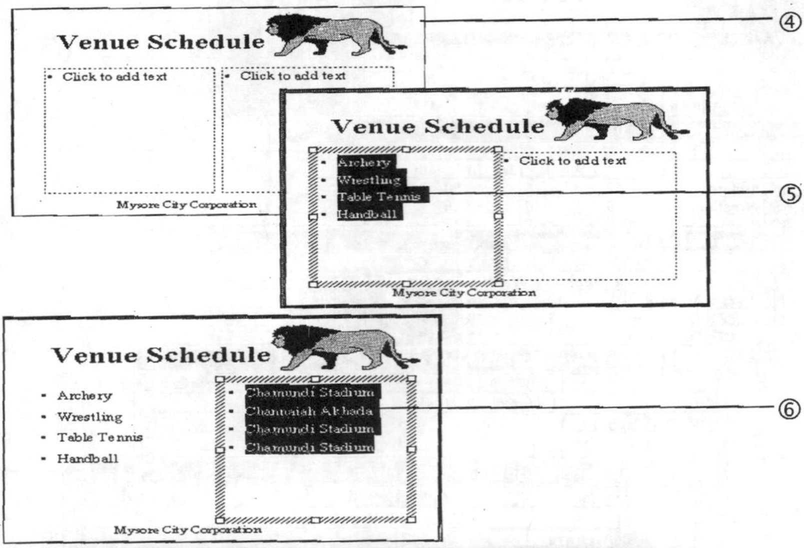

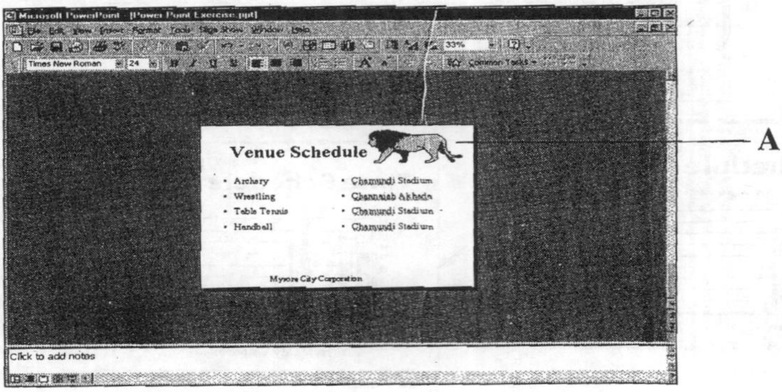

Creating the Seventh Slide

① Insert a new slide.

② Choose **Organising chart** from the **Autolayout** Box.

③ Click on the **OK** button to continue.

④ Add title, logo and footer.

⑤ Double click here to start creating the organisation chart.

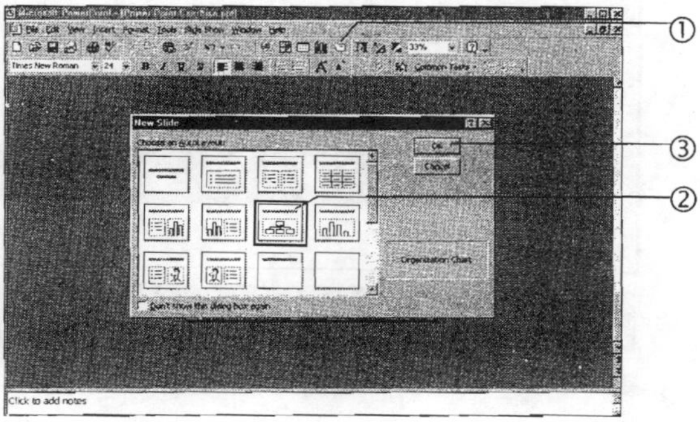

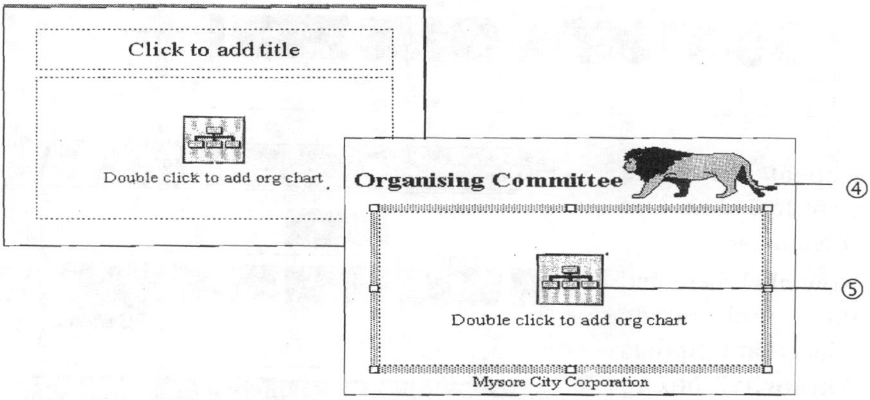

Organisation Chart

A This Window appears.

① Type the text.

② Click here and then click on the "**Commissioner MCC**" box to specify another subordinate for the Commissioner.

③ You will see that a box has been added for the other subordinate. You may now type his details.

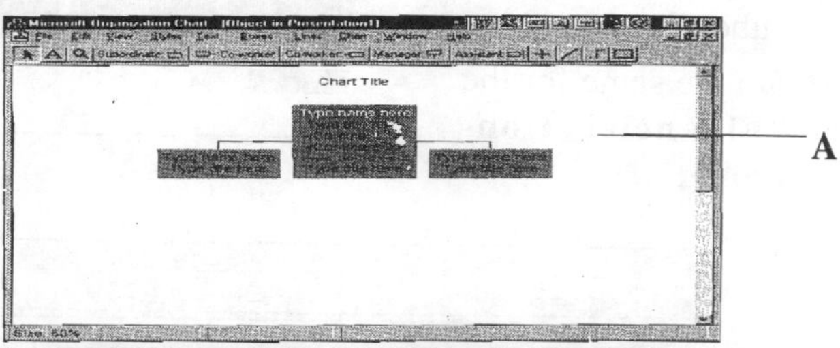

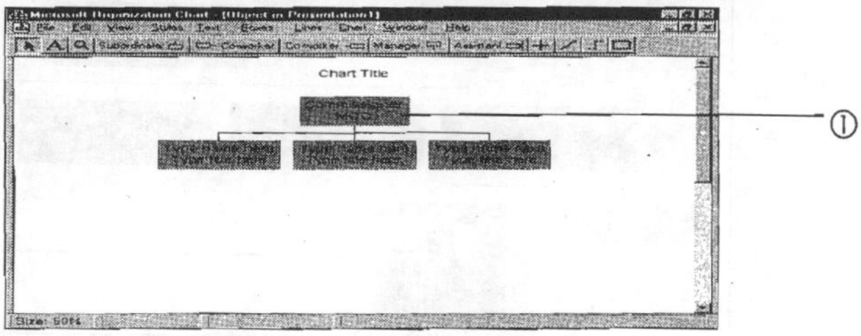

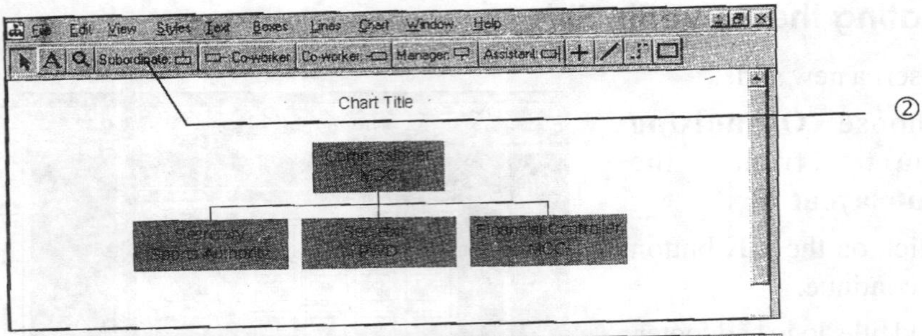

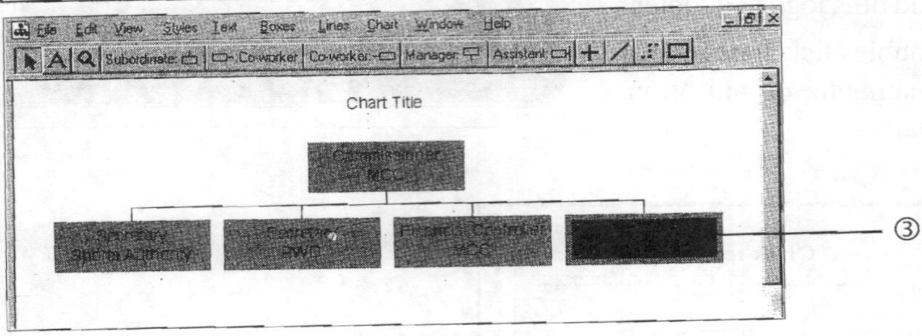

④ Repeat the same steps to add another subordinate.

⑤ Now click here and then click inside "**Secretary Sports Authority**" box to add his subordinate.

⑥ Repeat the same steps to add other subordinates.

⑦ Do the same for the "**Financial Controller**".

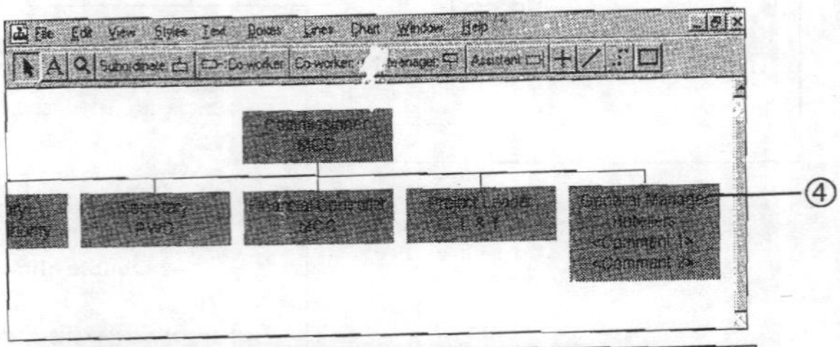

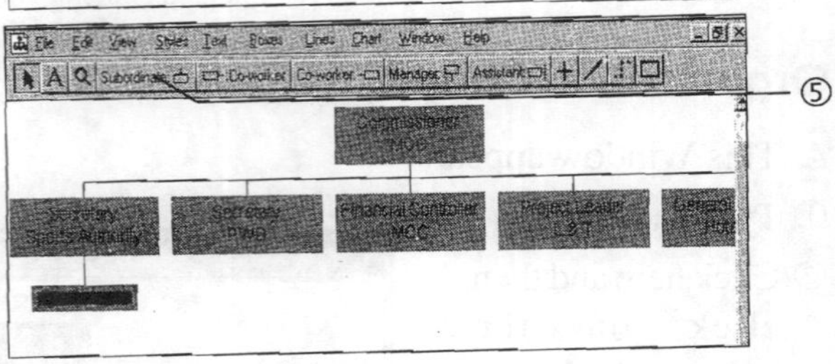

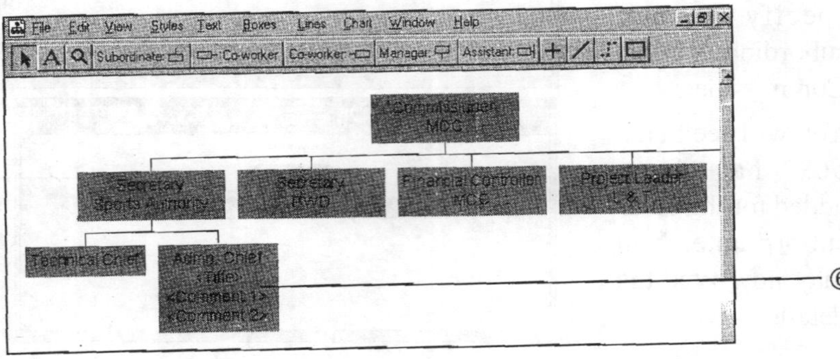

B Your organisation chart is now ready.

⑧ Choose **Exit and Return to Presentation** command from the **File** menu.

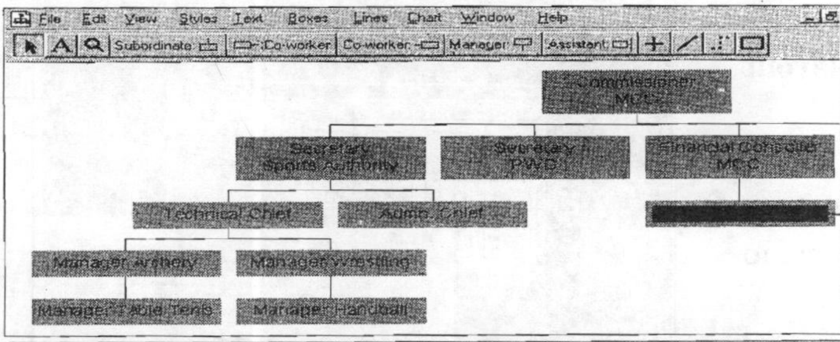

⑦

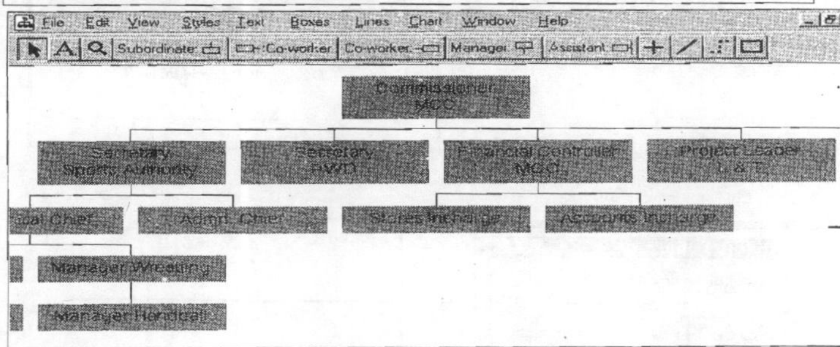

B

⑨ Click here to continue.

A Your seventh slide is complete.

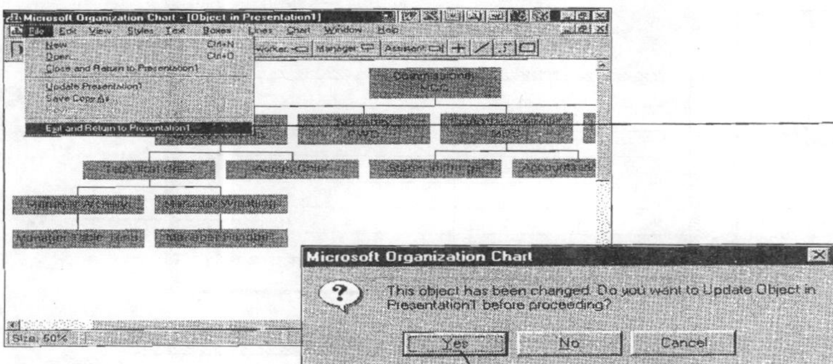

⑧

⑨

A

Creating the Eighth Slide

① Insert a new slide.

② Choose **table chart** from the **Autolayout** box.

③ Click the **OK** button once to continue.

④ Double click here to add table.

⑤ Specify the desired rows and columns.

A 2 Columns.

B 7 Rows.

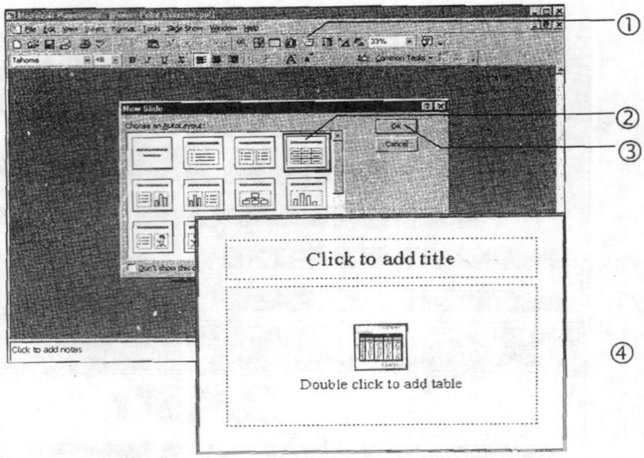

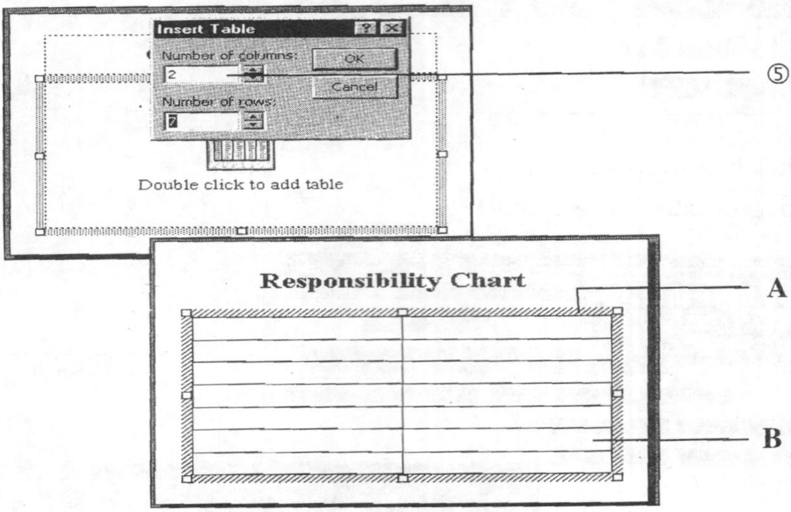

Table

① Type the text

A Your eighth slide is complete!

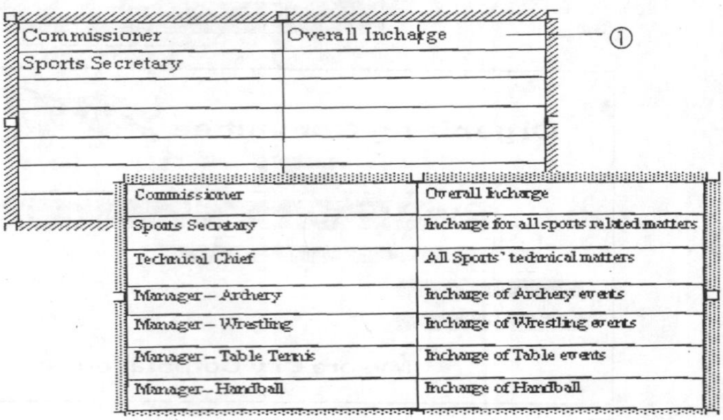

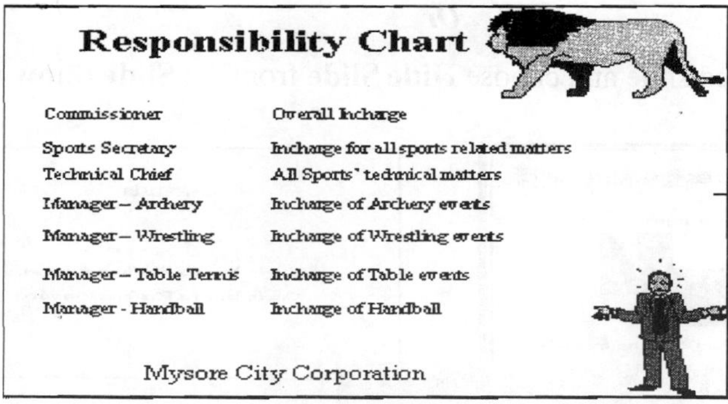

A

You would notice that the ninth and tenth slides can be created easily using the features explained earlier. So, this completes your presentation. You can save your masterpiece so that it can be used again.

Now to view your presentation, you can do any of the following:

i Press the function key **F5.**

ii Choose **Slide Show** from the **View** menu.

iii Click on the **Slide Show** icon, located at the lower-left of a Powerpoint window.

iv Choose **View Show** from the **Slide Show** menu.

Slide Show Controls

You can use the following shortcuts while running your slide show in full-screen mode.

- Press Enter, PageDown, Right Arrow, Down Arrow, Spacebar or N or click the mouse to advance to the next slide.
- Press PageUp, Left Arrow, Up Arrow, Backspace or P to return to the previous slide.
- Press <Number> simultaneously with the Enter key to go directly to the slide indicated by <Number>. For example, you can press <Enter> <9> key to go to the 9th slide of your presentation.
- Press Esc or 'Ctrl+Break' to end a slide show.

Hiding a Slide

You can hide a slide in a slide show. To hide a slide:

In slide sorter view, right click on the desired slide and choose **Hide Slide** from the popup menu. A null symbol ( ) appears on the slide number, indicating that the slide would be hidden in the slide show.

Or

Select the desired slide and choose **Hide Slide** from the **Slide Show** menu.

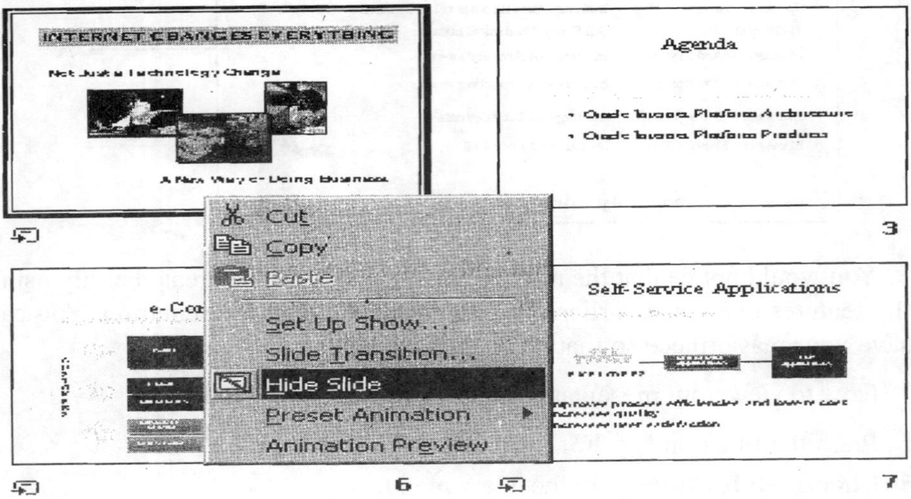

Checking Spelling and Correcting Typing Mistakes

You can check the spelling of your document automatically, either as you type or after completing your slides. When you check spelling automatically, red coloured wavy underlines indicate possible spelling errors. Spell Check component is common to all MS office programs. It can be accessed by choosing **Spelling** from the **Tools** menu (Refer to Word Processing chapter for further details).

You can correct common typing errors automatically as you work by using the **AutoCorrect** command of the **Tools** menu. You can customise the AutoCorrect entry list by creating a list of common errors you want to be corrected as you type. For instance, you can use Auto Correct to correct 'teh' to 'the'.

Adding an Entry to the AutoCorrect List

① Choose **AutoCorrect** from the **Tools** menu.

② Type the incorrect spelling of the word that you frequently mistype.

③ Type the correct spelling.

④ Click on the **Add** button and then click on the **OK** button.

A Select the desired options to apply the specified settings.

B AutoCorrect entry list.

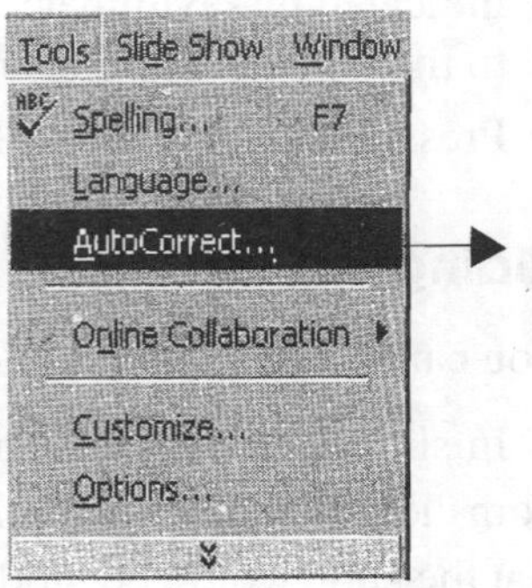

C Deletes the selected AutoCorrect entry.(The button is currently disabled because no entry is selected)

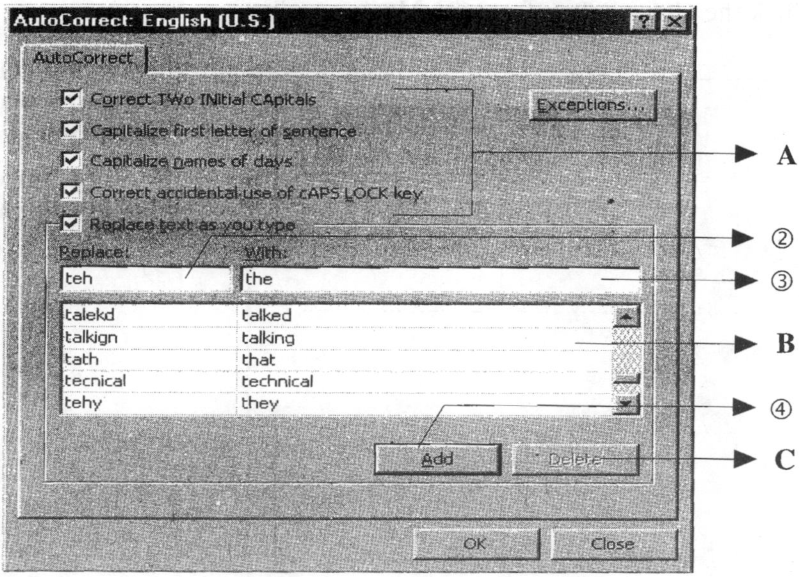

Making Notes Pages and Handouts

Notes: You can make notes corresponding to each slide of your presentation. Notes can be helpful to remember the key points of individual slides. As discussed earlier, Notes can be entered in the Notes pane. It may be kept in mind that notes can be printed while printing your presentation and viewed in the Normal view. You cannot view the notes when you run your presentation (Slide Show).

Handouts You can print the slides of your presentation as handouts, containing two, three, four, six or nine slides on a page. Handouts display only the slide contents; they do not include the corresponding notes. Similar to Slide Master, you have Notes and Handouts Master, where you can add items that you wish to appear on every slide of your presentation. To access Notes and Handouts master, choose **Notes Master** or **Handouts Master,** under **Masters** from the **View** menu.

Note: Any items (text or images) added to the Notes Master appear only when you print your presentation. They are not displayed in the Notes pane.

Creating Handouts

1. The window below appears when the Handouts Master is clicked. You can view 2, 3, 4, 6 or 9 slides per handout by clicking on the corresponding icons from the handouts master toolbar.

2. Add the desired items to the handout master, any item added to the handouts master appear only in the handouts, they do not affect the slide master.
3. Click the **Close** button from the **Master** toolbar.

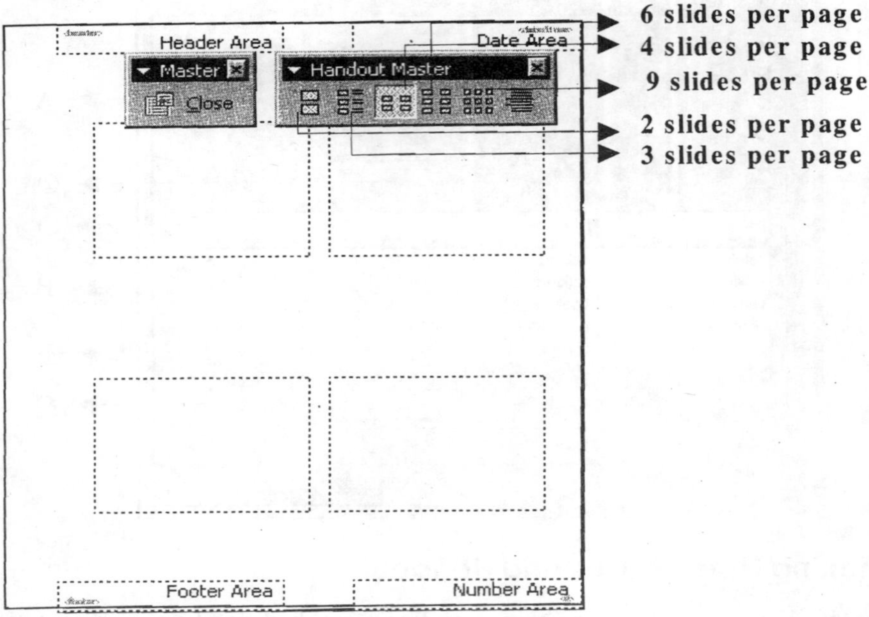

Printing Presentations

You can print your entire presentation–the slides, outline, notes and handouts. You can also print specific slides, handouts, notes pages, or outline pages. To print your presentation, choose **Print** from the **File** menu. Various print options can be specified using the Print dialogue box.

You can preview your presentation, as it will appear when printed.

- To preview the presentation in Grayscale mode, click the Grayscale Preview icon on the **Standard** toolbar.
- To preview the presentation in Black & White mode, press and hold the **Shift** key and then click the Pure Black & White Preview icon on the **Standard** toolbar.

① Use this option to print your entire presentation.

② Use this option to print your current slide (current slide is the one in which your cursor is currently placed).

③ Use this option to print specific slide(s). For example, you can print slides 3-5, 10-13 using this option.

④ Choose **Slides** if you wish to print the slides in your presentation. Choose **Handouts** if you wish to print the audience handouts. Once you select handouts from the drop down box, Handouts frame is enabled.You can then specify the number of slides you wish to print in a single page. You can also choose the orientation (Horizontal/ Vertical) of these slides on the page. Choose **Notes Pages** if you wish to print the notes. Choose **Outline View** to print the contents of the outline pane.

⑤ Use this option to print in **Grayscale** mode.

⑥ Use this option to print in **Pure Black and White** mode.

⑦ Click here to print your presentation with the specified settings.

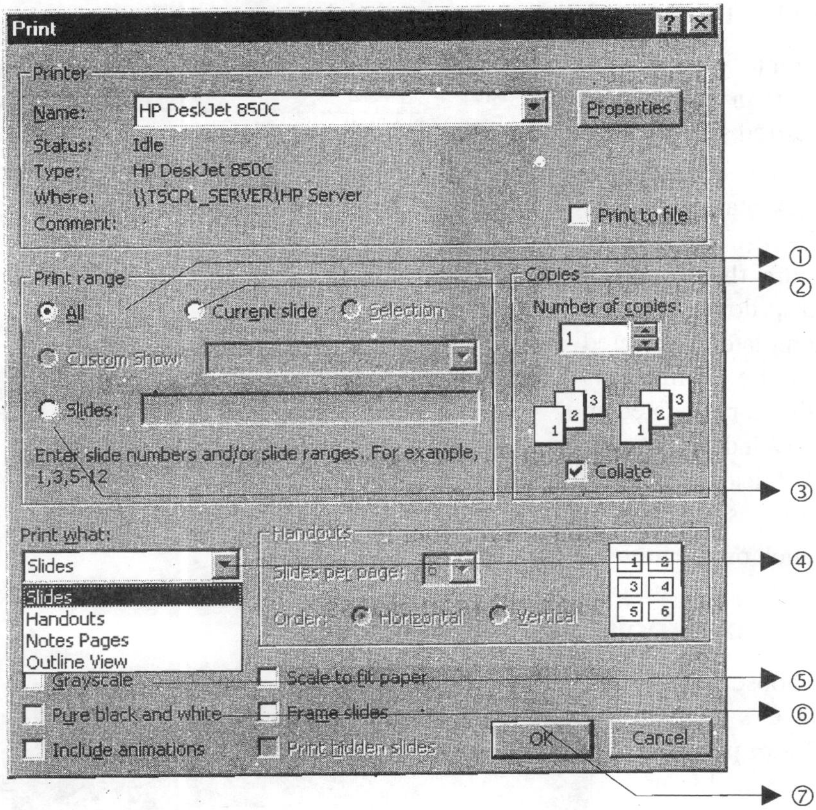

CUSTOMISING YOUR PRESENTATIONS

Creating the Look of Your Presentation

PowerPoint helps in creating eye-catching and effective presentations. It is designed to give your presentations a consistent appearance. PowerPoint automatically checks your presentation for consistency and style, and marks problems on a slide with a light bulb. You can either fix or ignore these errors. The light bulb appears only when the Office Assistant is turned on (**Office Assistant** can be turned On/Off from the **Help** menu). You can control the appearance of your presentation with the help of design templates, masters, color schemes, and slide layouts.

Design templates There are two types of templates in PowerPoint namely Design Templates and Content Templates. A Design Template determines the presentation's color scheme, fonts, and other design features. Content templates contain formats and color schemes just like design templates, plus slides with suggested text for specific subjects. PowerPoint has many inbuilt design templates. You can either choose from its inbuilt list or create your own templates.

Follow the steps below to create a template:

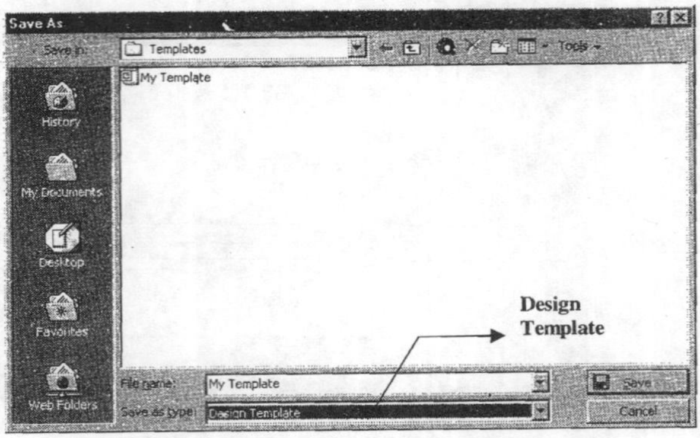

1. Create your presentation with the desired set of styles.
2. While saving your presentation, choose **Design Template** from the **Save As** drop down box. All templates are stored in the Templates directory located in C:\Windows_folder / Application Data/Microsoft (For Windows 95 or 98) so that they can be used as a base for creating other presentations.
3. Click on the **Save** button to save your template.

Using Powerpoint's Inbuilt Templates

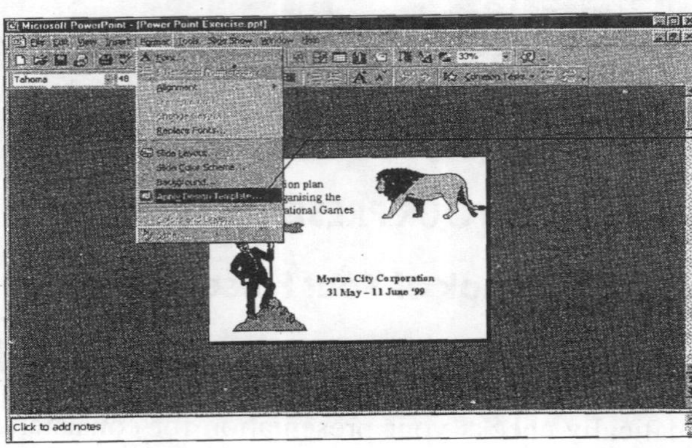

① Choose **Apply Design Template** command from the **Format** menu.

② Choose **Professional** (or any other design tem plate that you like after seeing a preview of the highlighted design).

③ Click here to continue.

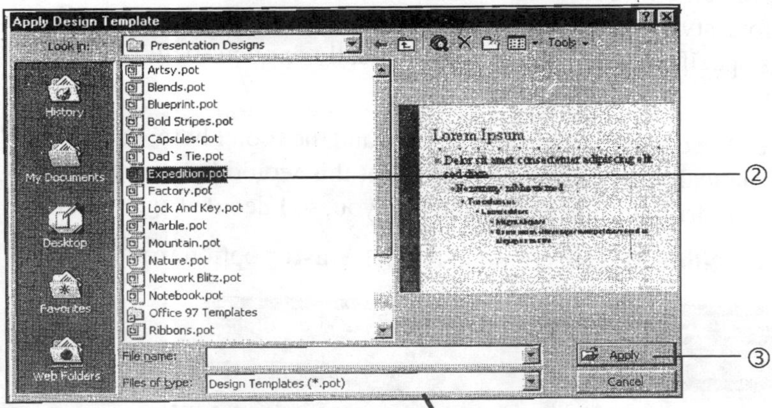

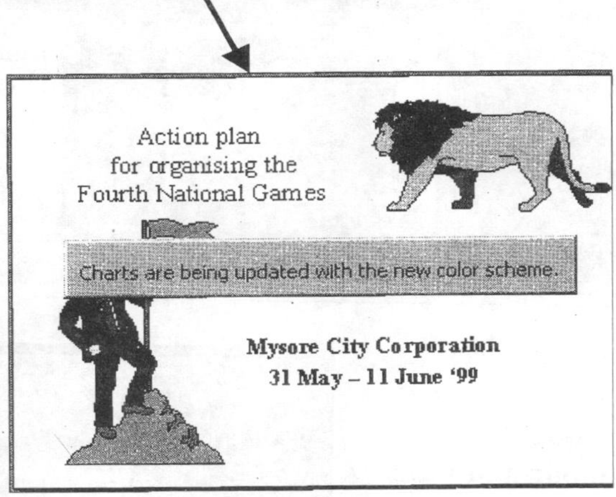

A Notice that the backgrounds of all the slides would have changed as per your chosen design template.

Master slide Master Slide is like a slide controller. You can specify the fonts, font styles, alignments, indentation and placement of text boxes. The settings specified here shall be automatically applied to all the slides in your presentation.

Note: We could have placed the logo and the footer here, in the Master slide to automatically appear on all slides. But this would have deprived me of the pleasure of drilling some command into you, so I decided against it!

① Choose **Slide Master** command under **Master** option from the **View** menu.

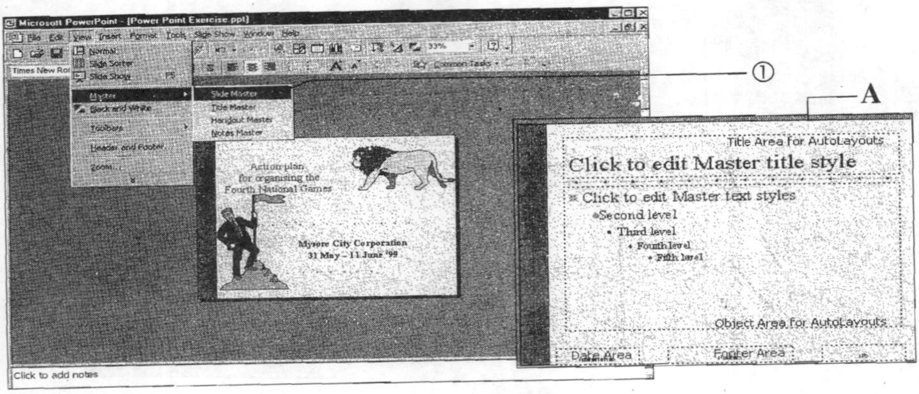

② Highlight this.

③ Choose **Text colour** under **Colour and Line** option from the **Format** menu.

④ Choose the desired colour by simply clicking it once and then click the **OK** button.

⑤ Repeat steps ② and ④ for changing the colour for the rest of slide text.

⑥ Choose **Slides** command from the **View** menu, go back to your slides and see the fruits of your great work.

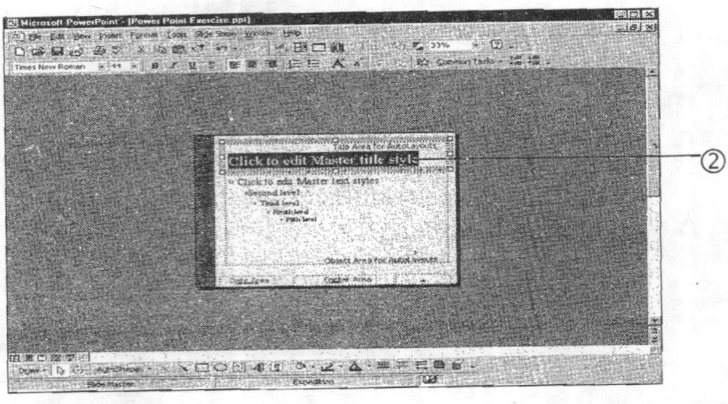

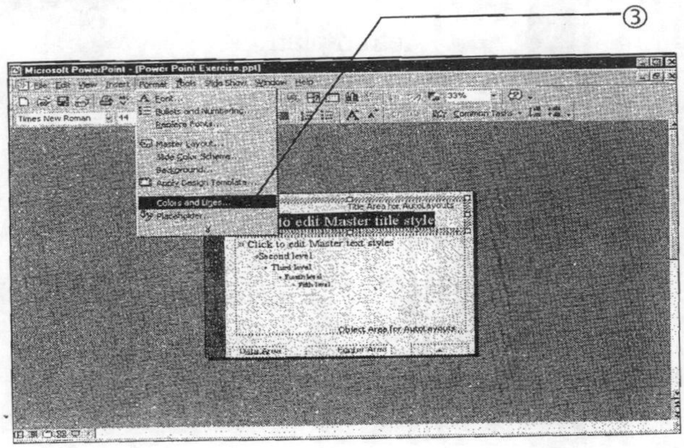

A The Slide Master appears on the screen. The settings specified here would be used by all the slides.

B Notice the changes in colour, not only of this, but all slides.

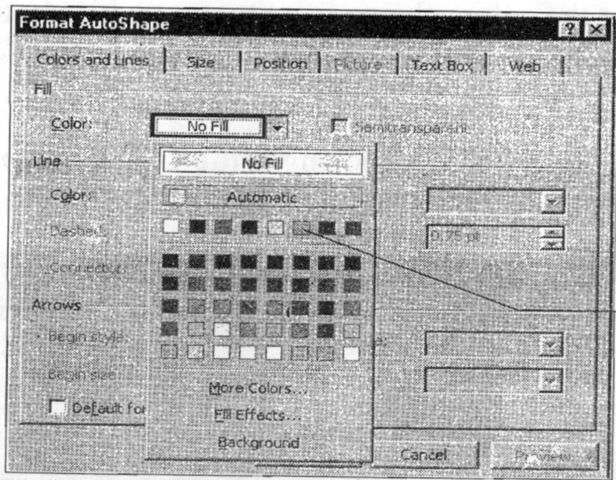

④

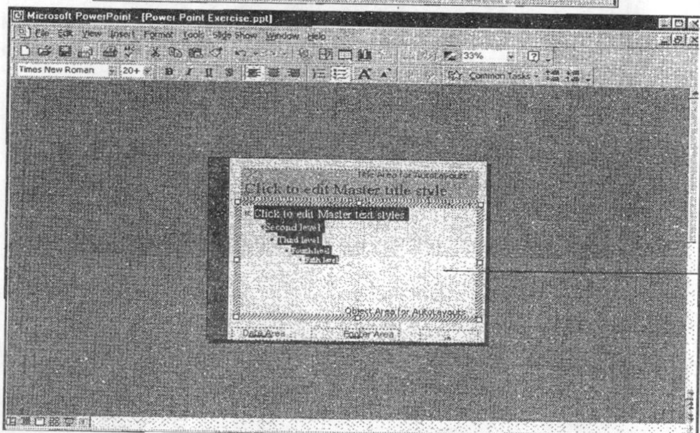

⑤

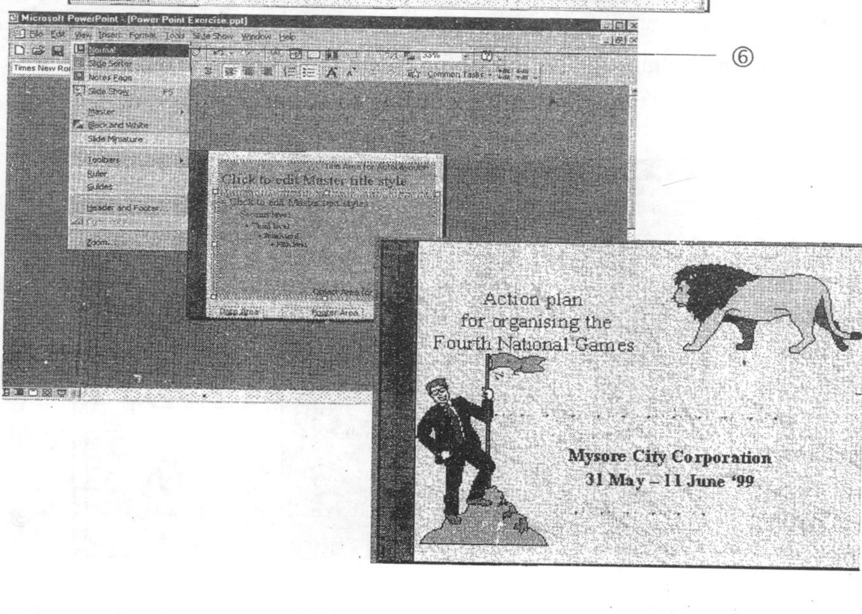

⑥

B

Color Schemes Color schemes are a set of eight coordinated colours that can be used for different elements (for text, background, fill, and so on) in your presentation. You can apply a color scheme for an individual slide or for an entire presentation. Each design template comes with a set of color schemes. However, you can change the color scheme to suit your requirement. After you apply a color scheme, the colours will be available for every element in your presentation.

Color schemes can be accessed by choosing **Slide Color Scheme** from the **Format** menu.

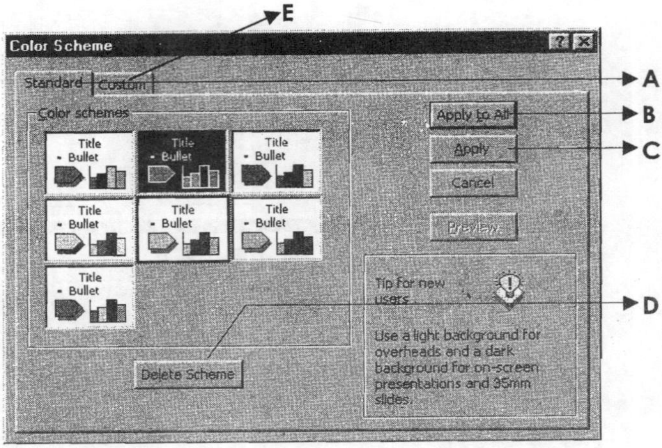

A Displays Powerpoint's inbuilt standard color schemes.

B Use this option if you wish to apply the selected color scheme to all the slides.

C Use this option to apply the selected color scheme to only selected slide(s).

D Deletes the selected scheme.

E Click here to modify the standard colour scheme. You can use the technique explained below to change the colour scheme of a design template as well.

① Use this option to change the colour of the selected element. You can change the colours of all the eight elements according to your requirement.

② Use this option to view your presentation with the selected settings. Settings will not be applied until you click on the **Apply** button.

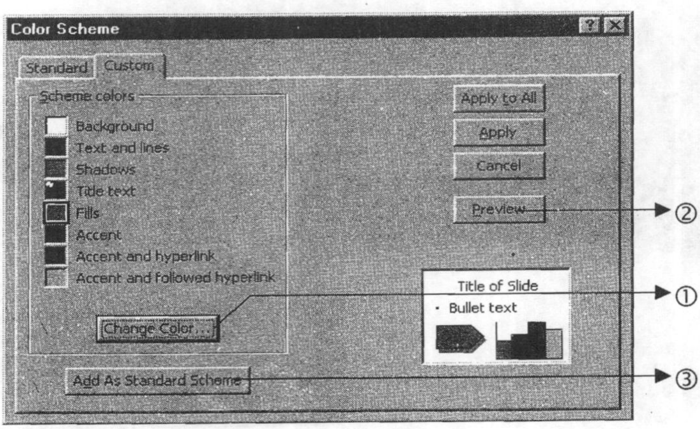

③ Use this option to add the changed scheme colours as a Standard Scheme. Once added, your color scheme will be displayed when you click on the Standard tab. This option will be enabled only when any of the scheme colours are changed.

Slide Layouts When you create a blank presentation, PowerPoint lets you choose from several predefined slide layouts. Titles, Bulleted List, 2 Column Text, Table, Chart, Organisation Chart, Clip Art & Text are examples of different slide layouts.

AutoContent Wizard

Now having done things the hard way, let us relax a bit and make PowerPoint sweat and do some work. Remember, right in the beginning I had mentioned AutoContent Wizard and Templates through which you can save considerable amount of work. Let us first see how it works.

The following window would be displayed on starting the PowerPoint:

① Click once on the **AutoContent Wizard** button.

② Now Click on the **OK** button to continue.

③ Click on **Next** button to select **Presentation Type** option.

④ Select **'Selling a Product or Service'** from Sales/Marketing option as Presentation Type.

⑤ Click on **'on-screen presentation'** button to get the type of output you would like to use.

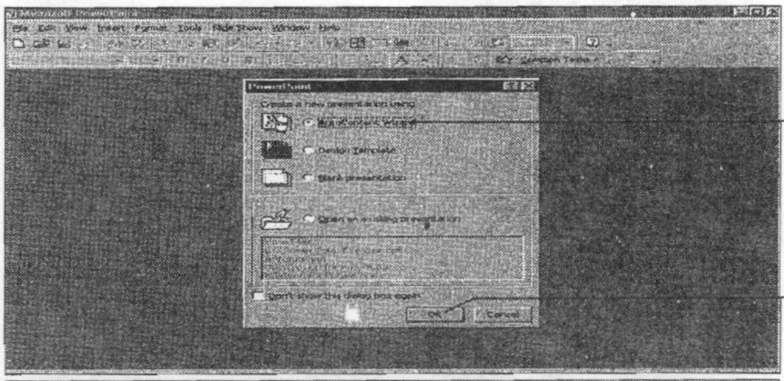

①

②

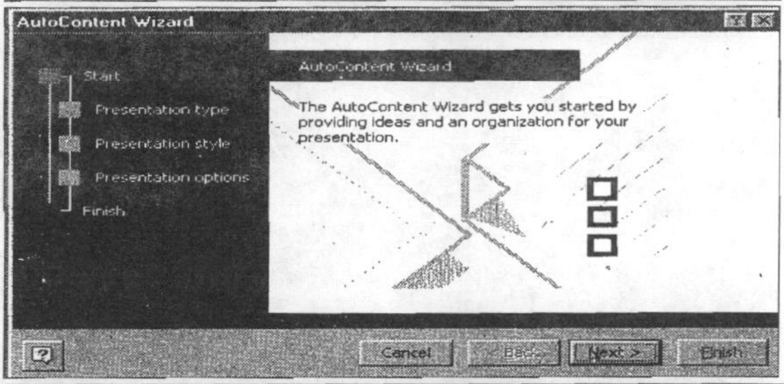

③

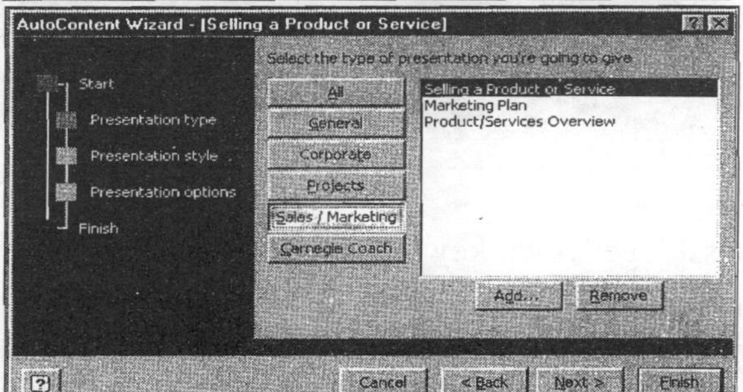

④

⑥ Type presentation title here.

⑦ Click once on the **Finish** button to see the output.

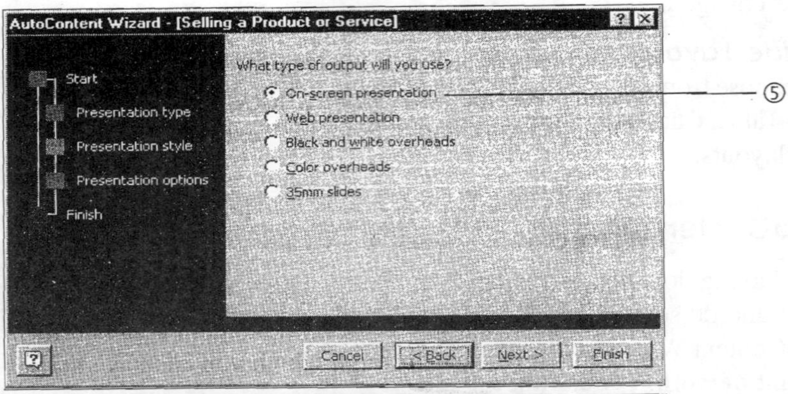

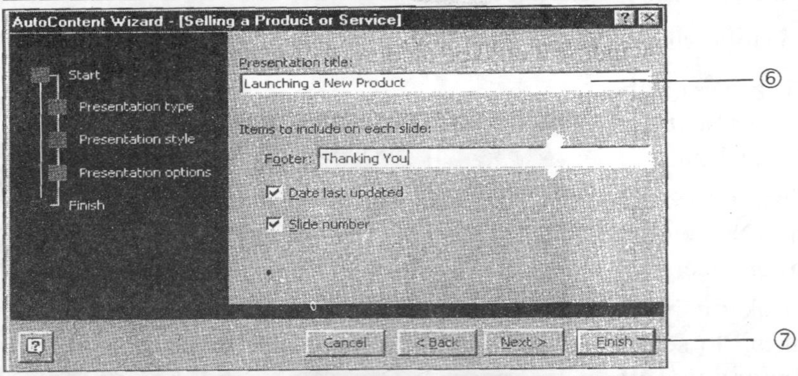

① Press Page Down key on your keyboard.

② In your next slide click on **State the desired Objectives** and start typing your presentation objective here after deleting the hint line(s) – the ones saying *State the desired objective* and *Use multiple points if necessary.*

③ In the third slide specify the client's requirements by typing over the hint lines.

④ In the fourth slide specify the list of products and features, and how each addresses a specific need or solves a specific problem. Since this section may require multiple slides use the **New Slide** option from the **Insert** menu to insert slides at this place.

①

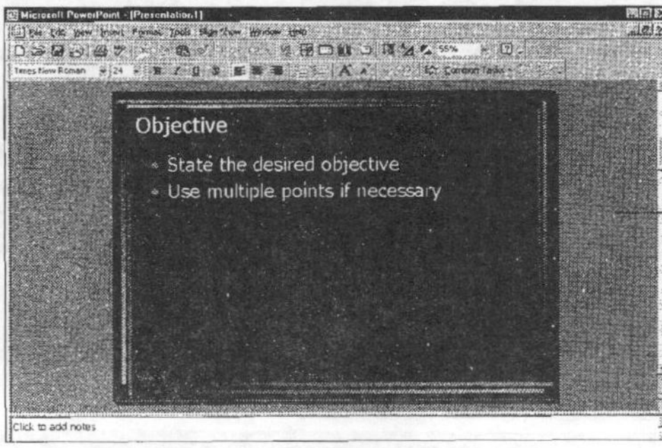

②

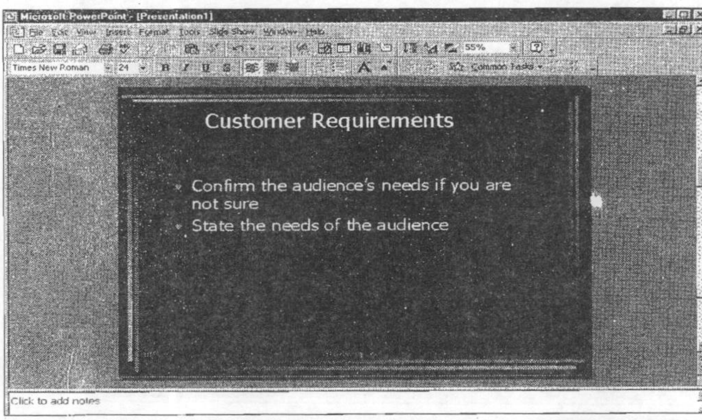

③

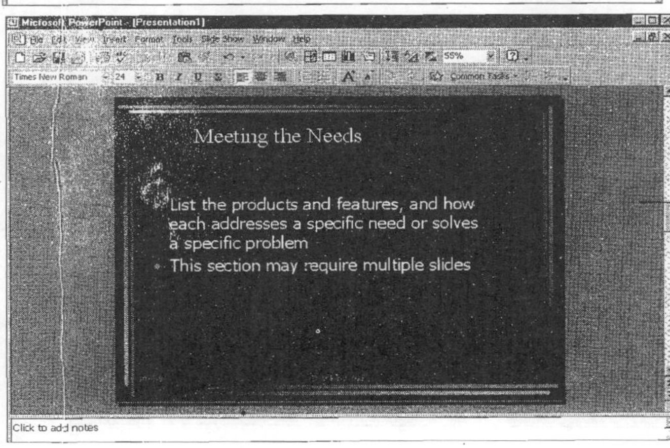

④

⑤ In the fifth slide, point out financial benefits of your product or services to the customer and compare cost – benefits between your product and its competitors. **Double Click** on the graph section to add a graph. In case graph is not required, simply click once in this section and press **Del** key on your keyboard.

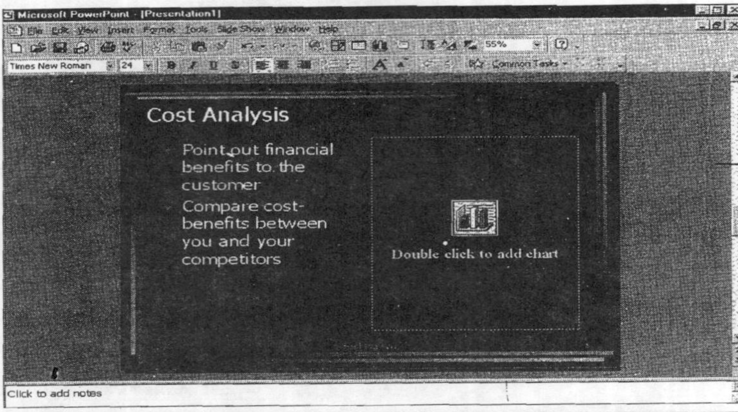

⑤

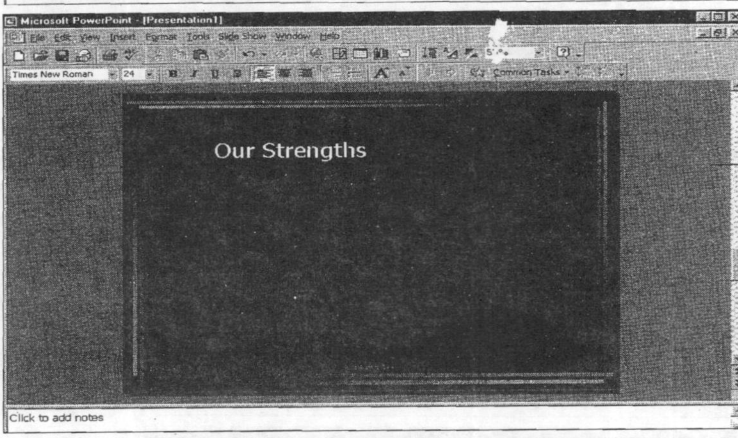

⑥

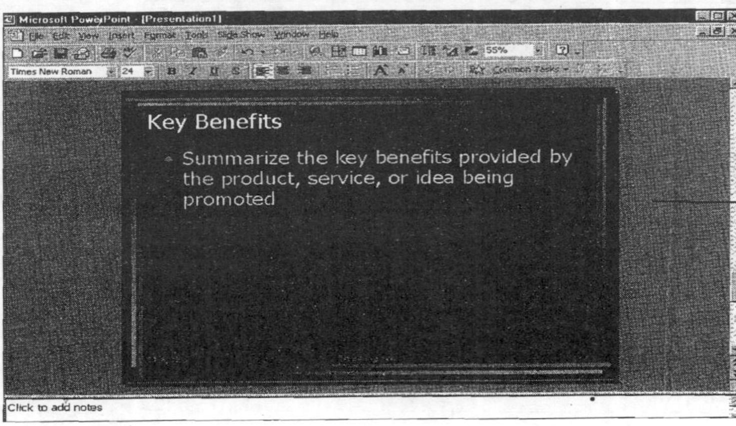

⑦

⑥ The sixth slide is a Table slide where you can either make a comparative chart showing the features of your product/service against its competitors, or simply specifying your strength areas.

⑦ In your seventh slide summarise the key benefits provided by the product, service, or idea being promoted.

⑧ The last slide, as usual, is the most important one. Here specify the actions required of your audience; simply put, how he is supposed to place the order!

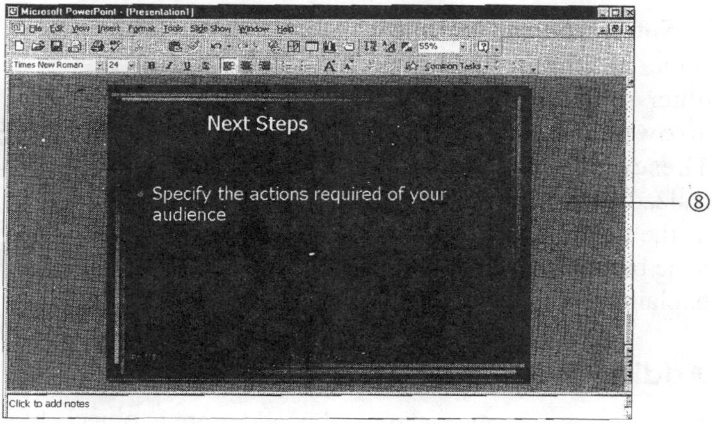

This and all other slides (which we shall soon work on) though predefined, are not sacrosant. You can add, delete or modify any component(s) of these slides, i.e., you can add or change text, change colour scheme, add clipart image – in short, do anything and everything that you could do if you were making a new presentation starting from the Blank Presentation option.

Inclusive of this slide, AutoContent Wizard has automatically prepared eight slides, (the number of slides depends on the Presentation Type chosen by you) which you can see one by one by pressing the **PageDown** key on your **Keyboard** or by scrolling by clicking and dragging the **mouse** over the **vertical scroll bar** shown to the right of your Window.

With this you have completed your second PowerPoint presentation using AutoContent Wizard. As you can appreciate, other than saving you a lot of time and effort in designing and beautifying your slides, it also helps you to structure your presentation with a sharp focus on all the key issues.

Working with Drawing Toolbar

PowerPoint comes with a set of readymade shapes that can be used in your presentations. They can be resized, rotated, coloured, and grouped with other shapes to make more complex shapes. You are already familiar with the Textbox object; let us explore some more options of the Drawing toolbar.

Adding an Oval

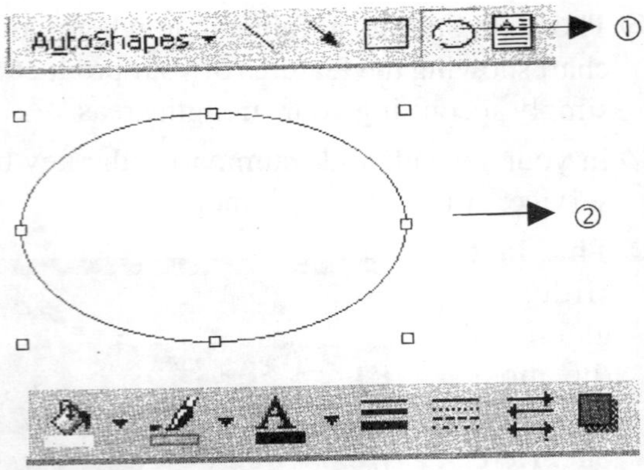

① Click the **Oval** icon from the **Drawing** toolbar.

② Drag with the mouse pointer to create an oval.

Note: You can use the same technique to draw other objects like lines, arrows and rectangles. These shapes can be resized in the same manner as the textbox was resized. You can also format the shapes by using various style buttons of the drawing toolbar. All the icons functions have already been explained in the beginning of the chapter; refer to them when in doubt.

Adding Predefined Shapes

You can use Autoshapes to quickly add graphic objects to your slide. You can edit or format the autoshapes, just as you can edit other drawing objects.

Adding an AutoShape

① Click on the desired **AutoShape** from the **Drawing** toolbar.

② Drag with the mouse pointer to create the selected autoshape.

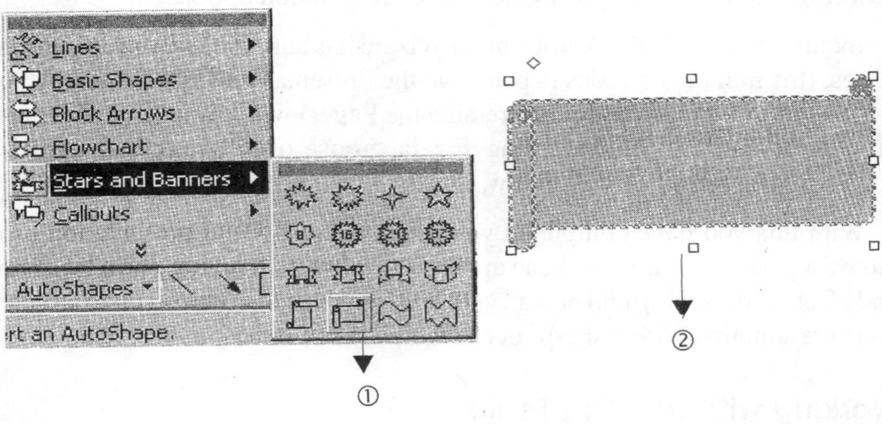

Rotating Objects

You can rotate an object 90 degrees to the left or right or to any other angle. If you rotate an object that has text attached to it, then the text also rotates along with the object.

To rotate an object

① Select the Object you wish to rotate and click on the **Free Rotate** icon from the **Drawing** toolbar.

② Drag a corner of the object in the direction you want to rotate it.

③ Click outside the object to confirm the new position of the objects.

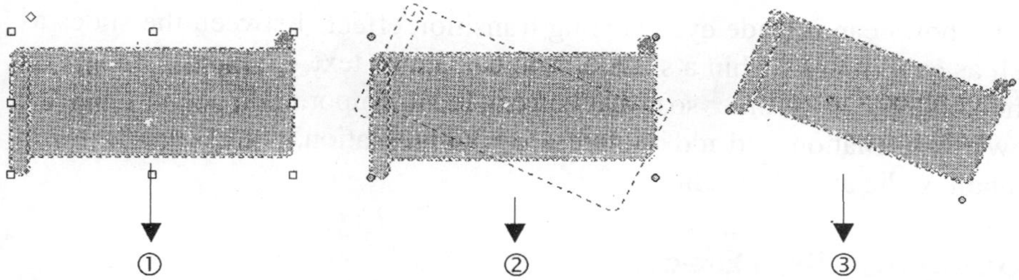

Grouping and Ungrouping Objects

You can group several objects to treat them as a single object. Groups can be composed of multiple sets of groups, i.e., it is possible to group 2 or more groups (each containing 2 or more objects) into a single group.

To group several objects

① Select the objects you wish to group using the **Shift** key.

② Choose **Group** under the **Draw** option from the **Drawing** toolbar.

A Both the objects are now grouped together.

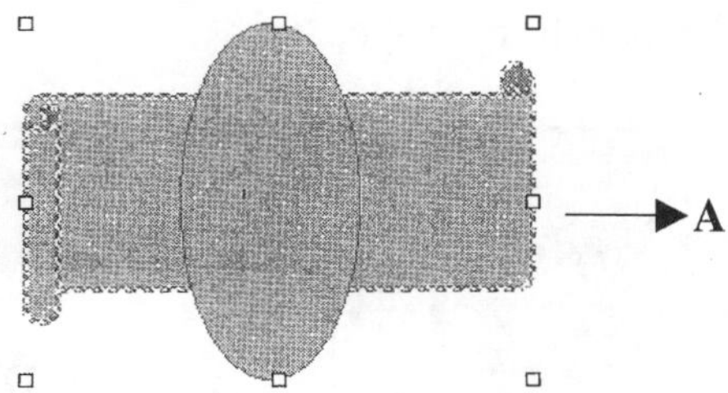

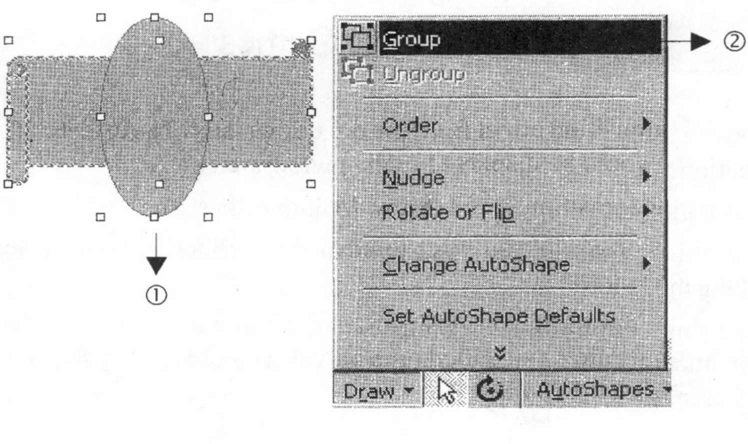

Notes:

1. You can apply any formatting features to the group as well.
2. You can ungroup the objects of a group by selecting the group and selecting **Ungroup** under the **Draw** option from the **Drawing** toolbar.

CREATING SLIDE SHOWS

Slide shows can include eye catching transition effects between the slides as well as animations within a slide. You can animate text, graphics, charts, and other objects in your slides so that you can focus on important points, control the flow of information, and add interest to your presentation. Slide shows can also contain Audio and Video clips.

Adding Transition Effects

A transition is a special effect (like dissolve, split, fade, wipe) that is used while changing over from one slide to the next.

To add a transition effect

① Open the presentation in which you wish to apply transition effects. Choose **Slide Transition** from the **Slide Show** menu, Slide Transition dialogue box would be displayed.

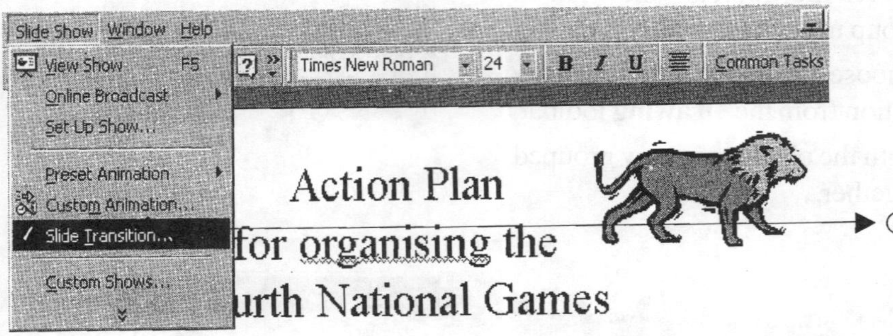

② Choose a transition effect from the drop down box. The effect of the selected transition would be displayed in the preview area (**'A'**).

③ Choose the transition speed (Slow, Medium or Fast).

④ Select this option if you wish to advance the slides in your presention by clicking the mouse.

⑤ Select this option if you wish to advance the slides in your presentation automatically after a specified time interval. You can specify the time interval by clicking on the spinner.

⑥ Select this option if you wish to add a sound effect. You can choose a sound effect from the drop down box.

⑦ Click here to apply the specified transition effect to the selected slide.

⑧ Click here to apply the specified transition effect to all the slides of your presentation.

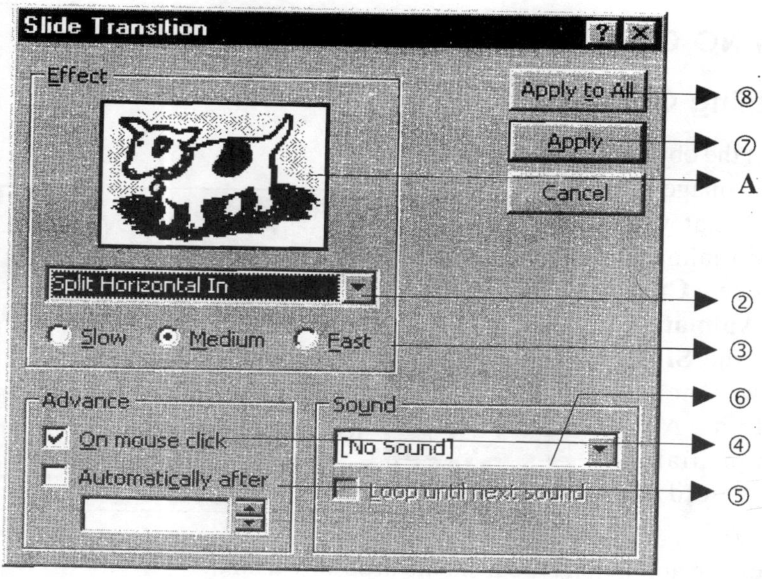

Adding Animation Effects

You can animate text, graphics, charts, and other objects on your slides. You can even animate the elements of a chart. For example, you can set the text to fly from left or right of a slide. Powerpoint allows you to control the order and timing of your animations; you can also set the animations to occur automatically without having to click the mouse.

Preset Animation Powerpoint allows you to animate various elements of your slide. To add animation to an object:

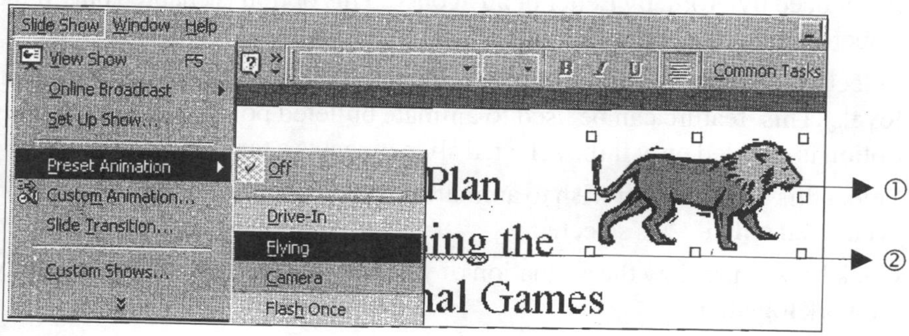

① Select the desired object.

② Choose an animation under **Preset Animation** option from the **Slide Show** menu. You can view the specified animation during the slide show.

To have more control on animating objects and controlling their order and timings during the slide show, you can choose **Custom Animation**.

CREATING CUSTOM ANIMATIONS

Animating Objects

① Select the object (Text, image or chart) that you wish to animate. Choose **Custom Animation** from the **Slide Show** menu, Custom Animation dialog box would be displayed.

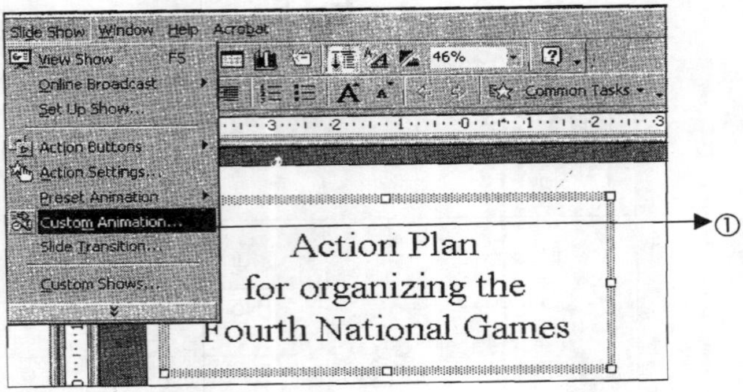

② Choose an animation type from the drop-down box.

③ Specify how the selected animation should appear. For example, if you have selected **Fly** as the animation type and **From Top** as the animation style then the selected object will have an effect of flying from the top of the slide.

④ Use this option if you wish to add a sound effect; choose the desired sound effect from the drop down box.

⑤ Use this option if you wish to modify the appearance of an object after animation. You can change the colour or hide the object after animation. Choose the desired action from the **After Animation** drop down box.

⑥ Choose the way you want Powerpoint to introduce your text. Text can be introduced by Word, by Letter or all at once. This option is enabled only if the selected slide object is a text object.

⑦ Select this option if you wish to introduce text according to the paragraph levels. This feature can be used to animate bulleted points one by one. This option is enabled only if the selected slide object is a text object.

⑧ Select this option if you wish to animate the text in reverse order. This option is enabled only if ⑦ is selected.

⑨ Click here to preview the animation of your text and objects, to see how they all work together.

⑩ Click on the **OK** button to apply your settings.

A Click on this tab if you wish to animate the elements of a chart.

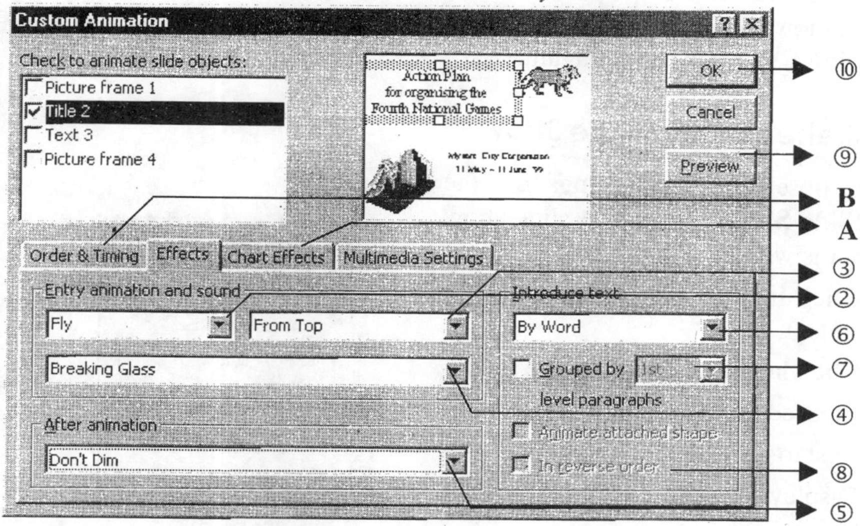

B Click on this tab to modify the animation order and timings.The following window would be displayed.

① Click on the Up and Down arrow keys to alter the animation order/sequence.

② Select this option if you wish to start the animation on mouse click.

③ Select this option if you wish to start animation after the specified time interval.You can specify the time interval by clicking on the spinner.

④ Click here to preview the animation order and timing of your slide objects.

⑤ Click on the **OK** button to apply your settings.

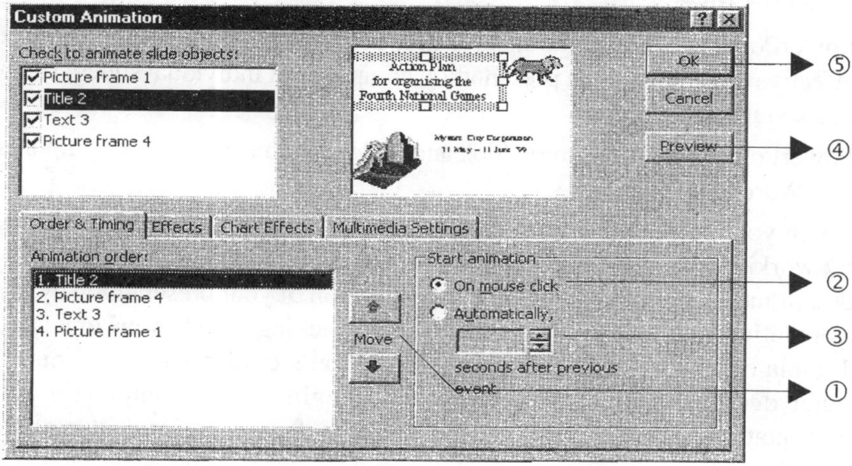

Rehearsing Slide Show Timings

Rehearse timings feature can be used to record the total time taken by your presentation. You can also adjust the timings you have already set (during animation) and then rehearse the new ones. When you finish, you can accept the timings or you can try again.

To Rehearse the Slide Show

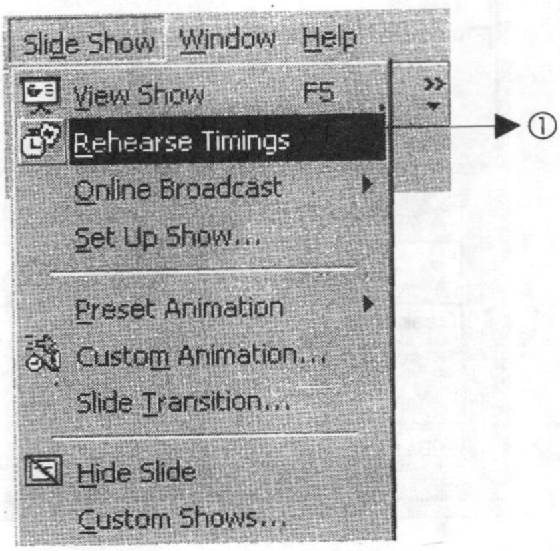

① Choose **Rehearse Timings** from the **Slide Show** menu. The slide show starts with the Rehearsal dialog box.

② Click here to advance to the next slide.

③ Click here to pause the slide show.

④ Elapsed time of current slide.

⑤ Restarts a slide.

⑥ Displays the elapsed time of the slide show.

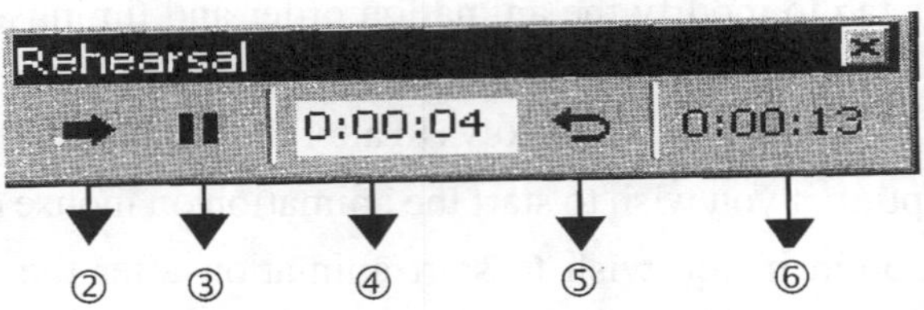

KEY POINTS

PowerPoint Basics

- PowerPoint is a presentation tool that helps in creating eye-catching and effective presentations. A presentation comprises of individual slides arranged in a sequential manner.
- PowerPoint shares a common look and feel with other MS Office components like Word and Excel.
- When you create a new presentation, you have three options: You can start by working with a wizard (called the AutoContent Wizard) that helps you determine the theme, contents and organisation of your presentation by using a predefined outline, or you can also start by picking out a PowerPoint Design Template, which determines the presentation's colour scheme, fonts, and other design features, or you can also begin with a completely blank presentation with the color scheme, fonts, and other design features set to default values.

- New slides can be inserted into a presentation, existing slides can be deleted from a presentation and slides within a presentation can be reordered. You can also number the slides in your presentation by making use of header and footer option.
- Whenever a presentation is saved, it is saved in the default directory. However, this default location can be changed using the Options command from the Tools menu. A PowerPoint presentation has .ppt as its extension name. You can use AutoSave option to save your presentation automatically at specified time intervals.
- Any PowerPoint presentation can be viewed in four different types of views namely Normal View, Outline View, Slide View and Slide Sorter View. By default, each new presentation opens in Normal View. It contains three panes, viz., the Outline Pane, the Slide Pane and the Notes Pane. Outline Pane displays a table of contents so that you can navigate through your presentation. Slide Pane allows viewing the contents of individual slides. Speaker notes or any information that you want to share with the audience can be added to Notes pane. Normal view permits you to work on all aspects of your presentation at one place. Slide Sorter view displays the thumbnail views of your presentation.

Designing Presentations

- The Auto Layout box that appears while creating a New presentation provides several slide layouts from which you can choose a slide that suits your need. Titles, Bulleted List, 2 Column Text, Table, Chart, Organization Chart, Clip Art and Text are examples of different slide layouts.
- Titles slide layout can be used if you wish to add only text to your slide. Bulleted List can be used if you want to create a bulleted list, 2 Column text can be used if you wish to place your text in two separate columns, Table can be used if you wish to insert tables into your slide. Chart can be used for creating charts, Organisation Chart is used to display the hierarchy of the employees of an organisation and Clipart is used if you wish to insert any images into your slide. You can either choose an auto layout or create a blank slide and then add the desired elements to it.
- You can apply different formatting features (like you can change the font style, size and alignment) to your text. You can also resize images and other drawing objects (like textboxes). Once these objects are inserted into your slide, you can drag them to the desired position in your slide.
- You can use the F5 key to view your presentation on the full screen. You can use the PageUp and PageDown keys for navigating the slides of your presentation.

- You can use the Spell Check component to check the spelling of your presentation. You can correct common typing errors automatically as you work by using the AutoCorrect command of the Tools menu. You can customise the AutoCorrect entry list by creating a list of common errors you want to be corrected as you type.
- You can print the slides of your presentation as handouts, containing two or three or four or six or nine slides on a page. Handouts display only the slide contents; they do not include the corresponding notes. Notes and Handouts Master can be used to add items that you wish to appear on every slide of your presentation.
- You can print your entire presentation – the slides, outline, notes and handouts. You can also print specific slides, handouts, notes pages, or outline pages. You can also preview your presentation, as it will appear when printed.

Customising Your Presentations

- You can control the appearance of your presentation with the help of design templates, masters, color schemes, and slide layouts.
- A Design Template determines the presentation's color scheme, fonts, and other design features. Content templates contain formats and color schemes just like design templates, plus slides with suggested text for specific subjects. All templates are stored in the Templates directory so that they can be used as a base for creating presentations.
- Master Slide is like a slide controller. You can specify the fonts, font styles, alignments, indentation and placement of text boxes. The settings specified here shall be automatically applied to all the slides in your presentation.
- Color schemes are a set of eight coordinated colours that can be used for different elements (text, background, fill, and so on) in your presentation. You can apply a color scheme for an individual slide or for an entire presentation. You can also change the colours in the color scheme.
- PowerPoint comes with a set of readymade shapes (like oval, rectangle, line, textbox and autoshapes) that can be used in your presentations. They can be resized, rotated, coloured, and grouped with other shapes to make more complex shapes.
- You can rotate a drawing object 90 degrees to the left or right or to any other angle using the Free rotate icon of the drawing toolbar. If you rotate an object that has attached text, then the text also rotates.
- You can group several objects to treat them as a single object. Groups can be composed of multiple sets of groups, i.e., it is possible to group 2 or more

groups (each containing 2 or more objects) into a single group. Grouped objects can be ungrouped at any time.

- Slide shows can include eye-catching transition effects between the slides as well as animations within a slide. A transition is a special effect (like dissolve, split, fade, wipe) that you can use to introduce a slide during the slide show. You can animate text, graphics, charts, and other objects on your slides. You can even animate the elements of a chart. For example, you can set the text to fly from left or right of a slide. PowerPoint allows you to control the order and timing of your animations; you can set the animations to occur automatically without having to click the mouse.
- Rehearse timings feature can be used to record the total time taken by your presentation. You can also adjust the timings you have already set (during animation) and then rehearse the new ones.

DO-IT-YOURSELF EXERCISES

Exercise I

Create a presentation for the senior executives of an organisation, highlighting the reasons and benefits of computerisation of an organisation. The presentation should include benefits, drawbacks, and steps involved for computerisation of an organisation. Key points of individual slides must be written in the Notes pane. Benefits and drawbacks should be written in the form of bullet points which should be animated automatically after 1 second. Each slide should be introduced with a transition effect.

Exercise II

Create a presentation for promoting the newly launched Sonata's Blue-i model mobile phone. The presentation should include overview, features of the product, distributors of the product, contact information etc. The presentation should contain the company logo on each slide, product photographs should be positioned against an appropriate background.

Exercise III

Create a presentation using PowerPoint's inbuilt design template for reporting the performance of engineering entrance test results. The presentation should include data for the last five years, number of students enrolled, number of students appeared, number of students cleared and number of students who joined the course for each of the five years. Use graphs to present these results and make comparative analysis of performance of candidates from north, south, east and west India.

REVIEW QUESTIONS

1. Choose the appropriate answer:

i. Extension name of PowerPoint presentations:

(a) .ppt (b) .xls
(c) .ppt (d) None of the above

ii. This pane can be used to add speaker's notes:

(a) Slide Pane (b) Outline Pane
(c) Notes Pane (d) None of the above

iii. You can choose this layout to display the hierarchies of the employees of an organisation:

(a) Chart (b) 2 Column text
(c) Table (d) Organisation Chart

iv. PowerPoint automatically checks your presentation for consistency and style, and marks the problems on a slide by making use of:

(a) Revision marks (b) Highlighting text
(c) Light bulb (d) None of the above

v. A special effect (like dissolve, split, fade, wipe) that you can use to introduce a slide during the slide show:

(a) Animation (b) Custom Animation
(c) Transition (d) None of the above

2. Enter True or False:

i. PowerPoint is a presentation tool that can be used to create effective presentations.

ii. You can reorder the slides in your presentation using the slide sorter view.

iii. A PowerPoint slide cannot contain any images.

iv. AutoCorrect can be used to correct common typing errors automatically as you work.

v. Handouts display only the slide contents; they do not include the corresponding notes.

vi. You cannot change the colours of a 'color scheme'.

vii. You cannot animate the elements of a chart.

3. Match the following:

X		Y
1. Displays the thumbnail views of your presentation	a.	Design Template
2. The settings specified here will be automatically applied to all the slides of your presentation.	b.	Color Scheme
3. This option can be used to save your presentation automatically at specified time intervals.	c.	Slide Master
4. A set of eight coordinated colors that can be used for different elements (for text, background, fill, and so on) in your presentation.	d.	Auto Save
5. Contains predesigned formats and color schemes that you can apply to any presentation to give it a particular look.	e.	Slide Sorter View

4. Fill in the blanks with the appropriate choices listed below:

(i) Color Scheme (ii) Normal (iii) Notes (iv) PageUp (v) Group (vi) Rehearse (vii) Array (viii) Slides (ix) Auto Content Wizard (x) PageDown (xi) Outline (xii) Slide Show (xiii) Slide (xiv) Color Group.

1. A presentation comprises of individual __________________ arranged in a sequential manner.
2. __________________ view permits you to work on all aspects of your presentation at one place.
3. __________________ helps you determine the theme, contents and organisation of your presentation by using a predefined outline.
4. __________________ can be used to view your presentation on the screen.
5. Any items added to the __________________ master appear only when printed.
6. You can use the ______________ key to view the next slide in your presentation during the slide show.
7. You can create a ______________ to treat several objects as a single object.
8. You can use ______________ option to record the timing of your presentation.

5. Write down a few characteristics of a good presentation.

CHAPTER 15

Networking

DATA TRANSMISSION

Analog Signal

The signals that we send to communicate with each other are referred to as data. Data can be represented in various forms, such as sound, letters, numbers and other characters (handwritten or printed), photos, graphics, and films. The nature of data can be of two types, analog and digital. You cannot use analog data in a PC, which can process only digital data in concise and simple data formats.

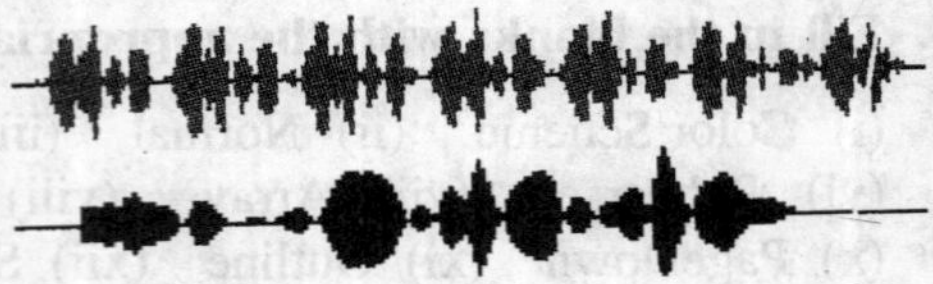

Figure 15.1 Analog waves

An analog or analogue signal is a signal whose amplitude and direction changes continuously. It differs from a digital signal in which amplitude remains constant. In digital signals, even very small fluctuations are meaningful. Analog signals are generally used in electrical context, however mechanical, pneumatic, hydraulic, and other systems may also use analog signals.

The word analog refers to an analogy between cause and effect, voltage in and voltage out, current in and current out, sound in and frequency out.

An analog signal uses some property of the medium to convey its information. For example, an aneroid barometer uses rotary position as a signal to convey pressure information. In electrical systems, the property that is used to convey information is voltage followed closely by frequency, current and charge.

An analog signal measures the changes in a physical phenomenon such as sound, light, temperature, position or pressure, using a transducer.

For example, during an analog sound recording, the variation in pressure of a sound that strikes a microphone creates a corresponding variation in the current passing through it. An increase in the volume of the sound causes the fluctuation of the current to increase while keeping the same rhythm.

The primary disadvantage of an analog signal is that it produces losses in the form of random variations called noise when it travels through a medium. As the signal is copied and recopied or transmitted over long distances, these random variations become dominant. In electrical systems, these variations are reduced by shielding, providing tight connections and using cable types such as coax and twisted pair.

It is very difficult to recover signal losses and distortion due to noise. When you amplify a signal to recover the attenuated parts of the signal, the noise is amplified as well.

Another method of conveying an analog signal is to use modulation. In this method, you alter any property such as amplitude or frequency, of a base signal (e.g., a sinusoidal carrier wave). For example, in amplitude modulation, you alter the amplitude of a sinusoidal voltage waveform. Similarly, frequency modulation involves changing the frequency of a signal. Other techniques such as changing the phase of the base signal also work.

Analog circuits do not involve quantization of information into digital format. Signal of sound, light, pressure or temperature are measured over the circuit.

For example, clocks with hands are called analog whereas clocks that display digits are called digital. However, many analog clocks are actually digital since the hands do not move in a smooth continuous motion, but in small steps after every second, half a second or every minute.

Digital Signal

PC is an electrical system, therefore, it can only deal with data associated with electricity.

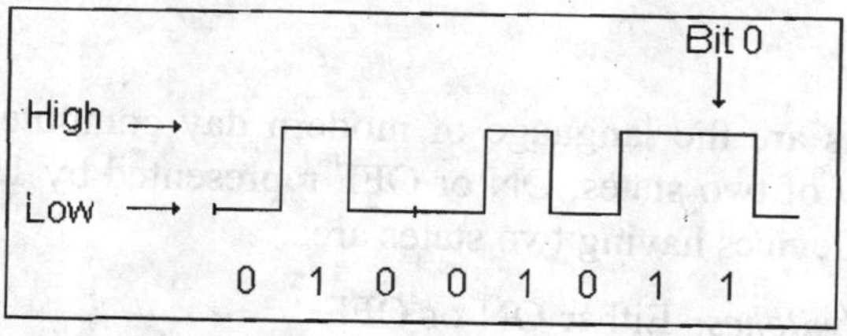

Figure 15.2 Digital signal

A digital signal is accomplished using electric switches, which are either off or on. You can consider an example of regular household switches. If a switch is off, the PC reads numeral 0 and if it the switch is on, it is read as numeral 1, as shown in the Figure 15.3.

Figure 15.3 Dataswitch

With our electric switches, we can write 0 or 1. A PC consists of a large number of switches in the form of transistors. There are literally millions of switches in the electronic components such as a PC or a TV. Each switch represents either a 0 or a 1, so we can process data using millions of 0s and 1s.

All the characters must be digitized and expressed in terms of 0s and 1s. Bits are organised in groups of 15. A group of 8 bits is called a byte.

A digital signal is a signal that is both discrete and quantized. Its primary counterpart is an analog signal. Digital signals usually occur in electronics, but may be found in other fields of engineering as well.

Digital signals may be divided into two categories:

- Signals that are inherently both discrete and quantized. For example, the number of people who visit a certain establishment every day.
- Signals that describe a phenomena, which is actually continuous in one way or another.

The signal must be discretized, quantized or both, in order to make it digital. This digitisation is required if the signal is to be processed in a computer or in any other digital device.

Because of the digital revolution, the usage of digital signals has increased significantly. Most household electronic devices are based entirely or almost entirely upon digital signals. The Internet is a network of digital signals, as is modern mobile phone communication.

Bandwidth

Digital signals are the language of modern day computers. Digital signal comprise only of two states, ON or OFF represented by 1 or 0, respectively Examples of devices having two states are:

- *Light Switches:* Either ON or OFF
- *Doors:* Either OPEN or CLOSED

Digital signals require greater bandwidth capacity than analogue signals, therefore, using digital signals to communicate is more expensive.

Signal Characteristics

• ***Baud Rate***

Baud rate is the speed of data transmission in terms of line changes that occur every second. For a digital signal of 20Hz, this is equivalent to 20 baud or 20 changes per second.

• ***Bits Per Second***

This is an expression of the number of bits per second. Where a digital signal is used, this is the same as the baud rate. When the signal is changed to another form, it will not be equal to the baud rate, as each line change can represent more than one bit (either two or four bits).

Digital signals sent via the PSTN need to be converted to analogue first by using a device called a modem. You can send digital signals without modifying them by using the IDSN.

• ***Transmission Speed***

This is a measure of how much information can be sent across the channel in a given time. For digital data communication, this is often expressed as the number of bits per second (bps). The higher the number of bits per second, the more information can be sent across the channel.

• ***Bandwidth***

Bandwidth is the frequency range of a channel, measured as the difference between the highest and lowest frequencies that the channel supports. The maximum transmission speed depends upon the available bandwidth. The larger the bandwidth, the higher the transmission speed.

A nominal voice channel has a bandwidth of 3.1KHz. In real life scenario, it is equivalent to about 1200 bps maximum for a binary digital signal.

• ***Current***

The amount of data transmitted across a point in one second. It is also called data rate, which is measured in terms of bits per second.

Grade of Communication Channels and Bandwidth

The term internal data transmission refers to the transfer of data within a computer, while external data transmission refers to the transfer of data to either local peripheral equipments such as printers, monitors or remote computers.

A data-communications channel is a path through which data travels in a medium. In other words, channels are data highways that carry signals between source and destination stations through predefined routes.

Bandwidth is the range of frequency, which a system can handle, or it is the maximum speed of data communication. Bandwidth is used in two main contexts in modern computing.

1. *Network or Communication Bandwidth:* Network or communication bandwidth is the maximum amount of data that can be handled by a network or other communications equipment such as a modem or a router. This is a slang term and should not be used by people who should know better. For more details, see the article on Shannon's law.

2. *Display Bandwidth:* Display bandwidth is the maximum frequency at which a monitor can accept an incoming signal to create a picture of a particular quality.

The grade or bandwidth of a channel determines the rate at which the channel can transmit data. A narrow bandwidth channel such as telegraph line transmits data at a rate between 45 to 90 baud. Telephone lines have a wider frequency rage and fall into the classification of voice-grade channels. They carry data at a rate between 300 to 9,600 baud. For high-speed transmission of large volumes of data, broad- band channels transmit data at rates of up to 120,000 baud. Coaxial cables, microwaves and fiber optic cables provide very high rates of data transmission.

Need of Data Transmission Over Distances

Communication is as old as civilization, but electrical communication effectively started with invent of telegraph in the early part of 19th century. Telegraphs revolutionized long-distance communications almost everywhere, reducing the time taken to communicate across a country from days to hours or minutes or from months to days between continents. The early telegraph was a very simple device as it used a direct current cell to operate an electromagnet.

At the time of invention of the telephone, most efforts were directed towards the development of a 'multiple' telegraph, one that could signal more than one code at a time. Despite digital communication getting a head start, voice telephony rapidly came to dominate the wide-area communications arena. It is only the last few decades that have seen the development of wide-area networks exclusively for data and only in the last few years that this technology, in the form of ISDN, has become available to home subscribers. Until very recently, if one wished to communicate between a home computer and a remote site, one had no choice but to use a modem to convert the computer signals into a form suitable for a voice communications medium.

The development of computer systems has been combined with improved communication facilities, which extend the power of the computer beyond the computer room and allow system benefits to be more widely available. This combination allows to use the computer facilities at remote sites, while having the expertise needed to operate the whole system at one site. The simplest example is dialling-up on the telephone network to connect a remote terminal with the computer and all its facilities.

For a large firm with numerous branch offices and several factories, a combination of computers and a communications network can be used for data transmission over long distances. Each of the factories can have its own medium-sized computer, linked to terminals within the factory and further terminals at adjacent branch offices. Communications links could also exist between adjacent branch offices. Communications links can also exist between the machines at branch offices and a larger machine at the corporate headquarters. The individual terminals can be used for collecting and disseminating the user data, with the satellite computer collating and editing this data and carrying out much of the total data processing. Major computation and corporate matters are passed to and handled by the large machine at headquarters.

This blend of computers and communications is now taken for granted as industry-standard in a number of rapidly growing business organisations. Even the most unsophisticated user may unknowingly be using very complex systems. For example, a small business may have a fairly simple terminal, which is connected to a local computer service bureau via telephone to use one of the facilities offered by that bureau.

This development was mobilised by the introduction of personal and office computing software such as word processors and desktop microcomputers. Opportunities are now being seized to take advantage of the economies of scale and added cost-efficiency offered by combining services. The convergence of voice, word processing and message systems is being capitalised on to the advantage of the user. The results are that a business manager will no longer have to turn separately to the:

- Information technology department for computer services.
- Private Automatic Branch Exchange (PABX) for telephones.
- Typing pool for document preparation.
- Mail room for document transmission.

More and more businesses and other governmental agencies are using computers in networks for basic business applications. A terminal computer is providing an economical method for distributing computing needs within an organization. Instead of using a computer terminal connected to the main computer system for performing these simple computing functions, a computer network consisting of small computers in conjunction with a larger central system with data base information is becoming a more feasible alternative.

In cases, where the offices/plants of an organisation are spread over large geographical area, it is felt that computerisation of offices/plants activities in isolation does not increase efficiency. In such cases, reliable data communication has to go hand in hand with computerisation to achieve the desired efficiency standards.

Over the period of time, the computer industry has developed numerous technologies to store and manipulate digital data. Digital information is essentially distortion-free, perfectly and infinitely replicable, instantly transportable (given fiber, cable, and future communication bandwidths), highly translatable, inherently editable, readily amenable to various forms of processing and compatible with other forms of digital information.

The network has been undergoing a process of digitization since the 1960's. Digital switching systems and their components offer, in total, an end-to-end network, which delivers more bandwidth, better error performance at lower power levels, and lower overall cost. Compression is relatively easily accomplished; yielding highly efficient utilization of bandwidth is easily enhanced through the use of data encryption techniques. Such a network is also more controllable and manageable on a centralized basis.

Digital networks also have the unique ability to treat all information streams as equals. All information is carried as a digital bit stream.

The primary factors responsible for the convergence of different forms of information are technological change and rapid diffusion of digital technology into an ever-wider array of information business. Beyond digitization, dramatic changes in the computing and telecommunications industries (primarily the faster microprocessors and increasing bandwidth) are also driving convergence. We examine each of these in turn.

Data Communication and Bandwidth

A communication or telecommunication process consists of three components:

- Source device
- Destination device
- Physical medium actively engaged in exchange of data.
- Logical medium like Protocol

Sending a message involves a device at source end and another device at the destination end. The message is communicated using a communication medium. To be more effective, you need to add one more process for getting feedback from the remote (destination) station. Therefore, there are four essential processes that are involved in a communication system.

(a) The sender creates the message.

(b) The medium carries the message.

(c) The receiver receives the message.

(d) Feedback verifies the message.

The field of data communications works as a link between the computer and the telecommunications industries. Computers are digital in nature and transfer information internally through parallel connections. Traditionally, telecommunications have been an analog process in which data is transmitted in a serial fashion.

You can transport a variety of multimedia objects over private and public networks that have data transmission facilities consisting of various types of analog and digital links and different bandwidth capabilities. The bandwidth may range from 10 Kbps of the traditional telephone lines to 1.2- Gbps capacity of high-speed ATM cell relay services.

Bandwidth capacities also depend on the nature of connecting media such as copper wire, coaxial cable, optical fiber and photonic networks in future. The bandwidth of a network also depends on the switching devices and network interfacing mechanisms. Therefore, they must also be taken into account in while designing a multimedia network

Data communication includes not only data transmission, but also data control and checking movement handling of information. In computer systems, data communication includes:

- The physical transmission circuits and networks.
- The hardware and software that support the data communication functions.
- Procedures for detecting and recovering errors.
- Rules and protocols to ensure the disciplined and comprehensible exchange of information.

Methods of Data-transmission: Communication Media

You use a variety of media to link devices in a communication network. The communication channels provided by the media can carry either analog or digital signals. All communication media fall into one of two broad classes: physical lines or wireless media.

The communication links are established using

- Paired wires and cables
- Co-axial cables
- Telephone lines
- Microwave links
- Fiber optic cables
- Satellite links

Types of Cable Media

Cables fall into two broad categories, electrical conductors and fiber optic, each containing various types of cables. Prior to an examination of fiber optic cables, this section examines two types of electrical cables: coaxial and twisted pair.

***NOTE**: Electrical cable types are frequently referred to as copper because that metal is the most frequently used conductor. You may hear fiber optic cables called simply fiber or glass.*

These types are compared in Table 15.1 and described in the following section

Table 15.1: *Characteristics of Cable Media*

TABLE	COST	MAX. DIST	MAXNUMBER	COMMON USAGE TYPE	METERS OFNODES
UTP	Very low	100	1024	Star network	2 to 155 Mbps
STP	Fairly expensive	100	270	IBM Tokenring	
Thinnet	Relatively inexpensive	185	30 per Thinnet		
Ethernet	less than STP or UTP segment				2 to 10 Mbps
Thicknet	Fairly expensive more than Thinnet, STP, or UTP; segment less than fiber-optic	500	100 per Thicknet-ethernet		2 to 10 Mbps
Fiber Optic	Most expensive, but costs are dropping	20km	No limit	FDDI	100 Mbps

You should consider the following characteristics when examining cables:

- Resistance to electrical magnetic interference (EMI).
- The Bandwidth range offered by the cable. LANs generally carry data at the rate between 1 to 100 megabits per second and require moderately high bandwidth.
- Attenuation characteristics of the cable. Attenuation describes how cables reduce the strength of a signal with distance. Resistance is one factor that contributes to signal attenuation.
- Cost of the cable.

***NOTE**: EMI can be a major headache for LAN technicians. Many electrical devices generate magnetic fields that produce unwanted electrical currents in data cables. The noise that results from these currents can degrade data signals, sometimes stopping communication altogether due to excessive error rates. Electrical motors and fluorescent lights are common sources of EMI, and it can be a genuine challenge to install cables in a network in an environment such as factories that contain many electrical devices.*

Networking of Computers

A network is nothing more than two or more computers connected together by a cable so that they can exchange information. In a computer network, all the computers in an office are connected through cables. You need to install a special network adapter card, which is an electronic circuit card that goes inside your computer to plug in the cable, set up and configure special network software.

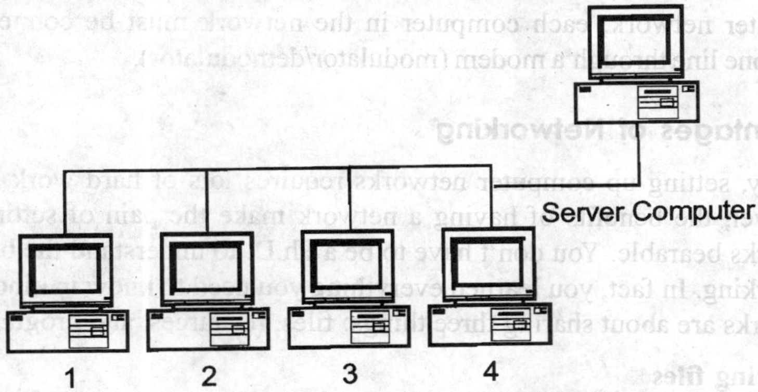

Figure 15.4 Networking of Computers

Shared Resources through Networking

Above figure shows a typical network with four PCs. You can see here that all four computers are connected together with a network cable. You can also see that the server computer has a laser printer attached to it. Because of the network, all the terminal computers can also use the laser printer attached to the server.

Technically, a computer connected to the network is called a node. A computer is said to be online, if it is turned on and is able to access the network. However, if the computer is unable to access the network, it is said to be offline. A computer can be offline due several reasons. It could be turned off, it could be broken, the cable that connects it to the network could be unplugged or there could be a wad of gum jammed into the disk drive.

In general terms, a computer network is an interconnection of various computer systems located at the same or different places. The interconnection is done through a communication link also known as the physical layer of the network. This link is totally transparent to the users of the network. The interfacing software known as protocol, which enables a user in one location to freely access a computer system in another location, provides the transparency of the communication link.

Computer networks include computers along with intelligent peripheral equipment such as automatic teller machines and point-of-sale terminals equipped with microprocessors. The computers are interconnected by telephone lines, microwave relays and other high-speed communication links for the purpose of exchanging data and sharing equipments. Networking has been implemented on all levels, from local to international, in diverse sectors of society. For example, networks are used by government organisations for rapid retrieval of information from databases at central locations and by banks and retail merchants for the transfer of funds or credit verification. If telephone lines are adopted for a computer network, each computer in the network must be connected to a telephone line through a modem (modulator/demodulator).

Advantages of Networking

Frankly, setting up computer networks requires lots of hard work and pain. However, the benefits of having a network make the pain of setting up the networks bearable. You don't have to be a Ph.D. to understand the benefits of networking. In fact, you learned everything you need to know in kindergarten. Networks are about sharing three things: files, resources, and programs.

- **Sharing files**

Networks enable you to share information with other computers connected to the network. Depending on how you set your network, you can share information using different ways. The most direct way is to send the files from your computer directly to your friend's computer. The second way is to send your file to an intermediate resting place where your friend can pick it up later. For example, you drop a bag full of ransom money at a phone booth. A third way is to permanently store the file at that intermediate place, where both of you can get the file whenever you want. One way or the other, the data travels to your friend's computer through the network cable.

- **Sharing resources**

This means that you can set up certain computer resources such as a disk drive or a printer, so that all of the computers on the network can access them. For example, the laser printer attached to server computer is a shared resource. That means that anyone on the network can use it.

Disk drives can also be shared resources. In fact, a disk drive must be set up as a shared resource in order to share files with other users. Suppose Computer

No. 3 wants to share a file with No. 4 and a shared disk drive has been set up on No. 2's computer. Computer No. 3 has to copy his file to the shared disk drive in No. 2's Computer and tell the No. 4 where he has put it. Then, when No. 4 gets around to it, he can copy the file from No1's computer to his own.

In addition, you can share other resources such as CD-ROM drives or modems, which let you access other computers that aren't on your network).

• **Sharing programs**

Sometimes, it is better to save programs that everyone uses on a shared disk, rather than keep separate copies of the programs on each computer. For example, if you have ten computer users who all use AutoCAD, you can store AutoCAD -on each computer or you can store AutoCAD on a shared disk.

• **Backups**

As all data is stored on the server, backing up critical data becomes a simple process.

• **Communication**

The biggest benefit, however, comes in the form of better communication facilities such as electronic mail and groupware applications. Through electronic mail or e-mail, members of a network can send messages and ensure safe delivery of data to other members, even when they are not there. Groupware applications allow users to work collectively on the same document.

Disadvantages of Networking

• **Crashes**

The biggest disadvantage is on a server-based network. When the server crashes, work gets disrupted as all network resources and its benefits are lost. Unless proper precautions are taken to ensure regular backups, the crash may result in the loss of critical data and time.

• **Data security problems**

As all the data resources are pooled together, it is possible for unauthorised personnel to access classified information if network security is weak or poorly implemented.

• **Lack of privacy**

A network may also result in loss of privacy, as anyone, especially your boss, with the right network privileges may read your private e-mail messages.

Some Examples of Networks

Because computers process data so quickly, you can justifiable say that they conquer time. With a computer, you can perform millions of calculations that would have taken days, weeks or even years by hand in seconds. Computer networks also enable us to conquer space problems. Here are some examples:

- Researches at a small state university need a supercomputer to calculate the results of a sophisticated bioinformatic problem. But they don't have the money to travel to a major supercomputer facility. In the past, these researchers would have given up. Today, they can send their data to a supercomputer centre through the Internet. The next day, they receive the results.
- A Tokyo-based insurance company has discovered a place where many young educated workers live. Even better, these workers do not mind taking clerical jobs such as processing insurance claim forms. The place is known as BHEL colony at Govindpura, Bhopal. The company sends forms from Tokyo to Bhopal through a satellite network. Workers process the forms there and send them back to Tokyo through the same network.
- You need some information from the MIT, but you don't have the time to visit it. With the aid of a program called Netscape Navigator, you can tour several MIT collections while sitting in front of your computer. You will see beautiful, full-colour graphic images of satellites, complex computer installations and research-ware.

Computer networks are also used for electronic mail, teleconferences and discussion groups such as those found on a computer bulletin board system (BBS).

TYPES OF NETWORKS

- *Local Area Network (LAN)* — A system of networked computers and other hardware resources spread in a small area such as a building.
- *Wide Area Network (WAN)* — A geographically dispersed communications network, with many owners, linking computers for the purpose of communicating with each other such as a national network for airline reservations or the Internet.
- *Metropolitan Area Network (MAN)* — WAN limited to only one metropolises.

LAN

A LAN consists of network interface cards that are fit inside the connected computers and cables (or an equivalent wireless connection) to connect these computers together. It also includes protocol software to move data from computer to computer, user interface software to connect the user and the network and operating system software to actually service users' needs for resources such as files and printers. Finally, you can say that a LAN runs end-user applications.

Once a network spans more than a few miles, such as a campus environment, it can be referred to as a Metropolitan Area Network (MAN). A MAN spans a region such as a city. A WAN brings companies into the sphere of networking by connecting computers in the entire enterprise, which may span over several cities, states and countries.

In the last 15 years, LANs have become a key business tool used by companies worldwide rather than just an experimental technology.. A LAN is a high-speed communications system designed to link computers and other data processing devices together within a small geographic area such as a workgroup, department or a single floor of a multi-storey building. Several LANs can also be interconnected within a building or campus of buildings to extend connectivity.

LANs have become popular because they allow users to share vital computing resources including expensive hardware such as printers and CD-ROM drives, application programs and most importantly, the information the users need to do their jobs. Prior to the development of LAN technology, individual computers were isolated from each other and limited in their range of applications. By linking these individual computers over LANs, their usefulness and productivity have been increased enormously. But a LAN is a local network by its very nature. It is confined to a fairly small area such as a building or even a single floor of a building. To realize the full benefit of computer networking, it is critical to link the individual LANs into an enterprise-wide backbone network that connects all the employees and computing resources of an enterprise, no matter how geographically dispersed they may be.

Today's LANs and LAN internetworks are powerful, flexible and easy to use, but they incorporate many sophisticated technologies that must work together flawlessly. For a LAN to really benefit an organization, it must be designed to meet the organization's changing communications requirements. Building a LAN is a process of choosing different pieces and matching them together. This course is designed to help students understand the fundamentals of how LANs operate, what are the different technology choices for building a LAN and the ramifications of choosing one option over another. We have also discussed the concept of internetworking or connecting disparate and geographically dispersed LANs together to form an enterprise system, the different technologies and products available to do so and the benefits and limitations of each.

NETWORK TOPOLOGIES

The word topology is commonly used to discuss the properties of various types of networks. Topology is the branch of mathematics that examines the characteristics of geometric shapes. Networks have shapes and the shape a network takes has much to do with the way it functions.

The physical topology of a network is the layout or actual appearance of the cabling scheme used on a network.

The logical topology of a network describes how the data flows through the physical topology. You soon discover that similar-looking networks can have quite different logical topologies.

Physical Topologies

All physical topologies are variations of two fundamental methods of connecting devices: point-to-point and multipoint. After examining these two fundamental topologies, several variations are examined.

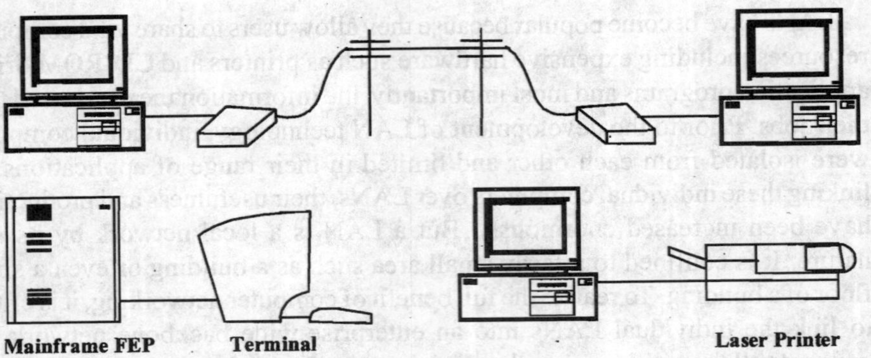

Figure 15.5 ptp

- ***Point-to-Point Topology***

Point-to-point (PTP) topology connects two nodes directly together.

The following examples are pure point-to-point links:

- Two computers communicating via modems.
- A mainframe terminal communicating with a front-end processor.
- A workstation communicating along a parallel cable to a printer.

In a point-to-point link, two devices monopolize a communication medium. Because the medium is not shared, a mechanism is not needed to identify the computers. Therefore, a simple, two-device point-to-point network has no need for addressing.

Point-to-point links can be simplex, half duplex, or full duplex. When devices must engage in bi-directional communication on a half-duplex link, some turnaround mechanisms must be in place to switch the roles of the sending and receiving devices.

- ***Multipoint Topology***

Multipoint topologies link three or more devices together through a single communication medium. Multipoint topologies work much like a party-line telephone service where several subscribers are connected to the same telephone line.

Because multipoint topologies share a common channel, each device needs a way to identify itself and the device to which it wants to send information. The method used to identify senders and receivers is called addressing.

Types of Physical Topologies

The following four types of physical topologies are frequently used in computer networking:

- Star
- Bus
- Ring
- Hybrid

(i) Star Topology

The star topology is a popular method of connecting the computers and resources through cables in a network. In star topology, each device connects to a central point via a point-to-point link. Depending on the logical architecture used, several names are used for the central point including the following:

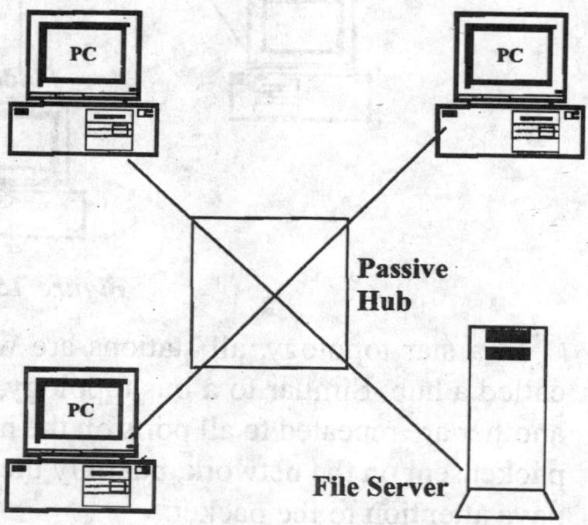

Figure 15.6 Star

Passive hub: A passive hub is a simple signal splitter. Its main function is to connect the arms of the star while maintaining the proper electrical characteristics.

A passive hub routes traffic to all nodes. This means that a tremendous load is created when much communication takes place between computers. Every computer has the additional burden of reading the address of each piece of information it receives to determine if the information is intended for that computer. Information containing other addresses is discarded.

Active hub: An active hub performs the same function as a passive hub, but contains electronic circuits that regenerate and retransmit the information. Thus, active hubs can be used to extend the size of a network.

Intelligent hub: Intelligent hubs perform the same functions as passive and active hubs; however, they can make informed path selections and perform some network management. Intelligent hubs route traffic only to the branch of the star on which the receiving node is located. If redundant paths exist, an intelligent hub can route information around normally used paths when cable problems occur.

Routers, bridges, & switches are examples of hub devices that can route data packets intelligently. Intelligent hubs can also incorporate diagnostic features that make it easier to troubleshoot network problems.

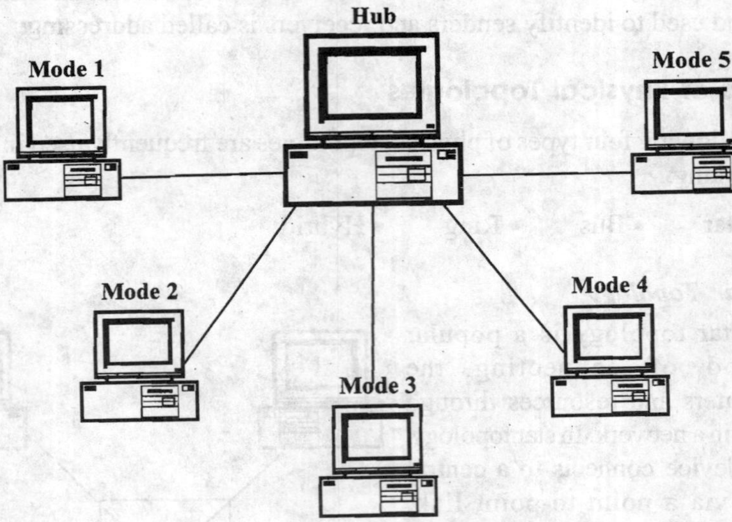

Figure 15.7 Star

In a star topology, all stations are wired to a central wiring concentrator called a hub. Similar to a bus topology, data packets sent from one station to another are repeated to all ports on the hub. This allows all stations to see each packet sent on the network, but only the station to which a packet is addressed pays attention to the packet.

The diagram illustrates a star topology LAN, which is a more robust topology than the bus topology. In a star topology, each station is connected to a central wiring concentrator or hub, by an individual length of twisted pair cable. The cable is connected to the Network Interface Cards (NIC) of a terminal computer at one end and to a port on the hub at the other end. The hubs are placed in wiring closets that are centrally located in a building.

Benefits of Stars

- Most modern cabling systems are designed in a star physical topology. The benefits of the star topology are many, including the following:
- Each device is isolated on its own cable. This makes it easy to isolate individual devices from the network by disconnecting them from the wiring hub.

- All data goes through the central point, which can be equipped with diagnostic devices that make it easy to trouble shoot and manage the network.
- Hierarchical organization allows isolation of traffic on the channel. This is beneficial when several, but not all, computers place a heavy load on the network. Traffic from those heavily used computers can be separated from the rest or dispersed throughout for a more even flow of traffic.

Disadvantages of Star Topology

Star topology has the following disadvantages:

- Because point-to-point wiring is utilized for each node, more cable is required.
- Hub failures can disable large segments of the network.

Examples of Star Topology

The following types of networks are examples of star topologies:

- ARCnet
- 10Base-T, 100Base-TX

  StarLAN

Token Ring is also wired in a physical star. However, as you will learn later in this lesson, physical wiring and the logical characteristics of Token Ring are quite different.

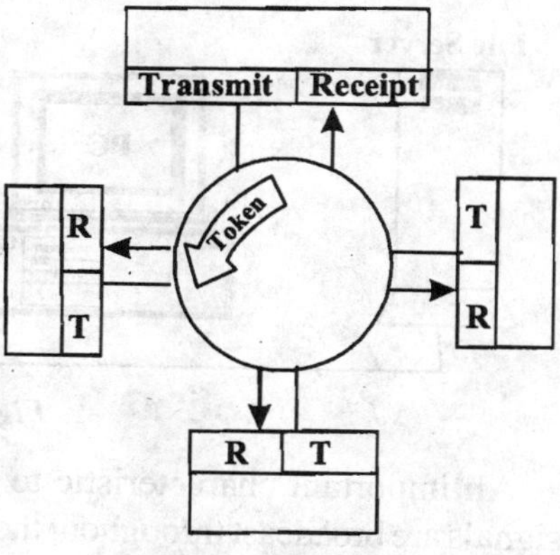

Figure 15.8 Ring

(ii) Ring Topology

Ring topology is a physical topology in which devices are connected in a closed loop using point-to-point links. In the diagram, you can see how each node on the ring acts as a repeater. It receives transmission from the previous node and amplifies it before passing it on.

Ring topology has the following advantage:

- Each repeater duplicates the data signals so that very little signal degradation occurs.

Ring topology has the following disadvantages:

- A break in the ring can disable the entire network. Many ring designs incorporate extra cabling that can be switched in if a primary cable fails.
- Because each node must have the capability of functioning as a repeater, the networking devices tend to be more expensive.

Examples of Ring Topology

The following are examples of ring topologies:

- IBM Token Ring (although wired as a star)
- Fiber Distributed Data Interface (FDDI)

(iii) Bus Topology

In a bus topology, all devices are attached to the same transmission medium. The medium has a physical beginning and end. All buses are implemented using electrical cables, usually coax and the ends of the cable must be terminated with a terminating resistor that matches the impedance of the cable. The terminating resistor prevents data reflections that come across as data corruption. The bus is considered a multipoint system because all devices tap into the same backbone cable.

Figure 15.9 Bus

An important characteristic to remember in bus topologies is that all data signals are broadcast throughout the entire bus structure. In the following diagram, if node B sends a signal to node C, the signal propagates for the length of the cable and is seen by nodes A and D as well. It is necessary to have an addressing mechanism so that each node understands which messages it is to receive and which to ignore.

Bus Type LAN

When Station B sends a packet to another station on the LAN, it passes by all of the stations connected to that LAN. On the bus network illustrated here, the electrical signal representing the packet travels away from the sending station in both the directions on the shared cable. All stations will see the packet, but only the station it is addressed to will pay attention to it.

Preamble	7 bytes
SFD	1 bytes
Destination Address	2 or 6 bytes
Source Address	2 or 6 bytes
Length Indicator	2 bytes
Data	
Padding	
FCS	4 bytes

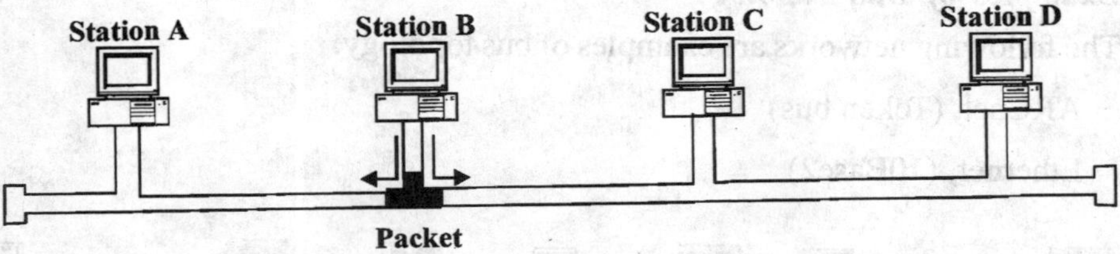

In a shared media network, when one station wishes to send a message to another station, it uses the software in the station to put the message in an envelope. This envelope, called a packet, consists of message data surrounded by a header and trailer that carry special information used by the network software to identify the destination station. One of the pieces of information placed in the packet header is the address of the destination station.

The NIC then transmits the packet onto the LAN. The packet is transmitted as a stream of data bits represented by two different voltages of electrical signals. As it travels along the shared cable, all the stations attached to it can see the packet. As it goes by the NIC in each station, the NIC checks the destination address in the packet header to determine if the packet is addressed to it. When the packet passes the station to which it is addressed, the NIC at that station copies the packet and then takes the data out of the envelope and gives it to the computer.

The diagram shows one source station sending a single message packet to one destination station. If the message that the source station wants to send is too big to fit into one packet, then the message is sent in a series of packets. On a shared access LAN, however, many stations share the same cable. Since each individual packet is small, it takes very little time to travel to the ends of the cable where the electrical signal dissipates. So after a packet carrying a message between one pair of stations passes along the cable, another station can transmit a packet to whatever station it needs to send a message. In this way, many devices can share the same LAN medium.

Benefits of Bus Topology

Bus topology has the following advantage:

- Cabling costs are minimized because of the common trunk.

Disadvantages of Bus topology

Disadvantages of Bus Topology are as Follows:

- Difficult to trouble shoot because no central distribution points exist.
- If the cable breaks, it can disable the entire segment of the network because they remove the required termination from each of the two cable fragments.

Examples of Bus Topology

The following networks are examples of bus topology:

ARCnet, (Token bus)

Ethernet, (10Base2)

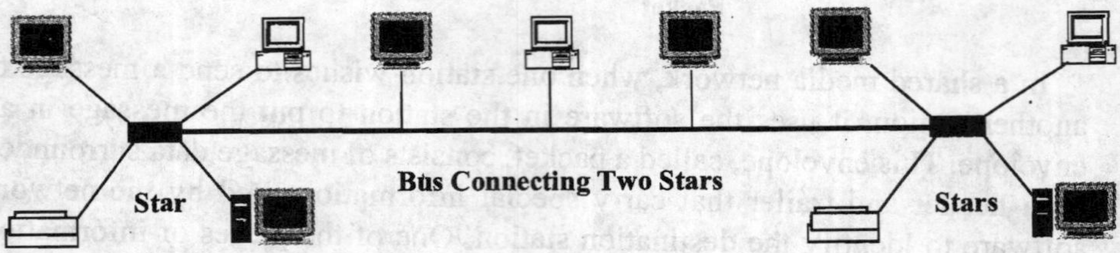

(iv) Hybrid Topology

The hybrid topology scheme combines multiple topologies into one large topology. The hybrid network is common in large wide-area networks. Because each topology has its own strengths and weaknesses, several different types can be combined for maximum effectiveness.

Benefits of Hybrid Topology

Hybrid topology has the following advantages:

- One company can combine the benefits of several different types of topologies.
- Workgroup efficiency and traffic can be customized.

Disadvantages of Hybrid Topology

The disadvantages of hybrid topology include the following:

- Devices on one topology cannot be placed into another topology without some hardware changes.

Examples of Hybrid Topology

- An example of a hybrid topology is as follows:

A company can place its accounting database users on a ring for better throughput, and its secretarial staff on a bus for ease of cabling.

***NOTE**: Throughput is the amount of data transferred per unit of time. It is viewed in terms of bits, bytes, or packets per second.*

PACKET TRANSMISSION

Historically, most communications systems started with point-to-point links, which directly connect the users wishing to communicate using a dedicated communications circuit. As the distance between users increases beyond the length of the cable (*e.g.*, the length of a telegraph wire), the connection between the users was formed by a number of sections, which were connected end-to-end in series to form the circuit. The connection between the users (A and D) in the figure below (*i.e.*, A and D) is represented by a series of links (AB, BC, and CD) and each link connects two entities known as nodes. For a point-to-point circuit, (also known as a permanent circuit) the nodes are patch panels, which provide a simple connection between the two links (*i.e.*, the two transmission circuits).

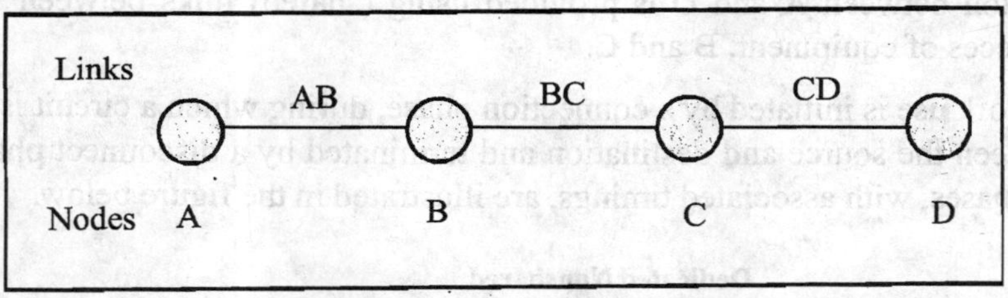

Figure 15.10 Switching

A connection between two systems A & D formed from 3 links.

As the number of connected users increased, it has become infeasible to provide a circuit, which connects every user to every other user and some sharing of the transmission circuits (known as "switching") has become necessary. To accomplish this goal, the data communications network evolved. A network is a set of nodes that are interconnected to permit the exchange of information. Three switching techniques have been proposed for building networks:

- Circuit switching
- Message switching
- Packet switching (both virtual circuit and datagram)

All these switching techniques allow sharing of communication facilities among multiple users (end systems), and use equipments located at the nodes (intermediate systems) to replace the patch-panels used in a point-to-point connection. Packet switching is most often used for data communication. Most networks consist of many links, which allow more than one path between nodes. A data communication network must be able to select an appropriate path for each required connection.

Any of these three approaches (circuit switching, message switching and packet switching) could yield minimum delay in a particular situation, though situations where message switching yields minimum delay are rare. The relative performance of circuit switching and packet switching depends strongly on the speed and cost of establishing a connection.

Circuit Switching

Circuit switching is the most familiar technique used to build a communications network. It is used for ordinary telephone calls. It allows communications equipment and circuits, to be shared among users. Each user has sole access to a circuit (functionally equivalent to a pair of copper wires) during network use. Consider communication between two points A and D in a network. The connection between A and D is provided using (shared) links between two other pieces of equipment, B and C.

Network use is initiated by a connection phase, during which a circuit is set up between the source and destination and terminated by a disconnect phase. These phases, with associated timings, are illustrated in the figure below.

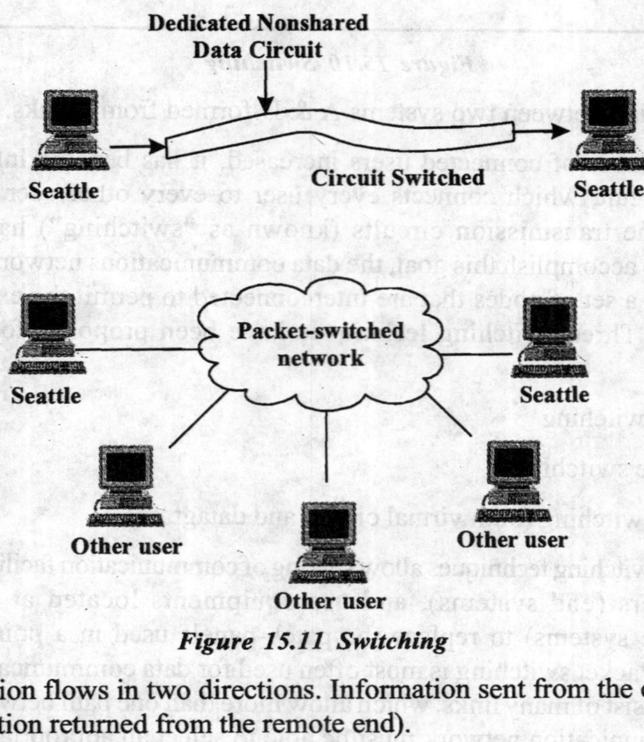

Figure 15.11 Switching

(Information flows in two directions. Information sent from the calling end and information returned from the remote end).

After a user requests a circuit, the desired destination address must be communicated to the local switching node (B). In a telephony network, this is achieved by dialling the number.

Node B receives the connection request and identifies a path to the destination (D) via an intermediate node (C). This is followed by a circuit connection phase handled by the switching nodes and initiated by allocating a free circuit to C (link BC), followed by transmission of a call request signal from node B to node C. In turn, node C allocates a link (CD) and the request is then passed to node D after a similar delay.

The circuit is then established and may be used. While it is available for use, resources (*i.e.,* in the intermediate equipment at B and C) and capacity on the links between the equipment are dedicated to the use of the circuit.

After the completion of the connection, a signal confirming circuit establishment (a connect signal in the diagram) is returned; this flows directly back to node A with no search delays since the circuit has been established. Transfer of the data in the message then begins. After data transfer, the circuit is disconnected and a simple disconnect phase is included after the end of the data transmission.

Phone networks use circuit switching; therefore, an end-to-end circuit must be set up before the call can begin. A fixed share of network resources is reserved for the call and no other call can use those resources until the original connection is closed. This means that a long silence between two teenagers uses the same resources as an active negotiation between two fast-talking lawyers. One advantage of circuit switching is that it enables performance guarantees such as guaranteed maximum delay, which is essential for real-time applications like voice conversations. It is also much easier to do detailed accounting for circuit-switched network usage.

Delays for setting up a circuit connection can be high, especially if ordinary telephone equipment is used. Call set up time with conventional equipment is typically on the order of 5 to 25 seconds after completion of dialling. New fast circuit switching techniques can however reduce delays to approximately 140 milliseconds. Trade-offs between circuit switching and other types of switching depend strongly on switching times.

Packet Switching Technologies

The telephone network is circuit switched, while data networks such as the Internet are packet switched. When a telephone call is made, a live circuit is set up through the network and a fixed amount of bandwidth, typically 64 Kbps, is reserved for the duration of the call.

Packet technology breaks data into small pieces, each containing an address. Sending a packet is much like mailing a letter; many envelopes of data enter the network at the same time, where they may travel over the same or different routes. Eventually, most of them arrive at the destination.

Packets are more efficient than circuits, because a single line can carry multiple messages simultaneously. The problem is 'real-time' communications, like voice or video, doesn't work well on packet networks because there is no way to know when the packets will arrive or in what order.

Packet technology is improving, however and it is only a matter of time before packet switched networks can support telephone calls, with an acceptable level of quality, at a fraction of the cost of a circuit switched call.

Packet switching refers to protocols in which messages are divided into packets before they are sent. Each packet is then transmitted individually and can even follow different routes to its destination. Once all the packets forming a message arrive at the destination, they are recompiled into the original message.

Most modern Wide Area Network (WAN) protocols, including TCP/IP, X.25 and Frame Relay, are based on packet-switching technologies. In contrast, normal telephone service is based on a circuit-switching technology, in which a dedicated line is allocated for transmission between two parties. Circuit switching is ideal when you need to transmit data quickly and you want the data packets arrive in the same order in which they are sent. This is the case with most real-time data such as live audio and video. Packet switching is more efficient and robust for data that can withstand some delays in transmission such as e-mail messages and Web pages.

A packet network is formed by links, which connect packet network equipments. Communication between A and D using circuits, which are shared using packet switching.

There are two important benefits of packet switching. The first and most important benefit is that since packets are short, the communication links between the nodes are only allocated to transferring a single message for a short period of time while transmitting each packet. Longer messages require a series of packets to be sent, but do not require the link to be dedicated between the transmission of each packet. The implication is that packets belonging to other messages may be sent between the packets of the message being sent from A to D. This provides a much fairer sharing of the resources of each of the links.

Another benefit of packet switching is known as pipelining. Pipelining is visible in the figure above. At the time packet 1 is sent from B to C, packet 2 is sent from A to B; packet 1 is sent from C to D while packet 2 is sent from B to C and packet 3 is sent from A to B and so forth. This simultaneous use of communications links represents a gain in efficiency, the total delay for transmission across a packet network may be considerably less than for message switching, despite the inclusion of a header in each packet rather than in each message.

The Internet uses the packet-switching technology. The term packet refers to the fact that the data stream from your computer is broken up into packets of about 200 bytes (on average), which are then sent out onto the network. Each packet contains a header with information necessary for routing the packet from source to destination. Thus each packet in a data stream is independent.

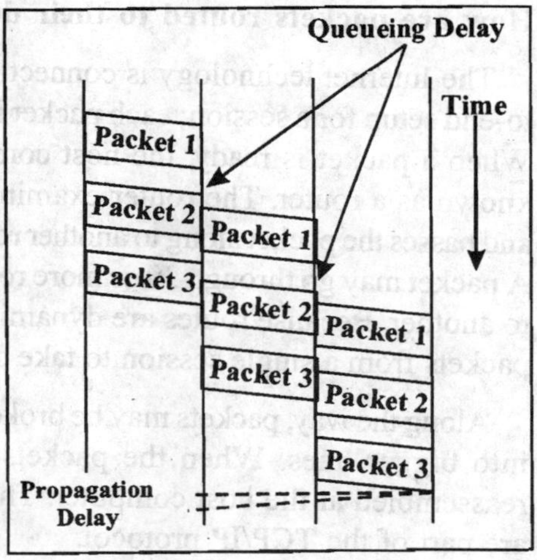

Figure 15.12 Packetsetup

The main advantage of packet switching is that it permits statistical multiplexing on the communications lines. This implies that the packets from many different sources can share a line, allowing for very efficient use of the fixed capacity. With current technology, packets are generally accepted onto the network on a first-come, first-served basis. If the network becomes overloaded, packets are delayed or discarded.

A new technology, ATM, attempts to combine the best of both worlds-the guaranteed delivery of circuit-switched networks and the robustness and efficiency of packet-switching networks.

Why do data networks use packet switching?

Economics can explain most of the preference for packet switching over circuit-switching on the Internet and other public networks. Circuit networks use lots of lines in order to economize on switching and routing. This means that once a call is set up, a line is dedicated to its use, regardless of its rate of data flow and no further routing calculations are needed. This network design makes sense when lines are cheap relative to switches.

The costs of both communications lines and computers have been declining exponentially for decades. However, since about 1970, switches (computers) have become relatively cheaper than lines. At this point, packet switching became economic. Also, lines are shared by multiple connections at the cost of many more routing calculations by the switches. This preference for using many relatively cheap routers to manage few expensive lines is evident in the topology of the backbone networks. For example, in NSFNET, any packet coming on to the backbone had to pass through two routers at its entry point and again at its exit point. A packet entering at Cleveland and exiting at New York traversed four routers but only one leased T-3 communications line.

How are packets routed to their destination?

The Internet technology is connectionless. This means that there is no end-to-end setup for a session; each packet is independently routed to its destination. When a packet is ready, the host computer sends it on to another computer, known as a router. The router examines the destination address in the header and passes the packet along to another router, chosen by a route-finding algorithm. A packet may go through 30 or more routers in its travel from one host computer to another. Because routes are dynamically updated, it is possible for different packets from a single session to take different routes to the destination.

Along the way, packets may be broken up into smaller packets or reassembled into bigger ones. When the packets reach their final destination, they are reassembled at the host computer. The instructions for doing this reassembly are part of the TCP/IP protocol.

Some packet switching networks are connection-oriented namely, X.25 networks, such as Tymnet and frame-relay networks. In such a network, a connection is set up before the transmission begins, just as in a circuit-switched network. A fixed route is defined and the information necessary to match packets to their session and defined route is stored in memory tables in the routers. Thus, connectionless networks economize on router memory and connection set-up time, while connection-oriented networks economize on routing calculations.

NETWORK APPLICATION

Ethernet

The Ethernet is the most widely used protocol for LANs. It strikes a good balance between speed, price, ease of installation and supportability. Approximately 80 percent of all LAN networks use Ethernet protocol.

The Ethernet standard is defined by the Institute of Electrical and Electronics Engineers (IEEE) in a specification commonly known as IEEE 802.3. The 802.3 specification covers rules for configuring Ethernet LANs, the types of media that can be used and how the elements of the network should interact. The Ethernet protocol provides the services for the Physical and Data Link layers of the OSI reference model.

One element of the 802.3 (or 802.3u) specification states that Ethernet networks run at a data rate of 10 million bits per second (10 Mbps) or 100 million bits per second (100 Mbps) in the case of Fast Ethernet.

Carrier Sense Multiple Access with Collision Detection (CSMA/CD) is another important element defined by the 802.3 specification. In this method, each station contends for access to the shared medium. It is possible for two stations to try sending packets at the same time, which results in a collision on the LAN. In Ethernet networks, collisions are considered normal events and the CSMA/CD access method is designed to quickly restore the network to normal activity after a collision occurs.

Ethernet Media and Topologies

An important part of designing and installing a LAN is the selection of appropriate medium and topology for the environment. Ethernet networks can be configured using either a star or a bus topology and installed using any of three different media.

Earlier, coaxial cable was the original LAN medium and used in a bus topology. In this topology, the coaxial cable forms a single bus to which all stations are attached. This topology is rarely used in new LAN installations today because it is relatively difficult to accommodate adding new users or moving existing users from one location to another. It is also difficult to troubleshoot problems on a bus LAN unless it is very small.

Ethernet networks can be built using three different types of media: shielded and unshielded twisted pair, coaxial and fiber optic cables. By far the most commonly used medium is twisted pair because it is associated with the very popular star topology. It is inexpensive, and very easy to install, troubleshoot and repair. Twisted pair cable comes in both unshielded and shielded forms. Unshielded twisted pair (UTP) cable used for LANs is similar to telephone cable but has somewhat more stringent specifications regarding its susceptibility to outside Electromagnetic Interference (EMI) than common telephone wire. Shielded Twisted Pair (STP), as its name implies, comes with a shielding around the cable to provide more protection against EMI.

Of the two types of twisted pair cable, UTP is by far the most commonly used. The specification for running Ethernet on UTP is called 10Base-T. This stands for 10 Mbps, baseband signaling (the signaling method used by Ethernet networks), over twisted pair cable. Other Ethernet specifications include 10Base5, which uses a thick coaxial cable, and 10Base2 that uses a thin coaxial cable media. Today, 10Base5 is seldom installed in new Ethernet networks and 10Base2 is used only in very small office networks or networks in high EMI areas. An additional standard, 10Base-FL, allows Ethernet to run on fiber optic link.

Fast Ethernet

An extension of the popular 10Base-T Ethernet standard, Fast Ethernet transports data at 100 Mbps. With rules defined by the IEEE 802.3u standard, Fast Ethernet leverages the familiar Ethernet technology and retains the CSMA/CD protocol of 10 Mbps Ethernet. Three types of Fast Ethernet are available: 100Base-TX, which runs over Category 5 UTP; 100Base-T4, which runs over existing Category 3 UTP and 100Base-FX, which operates over multimode fiber optic cabling.

Token Ring LANs

Another major LAN technology in use today is Token Ring. Token Ring rules are defined in the IEEE 802.5 specification. Like Ethernet, the Token Ring protocol provides services at the Physical and Data Link layers of the OSI model. Token Ring networks can be run at two different data rates, 4 Mbps or 16 Mbps.

The access method used on Token Ring networks is called token passing. Token passing is a deterministic access method in which collisions are prevented by assuring that only one station can transmit at any given time. This is accomplished by passing a special packet called a token from one station to another around a ring. A station can only send a packet when it gets the free token. When a station gets a free token and transmits a packet, it travels in one direction around the ring, passing all of the other stations along the way. As with Ethernet, the packet is usually addressed to a single station and when it passes by that station, the packet is copied. The packet continues to travel around the ring until it returns to the sending station, which removes it and sends a free token to the next station around the ring.

Token Ring Topology and Media

Token Ring networks use what is called a ring topology. However, it is actually implemented in what can best be described as a collapsed ring or star wired ring that looks like a physical star topology.

Basic Ring Topology LAN

The ring topology used in Token Ring networks is a collapsed ring that looks like a star topology. Each station is connected to a Token Ring wiring connector by a single twisted pair cable with two wire pairs. One pair serves as the inbound portion of the ring (also known as the receive pair) and the other pair serves as the outbound or transmit pair.

In Token Ring LANs, each station is connected to a Token Ring wiring concentrator, called a Multistation Access Unit (MAU), using an individual run of twisted pair cable. Like Ethernet hubs, MAUs are located in wiring closets.

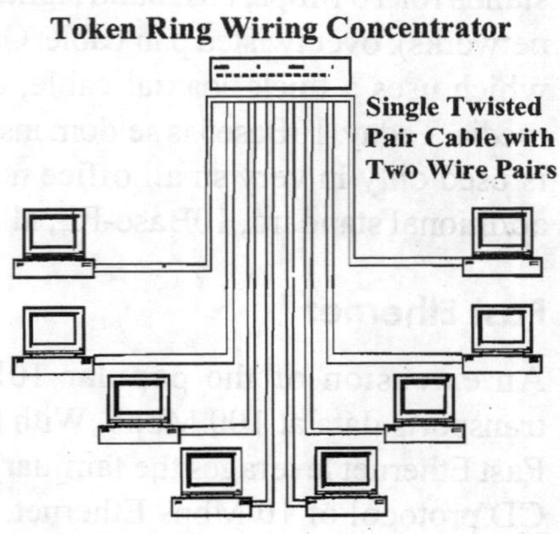

Figure 15.13 Ring

FDDI

Fiber Distributed Data Interface, commonly known as FDDI, provides data transport at 100 Mbps, a much higher data rate than Ethernet or Token Ring. Originally, FDDI networks required fiber optic cable, but today they can be run on UTP as well. Fiber is still preferred in many FDDI networks because it can be used over much greater distances than UTP cable. Like Token Ring, FDDI uses a token passing media access method. Also, it is usually configured in a collapsed ring, or star topology. FDDI is used primarily as a backbone, a segment of network that links several individual workgroup or department LANs together in a single building. It is also used to link several building LANs together in a campus environment.

WAN (Wide Area Network)

The term Wide Area Network (WAN) is used to describe a computer network spanning a regional, national or global area. For example, for a large company, the head quarters might be at Delhi and regional branches at Bombay, Madras, Bang lore and Calcutta. Here regional centres are connected to head quarters through WAN.

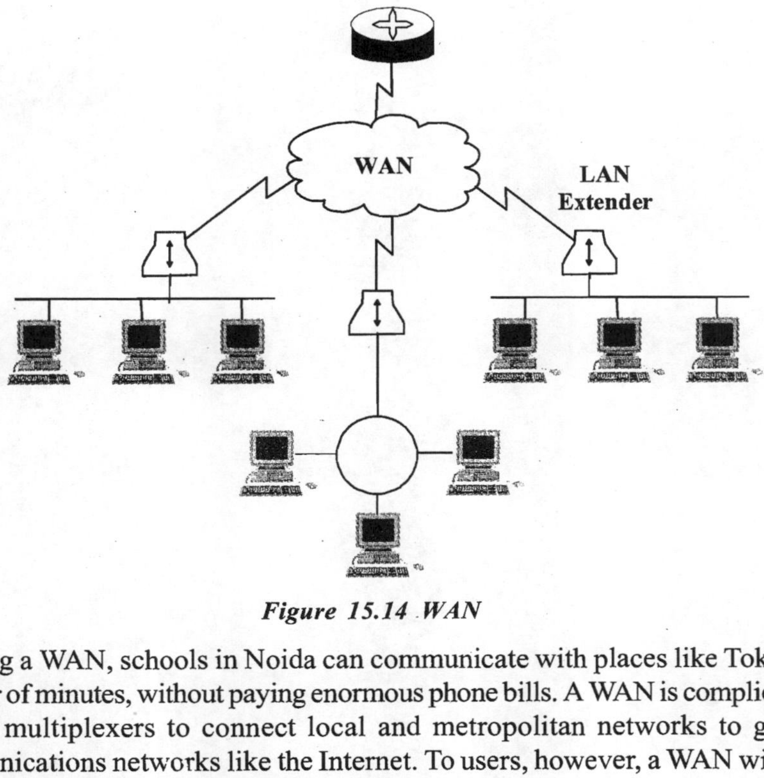

Figure 15.14 WAN

Using a WAN, schools in Noida can communicate with places like Tokyo in a matter of minutes, without paying enormous phone bills. A WAN is complicated. It uses multiplexers to connect local and metropolitan networks to global communications networks like the Internet. To users, however, a WAN will not appear to be much different than a LAN or a MAN.

The distance between computers connected to WAN is larger. Therefore the transmission medium used is normally telephone lines, microwaves or satellite links.

WAN may link the computers by means of cables, optical fibers or satellites, but their users commonly access the networks via a modem, which refers to a device that allows computers to communicate over telephone lines). The largest wide-area network is the Internet, a collection of networks and gateways linking millions of computer users on every continent.

CHAPTER 16 Database Management Systems

DATA AND INFORMATION

Data

Data refers to the basic facts and entities such as names and numbers. Examples of data are dates, weights, prices, costs, numbers of items sold, employee names, product names, addresses, tax codes, registration marks etc.

Data consists of a series of facts or statements that may have been collected, stored, processed and/or manipulated but have not been organized or placed into context. When data is organized, it becomes information. Information can be processed and used to draw generalised conclusions or knowledge.

Example: A file listing all the orders placed through an online service is an example of data. If we sort the data by ZIP code and summarize the number of orders that come from each city, we have created information. We can acquire knowledge by taking this information and making statements such as "Most orders for Widget X come from the north-eastern United States."

In a business, data input is a collection of facts about environmental elements such as consumers, suppliers, competitors and government. Data are refers to the raw materials consumed in production processes used in factories or industries.

Information

Information is the data that is converted into a more useful form. Information is used for direct utilisation of mankind, as it helps human beings in their decision making process. For example, time table, merit list, report card, headed tables, printed documents, pay slips, receipts, reports etc.

The information is obtained by assembling items of data into a meaningful form. Other forms of information are pay-slips, schedules, reports, work sheet, bar charts, invoices and account-returns. The information may further be processed and/or manipulated to form knowledge.

Sometimes, information obtained as an output from one system is used as input for another system. An information system is a set of processes, executed on raw data, to produce information that will be useful in decision making.

An information system must have a full range of functions to achieve its purpose, including observation, measurement, description, explanation, forecasting and decision making.

The heart of the integration of information needed in MIS (Management Information Systems) is a database. A database is an organized pool of information resources of an organisation, including raw materials and procedures. The idea is that the database consists of most of the data available, in the organisation and can be accessed by different managers for their varied uses. One manager may access the database for planning, another manager may need data for controlling, and generally all managers may need to access the database for decision making.

Difference between Information and Data

It is necessary to make distinction between the two terms namely, data and information that are usually used interchangeably. Data is the material on which computer programs work upon. It can be numbers, letters of the alphabet, words, special symbols but they themselves have no meaning. For example, the following sequence of digits 240343 is meaningless by itself since it could refer to date of birth, part number for a automobile, number of rupees spent on a project, population of a town, number of people employed in a large organisation etc. Once we know what the sequence refers to, then it becomes meaningful and can be called information. For example, when we write 24-03-43, it may mean date of birth as 24th March 1943.

A set of words would be data but text would be information. For example "annual-examination, amitabh, jyotsna, physics" is a set of data and "jyotsna scored the highest marks in physics in annual-examination" is information. Information may be processed or manipulated further and the information received from one source can be data for another source. For example, the scorecard of an individual is the information about the individual but is also the data for making merit list of the entire board or university.

Database Concept

A database is an organized collection of data. The term originated within the computer industry. In other words, a database is a collection of records stored on a computer in a systematic way. For better retrieval and sorting, each record is usually organised as a set of data elements or facts. The items retrieved from the database are the information that can be used for decision making. The computer program used to manage and query a database is known as a Database Management System (DBMS). The properties and design of database systems are included in the study of information science.

The central concept of a database is that of a collection of records or pieces of knowledge. The structural description of the type of facts held in a database is called a schema. The schema describes the objects that are represented in the database and the relationships among them. The schemas organized in a particular way are called the database models or data models. The most commonly used model is the relational model, which represents all the information in the form of table. There can be multiple tables in a relation model and each table comprises of a row and column. This model represents relationships by the use of values common to more than one table. Other models such as the hierarchical model and the network model use a more explicit representation of relationships.

Many professionals consider a collection of data to constitute a database only if it has certain properties such as if the data is managed to ensure its integrity and quality, if it allows shared access by a community of users, if it has a schema or if it supports a query language. However, there is no agreed definition of these properties.

Database management systems are usually categorized according to the data model that they support: relational, object-relational, network and so on. The data model tends to determine the query languages that are available to access the database. A great deal of the internal engineering of a DBMS, however, is independent of the data model and is concerned with managing factors such as performance, concurrency, integrity and recovery from hardware failures. In these areas, there are large differences between products.

Database Oriented Approach to Data Management

A database is a computerized record keeping system. It is a system involving data, the hardware that physically stores that data, the software that utilizes the hardware's file system in order to: (1) store the data and (2) provide a standardized method for retrieving or changing the data and finally, the users who turn the data into information.

Databases of 1960s were created to solve the problems with file-oriented systems. These databases were compact, fast, easy to use, and accurate, allowed the easy sharing of data between multiple users and were secure.

A database might be as complex and demanding as an account tracking system used by a bank to manage the constantly changing accounts of thousands of bank customers or it could be as simple as a collection of electronic business cards on your laptop.

The important thing is that a database allows you to store data and retrieve or modify that data according to your requirement. Traditionally, databases ran on large, powerful mainframes for business applications.

However, with the advent of small, powerful personal computers, databases have become more readily usable by the average computer user. Microsoft's Access is a popular PC-based engine. More importantly for our focus, databases have quickly become integral to the design, development and services offered by Web sites.

Databases

A database can be defined in various ways, for example:

- A database is a collection of structured data. The structure of the data is independent of any particular application.
- A database is a file of data structured in such a way that it may serve a number of applications without its structure being dictated by any one of those applications. The concept being that programs are written round the database rather than files being structured to meet the needs of particular programs.

Flat Databases

Flat database is a single kind of record with a fixed number of fields. Generally sorting for flat file databases is done at script level, however, distinct flat databases are combined in a way to emulate some of the behaviour of a relational database. Flat file databases are generally splitted by using a common delimiter.

CIMA

The centre of any information system is its database, which is a collection of the data resources of an organisation, designed to meet the requirements of the company for processing and retrieving information by decision makers. One important use of database is to target more precisely marketing efforts. In the USA, the latest trend in management information systems is the executive information system, which is used by senior managers. Quality software produces full colour display on large high quality monitors.

Briefly, a database is a collection of data supporting the operations of the organisation. It is, however, rather more than that because it must also:

- Be substantially non-redundant;
- Be program independent (data independence);
- Be usable by all the programs;

- Include all the necessary structural interrelations of data; have a common approach to the retrieval, insertion and amendment of data.

Let us consider these requirements individually.

Non-redundancy

As already suggested, non-redundancy is beneficial in eliminating the contradictions and in saving storage space. Occasionally, amount of redundancy is acceptable such as when the need for data security or rapid access is paramount.

Data Independence

This means that the data and the programs are independent, which means that the data can be moved or restructured without the need to make alterations to the programs. Similarly an enforced program change does not call for rearrangement of the data layout. If there is no data independency, then a program requiring more data items from a file necessitates rearranging it, and consequently other programs have to be modified to cope with the rearrangement of the file.

Program Usage

A database needs to be usable by not only all the existing applications but also by all foreseeable applications. These are ambitious aims, but nonetheless a database must be open-ended so as to accept new sets of data items and change to the existing data item sets.

Data Inter-relationships

Data inter-relationships are necessary because of the fact that various applications use data in different ways. For example, one application may demand a link between an employee's name and his pension contribution, another between his tax payment and his previous employer. Requirements such as these impose stringent demands upon the database's accuracy, security and flexibility.

Common Approach

Common approach is based on simplicity and understanding of data and programs. Although application programmers are not concerned with the database's structure and techniques, a common approach simplifies the database control programs and facilitates the database administrator's work.

Objectives of using a Database

- It should permit the establishment of a single area for common information that is used by all authorized users.
- It should allow important information to be recorded on floppy disk, magnetic disk, or mass storage, while secondary records are maintained on magnetic tape or other low-cost storage medium.

- It should guarantee accuracy of updating by an automatic maintenance feature for all segments of the data file.
- It should allow variable-length records in order to conserve space.
- It should have provision for expanding or reducing files; both the number of records in the file and the data elements in each record.
- It should allow security of files or segments of files.
- There must be a provision for some types of lockout feature so that certain files or areas of files or even individual records cannot be accessed during updating.

The important features of a database are:

- *Data Independence:* An item of data is stored for its own sake and not for one specific use. Thus the use of the data is generalised and is independent of the programs that are being used.
- *Data Integrity:* Data Integrity means the avoidance of conflicting, duplication of data. Consider an example where multiple application programs retrieve information regarding stock balance from a database. If the stock balance information in the database is updated, you need to update all the application programs that retrieve information from the database in order to maintain the integrity of data. For example, if a stock balance alters only once, .
- *Flexibility:* Flexibility means that data can be accessed in several ways and for various purposes. These can range from routine accesses for transaction processes to one-off queries by the chief executive.
- The database can grow and change and is built up stage by stage within an organisation. It will actually comprise of several databases, each providing the anticipated information for several logically related management information systems where the data can be accessed, retrieved and modified with reasonable flexibility.
- The data structures and relationships require highly technical software called the Data Base Management System (DBMS) to deal with them. Fortunately the user is shielded to a large extent from the complexity and is able to access the database with the minimum of technical knowledge.
- When the only possible form of data storage is unrelated, unique files for each application engender a narrow, parochial view of information. The reality is that management needs information which crosses functions, applications and levels and the flexibility of databases and the linkages possible make the concept a powerful one and essential for end user systems.

- An organisation is not confined to its own internal database. There are companies, which sell access to databases dealing with matters that an individual organisation would find expensive to collect. Examples of these public databases include those providing stock exchange and financial data, environmental data, legal matters including EU treaties and legislation, consumer research and marketing data and so on. In 1995 over 8000 external databases were available and the number was continually growing.

In the early days of computerisation, it was normal to maintain specific files for individual applications. Data was processed centrally in batches and there was little or no on-line interrogation of files.

This approach meant that there was duplication of data, inflexibility, concentration on the needs of the computer system rather than the difficulties of accessing files by on-line users. To overcome these problems, databases were developed.

Data Independence

We define data independence as the immunity of applications to changes in storage and access strategy, which implies that the applications concerned do not depend on any one particular storage or access strategy. In non-database implementations, knowledge of how data is organised and accessed is built into application programs. Examples of this exist in non-database applications and such knowledge could be:

- Representation of numeric data
- Representation of character data
- Data coding
- Data materialisation
- Stored record structure
- Stored file structure

All these possible manifestations of data dependence are eliminated with the use of database management system because with DBMS, it is possible for the DBA to change the storage structure or access methods without affecting the application programs.

Data independence is important because:

- Different applications will need to look at data in different ways.
- One must be able to change storage mechanisms and formats without having to modify all application programs. For example:

- Method of representation of numeric and alphanumeric data (e.g., Changing date format to avoid Y2000 problem)
- Units (e.g., metric vs. furlongs)
- Coding (e.g., ICD-9 vs. descriptive text)
- Record structure (example)
- File structure (sequential, sorted, indexed, etc.)

Data Independence is

1. The ability to modify a schema definition at one level without affecting a schema definition at a higher level.
2. There are two kinds:
   - Physical data independence
   - The ability to modify the physical schema without causing application programs to be rewritten.
   - Modifications at this level are usually to improve performance.
   - Logical data independence
   - The ability to modify the conceptual schema without causing application programs to be rewritten. Logical data independency is usually used when logical structure of database is altered.
3. Logical data independence is harder to achieve, as the application programs are usually dependent on the logical structure of the data. An analogy is made to abstract data types in programming languages.

DATABASE MANAGEMENT SYSTEMS

A Database Management System (DBMS), or simply a database system (DBS), consisting of a collection of interrelated and persistent data usually referred to as the database (DB).

A set of application programs used to access, update and manage that data forms the data management system.

The goal of a DBMS is to provide an environment that is both convenient and efficient to use in

- Retrieving information from the database.
- Storing information in the database.
- Manage large bodies of information.

- Providing for the safety of information in the database (crash recovery and security).
- Concurrency control if the system is shared by users.

Advantages of DBMS

The advantages of DBMS are as follows:

- Clear picture of logical organisation of data set.
- Centralisation for multi-users.
- Data independence.
- Monitoring database performance.
- Centralized data reduces management problems.
- Data redundancy and consistency are controllable.
- Program - data interdependency is diminished.
- Flexibility of data is increased.
- Reduction in data redundancy.
- Maintenance of data integrity and quality
- Data are self-documented or self-descriptive.
- Avoidance of inconsistency.
- Reduced cost of software development.
- Security restrictions.
- Application programs are independent of structure of database.
- Application programs share the same data.
- New programs are easier and cheaper to implement.

Types of Data Models

Data models are usually categorized by levels of abstraction:

- Conceptual
- Logical
- Physical

These have no agreed formal definitions.

Professional data modelers understand the approximate scope of each.

These layers may appear in different ways. Some approaches deal only with the physical or logical model. Others offer elements of all three but not necessarily in three separate views.

DATABASE MODELS

Besides differentiating databases according to function, databases can also be differentiated according to how they model the data.

A model defines the method of storing and retrieving data. A data model is defined as a set of guidelines for representing the logical organisation of data in a database. It also refers to a pattern according to which data and relationships can be organised. A data model consists of:

- A named logical unit (record type, data item)
- Relationships among logical units
- A data item is the smallest logical unit of data, an instance of which is known as a data item value.
- A record type is a collection of data items and a record is hence defined as an instance of a record type.

Well, essentially a data model is a "description" of both a container for data and a methodology for storing and retrieving data from that container. Actually, there isn't really a data model "thing". Data models are abstractions, which can be mathematical algorithms and concepts. You cannot really touch a data model. But nevertheless, they are very useful. The analysis and design of data models has been the cornerstone of the evolution of databases. As models have advanced so has database efficiency.

Modeling: Three Schema Architecture

In general, modeling is based on the three-schema architecture. A schema is an abstract definition of reality. The levels of schema architecture are:

- **Level 0:** Real World
- **Level 1:** Conceptual Model - E-R Model or Object-Oriented Model
- **Level 2:** Implementation Model - Relational Model
- **Level 3:** Physical Model - Physical Data Structures.

In designing a database, we begin with the development of a conceptual model. A number of different conceptual modeling approaches are used including:

- Hierarchical (legacy)
- Network (legacy)
- Entity-Relationship (linked to relational model)
- Object-Oriented (generally converted to a relational model)

Conceptual Level (or logical level)

- Conceptual view is the representation of the entire database of the data "as it really is". For example, the logical model of the whole database.
- Conceptual schema is a definition of the total database.
- Security checks are defined so only allowed users obtain access to the database. For example, passwords and grant permissions for each table.
- Integrity checks (validation) are also defined, which ensures that users do not harm the correctness of the database. For example, range checks on certain fields and referential integrity checks.
- Specifications should be data independent, with no reference to physical storage structure or access methods.
- Ideally, the conceptual schema describes the complete enterprise; including data flows from point to point, audit considerations etc.
- Once a good conceptual schema is developed, the rest is easy.
- Conceptual Data Definition Language (DDL) provides creation and maintenance of the full schema.

The database administrator is responsible for the maintenance of the conceptual schema.

Schema

Pronounced as skee-ma, the structure of a database system, described in a formal language and supported by the DBMS. In a relational database, the schema defines the tables, the fields in each table and the relationships between fields and tables.

Schemas are generally stored in a data dictionary. Although a schema is defined in text database language, the term is often used to refer to a graphical depiction of the database structure.

The use of database management systems does not eliminate the need for computer programs. The DBMS is a bridge between the application program and the operating system. The application program determines what data are needed and how they are processed and the operating system of the computer is responsible for placing data on the magnetic storage devices. A schema defines the database and a subschema defines the portion of the database that a specific program will use. Typically, programs use only a section of the database to retrieve data from the database:

- The application program determines what amount of data is needed and communicates the need to the database management system.

- The DBMS determines that the data requested is in fact stored in the database (even though it may be stored under a different name-an alias). The data must be defined in the subschema (possible only if the data is in the database).
- The DBMS provides instructions to the operating system to locate and retrieve the data from the specific location on the magnetic disk (or whatever device it is stored on).
- A copy of the data is given to the application program for processing.

The DBMS permits data independence, which means that the application program can change without affecting the stored data. Under ordinary master file arrangements, if the program changes in such a way that the arrangement of the data retrieved or stored is modified, the master files must be recreated and restructured. With data independence, changes may occur in one data store or data use without affecting the other. A data dictionary is embedded in the data management system through the schema and subschema to ensure that data is properly defined and described and that duplicate names (aliases) do not result in redundant data storage or loss of data integrity.

External Level

The External schema describes the external view.

- External schema is defined by the Data Definition Language (DDL)
- The Data Manipulation Language (DML) is used to access data.

A formal definition of the logical structure of the database is often represented as an Entity-Relationship diagram.

The schema for the external and internal levels is kept by the database in its data dictionary, also known as the Catalogue or System Tables.

Internal Level

Internal view is the representation of the actual storage of the database. Internal schema defines the records, indexes, files and other physical attributes. For every conceptual file there may be several actual storage files. It should be able to change, reorganise and optimise the physical characteristics without affecting the conceptual view.

Internal Data Definition Language is used to write the internal schema. This language does not specify the actual disk block sizes and disk pagesbut is performed by the operating system. So the database's internal level is removed from the computer's physical level.

Schema Integration

Schema integration, as defined by the authors, occurs in two contexts:

1. View integration (in database design), which produces a global conceptual description of a proposed database; and
2. Database integration (in distributed database management), which produces the global schema of a collection of databases.

Schema Objects

A schema is a collection of logical structures of data or schema objects. A schema is owned by a database user and has the same name as that of the user. Each user owns a single schema. Schema objects can be created and manipulated with SQL and include the following types of objects:

- Clusters
- Database links
- Stand-alone stored functions
- Indexes
- Packages
- Stand-alone procedures
- Sequences
- Snapshots
- Snapshot logs
- Synonyms
- Tables
- Database triggers
- Views

These objects are available only with Oracle's procedural and distributed options.

Other types of objects are also stored in the database and can be created and manipulated with SQL, but are not contained in a schema:

- Profiles
- Roles
- Rollback segments
- Tablespaces

Most of these objects occupy space in the database.

Overall System Structure

- Database systems are partitioned into modules for different functions. Some functions (e.g. file systems) may be provided by the operating system.
- Software Components include:
- File manager manages allocation of disk space and data structures that are used to represent information on disk.
- Database manager: Database manager is the interface between low-level data and application programs and queries.
- Query processor translates statements in a query language into low-level instructions the database manager understands. The query processor may also attempt to find an equivalent but more efficient form.
- DML pre-compiler converts the DML statements embedded in an application program into normal procedure calls in a host language. The precompiler interacts with the query processor.
- DDL compiler converts DDL statements to a set of tables containing metadata stored in a data dictionary.

In addition, several data structures are required for physical system implementation.

Data Files: Store the Database Itself

- *Data dictionary:* Stores information about the structure of the database. It is used heavily. Great emphasis should be placed on developing a good design and efficient implementation of the dictionary.
- *Indices:* Provide fast access to data items holding particular values.

The Relational Model

The relational data model is currently the most popular data model used in database management systems because it is conceptually simple and understandable by information systems professionals and many end users. It had evolved, since relationships need not be predefined; and it uses data values to imply relationships. The relational data model, developed in 1970 by E.F. Codd, is based on a relation, a two-dimensional table. Rows in the table represent the records and columns show the attributes of the entity. Relational databases use a model to show how data in a record is logically related.

The order of the data in the table is not significant and no order is implied when records are included in the relation. Similarly, the physical details of storage (whether random, indexed, or sequential organisation) are not of concern to the analyst. Relational table shows logical and not physical relationships.

When a request for information is made, the system produces a table containing the information. In the laundry example, if a manager wishes to determine who uses napkins, the systems will produce a table containing the names of all users of napkins.

Data items are individual units of information, e.g. name, and address, number of items in inventory, weekly sales total and grade in a course. A record normally consists of a set of related data items, for example an employee record would consist of various data items concerning a given employee. A file is a unified set of data, which is usually in the form of a collection of records. All files are not subdivided into records. For example, the government may keep a file consisting of all information on a particular airplane disaster.

Relation

Each record has a set of attributes, fields or items. The range of possible values or domain is defined for each attribute.

Records of each type form a table or relation. In a table, each row is a record or tuple and each column is an attribute or field.

Relation, Tuple and Field

The degree of a relation is the number of attributes in the table. A one-attribute table is a unary relation. A two-attribute table is a binary relation. An n-attribute table is an n-ary relation.

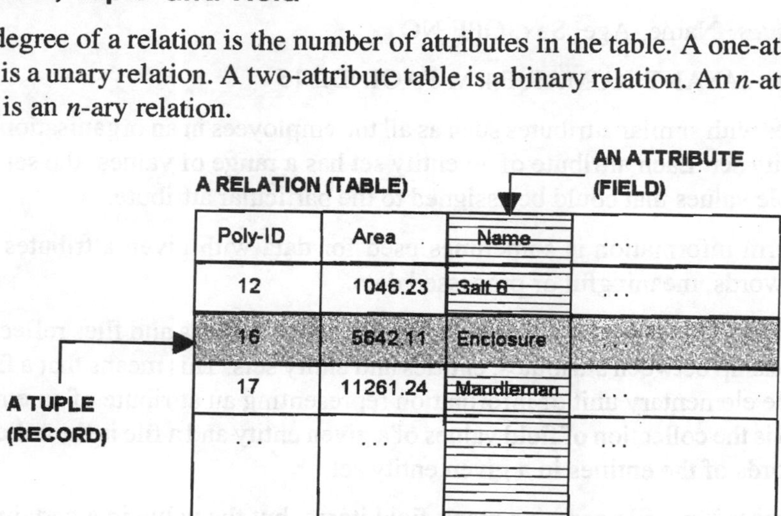

The degree of a relation

Keys

A key of a relation is a subset of attributes with the following properties:

- *Unique identification:* The value of a key is unique for each tuple.
- *Non-redundancy:* No attribute in the key can be discarded without destroying the uniqueness of the key.
- A prime attribute of a relation is an attribute, which participates in at least one key and all other attributes are non-prime.

Data are simply values or sets of values. A data item refers to a single unit of values. Data items that are divided into subitems are called group items. Those data items that are not subdivided into groups are called elementary items. For example, an employee's name may be divided into three subitems, first name, middle initial and last name, but the social security number would normally be treated as a single item.

An entity is something that has certain attributes or properties, which may be assigned values. The values themselves may be either numeric or nonnumeric. For example, following are the possible attributes and their corresponding values for an entity, an employee of a given organisation:

Attributes: Name, Age, Sex, GPF NO

Values: JAYANT KUMAR 34 M PAOIND2/15

Entities with similar attributes such as all the employees in an organisation form an entity set. Each attribute of an entity set has a range of values; the set of all possible values that could be assigned to the particular attribute.

The term information is sometimes used for data with given attributes or in other words, meaningful or processed data.

The way data is organised into hierarchy of fields, records and files reflects the relationship between attributes, entities and entity sets. This means that a field is a single elementary unit of information representing an attribute of an entity, a record is the collection of field values of a given entity and a file is the collection of records of the entities in a given entity set.

Each record in a file contains many field items, but the value in a certain field may uniquely determine the record in the file. Such a field is called a primary key.

Data and relationships are represented by a collection of tables. Each table has a number of columns with unique names, e.g. customer, account. A sample relational database.

The E-R Model

The entity-relationship model is based on the collection of basic objects called entities and relationships among these objects.

An entity is a distinguishable object that exists. Each entity has associated with it a set of attributes describing it. For example, number and balance for an account entity. However, a relationship is an association among several entities.

For example, a cust_acct relationship associates a customer with each account he or she has. The set of all entities or relationships of the same type is called the entity set or relationship set.

Another essential element of the E-R diagram is the mapping cardinalities, which express the number of entities to which another entity can be associated via a relationship set.

The overall logical structure of a database can be expressed graphically by an E-R diagram:

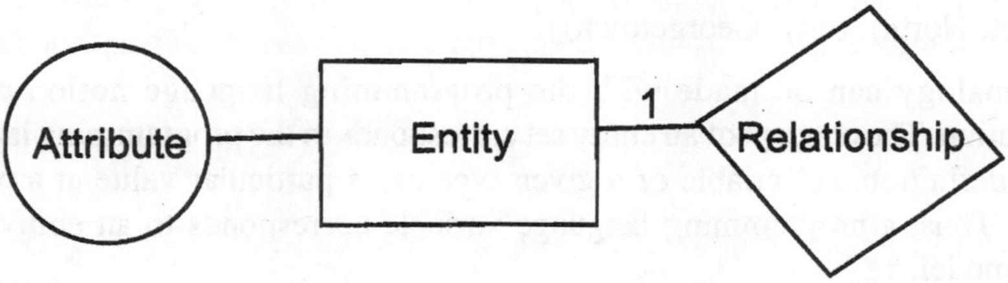

rectangles: Represent entity sets.

ellipses: Represent attributes.

diamonds: Represent relationships among entity sets.

lines: Link attributes to entity sets and entity sets to relationships.

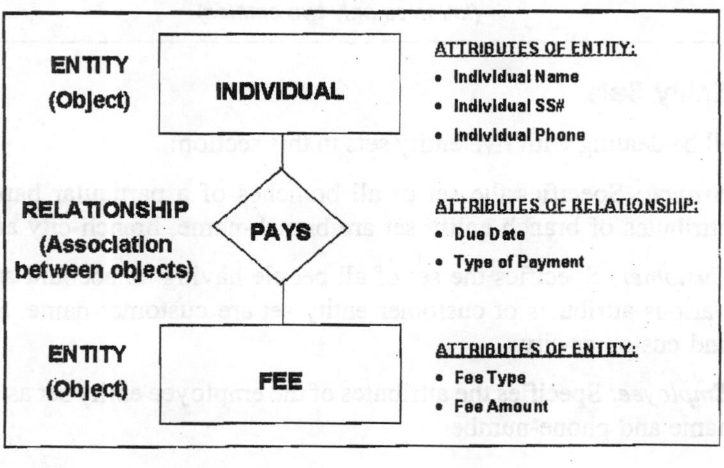

Entities and Entity Sets

An entity is an object that exists and is distinguishable from other objects. For instance, John Harris with S.I.N. 890-12-3456 is an entity, as he can be uniquely identified as one particular person in the universe.

An entity may be concrete, for example, a person or a book. or abstract, for example a holiday or a concept. An entity set is a set of entities of the same type, for example, all persons having an account at a bank.

Entity sets need not be disjoint. For example, the entity set employee (all employees of a bank) and the entity set customer (all customers of the bank) may have members in common. An entity is represented by a set of attributes. For example, S.I.N., street, city for "customer" entity. The domain of the attribute is a set of permitted values, for example, telephone number must be seven positive integers. Formally, an attribute is a function, which maps an entity set to a domain. Every entity is described by a set of attributes and data value pairs. There is one pair for each attribute of the entity set. For example, a particular customer entity is described by the set {(name, Harris), (S.I.N., 890-123-456), (street, North), (city, Georgetown)}.

An analogy can be made with the programming language notion of type definition. The concept of an entity set corresponds to the programming language type definition. A variable of a given type has a particular value at a point in time. Thus, a programming language variable corresponds to an entity in the E-R model.

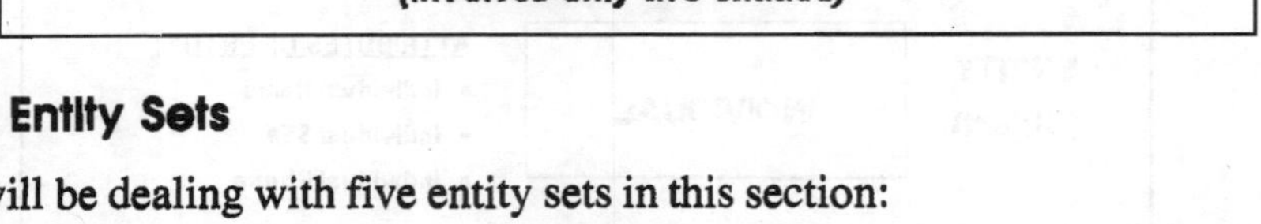

BINARY RELATIONSHIP
(Involves only two entities)

Five Entity Sets

We will be dealing with five entity sets in this section:

- *Branch:* Specifies the set of all branches of a particular bank. Various attributes of branch entity set are branch-name, branch-city and assets.
- *Customer:* Specifies the set of all people having an account at the bank. Various attributes of customer entity set are customer-name, SSN, street and customer-city.
- *Employee:* Specifies the attributes of the employee entity set as employee-name and phone-number.

- *Account:* Specifies the set of all accounts that are created and maintained in the bank. Various attributes of account entity set are account-number and balance.
- *Transaction:* Specifies the set of all account transactions that are executed in the bank. Various attributes of transaction entity set are transaction-number, date and amount.

Attributes

It is possible to define a set of entities and the relationships among them in a number of different ways. The main difference is in how we deal with attributes.

Consider the entity set, employee with attributes, employee-name and phone number. We could argue that the phone be treated as an entity itself with attributes, phone number and location. Then we have two entity sets, and the relationship set, EmpPhn defining the association between employees and their phones. This new definition allows employees to have several (or zero) phones. New definition may more accurately reflect the real world. We cannot extend this argument easily to make employee name an entity.

The question of what constitutes an entity and what constitutes an attribute depends mainly on the structure of the real world situation being modeled and the semantics associated with the attribute in question.

CHAPTER 17

Internet—Connecting the World

INTRODUCTION

Traditionally, computers were stand-alone systems. Transferring information from one computer to another could be done through mediums such as the floppy disk and tape. Resources such as printers, scanners and CD-ROM drives could not be shared across the computers. They had to be attached physically to the computers to use them. However, with the invention of networking, it became possible to share resources across computers. In addition, it enabled sharing the knowledge base thereby helping people take advantage of rich information base and work collectively.

The Internet is a 'network of networks'. It can be visualized as a number of interconnected computers located at physically disparate locations around the world. It is a global network of computers, cutting across barriers and boundaries of countries, class, race or sex. It comprises of tens and thousands of computer networks linked to each other.

These computer networks are categorised into following types:

Local Area Network (LAN)

LANs connect devices such as computers and printers, over short distances typically within an office premises or campus. Computers and devices are connected through cables within a distance of 2000 feet. Wireless Local Area Network (WLAN) and Bluetooth technology are also types of LANs.

Wide Area Network (WAN)

WANs span over areas larger than a single building or a campus. They can span over multiple buildings or different offices of an organization across physically different locations in the same city or across cities.

Metropolitan Area Networks (MAN)

MANs refer to the LANs connected through high-speed, seamless interconnection within a 'metropolitan' area. The word 'metropolitan' does not necessarily mean a city, but can be any area that is spread out but is treated as one entity e.g., a company having its buildings across a large area of land. MANs cover geographical areas that are larger than LANs but smaller than WANs.

Key Uses of the Internet

The Internet has made things simple. It can be used for following:

- *Direct Communication:* You can send messages to family and friends, business associates and acquaintances using the electronic mail facility. Using electronic mail, you can send and receive messages within few seconds anywhere in the world. Using Internet Relay Chat (IRC), you can have online communication with people over the Internet. You can log into a chat room and converse with others by typing messages that are instantly delivered. With the improvement of network technologies and increase in broadband, you cannot only use text messages but also graphics, audio, video for communication with other people.
- *Online Shopping:* Logically, the Internet has removed all barriers of distance and nationality. You can shop for products and services across the world by logging on to a Web portal. You can also pay your bills online using credit and debit cards. You can also transfer money between different accounts with a click of mouse.
- *Distance Education:* The Internet provides a perfect medium for knowledge sharing and information dissemination. Courses are available on the Internet. You can register and pay online, and can complete a course on different interest areas. You can now pursue specialized higher studies in the comfort of your own office or home.
- *Knowledge Base:* The Internet provides a rich information base that can be accessed by people around the globe. In fact, it is one of the richest information bases that can be accessed on the click of mouse. Using search engines, you can search for detailed information on any topic of your interest.
- *Banking:* Banks are using information technology to provide online banking facilities to their customers. Using the Internet, you can now view your account details, get drafts made, request for chequebooks and transfer money from one account to another. The use of ATMs has shifted the mundane back-office work to the customer himself. Instead of hiring an army of bank clerks, banks are using ATMs to considerably reduce time and operational costs.

- *Travel:* Using the Internet, travel agencies are publish their services on the Web along with the latest discounts, packages and availability details so that customers can compare rates, make online bookings and avail the discounts without having to run around multiple offices.
- *Bill Payments:* The government sector has also realized the benefits of IT. Now, you can make online payments for public utilities such as water, electricity and phones, using credit cards as the payment medium.

INTERNET CONNECTIVITY OPTIONS

You can use two options for connecting to the Internet.

Direct Connection

Through a direct connection, a machine is directly connected to the Internet backbone and acts like a gateway. Though a direct connection provides full access to all the Internet services, it is very expensive to implement and maintain. Direct connections are suitable only for very large organizations or companies.

Through Internet Service Provider (ISP)

You can also connect to the Internet through the gateways provided by ISPs. The range of the Internet services varies depending on the ISPs. Therefore, you should use the Internet services of the ISP that is best suitable for your requirements. You can connect to your ISP using two methods:

Remote dial-up Connection

A dial-up connection enables you to connect to your ISP using a modem. A modem converts the computer bits or digital signals to modulated or analogue signals that the phone lines can transmit and vice versa. Dial-up connection uses either SLIP (Serial Line Internet Protocol) or PPP (Point to Point Protocol) for transferring information over the Internet.

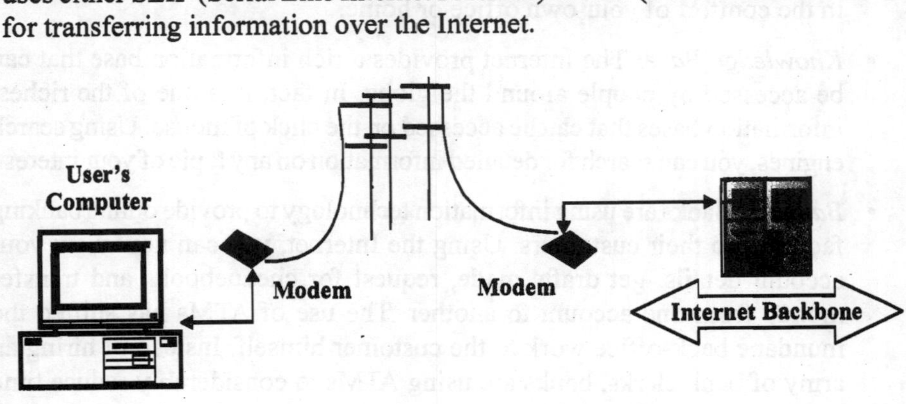

For dial-up connections, regular telephone lines are used. Therefore, the quality of connection is not always good.

Permanent Dedicated Connection

You can also have a dedicated Internet connection that typically connects you to ISP through a dedicated phone line. A dedicated Internet connection is a permanent telephone connection between two points. Computer networks that are physically separated are often connected using leased or dedicated lines. These lines are preferred because these are always open for communication traffic unlike the regular telephone lines that require a dialling sequence to be activated. Often this line is an ISDN (Integrated Services Digital Network) line that allows transmission of data, voice, video and graphics at very high speed. ISDN applications have revolutionized the way business communicates. ISDN lines support upward scalability, which means that you can transparently add more lines to get faster speeds – going up to 1.28 mbps (million bits per second).

T1 and T3 are the other two types of commonly used dedicated line types for Internet connections. Dedicated lines are becoming popular because of their faster data transfer rates. Dedicated lines are cost-effective for the business that uses Internet services extensively.

Internet Protocols

Internet protocols are required to transfer data over networks and/or the Internet in an efficient manner. When various computers are connected through a computer network, it becomes necessary to use a protocol to efficiently use network bandwidth and avoid collisions.

A network protocol defines a language that contains rules and conventions for reliable communication between different devices over the network. For example, it includes rules that specify how to package data into messages, how to acknowledge a message and how to compress data.

There are a number of Internet protocols used. The most commonly used protocols are:

— Transmission Control Protocol/Internet Protocol (TCP/IP)

— HyperText Transfer Protocol (HTTP)

— File Transfer Protocol (FTP)

— Telnet

(a) Transmission Control Protocol/Internet Protocol (TCP/IP)

It is a protocol suite used to transfer data over the Internet. Two main protocols in this protocol suite are:

TCP: It forms the higher layer of TCP/IP and divides a message or a file into smaller packets that are transmitted over the Internet. These packets are received by a TCP layer on the other side, which then reassembles the data packets into the original message.

IP: It is the lower layer that handles the address part of each packet so that it is delivered to the right destination. Usually, each gateway computer on the network checks this address to identify where to forward the message. This implies that all the packets of a message are delivered to the destination regardless of the route used for delivering the packets.

The working of TCP/IP can be compared with shifting your residence to a new location. This activity would involve packing your belongings in smaller boxes for easy transportation, with the new address and a number written on each of the boxes. You would then load them on multiple vehicles. These vehicles may take different routes to reach the same destination. The delivery time of vehicles depends on the amount of traffic and the length of the route. Once the boxes are delivered to the destination, you would check these to make sure that all have been delivered in good shape. After that, you need to unpack the boxes and reassemble your house.

(b) HyperText Transfer Protocol (HTTP)

HTTP is a protocol for transferring files (text, image, sound, video and other multimedia files) using the Internet. It is an application protocol that runs on the top of the TCP/IP protocol suite, which is the foundation protocol of the Internet. It defines how messages are formatted and transmitted and what actions Web servers and Web browsers should take in response to the commands issued. HTTP is based on a client/server architecture where your Web browser acts as a HTTP client making requests to the Web server machines. In addition to the Web pages, a server machine contains an HTTP daemon that handles the Web page requests. Typically, when a user types a URL (Uniform Resource Locator) or clicks on a hypertext link, the browser builds an HTTP request and sends it to the IP address indicated in the URL. The HTTP daemon on the destination server then receives this request and responds by sending back the requested Web page.

HTTP is a stateless protocol, which means each request is processed independently, without any knowledge of the previous request. This is the reason that the server side programming languages such as JSP, PHP and ASP .NET have gained popularity.

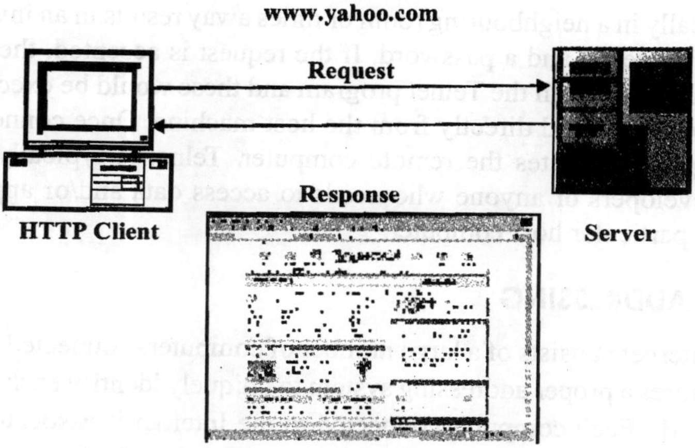

(C) File Transfer Protocol (FTP)

FTP is an application protocol for exchanging files between computers over the Internet. It is the simplest and most commonly used protocol for downloading / uploading a file from / to a server. For example, downloading a document or an article from a Web site. Like other protocols, FTP also uses TCP/IP protocol suite for data transfer.

FTP also works on a client/server architecture where an FTP client program is used to make a request to an FTP server (files can be stored on computers referred to as FTP servers). Basic FTP support is usually provided as part of the TCP/IP suite of programs. You can use FTP using a simple command line interface such as MS-DOS prompt or use a commercial program that provides a graphical user interface. Using FTP, you can update files on a server. Your Web browser could also make FTP requests to download documents or programs you request from your page. Typically, you would need a login to an FTP server. However, publicly available files can be easily accessed using anonymous FTP.

(d) Telnet

Telnet is a protocol that allows you to access a remote computer provided you have been given the permission to do so. It is typically referred to as 'remote login'. Telnet is based on a different concept from HTTP and FTP. HTTP and FTP allow you to request specific files from remote computers only, while with Telnet you log on as a regular user on a remote machine with whatever privileges you may have been granted on that computer to access specific application and data. A request for a connection to a remote host, which may be a computer lying physically in a neighbouring room or miles away results in an invitation to log on with a user id and a password. If the request is accepted, the user can enter commands through the Telnet program and these would be executed as if they were being entered directly from the host machine. Once connected, the user's computer emulates the remote computer. Telnet is typically used by program developers or anyone who needs to access data and/or applications located at a particular host computer.

INTERNET ADDRESSING

Since the Internet consists of a large number of computers connected with each other, it requires a proper addressing system to uniquely identify each computer in the network. Each computer connected to the Internet is associated with a unique number and/or a name called computer address. Before you wish to access any Web pages on a computer, you would require the computer address.

IP Address An IP address is a unique number associated with each computer making it uniquely identifiable within all the computers connected to the Internet. This is a 32 bit number and is divided into four octets such as 00001010 00000000 00000000 00000110. For human readability, it is represented in a decimal notation, separating each octet with a period. The above number would therefore be represented as: 10.0.0.6.

Each octet can range from 0 – 255, thus all IP addresses lie between 0.0.0.0 to 255.255.255.255 resulting in total 4294, 967,296 possible IP addresses. It may be worth noting that no two machines (or hosts) can have the same IP address.

Domain Naming System (DNS): In a network, computers and devices can be grouped as a unit with common rules and procedures. Such a group is called a Domain. Each domain name therefore corresponds to a group of IP addresses. Some examples of domain names include Yahoo.com, Microsoft.com and abcuniv.edu. The last portion of the domain name provides information on the kind of organization to which the address belongs.

Commonly used abbreviations in domain names:

Abbreviation	*What it represents*
com	Commercial organization
org	Non-profit organization
edu	Educational institution
net	Networking organizations
gov	Government agencies

A Domain Naming System (or DNS) is an Internet service that translates domain names to or from IP addresses, which is the actual basis of addressing on the Internet. A DNS is typically a database containing information about domain names and their corresponding IP addresses.

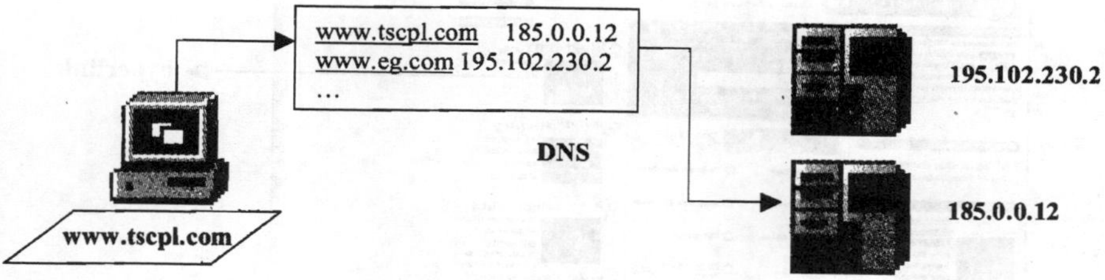

Starting the Internet

Before you start using the Internet, it may be useful to understand some terminology commonly used in the context of the Internet.

Common Terminology

World Wide Web (www) Commonly known as 'WWW', 'Web' or W3' consists of a number of distributed servers that are connected through hypermedia documents. These documents are created using HyperText Markup Language (HTML). Related text organised into units can be accessed by using a link called hyperlink. These links (or hyperlinks) allow the user to navigate from one document to another without having to worry about the actual physical location of the documents. WWW makes it possible to share information between disparate users, computers and operating systems. It is therefore the fastest growing application of the Internet.

Website

The Web can be understood as a collection of thousands of information locations connected with each other. Each such location is called a Web site and comprises of multiple Web pages. A Web page is created using HTML and is like any other computer document. It consists of text, pictures, sound, video and hyperlinks. You can navigate from one Web page to another using the hyperlinks. A Web site can be created by an individual or a company. Web sites are hosted on the Web servers accessible on the Internet. A URL (Uniform Resource Locator) defines the address of a Web site and is used to point to the homepage of the Web site. A homepage is the first page that is displayed when you access a Web site. It serves as a reference point and contains links to additional HTML pages or links to other Web sites. The screen below displays the homepage of the Web site britannica.com that is displayed on typing the URL **'http://www.britannica.com'**.

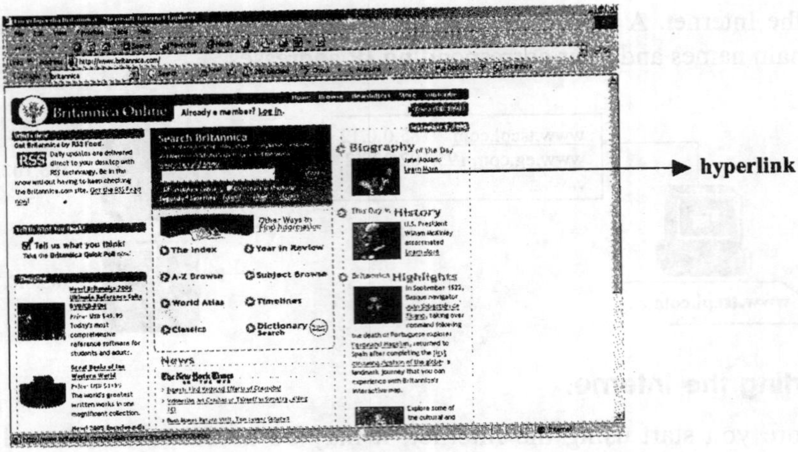

Uniform Resource Locator (URL)

A URL defines the address of a site on the Internet. They define the global addresses of documents and other resources on WWW.

Typically, the first part of a URL indicates the protocol to be used, while the second part specifies the domain name or IP address where the resource is located. Some examples of URLs are shown below:

URL	*Description*
http://mysite.com/index.html	Fetch a web page (index.html) using the HTTP **Protocol**
ftp://www.sharware/myzip.exe	Fetch an executable file (myzip.exe) using FTP **Protocol**

HyperText Markup Language (HTML)

HTML is the language for publishing hypertext or HTML pages on WWW. It is a non-proprietary format. You can use a large number of tools for creating HTML pages, ranging from simple editors to sophisticated authoring tools that work on the WYSIWYG principle. HTML provided various tags to structure text in a HTML page. For example you can use <p></p>, <li></li> and <a></a> tags to structure text into paragraphs, lists and hypertext links. Following is an HTML page showing various HTML tags:

```
<HTML>
<HEAD>
<TITLE> Welcome Page</TITLE>
</HEAD>
<BODY>
        <p align='center'><font color='black' face='Arial' size='6'>Welcome to Everybody's
Site</font>
<p align='center'><font color='red' face='Arial' size='5'>Thought for the day.</font>          ①
<p align='center'><font color='blue' face='Arial' size='5'><b>Don't like working on your
own?</font>
<p align='center'><font color='blue' face='Arial' size='5'>Hate making decisions?</font>       ②
<p align='center'><font color='blue' face='Arial' size='5'>Then call a meeting !!</font></b>
<p align='center'><img src='meeting.jpg' height='100' width='100' >                             ③
<p align='center'><a href='http://www.yahoo.com'> <font color='blue' face='Arial'
size='3'>Check Mail</font> </a>
</BODY>
</HTML>
```

The output of the HTML code is as following:

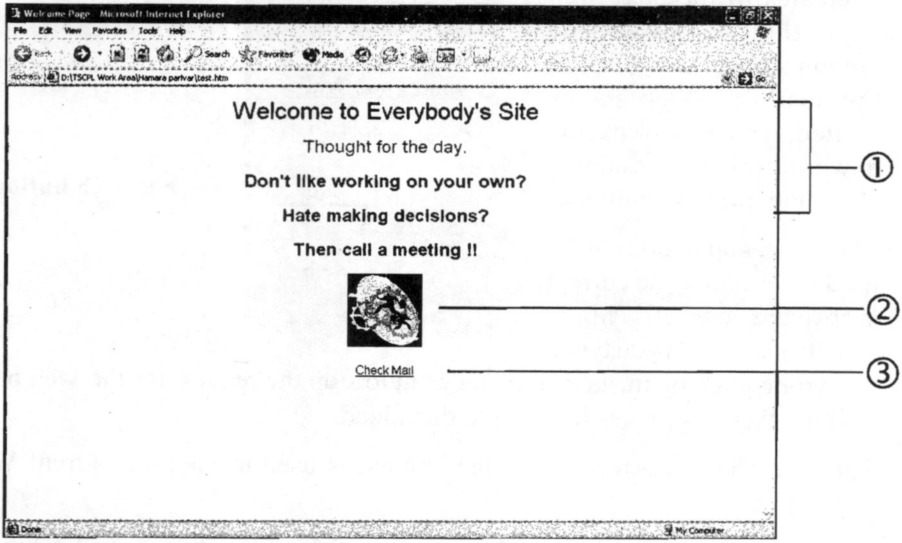

Web Browser

A Web browser, commonly known as browser, is a computer application that creates requests for HTML pages or Web pages and displays the processed HTML page. Web browsers use the HTTP (hypertext Transfer protocol) to request for information from Web servers. The two most commonly used Web browsers are:

— Netscape Navigator
— Microsoft Internet Explorer

Other examples of Web browsers include Mosaic, Cello, and Lynx.

Having knowledge of basic features of the browsers will be helpful to you them easily.

Toolbar of the Internet Explorer

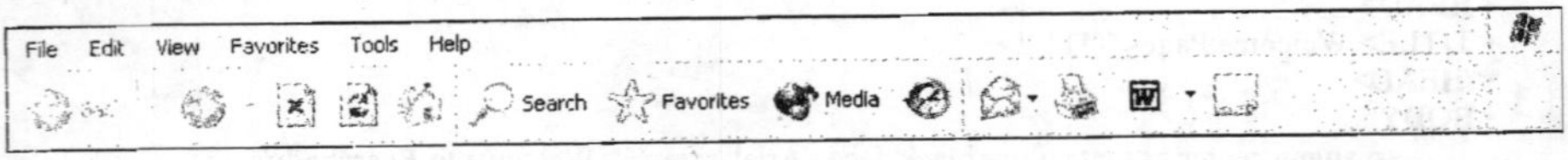

The toolbar consists of various icons that can be used to execute functions. In fact, most of the options available through the menu bar are also available through the icons in the toolbar. Some commonly used icons are:

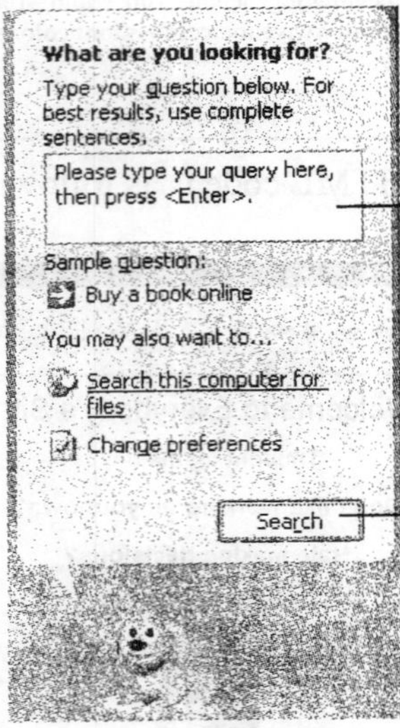

Search Text box

Search Button

Back: The back button allows you to navigate to the Web page you viewed last.

Forward: The forward button on the toolbar navigates to the next Web page that was accessed previously. To view a list of the last few Web pages visited, you can click the down arrow button beside the Back and Forward buttons.

Stop: The stop button can be used to terminate the current Web page request. This is usually used when you typed the wrong URL by mistake and you want to stop the request for the Web page or if the Web page takes too long to download.

Refresh: The Refresh or the Reload button is used to load the current Web page again.

In other words, it refreshes the contents of the current page by fetching a new copy of it.

Search: The Search button allows you to find information on the Web. You can find information by clicking on the Search button on the toolbar. This will activate the search text box as shown. You can then type in a word or phrase and click the 'search' button to start the search.

Favorites: The Favorites button is used to record the addresses of frequently visited Web sites. Once a Web site or a Web page is added to the favorites list, it can be revisited by simply clicking on the link in the list. This saves the effort of typing the URL each time the user wishes to visit the same site.

History: The History button is used to view the list of all the Web pages visited in the last few days, hours or minutes. To revisit any one of them, simply click on the address.

Print: The Print button is used to print contents of the current Web page.

Net Surfing

Net surfing, Internet browsing or exploring a network or the

World Wide Web is associated with visiting different Web sites on the Internet. It is typically finding places of interest on the click of a mouse. It is analogous to surfing TV channels with remote control.

Searching

Searching is one of the most common use of the Internet. You can search for any topic or information on the internet. This is possible by using Web sites that provide a search engine.

Search Engines

A search engine is a software system that enables the users to search information on the WWW using keywords. It is designed to help the Internet users locate Internet resources such as Web pages, documents, programs and images using a keyword search mechanism. Search engines typically use databases that contain references to a host of resources. Users interact with a search engine using an interface. There are many search engines available with different appearance and search mechanisms. Commonly used search engines are: Google, Yahoo, MSN, Altavista, AOL, Ask Jeeves, Lycos, Excite and HotBot.

Google (http://www.google.com) **Yahoo (http://www.yahoo.com)**

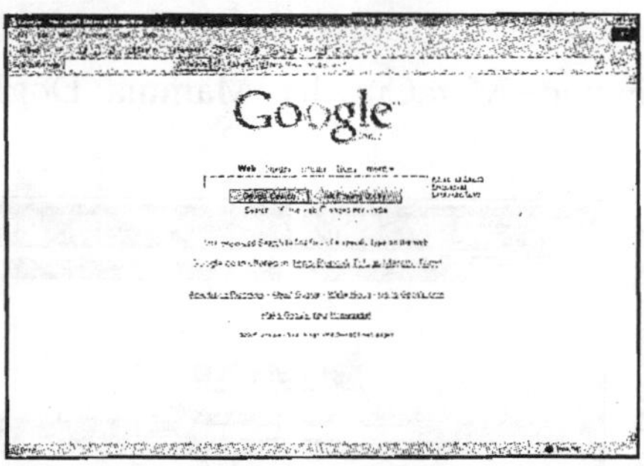

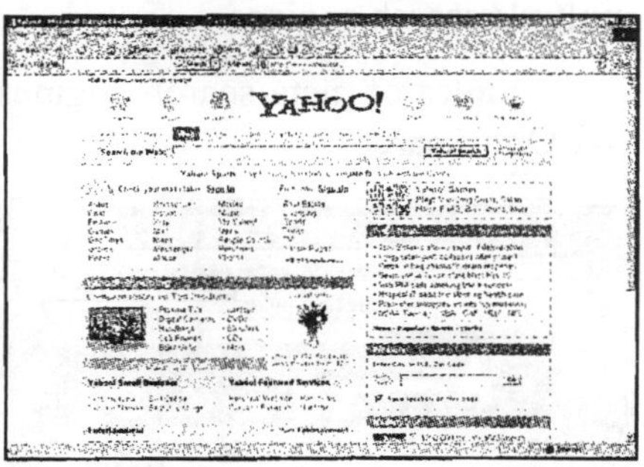

Useful Tips for Searching

- Type in the words such as Singapore in the search box to get the result pages

– You could also use multiple search terms that will produce more appropriate results. For example, if you are planning a vacation in Singapore, you may need to type both the terms in the search box, as shown:

"Vacation Singapore"

This will result in pages containing both the terms and will therefore be more specific for your search. You should, therefore, choose your search terms carefully.

– To restrict a search further, include more terms in your search criteria.

– You could also search using phrases, when you need the results to contain the exact phrases. If this is desired, include the search phrase in quotation marks as shown:

"Five star hotels in Singapore"

– Searches are usually not case sensitive.

Meta Search Engines

Since different search engines use different search algorithms, you may often get different results for the same search criterion when using different search engines. The user must therefore know which search engine is best suited for his/her specific query. Meta-search engines make the search task easy by providing a central location to type the keyword or phrase and then obtaining results from multiple search engines. They enable the user to use different search engines simultaneously for searching without having to worry about which search engine to be used for a specific query. Meta search engines do not have any database to search but only provide services to route a single query to multiple search engines.

Examples of meta-search engines include MetaCrawler, Mamma, DogPile and One Search.

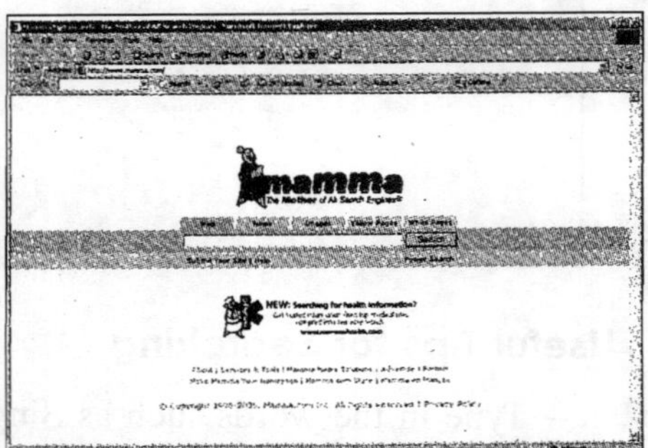

E-mailing

E-Mail, short for electronic mail enables you to send your correspondence instantaneously anywhere in the world via the Internet. E-mail has made the world a 'small place'.

The popularity of e-mail is because of its capability of sending and receiving messages anytime, anywhere without any cost. E-mail allows you to send and receive a variety of file types such as text, image, video, sound and graphics to a single recipient or multiple recipients using broadcasting. To use the e-mail feature, you just need to create an e-mail account for yourself using a Web site that offers such services. Various sites provide e-mail facility. Some of them such as Yahoo.com, Rediff.com, hotmail.com and lycos.com provide it free of cost while others charge for it.

Since by now you would be quite keen to use the e-mail facility, let us run through creating and using an e-mail account on Yahoo.com.

Creating an e-mail Account

Type the URL '**http://www.yahoo.com**' in the address bar of a Web browser such as Internet Explorer to visit the Yahoo homepage:

The page that is now displayed is the 'Sign in' page. If you are an existing user, you need to type in your user id and password to log on to your account. If you are a first time user, you need to first create an account for yourself.

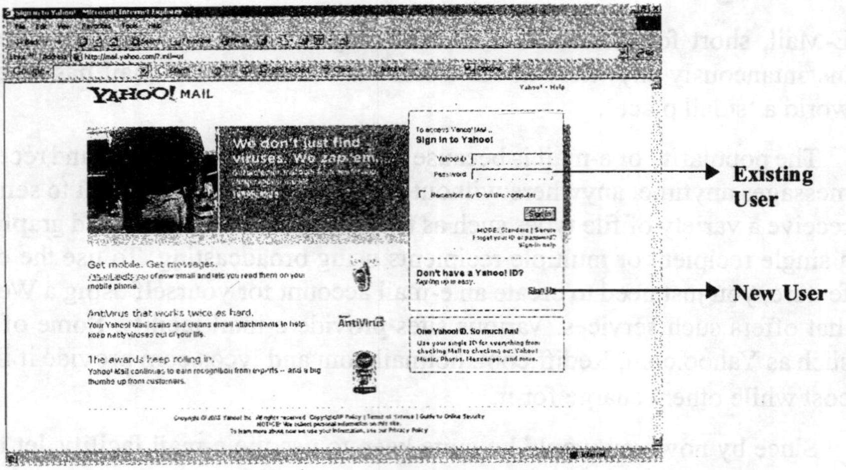

Click 'Sign Up' to create a new user. The page that is displayed is a registration form that requires you to fill in your details along with the user Id and password for your new e-mail account.

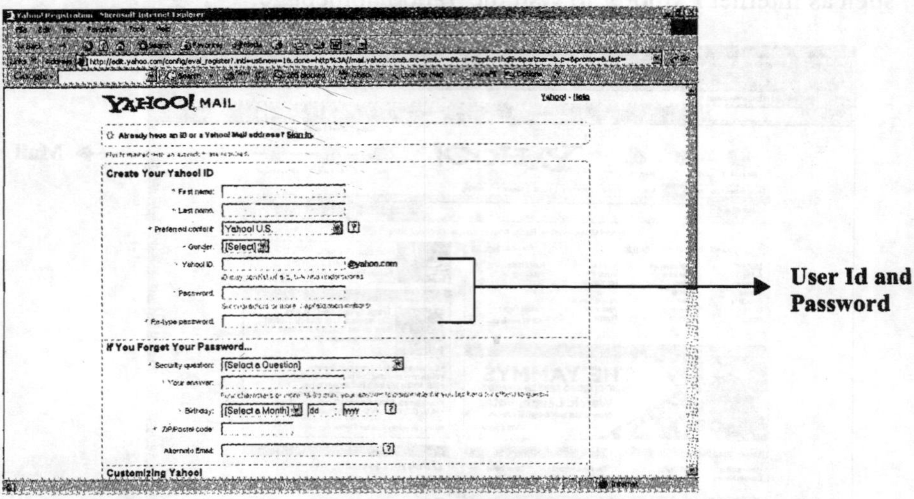

Once you have registered yourself on a Web site, you become a member and can simply log on to your mail account to start sending and receiving e-mails. For all future access, you would require to remember your user id and password because that is the key to your login.

Checking your e-mail

You can access your e-mail anytime by logging on to your mail. To do so, perform the following steps:

- Type the URL 'http://www.yahoo.com' in the address bar of a Web browser.
- Enter your user Id and password.

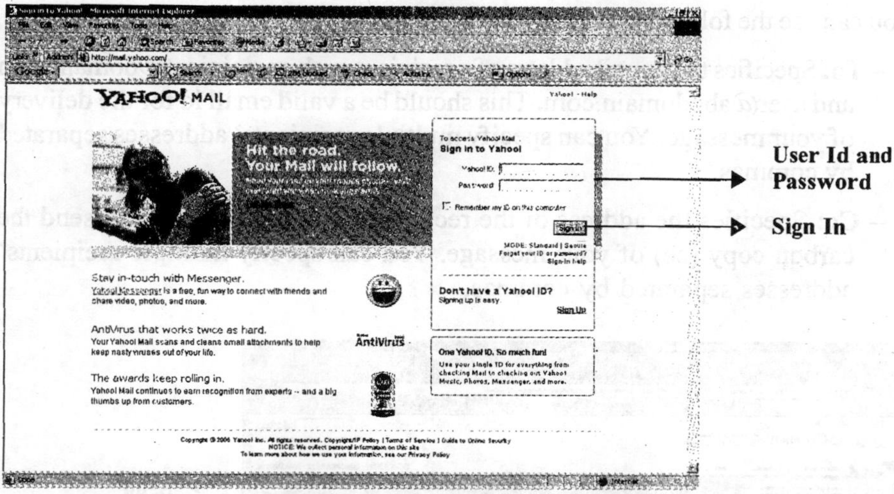

Once you have signed in successfully, you can access your e-mail account. You can access your 'Inbox' to view any incoming mail or to write a new mail.

Clicking the Inbox button displays all the received messages or mails.

You can read an e-mail by clicking the e-mail subject.

Clicking the e-mail subject displays the contents of your e-mail that can be read to take necessary action.

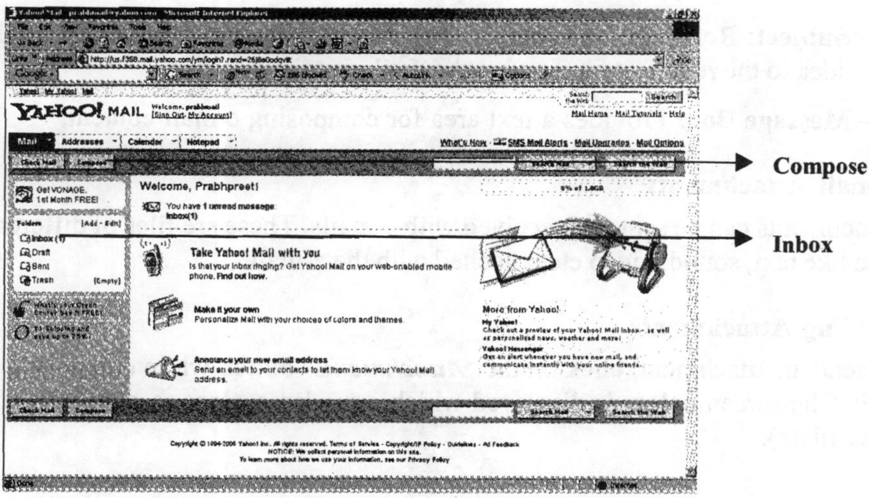

Sending an e-mail

The Compose option on the left corner of your screen allows you to write an e-mail message. You can also attach documents to your mail. When you select the Compose option, the following screen appears:

You can use the following option while composing or writing an e-mail message.

- **To:** Specifies the e-mail address of a recipient such as recipient@domain.com and user@abcdomain.com. This should be a valid email id for the delivery of your message. You can specify multiple recipients' addresses separated by commas.
- **Cc:** Specifies the address of the recipient to whom you want to send the carbon copy (cc) of your message. You can specify multiple recipients' addresses separated by commas.

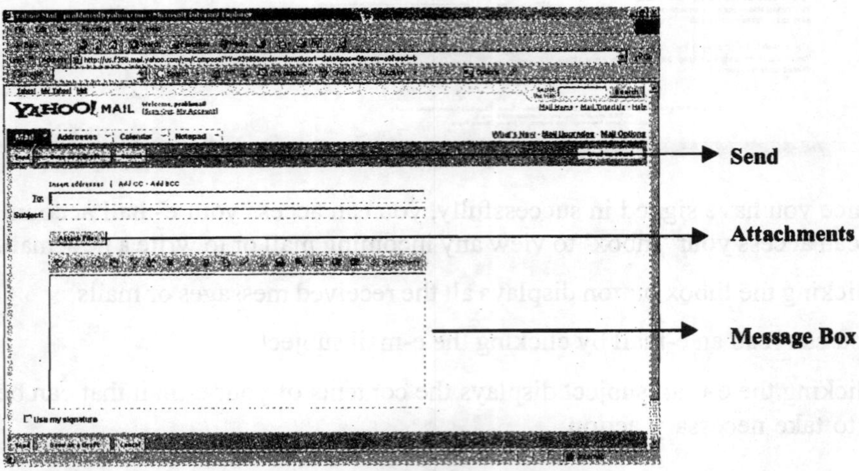

- **Subject:** Refers to the subject of the e-mail message. It provides a fair idea to the recipient about what the mail contains.
- **Message Box:** Provides a text area for composing e-mail content.

E-mail Attachments

Attachments can be sent and received with e-mails. These are files of different type like text, sound, video etc, attached with the e-mail.

Sending Attachments

To send an attachment, click on the '***Attachments***' button while composing a mail. The screen below is displayed which provides options to attach one or more file(s).

Clicking the ***'Browse'*** button against the box provided to enter the file name opens a standard file selection dialog box. This lets you browse through the files on your disk(s) and select the file you wish to attach. Once you select the file to attach, click the '***Open***' button. You can repeat this process if you wish to attach more file(s). Once you are done with selecting all the files, click the '***Attach Files***' button and then return to your message to proceed with sending the message with the attached file(s).

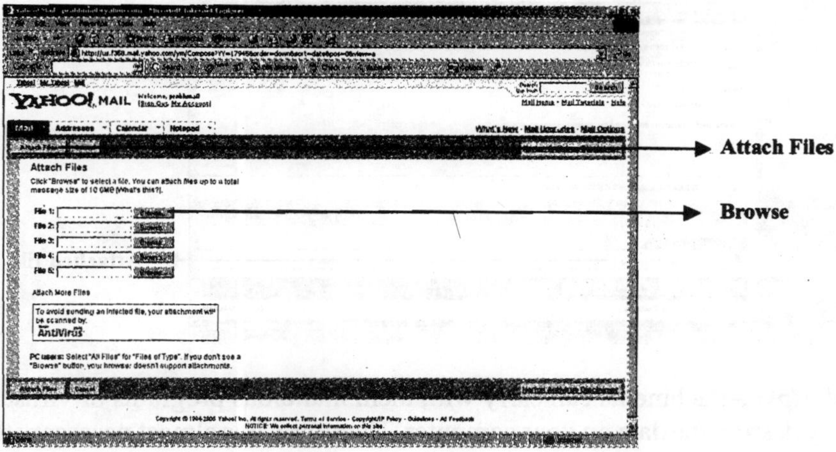

Opening Attachments

If you receive an e-mail message with an attachment(s), you could either download or save the attached files to the disk to be viewed later or view them on-line. To see an attachment, click the attached file(s).

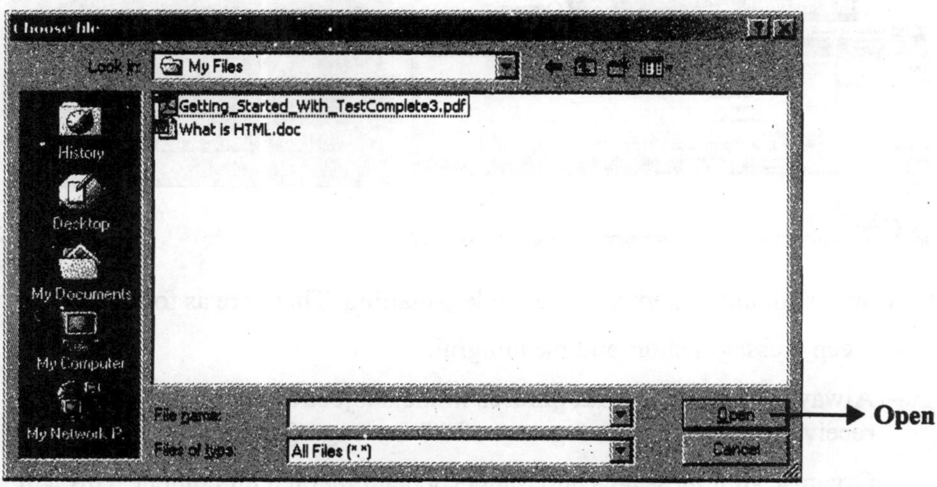

The following screen is displayed. Clicking the '*Download Attachment*' button displays the subsequent screen providing options to either open the attachment on-line and/or '***save*** it to disk for subsequent viewing.

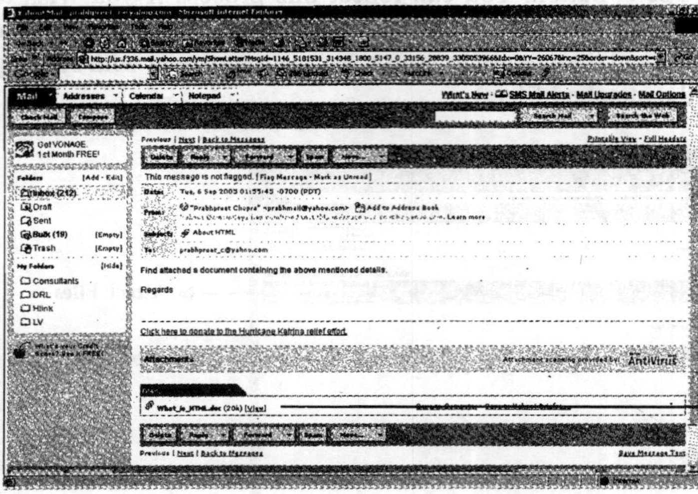

Useful Tips: Attachments can carry with them malicious programs or viruses that may destroy the data on your computer. Therefore, it is almost necessary to scan these files with anti-virus software before opening them.

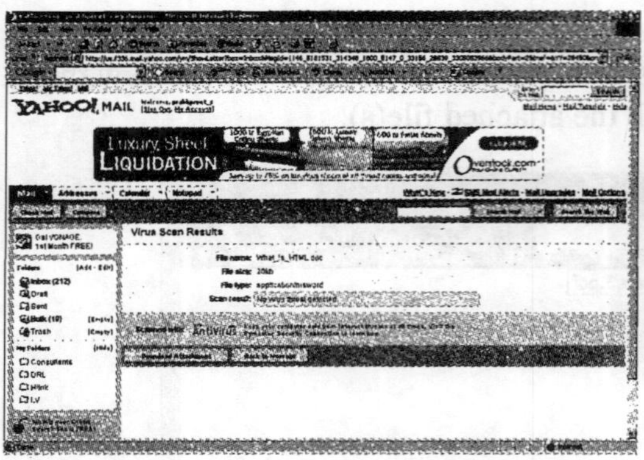

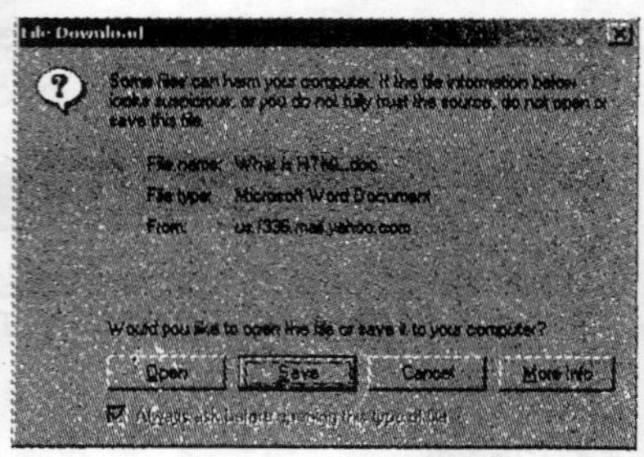

Few things should be kept in mind while e-mailing. These are as follows:

- Keep messages short and meaningful.
- Always write meaningful phrases in the subject of your mail to help the receiver understand the **urgency** of the message (if any).
- Organise your messages into folders depending on their content. This will make it easy to find and maintain your e-mail message.

- Restrict your attachments to the maximum permissible size limit.
- Use a compression software (like WinZip) to compress your file(s) before attaching them. Short messages are easier to handle.
- Scan your attachments before opening them.
- Periodically scan your messages to delete your old messages and avoid mail cluttering in your mailbox. This will help preserve your email account space.
- Always log out of your e-mail account once you wish to stop working with your e-mail.
- Last but not the least.

Periodically change your e-mail account password to protect it from unauthorized use.

Internet Chat

In the earlier days, the only way to get in touch with someone in another city was to either to write a letter or make a long distance call.

The Internet has connected the world. Letters have been replaced by emails. However, there is a time lag between sending the message, the receiver opening it at his/her end and then responding to the same. This can become a little frustrating in case you are running short of time. A solution for this lies in the Internet chat, which works much like the verbal chat.

The Internet Relay Chat (commonly known as the IRC), developed in Finland in 1988 by a programmer called Jarkko Oikarinen, is a multi-user chat system. It allows you to communicate with people anywhere in the world as long as they are logged on to the Internet at the same time. It allows you to type in a message, and your friend, anywhere in the world, if logged in would receive it almost instantaneously. He/she can then respond in the same way. Other than typing instead of speaking, chatting is as good as speaking to another person on a phone. There are free chat sites on the Web that can be used to communicate with one or more people from different locations. An illustration of using the Yahoo chat is show below:

Log on to the Yahoo site by typing the URL **'http://www.Yahoo.com'** and click the **"Chat'** link to move to the chat page.

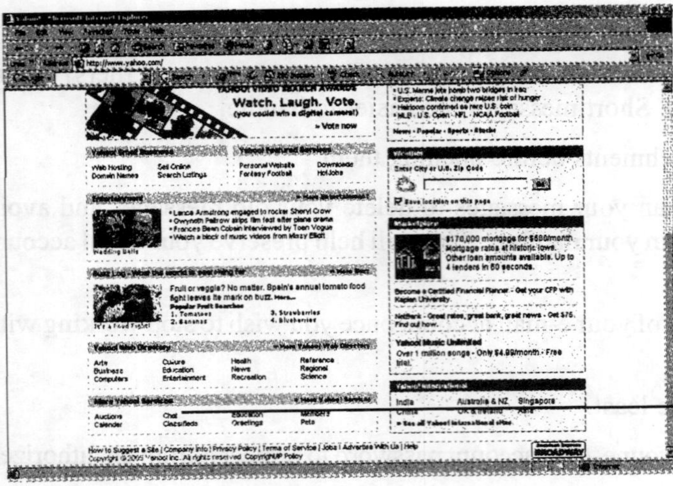

If you are a yahoo user, type in the user id and password and click ***'Sign In'***. This will check for your credentials as a valid user.

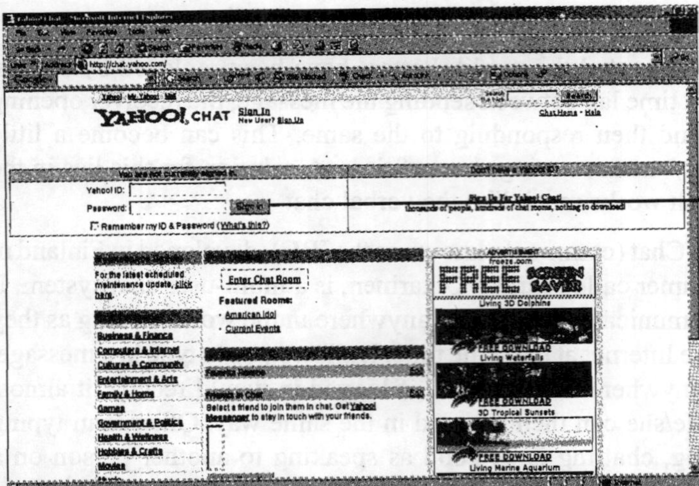

Once you are logged in, you can click *Enter Chat Room* to start chatting

Clicking this link will take you into a room called ***Chat Central*** where you can find many people chatting. You can just jump in and start chatting. Optionally, you could change your chat room by clicking the ***'Change Room'*** button available on the upper-left corner of your screen. This displays a list of chat rooms available to select from. You could choose the chat room of your interest.

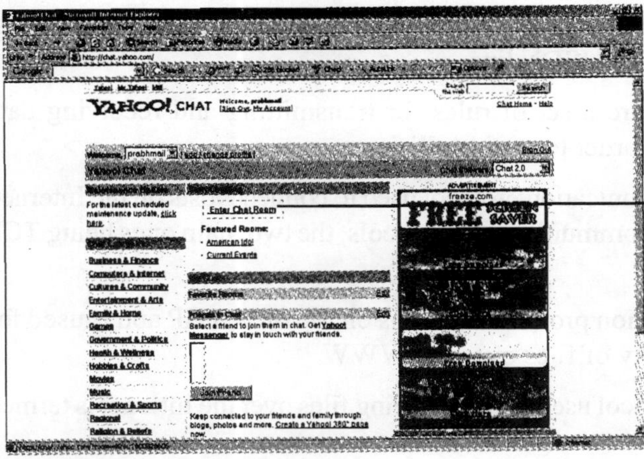

Enter Chat Room

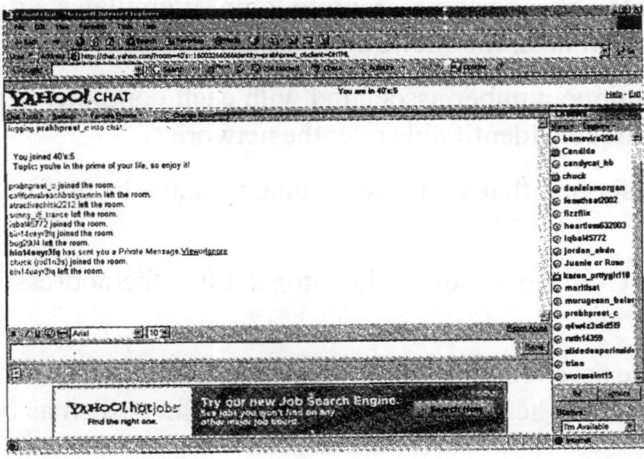

Change Room

KEY POINTS

- The Internet is called the 'network of networks' and connects computers networks all over the world.
- LAN is a network that connects devices over short distances, typically a building or a campus.
- WAN connects devices spread across wide geographical areas. These could be physically located in the same city or in different cities.
- Direct connection or connections through an ISP are the two methods for connecting to the Internet.
- A remote dial-up connection uses telephone lines and modems to connect to an ISP.

- Direct connections to an ISP can be made using dedicated phone lines. Typically this line is an ISDN line.
- Internet protocols are a set of rules for transmitting and receiving data over the Internet in order to avoid collision.
- TCP/IP is the communication protocol used to connect hosts on the Internet. It is a collection of communication protocols, the two main ones being TCP and IP.
- HTTP is an application protocol that runs on top of TCP/IP and is used for transferring a variety of files over the WWW.
- An application protocol used for exchanging files over the Internet is termed as FTP.
- The Telnet protocol lets you perform a remote login. It emulates a direct connection to a different host. Internet.Connecting the World 539
- An IP address is a unique number associated with each computer on the network making it uniquely identifiable over the network.
- DNS is an Internet service that translates domain names to or from IP addresses.
- URL, short form of Uniform Resource Locator defines the address of a Web site on the Internet.
- HTML is the language used for publishing Web pages. It defines the various aspects of a Web page like heading, text and special effects such as bold, underline, italics etc.
- A search engine allows users to search for information on the WWW using keywords.
- The application used to access and display HTML documents is termed as 'Web Browser'. Netscape Navigator and Microsoft Internet Explorer are the commonly used Web browsers.
- E-mail or electronic mail is commonly used to send and receive messages over the Internet. Most of the Web sites provide free e-mailing facilities.
- The Internet Relay Chat or IRC allows users anywhere in the world to communicate with each other, as long as they are logged in.

REVIEW QUESTIONS

1. Choose the appropriate answer:

i. Transistor-based computers are
  (a) Connects devices within short distances
  (b) Connects devices across cities
  (c) Is a network of networks
  (d) Both a and b

ii. The Protocol used to communicate over the Internet is
  (a) HTML (b) HTTP
  (c) FTP (d) TCP/IP

iii. The language used for publishing documents on the World Wide Web
  (a) HTML (b) HTTP
  (c) FTP (d) TCP/IP

iv. The search engine lets you
  (a) Send messages to others
  (b) Chat with others almost in real time
  (c) Search for information in a specific database
  (d) Search for information on the World Wide Web

2. State whether TRUE or FALSE:

(i) The Internet is not owned by any single individual, company or country.

(ii) It is the job of the DNS to match the domain names to the IP addresses.

(iii) Net surfing is the process of publishing web documents

(iv) A permanent dedicated connection can be either by way of SLIP or PPP

3. Match the following:

X	Y
1. Address of a site on the Internet	a. HTML
2. A language for publishing hypertext on the World Wide Web	b. WAN
3. Using a host on the Internet as if you are directly connected	c. URL
4. Application that displays HTML documents on the WWW	d. Web Browser
5. Network covering wide geographical areas	e. Telnet

4. Fill in the Blanks with the appropriate choices listed below

(i) IRC (ii) www.msn.com (iii) Tags (iv) Dial-up (v) MetaCrawler

1. ________________ is a meta search engine.

2. ________________ is a multi-user system that allows users to communicate in nearly real time.

3. Connecting to your ISP using a modem and your telephone line, is called a ______________ connection.

4. ________________ is a valid domain name.

5. HTML uses _____________ to structure contents on a web page.

CHAPTER 18

Information Technology and Society

Information Technology (or IT as it is popularly called) has dramatically changed the way of our life. After the discovery of electricity, the computer ranks as one of the most important breakthroughs of the modern era. Like electricity, IT has impacted all facets of life and in fact its usage is so ubiquitous that it is hard for today's generation to even visualise as to how our ancestors lived without computers. From medicine to transportation, from banking to the entertainment industry there is hardly any industry or sector that does not deploy IT in a fundamental manner to achieve one of the three goals:

(a) Reducing cost of operations by increasing operational efficiency and staff productivity

(b) Improving revenues and bottom lines by helping management in informed decision-making and focusing on priority areas

(c) Improving customer satisfaction by providing better, faster and value-added services

IT has opened up several allied industries and employment opportunities which never existed before. Whether it is Business Process Outsourcing (remote data processing) or Web enabled services (medical transcription, call centres etc.) IT has opened up new avenues for jobs. Thanks to the Internet, developing nations today can also participate in the global economy and help bridge the haves and have-nots divide.

In this chapter, we shall look at how IT has revolutionised major areas of human activity, transforming our lives in the process.

APPLICATION OF IT IN RAILWAYS

The railroad industry is an important driver for a country's economic growth. An efficient rail network means transportation of goods and people at low cost and in time; and thereby facilitates economic growth. However the size and complexity of problems, which the railways face, are also unique. For instance, let us consider Indian Railways, which is one of the largest rail networks in the world. It runs around 11000 trains everyday, out of which 7000 are passenger trains. It has over 7500 locomotives, 37000 coaches and over 2 lakh freight wagons. It operates from over 6800 railway stations and employs over 1.5 million people. The sheer scale of their operations poses numerous management and operational problems. Fortunately the key decision-makers in railways saw the tremendous potential of IT in solving some of these problems and embarked upon a major computerisation initiative. Some of these are:

- All India Centralised Reservations System – one of the most successful examples of computerisation in the country, the computerised reservations mean that anybody, even in a small town, can book tickets for any destination.
- Internet Booking – IRCTC has launched online ticketing facility which can be accessed through the website irctc.co.in. Currently these facilities are available at 758 locations in the country. Computerised reservation related enquiries about passenger status, train schedule, trains between pairs of stations, etc., are also provided on this site. Anybody with a credit card can book a ticket on any train through this website The site levies a small service fee and delivers the ticket to the passenger's home through courier within 24 hours. Timetables, network maps, freight information, fares and tariff are also available on the Indian Railways home page.
- Computerised unreserved ticketing–nearly 12 million unreserved passengers travel everyday on Indian Railways. To cater to this huge segment, computerised ticketing systems has been recently launched. Unreserved tickets can now be issued even from locations other than the boarding station, reducing long queues at booking offices and stations.
- A pilot project for issuing monthly and quarterly season tickets through Automated Teller Machines (ATMs) has been successfully launched in Mumbai recently. Another pilot project for purchasing tickets (including monthly and quarterly season tickets) through Smart Cards has also been launched.
- National Train Enquiry System has been introduced in order to provide upgraded passenger information and enquiries. This system provides train running position in real time – through various output devices such as terminals in the station enquiries and Interactive Voice Response System (IVRS) – at important railway stations. This project has been implemented at 98 stations so far.
- Railways have established their own intranet called 'Railnet'. It provides networking between Railway Board, Zonal Headquarters, Divisional headquarters, Production Units, Training Centres, etc., to facilitate inter and intra departmental communication and coordination.

Airlines

The air travel industry is one of the biggest users of Information Technology. There is hardly any aspect of the airline business in which computer systems have not been deployed for increasing revenues, reducing costs and enhancing customer satisfaction.

It is now almost inconceivable to book a ticket or get a seat confirmed across multiple sales counters (airline offices, travel agents, etc.) spread over numerous cities, without using computerised databases and e- networking. Like most other industries, the use of computerised systems in the air travel industry started with the front office and sales desk with back-office operations playing a oracial role in delivering a quality experience to consumers. What typically started as airlines intranet systems have now blossomed into vast web-based online systems which can be accessed by anybody from anywhere in the world.

Some of the interesting areas where IT has been used successfully are:

- **onlineticket reservation through Internet:** Today, most leading airlines like United Airlines, Delta, British Airways, etc., sell tickets through their websites. You can book the ticket through the Internet, pay online by giving your international credit card details and then collect the ticket (on the day of journey) boarding pass from e-ticket kiosks at the airport by simply furnishing your booking reference details.
- **flight and seats availability:** If you wish to travel from New Delhi to New York and do not know what your flight options are, simply log onto the airline site (or better still a travel site like 'msn' which offers information and tickets from many airlines and can therefore give you more options than a single airline's website), specify the cities of travel origin and destination along with preferred journey dates and the database would yield all the possible options. Once you have selected the flights, you could even go a step further (possible in case of a few airlines) and book a specific seat number in that flight along with the choice of meal.
- **last minute deals and auctions:** A seat is a perishable commodity. An unsold seat means a revenue opportunity lost forever. Therefore, most airlines, including Indian Airlines (and some specialised ticket auction sites like Razorfinish.com) have now started a facility on their website where potential customers can bid for last minute tickets in online auctions. Cases of people buying a ticket worth $1000 for as low as $100 are not uncommon. This is a case of win-win by effective use of IT – the passenger is happy at getting the ticket at a fraction of it's normal cost, and the airline is able to recover something from what might otherwise have been an unsold seat.

All these facilities/opportunities would have been impossible without integrated online computer systems.

Banking

In the sixties and seventies the banking industry–as fiercely competitive as ever–was losing the battle of providing good customer services due to impossibly heavy workloads. All major banks already had branches in most major locations and they simply had to recruit more and more staff to cope with the increasing number of customers. The accepted wisdom was that cost was the main basis for competition and so the banks were making strenuous efforts to reduce operational costs, kicking off the process by computerising customer accounts. Computerisation did lead to cost reductions by saving a lot of back office work, but banks still needed to employ large number of front office staff to deal with customers. To overcome this problem, one of the UK banks adopted a radical solution. Why not get the customers to do the clerical work? This idea–not unlike that behind the airline reservation systems–led to the development of Automatic Teller Machines (ATMs) which allowed customers to take advantage of specific banking services 24 hours a day, 7 days a week, without entering the bank. ATMs made it easy to deposit and withdraw money, check balances, request statements etc., and coupled with the added advantage of round the clock availability, they not only reduced staff workloads but save customers a new experience of hassle-free banking.

The banking sector has come a long way since then. It is now one of the largest users of information technology. Some of the areas where banks typically use IT are:

- **Back office computerisation:** Nowadays, almost all Indian and international banks run on fully integrated and online systems where all back office operations like accounts posting, reconciliation, clearing house operations, etc., are completely automated.
- **Front office computerization:** All banks provide facilities like instant account statement, making fixed deposits, electronic funds transfer, direct debit facility, etc. to their customers. None of these would be possible without the low transaction costs and efficiency offered by computerised systems.
- **Automatic Teller Machines (ATMs):** These computerised machines enable customers to do their regular bank transactions (like depositing and withdrawing money, ascertaining current account balance, etc.) without visiting a bank branch. ATMs considerably reduce costs for banks (employee cost, space cost, etc.) and provide better level of service to customers (by enabling 24 hour banking access at numerous locations).
- **Internet Banking:** Most banks like HSBC, Standard Chartered, HDFC, ICICI etc. have extremely user friendly websites where the typical banking transactions (like making request for cash and cheque pickup, cash delivery, generating account statements, requests for cheque books and drafts, etc.) can be carried out online without visiting the bank. This innovative use of IT

has meant that effectively, customers have no need to physically visit the bank for must routine banking transactions, an enormous convenience.

- **Credit Card Operations:** In a typical credit card operation, you purchase an article or a service and give your credit card to the vendor/service provider at the time of clearing the bill. The vendor (called 'Merchant' in banking language) swipes your credit card on a Point of Sale (POS) machine that instantly dials into the bank database to verify the authenticity and credit worthiness of the card. If both are satisfactory (in other words the transaction is covered by your credit card limit agreed between you and the bank) the POS prints an authentication receipt that authorises the Merchant to collect the transaction amount from the bank instead from the customers. Credit cards obviate the necessity of having to carry huge amounts of cash, and an option of spending more than one current cash status. On the other hand, banks earn money by charging a transaction fee from the merchant and interest on the credit facility. This entire operation is critically dependent on IT and would not have been possible otherwise.

Insurance

Like banking, the insurance sector has also to contend with a lot of routine paperwork–insurance policies, claims filed, survey or investigation reports, payment receipts etc. A perfect opportunity to use IT to reduce costs and processing times.

> *According to Insurance Journal "Eighty-eight per cent of insurers think that IT will become more important in driving efficiencies and cost-reductions in future, according to new research released by RebusIS, an insurance technology solutions provider. A further 55 per cent of respondents to the survey argued that IT is currently playing an 'important' role in driving efficiencies and cost-reductions, with 43 per cent contesting that IT is 'essential' to business efficiency."*

Typically, insurance companies use computerised databases to keep track of all insurance policies, generating premium due statements, premium received receipts, lodging claims for insurance recovery, etc. Basically all kind of transactions are recorded and processed through computerized systems. This not only enables insurance companies to provide quicker and more efficient service to it's clients, it also allows them to minimise their risks and maximise profits by enabling complex financial, economic and demographic analyses of their customers. Using sophisticated computer programs, an insurance company can determine which customer segments are growing the fastest, which are most profitable, and which are more risky than others.

Although a lot of processes have been automated, things like Insurance claims etc. are still filed on paper forms first. The volumes involved are quite intimidating prompting some insurance companies in US and Europe to outsource the entire data entry process to specialised offshore firms–many of them in India!

This is how the typical process works: an insurance agent or the insured party fills up a paper form somewhere in US. These forms are collected from multiple locations at one location – let's say the Insurance Company's head office. A team of professionals from the data entry agency (working in the Insurance company's head office) scan these forms through high speed scanners, generates image files for all the forms and then at the end of the day, using the Internet, transmits all these images to their data processing facility, let's say in New Delhi. Due to time difference, by the time this transmission is done at the end of day in US, it is morning in India. A team of trained data entry operators, using specialised software, views these forms (as images) on one portion of their screen and then types the same data in a database. Once the data has been properly verified and validated the database is then uploaded back to the US within a few hours. This means that the images that were sent from US the previous night could be available in US the next morning in the form of a computerised database! Of course, other than the effective use of IT, the time difference between US and India has helped tremendously to make this 'zero time lag' system a great success! This system of outsourcing one of the business functions is called 'BPO' or Business Process Outsourcing.

Another more sophisticated alternative to this is OCR – Optical Character Recognition where the images are run through OCR software that automatically converts these into text. OCR is only feasible where the text quality is very (typically typed or computer printed matter) high. Since OCR operations still produce only 90 to 95% accurate text, human intervention is still required to correct the mistakes made by OCR systems. In course of time, however, technological advancements will bring 100% reliability and further change the face of remote processing arrangements.

Financial Accounting

Financial Accounting was one of the first business functions for which software applications were developed. The importance of financial accounting and management for any business cannot be overemphasised, but the scale of transactions, the repetitive and structured nature of the data and the sheer volumes involved in the case of large corporates makes for an ideal case for computerisation. Computerizing accounts also takes the drudgery out of book-keeping, which means that accountants can now concentrate more on analysing information rather than devoting countless hours merely in filling out vouchers and updating registers and ledgers.

Typically this is how a computerised accounting system works. The accounting clerk makes the voucher directly on the computer using a financial accounting software package. The voucher on the screen looks very similar to a regular paper voucher and is in fact much simpler to fill because things like current date and voucher number are generated automatically. The appropriate account names that have to be debited or credited need not be typed but simply selected by the click of a mouse from a list of all ledger accounts. Appropriate checks and validations are also built into the accounting software which reduces the chances of errors. For example, unless the total of all debit accounts equals to the total of all credit accounts, software will not allow the voucher to be saved.

Once the basic data has been entered into the computer voucher, the accountant can print out as many copies as required. Unlike a manual accounting system where a the voucher–once prepared, has to be entered into the daybook and then posted in the relevant lager account, the computer software does this automatically. In fact the moment the voucher is entered and saved it is not only automatically posted to all the relevant daybooks and ledger but also up-to-date trial balance, profit and loss account and balance sheet can be generated instantly showing the downstream effects on each one of them. Since there is no time lag between voucher preparation and posting, the accounting software always shows up-to-date statement and final account.

Depending upon the size of the organisation and the complexity of its operation, different software packages are readily available in the market. At the bottom end are popular and inexpensive software such as Tally and EX which are quite sufficient for most small and medium scale organisations. Tally provides an excellent user friendly interface through which all accounting transactions can be entered or modified easily and the user can see the effects of each transaction in all financial statements.

At the top end of the market is ERP (Enterprise Resource Planning) software like ORACLE Financials, BAAN, SAP etc., which cater to the financial accounting and management needs of huge multi-location, multi-currency, multi-operations organisations like Nestlé, Pepsi, Coca Cola, Procter & Gamble etc. Such software, is called ERP software, since it provides completely integrated solutions for all functions of a business like financial accounting, inventory, payroll, production planning and control etc. Despite the fact that ERP solutions typically cost millions of rupees and are relatively much more complex to implement they provide an excellent platform for ensuring that the company's system and procedure are uniformly followed across multiple locations (or even countries). Such systems also make it very easy to consolidate huge amounts of information from different profit centres and locations.Thus, effective near real time management information can be generated to assist apex level decision-making.

Inventory Control

For any manufacturing firm, managing inventory is crucial. High inventory results in money being locked up unnecessarily, thereby reducing liquidity and indirectly profitability (if you offer immediate payment, most suppliers would be willing to offer you better rates). On the other hand, lower inventory of finished goods may lead to lost sales, or lower inventory of raw material may lead to disruption in production line. Optimum stock levels optimise operational efficiency.

Most large manufacturing units typically need hundreds (if not thousands) of raw material components and produce many products. Managing optimal inventory of such a large number of items is a difficult task. It is here that information technology again plays a very useful role. Inventory management software provides facility for specifying (and determining) the maximum, minimum and reorder levels for each item, so that appropriate levels of inventory can be maintained keeping in mind lead times and JIT systems (if any) for component suppliers.

Basically this is how a typical computerised inventory system works–a list of all the inventory items is prepared along with the maximum, minimum, reorder and current levels (quantity in hand as on a fixed date) for each item. This list is fed into the inventory software. Thereafter, all incomings (materials purchased or produced) and outgoings (sales or issues to production floor) are recorded through the inventory package. Since the computer knows all the ins and outs for each item, it can track the exact quantity in hand for each. The package also generates reports for all the fresh stocks that need to be procured (based upon the levels specified). A variety of other useful MIS reports like aging analysis, goods movement analysis, slow and fast moving stock report, valuation report etc. can also be generated which assists the store keeper and accountants.

Some of the more sophisticated inventory packages (or inventory modules of ERP packages like Oracle financials, BAAN, SAP etc.) automatically generate purchase orders (as soon as minimum level of any item is reached), provide automatic posting of accounting entries (as soon as any purchase or sale is carried out) and generate analytical reports which (italize) show the previous and future trends in inventory consumption.

Some interesting innovations in usage of IT for better inventory management are:

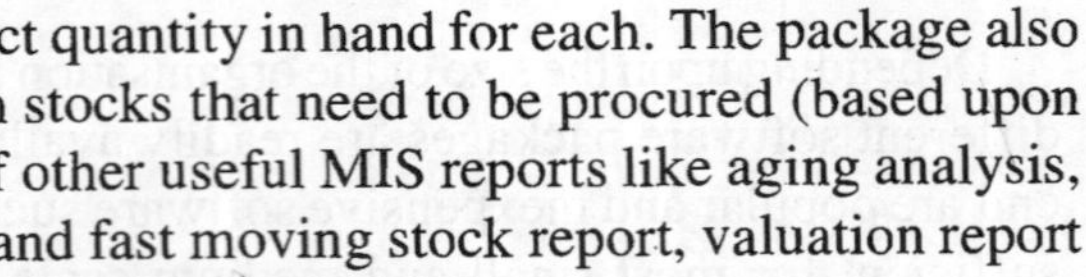

- Use of barcoding system– bar coding is a technique which allows data to be encoded in the form of a series of parallel and adjacent bars and spaces which represent a string of characters. A bar code printer encodes any data into these spaces and bars and then a bar code reader is used to decode the bar codes by scanning a light source across the bar code and measuring the intensity of light reflected back by the white spaces. Bar coding provides an excellent and fast method for identifying items, their batch nos. expiry dates etc. without having to manually type or read the data.

- Use of Hand Held Terminals (HHTs)–HHTs are simple devices used to communicate with any type of microprocessor-based device. The standard input device is the keyboard (typically more akin to the calculator, rather than the computer keyboard) and a small LCD display for the output. HHTs are compact, simple and rugged devices designed for outdoor applications like collecting the information about inventory from large warehouses, recording movement of goods in and out etc.
- Internet and Intranets – many organisations (specially those following 'Just In Time' techniques) now have a system whereby the moment they receive an order or a request for an item (which is not in stock or whose stock is low), the inventory package automatically generates a purchase or supply order electronically and mails it to the preferred supplier–all this without any human intervention!

Hotel Management

The hotel industry is an integral part of the tourism industry, which is a vital source of revenue and foreign exchange for a country's economy. A vibrant hotel industry means greater employment generation. However, since this industry relies on easy and quick availability of information, the role of IT in its development and growth cannot be over-stressed. In fact, IT has revolutionised the hotel and tourism industry. This is because the instant availability of information about the tourists spots, hotel infrastructure, room availability, traiff details, online looking etc. at a click of button. IT is playing a critical role in improving performance because of its potential of creating customer relationships and the flow of information between the people and customers.

There are numerous instances of use of IT in hotel industry. Some of these include:

- Today's hotel management software means that the moment a guest expresses interest in staying at the hotel, till the time he checks out, all transactions with him (room charges, food and laundry bills, business centre, heath centre, hiring cars etc.) are recorded electronically, making information available at the click of a button.
- Many leading hotels offer online booking facility for tourists and guests. This makes it very easy for the tourist as he has before hand knowledge of room availability and charges. There are several websites wholly devoted to this. Microsoft's MSN has a traveller's section where one can search for hotel

accommodation based on criteria like city, location, budget etc. For example, a tourist can specify the city and his budget. Based on this information, the search facility throws up a complete list of hotels available. Moreover, the tourist can even specify his preferred location. Once the hotel is identified, booking can be made online using an internationally valid credit card.

- Most of the hotels have computerised their records. It is very easy to know details of room availability at a particular time. The information about the occupant is also available instantly. This computerised system typically integrates all hotel MIS functions into one system. Cendant Corporation has successfully implemented this practice in its chain of hotels. The Barbizon Hotel and Empire Hotel, New York has eliminated logbooks and standardised record keeping by the use of customised software. Carlson Hospitality Worldwide has the most efficient and productive reservation system in US. IMPAC Hotel Group has lobby kiosk touch-screen guest-tracking system. Inter-Continental Hotels & Resorts use a global strategic marketing database. All these are examples of use of IT in hotel industry, which have made significantly transformed operations and profitability.
- Hotel Information Systems help users to access guest database information and use the information to create attractive one-to-one reservation confirmations, e-mail marketing and sales messages, custom reports and e-mail comment cards to reinforce guest relationships. The Balsams Grand Resort Hotel has a comprehensive guest history program that it has used successfully for productive purposes. Courtyard by Marriott has an intranet system by which it has replaced manuals and printed material.
- Information technology is being increasingly used by international hotel chains to formulate and align their corporate strategies. Marriott International is a successful example of alignment of Information Technology with Corporate Strategy.

Education

Teaching has traditionally been associated with classroom instructions on a blackboard with the instructor dependent almost entirely on his/her oratory and presentation skills for holding the attention of the class. From a student's perspective, she had to keep pace with the instructor's pace, which meant that the slower (though not necessarily less intelligent) student was at a natural disadvantage. Similarly some students were more interested in a more in-depth study than the others. Since access to information was neither easy nor inexpensive, these variables had always posed a major barrier to learning.

Ever since the advent of Information Technology, the scenario has changed dramatically. Today, the instructor has a repertoire of Information technologies. To make the lecture not only more interesting but also more informative, there are advanced electronic teaching tools available. These vary from simple slide presentations to full blown multimedia presentations which have video clippings, sound effects animation and graphics to explain even the most abstruse subjects in a simple and easy-to-understand manner. As an example, a medical student does not have to pore over boring textbooks to understand lets say, the human anatomy. Simple computer packages like 'Body Works' are available which explain the same using photographs, images and graphics that make in-depth learning fun rather than a chore. Moreover, learning is not only faster but is retained longer when test is supported by visuals and sound clips. Multimedia has transformed both classroom as well as online (distance) and packaged (CDs, VCDs, DVDs etc.) education, in terms of both content as well as interactivity.

Some of the interesting developments in IT for the education sector can be seen in:

- **Computer Based Training (CBT):** In most of the progressive institutes today, classroom sessions are complemented by CBTs. CBT typically comprises user-friendly software in which the course syllabi is broken up into a series of interactive sessions. These sessions involve imparting a slice of knowledge to the student and then quizzing him to reinforce his understanding. Students have the option of going through these sessions at a time most convenient to them and a pace best suited to them. CBTs also provide an excellent medium for the student to learn by exploration and discovery rather than by rote.

> *"Education software is often positioned as 'enriching' the learning process and not as a potential substitute for traditional teacher-based methods."*

- **Internet:** Thanks to the Internet, any and every type of information is available at the touch of a button. No longer have students to trudge long distances to visit a library and spend valuable time plodding through library catalogues to find the right information. Using a search engine, one can easily access the desired information. Also, knowledge is no longer restricted within the academic fraternity alone. Thanks to our networked world (Intranet / Internet) information dissemination is faster and widespread.
- **Distance Learning:** Information Technology has also made distance learning a reality. You need not be physically present in a Business School to do a management course from there. By innovative use of information technology, educational institutes have reached out to students who would otherwise never have been able to enroll with them.
- **Computerisation of Administrative Tasks:** Most academic institutes use computerised systems for student enrollment, fee management, examination administration, etc. For instance, enrollment forms are now available on institutional websites, and examination results are usually available on the

Internet. Some schools have also started collecting fees through Internet by using credit cards.

Telephone Exchanges

The first telephone service invented by Alexander Graham Bell was strictly 'point-to-point', i.e., each user had to be physically wired to every other user. There was no 'telephone exchange'. Needless to say, Bell immediately realised the need for an exchange, and made one. In this first exchange each subscriber had to be wired only upto his local exchange. An operator sitting in the exchange connected him to other subscribers upon request (earlier phones did not have dialing facility) by physically connecting the caller's wire to the recipient subscriber's telephone by using a hand actuated circuit switch. One does not need to stretch one's imagination to appreciate the fact that operator-controlled exchanges were not only extremely labour intensive but also highly error prone.

Now compare to this the digital, computerised telephone exchanges used today. These are electronic systems that do the switching operation based upon a 'stored program control'. The rules defined in the software assess which destination the caller is trying to reach, plot the most optimal path, intimate the called party, inform the caller about his call status and then if the called party accepts the call, establish the circuit. The call is monitored during its progress and the circuit disconnected once the call is terminated. Computerised exchanges improved and enhanced call-processing capacity, thereby lowering the cost of operations. They also opened up a dazzling array of IT-enabled subscibers services that have made modern telephany an indispensable service.

Bharat Sanchar Nigam Limited (BSNL) one of the main providers of telephony services extensively uses a product called INFOTEL for managing their telephone exchanges. This product provides facilities for:

- **Provision of facilities:** Activation, deactivation and modification of subscriber facilities such as ISD, STD, call waiting, call transfer, computer-generated bills etc.
- **Fault booking and restoration service:** To maintain a database of complaint calls either through an IVRS (Interactive Voice Response System) or a customer service cell. The system automatically creates the complaint docket and generates a range of statistical and exception reports.
- **Line data maintenance:** The system provides online data on cable codes, cable pair numbers, cabinet number, pillar numbers, etc., for all subscriber connections to facilitate and expedite line repair and maintenance.
- **Directory Enquiry:** The computerised subscriber database also allows extensive on line or voice-based directory enquiry based upon subscriber name, location, telephone number etc.

Mobile Phones

Statistically, major portions of the populations of any developing country still do not possess a telephone. Making a simple call to anybody requires locating the nearest telephone booth, waiting for ones' turn in the queue, and then paying for a short chat on (most often) a disturbed line.

In the developing countries the penetration of landline phones has been low largely due to the hassles of laying cables across long distances. Especially in the case of remote areas, the cost of connecting a few phones to the main land mass becomes disproportionately high. Maintaining these telephone cables across inhospitable terrain also poses a major challenge to network expansion planners and engineers.

It sometimes pays to be late! Thanks to the advances made in the telecommunications industry in the last two decades, mobile phones provide an excellent cost effective and efficient alternative to the land phones for developing countries like India.

A cellular phone (as mobile phones are also known) is primarily a radio – a very sophisticated variant of a radio telephone. The genius of a cellular system is the division of the city into small cells (hexagons on a big hexagonal grid). Each cell has a base station that consists of a tower and a small building containing the radio equipment. Wireless communication is possible within and across cells allowing a user complete mobility making communication much easier and less time consuming. Through switching devices in landline telephone exchanges, mobile phone users can also access the global landline network, effectively bringing everyone within speaking distance.

The mobile phone industry owes its growth to information technology which is in fact central and pivotal in any mobile system. Technologies like PCS, TDMA, CDMA, GSM are often associated with mobile phones.

PCS (personal communications services) is a wireless phone service somewhat similar to cellular telephone service but emphasising personal service and extended mobility. It is sometimes referred to as digital cellular (although cellular systems can also be digital). Like cellular, PCS is for mobile users and requires a number of antennas to blanket an area of coverage. As a user moves around, the user's phone signal is picked up by the nearest antenna and then forwarded to a base station that connects to the wired network.

TDMA (time division multiple access) is a technology used in digital cellular telephone communication that divides each cellular channel into three time slots in order to increase the amount of data that can be carried.

CDMA employs analog-to-digital conversion (ADC) in combination with spread spectrum technology. Audio input is first digitised into binary elements. The frequency of the transmitted signal is then made to vary according to a defined pattern (code), so it can be intercepted only by a receiver whose frequency response is programmed with the same code, so it follows exactly along with the transmitter frequency. There are trillions of possible frequency-sequencing codes; this enhances privacy and makes cloning difficult.

GSM (Global System for Mobile communication) is a digital mobile telephone system that is widely used in Europe and other parts of the world. GSM uses a variation of time division multiple access (TDMA) and is the most widely used of the three digital wireless telephone technologies (TDMA, GSM, and CDMA). GSM digitises and compresses data, then sends it down a channel with two other streams of user data, each in its own time slot. GSM is in fact the de facto wireless telephone standard in Europe.

Today, mobile phones are proliferating as handsets get cheaper and call rates decline, bringing them within the reach of the common man. They provide an array of functions (some very simple and others very sophisticated). Some of the popular functions which are based upon IT are:

- SMS (Short Messaging Service)–small text messages can be exchanged between people who do not believe in long verbal conversations over communication channels. In fact today SMS has gained popularity as a medium for sending and forwarding jokes!
- Address Book–is a store of contact information maintained on the mobile handset or the central server. It does away with the usual problem of maintaining a hard copy address book and allows the phone user to dial numbers without having to bother about carrying a bulky file-o-fax or telephone diary along.
- Schedules or to-do lists–you can store a list of important tasks that you wish to accomplish. Most mobile phones software also provide for appointments and reminders associated with these tasks.
- Send or receive e-mail–thanks to WAP technology it is now possible to access your e-mails using your mobile phone. Popular portals like Yahoo and Rediff offer a facility whereby users get automatic alerts on their mobile phones as soon as any new mail arrives. You can also use your mobile phone for chatting using your MSN or ICQ account.
- Get information updates–All mobile service providers now provide add-on facilities for their subscribers to receive regular updates on news, entertainment, stock market prices. This is done by integrating web-based databases with the mobile users' database. Service providers also use this capability to advertise for new products, services and schemes.

As you can appreciate, all the above facilities are based upon the usage of electronic databases and intelligent software available on the mobile phone. Due to the global trend of convergence the dividing line between information technology and telecommunications technology is getting increasingly blurred. Today's computers combine phone, fax, television, VCD/DVD drives, stereo – all in one seamless bundle.

Video Games

Games have been one of the most popular uses of computers. In fact, organisations like Attari, Nintendo, and Sony who were developers of video games have been instrumental in the improvements in the multimedia capabilities of desktop computers. Till about a decade ago when personal computers had severe limitations of disk storage, processing speed, and memory size, only very simple uni-dimensional video games were possible. But with the development of much faster Pentium series of CPUs with inbuilt multimedia capabilities coupled with improvement in digital storage and acoustics, today's games are limited only by their creators' imagination and not by any technological hindrances. Today's games like Doom, Pokeman, PlayStation, Galaxian, Defender, etc., use very sophisticated graphic and sound techniques to create three dimensional games.

Some of the interesting developments in this area have been:

- virtual reality
- improvements in specialised input devices like joysticks
- special game cards and enhanced graphic capability of CPU
- Web games (Casinos)

Information Kiosks

Traditionally, getting information from any large organisation or government department meant standing in a long queue and then having to deal the changing moods of the person sitting at the information desk. Not only did it take a lot of time but one invariably did not get the complete and authentic information in one go since even if the person responsible for giving information was available and willing, s/he invariably did not provide the complete information.

Proactive organisations decided to use information technology to solve this problem and provide better level of service to customers and citizens. Information kiosks are computer-based terminals that provide information of any kind. Typically these kiosks use a touch screen technology where the user does not have to type through the keyboard or click using a mouse but simply touch hot-spots on the computer monitor to select the desired option. These kiosks also use sound recorded in vernacular languages to make the content more user friendly and to reach out to the illiterate and literate alike.

The most popular applications of information kiosks can be seen in:

- **Public access areas**–shopping malls, holiday resorts, cinema halls, etc., use information kiosks with graphics and audio prompts that assist customers in accessing information about the desired products, services and Frequently Asked Questions (FAQs) about availability, price, attributes etc.
- **Public utilities**–one of the early users of information kiosks were public utility organisations (in USA and Europe). Most public companies receive enormous amount of requests for information about their services, lodging complaints, application status etc. Instead of employing an army of front office staff (and taking on the additional hassles of their constant training and ensuring that their motivation is at high levels!) most organisations opted for the information kiosks to provide hassle-free round the clock service to its customers. Information kiosks reduce personnel cost as well as the need for vast office space and costly support equipment.
- **Web kiosks**–Although the early usage of information kiosks was limited largely to static information (brochures, technical information and collaterals), information kiosks are being increasingly used to provide database driven, online information. For instance, information kiosks at the New York airport are linked to all the major hotels in the city and any traveller can do an online booking after confirming room availability.

Special Effects in Movies

Special effects in movies have come a long way since the early twentieth century. During the early years of movie making, special effects were limited to time-lapse cinematography–hand controlled dummies brought to life by stop motion filming which meant manually moving the animated model a fraction of an inch and taking a snapshot. For example, the1933 classic ***King Kong*** involved tedious photography of a life-size dummy model moved laboriously inch-by-inch between takes by a team of assistants.

Similarly, the early animation movies (popularly called cartoon films) involved a team of artists and painters who would painstakingly draw and paint each sketch frame by frame. The photography team would then click shots of these sketches at the rate of 24 frames a second of film and edit them into a story.

Cut to the twenty first century. If another version King-Kong were to be made in 2004 (and it has) what you would get is a completely authentic looking Gorilla (made fiercer by even better digitally created and enhanced sound effects) walking in a lush green forest (once again created by a clever mix of amazon rain forest pictures and computer technique commonly known as digital compositing). Not only would the ape look and behave completely naturally but would be able to perform stunts (like 360 degree flips or making 100 meter jumps) that would just not have been possible with any physical model.

Some of the interesting techniques used for creating special effects are:

- **digital compositing:** Typically done through a process called 'Bluescreen' where the actors perform the scene in a studio in front of a large blue screen. A separate team of computer designers and artists create a virtual background (by mixing multiple photographs and computer generated images). Later the actors' footage is superimposed on the top of the background to create a seamless 'composite picture'.
- **time slicing:** In this technique a series of cameras are placed around the object of concern. All these cameras shoot pictures at precisely the same time. When these pictures are played together it appears as if there is one camera moving around the object. Coupled with other special tricks (such as slow motion photography as used in the Matrix series) this creates an ethereal effect.
- **Computer-generated imaging (CGI):** CGI techniques are used to create scenes which are either not possible in real life or would be too expensive or dangerous to film. For instance to gather a crowd of 150,000 people in the Colosseum to shoot a gladiator fight sequence would cost an enormous amount of money besides creating nightmarish logistical problems. Doing the same though CGI would not only cost a fraction of the money, but also save precious time.

None of the above developments would have been possible without the fantastic developments in Information technology.

REVIEW QUESTIONS

1. Give some examples of how the Indian Railways has used Information Technology to provide better level of service to its customers.
2. Distinguish between an 'Offline' system and an 'Online' system.
3. How has the banking industry used IT to reduce its cost of operations?
4. Give examples of enhanced services offered by airlines and hotels by deploying information technology.
5. How have advances made in IT and web benefited a developing country like India?
6. How can information technology help improve operations in a departmental store?
7. If Mahabharata (the movie) was to be remade now, what role would IT play in making the **magnus opus** come to life.
8. Do you think that IT can help only large organisations–or does it have its application in small and medium sized organisations as well?
9. Discuss the possible uses of IT in the fields of space research, medicine, aerial mapping in defence and global weather forecasting.
10. Explore the latest contribution of IT to genetic research and the horizons of genetic engineering leading to clones, cyborg's and androids.

